WITHDRAWN

D1712288

THE ENGLISH NOVEL
Twentieth Century Criticism

American and British Literature
Reference Works from Swallow Press

The English Novel: Twentieth Century Criticism

Volume I: Defoe Through Hardy
edited by Richard J. Dunn

Volume II: Twentieth Century Novelists
edited by Paul Schlueter and
June Schlueter

Articles on American and British Literature

an Index to Selected
Periodicals, 1950-1977
edited by Larry B. and Sandra Corse

American Short-Fiction Criticism and Scholarship

1959-1977, A Checklist
edited by Joe Weixlmann

Fourth Directory of Periodicals

Publishing Articles on English
and American Literature and Language
edited by Donna Gerstenberger and
George Hendrick

The English Novel
Twentieth Century Criticism

Volume II, Twentieth Century Novelists

edited by
Paul Schlueter
and
June Schlueter

SWALLOW PRESS
OHIO UNIVERSITY PRESS
Chicago   Athens, Ohio   London

Swallow Press Books
are published by
Ohio University Press
Athens, Ohio 45701

Library of Congress Cataloging in Publication Data (Revised)
Main entry under title:

The English novel.

   Contents: v. 1. Defoe through Hardy. / Richard J. Dunn —
v. 2. Twentieth century novelists / Paul and June Schlueter.
   1. English fiction—History and criticism—Bibliography.
Z2014.F4E53   016.823′91′09   76-17741
ISBN 0-8040-0742-X (v. 1)   AACR2
ISBN 0-8040-0424-2 (v. 2)

Dedicated To
Ed and Elizabeth Huberman
and to the Memory of
Harry T. Moore (1908-1981)

CONTENTS

Introduction

This volume, one of a series, is, we believe, the most nearly complete bibliography of criticism of the twentieth century British novel yet published. Yet in trying to make the volume as definitive as possible, we have also had the onerous task of having to keep the volume within manageable limits. It is therefore a *selective* bibliography, with citations from 1900 through the end of 1975. Our choices were necessarily arbitrary, for reasons of both space and relevance, but we believe, all in all, that we have made an intelligent compilation of secondary criticism of the modern English novel.

We did, however, have to make a number of decisions regarding coverage and limitations. In general, we have followed the practice of the annual bibliography in *PMLA* regarding those authors to be included. This means, for example, that Samuel Beckett (cited by *PMLA* under French literature) is omitted, but James Joyce is included. Some writers normally identified with nations in the British Commonwealth are listed by *PMLA* under twentieth century English literature, but we have had to decide, again arbitrarily, to omit such writers. This means, for example, that Malcolm Lowry, usually considered Canadian rather than English, is excluded. We have also tried to include only those novelists considered in the "mainstream" of British fiction. Hence Agatha Christie is omitted while Dorothy Sayers and G. K. Chesterton are included because the latter writers wrote more than detective fiction; Arthur C. Clarke is omitted while H. G. Wells is included because Wells wrote more than science fiction. Other writers are excluded because they seem, overall, simply to be too "lightweight" for substantive criticism. All in all, we believe our selection to be representative of the state of British fiction in this century.

As arbitrary as our choices for authors to be included may seem, our judgment regarding articles and books to be cited under various novelists' names may seem even more arbitrary. Yet in order to make this volume as practical and useful as possible, we believe our criteria are justified. Perhaps it would be easier to indicate the kinds of material we have *not* included:

    a. theses and dissertations;
    b. encyclopedias, general and literary;
    c. material published in a language other than English and not available in translation;
    d. biographical and autobiographical works, memoirs and reminiscences, and collections of letters—unless substantive commen-

tary about the novelist as a writer or about his novels as works of literature is included;

e. most introductions to individual or collected works of a novelist, unless, once again, these are of particular importance;

f. student guides or analyses of a writer's work;

g. most book reviews, unless of essay length and/or of particular importance (as, for example, when one novelist reviews another's work);

h. most notes of one page (the sort regularly appearing in *Notes and Queries*, *Explicator*, and such specialized journals as *Wake Newslitter*);

i. material related to genres for which an author might be noted other than the novel (In practice, this is sometimes difficult, since some overlap does occur. And while it might be easy, for example, to distinguish between criticism about a writer's novels and his occasional forays into verse or art criticism, it is considerably more difficult regarding amorphous genres such as novellas. Hence we have included Conrad's *Heart of Darkness* but not his "The Secret Sharer"; we have included Lawrence's *The Fox*, but not his "The Princess.");

j. bibliographies or checklists of an author's work unless a listing of secondary criticism is also included (In general, we have tried to include bibliographies whenever we could, but whenever possible limiting these to collections of entries about an author's work.);

k. criticism of criticism, accounts of critical reception given various novels, and items referring to collections or library holdings.

On a more positive note, we have tried to include as representative an array of criticism as possible. A generous representation of criticism from earlier in this century, for example, seems to us necessary, even though by today's standards much of this would be termed "appreciative" rather than "critical." The various "schools" of criticism in the last generation or so are well represented, with abundant examples of the New Criticism, Marxist, Freudian, and Christian interpretations, textual and structural analyses, and, as appropriate, material related to the film as this applies to the novel.

We have also adopted some other operating principles for this volume, usually for bibliographic accuracy or to save space. These principles include the following:

a. The original source, whenever possible, is cited for all entries, even though, in some cases, the item may also be available in an author's selected essays or in various compendia of essays.

b. Accordingly, collections of essays about a novelist or a particular novel, such as Prentice-Hall's "Twentieth Century Interpretations" and "Twentieth Century Views" series, are cited only by the name of the full collection, not by individual essays in such collections. For one thing, such collections usually reprint essays previously published elsewhere; for another, the same essays seem to turn up endlessly, in collection after collection. On those few occasions where such a reprint collection does contain the first printing of an essay, we have cited that item. Collections of original essays are cited only by the title of the collection, not by individual essay titles. In the case of special issues of journals devoted to particular novelists and their work, we have not only listed that issue under a separate heading, "Special Issues," but analyzed the collection as well.

c. If a book deals with three or more works by a particular novelist, that book is cited under "General Studies" for that novelist, not broken down with citations for each of the novels discussed. Similarly, if an entry pertains to a novel for which there are not enough entries to justify a separate heading, we have included that entry under "General Studies."

d. If a book is cited for more than one novelist represented in these pages, full bibliographic information for the edition cited, along with data for editions with identical pagination, is provided in the "List of Works Cited and General Bibliography" concluding this volume, not under each such author. Some frequent y-cited general studies are merely referred to as "See also" items at the end of sections of sub-sections of the bibliography for a particular author. In these cases, we have provided as full a bibliographic entry as possible so that the interested reader is aware of various editions.

e. If a collection of essays by a critic is cited, only the appropriate page numbers in that volume, not individual essay titles, are cited.

f. We have in general followed *PMLA*'s style in abbreviations for journals indexed by *PMLA*, and have created similar short-forms for other journals; all such abbreviations are explained in full in the "Periodicals Cited" portion of this book. All Roman numerals normally used for volume numbers have been converted to Arabic for ease of usage and for conciseness. Whenever we have deviated from *PMLA* style, it has been in the interest of saving space.

One fact immediately evident from even a cursory glance at the contents of this volume is the disproportionate attention given some writers and the almost total disregard given others. While this might merely reflect the state of criticism today, it does seem to us that little if any

Introduction

attention has been given to a host of talented novelists in our day, writers who never seem to attract much critical attention. Such novelists could include Sybille Bedford, John Berger, John Bowen, Brigid Brophy, William Cooper, Nigel Dennis, Gabriel Fielding, Rumer Godden, Elizabeth Jane Howard, Pamela Hansford Johnson, Rosamund Lehmann, Colin MacInnes, L. H. Myers, Frederic Raphael, Simon Raven, Mary Renault, Jean Rhys, Robert Shaw, David Storey, Elizabeth Taylor, Honor Tracy, Paul West, and Keith Waterhouse. Some of these novelists are included in our bibliography, most are not; all of them, however, are promising areas of investigation for scholars who hesitate to add one more essay on *A Passage to India* or *Ulysses* or *Women in Love* to the many we cite.

Finally, we know that in a work of this sort errors and omissions have undoubtedly occurred. We have used every available bibliography in print in the preparation of this book, have cross-checked our references, and have examined the original sources for over 90% of all items included. Even so, with some 7,500 entries, covering three-fourths of this century, an occasional error is bound to occur. For these we apologize, and we ask that these errors—and obvious items that should have been included—be brought to our attention by writing to us in care of the publishers or at the academic address given for us in the annual *PMLA* directory.

We have used a number of libraries in the preparation of this bibliography, including the New York Public Library and the academic libraries at Kean College of New Jersey, Lafayette College, Lehigh University, Rutgers University, Princeton University, Columbia University, and Yale University. Special thanks are due Ronald Robbins and Richard Everett, reference librarians at Lafayette College, for their help in resolving a formidable range of problems, inconsistencies, searches for missing books, inter-library requests, and the many other kinds of help that librarians are especially able to provide. We also thank Lafayette College for a grant which helped us through the final stages of this project.

Paul and June Schlueter
Easton, PA, March 24, 1980

PERIODICALS CITED

A&L	*The Academy and Literature*
ABC	*American Book Collector*
ABR	*American Benedictine Review*
Accent	
ACLALSB	*ACLALS Bulletin* (Mysore, India)
AD	*A.D.* [*Anno Domini*]
Adam	*Adam International Review*
Adelphi, The	
Age	
Agenda	
Agora	*Agora: A Journal in the Humanities and Social Sciences*
AI	*American Imago*
AIR	*Anglo-Italian Review*
AL	*American Literature*
ALitASH	*Acta Litteraria Academiae Scientiarum Hungaricae*
Alphabet	
ALS	*Australian Literary Studies*
America	
American Prefaces	
AmerM	*American Mercury*
AmerR	*American Review*
AMH	*Annals of Medical History*
Analyst	
AN&Q	*American Notes and Queries*
Anonymous	*Anonymous: A Journal for the Woman Writer*
Antemurale	
AntigR	*Antigonish Review*
Aphra	
Approach	
AQ	*American Quarterly*
AR	*Antioch Review*
Arcadia	
Arena	
ArielE	*Ariel: A Review of International English Literature*
ArlQ	*Arlington Quarterly*
ArmD	*Armchair Detective*
ArQ	*Arizona Quarterly*
AS	*American Speech*
ASch	*American Scholar*

Periodicals Cited

AsianR	*Asian Review*
AsiaticR	*Asiatic Review*
ASJ	*Anglo-Soviet Journal*
ASoc	*Arts in Society*
Aspect	
AT	*Africa Today*
Athenaeum	
Atlantic	*Atlantic Monthly*
AUB-LG	*Analele Universitătii, Bucuresti, Limbi Germanice*
AUB-LUC	*Analele Universitătii, Bucuresti, Literaturĕ Universală si Comparată*
AUC-PPSE	*Acta Universitatis Carolinae. Philologica 5, Prague Studies in English*
Audience	
Audit	
AUMLA	*Journal of the Australasian Universities Language and Literature Association*
AusQ	*Australian Quarterly*
AW	*Anglica Wratislaviensia*
AWR	*The Anglo-Welsh Review*
BA	*Books Abroad*
Balcony	*Balcony: The Sydney Review*
BaumB	*The Baum Bugle: A Journal of Oz*
BB	*Bulletin of Bibliography and Magazine Notes*
BC	*Book Collector*
Bell, The	
BI	*Books at Iowa*
BJA	*British Journal of Aesthetics*
BJRL	*Bulletin of the John Rylands Library*
Blackfriars	
BLR	*Bodleian Library Record*
BMQ	*British Museum Quarterly*
BNYPL	*Bulletin of the New York Public Library*
BO	*Black Orpheus*
Bolt	
Bookguide	
BookJ	*Bookman's Journal*
Bookman (London) (now *London Mercury*)	
Bookman (N.Y.)	
Bookman's Journal and Print Collector	
Book News Monthly	
Books and Art	

Books and Bookmen
Boundary	*Boundary 2: A Journal of Postmodern Literature*
BP	*Banasthali Patrika*

Britain Today
BRMMLA	*Rocky Mountain Review of Language and Literature* (formerly *Bulletin of the Rocky Mountain Modern Language Association*)
BSE	*Bruno Studies in English*
BSTCF	*Ball State Teachers College Forum* (now *Ball State University Forum*)
BSUF	*Ball State University Forum* (formerly *Ball State Teachers College Forum*)
BUJ	*Boston University Journal*
BuR	*Bucknell Review*

Busara
BUSE	*Boston University Studies in English*
BWVACET	*The Bulletin of the West Virginia Association of College English Teachers*
BYUS	*Brigham Young University Studies*
CahiersI	*Cahiers Irlandais*
CairoSE	*Cairo Studies in English*
CalML	*Calendar of Modern Letters*
CalR	*Calcutta Review*
CambJ	*Cambridge Journal*
CambR	*Cambridge Review*
C&L	*Christianity and Literature*
CanF	*Canadian Forum*
CanL	*Canadian Literature. Littérature Canadienne*
CanLib	*Canadian Library*
CarlM	*Carleton Miscellany*
Carnegie	*Carnegie Magazine*
CarQ	*Carolina Quarterly*
Carrell	*The Carrell: Journal of the Friends of the University of Miami (Fla.) Library*
CathW	*Catholic World* (now *New Catholic World*)
CCC	*College Composition and Communication*
CE	*College English*
CEA	*CEA Critic*
CEJ	*California English Journal*
CentR	*The Centennial Review of Arts and Science*

Character and Personality
ChCen	*Christian Century*

Periodicals Cited

Chesterton Review
Chimera
ChiR   *Chicago Review*
ChS   *Christian Scholar* (now *Soundings*)
CimR   *Cimarron Review*
Cithara
CJ   *Classical Journal*
CJF   *Chicago Jewish Forum*
CJH   *Canadian Journal of History. Annales canadiennes*
                 d'histoire
CL   *Comparative Literature*
CLAJ   *College Language Association Journal*
CL&PM   *Current Literature and the Publisher's Miscellany*
ClareQ   *Claremont Quarterly*
ClasQ   *Classical Quarterly*
ClioW   *Clio: An Interdisciplinary Journal of Literature,*
                 History, and the Philosophy of History
CLC   *Columbia Library Columns*
CLQ   *Colby Library Quarterly*
CLS   *Comparative Literature Studies*
CollL   *College Literature*
Colophon
ColQ   *Colorado Quarterly*
Commentary
Complit-Litcomp
Confrontation
ConL   *Contemporary Literature* (formerly *Wisconsin*
                 Studies in Contemporary Literature)
ConnR   *Connecticut Review*
ConQ   *Congregational Quarterly*
Conradiana   *Conradiana: A Journal of Joseph Conrad*
ContempR   *Contemporary Review*
Cornhill   *Cornhill Magazine*
Costerus   *Costerus: Essays in English and American*
                 Language and Literature
CQ   *The Cambridge Quarterly*
CQR   *Church Quarterly Review*
CR   *The Critical Review*
CRCL   *Canadian Review of Comparative Literature*
Creative Reading
Cresset
Crit   *Critique: Studies in Modern Fiction*

Criterion
CritI   *Critical Inquiry: A Voice for Reasoned Inquiry into*
                  Significant Creations of the Human Spirit
Critic, The
Criticism
CritQ   *Critical Quarterly*
CritS   *Critical Survey*
Cross Currents
CSLBull   *Bulletin of the New York C. S. Lewis Society*
CSP   *Canadian Slavonic Papers*
CSR   *Christian Scholar's Review (formerly*
                  The Gordon Review)
CUF   *Columbia University Forum*
Culture
CW   *Classical World*
Cweal   *Commonweal* (New York)

Daedalus   *Daedalus: Journal of the American Academy of*
                  Arts and Sciences
Delaware Notes
DelLR   *Delaware Literary Review*
Delta   *Delta: The Cambridge Literary Review*
Descant
DHLR   *The D. H. Lawrence Review*
Diacritics   *Diacritics: A Review of Contemporary Criticism*
Dial
Dialogue
Dickensian
DilR   *Diliman Review*
Diplomat
Direction
Discourse
DM   *The Dublin Magazine*
Downside Review
DQR   *Dutch Quarterly Review of Anglo-American Letters*
DR   *Dalhousie Review*
Dreiser Newsletter
DSN   *Dickens Studies Newsletter*
DubR   *Dublin Review* (now *Wiseman Review*)
DUJ   *Durham University Journal*
Duquesne Review
DUS   *Drew University Studies*

Periodicals Cited

EA	*Études Anglaises*
E&S	*Essays and Studies by Members of the English Association*
EAS	*Essays in Arts and Sciences*
Edda	
Edinburgh	*Edinburgh Review*
EFT	*English Fiction in Transition* (now *English Literature in Transition*)
Egoist, The	
EIC	*Essays in Criticism*
EigoS	*Eigo Seinen* [*The Rising Generation*]
Eire	*Éire-Ireland: A Journal of Irish Studies*
EJ	*English Journal*
ElemE	*Elementary English*
ELH	*Journal of English Literary History*
ELLS	*English Literature and Language*
ELN	*English Language Notes*
ELT	*English Literature in Transition (1880-1920)* (formerly *English Fiction in Transition*)
ELUD	*Essays in Literature*
EM	*English Miscellany*
Encounter	
English	
EngR	*English Record*
EngRev	*English Review*
Envoy	
ER	*Études Rabelaisiennes*
ErasmusR	*Erasmus Review: A Journal of the Humanities*
ES	*English Studies*
ESA	*English Studies in Africa*
ES(A)	*English Studies* (Amsterdam)
ESC	*English Studies in Canada*
Esquire	
ET	*Expository Times*
EUQ	*Emory University Quarterly*
Europe	
Everyman	
EvR	*Evergreen Review*
EWN	*Evelyn Waugh Newsletter*
Explorations	
Extrapolation	

Feminist Studies
FHA   *Fitzgerald-Hemingway Annual*
First Person
FJS   *Fu Jen Studies*
FMLS   *Forum for Modern Language Studies*
FMod   *Filologia Moderna*
Focus
Folio   *Folio: Papers on Foreign Languages and Literature*
Folio of New Writing
Folklore
Foreground
Fortnightly   *Fortnightly Review*
Forum, The
ForumH   *Forum* (Houston)
Four Quarters
FP   *Filolõski Pregled*
FQ   *Florida Quarterly*
FR   *French Review*
FWF   *Far-Western Forum: A Review of Ancient and
                Modern Language*

GaR   *Georgia Review*
Gemini/Dialogue
Genre
GL&L   *German Life and Letters*
GorR   *The Gordon Review* (now *Christian Scholar's
                Review*)
GR   *Germanic Review*
Griffin, The
GSlav   *Germano-Slavica*
Guardian (Rangoon)
GyS   *Gypsy Scholar*

HAB   *The Humanities Association Review. La Revue de
                l'Association des Humanites* (formerly
                Humanities Association Bulletin)
Harper's
HarvA   *Harvard Advocate*
HarvM   *Harvard Monthly*
HC   *The Hollins Critic*
Here and Now
Hermathena   *Hermathena: A Dublin University Review*

Periodicals Cited

Hindustan	Hindustan Times
HJ	Hibbert Journal
HLQ	Huntington Library Quarterly
Holiday	
HopR	Hopkins Review
Horizon (L)	Horizon (London)
Horizon (N.Y.)	Horizon (New York)
Horizontes	Horizontes: Revista de la Universidad Católica de Puerto Rico
Hound & Horn	
HSE	Hungarian Studies in English
HSELL	Hiroshima Studies in English Language and Literature
HSL	Hartford Studies in Literature
HTR	Harvard Theological Review
HudR	Hudson Review
Humanist, The	
Humanist, The (London)	
Human World	
HUSL	Hebrew University Studies in Literature
Ibadan	
ICarbS	
IEY	Iowa English Bulletin: Yearbook
IFR	International Fiction Review
IH	ITA Humanidades
IJE	International Journal of Ethics
IJES	Indian Journal of English Studies
ILA	International Literary Annual
Ill. Quart.	Illinois Quarterly
Images of Truth	
Indl	Indian Literature
Innisfree	
InoL	Inostrannaya Literature
Intercollegiate Review	
Interp	Interpretations: Studies in Language and Literature
Inventario	
Invitation to Learning Reader	
IowaR	Iowa Review
IrD	Irish Digest
IrEccRec	Irish Ecclesiastical Record
IrM	The Irish Monthly
ISE	Ibadan Studies in English

Isis	
Italica	
IUR	*Irish University Review*
JA	*Jahrbuch für Amerikastudien*
JAAC	*Journal of Aesthetics and Art Criticism*
JAF	*Journal of American Folklore*
JAMA	*Journal of the American Medical Association*
JASt	*Journal of Asian Studies*
JCF	*Journal of Canadian Fiction*
JCH	*Journal of Contemporary History*
JEGP	*Journal of English and Germanic Philology*
JES	*Journal of European Studies*
JGE	*Journal of General Education*
JHI	*Journal of the History of Ideas*
JHR	*Journal of Human Relations*
JHS	*Journal of Historical Studies*
JIL	*Journal of Irish Literature*
JJQ	*James Joyce Quarterly*
JJR	*James Joyce Review*
JKUH	*Journal of Karnatak University, Humanities*
JKUR	*Jammu and Kashmir University Review*
JLN	*Jack London Newsletter*
JML	*Journal of Modern Literature*
JMSUB	*Journal of the Maharaja Sayajirao University of Baroda*
JNT	*Journal of Narrative Technique*
John O'London's Weekly	
Joliso	*Joliso: East African Journal of Literature and Society*
JPC	*Journal of Popular Culture*
JPol	*Journal of Politics*
JQ	*Journalism Quarterly*
JSCR	*Jackson [Miss.] State College Review*
Jubilee	
Junction	
Kalki	*Kalki: Studies in James Branch Cabell*
KanQ	*Kansas Quarterly* (formerly *Kansas Magazine*)
Kerygma	
KFLQ	*Kentucky Foreign Language Quarterly*
KGUAS	*Kwansei Gakuin University Annual Studies*
KM	*Kansas Magazine* (now *Kansas Quarterly*)

Periodicals Cited

KN	Kwartalnik Neofilologiczny
KPAB	Kentucky Philological Association Bulletin
KR	Kenyon Review
KSJ	Keats-Shelley Journal
L&I	Literature and Ideology
L&L	Linguistica et Litteraria
L&P	Literature and Psychology
Lang&L	Language and Literature
Lang&S	Language and Style
LanM	Les Langues Modernes
LB	Leuvense Bijdragen
LCrit	Literary Criterion
LCUP	Library Chronicle of the University of Pennsylvania (formerly University of Pennsylvania Chronicle)
LCUT	Library Chronicle of the University of Texas
LDIBR	Literary Digest International Book Review
LE&W	Literature East and West
LFQ	Literature/Film Quarterly
LHB	Lock Haven Bulletin (now Lock Haven Review)
LHR	Lock Haven Review (formerly Lock Haven Bulletin)
LHY	Literary Half-Yearly
Library, The	
Life	Life Magazine
Life and Letters	
Listener	
LitQ	Literary Quarterly
LitR	Literary Review
LittleR	Little Review
Living Age	
LM	Language Monographs
LNL	Linguistics in Literature
LonM	London Magazine
London Mercury (formerly Bookman [London])	
LonQR	London Quarterly Review
LQ&HR	London Quarterly and Holborn Review
LT	Levende Talen
MadQ	Madison Quarterly
Mad River Rev.	
Mahfil	
Mainstream	
ManchQ	Manchester Quarterly

Mandrake
ManR　　　　*Manchester Review*
MAQR　　　　*Michigan Alumnus Quarterly Review* (now *Michigan Quarterly Review*)
MarQ　　　　*Maryland Quarterly*
MarxQ　　　*Marxist Quarterly*
MCR　　　　*Melbourne Critical Review*
MDAC　　　*Mystery and Detection Annual*
Meanjin　　*Meanjin Quarterly*
Memoirs and Proceedings of the Manchester Literary and Philosophical Society
MFS　　　　*Modern Fiction Studies*
MHRev　　　*Malahat Review*
Midstream
Midway (Chicago)
Midwest　　*Midwest Journal*
Mind
MinnR　　　*Minnesota Review*
MLN　　　　*Modern Language Notes*
MLQ　　　　*Modern Language Quarterly*
MLR　　　　*Modern Language Review*
MLS　　　　*Modern Language Studies*
MN　　　　*Monumenta Nipponica*
ModA　　　*Modern Age*
ModQ　　　*Modern Quarterly*
ModR　　　*Modern Review*
ModSp　　　*Moderne Sprachen: Organ des Verbandes des Österreichischen Neuphilologen für Moderne Sprachen, Literatur, und Pädagogik*
Month
Mosaic　　*Mosaic: A Journal for the Comparative Study of Literature and Ideas*
Motive
MP　　　　*Modern Philology*
MQ　　　　*Midwest Quarterly*
MQR　　　*Michigan Quarterly Review* (formerly *Michigan Alumnus Quarterly Review*)
MR　　　　*Massachusetts Review*
Ms.
MSCS　　　*Mankato State College Studies*
MSE　　　　*Massachusetts Studies in English*
MSLC　　　*Modernist Studies: Literature and Culture 1920-1940*

Periodicals Cited

MSpr	Moderna Språk
MTQ	Mark Twain Quarterly

Mythlore [Incorporates Tolkien Journal]

Names
N&Q	Notes and Queries

Nation
National Observer
National Review (London)
National Review (New York)
Nation and Athenaeum
NC	Nineteenth Century and After
NCF	Nineteenth-Century Fiction
NConL	Notes on Contemporary Literature
NDEJ	Notre Dame English Journal
NDQ	North Dakota Quarterly

New Blackfriars
New Humanist
NewL	New Letters (formerly University of Kansas City Review and University Review)
NewLR	New Left Review

New Oxford Outlook
New Republic
New Review, The
New Society
New Statesman (formerly New Statesman and Nation)
New Worlds
New World Writing
Niekas
Nimbus (London)
Nine
NLauR	New Laurel Review
NLH	New Literary History
NLR	Navajo Language Review
NM	Neuphilologische Mitteilungen
NMQ	New Mexico Quarterly
NoAmR	North American Review

Norseman
Novel	Novel: A Forum on Fiction
NsM	Neusprachliche Mitteilungen aus Wissenschaft und Praxis
NWR	Northwest Review

NY	*New Yorker*
NYHTB	*New York Herald Tribune Books*
NYRB	*New York Review of Books*
NYTBR	*New York Times Book Review*
NYTM	*New York Times Magazine*
NZSJ	*New Zealand Slavonic Journal*
Observer	*Observer Magazine*
OhR	*Ohio Review*
OJES	*Osmania Journal of English Studies*
OL	*Orbis Litterarum*
Orcrist	*Orcrist: Bulletin of the University of Wisconsin*
	J. R. R. Tolkien Society
Orion	*Orion, A Miscellany*
OUR	*Ohio University Review*
Outlook, The	
Overland	
OW	*Orient/West*
Pacific Spectator	
PAPA	*Publications of the Arkansas Philological*
	Association
PAPS	*Proceedings of the American Philosophical Society*
Paragone	
Paris Review	
Paunch (Buffalo, N.Y.)	
PBA	*Proceedings of the British Academy*
PBSA	*Papers of the Bibliographical Society of America*
PCCTET	*Proceedings of the Conference of College Teachers*
	of English of Texas
PCL	*Perspectives on Contemporary Literature*
PCP	*Pacific Coast Philology*
PCTEB	*Pennsylvania Council of Teachers of English*
	Bulletin
PELL	*Papers on English Language and Literature*
	(now *Papers on Language and Literature*)
Per	*Perspective*
Person	*The Personalist*
Phi Kappa Phi Journ.	
Philobiblon	
PhilS	*Philological Studies*
Phoenix	

Periodicals Cited

PhoenixK	Phoenix (Korea U.)
PLL	Papers on Language and Literature (formerly Papers on English Language and Literature)
PMASAL	Papers of the Michigan Academy of Science, Arts, and Letters (now Michigan Academician)
PMLA	Publications of the Modern Language Association of America
PMLC	Papers of the Manchester Literary Club
Poetry	
PolP	Polish Perspectives
PolQ	Political Quarterly
PolR	Polish Review
PowysN	The Powys Newsletter
PP	Philologica Pragensia
PPNCFL	Proceedings of the Pacific Northwest Conference on Foreign Languages
PPR	Philosophy and Phenomenological Research
PQ	Philological Quarterly
PR	Partisan Review
Present Opinion	
Proof	Proof: Yearbook of American Bibliographical and Textual Studies
Prose	
PrS	Prairie Schooner
PSQ	Political Science Quarterly
PSSHR	Philippine Social Sciences and Humanities Review
PsyR	Psychoanalytic Review (formerly Psychoanalysis and the Psychoanalytic Review)
PUASAL	Proceedings of the Utah Academy of Sciences, Arts, and Letters
PULC	Princeton University Library Chronicle
Punch	
PURBA	Panjab University Research Bulletin (Arts)
QJS	Quarterly Journal of Speech
QJSE	Quarterly Journal of Speech Education
QQ	Queen's Quarterly
QR	Quarterly Review
QRL	Quarterly Review of Literature
Quadrant	
Quest (Bombay)	
Ramparts	

RANAM	*Rescherches Anglaises et Américaines*
ReAL	*RE: Arts and Letters*; now *RE: Artes Liberales*
RecL	*Recovering Literature*
REL	*Review of English Literature*
Religion in Life	
Renascence	
Rendezvous	*Rendezvous: Journal of Arts and Letters*
Reporter	
RES	*Review of English Studies*
Review of Reviews	
RevL	*Revista de Letras*
RevN	*La Revue Nouvelle*
RIP	*Rice Institute Pamphlets* (now *Rice U. Studies*)
RLC	*Revue de Littérature Comparée*
RLV	*Revue des Langues Vivantes*
RMS	*Renaissance and Modern Studies*
RQ	*Riverside Quarterly*
RR	*Romanic Review*
RS	*Research Studies*
RUO	*Revue de l'Université d'Ottawa*
RUS	*Rice University Studies* (formerly *Rice Institute Pamphlets*)
RUSEng	*Rajasthan University Studies in English*
RusR	*Russian Review*
SAB	*South Atlantic Bulletin*
SAQ	*South Atlantic Quarterly*
SB	*Studies in Bibliography: Papers of the Bibliographical Society of the University of Virginia*
SCB	*South Central Bulletin*
School Librarian, The	
Science and Society	
Scientific Monthly	
Scrutiny	
SDR	*South Dakota Review*
SEER	*Slavonic and East European Review*
SEL	*Studies in English Literature, 1500-1900*
SELit	*Studies in English Literature* (English Literary Society of Japan)
SELL	*Studies in English Literature and Language*
Serif	*The Serif*

Periodicals Cited

SFQ	Southern Folklore Quarterly
SFS	Science Fiction Studies
SGG	Studia Germanica Gandensia
ShAB	Shakespeare Association Bulletin
ShawR	Shaw Review
Shenandoah	
SHR	Southern Humanities Review
SHVBVGG	Spieghel Historiael Van de Bond Van Gentste Germanisten
SIH	Studies in the Humanities
SITC	Studies in the 20th Century
SLitI	Studies in the Literary Imagination
SLUSHTA	St. Louis University Studies in Honor of St. Thomas Aquinas
SN	Studia Neophilologica
SNL	Satire Newsletter
SNNTS	Studies in the Novel
SocR	Sociological Review
SoQ	The Southern Quarterly
SoR	Southern Review
SoRA	Southern Review: An Australian Journal of Literary Studies
Southerly (Sydney)	
SovL	Soviet Literature
SovR	Soviet Review
SP	Studies in Philology
Spectator	
Spectrum	
Speculum	
SPJ	St. Pancreas Journal
SQ	Shakespeare Quarterly
SR	Sewanee Review
SRAZ	Studia Romanica et Anglica Zagrabiensia
SRC	Studies in Religion/Sciences Religieuses
SRL	Saturday Review of Literature (now Saturday Review)
SSF	Studies in Short Fiction
Standard	
Standpunte	
Strand	Strand Magazine
Studies	Studies: An Irish Quarterly

StudiesÉ   *Studies in English* (now *Texas Studies in Literature and Language*)
Style (U. of Arkansas)
Sufi   *Sufi Quarterly*
Summary (London)
SUS   *Susquehanna University Studies*
SWR   *Southwest Review*
Symposium
Symposium(S) (Syracuse U. Press)

TamR   *Tamarack Review*
T&T   *Time and Tide*
TAr   *Theatre Arts*
TC   *Twentieth Century* (London)
TC(A)   *Twentieth Century* (Australia)
TCL   *Twentieth Century Literature*
TCS   *Twentieth Century Studies*
TCV   *Twentieth Century Verse*
TES   *Temple English Studies*
TES(L)   *Times Educational Supplement* (London)
TFSB   *Tennessee Folklore Society Bulletin* (Middle Tennessee State U.)
Theology
Theoria   *Theoria: A Journal of Studies in the Arts, Humanities and Social Sciences* (U. of Natal)
Thoth (Dept. of English, Syracuse U.)
Thought
Threshold
Time
Tirade
TLR   *Turnbull Library Record*
TLS   *Times Literary Supplement* (London)
Tolkien Journal [Incorporated into *Mythlore*]
Tomorrow
Topic
TP   *Terzo Programma*
TQ   *Texas Quarterly*
TR   *La Table ronde*
Trace
Transition
TriQ   *Tri-Quarterly*

Periodicals Cited

Triumph
Trivium
Trollopian
TSB   *Thoreau Society Bulletin*
TSE   *Tulane Studies in English*
TSL   *Tennessee Studies in Literature*
TSLL   *Texas Studies in Literature and Language* (formerly
                 Studies in English)
TWA   *Transactions of the Wisconsin Academy of Science,
                 Arts, and Letters*
Twin Circle
Two Cities

UA   *United Asia*
UCC   *University of California Chronicle*
UCPES   *University of California Publications in English
                 Studies*
UDR   *University of Dayton Review*
UES   *Unisa English Studies*
UKCR   *University of Kansas City Review* (later *University
                 Review*; now *New Letters*)
ULR   *University of Leeds Review*
UMSE   *University of Mississippi Studies in English*
Unicorn
Unilit
Unitas
Universitas
UPoR   *University of Portland Review*
UR   *University Review* (formerly *University of
                 Kansas City Review*; now *New Letters*)
URev   *University Review*
Use of English, The
UTQ   *University of Toronto Quarterly*
UWR   *University of Windsor Review*

Vanity Fair
Venture
Vinduet
Virginia Woolf Misc.
VLM   *Voprosi Literaturi*
VN   *Victorian Newsletter*
Vogue
VolR   *Volusia Review*

VQ	*Visvabharati Quarterly*
VQR	*Virginia Quarterly Review*
VS	*Victorian Studies*
VWQ	*Virginia Woolf Quarterly*
WAL	*Western American Literature*
WascanaR	*Wascana Review*
WaterR	*Waterloo Review*
WCR	*West Coast Review*
Wellsian	
WelshR	*Welsh Review*
Westerly	
WestmR	*Westminster Review*
WestR	*Western Review*
WF	*Western Folklore*
WGCR	*West Georgia College Review*
WHR	*Western Humanities Review*
WLWE	*World Literature Written in English*
WN	*A Wake Newslitter*
World Review	
World To-Day	
WuW	*Welt und Wort*
WR	*Wiseman Review* (formerly *Dublin Review*)
WS	*Word Study*
WSCL	*Wisconsin Studies in Contemporary Literature* (now *Contemporary Literature*)
WSL	*Wisconsin Studies in Literature*
WVUPP	*West Virginia University Philological Papers*
XR	*X, A Quarterly Review*
XUS	*Xavier University Studies*
Yale Literary Mag.	
YWES	*Year's Work in English Studies*
YCGL	*Yearbook of Comparative and General Literature*
YES	*Yearbook of English Studies*
YR	*Yale Review*
ZAA	*Zeitschrift für Anglistik und Amerikanistik*
ZRL	*Zagadnienia Rodzajów Literackich*

PART I: NOVELISTS

RICHARD ALDINGTON

GENERAL STUDIES

Baum, Paull F. "Mr. Richard Aldington." *SAQ*, 28 (1929), 201-08.

Benkovitz, Miriam J. "Nine for Reeves: Letters from Richard Aldington." *BNYPL*, 69 (1965), 249-374.

Bergonzi, Bernard. *Heroes' Twilight*, 61-62, 182-86.

Connolly, Cyril. *The Evening Colonnade*, 233-36.

Cunard, Nancy. *These Were the Hours*. Ed. and intro. Hugh Ford. Carbondale: Southern Illinois Univ. Press, 1969, 51-58, 156-60.

Dodd, Lee W. "Cursed Like Orestes." *SatR*, 6 (October 12, 1929), 232-33.

Gates, Norman T. "Richard Aldington and The Clerk's Press." *OhR*, 13 (1971), 21-27.

Kershaw, Alister. "Introduction." *Richard Aldington: Selected Critical Writings, 1928-1960*. Carbondale: Southern Illinois Univ. Press, 1970, xv-xx.

_____, and Frédéric-Jacques Temple, eds. *Richard Aldington: An Intimate Portrait*. Carbondale: Southern Illinois Univ. Press, 1965.

Megata, Morikima. "Richard Aldington's Letters, 1952-1962." *Kobe City University Journal*, 20 (1969), 23-39; 20 (1970), 95-111; 21 (1970), 65-73; 22 (1971), 107-16.

Moore, Harry T. "Preface." *Richard Aldington: Selected Critical Writings, 1928-1960*. Carbondale: Southern Illinois Univ. Press, 1970, vii-xiv.

_____. "Preface." Richard Aldington, *Soft Answers*. Carbondale: Southern Illinois Univ. Press, 1967, v-xii.

Reed, John R. *Old School Ties*, 185-87, 201-07.

Rosenfeld, Paul. *By Way of Art*, 236-49.

Rosenthal, Sidney. "Richard Aldington and the Excitement of Reason." *Twenty-Seven to One*. Ed. Bradford B. Broughton, 133-43.

Thatcher, David S. "Richard Aldington's Letters to Herbert Read." *MHRev*, 15 (1970), 5-44.

Urnov, Mikhail. "Foreword." *Richard Aldington: A Bibliographical Index*. Moscow: All-Union State Library of Foreign Literature, 1965, 4-15.

Vickery, John B. "Mythopoesis and Modern Literature." *The Shaken Realist*. Ed. Melvin J. Friedman and John B. Vickery, 219-23.

Waugh, Alec. *My Brother Evelyn and Other Portraits*, 60-72.

See also: Swinnerton, *Georgian*; Vines.

KINGSLEY AMIS

BIBLIOGRAPHIES

Firchow, Peter. *The Writer's Place*, 15-38.

Richard Aldington, continued

Vann, J. Donn, and James T. F. Tanner. "Kingsley Amis: A Checklist of Recent Criticism." *BB*, 26 (1969), 105, 111, 115-17.

INTERVIEWS
Amis, Kingsley. "My Kind of Comedy." *TC*, 170 (1961), 46-50.

GENERAL STUDIES
Allsop, Kenneth, *The Angry Decade*, 51-66.

Amis, Kingsley. "Real and Made-Up People." *TLS*, July 27, 1973, 847.

Bergonzi, Bernard. "Kingsley Amis." *LonM*, n.s. 3, 10 (January 1964), 50-65.

Bićanić, Sonia. "Cats, Birds and Freedom." *SRAZ*, 29-32 (1970-71), 515-22.

Caplan, Ralph "Kingsley Amis." *Contemporary British Novelists.* Ed. Charles Shapiro, 3-15.

Chase, Richard. "Middlebrow England: The Novels of Kingsley Amis." *Commentary*, 22, 3 (September 1956), 263-69.

Colville, Derek. "The Sane New World of Kingsley Amis." *BuR*, 9, 1 (1960), 46-57.

Davie, Donald. *Thomas Hardy and British Poetry*, 69-71, 83-90, 98-104.

"An Englishman's Bond." *TLS*, May 27, 1965, 408.

Gindin, James J. "The Reassertion of the Personal." *TQ*, 1, 4 (1958), 126-34.

Glicksberg, Charles I. "The Literature of the Angry Young Men." *ColQ*, 8 (1960), 293-303.

Gorer, Geoffrey. "The Perils of Hypergamy." *New Statesman*, 53 (1957), 566-68.

Green, Martin. "Amis and Salinger: The Latitude of Private Conscience." *ChiR*, 11, 4 (1958), 20-25.

————. "British Comedy and the British Sense of Humour: Shaw, Waugh, and Amis." *TQ*, 4, 3 (1961), 217-27.

Hamilton, Kenneth. "Kingsley Amis, Moralist." *DR*, 44 (1964), 339-47.

Heppenstall, Rayner. *The Fourfold Tradition*, 213-48.

Hilty, Peter. "Kingsley Amis and Mid-Century Humor." *Discourse*, 3 (1960), 26-45.

Holloway, John. "Tank in the Stalls: Notes on the 'School of Anger'." *HudR*, 10 (1957), 424-29.

Hopkins, Robert H. "The Satire of Kingsley Amis' *I Like It Here.*" *Crit*, 8, 3 (1966), 62-70.

Hurrell, John D. "Class and Conscience in John Braine and Kingsley Amis." *Crit*, 2, 1 (1958), 39-53.

"In a Buyer's Market." *TLS*, October 10, 1968, 1145.

James, Clive. "Profile 4: Kingsley Amis." *The New Review*, 1, 4 (1974), 21-28.

Lebowitz, Naomi. "Kingsley Amis: The Penitent Hero." *Per*, 10 (1958), 129-36.

Lodge, David. *Language of Fiction*, 243-67.

_____. "The Modern, the Contemporary, and the Importance of Being Amis." *CritQ*, 5 (1963), 335-54.

Macleod, Norman. " 'This familiar regressive series': Aspects of Style in the Novels of Kingsley Amis." *Edinburgh Studies in English and Scots*. Ed. A. J. Aitken, Angus McIntosh and Herman Pálsson, 121-43.

Marshment, Margaret. "Racism for Fun." *Joliso*, 2, 2 (1974), 61-68.

Meckier, Jerome. "Looking Back at Anger: The Success of a Collapsing Stance." *DR*, 52 (1972), 47-58.

Mehoke, James S. "Sartre's Theory of Emotion and Three English Novelists: Waugh, Green, and Amis." *WSL*, 3 (1966), 105-13.

Moberg, George. "Structure and Theme in Amis' Novels." *CEA*, 25, 6 (1963), 7, 10.

O'Connor, William Van. "The New University Wits." *KR*, 20 (1958), 38-50.

Orel, Harold. "The Decline and Fall of a Comic Novelist: Kingsley Amis." *KanQ*, 1, 3 (1969), 17-22.

Parker, R. B. "Farce and Society: The Range of Kingsley Amis." *WSCL*, 2, 3 (1961), 27-38.

Rippier, Joseph S. *Some Postwar English Novelists*, 138-58.

Ross, T. J. "Manners, Morals, and Pop: On the Fiction of Kingsley Amis." *SITC*, 4 (1969), 61-73.

Scott, J. D. "Britain's Angry Young Men." *SatR*, 40 (July 27, 1957), 8-11.

"The Turns of a Plain Man." *TLS*, April 6, 1973, 393.

Voorhees, Richard J. "Kingsley Amis: Three Hurrahs and a Reservation." *QQ*, 79 (1972), 38-46.

Wilson, Edmund. *The Bit Between My Teeth*, 274–81.

See also: Allen, *Tradition*; Bergonzi, *Situation*; Gindin, *Postwar*; W. O'Connor, *New*; Rabinovitz.

LUCKY JIM

Allen, Walter. "New Novels." *New Statesman*, 47 (1954), 136–37.

Boyle, Ted E., and Terence Brown. "The Serious Side of Kingsley Amis's *Lucky Jim*." *Crit*, 9, 1 (1967), 100-07.

Brophy, Brigid. *Don't Never Forget*, 217-22.

Conquest, Robert. "Christian Symbolism in *Lucky Jim*." *CritQ*, 7 (1965), 87-92.

Richard Aldington, continued

Cunliffe, W. Gordon. "Interesting Things." *Insight II.* Ed. John V. Hagopian and Martin Dolch, 11-12.
Noon, William T. "Satire: Poison and the Professor." *EngR*, 11 (1960), 53-56.
Proctor, Mortimer R. *The English University Novel*, 175-76.

ONE FAT ENGLISHMAN
Kelly, Edward. "Satire and Word Games in Amis' *Englishman.*" *SNL*, 9 (1972), 132–38.
Powell, Anthony. "Kingsley's Heroes." *Spectator*, 211 (November 29, 1963), 709-10.
Soule, George. "The High Cost of Plunging." *CarlM*, 5 (1964), 106-11.

TAKE A GIRL LIKE YOU
Coleman, John. "King of Shaft." *Spectator*, 205 (September 23, 1960), 445–46.
Moers, Ellen. "Still Angry." *Commentary*, 31, 6 (June 1961), 542-44.
Ross, T. J. "Lucky Jenny, or Affluent Times." *New Republic*, 144 (March 27, 1961), 21-23.
Sissman, L. E. "Kingsley Amis at Halfway House." *NY*, 45 (April 26, 1969), 163-70.

BRENDAN BEHAN
GENERAL STUDIES
Boyle, Ted E. *Brendan Behan.* New York: Twayne, 1969.
Gerdes, Peter R. *The Major Works of Brendan Behan.* Frankfurt: Lang, 1973.
McCann, Sean, ed. *The World of Brendan Behan.* London: New English Library, 1965; New York: Twayne, 1966.
MacInnes, Colin. "The Writings of Brendan Behan." *LonM*, n.s. 2, 5 (August 1962), 53-61.
O'Connor, Ulick. *Brendan Behan.* London: Hamilton, 1970.
Porter, Raymond J. *Brendan Behan.* New York: Columbia Univ. Press, 1973.

ARNOLD BENNETT
BIBLIOGRAPHIES
Gerber, Helmut E. [?]. "Arnold Bennett." *ELT*, 10, 4 (1967), 204-08.
Hepburn, James G. "Arnold Bennett." *EFT*, 1, 1 (1957), 7-12.
Kennedy, James G. "Arnold Bennett." *ELT*, 6, 1 (1963), 19-25.
Miller, Anita. "Arnold Bennett." *ELT*, 13, 1 (1970), 40-45; 14, 1 (1971), 55-59.

Riemer, Werner W. "Arnold Bennett: A Check List of Secondary Literature." *BNYPL*, 77 (1974), 342-57.

GENERAL STUDIES
Agate, James E. *Alarums and Excursions*, 259-64.
Allen, Walter. *Arnold Bennett*. London: Home and Van Thal, 1948; Denver: Swallow, 1949; New York: AMS, 1973.
Barker, Dudley. *Writer by Trade: A View of Arnold Bennett*. London: Allen and Unwin, 1966; *Writer by Trade: A Portrait of Arnold Bennett*. New York: Atheneum, 1966.
Bellamy, William. *The Novels of Wells, Bennett, and Galsworthy*, 71-87, 144-64, 211-16.
Bergonzi, Bernard. "The Novelist as Hero." *TC*, 164 (1958), 444-55.
Blanche, Jacques-Emile. *More Portraits of a Lifetime*, 178-83.
Braybrooke, Patrick. *Peeps at the Mighty*, 147-58.
Bullett, Gerald W. *Modern English Fiction*, 34-45.
Chesterton, G. K. *Fancies Versus Fads*, 101-09.
Collins, Norman. *The Facts of Fiction*, 258-75.
Conacher, W. M. "Arnold Bennett and the French Realists." *QQ*, 56 (1949), 409-17.
Cooper, Frederic T. *Some English Story Tellers*, 206-31.
Cross, Wilbur L. *Four Contemporary Novelists*, 63-98.
Curtin, Frank D. "Arnold Bennett and After." *If By Your Art*. Ed. Agnes L. Starrett, 117-36.
Darton, F. J. Harvey. *Arnold Bennett*. New York: Holt, 1915.
Davis, Oswald H. *The Master: A Study of Arnold Bennett*. London: Johnson, 1966.
Decker, Clarence R. *The Victorian Conscience*, 32-33, 164-67.
Drabble, Margaret. *Arnold Bennett: A Biography*. London: Weidenfeld and Nicolson; New York: Knopf, 1974.
_____. "The Fearful Fame of Arnold Bennett." *Observer*, May 21, 1967, 13-14.
Dutton, George B. "Arnold Bennett, Showman." *SR*, 33 (1925), 64-72.
Elwin, Malcolm. *Old Gods Falling*, 329-62.
Ervine, St. John G. *Some Impressions of My Elders*, 61-89.
Ford, Ford Madox. *It Was The Nightingale*, 18-20.
Fraser, John. "George Sturt's Apprenticeship." *REL*, 5, 1 (1964), 35-50.
Gardiner, Alfred G. *Portraits and Portents*, 98-105.
Guedalla, Philip. *A Gallery*, 70-76.
Hackett, Francis. "Arnold Bennett." *SatR*, 7 (May 2, 1931), 789-90.
_____. *Horizons*, 139-62.
Hall, James. *Arnold Bennett: Primitivism and Taste*. Seattle: Univ. of Washington Press, 1959.

7

Arnold Bennett, *continued*

Hepburn, James G. *The Art of Arnold Bennett*. Bloomington: Indiana Univ. Press, 1963.
———. "Manuscript Notes for *Lord Raingo*." *EFT*, 5, 1 (1962), 1-5.
Heywood, C. "D. H. Lawrence's *The Lost Girl* and Its Antecedents by George Moore and Arnold Bennett." *ES*, 47 (1966), 131-34.
Hoffmann, Richard S. "Proportion and Incident in Joseph Conrad and Arnold Bennett." *SR*, 32 (1924), 79-92.
Hynes, Samuel, ed. *THE AUTHOR'S CRAFT and Other Critical Writings of Arnold Bennett*. Lincoln: Univ. of Nebraska Press, 1968.
———. "The Whole Contention Between Mr. Bennett and Mrs. Woolf." *Novel*, 1 (1967), 34-44.
Jackson, Frank H. "Economics in Literature." *Duquesne Rev.*, 3 (1958), 80-85.
James, Henry. "The Younger Generation." *TLS*, March 19, 1914, 133-34; April 2, 1914, 157-58.
Kennedy, James G. "Arnold Bennett: *Künstler* and *Bürger*." *EFT*, 5, 2 (1962), 1-20.
———. "Reassuring Facts in *The Pretty Lady, Lord Raingo*, and Modern Novels." *ELT*, 7, 3 (1964), 131-42.
Knight, Grant C. *The Novel in English*, 326-32.
Kreutz, Irving. "Mr. Bennett and Mrs. Woolf." *MFS*, 8 (1962), 103-15.
Lafourcade, Georges. *Arnold Bennett, A Study*. London: Muller, 1939.
Lucas, John. *Arnold Bennett: A Study of His Fiction*. London: Methuen, 1974.
Lynd, Robert. "Arnold Bennett." *Post-Victorians*, by Various Authors, 69-82.
———. *Books and Authors*, 188-95.
Maugham, W. Somerset. *The Vagrant Mood*, 220-34.
———. "W. Somerset Maugham on Arnold Bennett." *Novelists on Novelists*. Ed. Louis Kronenberger, 347-54.
Mencken, H. L. *Prejudices*, 1st ser., 36-51.
Muir, Edwin. "Arnold Bennett." *Scrutinies*. Ed. Edgell Rickword, 15-28.
Munro, John M. "The Case for Compromise: Arnold Bennett's *Imperial Palace*." *ArielE* 2, 4 (1972), 18-29.
Mylett, Andrew, ed. *Arnold Bennett: THE EVENING STANDARD Years, "Books and Persons." 1926-1931*. Hamden, Conn.: Archon, 1974.
Nicholson, Norman. *Man and Literature*, 40-48.
Oates, Joyce Carol. "Bricks and Mortar." *Ms.*, 3, 2 (August 1974), 34-36.
Phelps, Gilbert. *The Russian Novel in English Fiction*, 110-12.
Pilkington, Frederick. "Methodism in Arnold Bennett's Novels." *ContempR*, 189 (1956), 109-15.

Priestley, J. B. *Figures in Modern Literature*, 3-30.

———. "Mr. Arnold Bennett." *London Mercury*, 9 (1924), 394-406.

Roberts, Thomas R. *Arnold Bennett's Five Towns Origins*. City of Stoke-on-Trent, Libraries, Museums and Information Committee, 1961.

Roby, Kinley. "Arnold Bennett: Shaw's Ten O'Clock Scholar." *ShawR*, 13 (1970), 96-104.

———. "Arnold Bennett's Social Conscience." *MFS*, 17 (1971-72), 513-24.

———. *A Writer at War: Arnold Bennett, 1914-1918*. Baton Rouge: Louisiana State Univ. Press, 1972.

Scarfe, Francis. "Arnold Bennett 'A Synthetic Impressionist'." *EA*, 25 (1972), 408-11.

Shaw, G. Bernard. *Selected Prose*, 996-1004.

Simons, J. B. *Arnold Bennett and His Novels*. Oxford: Blackwell, 1936.

Sitwell, Osbert. *Noble Essences*, 317-34.

Squire, John C. "Arnold Bennett: A Postscript." *Essays of the Year, 1930-1931*, by Various Authors, 126-34.

Swinnerton, Frank A. *Tokefield Papers*, 125-31.

Thompson, Edward R. *Portraits of the New Century*, 55-58.

Tillier, Louis. *Studies in the Sources of Arnold Bennett's Novels*. Paris: Didier, 1969.

Tully, Jim. "Arnold Bennett." *The American Spectator Year Book*. Ed. George Jean Nathan, et al., 109-15.

———. *A Dozen and One*, 155-66.

Wain, John. *Arnold Bennett*. New York: Columbia Univ. Press, 1967.

———. *Preliminary Essays*, 121-56.

Wallace, Archer. *Religious Faith of Great Men*, 30-55.

Waterhouse, Keith. "Hero: Arnold Bennett." *Punch*, 254 (May 15, 1968), 698-700.

West, Geoffrey [Geoffrey H. Wells]. *The Problem of Arnold Bennett*. London: Joiner and Steele, 1932.

West, Rebecca. *The Strange Necessity*, 215-31.

Wilson, Angus. "A Man from the Midlands." *TLS*, July 12, 1974, 737-38.

———. "Arnold Bennett's Novels." *LonM*, 1, 9 (October), 59-67.

Wilson, Harris, ed. *Arnold Bennett and H. G. Wells: A Record of a Personal and a Literary Friendship*. Urbana: Univ. of Illinois Press; London: Hart-Davis, 1960.

Woolf, Virginia. *Collected Essays*, v. 1, 319-37.

"The World of Wells and Bennett." *TLS*, August 28, 1953, xxvi.

Wright, Walter F. *Arnold Bennett: Romantic Realist*. Lincoln: Univ. of Nebraska Press, 1971.

_____. "The Comic Spirit in Arnold Bennett." *KanQ*, 1, 3 (1969), 35-40.
See also: Adcock, *Gods*; Aiken, *ABC*; Beach, *20th*; Beresford; Bradbury, *Social*; P. Braybrooke, *Philosophies*; A. Collins, *20th*; Cunliffe, *Half-Century, 20th Century*; Drew, *Modern*; Eagleton; Edgar, *Art*; Follett and Follett; Forster, *Aspects*; Frierson; Gindin, *Harvest*; Goldring, *Reputations*; J. Gray; C. Hamilton; Hind, *Authors*; Hynes, *Edwardian*; Kettle; Lacon; Lovett, *History*; MacCarthy, *Memories*; McCullough; Mackenzie; Marble; Maugham; Muller, *Modern*; Orage, *Essays*; Overton, *Authors*; W. Phelps; Pritchett, *Living*; Richards; Scott-James, *50, Personality*; Sherman, *Contemporary*; Swinden; Swinnerton, *Background, Foreground, Georgian*; Tillyard, *Epic*; Wagenknecht, *Cavalcade*; Ward, *20th*; Weygandt; H. Williams, *Modern*.

CLAYHANGER TRILOGY
[CLAYHANGER, HILDA LESSWAYS, THESE TWAIN]
Ball, David. "Some Sources for Bennett's *Clayhanger* Trilogy." *English*, 21 (1972), 13-17.
Harris, Wendell V. "Molly's 'Yes': The Transvaluation of Sex in Modern Fiction." *TSLL*, 10 (1968), 107-18.
Hepburn, James G. "The Two Worlds of Edwin Clayhanger." *BUSE*, 5 (1961), 246-55.

THE OLD WIVES' TALE
Siegel, Paul N. "Revolution and Evolution in Bennett's *The Old Wives' Tale*." *ClioW*, 4 (1975), 159-72.
See also: Brewster and Burrell; Swinden.

RICEYMAN STEPS
Durkin, Brian. "Some New Lights on *Riceyman Steps*." *ELT*, 10, 2(1967), 66-80.
Flory, Evelyn A. "*Riceyman Steps*": The Role of Violet and Elsie." *ELT*, 14, 2(1971), 93-102.
Hepburn, James G. "The Notebook for *Riceyman Steps*." *PMLA*, 78 (1963), 257-61.
_____. "Some Curious Realism in *Riceyman Steps*." *MFS*, 8 (1962), 116-26.

ELIZABETH BOWEN
BIBLIOGRAPHIES
Sellery, J'nan. "Elizabeth Bowen: A Check List." *BNYPL*, 74 (1970), 219-74.

INTERVIEWS
Breit, Harvey. *The Writer Observed*, 107-09.

GENERAL STUDIES
Austin, Allan E. *Elizabeth Bowen*. New York: Twayne, 1971.
Blodgett, Harriet. *Patterns of Reality: Elizabeth Bowen's Novels*. The Hague: Mouton, 1975.
Bowen, Elizabeth. *Seven Winters: Memories of a Dublin Childhood and Afterthoughts: Pieces on Writing*. New York: Knopf, 1962.
Brooke, Jocelyn. *Elizabeth Bowen*. London: Longmans, Green, 1952.
Cecil, David. "Chronicler of the Heart: The British Writer, Elizabeth Bowen." *Vogue*, 122 (November 1, 1953), 118-19.
Coles, Robert. *Irony in the Mind's Eye: Essays on Novels by James Agee, Elizabeth Bowen, and George Eliot*. Charlottesville: Univ. of Virginia Press, 1974.
Coles, William. "The Pattern of Responsibility in the Novels of Elizabeth Bowen." *HarvA*, 126, 2 (1952), 20-22, 37-40.
Daiches, David. "The Novels of Elizabeth Bowen." *EJ*, 38 (1949), 305-13.
Dorenkamp, Angela G. " 'Fall or Leap': Bowen's *The Heat of the Day*." *Crit*, 10, 3 (1968), 13-21.
Fitzsimmons, T. "World of Love." *SR*, 63 (1955), 323-30.
Gindin, James J. "Ethical Structures in John Galsworthy, Elizabeth Bowen, and Iris Murdoch." *Forms of Modern British Fiction*. Ed. Alan W. Friedman, 15-41.
Greene, George. "Elizabeth Bowen: Imagination as Therapy." *Per*, 14 (1965) 42-52.
Greene, Graham. "The Dark Backward: A Footnote." *London Mercury*, 32 (1935), 562-65.
Hall, James. *The Lunatic Giant in the Drawing Room*, 17-55.
Hardwick, Elizabeth. "Elizabeth Bowen's Fiction." *PR*, 16, 11 (1949), 1114-21.
Harkness, Bruce. "The Fiction of Elizabeth Bowen." *EJ*, 44 (1955), 499-506.
Heath, William W. *Elizabeth Bowen: An Introduction to Her Novels*. Madison: Univ. of Wisconsin Press, 1961.
Kenney, Edwin J. *Elizabeth Bowen*. Lewisburg, Pa.: Bucknell Univ. Press, 1974.
Kiely, Benedict. "Elizabeth Bowen." *IrM*, 78 (April 1950), 175-81.
_____. *Modern Irish Literature*, 151-59.
McDowell, Frederick P. W. "Elizabeth Bowen's *The Little Girls*." *Crit*, 7, 1 (1964), 139-43.

O'Faoláin, Seán. "Elizabeth Bowen." *Britain Today*, 143 (March 1948), 16-19.

Parrish, Paul A. "The Loss of Eden: Four Novels of Elizabeth Bowen." *Crit.* 15, 1 (1973), 86-100.

Pendry, E. D. *The New Feminism of English Fiction*, 120-52.

Prescott, Orville. *In My Opinion*, 92-109.

Pritchett, V. S. "The Future of English Fiction." *PR*, 15, 10 (1948), 1063-70.

Rowse, Alfred L. *The English Spirit*, 247-59.

Rupp, Richard Henry. "The Post-War Fiction of Elizabeth Bowen." *XUS*, 4 (1965), 55-67.

Sackville-West, Edward. "An Appraisal: Ivy Compton-Burnett and Elizabeth Bowen." *Horizon (L)*, 13 (June 1946), 367-85.

―――. *Inclinations*, 78-103.

Seward, Barbara. "Elizabeth Bowen's World of Impoverished Love." *CE*, 18 (1956), 30-37.

Sharp, Sister M. Corona, O.S.U. "The House as Setting and Symbol in Three Novels by Elizabeth Bowen." *XUS*, 2 (1963), 93-103.

Snow, Lotus. "The Uncertain 'I': A Study of Elizabeth Bowen's Fiction." *WHR*, 4 (1950), 299-310.

Stokes, Edward. "Elizabeth Bowen—Pre-Assumptions or Moral Angle?" *AUMLA*, 11 (1959), 35-47.

Strickhausen, Harry. "Elizabeth Bowen and Reality." *SR*, 73 (1965), 158-65.

Strong, L. A. G. "Elizabeth Bowen." *Living Writers*. Ed. Gilbert Phelps, 58-69.

―――. *Personal Remarks*, 132-45.

Sullivan, Walter. "A Sense of Place: Elizabeth Bowen and the Landscape of the Heart." *SR*, 84 (1975), 142-49.

Wagner, Geoffrey. "Elizabeth Bowen and the Artificial Novel." *EIC*, 13 (1963), 155-163.

Why Do I Write? An Exchange of Views Between Elizabeth Bowen, Graham Greene and V. S. Pritchett.

Wyndham, Francis. "Twenty-five Years of the Novel." *The Craft of Letters in England*. Ed. John Lehmann, 44-59.

See also: Allen, *Tradition*; A. Collins, *20th*; Fraser; Frierson; Gill; Karl; O'Faoláin; Marković; Prescott.

THE DEATH OF THE HEART

Bogan, Louise. *Selected Criticism*, 125-28.

Heinemann, Alison. "The Indoor Landscape in Bowen's *The Death of the Heart*." *Crit*, 10, 3 (1968), 5-12.

Van Duyn, Mona. "Pattern and Pilgrimage: A Reading of *The Death of the Heart.*" *Crit*, 4, 2 (1961), 52-66.

EVA TROUT
"Elizabeth Bowen's New Novel." *TLS*, January 30, 1969, 101.

Moss, H. "The Heiress Is an Outsider." *NYTBR*, October 13, 1968, 1, 28, 30.

Taylor, Elizabeth. "The Progress of Eva." *New Statesman*, 77 (1969), 119.

Wyndham, Francis. "Eva Trout." *LonM*, n.s. 8, 12 (March 1969), 89-91.

JOHN BRAINE

GENERAL STUDIES
Alayrac, Claude. "Inside John Braine's Outsider." *Caliban*, 8 (1971), 111-38.

Allsop, Kenneth. *The Angry Decade*, 86-93.

Glicksberg, Charles I. "The Literature of the Angry Young Men." *ColQ*, 8 (1960), 293-303.

Gorer, Geoffrey. "The Perils of Hypergamy." *New Statesman*, 53 (1957), 566-68.

Holloway, John. "Tank in the Stalls: Notes on the 'School of Anger'." *HudR*, 10 (1957), 424-29.

Hurrell, John D. "Class and Conscience in John Braine and Kingsley Amis." *Crit*, 2, 1 (1958), 39-53.

Jelly, Oliver. "Fiction and Illness." *REL*, 3, 1 (1962), 80-89.

Lee, James W. *John Braine*. New York: Twayne, 1968.

Meckier, Jerome. "Looking Back at Anger: The Success of a Collapsing Stance." *DR*, 52 (1972), 47-58.

"Rasping at Progs." *TLS*, August 29, 1968, 913.

Rippier, Joseph S. *Some Postwar English Novelists*, 178-92.

Scott, J. D. "Britain's Angry Young Men." *SatR*, 40 (July 27, 1957), 8-11.

Shestakov, Dmitri. "John Braine Facing His Fourth Novel." *SovL*, no. 8 (August 1964), 178-81.

See also: Fraser; Hall, *Tragic;* Karl.

ANTHONY BURGESS

INTERVIEWS
Bunting, Charles T. "An Interview in New York with Anthony Burgess." *SNNTS*, 5 (1973), 505-29.

Anthony Burgess, continued

Churchill, Thomas. "An Interview with Anthony Burgess." *MHRev*, 17 (January 1971), 103-27.
Cullinan, John. "Anthony Burgess." *Paris Review. Writers at Work*, 4th ser., 323-58.
Page, Malcolm. "Anthony Burgess: The Author as Performer." *WCR*, 4, 3 (1970), 21-24.
Reilly, Lemuel, "An Interview with Anthony Burgess." *DelLR*, 2 (1973), 48-55.

GENERAL STUDIES

Aggeler, Geoffrey. "Between God and Notgod: Anthony Burgess' *Tremor of Intent*." *MHRev*, 17 (January 1971), 90-102.
———. "The Comic Art of Anthony Burgess." *ArQ*, 25 (1969), 234-51.
———. "Pelagius and Augustine in the Novels of Anthony Burgess." *ES*, 55 (1974), 43-55.
———. "A Wagnerian Affirmation: Anthony Burgess' *The Worm and the Ring*." *WHR*, 27 (1973), 401-10.
Burgess, Anthony. "The Seventeenth Novel." *Page 2*. Ed. Francis Brown, 85-89.
Chalpin, Lila. "Anthony Burgess' Gallows Humor in Dystopia." *TQ*, 16, 3 (1973), 73-84.
Davis, Earle. " 'Laugh Now—Think Later!': The Genius of Anthony Burgess." *KM*, 1968, 7-12.
DeVitis, A. A. *Anthony Burgess*. New York: Twayne, 1972.
Evans, Robert O. "The *nouveau roman*, Russian Dystopias, and Anthony Burgess." *SLitI*, 6, 2 (1973), 27-37.
Fitzpatrick, William P. "Anthony Burgess' Brave New World: The Ethos of Neutrality." *SIH*, 3 (1972), 32-33.
———. "Black Marketeers and Manichees: Anthony Burgess' Cold War Novels." *WVUPP*, 21 (1974), 78-91.
Friedman, Melvin J. "Anthony Burgess and James Joyce: A Literary Confrontation." *LCrit*, 9, 4 (1971), 71-83.
Hicks, Granville. "The Fertile World of Anthony Burgess." *SatR*, 50 (July 15, 1967), 27-29, 36.
Horder, John. "Art that Pays." *Guardian*, October 10, 1964, 5.
Kennard, Jean E. *Number and Nightmare*, 131-54.
LeClair, Thomas. "Essential Opposition: The Novels of Anthony Burgess." *Crit*, 12, 3 (1971), 77-94.
Mitchell, Julian. "Reputations—X: Anthony Burgess." *LonM*, n.s. 3, 11 (February 1964), 48-54.
Morris, Robert K. *The Consolations of Ambiguity: An Essay on the Novels of Anthony Burgess*. Columbia: Univ. of Missouri Press, 1971.

Pritchard, William H. "The Novels of Anthony Burgess." *MR*, 7 (1966), 525-39.
Stinson, John J. "Anthony Burgess: Novelist on the Margin." *JPC*, 7 (1973), 136-51.
_____. "The Manichee World of Anthony Burgess." *Renascence*, 26 (1973), 37-47.
Sullivan, Walter. "Death Without Tears: Anthony Burgess and the Dissolution of the West." *HC*, 6, 2 (1969), 1-11.
See also: Bergonzi, *Situation*; Enright, *Onion*.

A CLOCKWORK ORANGE
Anderson, Ken. "A Note on *A Clockwork Orange*." *NConL*, 2, 5 (1972), 5-7.
Brophy, Elizabeth. "*A Clockwork Orange*: English and Nadsat." *NConL*, 2, 2 (1972), 4-6.
Connelly, Wayne C. "Optimism in Burgess' *A Clockwork Orange*." *Extrapolation*, 14 (1972), 25-29.
Cullinan, John. "Anthony Burgess' *A Clockwork Orange*: Two Versions." *ELN*, 9 (1972), 287-92.
Dimeo, Steven. "The Ticking of an Orange." *RQ*, 5 (1973), 318-21.
Evans, Robert O. "Nadsat: The Argot and Its Implications in Anthony Burgess' *A Clockwork Orange*." *JML*, 1 (1971), 406-10.
Fulkerson, Richard P. "Teaching *A Clockwork Orange*." *CEA*, 37, 1 (1974), 8-10.
Gilbert, Basil. "Kubrick's Marmalade: The Art of Violence." *Meanjin*, 33 (1974), 157-62.
Isaacs, Neil D. "Unstuck in Time: *Clockwork Orange* and *Slaughterhouse-Five*." *LFQ*, 1 (1973), 122-31.
McCracken, Samuel. "Novel into Film, Novelist into Critic: *A Clockwork Orange* Again." *AR*, 32 (1973), 427-36.
Plank, Robert. "The Place of Evil in Science Fiction." *Extrapolation*, 14 (1973), 100-11.

ENDERBY
Aggeler, Geoffrey. "Mr. Enderby and Mr. Burgess." *MHRev*, 10 (April 1969), 104-10.
Fitzpatrick, William P. "The Sworn Enemy of Pop: Burgess' Mr. Enderby." *BWVACET*, 1, 1 (1974), 28-37.
Hoffmann, Charles G., and A. C. Hoffmann. "Mr. Kell and Mr. Burgess: Inside and Outside Mr. Enderby." *The Shaken Realist*. Ed. Melvin J. Friedman and John B. Vickery, 300-10.
Solotaroff, Theodore. *The Red Hot Vacuum*, 269-75.

Anthony Burgess, continued

MF

Aggeler, Geoffrey. "Incest and the Artist: Anthony Burgess' *MF* as Summation." *MFS*, 18 (1972-73), 529-43.

Kennard, Jean. "*MF*: A Separable Meaning." *RQ*, 6 (1975), 200-06.

NOTHING LIKE THE SUN

Burgess, Anthony. "Genesis and Headache." *Afterwords*. Ed. Thomas McCormack, 28-47.

Schoenbaum, Samuel. *Shakespeare's Lives*. Oxford: Clarendon, 1970, 765-66.

THE WANTING SEED

Kateb, George. "Politics and Modernity: The Strategies of Desperation." *NLH*, 3 (1971), 93-111.

Murdoch, Brian. "The Overpopulated Wasteland: Myth in Anthony Burgess' *The Wanting Seed*." *RLV*, 39 (1973), 203-17.

JOYCE CARY

BIBLIOGRAPHIES

Beebe, Maurice, et al. "Criticism of Joyce Cary: A Selected Checklist." *MFS*, 9, 3 (1963), 284-88.

Reed, Peter J. "Joyce Cary: A Selected Checklist of Criticism." *BB*, 25 (1968), 133-34, 151.

INTERVIEWS

Breit, Harvey. *The Writer Observed*, 167-69.

Burrows, J., and A. Hamilton. "Joyce Cary." *Paris Review. Writers at Work*, 1st ser., 51-67.

Cohen, Nathan. "A Conversation with Joyce Cary." *TamR*, 3 (1957), 5-15.

"The Novelist at Work: A Conversation Between Joyce Cary and Lord David Cecil." *Adam*, 18, 212-13 (1950), 15-25.

SPECIAL ISSUES

Adam International Review [*Adam*], 18, 212-13 (1950).
Modern Fiction Studies [*MFS*], 9, 3 (1963).

GENERAL STUDIES

Acton, Harold, "The Artist." *Adam*, 31, 301-03 (1966), 9-14.

Adams, Hazard. "Joyce Cary's Swimming Swan." *ASch*, 29 (1960), 235-39.

Allen, Walter. *Joyce Cary*. London: Longmans, Green, 1953; rev. 1954, 1956, 1963.

Barr, Donald. "A Careful and Profound Thinker." *Adam*, 18, 212-13 (1950), 30-31.

Bloom, Robert. *The Indeterminate World: A Study of the Novels of Joyce Cary*. Philadelphia: Univ. of Pennsylvania Press, 1962.

Cary, Joyce. "A Novel is a Novel is a Novel." *Adam*, 18, 212-13 (1950), 1-3.

_____. "The Way a Novel Gets Written." *Adam*, 18, 212-13 (1950), 3-11.

Case, Edward. "The Free World of Joyce Cary." *ModA*, 3 (1959), 115-24.

Davin, Dan. "Five Windows Darken: Recollections of Joyce Cary." *Encounter*, 44 (June 1975), 24-33.

Echeruo, Michael J. C. "Mood and Meaning in Joyce Cary's *A House of Children*." *PURBA*, 6, 1 (1975), 3-8.

Fisher, Barbara. "Joyce Cary's Published Writings." *BLR*, 8 (1970), 213-28.

Foster, Malcolm. "Fell of the Lion, Fleece of the Sheep." *MFS*, 9, 3 (1963), 257-62.

_____. *Joyce Cary: A Biography*. Boston: Houghton Mifflin, 1968.

Friedman, Alan W. "Joyce Cary's Cubistic Morality." *ConL*, 14 (1973), 78-96.

Gardner, Helen. "The Novels of Joyce Cary." *E&S*, 28 (1975), 76-93.

Geering, R. G. "Joyce Cary: The Man and His Work." *Quadrant*, 3, 3 (Winter 1959), 45-51.

Hardy, Barbara. "Form in Joyce Cary's Novels." *EIC*, 4 (1954), 180-90.

Hoffmann, Charles G. "Joyce Cary and the Comic Mask." *WHR*, 13 (1959), 135-42.

_____. "Joyce Cary: Art and Reality. The Interaction of Form and Narrator." *UKCR*, 26 (1960), 273-83.

_____. *Joyce Cary: The Comedy of Freedom*. Pittsburgh: Univ. of Pittsburgh Press, 1964.

Holloway, John. "Joyce Cary's Fiction: Modernity and 'Sustaining Power'." *TLS*, Aug. 7, 1959, xiv-xv.

Johnson, Pamela Hansford. "Three Novelists and the Drawing of Character: C. P. Snow, Joyce Cary and Ivy Compton-Burnett." English Association, London. *Essays and Studies*, n.s., v. 3 (1950), 82-99.

Kanu, S. H. *A World of Everlasting Conflict: Joyce Cary's View of Man and Society*. Ibadan: Ibadan Univ. Press, 1974.

Karl, Frederick R. "Joyce Cary: The Moralist as Novelist." *TCL*, 5 (1960), 183-96.

Kennedy, Alan. *The Protean Self*, 99-149.

Joyce Cary, continued

Kennedy, Richard S. "Joyce Cary's Comic Affirmation of Life." *PCTEB*, 13 (1966), 3-14.

King, Carlyle. "Joyce Cary and the Creative Imagination." *TamR*, 10 (1959), 39-51.

Larsen, Golden L. *The Dark Descent: Social Change and Moral Responsibility in the Novels of Joyce Cary.* London: M. Joseph, 1965; New York: Roy, 1966.

Monas, Sidney. "What to Do with a Drunken Sailor." *HudR*, 3 (1950), 466-74.

Noble, Robert W. *Joyce Cary.* New York: Barnes and Noble; Edinburgh: Oliver and Boyd, 1973.

O'Connor, William Van. *Joyce Cary.* New York: Columbia Univ. Press, 1966.

Owen, B. Evan. "The Supremacy of the Individual in the Novels of Joyce Cary." *Adam*, 18, 212-13 (1950), 25-29.

Raskin, Jonah. *The Mythology of Imperialism*, 222-41, 294-331.

Rosenthal, Michael. "Joyce Cary's Comic Sense." *TSLL*, 13 (1971), 337-46.

Salz, Paulina J. "The Philosophical Principles in Joyce Cary's Work." *WHR*, 20 (1966), 159-65.

Seymour-Smith, Martin. "Zero and the Impossible." *Encounter*, 9 (November 1957), 38-51.

Simmons, James. "Joyce Cary in Ireland." *On the Novel.* Ed. Benedikt S. Benedikz, 140-60.

Starkie, Enid. "Joyce Cary: A Personal Portrait." *VQR*, 37 (1961), 110-34; Royal Soc. of Lit. of the U. K., London. *Essays by Divers Hands*, v. 32, 125-44.

Steinbrecher, George, Jr. "Joyce Cary: Master Novelist." *CE*, 18 (1957), 387-95.

Stevenson, Lionel. "Joyce Cary and the Anglo-Irish Tradition." *MFS*, 9, 3 (1963), 210-16.

Stewart, Douglas G. *The Ark of God*, 129-58.

Stewart, Robert. "Understanding English Conservatism, with Apologies to Joyce Cary." *CJH*, 6 (1971), 153-69.

Teeling, John. "Joyce Cary's Moral World." *MFS*, 9, 3 (1963), 276-83.

Van Horn, Ruth G. "Freedom and Imagination in the Novels of Joyce Cary." *Midwest*, 5 (1952-53), 19-30.

West, Anthony. "Footloose and Fancy-Free." *NY*, 36 (April 30, 1960), 170-76.

Wolkenfeld, Jack. *Joyce Cary: The Developing Style.* New York: New York Univ. Press, 1968.

Woodcock, George. "Citizens of Babel: A Study of Joyce Cary." *QQ*, 63 (1956), 236-42.

Wright, Andrew. *Joyce Cary: A Preface to His Novels.* London: Chatto and Windus, 1958.
_____. "Joyce Cary: Fragments of an *Oeuvre*." *ILA*, 1 (1958), 162-64.
_____. "Joyce Cary's Unpublished Work." *LonM*, 5, 1 (January 1958), 35-42.
_____. "A Note on Joyce Cary's Reputation." *MFS*, 9, 3 (1963), 207-09.
See also: Allen, *Tradition*; Gill; Gindin, *Harvest*; Hall, *Tragic*; Karl; Kettle; McCormick; Marković; Prescott; Webster.

AFRICAN NOVELS
[AISSA SAVED, AN AMERICAN VISITOR, THE AFRICAN WITCH, MR. JOHNSON]

Barba, Harry. "Cary's Image of the African in Transition." *UKCR*, 29 (1963), 215-21, 291-96.
Cary, Joyce. "My First Novel." *Listener*, 49 (1953), 637.
Collins, Harold R. "Joyce Cary's Troublesome Africans." *AR*, 13 (1953) 397-406.
Cosman, Max. "The Protean Joyce Cary." *Cweal*, 69 (1959), 596-98.
Echeruo, M. J. C. *Joyce Cary and the Novel of Africa.* London: Long-Green; New York: African Pub., 1973.
French, Warren G. "Joyce Cary's American Rover Girl." *TSLL*, 2 (1960), 281-91.
Fyfe, Christopher. "The Colonial Situation in *Mister Johnson*." *MFS*, 9, 3 (1963), 226-30.
Hall, Alan. "The African Novels of Joyce Cary." *Standpunte*, 12 (March-April 1958), 40-55.
Hoffmann, Charles G. "Joyce Cary's African Novels." *SAQ*, 62 (1963), 229-43.
Kamoli, Arthur. "The European Image of Africa and the African." *Busara*, 2 (1969), 51-53.
Killam, G. D. *Africa in English Fiction*, 123-69.
Larson, Charles R. "Mr. Johnson—Faithful African Portrait? *AT*, 16, 1 (1969), 19-20.
Mahood, Molly M. *Joyce Cary's Africa.* London: Methuen; Boston: Houghton Mifflin, 1965.
Majumdar, Bimalendu. "Joyce Cary's African Novels: Vision of an Artist." *Essays Presented to Prof. Amalendu Bose.* Ed. Dipendu Chakrabarti, 91-97.
Moody, P. R. "Road and Bridge in Joyce Cary's African Novels." *BRMMLA*, 21 (1967), 145-49.
Moore, Gerald. "*Mr. Johnson* Reconsidered." *BO*, 4 (1958), 16-23.
Sandison, Alan G. "Living Out the Lyric: *Mr. Johnson* and the Present Day." *English*, 20 (1971), 11-16.

Joyce Cary, continued

Smith, B. R. "Moral Evaluation in *Mister Johnson.*" *Crit*, 11, 2 (1969), 101-10.
Tucker, Martin. *Africa in Modern Literature*, 23-25, 37-47.

THE CAPTIVE AND THE FREE
Hicks, Granville. "Joyce Cary's Last Novel." *SatR*, 42 (January 24, 1959), 14.
Hoffmann, Charles G. "*The Captive and the Free*: Joyce Cary's Unfinished Trilogy." *TSLL*, 5 (1963), 17-24.
Miller, Richard Hugh. "Faith Healing and God's Love in Joyce Cary's *The Captive and the Free.*" *AntigR*, 21 (1975), 71-73.
Watson, Kenneth. "*The Captive and the Free*: Artist, Child, and Society in the World of Joyce Cary." *English*, 16 (1966), 49-54.

CASTLE CORNER
Hoffmann, Charles G. " 'They Want To Be Happy': Joyce Cary's Unfinished *Castle Corner* Series." *MFS*, 9, 3 (1963), 217-25.
Weintraub, Stanley. "*Castle Corner*: Joyce Cary's *Buddenbrooks.*" *WSCL*, 5 (1964), 54-63.

CHARLEY IS MY DARLING
Webb, Bernice L. "Animal Imagery and Juvenile Delinquents in Joyce Cary's *Charley Is My Darling.*" *SCB*, 32 (1972), 240-42.
———. "Joyce Cary's Redefinition of Car Theft, Illicit Sex, and Pornography in *Charley Is My Darling.*" *NLauR*, 2, 1 (1972), 19-22.
West, Anthony. "Footloose and Fancy-Free." *NY*, 36 (April 30, 1960), 170-76.

A FEARFUL JOY
Eastman, Richard M. "Historical Grace in Cary's *A Fearful Joy.*" *Novel*, 1 (1968), 150-57.
Pittock, Malcolm. "Joyce Cary: *A Fearful Joy.*" *EIC*, 13 (1963), 428-32.

FIRST (ARTISTIC) TRILOGY
[HERSELF SURPRISED, TO BE A PILGRIM, THE HORSE'S MOUTH]
Adams, Hazard. "Blake and Gulley Jimson: English Symbolists." *Crit*, 3, 1 (1959), 3-14.
———. "Joyce Cary's Three Speakers." *MFS*, 5 (1959), 108-20.
Adams, Robert H. "Freedom in *The Horse's Mouth.*" *CE*, 26 (1965), 451-54, 459-60.
Alter, Robert. *Rogue's Progress*, 129-32.

Brawer, Judith. "The Triumph of Defeat: A Study of Joyce Cary's *First Trilogy*." *TSLL*, 10 (1969), 629-34.

Cary, Joyce. "Three New Prefaces." *Adam*, 18, 212-13 (1950), 11-14.

Faber, Kathleen R., and M. D. Faber. "An Important Theme of Joyce Cary's Trilogy." *Discourse*, 11 (1968), 26-31.

Garant, Jeanne. "Joyce Cary's Portrait of the Artist." *RLV*, 24 (1958), 476-86.

Hamilton, Kenneth. "Boon or Thorn? Joyce Cary and Samuel Beckett on Human Life." *DR*, 38 (1959), 433-42.

Hoffmann, Charles G. "The Genesis and Development of Joyce Cary's First Trilogy." *PMLA*, 78 (1963), 431-39.

Jones, Ernest. "The Double View." *Nation*, 170 (1950), 184-86.

Kelly, Edward H. "The Meaning of *The Horse's Mouth*." *MLS*, 1, 2 (1971), 9-11.

Lyons, Richard S. "Narrative Method in Cary's *To Be a Pilgrim*." *TSLL*, 6 (1964), 269-79.

Messenger, Ann P. "A Painter's Prose: Similes in Joyce Cary's *The Horse's Mouth*." *ReAL*, 3, 2 (1970), 16-28.

Mitchell, Giles R. *The Art Theme in Joyce Cary's First Trilogy*. The Hague: Mouton, 1971.

Mustanoja, Tauno F. "Two Painters: Joyce Cary and Gulley Jimson." *NM*, 61 (1960), 221-44.

Petri, Lucretia. "A Tentative Analysis of 'Bourgeois' Substitutes and ' . . . Colour' Compounds in Joyce Cary's *The Horse's Mouth*." *AUB-LG*, 21 (1972), 35-44.

Ready, William B. "Joyce Cary." *Critic*, 18 (June-July 1960), 9-10, 59-60.

Reed, Peter J. " 'The Better the Heart': Joyce Cary's Sara Monday." *TSLL*, 15 (1973), 357-70.

_____. "Getting Stuck: Joyce Cary's Gulley Jimson." *TCL*, 16 (1970), 241-52.

_____. "Holding Back: Joyce Cary's *To Be a Pilgrim*." *ConL*, 10 (1969), 103-16.

Ryan, Marjorie. "An Interpretation of Joyce Cary's *The Horse's Mouth*." *Crit*, 2, 1 (1958), 29-38.

Seltzer, Alvin J. "Speaking Out of Both Sides of *The Horse's Mouth*: Joyce Cary vs. Gulley Jimson." *ConL*, 15 (1974), 488-502.

Shapiro, Stephen A. "Joyce Cary's *To Be A Pilgrim*: Mr. Facing-Both-Ways." *TSLL*, 8 (1966), 81-91.

_____. "Leopold Bloom and Gulley Jimson: The Economics of Survival." *TCL*, 10 (1964), 3-11.

Stockholder, Fred. "The Triple Vision in Joyce Cary's First Trilogy." *MFS*, 9, 3 (1963), 231-44.

Joyce Cary, continued

Wright, Andrew. "An Authoritative Text of *The Horse's Mouth*." *PBSA*, 61 (1967), 100-09.
See also: Allen, *Reading*.

POLITICAL TRILOGY
[PRISONER OF GRACE, EXCEPT THE LORD, NOT HONOUR MORE]
Battaglia, Francis J. "Spurious Armageddon: Joyce Cary's *Not Honour More*." *MFS*, 13 (1967), 479-91.
Bettman, Elizabeth R. "Joyce Cary and the Problem of Political Morality." *AR*, 17 (1957), 266-72.
Kerr, Elizabeth M. "Joyce Cary's Second Trilogy." *UTQ*, 29 (1960), 310-25.
King, Carlyle. "Joyce Cary and the Creative Imagination." *TamR*, 10 (1959), 39-51.
Mitchell, Giles R. "Joyce Cary's *Except the Lord*." *ArlQ*, 2, 2 (1969), 71-82.
_____. "Joyce Cary's *Prisoner of Grace*." *MFS*, 9, 3 (1963), 263-75.
Nyce, Benjamin. "Joyce Cary's Political Trilogy: The Atmosphere of Power." *MLQ*, 32 (1971), 89-106.
Rosenthal, Michael, "Joyce Cary's Ambiguous Chester Nimmo." *SAQ*, 70 (1971), 332-40.

G. K. CHESTERTON
BIBLIOGRAPHIES
Sullivan, John. *Chesterton Continued: A Bibliographical Supplement*. London: Univ. of London Press, 1968.
_____. *G. K. Chesterton: A Bibliography*. London: Univ. of London Press; New York: Barnes and Noble, 1958.

SPECIAL ISSUES
Mark Twain Quarterly, [MTQ], 1, 3 (1937), 1-24.

GENERAL STUDIES
Agar, Herbert. "A Great Democrat." *SoR*, 3 (1937), 95-105.
Alexander, Calvert. *The Catholic Literary Revival*, 233-54.
Amis, Kingsley. "Four Fluent Fellows: An Essay on Chesterton's Fiction." *Encounter*, 41 (October 1973), 94-100.
Batchelor, John. "Chesterton as an Edwardian Novelist." *Chesterton Rev.*, 1 (1974), 23-35.
Belloc, Hilaire. "Gilbert Keith Chesterton." *SatR*, 14 (July 4, 1936), 3-4, 14.

_____. *On the Place of Gilbert Chesterton in English Letters.* London; Sheed and Ward, 1940.

Bergonzi, Bernard. "Chesterton and/or Belloc." *CritQ*, 1 (1959), 64-71.

Bogaerts, Anthony M. A. *Chesterton and the Victorian Age.* Hilversum: Rosenbeek En Venemans Uitgeversbedr. N. V., 1940.

Bond, Raymond T., ed. *The Man Who Was Chesterton.* New York: Dodd, Mead, 1937; New York: Arno, 1973.

Boyd, Ernest A. *Portraits,* 193-96.

Boyd, Ian. *The Novels of G. K. Chesterton: A Study in Art and Propaganda.* New York: Barnes and Noble, 1975.

Bradbrook. B. R. "The Literary Relationship Between G. K. Chesterton and Karel Čapek." *SEER,* 39 (1961), 327-38.

Braybrooke, Patrick. *Gilbert Keith Chesterton.* Philadelphia: Lippincott, 1922.

_____. *Some Catholic Novelists,* 3-33.

Bridges, Horace J. *Criticisms of Life,* 42-76.

Cammaerts, Emile. *The Laughing Prophet: The Seven Virtues and G. K. Chesterton.* London: Methuen, 1937.

Chambers, Leland H. "Gide, Santayana, Chesterton, and Browning." *CLS,* 7 (1970), 216-28.

Chesterton, Cecil. *Gilbert K. Chesterton: A Criticism.* New York: Lane, 1909.

Churchill, R. C. "The Man Who Was Sunday: G. K. Chesterton, 1874-1936." *ContempR,* 224 (1974), 12-15.

Clarke, Margaret. "Chesterton the Classicist." *DubR,* 229 (1955), 51-67.

Clipper, Lawrence J. *G. K. Chesterton.* New York: Twayne, 1974.

Cunningham, Lawrence S. "Chesterton as Mystic." *ABR,* 26 (1975), 16-24.

_____. "Chesterton Reconsidered." *Thought,* 47 (1972), 271-79.

Eaker, J. Gordon. "G. K. Chesterton Among the Moderns." *GaR,* 13 (1959), 152-60.

Edwards, Dorothy. "G. K. Chesterton." *Scrutinies.* Ed. Edgell Rickword, 29-40.

Ervine, St. John G. *Some Impressions of My Elders,* 90-112.

Evans, Maurice. *G. K. Chesterton.* New York: Haskell House, 1972.

Feeney, Leonard. "The Metaphysics of Chesterton." *Thought,* 17 (1942), 22-36.

Fielding, K. J. "Chesterton Revisited." *DSN,* 6 (1975), 14-15.

Freeman, John. *English Portraits and Essays,* 1-32.

Gassman, Janet. "A Second Look at G. K. Chesterton." *Religion in Life,* 28 (1959), 443-54.

G. K. Chesterton, continued

Gilkes, A. N. "G. B. S., G. K. C. and Paradox." *Fortnightly*, n.s. 168 (1950), 266-70.
Green, V. H. H. "Gilbert Keith Chesterton: I. The Challenge of the Age." *Theology*, 43 (1941), 93-101; "II. The Response of G. K. C." *Theology*, 43 (1941), 150-55.
Hamilton, Kenneth M. "G. K. Chesterton and George Orwell: A Contrast in Prophecy." *DR*, 31 (1951), 198-205.
Hamilton, Robert. "The Rationalist from Fairyland." *QR*, 305 (1967), 444-53.
Hardie, W. F. R. "The Philosophy of G. K. Chesterton." *HJ*, 29 (1931), 449-64.
Harris, Frank. *Contemporary Portraits*, 3d ser., 61-69.
Hart, Jeffrey. "In Praise of Chesterton." *YR*, 53 (1963), 49-60.
Hetzler, Leo A. "Chesterton and the Man in the Forest." *Chesterton Rev.*, 1 (1974), 11-18.
Hollis, Christopher. *Gilbert Keith Chesterton*. London: Longmans, Green, 1954.
————. *The Mind of Chesterton*. London: Hillis and Carter; Coral Gables, Fla.: Univ. of Miami Press, 1970.
Jago, David. "The Metaphysician as Fiction-Writer: G. K. Chesterton's Narrative Techniques." *AntigR*, 22 (1975), 84-99.
John, V. V. "The Chestertonian Style." *CathW*, 184 (1957), 369-74.
Kelly, Hugh. "G. K. Chesterton: His Philosophy of Life." *Studies*, 31 (1942), 83-97.
Kenner, Hugh. *Paradox in Chesterton*. New York: Sheed and Ward, 1947.
Kirk, Russell. "Chesterton, Madmen, and Madhouses." *ModA*, 15 (1971), 6-16.
Knox, Ronald A. "Chesterton in His early Romances." *DubR*, 199 (1936), 351-65.
Kunkel, Francis L. "The Priest as Scapegoat in the Modern Catholic Novel." *Ramparts*, 1 (1963), 72-78.
Las Vergnas, Raymond. *Chesterton, Belloc, Baring*. Tr. C. C. Martindale. New York: Sheed and Ward, 1938.
Lea, F. A. "G. K. Chesterton." *Modern Christian Revolutionaries*. Ed. Donald Attwater, 89-157.
————. *The Wild Knight of Battersea*. London: James Clarke, 1945.
Lewis, C. S. "Notes on the Way." *T&T*, 26 (1946), 1070-71.
Lowther, F. H. "G. K. Chesterton: The Man and his Work." *LonQR*, 168 (1943), 335-41.
Lunn, Arnold H. M. *Roman Converts*, 209-65.
McGovern, Eugene. "Some Notes on Chesterton." *CSLBull*, 5, 7 (1974), 6-8.

McLuhan, Marshall. "G. K. Chesterton: A Practical Mystic." *DR*, 15 (1936), 455-64.

Marcu, Valeriu. *Men and Forces of Our Time*, 163-74.

Mason, Michael. "Chesterbelloc." *TC*, 176-77 (1968-69), 84-87.

Monod, Sylvère. "1900-1920: The Age of Chesterton." *Dickensian*, 66 (1970), 101-20.

Morley, Christopher. *Powder of Sympathy*, 218-22.

Noyes, Alfred. "The Centrality of Chesterton." *QR*, 291 (1953), 43-50.

Pfleger, Karl. *Wrestlers with Christ*, 157-81.

Scott, William T. *Chesterton and Other Essays*. New York: Eaton and Mains, 1912.

Sewell, Elizabeth, "G. K. Chesterton: The Giant Upside Down." *Thought*, 30 (1955), 555-76.

Sheed, Wilfred. *The Morning After*, 259-75.

Sherman, Stuart P. *Emotional Discovery of America*, 165-80.

Slosson, Edwin E. *Six Major Prophets*, 129-89.

Sprug, Joseph W., ed. *An Index to G. K. Chesterton*. Washington, D. C.: Catholic Univ. Press, 1966.

Sullivan, John, ed. *G. K. Chesterton: A Centenary Appraisal*. New York: Barnes and Noble, 1974.

Versfeld, M. "Chesterton and St. Thomas." *ESA*, 4 (1961), 128-46.

Ward, Leo R. "The Innocence of G. K. Chesterton." *ModA*, 19 (1975), 146-56.

Ward, Maisie. *Gilbert Keith Chesterton*. New York: Sheed and Ward, 1943.

――――. *Return to Chesterton*. London: Sheed and Ward, 1952.

West, Julius. *G. K. Chesterton*. New York: Dodd, Mead, 1916.

Wills, Garry. *Chesterton: Man and Mask*. New York: Sheed and Ward, 1961.

Woodruff, Douglas. "On Newman, Chesterton, and Exorbitance." *For Hilaire Belloc*. Ed. Douglas Woodruff, 30-48.

Woolf, Samuel Johnson. *Drawn From Life*, 321-29.

See also: Adcock, *Glory*; Bergonzi, *Turn*; A. Collins, *20th*; Cunliffe, *20th Century*; Hamilton; Hind, *Authors*; Hynes, *Edwardian*; Lacon; Lodge, *Novelist*; Lynd, *Old*; Maurois; Orage, *Readers*; Scott-James, *50*; Swinnerton, *Background, Georgian*; Vines; H. Williams, *Modern*.

IVY COMPTON-BURNETT

INTERVIEWS

"A Conversation Between I. Compton-Burnett and M. Jourdain." *Orion*, 1 (1945), 20-28.

"Interview with Miss Compton-Burnett." *REL*, 3, 4 (1962), 96-112.
Kermode, Frank. "The House of Fiction: Interviews with Seven English Novelists." *PR*, 30 (1963), 61-82.

GENERAL STUDIES

Amis, Kingsley. "One World and Its Way." *TC*, 158 (1955), 168-75.
Baldanza, Frank. *Ivy Compton-Burnett*. New York: Twayne, 1964.
Balutowa, Bronislawa. "The Group Dynamics in the Plots of Ivy Compton-Burnett." *ZRL*, 13, 1 (1970), 75-94.
————. "Type Versus Character in the Novels of Ivy Compton-Burnett." *KN*, 17 (1970), 377-98.
Bogan, Louise. *Selected Criticism*, 189-90.
Brophy, Bridget. *Don't Never Forget*, 167-70.
Burkhart, Charles, ed. *The Art of I. Compton-Burnett: A Collection of Critical Essays*. London: Gollancz, 1972.
————. *I. Compton-Burnett*. London: Gollancz, 1965.
Curtis, Mary M. "The Moral Comedy of Miss Compton-Burnett." *WSCL*, 5 (1964), 213-21.
Ginger, John. "Ivy Compton-Burnett." *LonM*, 9, 10 (January 1970), 58-71.
Gold, Joseph. "Exit Everybody: The Novels of Ivy Compton-Burnett." *DR*, 42 (1962), 227-38.
Greenfield, Stanley B. "*Pastors and Masters*: The Spoils of Genius." *Criticism*, 2 (1960), 66-80.
Iser, Wolfgang. *The Implied Reader*, 152-63, 234-56.
Jefferson, D. W. "A Note on Ivy Compton-Burnett." *REL*, 1, 2 (1960), 19-24.
Johnson, Pamela Hansford. *I. Compton-Burnett*. London: Longmans, Green, 1951.
————. "Three Novelists and the Drawing of Character: C. P. Snow, Joyce Cary and Ivy Compton-Burnett." English Association, London. *Essays and Studies*, n.s., v. 3 (1950), 82-99.
Levinsky, Ruth. "Literary Trends and Two Novelists: Nathalie Sarraute and Ivy Compton-Burnett." *PCCTET*, 37 (1972), 25-28.
Liddell, Robert. *The Novels of Ivy Compton-Burnett*. New York: R. West; London: Gollancz, 1955.
————. *A Treatise on the Novel*, Appendix III, 146-163.
McCabe, Bernard. "Ivy Compton-Burnett: An English Eccentric." *Crit*, 3, 2 (1960), 47-63.
McCarthy, Mary. "The Inventions of I. Compton-Burnett." *Encounter*, 27 (November 1966), 19-31.
————. *The Writings on the Wall*, 145-52.

MacSween, Roderick J. "Ivy Compton-Burnett: Merciless Understanding." *AntigR*, 7 (1971), 39-46.

May, James Boyer. "Ivy Compton-Burnett: A Time Exposure." *Trace*, 49 (1963), 92-99.

Nevius, Blake. *Ivy Compton-Burnett*. New York: Columbia Univ. Press, 1970.

Pendry, E. D. *The New Feminism of English Fiction*, 90-119.

Pittock, Malcolm. "Ivy Compton-Burnett's Use of Dialogue." *ES*, 51 (1970), 43-46.

Prescott, Orville. *In My Opinion*, 92-109.

Preston, John. "The Matter in a Word." *EIC*, 10 (1960), 348-56.

Reaney, James. "The Novels of Ivy Compton-Burnett." *CanF*, 29 (1949), 11-12.

Sackville-West, Edward. "An Appraisal: Ivy Compton-Burnett and Elizabeth Bowen." *Horizon (L)*, 13 (June 1946), 367-85.

_____. *Inclinations*, 78-103.

_____. "Ivy Compton-Burnett." *Living Writers*. Ed. Gilbert Phelps, 79-93.

Sarraute, Nathalie. *The Age of Suspicion* 112-17.

Snow, Lotus. " 'Good is Bad Condensed': Ivy Compton-Burnett's View of Human Nature." *WHR*, 10 (1956), 271-76.

Sprigge, Elizabeth. *The Life of Ivy Compton-Burnett*. New York: Braziller, 1973.

Spurling, Hilary. *Ivy When Young: The Early Life of I. Compton-Burnett, 1884-1919*. London: Gollancz, 1974.

Strachey, Richard. "The Works of Ivy Compton-Burnett." *Life and Letters*, 12, 64 (1935), 30-36.

"When an Age Is Ended." *TLS*, February 5, 1971, 145.

Wilson, Angus. "Evil in the English Novel." *KR*, 29 (1967), 167-94.

_____. "Ivy Compton-Burnett." *LonM*, 2, 7 (August 1955), 64-70.

See also: Allen, *Tradition*; Bowen, *Impressions*; Gillie, *Movements*; Karl; Kettle; Prescott; Webster; A. West, *Principles*.

JOSEPH CONRAD

BIBLIOGRAPHIES

Beebe, Maurice. "Criticism of Conrad: A Selected Checklist." *MFS*, 1 (1955), 30-45; 10 (1964), 81-106.

Bojarski, Edmund A., and H. R. Stevens, eds. *Conrad in Academe: A Bibliography*. Ann Arbor: Pierian, 1970.

Chapple, J. A. V. "Conrad." *The English Novel*. Ed. A. E. Dyson, 300-13.

Joseph Conrad, continued

Conradiana. (publishes an annual bibliography of criticism)
Ehrsam, Theodore. *A Bibliography of Joseph Conrad.* Metuchen, N.J.: Scarecrow, 1969.
Lohf, Kenneth A., and Eugene P. Sheehy. *Joseph Conrad at Mid-Century: Editions and Studies, 1895-1955.* Minneapolis: Univ. of Minnesota Press, 1957.
Monteiro, George. "Addenda to the Bibliographies of Conrad, Cooke, Damon, Ford, Glasgow, Holmes, Jewett, Lewis, Mumford, Robinson, and Scott." *PBSA*, 69 (1975), 273-75.
Teets, Bruce E., and Helmut E. Gerber, eds. *Joseph Conrad: A Bibliography of Writings about Him.* DeKalb: Northern Illinois Univ. Press, 1971.

INTERVIEWS
Clemens, Cyril. "A Chat with Joseph Conrad." *Conradiana*, 2, 2 (1970), 97-103.
Rascoe, Burton. *We Were Interrupted*, 291-95.

SPECIAL ISSUES
London Magazine [LonM], 4, 11 (November 1957), 21-49.
Modern Fiction Studies [MFS], 1, 1 (1955).
Modern Fiction Studies [MFS], 10, 1 (1964).
Polish Review [PolR], 20, 2-3 (1975), 5-222.

GENERAL STUDIES
Adicks, Richard. "Conrad and the Politics of Morality." *HAB*, 23, 2 (1972), 3-7.
Allen, Jerry. "Conrad's River." *CUF*, 5, 1 (1962), 29-35.
————. *The Sea Years of Joseph Conrad.* Garden City, N. Y.: Doubleday, 1965.
Allen, Mary. "Melville and Conrad Confront Stillness." *RS*, 40 (1972), 122-30.
Allen, Walter. *Six Great Novelists*, 135-82.
Anderson, James A. "Conrad and Baroja: Two Spiritual Exiles." *KN*, 20 (1973), 363-71.
Andreach, Robert J. *The Slain and Resurrected God*, 29-119.
Andreas, Osborn. *Joseph Conrad: A Study in Non-Conformity.* New York: Philosophical Library, 1959.
Anthony, Irvin. "The Illusion of Joseph Conrad." *Bookman* (N.Y.), 74 (1932), 648-53.
Baines, Jocelyn. *Joseph Conrad: A Critical Biography.* New York: McGraw-Hill; London: Weidenfeld and Nicolson, 1960.

Bancroft, William W. *Joseph Conrad: His Philosophy of Life.* Boston: Stratford, 1933.

Bantock, G. H. "Conrad and Politics." *ELH*, 25 (1958), 122-36.

———. "The Two 'Moralities' of Joseph Conrad." *EIC*, 3 (1953), 125-42.

Bates, H. S. "Joseph Conrad and Thomas Hardy." *The English Novelists.* Ed. Derek Verschoyle, 249-63.

Beebe, Maurice. *Ivory Towers and Sacred Founts*, 165-71, 300-03.

———. "The Masks of Conrad." *BuR*, 11, 4 (1963), 35-53.

Beeton, D. Ridley. "Joseph Conrad and George Eliot: An Indication of the Possibilities." *PolR*, 20, 2-3 (1975), 78-86.

Beker, Miroslav. "Virginia Woolf's Appraisal of Joseph Conrad." *SRAZ*, 12 (1961), 17-22.

Bender, Todd K. "Computer Analysis of Conrad." *PolR*, 20, 2-3 (1975), 123-32.

Bendz, Ernst. *Joseph Conrad: An Appreciation.* Gothenburg: Gumbert, 1923.

Bennett, Arnold. *Books and Persons*, 36-40.

Berman, Jeffrey. "Writing as Rescue: Conrad's Escape from the Heart of Darkness." *L&P*, 25 (1975), 65-78.

Björkman, Edwin August. *Voices of Tomorrow*, 240-59.

Bojarski, Edmund A. "Conrad at the Crossroads: From Navigator to Novelist With Some New Biographical Mysteries." *TQ*, 11, 4 (1968), 15-29.

———. "Joseph Conrad's Polish Soul." *ES*, 44 (1963), 431-37.

———, and Harold R. Stevens. "Joseph Conrad and the *Falconhurst*." *JML*, 1 (1970), 192-208.

Bonney, William W. "Joseph Conrad and the Discontinuous Point of View." *JNT*, 2 (1972), 99-115.

Bowen, Robert O. "Loyalty and Tradition in Conrad." *Renascence*, 12 (1960), 125-31.

Boyle, Ted E. *Symbol and Meaning in the Fiction of Joseph Conrad.* The Hague: Mouton, 1965.

Braun, Andrzej. "In Conrad's Footsteps." *Conradiana*, 4, 2 (1972), 33-46.

Braybrooke, Patrick. *Some Victorian and Georgian Catholics*, 137-68.

Brennan, Joseph X., and Seymour L. Gross. "The Problem of Moral Values in Conrad and Faulkner." *Person*, 41 (1960), 60-70.

Bridges, Horace J. *The God of Fundamentalism*, 297-319.

Bross, Addison C. "The Unextinguishable Light of Belief: Conrad's Attitude Toward Woman." *Conradiana*, 2, 3 (1970), 39-46.

Brown, Douglas. "From *Heart of Darkness* to *Nostromo*: An Approach to Conrad." *The Pelican Guide to English Literature*, v. 7. Ed. Boris Ford, 127-145.

Joseph Conrad, continued

Brown, E. K. "James and Conrad." *YR*, 35 (1945), 265-85.

Buczkowski, Yvonne. "Female Characters in Conrad's Novels and Short Stories: A Bibliographical Note." *MSLC*, 1, 3 (1974-75), 51-57.

Bullett, Gerald W. *Modern English Fiction*, 54-69.

Burgess, O. N. "Joseph Conrad: The Old and the New Criticism." *AusQ*, 29, 1 (1957), 85-92.

Burkhart, Charles. "Conrad the Victorian." *ELT*, 6, 1 (1963), 1-8.

Busza, Andrzej. "Conrad's Polish Literary Background and Some Illustrations of the Influence of Polish Literature on His Work." *Antemurale* (Roma), 10 (1966), 109-255.

Canby, Henry S. *Definitions*, ser. 1, 257-68.

Carroll, Welsey. "The Novelist as Artist." *MFS*, 1, 1 (1955), 2-8.

Cecil, David. *Fine Art of Reading*, 179-215.

Chubb, Edwin. *Stories of Authors*, 393-400.

Clemens, Florence. "Conrad's Malaysia." *CE*, 2 (1941), 338-46.

Clifford, Hugh C. "The Art of Mr. Joseph Conrad." *Spectator*, 89 (November 29, 1902), 827-28.

Conrad, Jessie. *Joseph Conrad and His Circle.* London: Jarrold's; New York: Dutton, 1935; Port Washington, N.Y.: Kennikat, 1964.

Conrad, Joseph. *Conrad's Prefaces to His Works.* London: Dent, 1937.

Cook, Albert. "Conrad's Void." *NCF*, 12 (1958), 326-30.

Coolidge, Olivia E. *The Three Lives of Joseph Conrad.* Boston: Houghton Mifflin, 1972.

Cooper, Christopher. *Conrad and the Human Dilemma.* New York: Barnes and Noble; London: Chatto and Windus, 1970.

Cooper, Frederic T. *Some English Story Tellers*, 1-30.

Cox, C. B. "Joseph Conrad and the Question of Suicide." *BJRL*, 55 (1973), 285-99.

————. *Joseph Conrad: The Modern Imagination.* London: Dent; Totowa, N.J.: Rowman and Littlefield, 1974.

Cox, Sidney. "Joseph Conrad: The Teacher as Artist." *EJ*, 19 (1930), 781-95.

Crankshaw, Edward. *Joseph Conrad: Some Aspects of the Art of the Novel.* London: Lane, 1936; New York: Russell and Russell, 1963.

Crews, Frederick C. *Out of My System*, 41-62.

————. "The Power of Darkness." *PR*, 34 (1967), 507-25.

Cross, Wilbur L. *Four Contemporary Novelists*, 9-60.

————. "The Illusions of Joseph Conrad." *YR*, 17 (1928), 464-82.

Curle, Richard. *Caravansary and Conversation*, 155-63.

————. *Joseph Conrad and His Characters: A Study of Six Novels.* London: Heinemann, 1957; Fair Lawn, N.J.: Essential Books, 1958.

_____. *Joseph Conrad: A Study*. London: Routledge and K. Paul; Garden City, N.Y.: Doubleday, 1914.

Davidson, Donald. "Joseph Conrad's Directed Indirections." *SR*, 33 (1925), 163-77.

Davis, Harold E. "Shifting Rents in a Thick Fog: Point of View in the Novels of Joseph Conrad." *Conradiana*, 2, 2 (1970), 23-38.

Dowden, Wilfred S. *Joseph Conrad: The Imaged Style*. Nashville, Tenn.: Vanderbilt Univ. Press, 1970.

Duffin, Henry Charles. "Conrad: A Centenary Survey." *ContempR*, 192 (1957), 319-23.

Duffy, J. J. "Conrad and Pater: Suggestive Echoes." *Conradiana*, 1, 1 (1968), 45-47.

Ellis, Havelock. *From Marlowe to Shaw*, 303-13.

_____. *The Philosophy of Conflict*, 246-56.

_____. *Views and Reviews*, 2d ser., 116-20.

Farrell, James T. "On Joseph Conrad." *Conradiana*, 1, 1 (1968), i-ii.

Feaster, John. "Joseph Conrad: The Limits of Humanism." *Cresset*, 35, 3 (1972), 9-12.

Fernandez, Ramon. *Messages*, 137-51.

Fleishman, Avrom. *Conrad's Politics: Community and Anarchy in the Fiction of Joseph Conrad*. Baltimore: Johns Hopkins Univ. Press, 1967.

Fletcher, James V. "Ethical Symbolism in Conrad." *CE*, 2 (1940), 19-26.

Follett, Helen T., and Wilson J. Follett. "Contemporary Novelists: Joseph Conrad." *Atlantic*, 119 (1917), 233-43.

Follett, Wilson. *Joseph Conrad: A Short Study*. Garden City, N. Y.: Doubleday, 1915, 1966.

Ford, Ford Madox. *It Was The Nightingale*, 308-11.

_____. *Joseph Conrad: A Personal Remembrance*. Boston: Little, Brown, 1924.

_____. *Portraits from Life*, 57-69.

Freislich, Richard. "Marlow's Shadow Side." *LonM*, 4, 11 (November 1957), 31-36.

Friedman, Norman. "Criticism and the Novel: Hardy, Hemingway, Crane, Woolf, and Conrad." *AR*, 18 (1958), 343-70.

Garnett, Edward. *Friday Nights*, 83-101.

Garrett, Peter. *Scene and Symbol from George Eliot to James Joyce*, 160-80.

Gaston, Paul. "The Gospel of Work According to Joseph Conrad." *PolR*, 20, 2-3 (1975), 203-10.

Geddes, Gary. "Conrad and the Darkness before Creation." *AntigR*, 7 (1971), 92-104.

Joseph Conrad, continued

_____. "Conrad and the Fine Art of Understanding." *DR*, 47 (1967), 492-503.

_____. "That Extra Longitude: Conrad and the Art of Fiction." *UWR*, 3, 2 (1968), 65-81.

Gillon, Adam. "Betrayal and Redemption in Joseph Conrad." *PolR*, 5, 2 (1960), 18-35.

_____. "Conrad and Sartre." *DR*, 40 (1960), 61-71.

_____. "Cosmopolitanism in Conrad's Work." *Proceedings of IVth Congress of the Int'l. Comp. Lit. Ass'n.* Ed. François Jost, 94-99.

_____. *The Eternal Solitary: A Study of Joseph Conrad.* New York: Bookman, 1960.

_____. "The Jews in Joseph Conrad's Fiction." *CJF*, 22 (1963), 34-40.

_____. "Joseph Conrad and Shakespeare." *Conradiana*, 1, 1 (1968), 19-25; 2 (1968), 15-22; 3 (1969), 7-27. [For Part 4, see *Victory*; for Part 5, see *Heart of Darkness*.]

Goldknopf, David. "What's Wrong with Conrad: Conrad on Conrad." *Criticism*, 10 (1968), 54-64.

Goonetilleke, D. C. R. A. "On Conrad's Portrayal of Malayans." *ACLALSB*, 1974, 6-9.

Gordan, John Dozier. *Joseph Conrad: The Making of a Novelist.* Cambridge, Mass.: Harvard Univ. Press, 1940.

Gose, Elliott B. *Imagination Indulged*, 127-40.

Graver, Lawrence. *Conrad's Short Fiction.* Berkeley: Univ. of California Press, 1969.

Green, Jesse D. "Diabolism, Pessimism, and Democracy: Notes on Melville and Conrad." *MFS*, 8 (1962), 287-305.

Greene, Graham. *Collected Essays*, 182-84.

Guedalla, Philip. *A Gallery*, 77-84.

Guerard, Albert J. *Conrad the Novelist.* Cambridge, Mass.: Harvard Univ. Press, 1958.

_____. "Joseph Conrad." *Direction*, 1 (1947), 7-92.

Guetti, James. *The Limits of Metaphor: A Study of Melville, Conrad, and Faulkner.* Ithaca, N.Y.: Cornell Univ. Press, 1967.

_____. *The Rhetoric of Joseph Conrad.* Amherst, Mass.: Amherst Coll. Press, 1960.

Gurko, Leo. "Joseph Conrad at the Crossroads." *UKCR*, 25 (1958), 97-100.

_____. *Joseph Conrad: Giant in Exile.* New York: Macmillan, 1962.

_____. *The Two Lives of Joseph Conrad.* New York: Crowell, 1965.

Hall, James N. "My Conrad." *Atlantic*, 169 (May 1942), 583-87.

_____. *Under a Thatched Roof*, 170-87.

Hall, Leland. "Joseph Conrad." *English Literature During the Last Half-Century*, by J. W. Cunliffe, 2d ed., 179-99.

Hamill, Paul. "Conrad, Wells, and the Two Voices." *PMLA*, 89 (1974), 581-82.

Hardy, Barbara. *Tellers and Listeners*, 154-61.

Harper, George Mills. "Conrad's Knitters and Homer's Cave of the Nymphs." *ELN*, 1 (1963), 53-57.

Haugh, Robert F. *Joseph Conrad: Discovery in Design.* Norman: Oklahoma Univ. Press, 1957.

Hay, Eloise. "Joseph Conrad and Impressionism." *JAAC*, 34 (1975), 137-44.

———. *The Political Novels of Joseph Conrad: A Critical Study.* Chicago: Univ. of Chicago Press, 1963.

Heimer, Jackson W. "Patterns of Betrayal in the Novels of Joseph Conrad." *BSUF*, 8, 3 (1967), 30-39.

Henig, Suzanne, and Florence Talamantes. "Conrad and Balzac: A Trio of Balzacian Interrelationships." *PolR*, 20, 2-3 (1975), 58-70.

Hervouet, Yves. "Conrad and Anatole France." *ArielE*, 1, 1 (1970), 84-99.

Hewitt, Douglas J. *Conrad: A Reassessment.* Cambridge: Bowes and Bowes, 1952; Chester Springs, Pa.: Dufour, 1969, 1975; Totowa, N.J.: Rowman and Littlefield, 1975.

Hodges, Robert R. *The Dual Heritage of Joseph Conrad.* The Hague: Mouton, 1967.

Hoffman, Frederick J. *The Mortal No*, 50-64.

Hoffman, Stanton de Voren. "Conrad's Menagerie: Animal Imagery and Theme." *BuR*, 12, 3 (1964), 59-71.

———. *Comedy and Form in the Fiction of Joseph Conrad.* The Hague: Mouton; New York: Humanities, 1969.

Hoffmann, Richard. "Proportion and Incident in Joseph Conrad and Arnold Bennett." *SR*, 32 (1924), 79-87.

Hollingsworth, Alan M. "Freud, Conrad, and the Future of an Illusion." *L&P*, 5 (1955), 78-83.

Hosillos, Lucila. "A Reliable Narrator: Conrad's Distance and Effects Through Marlow." *DilR*, 18 (1970), 154-72.

Howe, Irving. "Order and Anarchy: The Political Novels." *KR*, 15 (1953), 505-521; "The Political Novels." *KR*, 16 (1954), 1-19.

———. *Politics and the Novel*, 76-113.

Huneker, James G. *Ivory Apes and Peacocks*, 1-21.

Hussey, William R. M. " 'He Was Spared that Annoyance'." *Conradiana*, 3, 2 (1971-72), 17-25.

Hutchinson, P. A. "Joseph Conrad, Alchemist of the Sea." *Essays in Memory of Barrett Wendell*, by his Assistants, 291-99.

Inniss, Kenneth. "Conrad's Native Girl: Some Social Questions." *PCP*, 5 (1970), 39-45.

Jablowski, Roza. *Joseph Conrad. 1857-1924*. Wroclaw: Ossolineum, 1961.

Jacobs, Robert G. "Comrade Ossipon's Favorite Saint: Lombroso and Conrad." *NCF*, 23 (1968), 74-84.

——. "H. G. Wells, Joseph Conrad, and the Relative Universe." *Conradiana*, 1, 1 (1968), 51-55.

James, Henry. "The Younger Generation." *TLS*, March 19, 1914, 133-34; April 2, 1914, 157-58.

Jean-Aubry, Gerard. *The Sea-Dreamer: A Definitive Biography of Joseph Conrad*. Tr. Helen Sebba. Garden City, N. Y.: Doubleday, 1957.

Jesse, F. T. "Joseph Conrad." *Post-Victorians*, by Various Authors, 117-28.

Johnson, Bruce. *Conrad's Models of Mind*. Minneapolis: Univ. of Minnesota Press, 1971.

——. "Joseph Conrad and Crane's *The Red Badge of Courage*." *PMASAL*, 48 (1963), 649-55.

Kaplan, Harold. *The Passive Voice*, 131-57.

Karl, Frederick R. "Conrad's Debt to Dickens." *N&Q*, 4 (1957), 398-400.

——. "Conrad, Wells, and the Two Voices." *PMLA*, 88 (1973), 1049-65.

——, ed. *Joseph Conrad: A Collection of Criticism*. New York: McGraw-Hill, 1974.

——. "Joseph Conrad: A *fin de siècle* Novelist—A Study in Style and Method." *LitR*, 2 (1959), 565-76.

——. "Joseph Conrad, Norman Douglas, and the *English Review*." *JML*, 2 (1972), 342-56.

——. *A Reader's Guide to Joseph Conrad*. New York: Noonday, 1960, 1969.

Keating, George T., ed. *A Conrad Memorial Library*. Garden City, N.Y.: Doubleday, 1929.

Kellett, Ernest E. *Reconsiderations*, 243-61.

Kenner, Hugh. *Gnomon*, 162-70.

Kerf, René. "Ethics Versus Aesthetics: A Clue to the Deterioration of Conrad's Art." *RLV*, 31 (1965), 240-49.

——. "Symbol Hunting in Conradian Land." *RLV*, 32 (1966), 266-77.

Kirschner, Paul. "Conrad and Maupassaunt." *REL*, 6, 4 (1965), 37-51.

——. *Conrad: The Psychologist as Artist*. Edinburgh: Oliver and Boyd, 1968.

Kisner, Sister M. Roseline, A.S.C. "The Lure of the Abyss for the Hollow Man: Conrad's Notion of Evil." *Conradiana*, 2, 3 (1970), 85-99.

Kleiner, Elaine L. "Joseph Conrad's Forgotten Role in the Emergence of Science Fiction." *Extrapolation*, 15 (1973), 25-34.

Knight, Grant C. *The Novel in English*, 305-13.

Knowles, Owen. "Commentary as Rhetoric: An Aspect of Conrad's Art." *Conradiana*, 5, 3 (1973), 5-27.

———. " 'To Make You Hear . . .': Some Aspects of Conrad's Dialogue." *PolR*, 20, 2-3 (1975), 164-80.

Kocmanova, Jessie. "The Revolt of the Workers in the Novels of Gissing, James, and Conrad." *BSE*, 1 (1959), 119-39.

Kreisel, Henry. "Joseph Conrad and the Dilemma of the Uprooted Man." *TamR*, 7 (1958), 78-85.

Krenn, Sister Heliena, S.Sp.S. "*Vae soli*: Joseph Conrad's Predilection for Isolated Characters." *FJS*, 3 (1970), 63-85.

Krieger, Murray. *The Play and Place of Criticism*, 92-101.

———. *The Tragic Vision*, 154-94.

Krzyzanowski, Ludwik, ed. *Joseph Conrad: Centennial Essays*. New York: Polish Institute of Arts and Sciences in America, 1960.

Leavis, F. R. *The Great Tradition*, 211-72.

———. "Joseph Conrad." *SR*, 66 (1958), 179-200.

Lee, Robert F. *Conrad's Colonialism*. The Hague: Mouton, 1969.

Levin, Harry. "Literature and Exile." *Listener*, 62 (1959), 613-17.

Levine, Paul. "Joseph Conrad's Blackness." *SAQ*, 63 (1964), 198-206.

Lillard, Richard G. "Irony in Hardy and Conrad." *PMLA*, 50 (1935), 316-22.

Lincoln, Kenneth R. "Conrad's Mythic Humor." *TSLL*, 17 (1975), 635-51.

———. "Voice and Vision in Joseph Conrad." *Conradiana*, 1, 3 (1969), 95-100.

Lorch, Thomas M. "The Barrier Between Youth and Maturity in the Works of Joseph Conrad." *MFS*, 10, 1 (1964), 73-80.

Lynd, Robert. *Books and Authors*, 196-205.

McDonald, Walter R. "Conrad as a Novelist of Moral Conflict and Isolation." *IEY*, 13 (1968), 34-43.

McFee, William. *Harbours of Memory*, 278-92.

———. *Swallowing the Anchor*, 85-112.

McIntyre, Allan O. "Conrad on Conscience and the Passions." *UR*, 31 (1964), 69-74.

———. "Conrad on the Functions of the Mind." *MLQ*, 25 (1964), 187-97.

———. "Conrad on Writing and Critics." *ForumH*, 4, 5 (1964), 37-42.

Madden, William A. "The Search for Forgiveness in Some Nineteenth Century English Novels." *CLS*, 3 (1966), 139-53.

Joseph Conrad, continued

Marković, Vida E. "The Emerging Character." *NWR*, 7 (1965-66), 80-97.

Martin, Joseph J. "Edward Garnett and Conrad's Plunge into the 'Destructive Element'." *TSLL*, 15 (1973), 517-36.

——. "Edward Garnett and Conrad's Reshaping of Time." *Conradiana*, 6, 2 (1974), 89-105.

Martin, W. R. "Beginnings and Endings in Conrad." *Conradiana*, 5, 1 (1973), 43-51.

Maser, Frederick E. "The Philosophy of Joseph Conrad." *HJ*, 56 (1957), 69-78.

Matlaw, Ralph. "Dostoevski and Conrad's Political Novels." *American Contributions to the Fifth Int'l. Congress of Slavists, Sofia, September 1963.* The Hague: Mouton, 1963, 213-31.

Mégroz, Rodolphe L. *Joseph Conrad's Mind and Method.* London: Faber and Faber, 1931, 1964.

Mencken, H. L. *Book of Prefaces*, 11-64.

——. *Prejudices*, 5th ser., 34-41.

Messenger, William E. "Conrad and His 'Sea Stuff.' " *Conradiana*, 6, 1 (1974), 3-18.

——. "Conrad and Melville Again." *Conradiana*, 2, 2 (1970), 53-64.

Meyer, Bernard C. *Joseph Conrad: A Psychoanalytic Biography.* Princeton, N. J.: Princeton Univ. Press, 1967.

Michel, Laurence. *The Thing Contained*, 86-106.

Michel, Lois A. "The Absurd Predicament in Conrad's Political Novels." *CE*, 23 (1961), 131-36.

Miller, J. Hillis. *Poets of Reality*, 13-67.

Moore, Carlisle. "Conrad and the Novel as Ordeal." *PQ*, 42 (1963), 55-74.

Morley, Christopher. *Internal Revenue*, 185-99.

——. *Romany Stain*, 218-22.

——. *Shandygaff*, 238-45.

Morley, Patricia A. "Conrad's Vision of the Absurd." *Conradiana*, 2, 1 (1970), 59-68.

Morris, Robert L. "The Classical Reference in Conrad's Fiction." *CE*, 7 (1946), 312-18.

Moser, Thomas. *Joseph Conrad: Achievement and Decline.* Cambridge, Mass.: Harvard Univ. Press, 1957.

Mroczkowski, Przemyslaw. *Conradiana Commentaries.* Krakow: Jagellonian Univ. Press, 1970.

——. "The Gnomic Element in Conrad." *KN*, 6 (1959), 193-209.

——. "Joseph Conrad the European." *PolR*, 20, 2-3 (1975), 87-96.

Mudrick, Marvin, ed. *Conrad: A Collection of Critical Essays.* Englewood Cliffs, N. J.: Prentice-Hall, 1966.

_____. "Conrad and the Terms of Modern Criticism." *HudR*, 7 (1954), 419-26.

_____. *On Culture and Literature*, 93-107.

_____. "The Originality of Conrad." *HudR*, 11 (1959), 545-53.

Muir, Edwin. *Latitudes*, 47-56.

Najder, Zdzislaw. "Conrad in His Historical Perspective." *ELT*, 14, 3 (1971), 157-66.

Nettels, Elsa. "The Grotesque in Conrad's Fiction." *NCF*, 29 (1974), 144-63.

_____. "James and Conrad on the Art of Fiction." *TSLL*, 14 (1972), 529-43.

Newhouse, Neville H. *Joseph Conrad*. London: Evans, 1966.

Newman, Paul B. "Joseph Conrad and the Ancient Mariner." *KM*, 10 (1960), 79-83.

O'Brien, Justin. "Camus and Conrad: An Hypothesis." *RR*, 58 (1967), 196-99.

Ordones, Elmer A. "The Early Joseph Conrad: Revisions and Style." *PSSHR*, 33 (1968), 1-192.

Palmer, John A. *Joseph Conrad's Fiction: A Study in Literary Growth*. Ithaca, N. Y.: Cornell Univ. Press, 1968.

Paris, Bernard J. *A Psychological Approach to Fiction: Studies in Thackeray, Stendhal, George Eliot, Dostoevsky, and Conrad*. Bloomington: Indiana Univ. Press, 1974, 215-74.

Perry, John Oliver. "Action, Vision, or Voice: The Moral Dilemmas in Conrad's Tale Telling." *MFS*, 10, 1 (1964), 3-14.

Phelps, Gilbert. *The Russian Novel in English Fiction*, 125-37.

Pritchett, V. S. *The Working Novelist*, 193-201.

Purdy, Strother B. "On the Relevance of Conrad: Lord Jim Over Sverdlovsk." *MQ*, 9 (1967), 43-51.

Rajiva, Stanley F. "The Singular Person: An Essay on Conrad's Use of Marlow as Narrator." *LCrit*, 8, 2 (1968), 35-45.

Ramsey, Roger. "The Available and the Unavailable 'I': Conrad and James." *ELT*, 14, 2 (1971), 137-45.

Rapin, René. "Reality and Imagination in the Works of Joseph Conrad, Parts I and II." *Conradiana*, 4, 3 (1972), 22-33; 5, 3 (1973), 46-59.

Raskin, Jonah. *The Mythology of Imperialism*, 126-95, 206-21.

Renner, Stanley. "The Garden of Civilization: Conrad, Huxley, and the Ethics of Evolution." *Conradiana*, 7, 2 (1975), 109-20.

_____. "A Note on Joseph Conrad and the Objective Correlative." *Conradiana*, 6, 1 (1974), 53-56.

Rhome, Frances D. "Headgear as Symbol in Conrad's Novels." *Conradiana*, 2, 3 (1970), 180-86.

Joseph Conrad, continued

Robertson, J. M. "The Novels of Joseph Conrad." *NoAmR*, 208 (1918), 439-53.

Robson, W. W. "The Politics of Solitude." *LonM*, 4, 11 (November 1957), 26-31.

Rogers, Robert. *A Psychoanalytic Study*, 42-46.

Rose, Alan M. "Conrad and the Sirens of the Decadence." *TSLL*, 11 (1969), 795-810.

Rosenfield, Claire. *Paradise of Snakes: An Archetypal Analysis of Conrad's Political Novels.* Chicago: Univ. of Chicago Press, 1967.

Roussel, Royal. *The Metaphysics of Darkness: A Study in the Unity and Development of Conrad's Fiction.* Baltimore: Johns Hopkins Univ. Press, 1971.

Russell, Bertrand. *Portraits from Memory*, 86-91.

Ryf, Robert S. *Joseph Conrad.* New York: Columbia Univ. Press, 1970.

Sackville-West, Edward. *Inclinations*, 72-77.

Said, Edward W. *Conrad, the Later Moralist.* Amsterdam: Rodopi, 1974.

———. "Conrad: The Presentation of Narrative." *Novel*, 7 (1974), 116-32.

———. *Joseph Conrad and the Fiction of Autobiography.* Cambridge, Mass.: Harvard Univ. Press, 1966.

Sandison, Alan. *The Wheel of Empire*, 120-48.

Sandstrom, Glenn. "The Roots of Anguish in Conrad and Dostoevsky." *PolR*, 20, 2-3 (1975), 71-77.

Saveson, John E. *Joseph Conrad: The Making of a Moralist.* Amsterdam: Rodopi, 1972.

———. "Spencerian Assumptions in Conrad's Early Fiction." *Conradiana*, 1, 3 (1969), 29-40.

Schneider, Daniel J. *Symbolism: The Manichean Vision*, 40-61.

Seltzer, Leon F. "Like Repels Like: The Case of Conrad's Antipathy for Melville." *Conradiana*, 1, 3 (1969), 101-05.

———. *The Vision of Melville and Conrad: A Comparative Study.* Athens: Ohio Univ. Press, 1970.

Shanks, Edward. *Second Essays on Literature*, 23-40.

Sherry, Norman. *Conrad and His World.* New York: Scribner's, 1973.

———. "Conrad and the Bangkok *Times*." *NCF*, 20 (1965), 255-66.

———. "Conrad and the S. S. *Vidar*." *RES*, 14 (1963), 157-63.

———. *Conrad's Eastern World.* London: Cambridge Univ. Press, 1966.

———, ed. *Conrad: The Critical Heritage.* London: Routledge & K. Paul, 1973.

_____. *Conrad's Western World.* Cambridge: Cambridge Univ. Press, 1971.

_____. "The Essential Conrad." *E&S*, 27 (1974), 98-113.

Slade, Joseph W. "The World's Greatest Fiction Writer." *Conradiana*, 5, 1 (1973), 5-11.

Smoller, Sanford J. "A Note on Joseph Conrad's Fall and Abyss." *MFS*, 15 (1969), 261-64.

Stallman, R. W., ed. *The Art of Joseph Conrad: A Critical Symposium.* East Lansing: Michigan State Univ. Press, 1960.

Stavrou, C. N. "Conrad, Camus, and Sisyphus." *Audience*, 7 (1960), 80-96.

Stawell, F. M. "Conrad." English Association, London. *Essays and Studies*, v. 6 (1920), 88-111.

Stegner, Wallace. "Variations on a Theme by Conrad." *YR*, 39 (1950), 512-23.

Stein, William Bysshe. "Conrad's East: Time, History, Action, and *Maya*." *TSLL*, 7 (1965), 265-83.

_____. "The Eastern Matrix of Conrad's Art." *Conradiana*, 1, 2 (1968), 1-14.

Stewart, J. I. M. *Eight Modern Writers*, 184-222.

_____. *Joseph Conrad.* New York: Dodd, Mead, 1968.

Sullivan, Walter. "The Dark Beyond the Sunrise: Conrad and the Politics of Despair." *SoR*, n.s. 8 (1972), 507-19.

Symons, Arthur. *Dramatis Personae*, 1-23.

Thomas, Edward. " 'Truer than History'." *ArielE*, 1, 1 (1970), 65-72.

Thompson, Alan R. "The Humanism of Joseph Conrad." *SR*, 37 (1929), 204-20.

Thomson, George H. "Conrad's Later Fiction." *ELT*, 12, 4 (1969), 165-74.

Thorburn, David. *Conrad's Romanticism.* New Haven, Conn.: Yale Univ. Press, 1974.

_____. "Conrad's Romanticism: Self-Consciousness and Community." *Romanticism: Vistas, Instances, Continuities.* Ed. David Thorburn and Geoffrey Hartman, 221-54.

Tindall, William York. "Apology for Marlow." *From Jane Austen to Joseph Conrad.* Ed. Robert C. Rathburn and Martin Steinmann, Jr., 274-85.

Tucker, Martin. *Joseph Conrad.* New York: Ungar, 1975.

Ure, Peter. "Character and Imagination in Conrad." *CambJ*, 3 (1950), 727-40.

Van Domelen, John E. "In the Beginning Was the Word, or Awful Eloquence and Right Expression in Conrad." *SCB*, 30 (1970), 228-31.

Verschoor, Edith E. "Joseph Conrad's World." *UES*, 8, 2 (1970), 12-18.

Joseph Conrad, continued

Voytovich, Edward R. "The Problem of Identity for Conrad's Women." *ELUD*, 2, 2 (1974), 51-68.

Wagenknecht, Edward C. " 'Pessimism' in Hardy and Conrad." *CE*, 3 (1942), 546-54.

Wain, John. "The Test of Manliness." *LonM*, 4, 11 (November 1957), 23-26.

Walpole, Hugh. *Joseph Conrad.* London: Hutchinson, 1929.

Walt, James. "Conrad and Katherine Mansfield." *Conradiana*, 4, 1 (1972), 41-52.

———. "Mencken and Conrad." *Conradiana*, 2, 2 (1970), 9-21; "Part II." 2, 3 (1970), 100-10.

Walton, James. "Conrad, Dickens, and the Detective Novel." *NCF*, 23 (1969), 446-62.

Warner, Oliver. *Joseph Conrad.* London: Longmans, Green, 1951.

———. "The Sea Writer." *LonM*, 4, 11 (November 1957), 21-23.

Watt, Ian. "Joseph Conrad: Alienation and Commitment." *The English Mind.* Ed. Hugh Sykes Davies and George Watson, 257-78.

Watts, C. T. "Joseph Conrad and the Ranee of Sarawak." *RES*, 15 (1964), 404-07.

Webster, H. T. "Joseph Conrad: A Reinterpretation of Five Novels." *CE*, 7 (1945), 125-34.

Weinstein, Arnold L. *Vision and Response in Modern Fiction*, 50-57.

Weygandt, Cornelius. "The Art of Joseph Conrad." *Schelling Anniversary Papers*, by his Former Students, 319-41.

Whitehead, Lee M. "Conrad's 'Pessimism' Re-Examined." *Conradiana*, 2, 3 (1970), 25-38.

Whittemore, Reed. *The Fascination of the Abomination*, 129-66.

Widmer, Kingsley. "Conrad's Pyrrhonistic Conservativism: Ideological Melodrama Around 'Simple Ideas'." *Novel*, 7 (1973), 133-42.

Wiley, Paul. L. *Conrad's Measure of Man.* Madison: Univ. of Wisconsin Press, 1954; New York: Gordian, 1966.

Williams, Harold H. *Modern English Writers*, 387-93.

Wilson, Arthur H. "The Complete Narrative of Joseph Conrad." *SUS*, 4 (1951), 229-62.

———. "The Great Theme in Conrad." *SUS*, 5 (1953), 51-84.

Wohlfarth, Paul. "Joseph Conrad and Germany." *GL&L*, 16 (1963), 81-87.

Woolf, Leonard. *Essays on Literature, History, Politics, etc.*, 57-71.

Woolf, Virginia. *Collected Essays*, v. 1, 302-08.

Wright, Edgar. "Joseph Conrad and Bertrand Russell." *Conradiana*, 2, 1 (1970), 7-16.

Wright, Walter F. "Ambiguity of Emphasis in Joseph Conrad." *On*

Stage and Off. Ed. John W. Ehrstine, John R. Elwood, and Robert C. McLean, 90-96.

_____. "How Conrad Tells a Story." *PrS*, 21 (1947), 290-95.

_____, ed. *Joseph Conrad on Fiction*. Lincoln: Univ. of Nebraska Press, 1964.

_____. *Romance and Tragedy in Joseph Conrad*. Lincoln: Univ. of Nebraska Press, 1949.

_____. " 'The Truth of My Own Sensations'." *MFS*, 1, 1 (1955), 26-29.

Yelton, Donald C. *Mimesis and Metaphor: An Inquiry into the Genesis and Scope of Conrad's Symbolic Imagery*. The Hague: Mouton, 1967.

Young, Vernon. "Joseph Conrad: Outline for a Reconsideration." *HudR*, 2 (1949), 5-19.

Young, W. J. "Conrad Against Himself." *CR*, 11 (1968), 32-47.

Zabel, Morton Dauwen. "Joseph Conrad: Chance and Recognition." *SR*, 53 (1945), 1-22.

Zellar, Leonard E. "Conrad and Dostoyevsky." *The English Novel in the Nineteenth Century*. Ed. George V. Goodin, 214-23.

Zyla, Wolodymyr T., and Wendell M. Aycock, eds. *Joseph Conrad: Theory and World Fiction*.

See also: Beach, *20th*; Beja; Beresford; Bowen, *Impressions*; A. Collins, *20th*; Cook; Cunliffe, *20th Century*, *Leaders*; Daiches, *Novel*; Donoghue, *Universe*; Drew, *Modern*; Edgar, *Art*; Fleishman; Follett and Follett; A. Friedman, *Turn*; Gerould; Gillie, *Movements*; Hamilton; Hind, *Authors*; Hoare; Hynes, *Edwardian*; Karl and Magalaner; Kettle; Lovett; Lynd, *Old*; MacCarthy, *Portraits*; McCullough; Mackenzie; Macy; Marble; Marković; Maurois; Muller, *Modern*; Overton, *Authors*; Pritchett, *Living*; Routh, *Towards*; Scott-James, *50*; Swinnerton, *Georgian*, *Background*; Tindall, *Forces*; Wagenknecht, *Cavalcade*; Ward, *20th*; Weygandt; H. Williams, *Modern*; R. Williams, *Novel*; Zabel, *Craft*.

ALMAYER'S FOLLY

Dowden, Wilfred S. "*Almayer's Folly* and *Lord Jim*: A Study in the Development of Conrad's Imagery." *RUS*, 51, 1 (1965), 13-27.

Gurko, Leo. "Conrad's First Battleground: *Almayer's Folly*." *UKCR*, 25 (1959), 189-94.

Hicks, John H. "Conrad's *Almayer's Folly*: Structure, Theme, and Critics." *NCF*, 19 (1964), 17-31.

King, Russell S. "Conrad's *Almayer's Folly* and Lenormand's *Le Simoun*: Some Aspects of Characterization." *RLC*, 49 (1975), 302-11.

O'Connor, Peter D. "The Function of Nina in *Almayer's Folly*." *Conradiana*, 7, 3 (1975), 225-32.

Sherry, Norman. " 'Rajah Laut': A Quest for Conrad's Source." *MP*, 62 (1964), 22-41.

Squire, John C. *Books in General*, 1st ser., 168-72.

Stein, William B. "*Almayer's Folly*: The Terror of Time." *Conradiana*, 1, 1 (1968), 27-34.

Watt, Ian. "*Almayer's Folly*: Memories and Models." *Mosaic*, 8, 1 (1973), 165-82.

THE ARROW OF GOLD

Begnal, Michael H. "The Ideals of Despair: A View of Joseph Conrad's *The Arrow of Gold*." *Conradiana*, 3, 3 (1971-72), 37-40.

Kirschner, Paul. "Conrad's Strong Man." *MFS* 10, 1 (1964), 31-36.

Mansfield, Katherine. *Novels and Novelists*, 57-61.

Rude, Donald W. "Conrad's Revision of the First American Edition of 'The Arrow of Gold'." *PolR*, 20, 2-3 (1975), 106-22.

Toliver, Harold E. "Conrad's *Arrow of Gold* and Pastoral Tradition." *MFS*, 8 (1962), 148-58.

CHANCE

Cagle, William R. "The Publication of Joseph Conrad's *Chance*." *BC*, 16 (1967), 305-22.

Coleman, A. P. "Polonisms in the English of Conrad's *Chance*." *MLN*, 46 (1931), 463-68.

Duncan-Jones, E. E. "Some Sources of *Chance*." *RES*, 20 (1969), 468-71.

Fleischmann, Wolfgang B. "Conrad's *Chance* and Bergson's *Laughter*." *Renascence*, 14 (1962), 66-71.

Geddes, Gary. "The Structure of Sympathy: Conrad and the *Chance* That Wasn't." *ELT*, 12, 4 (1969), 157-88.

Grabo, Carl H. *The Technique of the Novel*, 66-71.

Harkness, Bruce. "The Epigraph of Conrad's *Chance*." *NCF*, 9 (1954), 209-22.

Haugh, Robert F. "Conrad's *Chance*: *Progression d'Effet*." *MFS*, 1, 1 (1955), 9-15.

Hough, Graham. "*Chance* and Joseph Conrad." *Listener*, 58 (1957), 1063-65.

———. *Image and Experience*, 211-22.

Hudspeth, Robert N. "Conrad's Use of Time in *Chance*." *NCF*, 21 (1966), 283-89.

Johnson, J. W. "Marlow and *Chance*: A Reappraisal." *TSLL*, 10 (1968), 91-105.

Levin, Gerald H. "An Allusion to Tasso in Conrad's *Chance.*" *NCF*, 13 (1958), 145-51.

Moser, Thomas C. "Conrad, Ford, and the Sources of *Chance.*" *Conradiana*, 7, 3 (1975), 207-24.

Smith, Curtis C. "Conrad's *Chance*: A Dialectical Novel." *Thoth*, 6, 2 (1965), 16-24.

Watt, Ian. "Conrad, James and *Chance.*" *Imagined Worlds.* Ed. Maynard Mack and Ian Gregor, 301-22.

Zuckerman, Jerome. "Contrapuntal Structure in Conrad's *Chance.*" *MFS*, 10, 1 (1964), 49-54.

CONRAD-FORD COLLABORATIONS
[THE INHERITORS, ROMANCE, NATURE OF A CRIME]

Bender, Todd K. "Fictional Time and the Problem of Free Will." *WSL*, 5 (1968), 12-22.

Brebach, Raymond T. "The Making of *Romance*, Part Fifth." *Conradiana*, 6 (1974), 171-81.

Esslinger, Pat M. "A Theory and Three Experiments: The Failure of the Conrad-Ford Collaboration." *WHR*, 22 (1968), 59-67.

Goldring, Douglas. *South Lodge*, 165-77.

Higdon, David L. "The Conrad-Ford Collaboration." *Conradiana*, 6 (1974), 155-56.

Jacobs, Robert G. "H. G. Wells, Joseph Conrad, and the Relative Universe." *Conradiana*, 1, 1 (1968), 51-55.

Karl, Frederick R. "Conrad, Ford, and the Novel." *Midway*, 10, 2 (1969), 17-34.

Kenner, Hugh. "Conrad and Ford: The Artistic Conscience." *Shenandoah*, 3 (1952), 53-55.

Meixner, John A. "Ford and Conrad." *Conradiana*, 6 (1974), 157-69.

Rose, Charles. "*Romance* and the Maiden Archetype." *Conradiana*, 6 (1974), 183-88.

Watts, C. T. "Joseph Conrad, Dr. Macintyre, and *The Inheritors.*" *N&Q*, 14 (1967), 245-47.

HEART OF DARKNESS

Amur, G. S. "*Heart of Darkness* and 'The Fall of the House of Usher': The Tale as Discovery." *LCrit*, 9 (1971), 59-70.

Baum, Joan. "The 'Real' *Heart of Darkness.*" *Conradiana*, 7, 2 (1975), 183-87.

Benson, Donald R. "*Heart of Darkness*: The Grounds of Civilization in an Alien Universe." *TSLL*, 7 (1966), 339-47.

Boyle, Ted E. "Marlow's 'Lie' in '*Heart of Darkness*'." *SSF*, 1 (1964), 159-63.

Joseph Conrad, continued

Brady, Marion B. "Conrad's Whited Sepulcher." *CE*, 24 (1962), 24-29.
Brashers, H. C. "Conrad, Marlow, and Gautama Buddha: On Structure and Theme in *Heart of Darkness.*" *Conradiana*, 1, 3 (1969), 63-71.
Bruffee, Kenneth A. "The Lesser Nightmare: Marlow's Lie in *Heart of Darkness.*" *MLQ*, 25 (1964), 322-29.
Burgess, C. F. "Conrad's Pesky Russian." *NCF*, 18 (1963), 189-93.
Canario, John W. "The Harlequin in *Heart of Darkness.*" *SSF*, 4 (1967), 225-33.
Chiampi, Rubens. "*Heart of Darkness.*" *IH*, 5 (1969), 52-68.
Collins, Harold R. "Kurtz, the Cannibals, and the Second-Rate Helmsman." *WHR*, 8 (1954), 299-310.
Cook, William J. "More Light on *Heart of Darkness.*" *Conradiana*, 3, 3 (1971-72), 4-14.
Dahl, James C. "Kurtz, Marlow, Conrad and the Human Heart of Darkness." *SLitI*, 1, 2 (1968), 33-40.
D'Avanzo, Mario L. "Conrad's Motley as an Organizing Metaphor in *Heart of Darkness.*" *CLAJ*, 9 (1966), 289-91.
Dean, Leonard F. "Tragic Pattern in Conrad's *Heart of Darkness.*" *CE*, 6 (1944), 100-04.
——, ed. *HEART OF DARKNESS: Backgrounds and Criticisms.* Englewood Cliffs, N. J.: Prentice-Hall, 1960.
Dowden, Wilfred S. "The Light and the Dark: Imagery and Thematic Development in Conrad's *Heart of Darkness.*" *RIP*, 44, 1 (1957), 33-51.
Edwards, Paul. "Clothes for the Pilgrimage: A Recurrent Image in *Heart of Darkness.*" *Mosaic*, 4, 3 (1971), 67-74.
Emmett, V. J., Jr. "Carlyle, Conrad, and the Politics of Charisma: Another Perspective on *Heart of Darkness.*" *Conradiana*, 7, 2 (1975), 145-53.
Evans, Robert O. "Conrad's Underworld." *MFS*, 2 (1956), 56-62.
——. "Further Comment on *Heart of Darkness.*" *MFS*, 3 (1957), 358-60.
Faulkner, Peter. "Vision and Normality: Conrad's *Heart of Darkness.*" *ISE*, 1 (1969), 36-47.
Feder, Lillian. "Marlow's Descent into Hell." *NCF*, 9 (1955), 280-92.
Garnett, Edward. "Mr. Conrad's New Book: *YOUTH: A Narrative; and Two Other Stories.*" *A&L*, 1596 (1902), 606-07.
Gertzman, Jay A. "Commitment and Sacrifice in *Heart of Darkness*: Marlow's Response to Kurtz." *SSF*, 9 (1972), 187-96.
Gillon, Adam. "Joseph Conrad and Shakespeare: Part Five—King Lear and 'Heart of Darkness'." *PolR*, 20, 2-3 (1975), 13-30.

Godshalk, William L. "Kurtz as Diabolical Christ." *Discourse*, 12 (1969), 100-07.

Green, R. "Messrs. Wilcox and Kurtz: Hollow Men." *TCL*, 14 (1969), 231-39.

Gross, Harvey. "Aschenbach and Kurtz: The Cost of Civilization." *CentR*, 6 (1962), 131-43.

Gross, Seymour L. "A Further Note on the Function of the Frame in *Heart of Darkness*." *MFS*, 3 (1957), 167-70.

Guerard, Albert J. "Introduction." *HEART OF DARKNESS and THE SECRET SHARER*, by Joseph Conrad. New York: New American Library, 1950, 7-15.

Guetti, James. "*Heart of Darkness* and the Failure of the Imagination." *SR*, 73 (1965), 488-504.

Harkness, Bruce. *Conrad's HEART OF DARKNESS and the Critics*. San Francisco: Wadsworth, 1960.

Helder, Jack. "Fool Convention and Conrad's Hollow Harlequin." *SSF*, 12 (1975), 361-68.

Hoffman, Stanton de Voren. "The Hole in the Bottom of the Pail: Comedy and Theme in *Heart of Darkness*." *SSF*, 2 (1963), 113-23.

Hopwood, Alison L. "Carlyle and Conrad: Past, Present and 'Heart of Darkness'." *RES*, 23 (1972), 162-72.

Johnson, Bruce. " 'Heart of Darkness' and the Problem of Emptiness." *SSF*, 9 (1972), 387-400.

———. "Names, Naming, and the 'Inscrutable' in Conrad's *Heart of Darkness*." *TSLL*, 12 (1971), 675-88.

Karl, Frederick R. "Introduction to the *Danse Macabre*: Conrad's *Heart of Darkness*." *MFS*, 14 (1968), 143-56.

Ketterer, David A. " 'Beyond the Threshold' in Conrad's *Heart of Darkness*." *TSLL*, 11 (1969), 1013-22.

Killam, C. Douglas. "Kurtz's Country." *LHR*, 7 (1965), 31-42.

Kimbrough, Robert, ed. *HEART OF DARKNESS: An Authoritative Text, Backgrounds and Sources, Essays in Criticism*. New York: Norton, 1963.

Kitonga, Ellen M. "Conrad's Image of African and Coloniser in *Heart of Darkness*." *Busara*, 3, 1 (1970), 33-35.

Lemon, Lee. "Readers, Teachers, and Critics and the Nature of Literature." *PAPA*, 1, 2 (1975), 2-13.

Lincoln, Kenneth R. "Comic Light in *Heart of Darkness*." *MFS*, 18 (1972), 183-97.

Low, Anthony. "*Heart of Darkness*: The Search for an Occupation." *ELT*, 12, 1 (1969), 1-9.

McIntyre, Allan J. "Psychology and Symbol: Correspondences between *Heart of Darkness* and *Death in Venice*." *HSL*, 7 (1975), 216-35.

McLauchlan, Juliet. "Conrad's 'Three Ages of Man': The 'Youth' Volume." *PolR*, 20, 2-3 (1975), 189-202.

Martin, David M. "The Diabolic Kurtz: The Dual Nature of His Satanism in *Heart of Darkness*." *Conradiana*, 7, 2 (1975), 175-77.

———. "The Function of the Intended in Conrad's 'Heart of Darkness'." *SSF*, 11 (1974), 27-33.

Maud, Ralph. "The Plain Tale of *Heart of Darkness*." *HAB*, 17, 2 (1966), 13-17.

Mellard, James. "Myth and Archetype in *Heart of Darkness*." *TSL*, 13 (1968), 1-15.

Meyers, Jeffrey. "Savagery and Civilization in *The Tempest, Robinson Crusoe*, and *Heart of Darkness*." *Conradiana*, 2, 3 (1970), 171-79.

Montag, George E. "Marlow Tells the Truth: The Nature of Evil in *Heart of Darkness*." *Conradiana*, 3, 2 (1971-72), 93-97.

Na, Yong-Gyun. "The Original Sin Motif in *Heart of Darkness*." *SE-Lit*, 48 (1972), 97-107.

Nettels, Elsa. " 'Heart of Darkness' and the Creative Process." *Conradiana*, 5, 2 (1973), 66-73.

Ober, Warren U. "*Heart of Darkness*: 'The Ancient Mariner' a Hundred Years Later." *DR*, 45 (1965), 333-37.

Owen, Guy, Jr. "A Note on *Heart of Darkness*." *NCF*, 12 (1957), 168-69.

Pavlov, Grigor. "Two Studies in Bourgeois Individualism by Joseph Conrad." *ZAA*, 17 (1969), 229-38.

Peirce, William P. "An Artistic Flaw in *Heart of Darkness*." *Conradiana*, 1, 3 (1969), 73-80.

Pérez Firmat, Gustavo. "Don Quixote in *Heart of Darkness*." *CLS*, 12 (1975), 374-83.

Pinsker, Sanford. "Language, Silence, and the Existential Whisper: Once Again at the *Heart of Darkness*." *MLS*, 2, 2 (1972), 53-59.

Raskin, Jonah. "*Heart of Darkness*: The Manuscript Revisions." *RES*, 18 (1967), 30-39.

Reid, Stephen A. "The 'Unspeakable Rites' in *Heart of Darkness*." *MFS*, 9 (1964), 347-56.

Ridd, Carl. "Saving the Appearances in Conrad's *Heart of Darkness*." *SRC*, 2 (1972), 93-113.

Ridley, Florence H. "The Ultimate Meaning of 'Heart of Darkness'." *NCF*, 18 (1963), 43-53.

Rogers, William N., II. "The Game of Dominoes in *Heart of Darkness*." *ELN*, 13 (1975), 42-45.

Ruthven, K. K. "The Savage God: Conrad and Lawrence." *CritQ*, 10 (1968), 39-54.

Saveson, John E. "Conrad's View of Primitive Peoples in *Lord Jim* and *Heart of Darkness*." *MFS*, 16 (1970), 163-83.

Spinner, Kaspar. "Embracing the Universe: Some Annotations to Joseph Conrad's *Heart of Darkness*." *ES*, 43 (1962), 420-23.

Stark, Bruce R. "Kurtz's Intended: The Heart of *Heart of Darkness*." *TSLL*, 16 (1974), 535-55.

Stein, William Bysshe. "Buddhism and *The Heart of Darkness*." *WHR*, 11 (1957), 281-85.

———. *"The Heart of Darkness*: A Bodhisattva Scenario." *OW*, 9, 5 (1964), 37-46. [Also in *Conradiana*, 2, 2 (1970), 39-52]

———. "The Lotus Posture and *The Heart of Darkness*." *MFS*, 2 (1956), 235-37.

Stephens, R. C. *"Heart of Darkness*: Marlow's 'Spectral Moonshine'." *EIC*, 19 (1969), 273-84.

Sugg, Richard P. "The Triadic Structure of 'Heart of Darkness'." *Conradiana*, 7, 2 (1975), 179-82.

Thale, Jerome. "Marlow's Quest." *UTQ*, 24 (1955), 351-58.

———. "The Narrator as Hero." *TCL*, 3 (1957), 69-73.

Vernon, John E. *The Garden and the Map*, 29-38.

Wasserman, Jerry. "Narrative Presence: The Illusion of Language in *Heart of Darkness*." *SNNTS*, 6 (1973), 327-38.

Watts, C. T. *"Heart of Darkness*: The Covert Murder-Plot and the Darwinian Theme." *Conradiana*, 7, 2 (1975), 137-43.

Whitehead, Lee M. "The Active Voice and the Passive Eye: *Heart of Darkness* and Nietzsche's *The Birth of Tragedy*." *Conradiana*, 7, 2 (1975), 121-35.

Wilcox, Stewart C. "Conrad's 'Complicated Presentations' of Symbolic Imagery in *Heart of Darkness*." *PQ*, 39 (1960), 1-17.

Williams, George Walton. "The Turn of the Tide in 'Heart of Darkness'." *MFS*, 9 (1963), 171-73.

Yarrison, Betsy C. "The Symbolism of Literary Allusion in *Heart of Darkness*." *Conradiana*, 7, 2 (1975), 155-64.

Yoder, Albert C. "Oral Artistry in Conrad's *Heart of Darkness*: A Study of Oral Aggression." *Conradiana*, 2, 2 (1970), 65-78.

Zak, William F. "Conrad, F. R. Leavis, and Whitehead: 'Heart of Darkness' and Organic Holism." *Conradiana*, 4, 1 (1972), 5-24.

LORD JIM

Bass, Eben. "The Verbal Failure of Lord Jim." *CE*, 26 (1965), 438-44.

Bellis, George. "Fidelity to a Higher Ideal: A Study of the Jump in Conrad's *Lord Jim*." *ErasmusR*, 1, 1 (1971), 63-71.

Bolton, W. F. "The Role of Language in *Lord Jim.*" *Conradiana*, 1, 3 (1969), 51-59.

Brady, M. B. "The Collector-Motif in *Lord Jim.*" *BuR*, 16, 2 (1968), 66-85.

Bruffee, Kenneth A. "Elegiac Romance." *CE*, 32 (1971), 465-76.

Bruss, Paul S. "Marlow's Interview with Stein: The Implications of the Metaphor." *SNNTS*, 5 (1973), 491-503.

Burstein, Janet. "On Ways of Knowing in *Lord Jim.*" *NCF*, 26 (1972), 456-68.

Clark, Charles C. "The Brierly Suicide: A New Look at an Old Ambiguity." *ArlQ*, 1, 2 (1967-68), 259-65.

Cook, William J., Jr. *"Lord Jim* as Metaphor." *Conradiana*, 1, 2 (1968) 45-53.

Cox, C. B. "The Metamorphoses of Lord Jim." *CritQ*, 15 (1973), 9-31.

Day, A. Grove. "Pattern in *Lord Jim*: One Jump After Another." *CE*, 13 (1952), 396-97.

Dowden, Wilfred S. *"Almayer's Folly* and *Lord Jim*: A Study in the Development of Conrad's Imagery." *RUS*, 51, 1 (1965), 13-27.

Engelberg, Edward. *The Unknown Distance*, 172-85.

Epstein, Harry S. *"Lord Jim* as a Tragic Action." *SNNTS*, 5 (1973), 229-47.

Eschbacher, Robert L. *"Lord Jim*, Classical Rhetoric, and the Freshman Dilemma." *CE*, 25 (1963), 22-25.

Fichter, Andrew. "Dramatic Voice in *Lord Jim* and *Nostromo.*" *Thoth*, 12, 3 (1972), 3-19.

Flamm, Dudley. "The Ambiguous Nazarene in *Lord Jim.*" *ELT*, 11, 1 (1968), 35-37.

Fraser, G. S. *"Lord Jim*: The Romance of Irony." *CritQ*, 8 (1966), 231-41.

Garmon, Gerald M. *"Lord Jim* as Tragedy." *Conradiana*, 4, 1 (1972), 34-40.

Gold, Joseph. "Two Romantics: Jim and Stein." *CEA*, 24, 5 (1962), 1, 11-12.

Gordan, John D. "The Rajah Brook and Joseph Conrad." *SP*, 35 (1938), 613-34.

Gose, Elliott B. *Imagination Indulged*, 141-66.

―――. "Pure Exercise of Imagination: Archetypal Symbolism in *Lord Jim.*" *PMLA*, 79 (1964), 137-47.

Gossman, Ann M., and George W. Whiting. "The Essential Jim." *NCF*, 16 (1961), 75-80.

Greenberg, Alvin. "Lord Jim and the Rock of Sisyphus." *ForumH*, 6, 3 (1968), 13-17.

Greene, Graham. *"Lord Jim." TLS*, December 6, 1974, 1389.

Haugh, Robert F. "Joseph Conrad and Revolution." *CE*, 10 (1949), 273-77.

———. "The Structure of *Lord Jim." CE*, 13 (1951), 137-41.

Hay, Eloise. *"Lord Jim*: From Sketch to Novel." *CL*, 12 (1960), 289-309.

Heimer, Jackson W. "Betrayal, Guilt, and Attempted Redemption in *Lord Jim." BSUF*, 9, 2 (1968), 31-43.

Hoben, John B. "Lord Jim: Marlow's Bewildered Voice." *Philobiblon*, 9 (1972), 3-8.

Hodges, Robert R. "The Four Fathers of Lord Jim." *UR*, 31 (1964), 103-10.

Hoffman, Stanton de Voren. " 'Scenes of Low Comedy': The Comic in *Lord Jim." BSTCF*, 5, 2 (1964), 19-27.

Holmes, Karen Sue. "Lord Jim, Conrad's Alienated Man." *Descant*, 4 (1960), 33-40.

Hunt, Kellogg W. *"Lord Jim* and *The Return of the Native*: A Contrast." *EJ*, 49 (1960), 447-56.

Jacobs, Robert G. *"Gilgamesh*: The Sumerian Epic that Helped *Lord Jim* to Stand Alone." *Conradiana*, 4, 2 (1972), 23-32.

Johnson, Bruce M. "Conrad's 'Karain' and *Lord Jim." MLQ*, 24 (1963), 13-20.

Karl, Frederick R. "Conrad's Stein: The Destructive Element." *TCL*, 3 (1958), 163-69.

Karrfalt, David H. "Accepting Lord Jim on His Own Terms: A Structural Approach." *Conradiana*, 2, 1 (1970), 37-47.

Kramer, Dale. "Marlow, Myth, and Structure in *Lord Jim." Criticism*, 8 (1966), 263-79.

Krieger, Murray. *The Play and Place of Criticism*, 98-104.

Kuehn, Robert E., ed. *LORD JIM: A Collection of Critical Essays.* Englewood Cliffs, N. J.: Prentice-Hall, 1969.

Levin, Gerald. "The Scepticism of Marlow." *TCL*, 3 (1958), 177-84.

McAlpin, Edwin A. *Old and New Books as Life Teachers*, 50-65.

McCann, Charles J. "Lord Jim vs. the Darkness: The Saving Power of Human Involvement." *CE*, 27 (1965), 240-43.

Malbone, Raymond Gates. " 'How to Be': Marlow's Quest in *Lord Jim." TCL*, 10 (1965), 172-80.

Messenger, Ann P., and William E. " 'One of Us': A Biblical Allusion in Conrad's *Lord Jim." ELN*, 9 (1971), 129-32.

Miller, J. Hillis. "The Interpretation of *Lord Jim." The Interpretation of Narrative.* Ed. Morton W. Bloomfield, 211-28.

Moseley, Edwin M. *Pseudonyms of Christ in the Modern Novel*, 15-35.

Joseph Conrad, continued

Moser, Thomas, ed. *Lord Jim.* Authoritative Text. "Sources," ed. Norman Sherry. "Backgrounds" and "Essays in Criticism," ed. Thomas Moser. New York: Norton, 1968.

Muccigrosso, Robert M. "Conrad's *Lord Jim*: Teaching the First Chapter." *EJ*, 55 (1966), 1039-41.

Najder, Zdzislaw. "*Lord Jim*: A Romantic Tragedy of Honor." *Conradiana*, 1, 1 (1968), 1-7.

Nelson, Carl. "The Ironic Allusive Texture of *Lord Jim*: Coleridge, Crane, Milton, and Melville." *Conradiana*, 4, 2 (1972), 47-59.

Nettels, Elsa. "Vision and Knowledge in *The Ambassadors* and *Lord Jim*." *ELT*, 18, 3 (1975), 181-93.

Newell, Kenneth B. "The Destructive Element and Related 'Dream' Passages in the *Lord Jim* Manuscript." *JML*, 1 (1970), 31-44.

_____. "The Yellow-Dog Incident in Conrad's *Lord Jim*." *SNNTS*, 3 (1971), 26-33.

Newman, Paul B. "The Drama of Conscience and Recognition in *Lord Jim*." *MQ*, 6 (1965), 351-66.

Paulding, Gouverneur, et al. "Conrad's *Lord Jim*." *Invitation to Learning Reader*, 2 (Fall 1952), 236-42.

Pavlov, Grigor. "Two Studies in Bourgeois Individualism by Joseph Conrad." *ZAA*, 17 (1969), 229-38.

Phillipson, John S. "Conrad's Pink Toads: The Working of the Unconscious." *WHR*, 14 (1960, 437-38.

Reichard, Hugo M. "The Patusan Crises: A Revaluation of Jim and Marlow." *ES*, 49 (1968), 547-52.

Sadoff, Ira. "Sartre and Conrad: Lord Jim as Existentialist Hero." *DR*, 49 (1969), 518-25.

Saveson, John E. "Conrad's View of Primitive Peoples in *Lord Jim* and *Heart of Darkness*." *MFS*, 16 (1970), 163-83.

_____. "The Intuitionist Hero of *Lord Jim*." *Conradiana*, 4, 3 (1972), 34-47.

_____. "Marlow's Psychological Vocabulary in *Lord Jim*." *TSLL*, 12 (1970), 457-70.

Schneider, Daniel J. "Symbolism in Conrad's *Lord Jim*: The Total Pattern." *MFS*, 12 (1966), 427-38.

Schultheiss, Thomas. "Cornelius the Nazarene: Ambi-Ambiguity in *Lord Jim*." *ELT*, 12, 4 (1969), 195-96.

Schwarz, Daniel R. "The Journey to Patusan: The Education of Jim and Marlow in Conrad's *Lord Jim*." *SNNTS*, 4 (1972), 442-58.

Seltzer, Alvin J. *Chaos in the Novel*, 80-91.

Sherry, Norman. "Conrad's Eastern Port: The Setting of the Inquiry in *Lord Jim*." *REL*, 6, 4 (1965), 52-61.

_____. "*Lord Jim* and *The Secret Sharer.*" *RES*, 16 (1965), 378-92.
_____. "The Pilgrim Ship in *Lord Jim*: Conrad's Two Sources." *PQ*, 44 (1965), 88-99.
Spalding, Alex. "*Lord Jim*: The Result of Reading Light Holiday Literature." *HAB*, 19, 1 (1968), 14-22.
Squire, John C. *Life and Letters*, 139-45.
Stegmaier, E. "The 'Would-scene' in Joseph Conrad's *Lord Jim* and *Nostromo.*" *MLR*, 67 (1972), 517-23.
Steinmann, Theo. "Lord Jim's Progression Through Homology." *ArielE*, 5, 1 (1974), 81-93.
Stevenson, Richard C. "Stein's Prescription for 'How to Be' and the Problem of Assessing Lord Jim's Career." *Conradiana*, 7, 3 (1975), 233-43.
Szczepanski, Jan Jozef. "In Lord Jim's Boots." *PolP*, 18, 1 (1975), 31-44.
Tanner, J. E. "The Chronology and the Enigmatic End of Lord Jim." *NCF*, 21 (1967), 369-80.
Tanner, Tony. "Butterflies and Beetles: Conrad's Two Truths." *ChiR*, 16, 1 (1963), 123-40.
_____. *Conrad: LORD JIM*. London: E. Arnold; Great Neck, N. Y.: Barron's Educational Series, 1963.
Webb, Michael. "Conrad's Use of the Motto 'Usque Ad Finem' in *Lord Jim* and in a Letter to Bertrand Russell." *Conradiana*, 5, 2 (1973), 74-80.
Whiting, George W. "Conrad's Revision of *Lord Jim.*" *EJ*, 23 (1934), 824-32.
See also: Drew, *Novel*; Van Ghent.

THE NIGGER OF THE "NARCISSUS"
Bernard, Kenneth. "Conrad's Fools of Innocence in *The Nigger of the 'Narcissus'.*" *Conradiana*, 2, 1 (1970), 49-57.
Biles, Jack I. " 'Its Proper Title': Some Observations on 'The Nigger of the "Narcissus" '." *PolR*, 20, 2-3 (1975), 181-88.
Bloch, Tuvia. "The Wait-Donkin Relationship in *The Nigger of the 'Narcissus'.*" *Conradiana*, 4, 2 (1972), 62-66.
Bonney, William W. "Semantic and Structural Indeterminacy in *The Nigger of the 'Narcissus'*: An Experiment in Reading." *ELH*, 40 (1974), 564-83.
Bruss, Paul S. "Conrad's *The Nigger*: The Narrator and the Crew." *EngR*, 23, 1 (Fall 1972), 16-26.
Burgess, C. F. "Of Men and Ships and Mortality: Conrad's *The Nigger of the 'Narcissus'.*" *ELT*, 15, 3 (1972), 221-31.

Joseph Conrad, continued

Daleski, H. M. "Hanging On and Letting Go: Conrad's *The Nigger of the 'Narcissus'*." *HUSL*, 2, 2 (1974), 171-96.

Davis, Harold E. "Symbolism in *The Nigger of the 'Narcissus'*." *TCL*, 2 (1956), 26-29.

Davis, Kenneth W., Lynn F. Henry, and Donald W. Rude. "Conrad's Trashing/Thrashing Sails: Orthography and a Crux in *The Nigger of the 'Narcissus'*." *Conradiana*, 6, 2 (1974), 131-33.

———, and Donald W. Rude. "The Transmission of the Text of *The Nigger of the 'Narcissus'*." *Conradiana*, 5, 2 (1973), 20-45.

Echeruo, W. J. C. "James Wait and *The Nigger of the 'Narcissus'*." *ESA*, 8 (1965), 166-80.

Foulke, Robert. "Postures of Belief in *The Nigger of the Narcissus*." *MFS*, 17 (1971), 249-62.

Guerard, Albert J. "*The Nigger of the Narcissus*." *KR*, 19 (1957), 205-32.

Gurko, Leo. "Death Journey in *The Nigger of the 'Narcissus'*." *NCF*, 15 (1961), 301-11.

Hammes, Kenneth W., Jr. "Melville, Dana, and Ames: Sources for Conrad's *The Nigger of the 'Narcissus'*." *PolR*, 19, 3-4 (1974), 29-33.

Haugh, Robert F. "Death and Consequences: Joseph Conrad's Attitude Toward Fate." *UKCR*, 18 (1952), 191-97.

Hodgson, John A. "Left-Right Opposition in *The Nigger of the 'Narcissus'*." *PLL*, 8 (1972), 207-10.

Kerf, René. "*The Nigger of the 'Narcissus'* and the MS. Version of *The Rescue*." *ES*, 44 (1963), 437-43.

Kinney, Arthur F. "Jimmy Wait: Joseph Conrad's Kaleidoscope." *CE*, 26 (1965), 475-78.

Martin, W. R. "The Captain of the *Narcissus*." *ESA*, 6 (1963), 191-97.

Masback, Frederic J. "Conrad's Jonahs." *CE*, 22 (1960), 328-33.

Miller, James E., Jr. "*The Nigger of the 'Narcissus'*: A Reexamination." *PMLA*, 66 (1951), 911-18.

Molinoff, Katherine. "Conrad's Debt to Melville: James Wait, Donkin and Belfast of the 'Narcissus'." *Conradiana*, 1, 3 (1969), 119-22.

Moorthy, P. Rama. "*The Nigger of the Narcissus*." *LCrit*, 7, 1 (1965), 49-58.

Morgan, Gerald. "Narcissus Afloat." *HAB*, 15, 2 (1964), 45-57.

Mudrick, Marvin. "The Artist's Conscience and *The Nigger of the Narcissus*." *NCF*, 11 (1957), 288-97.

Nelson, Harland S. "Eden and Golgotha: Conrad's Use of the Bible in *The Nigger of the 'Narcissus'*." *IEY*, 8 (1963), 63-67.

Palmer, John A., ed. *THE NIGGER OF THE "NARCISSUS": A Collection of Critical Essays.* Englewood Cliffs, N.J.: Prentice-Hall, 1969.

Pinsker, Sanford. "Joseph Conrad and the Language of the Sea." *Conradiana*, 3, 3 (1971-72), 15-21.

_____. "Selective Memory, Leisure and the Language of Joseph Conrad's *The Nigger of the 'Narcissus'*." *Descant*, 15 (1971), 38-48.

Pulc, I. P. "Two Portrayals of a Storm: Some Notes on Conrad's Descriptive Style in *The Nigger of the 'Narcissus'* and 'Typhoon'." *Style*, 4 (1970), 49-57.

Saveson, John E. "Contemporary Psychology in *The Nigger of the 'Narcissus'*." *SSF*, 7 (1970), 219-31.

Scrimgeour, Cecil. "Jimmy Wait and the Dance of Death: Conrad's *Nigger of the 'Narcissus'*." *CritQ*, 7 (1965), 339-52.

Smith, David R. " 'One Word More' About *The Nigger of the 'Narcissus'*." *NCF*, 23 (1968), 201-16.

Steinmann, Theo. "The Perverted Pattern of *Billy Budd* in *The Nigger of the 'Narcissus'*." *ES*, 55 (1973), 239-46.

Sutton, Maurice, ed. *Joseph Conrad: THE NIGGER OF THE "NARCISSUS."* New York: Barnes and Noble, 1968.

Torchiana, Donald T. "*The Nigger of the Narcissus*: Myth, Mirror, and Metropolis." *WascanaR*, 2, 2 (1967), 29-41.

Watt, Ian. "Conrad Criticism and *The Nigger of the 'Narcissus'*." *NCF*, 12 (1958), 257-83.

_____. "Conrad's Preface to *The Nigger of the 'Narcissus'*." *Novel*, 7 (1974), 101-15.

Wiley, P. L. "Two Tales of Passion." *Conradiana*, 6 (1974), 189-95.

Worth, George J. "Conrad's Debt to Maupassant in the Preface to *The Nigger of the 'Narcissus'*." University of Illinois, English Dept. *Studies by Members of the English Dept., in Memory of John Jay Parry*, 219-23.

Yates, Norris W. "Social Comment in *The Nigger of the 'Narcissus'*." *PMLA*, 79 (1964), 183-85.

Young, Vernon. "Trial by Water: Joseph Conrad's *The Nigger of the Narcissus*." *Accent*, 12 (1952), 67-81.

NOSTROMO

Brown, Ruth C. " 'Plung'd in that Abortive Gulf': Milton in *Nostromo*." *PolR*, 20, 2-3 (1975), 31-57.

Bufkin, Ernest C. "Conrad, Grand Opera, and *Nostromo*." *NCF*, 30 (1975), 206-14.

Curle, Richard. *Caravansary and Conversation*, 209-21.

Emmett, V. J., Jr. "The Aesthetics of Anti-Imperial Ironic Distortions of the Vergilian Epic Mode in Conrad's *Nostromo*." *SNNTS*, 4 (1972), 459-72.

Fichter, Andrew. "Dramatic Voice in *Lord Jim* and *Nostromo*." *Thoth*, 12, 3 (1972), 3-19.

Freeman, Rosemary. "Conrad's *Nostromo*: A Source and Its Use." *MFS*, 7 (1961), 317-26.

Gillon, Adam. "The Merchant of Esmeralda—Conrad's Archetypal Jew." *PolR*, 9, 4 (1964), 3-20.

Greiff, Louis K., and Shirley A. Greiff. "Sulaco and Panama: A Geographical Source in Conrad's *Nostromo*." *JML*, 3 (1973), 102-05.

Hainsworth, J. D. "An Approach to *Nostromo*." *Use of English*, 10 (1959), 181-86.

Haltresht, Michael. "The Gods of Conrad's *Nostromo*." *Renascence*, 24 (1972), 207-12.

Halverson, John, and Ian Watt. "The Original *Nostromo*: Conrad's Source." *RES*, 10 (1959), 45-52.

Harris, Wendell V. "Of Time and the Novel." *BuR*, 16, 1 (1968), 114-29.

Heimer, Jackson W. "Betrayal, Confession, Attempted Redemption, and Punishment in *Nostromo*." *TSLL*, 8 (1967), 561-79.

Karl, Frederick R. "The Significance of the Revisions in the Early Versions of *Nostromo*." *MFS*, 5 (1959), 129-44.

Kartiganer, Donald M. "Process and Product: A Study of Modern Literary Form." *MR*, 12 (1971), 297-328, 789-816.

Kimpel, Ben, and T. C. Duncan Eaves. "The Geography and History in *Nostromo*." *MP*, 56 (1958), 45-54.

King, William E. "Conrad's *Weltanschauung* and the God of Material Interests in *Nostromo*." *Conradiana*, 3, 3 (1971-72), 41-45.

Leech, Clifford. "The Shaping of Time: *Nostromo* and *Under the Volcano*." *Imagined Worlds*. Ed. Maynard Mack and Ian Gregor, 323-41.

Lynskey, Winifred. "The Role of the Silver in *Nostromo*." *MFS*, 1, 1 (1955), 16-21.

McCann, Charles J., and Victor Comerchero. "Setting as a Key to the Structure and Meaning of *Nostromo*." *RS*, 34 (1966), 66-84.

McLauchlan, Juliet. "The Politics of *Nostromo*." *EIC*, 18 (1968), 475-77.

Maclennan, D. A. C. "Conrad's Vision." *ESA*, 7 (1964), 195-201.

McMillan, Dougald. "*Nostromo*: The Theology of Revolution." *The Classic British Novel*. Ed. Howard M. Harper, Jr. and Charles Edge, 166-82.

Marten, Harry. "Conrad's Skeptic Reconsidered: A Study of Martin Decoud." *NCF*, 27 (1972), 81-94.

Mueller, William R. "Man and Nature in Conrad's *Nostromo*." *Thought*, 45 (1970), 559-76.

Muller, Herbert. *In Pursuit of Relevance*, 164-76.

Oates, Joyce Carol. " 'The Immense Indifference of Things': The Tragedy of Conrad's *Nostromo*." *Novel*, 9 (1975), 5-22.

Pinsker, Sanford. "The Conradian Hero and the Death of Language: A Note on *Nostromo*." *Conradiana*, 1, 1 (1968), 49-50.

Raskin, Jonah. "*Nostromo*: The Argument from Revision." *EIC*, 18 (1968), 183-92.

Rosa, Alfred F. "The Counterforce of Technology on the Pastoral Ideal in *Nostromo*." *MSE*, 1 (1968), 88-93.

Rosenfield, Claire. "An Archetypal Analysis of Conrad's *Nostromo*." *TSLL*, 3 (1962), 510-34.

Said, Edward W. "Conrad, *Nostromo*: Record and Reality." *Approaches to the Twentieth-Century Novel*. Ed. John Unterecker, 108-52.

Saunders, William S. "The Unity of *Nostromo*." *Conradiana*, 5, 1 (1973), 27-36.

Saveson, John E. "*Nostromo* and the London *Times*." *RES*, 24 (1973), 52-58.

_____. "Sources of *Nostromo*." *N&Q*, 19 (1972), 331-34.

Singh, Ramchander. "*Nostromo*: The Betrayed Self." *LCrit*, 10, 4 (1973), 61-66.

Smith, David R. "*Nostromo* and the Three Sisters." *SEL*, 2 (1962), 497-508.

Stegmaier, E. "The 'Would-scene' in Joseph Conrad's *Lord Jim* and *Nostromo*." *MLR*, 67 (1972), 517-23.

Tartella, Vincent P. "Symbolism in Four Scenes in *Nostromo*." *Conradiana*, 4, 1 (1972), 63-70.

Tick, Stanley. "The Gods of *Nostromo*." *MFS*, 10, 1 (1964), 15-26.

Tomlinson, Maggie. "Conrad's Integrity: *Nostromo, Typhoon, The Shadow-Line*." *MCR*, 5 (1962), 40-53.

Tomlinson, T. B. "Conrad's Trust in Life: *Nostromo*." *CR*, 14 (1971), 62-81.

Vidan, Ivo. "One Source of Conrad's *Nostromo*." *RES*, 7 (1956), 287-93.

_____. "Perspective of *Nostromo*." *SRAZ*, 13-14 (1962), 43-54.

_____. "Rehearsal for *Nostromo*." *SRAZ*, 10 (1961), 9-16.

_____, and Juliet McLauchlan. "The Politics of *Nostromo*." *EIC*, 17 (1967), 392-406.

Warren, Robert Penn. "Nostromo." *SR*, 59 (1951), 363-91.

Joseph Conrad, continued

Whitehead, Lee M. *"Nostromo*: The Tragic 'Idea'." *NCF,* 23 (1969), 463-75.
Whiting, George W. "Conrad's Revision of 'The Lighthouse' in *Nostromo." PMLA,* 52 (1937), 1183-90.
Wilding, Michael. "The Politics of *Nostromo." EIC,* 16 (1966), 441-56, and *EIC,* 18 (1968), 234-36.
See also: Brewster and Burrell; Mueller, *Celebration*; Tillyard, *Epic.*

AN OUTCAST OF THE ISLANDS
Gekoski, R. A. *"An Outcast of the Islands*: A New Reading." *Conradiana,* 2, 3 (1970), 47-58.
Gurko, Leo. "Conrad's First Battleground." *UKCR,* 25 (1959), 190-94.
Ordonez, Elmer A. "Notes on the Revisions in *An Outcast of the Islands." N&Q,* 15 (1968), 287-89.
Pinsker, Sanford. "Desire Under the Conradian Elms: A Note on *An Outcast of the Islands." Conradiana,* 5, 3 (1973), 60-63.
Resink, G. J. "Samburan Encantada." *Conradiana,* 1, 2 (1968), 37-44.

THE RESCUE
Bruccoli, Matthew J., and Charles A. Rheault, Jr. "Imposition Figures and Plate Gangs in *The Rescue." SB,* 14 (1961), 258-62.
Cross, Wilbur. "Some Novels of 1920." *YR,* n.s. 10 (1921), 396-411.
Geddes, Gary. *"The Rescue*: Conrad and the Rhetoric of Diplomacy." *Mosaic,* 7, 3 (1974), 107-25.
Gordon, John D. "The Rajah Brooke and Joseph Conrad." *SP,* 35 (1938), 613-34.
Howarth, Herbert. "Conrad and Imperialism: The Difference of *The Rescue." OhR,* 13, 1 (1971), 62-72.
Kehler, Joel R. "A Note on the Epigraph to Conrad's *The Rescue." ELN,* 12 (1975), 184-87.
Kerf, René. *"The Nigger of the 'Narcissus'* and the MS. Version of *The Rescue." ES,* 44 (1963), 437-43.
Liljegren, S. Bodvar. *Joseph Conrad as a "Prober of Feminine Hearts": Notes on the Novel THE RESCUE.* Uppsala: Lundequistska, 1968.
Mansfield, Katherine. *Novels and Novelists,* 213-17.
Morf, Gustav. " 'The Rescue' as an Expression of Conrad's Dual Personality." *PolR,* 20, 2-3 (1975), 211-16.
Wright, Walter F. "Conrad's *The Rescue* from Serial to Book." *RS,* 13 (1945), 203-24.
Young, Vernon. "Lingard's Folly: the Lost Subject." *KR,* 15 (1953), 522-39.

THE ROVER
Boyles, John. "Joseph Conrad's *The Rover.*" *Use of English*, 18 (1966), 124-28.

Fleishman, Avrom. "Conrad's Last Novel." *ELT*, 12, 4 (1969), 189-94.

Higdon, David L. "Conrad's *The Rover*: The Grammar of a Myth." *SNNTS*, 1 (1969), 17-26.

Howarth, Herbert. "The Meaning of Conrad's *The Rover.*" *SoR*, n.s. 6 (1970), 682-97.

Laine, Michael. "Conrad's *The Rover*: The Rejection of Despair." *QQ*, 80 (1973), 246-55.

Lippincott, H. F. "Sense of Place in Conrad's *The Rover.*" *Conradiana*, 6, 2 (1974), 106-12.

Martin, R. W. "Allegory in Conrad's *The Rover.*" *ESA*, 10 (1967), 186-94.

Wright, Elizabeth Cox. "The Defining Function of Vocabulary in Conrad's *The Rover.*" *SAQ*, 59 (1960), 265-77.

THE SECRET AGENT
Anderegg, Michael A. "Conrad and Hitchcock: *The Secret Agent* Inspires *Sabotage.*" *LFQ*, 3 (1975), 215-25.

Baird, Newton. "Conrad's Probe to Absolute Zero." *ArmD*, 9 (1975), 43-49.

Cheney, Lynne. "Joseph Conrad's *The Secret Agent* and Graham Greene's *It's a Battlefield:* A Study in Structural Meaning." *MFS*, 16 (1970), 117-31.

Cox, C. B. "Joseph Conrad's *The Secret Agent*: The Irresponsible Piano." *CritQ*, 15 (1973), 197-212.

Davis, Harold E. "Conrad's Revisions of *The Secret Agent*: A Study in Literary Impressionism." *MLQ*, 19 (1958), 244-54.

Dowden, Wilfred S. "The 'Illuminating Quality': Imagery and Theme in *The Secret Agent.*" *RIP*, 47, 3 (1960), 17-33.

Fleishman, Avrom. "The Symbolic World of *The Secret Agent.*" *ELH*, 32 (1965), 196-219.

Fradin, Joseph I. "Anarchist, Detective, and Saint: The Possibilities of Action in *The Secret Agent.*" *PMLA*, 83 (1968), 1414-22.

――――. "Conrad's Everyman: *The Secret Agent.*" *TSLL*, 11 (1969), 1023-38.

――――, and Jean W. Creighton. "The Language of *The Secret Agent*: The Art of Non-Life." *Conradiana*, 1, 2 (1968), 23-35.

Gilmore, Thomas B., Jr. "Retributive Irony in Conrad's *The Secret Agent.*" *Conradiana*, 1, 3 (1969), 41-50.

Gose, Elliott B., Jr. " 'Cruel Devourer of the World's Light': *The Secret Agent.*" *NCF*, 15 (1960), 39-51.

Guilhamet, Leon. "Conrad's 'The Secret Agent' as the Imitation of an Action." *PolR*, 20, 2-3 (1975), 145-53.

Gurko, Leo. "*The Secret Agent*: Conrad's Vision of Megalopolis." *MFS*, 4 (1958), 307-18.

Hagan, John, Jr. "The Design of Conrad's *The Secret Agent.*" *ELH*, 22 (1955), 148-64.

Haltresht, Michael. "Disease Imagery in Conrad's *The Secret Agent.*" *L&P*, 21 (1971), 101-05.

———. "The Dread of Space in Conrad's *The Secret Agent.*" *L&P*, 22 (1972), 89-97.

Hartsell, Robert L. "Conrad's Left Symbolism in *The Secret Agent.*" *Conradiana*, 4, 1 (1972), 57-59.

Heimer, Jackson W. "Betrayal in *The Secret Agent.*" *Conradiana*, 7, 3 (1975), 245-51.

Hertz, Robert N. "The Scene of Mr. Verloo's Murder in *The Secret Agent*: A Study of Conrad's Narrative and Dramatic Method." *Person*, 43 (1962), 214-25.

Hoff, Peter Sloat. " 'The Secret Agent': A Typical Conrad Novel?" *PolR*, 20, 2-3 (1975), 154-63.

Holland, Norman N. "Style as Character: *The Secret Agent.*" *MFS*, 12 (1966), 221-31.

Johnston, John H. "*The Secret Agent* and *Under Western Eyes*: Conrad's Two Political Novels." *WVUPP*, 17 (1970), 57-71.

Kilroy, James. "Conrad's 'Succès de Curiosité': The Dramatic Version of *The Secret Agent.*" *ELT*, 10, 2 (1967), 81-88.

Knoepflmacher, U. C. *Laughter and Despair*, 240-73.

Kubal, David L. "*The Secret Agent* and the Mechanical Chaos." *BuR*, 15, 3 (1967), 65-77.

Langbaum, Robert. "Thoughts for Our Time: Three Novels on Anarchism." *ASch*, 42 (1973), 227-50.

Lee, Robin. "*The Secret Agent*: Structure, Theme, Mode." *ESA*, 11 (1968), 185-93.

Luecke, Sister Jane Marie. "Conrad's Secret and Its Agent." *MFS*, 10, 1 (1964), 37-48.

Magnuson, Harold M. "Anarchism in Conrad's *The Secret Agent.*" *WSL*, 4 (1967), 75-88.

Mann, Thomas. *Past Masters*, 231-47.

Marsh, D. R. C. "Moral Judgments in *The Secret Agent.*" *ESA*, 3 (1960), 57-70.

Meyers, Jeffrey. "The Agamemnon Myth and *The Secret Agent.*" *Conradiana*, 1, 1 (1968), 57-59.

Michael, Marion C. "Conrad's 'Definite Intention' in *The Secret Agent.*" *Conradiana*, 1, 1 (1968), 9-17.

Moore, Harry T. "Leitmotif Symbolism in 'The Secret Agent'." *PolR*, 20, 2-3 (1975), 141-44.

Nash, Christopher. "More Light on *The Secret Agent.*" *RES*, 20 (1969), 322-27.

O'Grady, Walter. "On Plot in Modern Fiction: Hardy, James and Conrad." *MFS*, 11 (1965), 107-15.

Pritchett, V. S. "Conrad: The Exile, the Isolated Man." *New Statesman*, 40 (1950), 72-73.

Shadoian, Jack. "Irony Triumphant: Verloc's Death." *Conradiana*, 3, 2 (1971-72), 82-86.

Sherry, Norman. "Conrad's Ticket-of-Leave Apostle." *MLR*, 64 (1969), 749-58.

――――. "The Greenwich Bomb Outrage and *The Secret Agent.*" *RES*, 18 (1967), 412-28.

――――. "Sir Ethelred in *The Secret Agent.*" *PQ*, 48 (1969), 108-15.

Spector, Robert D. "Irony as Theme: Conrad's *Secret Agent.*" *NCF*, 13 (1958), 69-71.

Stallman, Robert W. "Checklist of Some Studies of Conrad's *The Secret Agent* Since 1960." *Conradiana*, 6, 1 (1974), 31-45.

――――. "Time and *The Secret Agent.*" *TSLL*, 1 (1959), 101-22.

Sullivan, Walter. "Irony and Disorder: *The Secret Agent.*" *SR*, 81 (1973), 124-31.

Thornton, Weldon. "An Episode from Anglo-Irish History in Conrad's *The Secret Agent.*" *ELN*, 10 (1973), 286-89.

Tillyard, E. M. W. *Essays, Literary and Educational*, 144-53.

――――. "*The Secret Agent* Reconsidered." *EIC*, 11 (1961), 309-18.

Walton, James. "Conrad and Naturalism: *The Secret Agent.*" *TSLL*, 9 (1967), 289-301.

――――. "Conrad and *The Secret Agent*: The Genealogy of Mr. Vladimir." *PolR*, 12, 3 (1967), 28-42.

Wiesenfarth, Joseph. "Stevie and the Structure of *The Secret Agent.*" *MFS*, 13 (1967), 513-17.

Zuckerman, Jerome. "The Motif of Cannibalism in *The Secret Agent.*" *TSLL*, 10 (1968), 295-99.

THE SHADOW-LINE

Bakker, J. "Crossing the Shadow-Line." *DQR*, 5 (1975), 195-205.

Joseph Conrad, continued

Benson, Carl. "Conrad's Two Stories of Initiation." *PMLA*, 69 (1954), 46-56.

Masbock, Frederic J. "Conrad's Jonahs." *CE*, 22 (1961), 328-33.

Sherry, Norman. " 'Exact Biography' and *The Shadow-Line.*" *PMLA*, 79 (1964), 620-25.

Tomlinson, Maggie. "Conrad's Integrity: *Nostromo, Typhoon, The Shadow-Line.*" *MCR*, 5 (1962), 40-53.

Watt, Ian. "Story and Idea in Conrad's 'The Shadow Line'." *CritQ*, 2 (1960), 133-48.

Waugh, Arthur. *Tradition and Change*, 276-84.

Zuckerman, Jerome. "The Architecture of *The Shadow-Line.*" *Conradiana*, 3, 2 (1971-72), 87-92.

SUSPENSE

Aubry, G. Jean. "The Inner History of Conrad's *Suspense.*" *BookJ*, 13 (1925), 3-10.

Mackenzie, Manfred. "Fenimore Cooper and Conrad's *Suspense.*" *N&Q*, 10 (1963), 373-75.

Wood, Miriam H. "A Source for Conrad's *Suspense.*" *MLN*, 50 (1935), 390-94.

UNDER WESTERN EYES

Adams, Barbara B. "Sisters Under Their Skins: The Women in the Lives of Raskolnikov and Razumov." *Conradiana*, 6, 2 (1974), 113-24.

Cady, Louise Lamar. "On Conrad's Compositional Effects in Razumov's Decision to Betray Haldin." *WVUPP*, 22 (1975), 59-62.

Fries, Maureen. "Feminism—Antifeminism in *Under Western Eyes.*" *Conradiana*, 5, 2 (1973), 56-65.

Goodin, George. "The Personal and the Political in *Under Western Eyes.*" *NCF*, 25 (1970), 327-42.

Gurko, Leo. "*Under Western Eyes*: Conrad and the Question of 'Where To?' " *CE*, 21 (1960), 445-52.

Hagan, John. "Conrad's *Under Western Eyes*: The Question of Razumov's 'Guilt' and 'Remorse'." *SNNTS*, 1 (1969), 310-22.

Heimer, Jackson W. "The Betrayer as Intellectual: Conrad's *Under Western Eyes.*" *PolR*, 12, 4 (1967), 57-68.

Herling-Grudzinski, Gustaw. "Under Conrad's Eyes." *Kultura Essays.* Ed. Leopold Tyrmand, 174-91.

Higdon, David L. "Chateau Borel, Petrus Borel, and Conrad's *Under Western Eyes.*" *SNNTS*, 3 (1971), 99-102.

———. "Pascal's *Pensée* 47 in *Under Western Eyes.*" *Conradiana*, 5, 2 (1973), 81-83.

Izsak, Emily K. "*Under Western Eyes* and the Problems of Serial Publication." *RES*, 23 (1972), 429-44.

Johnson, Bruce. "*Under Western Eyes*: Politics as Symbol." *Conradiana*, 1, 1 (1968), 35-44.

Johnston, John H. "*The Secret Agent* and *Under Western Eyes*: Conrad's Two Political Novels." *WVUPP*, 17 (1970), 57-71.

Karl, Frederick R. "The Rise and Fall of *Under Western Eyes*." *NCF*, 13 (1959), 313-27.

Kaye, Julian B. "Conrad's *Under Western Eyes* and Mann's *Doctor Faustus*." *CL*, 9 (1957), 60-65.

Kelley, Robert E. " 'This Chance Glimpse': The Narrator in *Under Western Eyes*." *UR*, 37 (1971), 285-90.

Martin, W. R. "Compassionate Realism in Conrad and *Under Western Eyes*." *ESA*, 17 (1974), 89-100.

Mukerji, N. "The Problem of Point of View in *Under Western Eyes*." *Essays Presented to Prof. Amalendu Bose*. Ed. Dipendu Chakrabarti, 73-80.

Saveson, John E. "The Moral Discovery of *Under Western Eyes*." *Criticism*, 14 (1972), 32-48.

Tanner, Tony. "Nightmare and Complacency: Razumov and the Western Eye." *CritQ*, 4 (1962), 197-214.

Viswanathan, Jacqueline. "Point of View and Unreliability in Bronte's *Wuthering Heights*, Conrad's *Under Western Eyes*, and Mann's *Doktor Faustus*." *OL*, 29 (1974), 42-60.

Watson, John Gillard. "The Role of the Writer." *HJ*, 56 (1958), 371-76.

Zabel, Morton Dauwen. "Introduction." *Under Western Eyes*, by Joseph Conrad. Garden City, N.Y.: Doubleday, 1963, xi-xxxvi.

See also: Eagleton; Pritchett, *Books*.

VICTORY

Bluefarb, Sam. "Samburan: Conrad's Mirror Image of Eden." *Conradiana*, 1, 3 (1969), 89-94.

Bonney, William W. "Narrative Perspective in *Victory*: The Thematic Relevance." *JNT*, 5 (1975), 24-39.

Butler, Richard E. "Jungian and Oriental Symbolism in Joseph Conrad's *Victory*." *Conradiana*, 3, 2 (1971-72), 36-54.

Curle, Richard. "Mr. Joseph Conrad and *Victory*." *Fortnightly*, n.s. 98 (1915), 670-78.

de la Mare, Walter. *Private View*, 19-22.

Dike, Donald A. "The Tempest of Axel Heyst." *NCF*, 17 (1962), 95-113.

Downing, Francis. "The Meaning of Victory in Joseph Conrad." *Cweal*, 55 (1952), 613-14.

Gatch, Katherine H. "Conrad's Axel." *SP*, 48 (1951), 98-106.

Joseph Conrad, continued

Gillon, Adam. "Joseph Conrad and Shakespeare, Part Four: A New Reading of *Victory.*" *Conradiana*, 7 (1975), 263-81.

Goens, Mary B. "The 'Mysterious and Effective Star': The Mythic World-View in Conrad's *Victory.*" *MFS*, 13 (1967), 455-63.

Greenberg, Robert A. "The Presence of Mr. Wang." *BUSE*, 4 (1960), 129-37.

Gross, Seymour L. "The Devil in Samburan: Jones and Ricardo in *Victory.*" *NCF*, 16 (1961), 81-85.

Heimer, Jackson W. " 'Look On—Make No Sound': Conrad's *Victory.*" *SIH*, 1 (1969), 8-13.

Hollahan, Eugene. "Beguiled into Action: Silence and Sound in *Victory.*" *TSLL*, 16 (1974), 349-62.

Howell, Elmo. "The Concept of Evil in Conrad's *Victory.*" *BSUF*, 12, 2 (1971), 76-79.

Kaehele, Sharon, and Howard German. "Conrad's *Victory*: A Reassessment." *MFS*, 10, 1 (1964), 55-72.

Kennard, Jean E. "Emerson and Dickens: A Note on Conrad's *Victory.*" *Conradiana*, 6 (1974), 215-19.

Lewis, R. W. B. "The Current of Conrad's *Victory.*" *Twelve Original Essays on Great English Novels.* Ed. Charles Shapiro, 203-31.

Lodge, David. "Conrad's *Victory* and *The Tempest*: An Amplification." *MLR*, 59 (1964), 195-99.

Lordi, R. J. "The Three Emissaries of Evil: Their Psychological Relationship in Conrad's *Victory.*" *CE*, 23 (1961), 136-40.

Page, Norman. "Dickensian Elements in *Victory.*" *Conradiana*, 5, 1 (1973), 37-42.

Raphael, Alice P. *Goethe, the Challenger*, 39-83.

Reinecke, George F. "Conrad's *Victory*: Psychomachy, Christian Symbols, and Theme." *Explorations of Literature.* Ed. Rima D. Reck, 70-80.

Renner, Stanley. "Affirmations of Faith in *Victory* and *Murder in the Cathedral.*" *CSR*, 4 (1974), 110-19.

Resink, G. J. "Axel Heyst and the Second King of the Cocos Islands." *ES*, 44 (1963), 443-47.

———. "Samburan Encantada." *Conradiana*, 1, 2 (1968), 37-44.

Roberts, Mark. *The Tradition of Romantic Morality*, 259-87.

Saveson, John E. "Conrad as Moralist in *Victory.*" *Costerus*, 8 (1973), 177-92.

———. "Conrad's Acis and Galatea: A Note on *Victory.*" *MLS*, 2, 2 (1972), 59-62.

Secor, Robert. *The Rhetoric of Shifting Perspectives: Conrad's VICTORY.* University Park: Penn. State Univ. Press, 1971.

Stallman, Robert W. "The Structure and Symbolism of Conrad's *Victory.*" *WestR*, 13 (1949), 146-57.

Tanner, Tony. "Conrad's *Victory*: An Answer to Schopenhauer." *LonM*, n.s. 5, 4 (July 1965), 85-90.

Webster, H. T. "Conrad's Changes in Narrative Conception in the Manuscripts of *"Typhoon" and Other Stories* and *Victory.*" *PMLA*, 64 (1949), 953-62.

Widmer, Kingsley. "Conrad's Pyrrhic *Victory.*" *TCL*, 5 (1959), 123-30.

See also: Walcutt.

WILLIAM COOPER

GENERAL STUDIES

Deakin, Nicholas. "An Appraisal of William Cooper: In Search of Banality." *T&T*, 42 (1961), 140-41.

Enright, D. J. "The New Pastoral-Comical." *Spectator*, 206 (February 3, 1961), 154-55.

Johnson, Pamela Hansford. "Smart Chap Grows Up." *Reporter*, 24 (March 16, 1961), 55-56.

Moers, Ellen. "Still Angry." *Commentary*, 31, 6 (June 1961), 542-44.

See also: Allen, *Tradition*.

NIGEL DENNIS

GENERAL STUDIES

Allsop, Kenneth. *The Angry Decade*, 147-55.

Dooley, D. J. "The Satirist and the Contemporary Nonentity." *SNL*, 10 (1972), 1-9.

Ewart, Gavin. "Nigel Dennis—Identity Man." *LonM*, n.s. 3, 8 (November 1963), 35-46.

Olney, James. "*Cards of Identity* and the Satiric Mode." *SNNTS*, 3 (1971), 374-89.

Peake, Charles. "*Cards of Identity*: An Intellectual Satire." *LHY*, 1 (1960), 49-57.

See also: Allen, *Tradition*; Bergonzi, *Situation*; Gindin, *Postwar*; Karl.

NORMAN DOUGLAS

BIBLIOGRAPHIES

McDonald, Edward D. *A Bibliography of Norman Douglas.* Philadelphia: Centaur Book Shop, 1927.

Woolf, Cecil. *A Bibliography of Norman Douglas.* London: Hart-Davis, 1954.

Norman Douglas, continued

GENERAL STUDIES

Aldington, Richard. *Pinorman: Personal Recollections of Norman Douglas, Pino Orioli, and Charles Prentice*. London: Heinemann, 1954.

Cunard, Nancy. *Grand Man: Memories of Norman Douglas*. London: Secker and Warburg, 1954.

Davenport, John. "Introduction." *Old Calabria*, by Norman Douglas. New York: Harcourt, 1956.

———. "Norman Douglas." *TC*, 151 (1952), 359-67.

Dawkins, R. M. *Norman Douglas*. London: Hart-Davis, 1952. [First ed., Florence, 1933, under the pseudonym R. MacGillivray]

Eckersley, Arthur. "The Work of Mr. Norman Douglas." *AIR*, 3 (1919), 40-44.

Fitzgibbon, Constantine. *Norman Douglas*. London: Longmans, Green, 1957.

———. *Norman Douglas: A Pictorial Record*. London: Richards, 1953.

Flint, R. W. "Norman Douglas." *KR*, 14 (1952), 660-68.

Flory, Evelyn A. "Norman Douglas and the Scientific Spirit." *ELT*, 14, 3 (1971), 167-77.

Greenlees, Ian. *Norman Douglas*. London: Longmans, Green, 1957.

Hueffer [Ford], Ford Madox. "A Haughty and Proud Generation." *YR*, n.s. 11 (1922), 703-17.

Karl, Frederick R. "Joseph Conrad, Norman Douglas, and the *English Review*." *JML*, 2 (1972), 342-56.

Leary, Lewis. *Norman Douglas*. New York: Columbia Univ. Press, 1968.

Lindeman, Ralph D. *Norman Douglas*. New York: Twayne, 1965.

Low, D. M. "Introduction." *Norman Douglas: A Selection from His Works*. London: Chatto and Windus; London: Secker and Warburg, 1955.

Lynd, Robert. *Books and Authors*, 285-92.

McDonald, Edward D. "The Early Work of Norman Douglas." *Bookman* (N.Y.), 66 (1927), 42-46.

Swan, Michael. *A Small Part of Time*, 27-39.

Szladits, Lola L. "Norman Douglas, *Gymnasiast*." *BNYPL*, 63 (1959), 309-17.

Tomlinson, H. M. *Norman Douglas*. London: Hutchinson, 1952.

Webster, H. T. "Norman Douglas: A Reconsideration." *SAQ*, 49 (1950), 226-36.

Wheatley, Elizabeth D. "Norman Douglas." *SR*, 40 (1932), 55-67.

Wilson, Edmund. *The Shores of Light*, 485-91.

See also: Forster, *Aspects*; Swinnerton, *Georgian*; Vines.

SOUTH WIND
Mais, Stuart P. B. *Books and Their Writers*, 27-36.
Matthews, Jack. "Jack Matthews on Norman Douglas's *South Wind.*" *Rediscoveries*. Ed. David Madden, 190-96.
Swan, Michael. "The Living Dead—II. Norman Douglas and the Southern World." *LonM*, 3, 6 (June 1956), 49-55.
See also: Frierson; Greene; Mackenzie; V. Woolf, *Contemporary*.

MARGARET DRABBLE

INTERVIEWS
Firchow, Peter. *The Writer's Place*, 102-121.
Hardin, Nancy S. "An Interview with Margaret Drabble." *ConL*, 14 (1973), 273-95.
Poland, Nancy. "Margaret Drabble: 'There Must Be a Lot of People Like Me'." *MQ*, 16 (1975), 255-67.

GENERAL STUDIES
Beards, Virginia K. "Margaret Drabble: Novels of a Cautious Feminist." *Crit*, 15, 1 (1973), 35-47.
Bonfond, François. "Margaret Drabble: How to Express Subjective Truth Through Fiction." *RLV*, 40 (1974), 41-55.
"Female and Male Subjects." *TLS*, May 22, 1969, 549.
Hardin, Nancy S. "Drabble's *The Millstone*: A Fable for Our Times." *Crit*, 15, 1 (1973), 22-34.
Libby, Marion V. "Fate and Feminism in the Novels of Margaret Drabble." *ConL*, 16 (1975), 175-92.
Mannheimer, Monica Lauritzen. "The Search for Identity in Margaret Drabble's *The Needle's Eye.*" *DQR*, 5 (1975), 24-35.
Myer, Valerie G. *Margaret Drabble: Puritanism and Permissiveness.* London: Vision, 1974; New York: Barnes and Noble, 1975.
Oates, Joyce Carol. "Bricks and Mortar." *Ms.*, 3, 2 (August 1974), 34-36.
Rose, Ellen C. "Margaret Drabble: Surviving the Future." *Crit*, 15, 1 (1973), 5-21.
Schaefer, J. O'Brien. "The Novels of Margaret Drabble." *New Republic*, 172 (April 26, 1975), 21-23.
Wikborg, Eleanor. "A Comparison of Margaret Drabble's *The Millstone* with Its *Veco-Revyn* Adaptation, 'Barnet Du Gav Mig'." *MSpr*, 65 (1971), 305-11.

LAWRENCE DURRELL

BIBLIOGRAPHIES

Beebe, Maurice. "Criticism of Lawrence Durrell: A Selected Checklist." *MFS*, 13 (1967), 417-21.

Lebas, Gerard. "Lawrence Durrell's *Alexandria Quartet* and the Critics: A Survey of Published Criticism." *Caliban*, 6 (1969), 91-114.

INTERVIEWS

"Durrell Answers a Few Questions." *Two Cities* (Paris), 1, 1 (1959), 25-28.

Durrell, Lawrence. *The Big Supposer: Lawrence Durrell, a Dialogue with Marc Alyn*. Tr. Francine Barker. New York: Grove, 1973.

Goulianos, Joan. "A Conversation with Lawrence Durrell About Art, Analysis, and Politics." *MFS*, 17 (1971), 159-66.

Henig, Suzanne. "Lawrence Durrell: The Greatest of Them All." *VWQ*, 2, 1-2 (1975), 4-12.

Mitchell, Julian, and Gene Andrewski. "Lawrence Durrell." *Paris Review. Writers at Work*, 2d ser., 257-82.

Young, Kenneth. "A Dialogue with Durrell." *Encounter*, 13 (December 1959), 61-68.

SPECIAL ISSUES

Modern Fiction Studies [*MFS*], 13, 3 (1967).

Two Cities (Paris), 1, 1 (1959), 3-28.

GENERAL STUDIES

Aldington, Richard. "A Note on Lawrence Durrell." *Two Cities* (Paris), 1, 1 (1959), 13-20.

_____. *Selected Critical Writings*, 121-29.

Arthos, John. "Lawrence Durrell's Gnosticism." *Person*, 43 (1962), 360-73.

Baldanza, Frank. "Lawrence Durrell's 'Word Continuum'." *Crit*, 4, 2 (1961), 3-17.

Bergonzi, Bernard. "Stale Incense." *NYRB*, (July 11, 1968), 37-39.

Bork, Alfred M. "Durrell and Relativity." *CentR*, 7 (1963), 191-203.

Bowen, John. "One Man's Meat: The Idea of Individual Responsibility." *TLS*, August 7, 1959, xii-xiii.

Brown, Sharon Lee. "*The Black Book*: A Search for Method." *MFS*, 13, 3 (1967), 319-28.

Corke, Hilary. "Lawrence Durrell." *LHY*, 2 (1961), 43-49.

Cortland, Peter. "Durrell's Sentimentalism." *EngR*, 14 (1964), 15-19.

Crowder, Richard. "Durrell, Libido, and Eros." *BSTCF*, 3, 2 (1962), 34-39.

Dennis, Nigel. "New Four-Star King of Novelists." *Life*, 49 (November 21, 1960), 96-109.

Durrell, Lawrence. "Introduction." *The Book of the It*, by George Groddeck. New York: Vintage, 1961.

Flint, R. W. "A Major Novelist." *Commentary*, 27, 4 (April 1959), 353-56.

Fraser, George S. *Lawrence Durrell: A Critical Study*. London: Faber and Faber; New York: Dutton, 1968; London: Longmans, Green, 1970; rev. ed. London: Faber and Faber, 1973.

Friedman, Alan W. "A 'Key' to Lawrence Durrell." *WSCL*, 8 (1967), 31-42.

―――. "Place and Durrell's Island Books." *MFS*, 13, 3 (1967), 329-42.

Gaster, Beryl. "Lawrence Durrell." *ContempR*, 205 (1964), 375-79.

Glicksberg, Charles I. "The Fictional World of Lawrence Durrell." *BuR*, 11, 2 (1963), 118-33.

Gossman, Ann. "Some Characters in Search of a Mirror." *Crit*, 8, 3 (1966), 79-84.

Green, Martin. "Lawrence Durrell, II: A Minority Report." *YR*, 49 (1960), 496-508.

Hagopian, John V. "Lawrence Durrell: 'The Halcyon Summer'." *Insight II*. Ed. John V. Hagopian and Martin Dolch, 94-104.

Hamard, Jean. "Lawrence Durrell: A European Writer." *DUJ*, 29 (1968), 171-81.

Howarth, Herbert. "Lawrence Durrell and Some Early Masters." *BA*, 37 (1963), 5-11.

Kameyama, Masako. "Lawrence Durrell: A Sketch." Kyoritsu Women's Junior College, Tokyo. *Collected Essays by the Members of the Faculty*, 32-49.

Kelly, John C. "Lawrence Durrell's Style." *Studies*, 52 (1963), 199-204.

Leslie, Ann. "This Infuriating Man: Lawrence Durrell." *IrD*, 82 (February 1965), 67-70.

Littlejohn, David. *Interruptions*, 73-90.

―――. "Lawrence Durrell: The Novelist as Entertainer." *Motive*, 23 (November 1962), 14-16.

―――. "The Permanence of Durrell." *ColQ*, 14 (1965), 63-71.

"The Long Arm of the Firm." *TLS*, March 26, 1970, 328.

Lund, Mary Graham. "The Big Rock Crystal Mountain." *Four Quarters*, 11, 4 (May 1962), 15-18.

―――. "Durrell: Soft Focus on Crime." *PrS*, 35 (1961), 339-44.

―――. "Eight Aspects of Melissa." *ForumH*, 3, 9 (1962), 18-22.

Lawrence Durrell, continued

―――. "Submerge for Reality: The New Novel Form of Lawrence Durrell." *SWR*, 44 (1959), 229-35.
Mackworth, Cecily. "Lawrence Durrell and the New Romanticism." *TC*, 167 (1960), 203-13.
Miller, Henry. "The Durrell of the Black Book Days." *Two Cities* (Paris), 1, 1 (1959), 3-6.
Moore, Harry T., ed. *The World of Lawrence Durrell.* Carbondale: Southern Illinois Univ. Press, 1962.
Morgan, Thomas B. "The Autumnal Arrival of Lawrence Durrell." *Esquire*, 54 (September 1960), 108-11.
O'Brien, R. A. "Time, Space and Language in Lawrence Durrell." *WaterR*, 6 (1961), 16-24.
"The Old Firm." *TLS*, April 25, 1968, 413.
Perlès, Alfred. *My Friend Lawrence Durrell.* Northwood, Middlesex: Scorpion, 1961.
Powell, Lawrence C. *The Little Package*, 122-24.
Rexroth, Kenneth. "The Artifice of Convincing Immodesty." *Griffin*, 9 (September 1960), 3-9.
―――. *Assays*, 118-30.
Rippier, Joseph S. *Some Postwar English Novelists*, 106-37.
Steiner, George. "Lawrence Durrell, I: The Baroque Novel." *YR*, 49 (1960), 488-95.
Sullivan, Nancy. "Lawrence Durrell's Epitaph for the Novel." *Person*, 44 (1963), 79-88.
Trail, George Y. "Durrell's Io: A Note on *Tunc* and *Nunquam*." *NConL*, 5, 3 (1975), 9-11.
Unterecker, John. "Fiction at the Edge of Poetry: Durrell, Beckett, Green." *Forms of Modern British Fiction.* Ed. Alan W. Friedman, 165-99.
―――. *Lawrence Durrell.* New York: Columbia Univ. Press, 1964.
Weigel, John A. *Lawrence Durrell.* New York: Twayne, 1966.
―――. "Lawrence Durrell's First Novel." *TCL*, 14 (1968), 75-83.
Wickes, George, ed. *Lawrence Durrell and Henry Miller: A Private Correspondence.* New York: Dutton, 1963.
See also: Allen, *Tradition*; Beja; Enright, *Conspirators*; Gindin, *Postwar*; Karl; Kazin, *Contemporaries*; Kermode; Pritchett, *Living*.

THE ALEXANDRIA QUARTET
[JUSTINE, BALTHAZAR, MOUNTOLIVE, CLEA]
Bliven, Naomi. "Alexandrine in Tetrameter." *NY*, 36 (August 13, 1960), 97-103.

Bode, Carl. "Durrell's Way to Alexandria." *CE*, 22 (1961) 531-38.

Burns, J. Christopher. "Durrell's Heraldic Universe." *MFS*, 13, 3 (1967), 375-88.

Cate, Curtis. "Lawrence Durrell." *Atlantic*, 208 (December 1961), 63-69.

Chapman, R. T. "Dead, or Just Pretending? Reality in *The Alexandria Quartet*." *CentR*, 16 (1972), 408-18.

Coleman, John. "Mr. Durrell's Dimensions." *Spectator*, 204 (February 19, 1960), 256-57.

Corke, Hilary. "Mr. Durrell and Brother Criticus." *Encounter*, 14 (May 1960), 65-70.

Creed, Walter G. "Pieces of the Puzzle: The Multiple-Narrative Structure of *The Alexandria Quartet*." *Mosaic*, 6, 2 (1973), 19-35.

———. " 'The Whole Pointless Joke'? Darley's Search for Truth in *The Alexandria Quartet*." *EA*, 28 (1975), 165-73.

Dare, H. "The Quest for Durrell's Scobie." *MFS*, 10 (1965), 379-83.

Dawson, Carl. "From Einstein to Keats: A New Look at the *Alexandria Quartet*." *FWF*, 1 (1974), 109-28.

Decancq, Roland. "What Lies Beyond? An Analysis of Darley's 'Quest' in Lawrence Durrell's *Alexandria Quartet*." *RLV*, 34 (1968), 134-50.

De Mott, Benjamin. "Grading the Emanglons." *HudR*, 13 (1960), 457-64.

Dobrée, Bonamy. "Durrell's Alexandrian Series." *SR*, 69 (1961), 61-79.

Enright, D. J. "Alexandrian Nights' Entertainments: Lawrence Durrell's *Quartet*." *ILA*, 3 (1961), 30-39.

Eskin, Stanley G. "Durrell's Themes in *The Alexandria Quartet*." *TQ*, 5, 4 (1962), 43-60.

Fraiberg, Louis. "Durrell's Dissonant Quartet." *Contemporary British Novelists*. Ed. Charles Shapiro, 16-35.

Friedman, Alan W. *Lawrence Durrell and the ALEXANDRIA QUARTET: Art for Love's Sake*. Norman: Univ. of Oklahoma Press, 1970.

Glicksberg, Charles I. *The Self in Modern Literature*, 89-94.

Godshalk, William L. "Some Sources of Durrell's *Alexandria Quartet*." *MFS*, 13, 3 (1967), 361-74.

Goldberg, Gerald J. "The Search for the Artist in Some Recent British Fiction." *SAQ*, 62 (1963), 387-401.

Gordon, Ambrose, Jr. "Time, Space, and Eros: The *Alexandria Quartet* Rehearsed." *Six Contemporary Novels*. Ed. William O. S. Sutherland, 6-21.

Lawrence Durrell, continued

Gossman, Ann. "Love's Alchemy in the *Alexandria Quartet*." *Crit*, 13, 2 (1971), 83-96.

Goulianos, Joan. "Lawrence Durrell and Alexandria." *VQR*, 45 (1969), 664-73.

Hagopian, John V. "The Resolution of the *Alexandria Quartet*." *Crit*, 7, 1 (1964), 97-106.

Harris, Wendell V. "Molly's 'Yes': The Transvaluation of Sex in Modern Fiction." *TSLL*, 10 (1968), 107-18.

Highet, Gilbert. "The Alexandrians of Lawrence Durrell." *Horizon (N.Y.)*, 2, 4 (March 1960), 113-18.

Howarth, Herbert. "A Segment of Durrell's *Quartet*." *UTQ*, 32 (1963), 282-93.

Hutchens, Eleanor H. "The Heraldic Universe in *The Alexandria Quartet*." *CE*, 24 (1962), 56-61.

Inglis, Fred. *An Essential Discipline*, 197-99.

Katope, Christopher G. "Cavafy and Durrell's 'The Alexandria Quartet'." *CL*, 21 (1969), 125-37.

Kelly, John C. "Lawrence Durrell: *The Alexandria Quartet*." *Studies*, 52 (1963), 52-68.

Kermode, Frank. "Fourth Dimension." *REL*, 1, 2 (1960), 73-77.

Kothandaraman, Bala. "The Comic Dimension in *The Alexandria Quartet*." *OJES*, 9, 1 (1972), 27-37.

Kruppa, Joseph A. "Durrell's *Alexandria Quartet* and the 'Implosion' of the Modern Consciousness." *MFS*, 13, 3 (1967), 401-16.

Lebas, Gérard. "The Fabric of Durrell's *Alexandria Quartet*." *Caliban*, 8 (1971), 139-50.

————. "The Mechanisms of Space-Time in *The Alexandria Quartet*." *Caliban*, 7 (1970), 79-97.

Lemon, Lee T. "*The Alexandria Quartet*: Form and Fiction." *WSCL*, 4 (1963), 327-38.

Levidova, I. "A Four-Decker in Stagnant Waters." *ASJ*, 23 (1962), 39-41.

Levitt, Morton P. "Art and Correspondences: Durrell, Miller, and *The Alexandria Quartet*." *MFS*, 13, 3 (1967), 299-318.

Lund, Mary Graham. "The Alexandrian Projection." *AR*, 21 (1961), 193-204.

Maclay, Joanna Hawkins. "The Interpreter and Modern Fiction: Problems of Point of View and Structural Tensiveness." *Studies in Interpretation*. Ed. Esther M. Doyle and Virginia Hastings Floyd, 155-69.

Manzalaoui, Mahmoud. "Curate's Egg; An Alexandrian Opinion of Durrell's *Quartet*." *EA*, 15 (1962), 248-60.

Mellard, Joan. "The Unity of Lawrence Durrell's *Alexandria Quartet* (1)." *LNL*, 1, 1 (1975), 77-143.

Michot, Paulette. "Lawrence Durrell's *Alexandria Quartet*." *RLV*, 26 (1960), 361-67.

Morcos, Mona L. "Elements of the Autobiographical in *The Alexandria Quartet*." *MFS*, 13, 3 (1967), 343-60.

Mullins, Edwin. "On Mountolive." *Two Cities* (Paris), 1, 1 (1959), 21-24.

Pritchett, V. S. *The Working Novelist*, 30-35.

Proser, Matthew N. "Darley's Dilemma: The Problem of Structure in Durrell's *Alexandria Quartet*." *Crit*, 4, 2 (1961), 18-28.

Read, Phyllis J. "The Illusion of Personality: Cyclical Time in Durrell's *Alexandria Quartet*." *MFS*, 13, 3 (1967), 389-400.

Robinson, W. R. "Intellect and Imagination in *The Alexandria Quartet*." *Shenandoah*, 18, 4 (1967), 55-68.

Romberg, Bertil. *Studies in the Narrative Technique of the First-Person Novel*, 277-308.

Russo, John Paul. "Love in Lawrence Durrell." *PrS*, 43 (1970), 396-407.

Scholes, Robert. *The Fabulators*, 17-28.

––––––. "Return to Alexandria: Lawrence Durrell and Western Narrative Tradition." *VQR*, 40 (1964), 411-20.

Steiner, George. *Language and Silence*, 280-87.

Taylor, Chet. "Dissonance and Digression: The Ill-Fitting Fusion of Philosophy and Form in Lawrence Durrell's *Alexandria Quartet*." *MFS*, 17 (1971), 167-79.

Weatherhead, A. K. "Romantic Anachronism in *The Alexandria Quartet*." *MFS*, 10 (1964), 128-36.

Wedin, Warren. "The Artist as Narrator in *The Alexandria Quartet*." *TCL*, 18 (1972), 175-80.

See also: Edel; R. Morris, *Continuance*; Walcutt.

GABRIEL FIELDING

INTERVIEWS
Newquist, Roy, ed. *Counterpoint*, 196-207.

GENERAL STUDIES
Borrello, Alfred. *Gabriel Fielding*. New York: Twayne, 1974.

Bowers, Frederick. "Gabriel Fielding's *The Birthday King*." *QQ*, 74 (1967), 149-58.

––––––. "The Unity of Fielding's *Greenbloom*." *Renascence*, 18 (1966), 147-55.

Grande, Luke M. "Gabriel Fielding, New Master of the Catholic Classic?" *CathW*, 197 (1963), 172-79.
Kunkel, Francis L. "Clowns and Saviors: Two Contemporary Novels." *Renascence*, 18 (1965), 40-44.
"Itch and Incense." *TLS*, June 23, 1966, 549.
Stanford, Derek. "Gabriel Fielding and the Catholic Novel." *Month*, 26 (1961), 352-56.
Towne, Frank. "The Tragicomic Moment in the Art of Gabriel Fielding." *To Find Something New*. Ed. Henry Grosshaus, 102-16.

RONALD FIRBANK

BIBLIOGRAPHIES
Davis, Robert Murray. "Ronald Firbank: A Selected Bibliography of Criticism." *BB*, 26 (1969), 108-11.

GENERAL STUDIES
Alford, Norman W. "Seven Notebooks of Ronald Firbank." *LCUT*, 8, 3 (1967), 33-39.
Auden, W. H. "Ronald Firbank and an Amateur World." *Listener*, 65 (1961), 1004-5, 1008.
Benkovitz, Miriam J. *Ronald Firbank*. New York: Knopf, 1969; London, Weidenfeld and Nicolson, 1970.
————. "Ronald Firbank in New York." *BNYPL*, 63 (May 1959), 247-59.
Braybrooke, Neville. "Ronald Firbank, 1886-1926." *DR*, 42 (1962), 38-49.
————. "Thorns and Vanities: Ronald Firbank Revisited." *Encounter*, 31 (September 1968), 66-74.
Brooke, Jocelyn. *Ronald Firbank*. New York: Roy, 1951.
————. *Ronald Firbank and John Betjeman*. London and New York: Longmans, Green, 1962.
Brophy, Brigid. *Prancing Novelist: A Defense of Fiction in the Form of A Critical Biography in Praise of Ronald Firbank*. New York: Barnes and Noble, 1973.
Connolly, Cyril. *Enemies of Promise*, 33-38.
Davis, Robert M. " 'Hyperaesthesia with Complications': The World of Ronald Firbank." *Rendezvous*, 3, 1 (1968), 5-15.
————. "From Artifice to Art: The Technique of Firbank's Novels." *Style*, 2 (1968), 33-47.
Forster, E. M. *Abinger Harvest*, 115-21.
Hafley, James. "Ronald Firbank." *ArQ*, 12 (1956), 161-71.
Kiechler, John A. *The Butterfly's Freckled Wings: A Study of Style in*

the Novels of Ronald Firbank. Schweizer Anglistische Arbeiten, 60. Berne: Francke, 1969.

Merritt, James D. *Ronald Firbank.* New York: Twayne, 1969.

Potoker, Edward M. *Ronald Firbank.* New York: Columbia Univ. Press, 1969.

Sitwell, Osbert. *Noble Essences,* 77-100.

Tyler, Parker. "The Prince Zoubaroff: Praise of Ronald Firbank. Part One." *Prose,* 1 (1970), 135-52. "Part Two." *Prose,* 2 (1971), 155-69.

Waugh, Evelyn. "Ronald Firbank." *Life and Letters,* 2 (1929), 191-96.

Wilson, Edmund. *Classics and Commercials,* 486-502.

———. *The Shores of Light,* 69-72, 264-66.

Woodward, A. G. "Ronald Firbank." *ESA,* 11 (1968), 1-9.

See also: McCormick; Pritchett, *Books*; Richards; Vines.

VAINGLORY

Davis, Robert M. "The Ego Triumphant in Firbank's *Vainglory.*" *PLL,* 9 (1973), 281-96.

———. "The Text of Firbank's *Vainglory.*" *PBSA,* 63 (1969), 36-41.

FORD MADOX FORD

BIBLIOGRAPHIES

Gerber, Helmut E. "Ford Madox Ford: An Annotated Checklist of Writings About Him." *EFT,* 1, 2 (1958), 2-19.

Harvey, David D. *Ford Madox Ford, 1873-1939: A Bibliography of Works and Criticism.* Princeton, N.J.: Princeton Univ. Press, 1962.

MacShane, Frank, "Supplement." *EFT,* 4, 2 (1961), 19-29; *ELT,* 6, 3 (1963), 154-61; 9, 4 (1966), 216-19.

Monteiro, George. "Addenda to the Bibliographies of Conrad, Cooke, Damon, Ford, Glasgow, Holmes, Jewett, Lewis, Mumford, Robinson, and Scott." *PBSA,* 69 (1975), 273-75.

Naumberg, Edward, Jr. "A Catalogue of a Ford Madox Ford Collection." *PULC,* 9 (April 1948), 134-65.

Schweik, Robert C. "Supplement." *ELT,* 13, 1 (1970), 46-50; 14, 3 (1971), 201-04.

SPECIAL ISSUES

"Homage to Ford Madox Ford—A Symposium." *New Directions in Prose and Poetry, 1942.* Ed. James Laughlin, 441-94.

Modern Fiction Studies [MFS], 9, 1 (1963).

Princeton University Library Chronicle [PULC], 9 (April 1948), 104-65.

Ford Madox Ford, continued

GENERAL STUDIES

Aldington, Richard. "Homage to Ford Madox Ford." *New Directions in Prose and Poetry, 1942.* Ed. James Laughlin, 456-58.

Aldridge, John W. "Alienated, Alienating Victorian Man of Letters." *SatR*, 54 (April 3, 1971), 23-25, 36.

Anderson, Sherwood. "Homage to Ford Madox Ford." *New Directions in Prose and Poetry, 1942.* Ed. James Laughlin, 458-59.

Andreach, Robert J. *The Slain and Resurrected God*, 120-207.

Arnold, Aerol. "Why Structure in Fiction: A Note to Social Scientists." *AQ*, 10 (1958), 325-37.

Bartlett, Paul. "Ford Madox Ford: A Profile." *QQ*, 74 (1967), 323-27.

Benét, William Rose. "Homage to Ford Madox Ford." *New Directions in Prose and Poetry, 1942.* Ed. James Laughlin, 459-60.

Bergonzi, Bernard. *Heroes' Twilight*, 79-81, 172-82.

Bishop, John Peale. "Homage to Ford Madox Ford." *New Directions in Prose and Poetry, 1942.* Ed. James Laughlin, 460-62.

Blackmur, R. P. "The King Over the Water: Notes on the Novels of F. M. Hueffer." *PULC*, 9 (April 1948), 123-27.

Borowitz, Helen Osterman. "The Paint beneath the Prose: Ford Madox Ford's Pre-Raphaelite Ancestry." *MFS*, 21 (1975), 483-98.

Braybrooke, Neville. "The Walrus and the Windmill: A Study of Ford Madox Ford." *SR*, 74 (1966), 810-31.

————. "Ford Madox Ford: A Reappraisal." *DM*, 8, 1-2 (1969), 67-77.

Brewer, Joseph. "Homage to Ford Madox Ford." *New Directions in Prose and Poetry, 1942.* Ed. James Laughlin, 462-66.

Cassell, Richard A. *Ford Madox Ford: A Study of His Novels.* Baltimore: Johns Hopkins Univ. Press, 1961.

————. "The Two Sorrells of Ford Madox Ford." *MP*, 59 (1961), 114-21.

Crankshaw, Edward. "Ford Madox Ford." *National Review* (L), 131 (August 1948), 160-67.

————. *Joseph Conrad*, 150-51, 168-70, 174-75, 200-204.

Dahlberg, Edward. "Homage to Ford Madox Ford." *New Directions in Prose and Poetry, 1942.* Ed. James Laughlin, 466-69.

Dillon, George. "Homage to Ford Madox Ford." *New Directions in Prose and Poetry, 1942.* Ed. James Laughlin, 469-70.

Dransfield, Jane. "Homage to Ford Madox Ford." *New Directions in Prose and Poetry, 1942.* Ed. James Laughlin, 470-71.

Engle, Paul. "Homage to Ford Madox Ford." *New Directions in Prose and Poetry, 1942.* Ed. James Laughlin, 471-72.

Fletcher, John Gould. "Homage to Ford Madox Ford." *New Directions in Prose and Poetry, 1942.* Ed. James Laughlin, 472-74.

Gabbay, Lydia Rivlin. "The Four Square Coterie: A Comparison of Ford Madox Ford and Henry James." *SNNTS*, 6 (1974), 439-53.

Goldring, Douglas. *The Last Pre-Raphaelite*. London: Macdonald, 1948; New York: Dutton, 1949. [Dutton ed. entitled *Trained for Genius: The Life and Writings of Ford Madox Ford*]

Gordon, Ambrose, Jr. *The Invisible Tent: The War Novels of Ford Madox Ford*. Austin: Univ. of Texas Press, 1964.

Gordon, Caroline. *A Good Soldier: A Key to the Novels of Ford Madox Ford*. Davis: Univ. of California Library, 1963.

———. "Homage to Ford Madox Ford." *New Directions in Prose and Poetry, 1942*. Ed. James Laughlin, 474-75.

———. "The Story of Ford Madox Ford." *Highlights of Modern Literature*. Ed. Francis Brown, 113-18.

Greene, Graham. "The Dark Backward: A Footnote." *London Mercury*, 32 (1935), 562-65.

Harvey, David D. *"Pro Patria Mori*: The Neglect of Ford's Novels in England." *MFS*, 9, 1 (1963), 3-16.

Hays, Peter L. *The Limping Hero*, 148-55.

Hicks, Granville. "Ford Madox Ford." *Bookman* (N.Y.), 72 (1930), 364-70; reprinted as "Homage to Ford Madox Ford." *New Directions in Prose and Poetry, 1942*. Ed. James Laughlin, 443-56.

Hill, A. G. "The Literary Career of Ford Madox Ford." *CritQ*, 5 (1963), 369-79.

Hoffmann, Charles G. *Ford Madox Ford*. New York: Twayne, 1967.

Hunt, Violet. *The Flurried Years*. London: Hurst and Blackett; New York: Boni and Liveright, 1926. [American ed. entitled *I Have This to Say*]

Huntley, H. Robert. *The Alien Protagonist of Ford Madox Ford*. Chapel Hill: Univ. of North Carolina Press, 1970.

———. "Flaubert and Ford: The Fallacy of 'Le Mot Juste'." *ELN*, 4 (1967), 283-87.

———. "Ford, Holbein and Dürer." *SAB*, 30, 3 (1965), 4-6.

Hynes, Samuel. "Ford and the Spirit of Romance." *MFS*, 9, 1 (1963), 17-24.

Leer, Norman. *The Limited Hero in the Novels of Ford Madox Ford*. East Lansing: Michigan State Univ. Press, 1966.

Lid, R. W. "Ford Madox Ford and His Community of Letters." *PrS*, 35 (1961), 132-36.

———. *Ford Madox Ford: The Essence of His Art*. Berkeley: Univ. of California Press, 1964.

———. "Ford Madox Ford, Flaubert, and the English Novel." *Spectrum*, 6 (1962), 10-19.

———. "Return to Yesterday." *Jubilee*, 9 (1962), 37-40.

Ludwig, Richard M. "The Reputation of Ford Madox Ford." *PMLA*, 76 (1961), 544-51.

Ford Madox Ford, continued

McLaughlin, Richard. "Ford Madox Ford: Historian of His Time." *America*, 84 (October 21, 1950), 79-81.

MacShane, Frank. "A Conscious Craftsman: Ford Madox Ford's Manuscript Revisions." *BUSE*, 5 (1961), 178-84.

————, ed. *Critical Writings of Ford Madox Ford*. Lincoln: Univ. of Nebraska Press, 1964.

————. "The *English Review*." *SAQ*, 60 (1961), 311-20.

————. "Ford Madox Ford and His Contemporaries: The Techniques of the Novel." *EFT*, 4, 1 (1961), 2-11.

————, ed. *Ford Madox Ford: The Critical Heritage*. London: Routledge and K. Paul, 1972.

————. *The Life and Work of Ford Madox Ford*. London: Routledge and K. Paul; New York: Horizon, 1965.

————. " 'To Establish the Facts': A Communication on Mr. A. R. Jones and Ford Madox Ford." *SAQ*, 61 (1962), 260-65.

Meixner, John A. *Ford Madox Ford's Novels: A Critical Study*. Minneapolis: Univ. of Minnesota Press, 1962.

Mizener, Arthur. *The Saddest Story: A Biography of Ford Madox Ford*. New York: World, 1971.

Mohay, Bela. "F. M. Ford's Contribution to the Theory of the Novel." *HSE*, 8 (1974), 51-66.

Morley, Christopher. "Homage to Ford Madox Ford." *New Directions in Prose and Poetry, 1942*. Ed. James Laughlin, 476-77.

Morris, Lloyd. "Homage to Ford Madox Ford." *New Directions in Prose and Poetry, 1942*. Ed. James Laughlin, 477.

Naumberg, Edward, Jr. "A Collector Looks at Ford Madox Ford." *PULC*, 9 (April 1948), 105-18.

Ohmann, Carol. *Ford Madox Ford: From Apprentice to Craftsman*. Middletown, Conn.: Wesleyan Univ. Press, 1964.

Poli, Bernard. *Ford Madox Ford and the TRANSATLANTIC REVIEW*. Syracuse, N.Y.: Syracuse Univ. Press, 1967.

————. "Cavalier and Cowboy: Goodbye to All That, Mr. Ford Braddocks Ford!" *Hemingway and THE SUN Set*. Ed. Bertram D. Sarason, 275-79.

Porter, Katherine Anne. *The Collected Essays*, 249-50.

————. "Homage to Ford Madox Ford." *New Directions in Prose and Poetry, 1942*. Ed. James Laughlin, 478-79.

Pound, Ezra. "Homage to Ford Madox Ford." *New Directions in Prose and Poetry, 1942*. Ed. James Laughlin, 479-83.

Roberts, R. Ellis. "Homage to Ford Madox Ford." *New Directions in Prose and Poetry, 1942*. Ed. James Laughlin, 483-86.

Schweik, Robert C. "Ford Madox Ford." *ELT*, 14, 3 (1971), 201-04.

Scott, Evelyn. "Homage to Ford Madox Ford." *New Directions in Prose and Poetry, 1942.* Ed. James Laughlin, 486-87.
Scott-James, Rolfe A. "Ford Madox Ford When He Was Heuffer." *SAQ,* 57 (1958), 236-53.
Shanks, Edward. "Ford Madox Ford: The Man and His Work." *World Review,* June 1948, 58-62.
Shaw, Peter. "On Ford Madox Ford." *Commentary,* 52, 3 (September 1971), 79-82.
Smith, Grover. *Ford Madox Ford.* New York: Columbia Univ. Press, 1972.
Stevens, George. "Homage to Ford Madox Ford." *New Directions in Prose and Poetry, 1942.* Ed. James Laughlin, 487.
Tate, Allen. "Homage to Ford Madox Ford." *New Directions in Prose and Poetry, 1942.* Ed. James Laughlin, 487-90.
Thornton, Lawrence. "Ford Madox Ford and *The Great Gatsby.*" *FHA,* 1975, 89-91.
Van Doren, Carl. "Homage to Ford Madox Ford." *New Directions in Prose and Poetry, 1942.* Ed. James Laughlin, 470.
Wagner, Geoffrey. "Ford Madox Ford: The Honest Edwardian." *EIC,* 17 (1967), 75-88.
Walter, E. V. "The Political Sense of Ford Madox Ford." *New Republic,* 134 (March 26, 1956), 17-19.
Wescott, Glenway. "Memories and Opinions." *Prose,* 5 (1972), 177-202.
Whittemore, Reed. *The Fascination of the Abomination,* 129-66.
Wiley, Paul L. *Novelist of Three Worlds: Ford Madox Ford.* Syracuse, N.Y.: Syracuse Univ. Press, 1962.
Williams, William Carlos. "Homage to Ford Madox Ford." *New Directions in Prose and Poetry, 1942.* Ed. James Laughlin, 490-91.
Winegarten, Renée. "Ford Madox Ford—Zionist." *Midstream,* 12 (August-September 1966), 71-75.
Young, Kenneth, *Ford Madox Ford.* London: Longmans, Green, 1955; rev. 1970.
See also: Allen, English, Tradition; Beach, *20th*; Bergonzi, *Turn*; Bradbury, *Possibilities*; Gill; Goldring, *Reputations*; Greene; Hind, *More*; Hynes, *Edwardian*; McCormick; Mackenzie; Mais, *Why*; Pritchett, *Living*; Scott-James, *50*; Swinnerton, *Georgian*; Vines; Zabel, *Craft.*

THE FIFTH QUEEN
Flint, R. W. "The Happy Breed." *NYRB,* 1 (January 9, 1964), 12-13.
Hoffmann, Charles G. " 'The Life and Times of Henry VIII': An Original for Ford Madox Ford's Fifth Queen Trilogy." *N&Q,* 14 (1967), 248-50.

THE GOOD SOLDIER

Andreach, Robert J. "Ford's *The Good Soldier*: The Quest for Permanence and Stability." *TSL*, 10 (1965), 81-92.

Aswell, Duncan. "The Saddest Storyteller in Ford's *The Good Soldier*." *CLAJ*, 14 (1970), 187-96.

Baernstein, Jo-Ann. "Image, Identity, and Insight in *The Good Soldier*." *Crit*, 9, 1 (1967), 19-42.

Barnes, Daniel R. "Ford and the 'Slaughtered Saints': A New Reading of *The Good Soldier*." *MFS*, 14 (1968), 157-70.

Bender, Todd K. "The Sad Tale of Dowell: Ford Madox Ford's *The Good Soldier*." *Criticism*, 4 (1962), 353-68.

Bort, Barry D. "*The Good Soldier*: Comedy or Tragedy?" *TCL*, 12 (1967), 194-202.

Braybrooke, Neville. "Fiction's Long Shadow: *The Good Soldier*." *ContempR*, 209 (1966), 261-64.

Bruffee, Kenneth A. "Elegiac Romance." *CE*, 32 (1971), 465-76.

Cassell, Richard A. "Notes on the Labyrinth of Design in *The Good Soldier*." *Modern British Fiction*. Ed. Mark Schorer, 160-75.

Cohen, Mary. "*The Good Soldier*: Outworn Codes." *SNNTS*, 5 (1973), 284-97.

Cox, James T. "The Finest French Novel in the English Language." *MFS*, 9, 1 (1963), 79-93.

———. "Ford's 'Passion for Provence'." *ELH*, 28 (1961), 383-98.

Goldring, Douglas. *South Lodge*, 116-22.

Gordon, Ambrose, Jr. "At the Edge of Silence: *The Good Soldier* as 'War Novel'." *MFS*, 9, 1 (1963), 67-78.

Gose, Elliott B., Jr. "The Strange Irregular Rhythm: An Analysis of *The Good Soldier*." *PMLA*, 72 (1957), 494-509.

Hafley, James. "The Moral Structure of *The Good Soldier*." *MFS*, 5 (1959), 121-28.

Hanzo, T. A. "Downward to Darkness." *SR*, 74 (1966), 832-55.

Henighan, T. J. "*The Desirable Alien*: A Source for Ford Madox Ford's *The Good Soldier*." *TCL*, 11 (1965), 25-29.

Hoffmann, Charles G. "Ford's Manuscript Revisions of *The Good Soldier*." *ELT*, 9, 3 (1966), 145-52.

Huntley, H. Robert. "*The Good Soldier* and *Die Wahlverwandtschaften*." *CL*, 19 (1967), 133-41.

Hynes, Samuel. "The Epistemology of *The Good Soldier*." *SR*, 69 (1961), 225-35.

Isaacs, Neil D. "The Narrator of *The Good Soldier*." *ELT*, 6, 1 (1963), 14-15.

Johnson, Ann S. "Narrative Form in *The Good Soldier*." *Crit*, 11, 2 (1969), 70-80.

Jones, Lawrence W. "The Quality of Sadness in Ford's *The Good Soldier*." *ELT*, 13, 4 (1970), 296-302.

Lehan, Richard. "Ford Madox Ford and the Absurd: *The Good Soldier*." *TSLL*, 5 (1963), 219-31.

Lentz, Vern B. "Ford's Good Narrator." *SNNTS*, 5 (1973), 483-90.

Lid, R. W. "Ford's 'Good Soldier': A Triumph of Narrative." *First Person*, 1 (1960), 45-56.

———. "On the Time-Scheme of *The Good Soldier*." *EFT*, 4, 2 (1961), 9-10.

Loeb, Harold. "Ford Madox Ford's *The Good Soldier*: A Critical Reminiscence." *CarlM*, 6, 2 (1965), 27-41.

McCaughey, G. S. "The Mocking Bird and the Tomcat: An Examination of Ford Madox Ford's *The Good Soldier*." *HAB*, 16, 1 (1965), 49-58.

McFate, Patricia, and Bruce Golden. "*The Good Soldier*: A Tragedy of Self Deception." *MFS*, 9, 1 (1963), 50-60.

McLaughlin, Agnes Veronica. "Dowell's Doubt: The Tragic Flaw in *The Good Soldier*." *Horizontes*, 35 (1974), 17-18.

McLaughlin, Marilou B. "Adjusting the Lens for *The Good Soldier*." *EngR*, 22, 3 (Spring 1972), 41-48.

Meixner, John A. "The Saddest Story." *KR*, 22 (1960), 234-64.

Mizener, Arthur. "*The Good Soldier*." *SoR*, n.s. 6 (1970), 589-602.

Moser, Thomas C. "Conrad, Marwood, and Ford: Biographical Speculations on the Genesis of *The Good Soldier*." *Mosaic*, 8, 1 (1974), 217-27.

———. "Towards *The Good Soldier*: Discovery of a Sexual Theme." *Daedalus*, 92 (1963), 312-25.

Mosher, Harold F., Jr. "Wayne Booth and the Failure of Rhetoric in *The Good Soldier*." *Caliban*, 6 (1969), 49-52.

Peirce, William P. "The Epistemological Style of Ford's *The Good Soldier*." *Lang&S*, 8 (1975), 34-46.

Ray, Robert J. "Style in *The Good Soldier*." *MFS*, 9, 1 (1963), 61-66.

Schorer, Mark. "The Good Novelist in *The Good Soldier*." *PULC*, 9 (April 1948), 128-33; *Horizon(L)*, 20 (August 1949), 132-38.

Schow, H. Wayne. "Ironic Structure in *The Good Soldier*." *ELT*, 18, 3 (1975), 203-11.

Siemens, Reynold. "The Juxtaposition of Composed Renderings in Ford's *The Good Soldier*." *HAB*, 23, 3 (1972), 44-49.

Stang, Sondra J. "A Reading of Ford's *The Good Soldier*." *MLQ*, 30 (1969), 545-63.

Thornton, Lawrence. "Escaping the Impasse: Criticism and the Mitosis of *The Good Soldier*." *MFS*, 21 (1975), 237-41.

Ford Madox Ford, continued

Tytell, John. "The Jamesian Legacy in *The Good Soldier.*" *SNNTS*, 3 (1971), 365-73.

Weinstein, Arnold L. *Vision and Response in Modern Fiction*, 57-69, 261-63.

Wiesenfarth, Joseph. "Criticism and the Semiosis of *The Good Soldier.*" *MFS*, 9, 1 (1963), 39-49.

Wiley, P. L. "Two Tales of Passion." *Conradiana*, 6 (1974), 189-95.

See also: Swinden.

PARADE'S END
[SOME DO NOT . . . , NO MORE PARADES, A MAN
COULD STAND UP, THE LAST POST]

Chapple, J. A. V. *Documentary and Imaginative Literature*, 328-31.

Core, George. "Ordered Life and the Abysses of Chaos: *Parade's End.*" *SoR*, n.s. 8 (1972), 520-32.

Delbaere-Grant, J. " 'Who shall inherit England?': A Comparison Between *Howards End, Parade's End,* and *Unconditional Surrender.*" *ES*, 50 (1969), 101-05.

Firebaugh, Joseph J. "Tietjens and the Tradition." *PS*, 6 (1952), 23-32.

Gordon, Ambrose, Jr. "A Diamond of Pattern: The War of F. Madox Ford." *SR*, 70 (1962), 464-83.

———. "*Parade's End*: Where War Was Fairy Tale." *TSLL*, 5 (1963), 25-41.

Gose, Elliot B., Jr. "Reality to Romance: A Study of Ford's *Parade's End.*" *CE*, 17 (1956), 445-50.

Grainger, J. H. "A Presentment of Englishry." *ContempR*, 213 (1968), 151-56.

Griffith, Marlene. "A Double Reading of *Parade's End.*" *MFS*, 9, 1 (1963), 25-38.

Heldman, James M. "The Last Victorian Novel: Technique and Theme in *Parade's End.*" *TCL*, 18 (1972), 271-84.

Henighan, T. J. "Tietjens Transformed: A Reading of *Parade's End.*" *ELT*, 15, 2 (1972), 144-57.

Hynes, Samuel. "Ford Madox Ford: 'Three Dedicatory Letters to *Parade's End*' with Commentary and Notes." *MFS*, 16 (1970), 515-28.

Isaacs, Neil D. "Ford Madox Ford and the Tietjens Fulfillment." *LHB*, 1, 1 (1959), 58-65.

Kashner, Rita J. "Tietjens' Education: Ford Madox Ford's Tetralogy." *CritQ*, 8 (1966), 150-63.

Kennedy, Alan. "Tietjens' Travels: *Parade's End* as Comedy." *TCL*, 16 (1970), 85-95.

Ford Madox Ford, continued

Kenner, Hugh. *Gnomon*, 144-61.
Levin, Gerald. "Character and Myth in Ford's *Parade's End.*" *JML*, 1 (1970), 183-96.
Lid, R. W. "Tietjens in Disguise." *KR*, 22 (1960), 265-76.
Macauley, Robie. "The Good Ford." *KR*, 11 (1949), 269-88.
MacShane, Frank. "The Pattern of Ford Madox Ford." *New Republic*, 132 (April 4, 1955), 16-17.
Mizener, Arthur. "A Large Fiction." *KR*, 13 (1951), 142-47.
Rexroth, Kenneth. *The Elastic Retort*, 124-27.
Seiden, Melvin. "The Living Dead—VI. Ford Madox Ford and His Tetralogy." *LonM*, 6, 8 (August 1959), 45-55.
———. "Persecution and Paranoia in *Parade's End.*" *Criticism*, 8 (1966), 246-62.
Solomon, Eric. "From *Christ in Flanders* to *Catch 22*: An Approach to War Fiction." *TSLL*, 11 (1969), 851-66.
Tobyansen, John R. "*Parade's End.*" *Shenandoah*, 1 (1950), 29-36.
Washburn, Claude C. *Opinions*, 53-68.
Williams, William Carlos. "*Parade's End.*" *SR*, 59 (1951), 154-61.
———. *Selected Essays*, 315-23.

E. M. FORSTER

BIBLIOGRAPHIES
Beebe, Maurice, and Joseph Brogunier. "Criticism of E. M. Forster: A Selected Checklist." *MFS*, 7 (1961), 284-92.
Borrello, Alfred. *E. M. Forster: An Annotated Bibliography of Secondary Materials*. Metuchen, N. J.: Scarecrow, 1973.
Bradbury, Malcolm. "Forster." *The English Novel*. Ed. A. E. Dyson, 314-33.
Gerber, Helmut E. "E. M. Forster: An Annotated Checklist of Writings About Him." *EFT*, 2, 1 (1959), 4-27; 4, 3 (1961), 41-47; [with Edwin Nierenberg and S. H. Hussain] *ELT*, 5, 1 (1962), 38-43; [and others] 5, 4 (1962), 25-32.
Kennedy, James G. "E. M. Forster." *ELT*, 6, 2 (1963), 97-105; 6, 4 (1963), 229-33; [and others] 8, 5 (1965), 278-83.
McDowell, Frederick P. W. "E. M. Forster." *ELT*, 10, 1 (1967), 47-64; 10, 4 (1967), 219-38; 11, 4 (1968), 206-16; 13, 2 (1970), 89-173.
———. *E. M. Forster*. Dekalb: Northern Illinois Univ. Press, 1976.

INTERVIEWS
Breit, Harvey. *The Writer Observed*, 53-56.
Furbank, P. N., and F. J. H. Haskell. "E. M. Forster." *Paris Review*. *Writers at Work*, 1st ser., 23-35.

E. M. Forster, continued

Gransden, K. W. "E. M. Forster at Eighty." *Encounter*, 12 (January 1959), 77-81.
Hasan, Aley. "The Life and Thought of E. M. Forster." *Hindustan*, 37 (1960), 4.
O'Connor, William Van. "A Visit with E. M. Forster." *WestR*, 19 (1955), 215-19.
Shahane, V. A. "A Visit to Mr. E. M. Forster." *Quest*, 53 (1967), 43-46.
Toynbee, Philip. "E. M. Forster at Eighty." *Observer*, December 20, 1958, 8, 10.
Wilson, Angus. "A Conversation with E. M. Forster." *Encounter*, 9 (November 1957), 52-57.

SPECIAL ISSUES
English Literature in Transition, 1880-1920 [*ELT*], 16, 4 (1973). 245-306.
The Literary Half-Yearly [*LHY*], 10 (1969), 1-123.
Modern Fiction Studies [*MFS*], 7, 3 (1961).

GENERAL STUDIES
Ackerley, Joe R. *E. M. Forster: A Portrait*. London: Ian McKelvie, 1970.
Alcalay, Valeria M. "Character Typology in E. M. Forster's Novels." *AUB-LG*, 22 (1972), 127-39.
Anand, Mulk Raj. "Profile of E. M. Forster." *LHY*, 10 (1969), 3-7.
Armand, Laura M. "Forster's Fallible Narrator." *EA*, 28 (1975), 269-80.
Ault, Peter. "Aspects of E. M. Forster." *DubR*, 219 (1946), 109-34.
Austin, Don. "The Problem of Continuity in Three Novels of E. M. Forster." *MFS*, 7, 3 (1961), 217-28.
Beaumont, Ernest. "Mr. E. M. Forster's Strange Mystics." *DubR*, 225, 3 (1951), 41-51.
Bedient, Calvin. *Architects of the Self*, 217-33, 250-65.
Beer, John B. *The Achievement of E. M. Forster*. London: Chatto and Windus; New York: Barnes and Noble, 1962.
Belgion, Montgomery. "The Diabolism of E. M. Forster." *Criterion*, 14 (1934), 54-73.
Bentley, Phyllis. "The Novels of E. M. Forster." *EJ*, 37 (1948), 163-70.
Borrello, Alfred. *An E. M. Forster Dictionary*. Metuchen, N. J.: Scarecrow, 1971.
_____. *An E. M. Forster Glossary*. Metuchen, N. J.: Scarecrow, 1972.
Boyle, Alexander. "The Novels of E. M. Forster." *IrM*, 78 (September 1950), 405-15.
Bradbury, Malcolm, ed. *E. M. Forster: A Collection of Critical Essays*. Englewood Cliffs, N. J.: Prentice-Hall, 1966.

Brander, Laurence. "Aspects of E. M. Forster." *LHY*, 10 (1969), 95-104
———. *E. M. Forster: A Critical Study.* London: Hart-Davis, 1968; Lewisburg, Pa.: Bucknell Univ. Press, 1970.
Brewer, D. S. *Proteus*, 198-232.
Brower, Reuben A. "Beyond E. M. Forster: Part 1—The Earth." *Foreground*, 1 (1946), 164-74.
———. "Beyond E. M. Forster: The Unseen." *ChiR*, 2 (1948), 102-12.
Brown, E. K. "E. M. Forster and the Contemplative Novel." *UTQ*, 3 (1934), 349-61.
———. "The Revival of E. M. Forster." *YR*, 33 (1944), 668-81; *Forms of Modern Fiction*. Ed. William Van O'Connor, 161-74.
Bullett, Gerald W. *Modern English Fiction*, 70-85.
Burra, Peter. "The Novels of E. M. Forster." *NC*, 116 (1934), 581-94.
Cecil, David. "E. M. Forster." *Atlantic*, 183 (January 1949), 60-65.
———. *Poets and Storytellers*, 181-201.
Chapple, J. A. V. *Documentary and Imaginative Literature*, 212-19, 332-38.
Colmer, John. *E. M. Forster: The Personal Voice.* London: Routledge and K. Paul, 1975.
Cox, Charles B. *The Free Spirit*, 74-102.
Crews, Frederick C. "E. M. Forster: The Limitations of Mythology." *CL*, 12 (1960), 97-112.
———. *E. M. Forster: The Perils of Humanism.* Princeton, N. J.: Princeton Univ. Press, 1962.
Curtis, Anthony. "E. M. Forster: The Man and His Work." *World Review*, May 1948, 44-47.
Dangerfield, George. "E. M. Forster: A Man with a View." *SatR*, 18 (August 27, 1938), 3-4, 14-16.
Dataller, Roger [A. A. Eaglestone]. *The Plain Man and the Novel*, 165-69.
Delany, Paul. "Lawrence and E. M. Forster: Two Rainbows." *DHLR*, 8 (1975), 54-62.
Dobrée, Bonamy. *The Lamp and the Lute*, 66-85.
———. *Modern Prose Style*, 66-85.
Doughty, Howard M., Jr. "The Novels of E. M. Forster." *Bookman* (N. Y.), 75 (1932), 542-49.
Echeruo, M. J. C. "E. M. Forster and the 'Undeveloped Heart'." *ESA*, 5 (1962), 151-55.
Ellem, Elizabeth. "E. M. Forster's 'Arctic Summer.' " *TLS*, September 21, 1973, 1087-89.
Enright, D. J. "A Passage to Alexandria." *LHY*, 10 (1969), 49-50.
———. *The Apothecary's Shop*, 168-86.

Evans, B. Ifor. *English Literature Between the Wars*, 27-39.

Ferry, David. "The Miracles of E. M. Forster." *HarvA*, 126, 2 (1952), 8-10, 34-35.

Fielding, K. J. "1870-1900: Forster and Reaction." *Dickensian*, 66 (1970), 85-100.

Finkelstein, Bonnie B. *Forster's Women: Eternal Differences.* New York: Columbia Univ. Press, 1975.

Friedman, Albert B. "Forster, Dostoyevsky, Akutagawa, and 'St. Peter and His Mother'." *ELN*, 1 (1964), 286-91.

Gardner, Philip, ed. *E. M. Forster: The Critical Heritage.* London: Routledge and K. Paul, 1973.

Garnett, David. "E. M. Forster and John Galsworthy." *REL*, 5, 1 (1964), 7-18.

――――. "Some Writers I Have Known: Galsworthy, Forster, Moore, and Wells." *TQ*, 4, 3 (1961), 190-202.

Gerber, Richard. "The English Island Myth: Remarks on the Englishness of Utopian Fiction." *CritQ*, 1 (1959), 36-43.

Gilomen, W. "Fantasy and Prophecy in E. M. Forster's Work." *ES*, 27 (1946), 97-112.

Godfrey, Denis. *E. M. Forster's Other Kingdom.* Edinburgh: Oliver and Boyd; New York: Barnes and Noble, 1968.

Goldman, Mark. "Virginia Woolf and E. M. Forster: A Critical Dialogue." *TSLL*, 7 (1966), 387-400.

Gransden, Karl W. *E. M. Forster.* Edinburgh: Oliver and Boyd; New York: Grove, 1962; rev. 1970.

――――. "E. M. Forster and 'Morgan'." *Encounter*, 36 (May 1971), 59-62.

Grubb, Frederick. "Homage to E. M. Forster." *ContempR*, 195 (1959), 20-23.

Hall, James. "Forster's Family Reunions." *ELH*, 25 (1958), 60-78.

Hall, Margaret A. "The Impact of Exotic Cultures on D. H. Lawrence and E. M. Forster." Doshisha Women's College of Liberal Arts. *Annual Reports of Studies*, v. 22, 246-61.

Hamill, Elizabeth. *These Modern Writers*, 137-44.

Hampshire, Stuart N. *Modern Writers*, 47-55.

――――. "Two Cheers for Mr. Forster." *NYRB*, 6 (May 12, 1966), 14-16.

Hannah, Donald. "The Limitations of Liberalism in E. M. Forster's Work." *EM*, 13 (1962), 165-78.

Hardy, Barbara. *The Appropriate Form*, 73-82.

Harrison, Gilbert A. "The Modern Mr. Forster." *New Republic*, 150 (January 11, 1964), 15-16.

Heilbrun, Carolyn. "A Modern Among Contemporaries." *Page 2.* Ed. Francis Brown, 241-44.

Heine, Elizabeth. "The Significance of Structure in the Novels of E. M. Forster and Virginia Woolf." *ELT*, 16 (1973), 289-306.

Hickley, Dennis. "Ou-Boum and Verbum." *Downside Rev.*, 72 (1954), 172-80.

Hoffman, Frederick J. *The Mortal No*, 9-10, 77-87.

Holt, Lee E. "E. M. Forster and Samuel Butler." *PMLA*, 61 (1946), 804-19.

Howarth, Herbert. "E. M. Forster and the Contrite Establishment." *JGE*, 17 (1965), 196-206.

Hynes, Samuel. "Forster at Eighty-Five: The Old Man at King's." *Cweal*, 79 (1964), 635-38.

Johnson, Elaine H. "The Intelligent Mr. E. M. Forster." *Person*, 35 (1954), 50-58.

Johnstone, J. K. "E. M. Forster." *The Politics of Twentieth-Century Novelists*. Ed. George A. Panichas, 15-29.

Jones, E. B. C. "E. M. Forster and Virginia Woolf." *The English Novelists*. Ed. Derek Verschoyle, 281-97.

Jones, Howard Mumford. "E. M. Forster and the Liberal Imagination." *SatR*, 26 (August 28, 1943), 6-7.

Kelvin, Norman. *E. M. Forster*. Carbondale: Southern Illinois Univ. Press, 1967.

Kermode, Frank. "Mr. E. M. Forster as a Symbolist." *Listener*, 59 (1958), 17-18.

Klingopulos, G. D. "E. M. Forster's Sense of History: and Cavafy." *EIC*, 8 (1958), 156-65.

———. "Mr. Forster's Good Influence." *The Pelican Guide to English Literature*, v. 7. Ed. Boris Ford, 263-274.

Koljevic, Svetozar. "E. M. Forster: Sceptic as Novelist." *Mad River Rev.*, 1 (1965), 3-15.

Lakshmi, Vijay. "Virginia Woolf and E. M. Forster: A Study of Their Critical Relations." *LHY*, 12, 2 (1971), 39-49; "Virginia Woolf and E. M. Forster: A Study in Inter-Criticism." *BP*, 16 (1971), 8-18.

Langbaum, Robert W. "A New Look at E. M. Forster." *SoR*, n.s. 4 (1968), 33-49.

Leavis, F. R. "E. M. Forster." *Scrutiny*, 7 (1938), 185-202.

Leavis, Q. D. "Mr. E. M. Forster." *Scrutiny*, 5 (1936), 100-05.

Lebowitz, Naomi. *Humanism and the Absurd in the Modern Novel*, 67-83.

Lehmann, John. "E. M. Forster: A Refusal to Be Great?" *LonM*, n.s. 2, 7 (October 1962), 74-78.

Liddell, Robert. *A Treatise on the Novel*, 64-70.

Lunan, N. M. "The Novels of E. M. Forster." *DUJ*, n.s. 6 (1945), 52-57.

E. M. Forster, continued

Macauley, Rose. "E. M. Forster." *Living Writers*. Ed. Gilbert Phelps, 94-105.
———. *The Writings of E. M. Forster*. London: Hogarth, 1938; New York: Barnes and Noble, 1970.
McConkey, James. *The Novels of E. M. Forster*. Ithaca, N. Y.: Cornell Univ. Press, 1957.
Macdonald, Alastair A. "Class-Consciousness in E. M. Forster." *UKCR*, 27 (1961), 235-40.
McDowell, Frederick P. W. *E. M. Forster*. New York: Twayne, 1969.
———. "E. M. Forster's Conception of the Critic." *TSL*, 10 (1965), 93-100.
———. "E. M. Forster's Theory of Literature." *Criticism*, 8 (1966), 19-43.
———. "E. M. Forster: Romancer or Realist?" *ELT*, 11, 2 (1968), 103-22.
McLuhan, Marshall. "Kipling and Forster." *SR*, 52 (1944), 332-43.
Martin, Richard. *The Love that Failed: Ideal and Reality in the Writings of E. M. Forster*. The Hague: Mouton, 1974.
Maskell, Duke. "Mr. Forster's Fine Feelings." *CQ*, 5 (1971), 222-35.
Mendilow, A. A. "The Triadic World of E. M. Forster." *Studies in English Language and Literature*. Ed. Alice Shalvi and A. A. Mendilow, 280-91.
Meyers, Jeffrey. "E. M. Forster and T. E. Lawrence: A Friendship." *SAQ*, 69 (1970), 205-16.
———. "The Paintings in Forster's Italian Novels." *LonM*, 13, 6 (February-March 1974), 46-62.
Missey, James L. "Forster's Redemptive Siren." *MFS*, 10 (1965), 383-85.
Moore, Geoffrey. "The Significance of Bloomsbury." *KR*, 17 (1955), 119-29.
Moore, Harry T. *E. M. Forster*. New York: Columbia Univ. Press, 1965.
Morley, Patricia A. "E. M. Forster's 'Temple': Eclectic or Visionary?" *UTQ*, 39 (1970), 229-41.
Mukherjee, Asim K. "The Split Personality of E. M. Forster." *Quest*, 56 (1968), 49-55.
Müllenbrock, Heinz-Joachim. "Modes of Opening in the Work of E. M. Forster: A Contribution to the Poetics of His Novels." *MP*, 70 (1973), 216-29.
Nicholson, Norman. *Man and Literature*, 157-60.
Nierenberg, Edwin. "The Prophecy of E. M. Forster." *QQ*, 71 (1964), 189-202.
O'Brien, M. D. "E. M. Forster's Intellectual Heritage." *ELLS*, 8 (1971), 27-36.

86

O'Connor, William Van. "Toward a History of Bloomsbury." *SWR*, 40 (1955), 36-52.

Oliver, Harold J. *The Art of E. M. Forster*. Melbourne: Melbourne Univ. Press, 1960.

_____. "Aspects of the Novel." *LHY*, 10 (1969), 83-89.

_____. "E. M. Forster: The Early Novels." *Crit* 1, 2 (1957), 15-33.

Onodera, Takeshi. "Forster to Lawrence." *EigoS*, 119 (1973) 454-55.

Ozick, Cynthia. "Forster as Homosexual." *Commentary*, 52, 6 (December 1971), 81-85.

Panichas, George A. "E. M. Forster and D. H. Lawrence: Their Views on Education." *Renaissance and Modern Essays*. Ed. G. R. Hibbard, 199-213.

_____. *The Reverent Discipline*, 157-69.

Panter-Downes, Mollie. "Kingsman." *NY*, 35 (Sept. 19, 1959), 51-86.

Pellow, J. D. C. "The Beliefs of E. M. Forster." *Theology*, 40 (April 1940), 278-85.

Peskin, S. G. "An Examination of Some Themes in the Novels of E. M. Forster." *UES*, 1 (1967), 1-22; 2 (1967), 1-14.

Plomer, William. *At Home*, 107-14, 144-46.

Porter, Katherine Anne. *The Collected Essays*, 72-74.

Priestley, J. B. "The Younger Novelists." *EJ*, 14 (1925), 435-43.

Pritchett, V. S. "Mr. Forster's New Year." *New Statesman*, 56 (1958), 912-13.

_____. *The Working Novelist*, 13-18.

Putt, S. Gorley. *Scholars of the Heart*, 35-42.

Rajiva, Stanley F. "E. M. Forster on Music." *LHY*, 10 (1969), 55-68.

Raleigh, John Henry. "Victorian Morals and the Modern Novel." *PR*, 25, 2 (1958), 241-64.

Ransom, John Crowe. "E. M. Forster." *KR*, 5 (1943), 618-23.

Raskin, Jonah. *The Mythology of Imperialism*, 222-41.

Rawlings, Donn. "E. M. Forster, 'Prophecy,' and the Subversion of Myth." *Paunch*, 30 (1967), 17-36.

Reed, John R. *Old School Ties*, 125-54.

Richards, I. A. "A Passage to Forster: Reflections on a Novelist." *Forum*, 78 (1927), 914-20.

Rosenbaum, S. P. "E. M. Forster and George Meredith." *PMLA*, 86 (1971), 1037-38.

Savage, Derek S. *The Withered Branch*, 44-69.

Savidis, George. "Cavafy and Forster." *TLS*, November 14, 1975, 1356.

Seymour, William K. "E. M. Forster: Some Observations and a Memory." *ContempR*, 217 (1970), 84-86.

E. M. Forster, continued

Shahane, V. A. *E. M. Forster: A Reassessment*. Mysore: Kitab Mahal (W.S.D.) Pvt. Ltd., 1962.

———. "Formative Influences on E. M. Forster: Henry James—A Study in Ambivalence." *OJES*, 1 (1961), 39-53.

Shanks, Edward. "Mr. E. M. Forster." *London Mercury*, 16 (1927), 265-74.

Shusterman, David. *The Quest for Certitude in E. M. Forster's Fiction*. Bloomington: Indiana Univ. Press, 1965.

Smith, H. A. "Forster's Humanism and the Nineteenth Century." *Forster: A Collection of Critical Essays*. Ed. Malcolm Bradbury, 106-16.

Sorenson, Philip E. "E. M. Forster: A Brief Memoir." *ClareQ*, 9, 1 (1963), 5-9.

Spence, Jonathan. "E. M. Forster at Eighty." *New Republic*, 141 (October 5, 1959), 17-21.

Spratt, P. "The World Citizen." *LHY*, 10 (1969), 91-94.

Stallybrass, Oliver, ed. *Aspects of E. M. Forster: Essays and Recollections Written for His Ninetieth Birthday, January 1, 1969*. New York: Harcourt; London: E. Arnold, 1969.

Stone, Wilfred. *The Cave and the Mountain: A Study of E. M. Forster*. Stanford, Cal.: Stanford Univ. Press, 1966.

Strong, L. A. G. *Personal Remarks*, 205-09.

Thomson, George H. "E. M. Forster and Howard Sturgis." *TSLL*, 10 (1968), 423-33.

———. "E. M. Forster, Gerald Heard, and Bloomsbury." *ELT*, 12, 2 (1969), 87-91.

———. *The Fiction of E. M. Forster*. Detroit: Wayne State Univ. Press, 1967.

———. "Symbolism in E. M. Forster's Earlier Fiction." *Criticism*, 3 (1961), 304-20.

Tillotson, Geoffrey. *Criticism and the Nineteenth Century*, 244-69.

Traversi, D. A. "The Novels of E. M. Forster." *Arena*, 1 (1937), 28-40.

Trilling, Lionel. "E. M. Forster." *KR*, 4 (1942), 160-73.

———. *E. M. Forster*. Norfolk, Conn.: New Directions, 1943.

Truitt, Willis H. "Thematic and Symbolic Ideology in the Works of E. M. Forster, In Memoriam." *JAAC*, 30 (1971), 101-09.

Turk, Jo M. "The Evolution of E. M. Forster's Narrator." *SNNTS*, 5 (1973), 428-40.

Turnell, Martin. *Modern Literature and Christian Faith*, 25-45.

Voorhees, Richard J. "The Novels of E. M. Forster." *SAQ*, 53 (1954), 89-99.

Waggoner, Hyatt H. "Exercises in Perspective: Notes on the Uses of Coincidence in the Novels of E. M. Forster." *Chimera*, 3, 4 (1945), 3-14.

Warner, Rex. *E. M. Forster*. London: Longmans, Green, 1950.

Warren, Austin. "The Novels of E. M. Forster." *AmerR*, 9 (1937), 226-51.

_____. *Rage for Order*, 119-41.

Watson, Ian. "E. M. Forster: Whimsy and Beyond." *EigoS*, 115 (1969), 282-85.

Watt, Donald J. "G. E. Moore and the Bloomsbury Group." *ELT*, 12, 3 (1969), 119-34.

Webner, Hélène L. "E. M. Forster's Divine Comedy." *Renascence*, 23 (1971), 98-110.

Wilde, Alan. *Art and Order: A Study of E. M. Forster*. New York: New York Univ. Press, 1964.

_____. "Depths and Surfaces: Dimensions of Fosterian [*sic*] Irony." *ELT*, 16 (1973), 257-74.

Wilson, Angus. "Evil in the English Novel." *KR*, 29 (1967), 167-94.

Woodward, A. "The Humanism of E. M. Forster." *Theoria*, 20 (1963), 17-33.

Woolf, Virginia. *Collected Essays*, v. 1, 342-51; v. 2, 51-55.

Wright, Cuthbert. "The Damned and the Saved." *Cweal*, 38 (1943), 557-61.

Zabel, Morton Dauwen. "E. M. Forster." *Nation*, 147 (October 22, 1938), 412-13, 416.

Zwerdling, Alex. "The Novels of E. M. Forster." *TCL*, 2 (1957), 171-81.

See also: Allen, *English*, *Tradition*; Bowen, *Impressions*; Bradbury, *Possibilities*; A. Collins, *20th*; Connolly, *Playground*; Eagleton; Fraser; A. Friedman, *Turn*; Frierson; Gillie, *Movements*; Gindin, *Harvest*; Gould; Hall, *Tragic*; Hoare; Hynes, *Edwardian*; R. Johnson, *Men*; Karl and Magalaner; Kermode; Lovett, *History*; Mais, *Why*; Neill; Pritchett, *Living*; Routh; Scott-James, *50*; Spender, *Creative*, *Love-Hate*; Stevenson, *History*; Swinnerton, *Georgian*; Tindall, *Forces*, *Symbol*; Vines; H. Williams, *Modern*; Zabel, *Craft*.

HOWARDS END

Allen, Walter. "Reassessments: *Howards End*." *New Statesman*, 49 (1955), 407-08.

Armstrong, Paul B. "E. M. Forster's *Howards End*: The Existential Crisis of the Liberal Imagination." *Mosaic*, 8, 1 (1974), 183-99.

E. M. Forster, continued

Bensen, Alice R. "E. M. Forster's Dialectic: *Howards End.*" *MFS*, 1, 4 (1955), 17-22.

Bergonzi, Bernard. "Before 1914: Writers and the Threat of War." *CritQ*, 6 (1964), 126-34.

Berland, Alwyn. "James and Forster: The Morality of Class." *CambJ*, 6 (1953), 259-80.

Bradbury, Malcolm. "E. M. Forster's *Howards End.*" *CritQ*, 4 (1962), 229-41.

Brown, E. K. *Rhythm in the Novel*, 46-55.

Churchill, Thomas. "Place and Personality in *Howards End.*" *Crit*, 5, 1 (1962), 61-73.

Colmer, John. "*Howards End* Revisited." *LHY*, 10 (1969), 9-22.

Delbaere-Garant, J. " 'Who shall inherit England?': A Comparison Between *Howards End, Parade's End* and *Unconditional Surrender.*" *ES*, 50 (1969), 101-05.

Dobrée, Bonamy. *Modern Prose Style*, 35-38.

Ebbatson, J. R. "The Schlegels' Family Tree." *ELT*, 18, 3 (1975), 195-201.

Gillen, Francis. "*Howards End* and the Neglected Narrator." *Novel*, 3 (1970), 139-52.

Green, R. "Messrs. Wilcox and Kurtz: Hollow Men." *TCL*, 14 (1969), 231-39.

Hagopian, John V., and Anne Beltran. "*Howard's End.*" *Insight II*. Ed. John V. Hagopian and Martin Dolch, 130-40.

Hoffman, Frederick J. "*Howards End* and the Bogey of Progress." *MFS*, 7, 3 (1961), 243-57.

Hoy. Cyrus. "Forster's Metaphysical Novel." *PMLA*, 75 (1960), 126-36.

McDowell, Frederick P. W. " 'The Mild, Intellectual Light': Idea and Theme in *Howards End.*" *PMLA*, 74 (1959), 453-63.

McGurk, E. Barry. "Gentlefolk in Philistia: The Influence of Matthew Arnold on E. M. Forster's *Howards End.*" *ELT*, 15, 3 (1972), 213-19.

Maskell, Duke. "Style and Symbolism in *Howards End.*" *EIC*, 19 (1969), 292-308.

Missey, James. "The Connected and the Unconnected in *Howards End.*" *WSL*, 6 (1969), 72-89.

Moseley, Edwin M. "A New Correlative for *Howards End*: Demeter and Persephone." *LHB*, 1, 3 (1961), 1-6.

Portnoy, Howard N. "The Imperialist vs. The Yeoman: Forster's *Howards End.*" *Junction*, 1972, 73-76.

Raina, M. L. "The Symbol and the Story: The Case of *Howards End.*" *PURBA*, 2, 2 (1971), 11-26.

Roby, Kinley E. "Irony and the Narrative Voice in *Howards End.*"
    JNT, 2 (1972), 116-24.
Schneider, Daniel J. *Symbolism: The Manichean Vision*, 124-26.
Shahane, V. A. "Beethoven's Fifth Symphony in *Howards End.*"
    IJES, 1 (1960), 100-03.
Thomson, George H. "Theme and Symbol in *Howards End.*" *MFS* ⌐ 3
    (1961), 229-42.
Wakefield, G. P. *Howards End* (E. M. Forster). Oxford: Basil Black-
    well, 1968.
Westburg, Barry R. "Forster's Fifth Symphony: Another Aspect ⌐f
    Howards End." *MFS*, 10 (1965), 359-65.
See also: Eagleton; Gill; J. Hardy.

THE LONGEST JOURNEY
Baker, James R. "Forster's Voyage of Discovery." *TQ*, 18, 2 (1975),
    99-118.
Cahill, Daniel J. "E. M. Forster's *The Longest Journey* and Its Crit-
    ics." *IEY*, 15 (1970), 39-49.
Crews, Frederick C. "*The Longest Journey* and the Perils of Human-
    ism." *ELH*, 26 (1959), 575-96.
Hanquart, Evelyne. "The Manuscript of Forster's *The Longest Jour-
    ney.*" *RES*, 25 (1974), 152-62.
Harvey, John. "Imagination and Moral Theme in E. M. Forster's *The
    Longest Journey.*" *EIC*, 6 (1956), 418-33.
Heine, Elizabeth. "Rickie Elliot and the Cow: The Cambridge Apostles
    and *The Longest Journey.*" *ELT*, 15, 2 (1972), 116-34.
McDowell, Frederick P. W. "Forster's Many-Faceted Universe: Idea
    and Paradox in *The Longest Journey.*" *Crit*, 4, 1 (1961), 41-63.
Magnus, John. "Ritual Aspects of E. M. Forster's *The Longest Jour-
    ney.*" *MFS*, 13 (1967), 195-210.
Shahane, V. A. "*The Longest Journey.*" *LCrit*, 4, 3 (1960), 1-8.

MAURICE
Bolling, Douglass. "The Distanced Heart: Artistry in E. M. Forster's
    Maurice." *MFS*, 20 (1974), 157-67.
"A Chalice for Youth." *TLS*, October 8, 1971, 1215.
Harvey, C. J. D. "*Maurice*: E. M. Forster's 'Homosexual' Novel."
    Standpunte, 97 (1971), 29-33.
Hotchkiss, Joyce. "Romance and Reality: The Dualistic Style of E. M.
    Forster's *Maurice.*" *JNT*, 4 (1974), 163-75.
Kondo, Ineko. "Denki to Sakuhin—E. M. Forster to *Maurice.*" *EigoS*,
    118 (1972), 14-16.

E. M. Forster, continued

McDowell, Frederick P. W. "Second Thoughts on E. M. Forster's *Maurice.*" *VWQ*, 1, 1 (1972), 46-59.

Meyers, Jeffrey. "Forster's Secret Sharer." *SoRA*, 5 (1972), 58-62.

Orr, Christopher. "D. H. Lawrence and E. M. Forster: From *The White Peacock* to *Maurice.*" *BWVACET*, 2, 2 (1975), 22-28.

Rising, C. "E. M. Forster's *Maurice*: A Summing Up." *TQ*, 17, 1 (1974), 84-96.

Salter, Donald. "That Is My Ticket: The Homosexual Writings of E. M. Forster." *LonM*, 14, 6 (February-March 1975), 5-33.

Spender, Stephen. "Forster's Queer Novel." *PR*, 39 (1972), 113-17.

A PASSAGE TO INDIA

Allen, Glen O. "Structure, Symbol, and Theme in E. M. Forster's *A Passage to India.*" *PMLA*, 70 (1955), 934-54.

Anand, Mulk Raj. "English Novels of the Twentieth Century on India." *AsianR*, 39 (1943), 244-51.

Appasamy, J. B. "The Hill of Devi." *LHY*, 10 (1969), 51-53.

Austin, Edgar A. "Rites of Passage in *A Passage to India.*" *OW*, 9, 3 (1964), 64-72.

Babu, M. Sathya. "Godbole in 'The Temple'." *LCrit*, 9, 2 (1970), 70-78.

Bell, Vereen M. "Comic Seriousness in *A Passage to India.*" *SAQ*, 66 (1967), 606-17.

Boyle, Ted E. "Adela Quested's Delusion: The Failure of Rationalism in *A Passage to India.*" *CE*, 26 (1965), 478-80.

Bradbury, Malcolm, ed. *A PASSAGE TO INDIA: A Casebook.* London: Macmillan, 1970.

Brander, Laurence. "E. M. Forster and India." *REL*, 3, 4 (1962), 76-84.

Brooks, Benjamin Gilbert. "Three English Novelists and the Pakistani Scene." *Crescent and Green: A Miscellany of Writings on Pakistan*, 120-30

Brower, Reuben A. *The Fields of Light*, 182-98.

Brown, E. K. *Rhythm in the Novel*, 89-115.

Burke, Kenneth. *Language as Symbolic Action*, 223-39.

Cammarota, Richard S. "Musical Analogy and Internal Design in *A Passage to India.*" *ELT*, 18, 1 (1975), 38-46.

Carnie, Daniel. "The Modern Middle Class: In Prem Chand and in Forster." *IndL*, 17, 1-2 (1974), 25-33.

Chaudhuri, Nirad C. "Passage from India." *Encounter*, 2 (June 1954), 19-24.

Clubb, Roger L. "*A Passage to India*: The Meaning of the Marabar Caves." *CLAJ*, 6 (1963), 184-93.

Collins, J. A. "Novels into Plays." *LHY*, 10 (1969), 77-81.

Colmer, John A., ed. *A PASSAGE TO INDIA*. London: E. Arnold, 1967.

Cooperman, Stanley. "The Imperial Posture and the Shrine of Darkness: Kipling's *The Naulahka* and E. M. Forster's *A Passage to India*." *ELT*, 6, 1 (1963), 9-13.

Daleski, H. M. "Rhythmic and Symbolic Patterns in *A Passage to India*." *Studies in English Language and Literature*. Ed. Alice Shalvi and A. A. Mendilow, 258-79.

Danna, Louise. "What Happened in the Cave? Reflections on *A Passage to India*." *MFS*, 7, 3 (1961), 258-70.

Deacon, Andrew. "*A Passage to India*: Forster's Confidence." *CR*, 14 (1971), 125-36.

Emmett, V. J., Jr. "Verbal Truth and Truth of Mood in E. M. Forster's *A Passage to India*." *ELT*, 15, 3 (1972), 199-212.

Fleishman, Avrom. "Being and Nothing in *A Passage to India*." *Criticism*, 15 (1973), 109-25.

Fleissner, Robert F. "Passage from 'Kubla Khan' to Forster's 'India'." *IndL*, 14, 3 (1972), 79-84.

Friend, Robert. "The Quest for Rondure: A Comparison of Two Passages to India." *HUSL*, 1, 1 (1973), 76-85.

Fussell, Paul, Jr. "E. M. Forster's Mrs. Moore: Some Suggestions." *PQ*, 32 (1953), 388-95.

Gaines, Clarence H. "Some Philosophers in Fiction." *NoAmR*, 220 (1924), 375-84.

Gish, Robert. "Forster as Fabulist: Proverbs and Parables in *A Passage to India*." *ELT*, 15, 4 (1972), 245-56.

Goonetilleke, D. C. R. A. "Colonial Neuroses: Kipling and Forster." *ArielE*, 5, 4 (1974), 56-68.

Gowda, H. H. Anniah. "E. M. Forster's India." *LHY*, 4, 1 (1963), 45-52.

——. " 'To The Caves'." *LHY*, 10 (1969), 23-34.

Hale, Nancy. "A Passage to Relationship." *AR*, 20 (1960), 19-30.

Harris, Wilson. "A Comment on *A Passage to India*." *LHY*, 10 (1969), 35-39.

Henderson, Philip. *The Novel Today*, 87-96.

Hewett, R. P. *Reading and Response*, 155-62.

Hollingsworth, Keith. "*A Passage to India*: The Echoes in the Marabar Caves." *Criticism*, 4 (1962), 210-224.

Horowitz, Ellin. "The Communal Ritual and the Dying God in E. M. Forster's *A Passage to India*." *Criticism*, 6 (1964), 70-88.

Hunt, John D. "Muddle and Mystery in *A Passage to India*." *ELH*, 33 (1966), 497-517.

Hynes, Joseph. "After Marabar: Reading Forster, Robbe-Grillet, Spark." *IowaR*, 5, 1 (1974), 120-26.

Italia, Paul G. "On Miss Quested's Given Name in E. M. Forster's *A Passage to India.*" *ELN,* 11 (1973), 118-20.

Iyengar, K. R. Srinivasa. "India in Anglo-American Fiction." *TSL,* 3 (1958), 107-16.

Jacobson, Dan. "Forster's Cave." *New Statesman,* 72 (1966), 560.

Kain, Richard M. "Vision and Discovery in E. M. Forster's *A Passage to India.*" *Twelve Original Essays on Great English Novels.* Ed. Charles Shapiro, 253-75.

Keir, W. A. S. "*A Passage to India* Reconsidered." *CambJ,* 5 (1952), 426-35.

Kennard, Jean E. "*A Passage to India* and Dickinson's Saint at Benares." *SNNTS,* 5 (1973), 417-27.

Kilner, G. "Some Questions of Interpretation in *A Passage to India.*" *Use of English,* 16 (1965), 302-07.

Levine, June P. "An Analysis of the Manuscripts of *A Passage to India.*" *PMLA,* 85 (1970), 284-94.

————. *Creation and Criticism: A PASSAGE TO INDIA.* Lincoln: Univ. of Nebraska Press, 1971.

Lewis, Robin J. "Orwell's *Burmese Days* and Forster's *A Passage to India:* Two Novels of Human Relations in the British Empire." *MSE,* 4, 3 (1974), 1-36.

Liang, Ting-Chi. "Connexions and Separations in *A Passage to India.*" *FJS,* 8 (1975), 47-64.

Lovett, Robert M. "*A Passage to India.*" *New Republic.* 39 (August 27, 1924), 393-94.

Ludowyk, E. F. C. "Return to *A Passage to India.*" *LHY,* 10 (1969), 41-47.

McDonald, Walter R. "The Unity of *A Passage to India.*" *CEA,* 36, 1 (1973), 38-42.

Maclean, Hugh. "The Structure of *A Passage to India.*" *UTQ,* 23 (1953), 157-71.

Mahood, M. M. "Amritsar to Chandrapore: E. M. Forster and the Massacre." *Encounter,* 41 (September 1973), 26-29.

Martin, John S. "Mrs. Moore and the Marabar Caves: A Mythological Reading." *MFS,* 11 (1966), 429-33.

Mason, William H. *A PASSAGE TO INDIA, by E. M. Forster.* New York: Barnes and Noble, 1965.

Meyers, Jeffrey. "The Politics of *A Passage to India.*" *JML,* 1 (1971), 329-38.

Moody, Phillipa. *A Critical Commentary on E. M. Forster's A PASSAGE TO INDIA.* London: Macmillan; New York: St. Martin's, 1968.

Moran, Ronald. " 'Come, Come,' 'Boum, Boum': 'Easy' Rhythm in E. M. Forster's *A Passage to India.*" *BSUF*, 9, 2 (1968), 3-9.

Morton, A. L. *The Matter of Britain*, 150-54.

Moseley, Edwin M. *Pseudonyms of Christ in the Modern Novel*, 153-61.

Muir, Edwin. "Mr. Forster Looks at India." *Nation*, 119 (October 8, 1924), 379-80.

Mukherjee, Sujit. "India's Entry into English Fiction." *Quest*, 47 (1965), 51-55.

――――. "The Marabar Mystery: An Addition to the Case-Book on the Caves." *CE*, 27 (1966), 501-03.

Naik, M. K. "Passage to Less than India: Some Limitations of *A Passage to India.*" *JKUH*, 18 (1974), 30-38.

Naslund, Sena Jeter. "Fantasy, Prophecy, and Point of View in *A Passage to India.*" *SNNTS*, 7 (1975), 258-76.

Natwar-Singh, K., ed. *E. M. Forster: A Tribute, with Selections from His Writings on India*. New York: Harcourt, 1964.

Nelson, Harland S., and G. K. Das. "Shonfield and Forster's India: A Controversial Exchange." *Encounter*, 30 (June 1968), 94-95.

Nierenberg, Edwin. "The Withered Priestess: Mrs. Moore's Incomplete Passage to India." *MLQ*, 25 (1964), 198-204.

Parry, Benita. *Delusions and Discoveries*, 260-320.

――――. "Passage to More than India." *E. M. Forster: A Collection of Critical Essays*. Ed. Malcolm Bradbury, 160-74.

Pedersen, Glenn. "Forster's Symbolic Form." *KR*, 21 (1959), 231-49.

Pradhan, S. V. "A 'Song' of Love: Forster's *A Passage to India.*" *CentR*, 17 (1973), 297-320.

Price, Martin. "People of the Book: Character in Forster's *A Passage to India.*" *CritI*, 1 (1975), 605-22.

Rahman, Kalimur. "Race-Relations in *A Passage to India.*" *Venture*, 2 (1961), 56-69.

Ramsaran, J. A. "An Indian Reading of E. M. Forster's Classic." *ISE*, 1 (1969), 48-55.

Rodrigues, E. L. "Towards an Understanding of E. M. Forster." *JMSUB*, 9, 1 (1962), 91-105.

Rutherford, Andrew, ed. *A PASSAGE TO INDIA: A Collection of Critical Essays*. Englewood Cliffs, N. J.: Prentice-Hall, 1970.

Scott, Paul. "India: A Post-Forsterian View." Royal Soc. of Lit. of the U. K., London. *Essays by Divers Hands*, v. 36, 113-32.

Shahane, V. A. "The Marabar Caves: Fact and Fiction." *AN&Q*, 5 (1966), 3-4, 20-21, 36-37, 54-55.

――――. "A Note on the Marabar Caves in E. M. Forster's *A Passage to India.*" *OJES*, 2 (1962), 67-75.

E. M. Forster, continued

_____, ed. *Perspectives on E. M. Forster's A PASSAGE TO INDIA: A Collection of Critical Essays.* New York: Barnes and Noble, 1968.

_____. "Symbolism in E. M. Forster's *A Passage to India. TES,* 44 (1963), 423-31.

Shahani, Ranjee G. "Some British I Admire, V: Mr. E. M. Forster." *AsiaticR,* n.s. 42 (1946), 270-73.

Shonfield, Andrew. "The Politics of Forster's India." *Encounter,* 30 (January 1968), 62-69.

Shusterman, David. "The Curious Case of Professor Godbole: *A Passage to India* Re-examined." *PMLA,* 76 (1961), 426-35.

Singh, Bhupal. *A Survey of Anglo-Indian Fiction,* 221-40.

Singh, K. Natwar. "Only Connect . . . E. M. Forster and India." *LHY,* 10 (1969), 105-14.

Singh, St. Nihal. "Indians and Anglo-Indians: as Portrayed to Britons by British Novelists." *ModR,* 36 (September 1924), 251-56.

Spencer, Michael. "Hinduism in E. M. Forster's *A Passage to India." JASt,* 27 (1968), 281-95.

Stern, Frederick C. " 'Never Resemble M. de Lesseps': A Note on *A Passage to India." ELT,* 14, 2 (1971), 119-21.

Stewart, Douglas Alexander. *The Flesh and the Spirit,* 17-24.

Taraporewala, M. P. "*A Passage to India*: Symphonic Symmetry." *Siddha III.* Ed. Frank D'Souza and Jagdish Shivpuri, 58-86.

Thomas, Roy, and Howard Erskine-Hill. "*A Passage to India*: Two Points of View." *AWR,* 15, 35 (1965), 44-50.

Thomson, George H. "Thematic Symbol in *A Passage to India." TCL,* 7 (1961), 51-63.

_____. "A Note on the Snake Imagery of *A Passage to India." ELT,* 9, 2 (1966), 108-10.

Viswanathan, K. *India in English Fiction,* 90-120.

Wagner, C. Roland. "The Excremental and the Spiritual in *A Passage to India." MLQ,* 31 (1970), 359-71.

Watts, Stephen. "Forster on 'India'—Author talks about Novel-into-Play." *NYT,* January 28, 1962, sec. 2, 1, 3.

Werry, Richard R. "Rhythm in Forster's *A Passage to India." Studies in Honor of John Wilcox.* Ed. A. Dayle Wallace and Woodburn O. Ross, 227-37.

White, Gertrude M. "*A Passage to India*: Analysis and Revaluation." *PMLA,* 68 (1953), 641-57.

See also: Kermode; Kettle.

A ROOM WITH A VIEW

Beer, John. "A Room with a View." *TLS*, June 11, 1971, 677.

Ellem, Elizabeth. "E. M. Forster: The Lucy and New Lucy Novels—Fragments of Early Versions of *A Room with a View*." *TLS*, May 28, 1971, 623-25.

Finkelstein, Bonnie B. "Forster's Women: *A Room With a View*." *ELT*, 16 (1973), 275-87.

Forster, E. M. "A View Without a Room: Old Friends Fifty Years Later." *NYTBR*, July 27, 1958, 4.

Lucas, John. "Wagner and Forster: *Parsifal* and *A Room with a View*." *ELH*, 33 (1966), 92-117.

Meyers, Jeffrey. " 'Vacant Heart and Hand and Eye': The Homosexual Theme in *A Room with a View*." *ELT*, 13, 3 (1970), 181-92.

See also: V. Woolf, *Contemporary*.

WHERE ANGELS FEAR TO TREAD

Delbaere-Garant, Jeanne. "The Call of the South: *Where Angels Fear to Tread* and *The Lost Girl*." *RLV*, 29 (1963), 336-57.

Meyers, Jeffrey. *Painting and the Novel*, 31-45.

Wilde, Alan. "The Aesthetic View of Life: *Where Angels Fear to Tread*." *MFS*, 7, 3 (1961), 207-16.

JOHN FOWLES

BIBLIOGRAPHIES

Evarts, Prescott, Jr. "John Fowles: A Checklist." *Crit*, 13, 3 (1972), 105-07.

INTERVIEWS

Newquist, Roy, ed. *Counterpoint*, 218-25.

GENERAL STUDIES

Allen, Walter. "The Achievement of John Fowles." *Encounter*, 35 (August 1970), 64-67.

Binns, Ronald. "John Fowles: Radical Romancer." *CritQ*, 15 (1973), 317-34.

Churchill, Thomas. "Waterhouse, Storey, and Fowles: *Which Way Out of the Room?*" *Crit*, 10, 3 (1968), 72-87.

Detweiler, Robert. "The Unity of John Fowles' Fiction." *NConL*, 1, 2 (1971), 3-4.

Dixon, Terrell F. "Expostulation and a Reply: The Character of Clegg in Fowles and Sillitoe." *NConL*, 4, 2 (1974), 7-9.

John Fowles, continued

Laughlin, Rosemary M. "Faces of Power in the Novels of John Fowles." *Crit*, 13, 3 (1972), 71-88.

Mathews, James W. "Fowles's Artistic Freedom: Another Stone from James's House." *NConL*, 4, 2 (1974), 2-4.

Palmer, William J. *The Fiction of John Fowles: Tradition, Art, and the Loneliness of Selfhood.* Columbia: Univ. of Missouri Press, 1974.

Rackham, Jeff. "John Fowles: The Existential Labyrinth." *Crit*, 13, 3 (1972), 89-103.

Scholes, Robert. "The Orgastic Fiction of John Fowles." *HC*, 6, 5 (1969), 1-12.

Tatham, Michael. "Two Novels: Notes on the Work of John Fowles." *New Blackfriars*, 52 (September 1971), 404-11.

THE FRENCH LIEUTENANT'S WOMAN

Brantlinger, Patrick, Ian Adam, and Sheldon Rothblatt. "*The French Lieutenant's Woman*: A Discussion." *VS*, 15 (1972), 339-56.

Costa, Richard Hauer. "Trickery's Mixed Bag: The Perils of Fowles' *French Lieutenant's Woman*." *BRMMLA*, 29 (1975), 1-9.

DeVitis, A. A., and William J. Palmer. "*A Pair of Blue Eyes* Flash at *The French Lieutenant's Woman*." *ConL*, 15 (1974), 90-101.

Evarts, Prescott, Jr. "Fowles' *The French Lieutenant's Woman* as Tragedy." *Crit*, 13, 3 (1972), 57-69.

Fowles, John. "Notes on an Unfinished Novel." *Afterwords*. Ed. Thomas McCormack, 160-75.

Kane, Patricia. "The Fallen Woman as Free-Thinker in *The French Lieutenant's Woman* and *The Scarlet Letter*." *NConL*, 2, 1 (1972), 8-10.

Kaplan, Fred. "Victorian Modernists: Fowles and Nabokov." *JNT*, 3 (1973), 108-20.

McGregor, Barbara R. "Existentialism in *The French Lieutenant's Woman*." *ReAL*, 1, 2 (1975), 39-46.

Rankin, Elizabeth D. "Cryptic Coloration in *The French Lieutenant's Woman*." *JNT*, 3 (1974), 193-207.

Rose, Gilbert J. "*The French Lieutenant's Woman*: The Unconscious Significance of a Novel to Its Author." *AI*, 29 (1972), 165-76.

THE MAGUS

Berets, Ralph. "*The Magus*: A Study in the Creation of a Personal Myth." *TCL*, 19 (1973), 89-98.

Bradbury, Malcolm. "John Fowles's *The Magus*." *Sense and Sensibility in Twentieth-Century Writing*. Ed. Brom Weber, 26-38.

Presley, Delma E. "The Quest of the Bourgeois Hero: An Approach to Fowles' *The Magus*." *JPC*, 6 (1972), 394-98.

Rubenstein, Roberta. "Myth, Mystery, and Irony: John Fowles's *The Magus*." *ConL*, 16 (1975), 328-39.

See also: Bradbury, *Possibilities*.

JOHN GALSWORTHY

BIBLIOGRAPHIES

Gerber, Helmut E. "John Galsworthy: An Annotated Checklist of Writings About Him." *EFT*, 1, 3 (1958), 7-29.

Goetsch, Paul. "Supplement." *ELT*, 8, 5 (1965), 284-90.

Stevens, Earl Eugene. "Supplement." *ELT*, 7, 2 (1964), 93-110; 10, 4 (1967), 238-40.

INTERVIEWS

Rascoe, Burton. *We Were Interrupted*, 320-22.

SPECIAL ISSUES

Bookman (London), 75 (December 1928), 147-58.

Bookman (London), 83 (March 1933), 473-506 [obituary issue].

GENERAL STUDIES

Adcock, A. St. John. *Gods of Modern Grub Street*, 113-20.

Austin, Hugh P. "John Galsworthy." *DubR*, 189 (1931), 95-106.

Barker, Dudley. *The Man of Principle: A View of John Galsworthy*. New York: London House and Maxwell, 1963.

Bartlett, Robert M. *They Dared to Live*, 39-42.

Bateman, May. "John Galsworthy." *CathW*, 114 (1922), 732-47.

Bates, Ernest S. "John Galsworthy." *EJ*, 22 (1933), 437-46.

Bellamy, William. *The Novels of Wells, Bennett, and Galsworthy*, 80-102, 165-204, 211-16.

Bloor, R. H. U. *The English Novel from Chaucer to Gulsworthy*, 242-46.

Bodgener, J. H. "John Galsworthy Looks at Life." *LonQR*, 152 (1929), 73-81.

Brash, W. Bardsley. "John Galsworthy." *LQ&HR*, 160 (1935), 460-71.

Bullett, Gerald W. *Modern English Fiction*, 46-53.

Canby, Henry S. "Galsworthy: An Estimate." *SatR*, 9 (March 18, 1933), 485-87.

———. *Seven Years' Harvest*, 30-39.

John Galsworthy, continued

Chevrillon, André. *Three Studies in English Literature: Kipling, Galsworthy, Shakespeare.* Tr. Florence Simmonds. Port Washington, N.Y.: Kennikat, 1967, 153-219.

Chubb, Edwin W. *Stories of Authors,* 401-04.

Clark, Barrett H. *Intimate Portraits,* 27-44.

Cobley, W. D. "John Galsworthy." *ManchQ,* 42 (1923), 187-211.

Colenutt, R. "The World of Mr. Galsworthy's Fiction." *Cornhill,* 149 (1934), 55-64.

Collins, Norman. *Facts of Fiction,* 258-75.

Conrad, Joseph. *Last Essays,* 125-37.

Cooper, Frederick T. *Some English Story Tellers,* 177-205.

Core, George. "Author and Agency: Galsworthy and the Pinkers." *LCUT,* 6 (1974), 61-73.

Croman, Natalie. *John Galsworthy: A Study in Continuity and Contrast.* Cambridge, Mass.: Harvard Univ. Press, 1933.

Cross, Wilbur L. *Four Contemporary Novelists,* 101-53.

———. "Some Novels of 1920." *YR,* n.s. 10 (1921), 396-411.

Cunliffe, J. W. *English Literature During the Last Half-Century,* 2d ed., 220-36.

Curle, Richard. *Caravansary and Conversation,* 155-63.

Eaker, J. Gordon. "Galsworthy and The Modern Mind." *PQ,* 29 (1950), 31-48.

Elwin, Malcolm. *Old Gods Falling,* 363-90.

Ervine, St. John. "John Galsworthy." *Great Democrats.* Ed. A. Barratt Brown. London: Nicholson and Watson, 1934, 277-95.

———. *Some Impressions of My Elders,* 113-60.

Follett, Helen T., and Wilson J. Follett. "Contemporary Novelists: John Galsworthy." *Atlantic,* 118 (December 1916), 757-67.

Ford, Ford Madox. "Galsworthy." *AmerM,* 37 (April 1936), 448-59.

———. *It Was The Nightingale,* 41-62.

———. "John Galsworthy and George Moore." *EngRev,* 57 (1933), 130-42.

———. *Portraits from Life,* 124-42.

Freeman, James C. "Whyte-Melville and Galsworthy's 'Bright Beings'." *NCF,* 5 (1950), 85-100.

"Galsworthy and Proust." *TLS,* December 8, 1950, 777-78.

Garnett, David. "E. M. Forster and John Galsworthy." *REL,* 5, 1 (1964), 7-18.

———. "Some Writers I Have Known: Galsworthy, Forster, Moore, and Wells." *TQ,* 4, 3 (1961), 190-202.

Gay, N. K. "Truth in Art and Truth in Life." *Preserve and Create.* Ed. Gaylord C. LeRoy and Ursula Beitz, 76-93.

100

Gindin, James J. "Ethical Structure in John Galsworthy, Elizabeth Bowen, and Iris Murdoch." *Forms of Modern British Fiction.* Ed. Alan W. Friedman, 15-41.

Gould, Gerald. "John Galsworthy as a Novelist." *Bookman* (London), 65 (1923), 131-38.

Greenough, Chester Noyes. *Collected Studies.* Cambridge: Merrymount Press, Harvard Coop. Soc. Distributors, 1940, 246-49.

Gretton, Mary S. "John Galsworthy." *ContempR*, 143 (1933), 319-25.

Guedalla, Philip. *A Gallery*, 85-97.

Hale, Edward E. "John Galsworthy." *Dial*, 59 (June 24-December 23, 1915), 201-03.

Hamilton, Robert. "John Galsworthy: A Humanitarian Prophet." *QR*, 291 (1953), 72-80.

Harkness, Bruce. "Conrad on Galsworthy: The Time Scheme of *Fraternity*." *MFS*, 1, 2 (1955), 12-18.

Harris, Frank. *Contemporary Portraits,* 3d ser., 31-43.

Hawkes, Carol A. "Galsworthy: The Paradox of Realism." *ELT*, 13, 4 (1970), 288-95.

Henderson, Philip. *The Novel Today*, 103-09.

James, Stanley B. "A Contrast in Sagas: Sigrid Undset and John Galsworthy." *Month*, 161 (1933), 520-26.

Kain, Richard M. "Galsworthy, The Last Victorian Liberal." *MadQ*, 4 (1944), 84-94.

Kaye-Smith, Sheila. *John Galsworthy.* London: Hutchinson, 1916.

Knight, Grant C. *The Novel in English*, 320-26.

Lawrence, D. H. "John Galsworthy." *Scrutinies.* Ed. Edgell Rickword, 51-72.

———. *Selected Literary Criticism*, 118-31.

Linn, James W., and H. W. Taylor. *A Foreword to Fiction*, 69-70, 81-85.

Lockert, Lacy. "Some of Mr. Galsworthy's Heroines." *NoAmR*, 215 (1922), 255-66.

Macartney, M. H. H. "The Novels of Mr. John Galsworthy." *WestmR*, 171 (1909), 682-93.

Mais, Stuart P. B. *Some Modern Authors*, 57-62.

Martin, Dorothy. "Mr. Galsworthy as Artist and Reformer." *YR*, 14 (1924), 126-39.

Masur, Gerhard. *Prophets of Yesterday*, 245-50.

Moses, Montrose J. "John Galsworthy." *NoAmR*, 235 (1933), 537-45; *Opinions and Attitudes in the Twentieth Century.* Ed. Stewart S. Morgan and William H. Thomas, 210-20.

Mottram, R. H. *John Galsworthy.* London: Longmans, Green, 1953.

Muir, Edwin. *The Structure of the Novel*, 116-25.

John Galsworthy, continued

Myers, Walter L. *The Later Realism*, 114-18, 131-34, 146-47.
Ould, Hermon. *John Galsworthy*. London: Chapman and Hall, 1934.
Overton, Grant M. *American Nights Entertainment*, 13-33.
_____. "Mr. Galsworthy's Secret Loyalties." *Bookman* (N.Y.), 57 (1923), 153-59.
Pallette, Drew B. "Young Galsworthy: The Forging of a Satirist." *MP*, 56 (1959), 178-86.
Phelps, Gilbert. *The Russian Novel in English Fiction*, 112-25, 145-46, 153-54.
Priestley, J. B. "John Galsworthy." *EJ*, 14 (1925), 347-55.
Reilly, Joseph J. *Dear Prue's Husband*. New York: Macmillan, 1932, 45-67.
Robertson, Stuart. "American Speech According to Galsworthy." *AS*, 6 (1932), 297-301.
Ross, Woodburn O. "John Galsworthy: Aspects of an Attitude." *Studies in Honor of John Wilcox*. Ed. A. Dayle Wallace and Woodburn O. Ross, 195-208.
Russell, Frances T. "Ironic John Galsworthy." *UCC*, 32 (1930), 78-87.
Sauter, Rudolf. *Galsworthy the Man: An Intimate Portrait*. London: Peter Owen, 1967.
Semper, Isidore J. *Return of the Prodigal*, 112-34.
Shanks, Edward. "Mr. John Galsworthy." *London Mercury*, 8 (1923), 393-404.
_____. *Second Essays in Literature*, 41-61.
Simrell, V. E. "John Galsworthy: The Artist as Propagandist." *QJSE*, 13 (1927), 225-36.
Swinnerton, Frank. "John Galsworthy." *Bookman* (London), 75 (December 1928), 147-51.
Takada, Mineo. "The Difficulties Lie in His Englishness: A Study of John Galsworthy." Doshisha Women's College of Liberal Arts. *Annual Reports of Studies*, v. 21, 197-227.
Takahashi, Genji. *Studies in the Works of John Galsworthy, with Special Reference to His Visions of Love and Beauty*. Tokyo: Shinozaki Shorin, 1954; rev. 1956.
Thompson, Edward R. *Portraits of the New Century*, 46-49.
Wagenknecht, Edward C. "The Selfish Heroine: Thackeray and Galsworthy." *CE*, 4 (1943), 293-98.
Walpole, Hugh. "John Galsworthy." *Post-Victorians*, by Various Authors, 173-85.
Watkin, Edward. *Men and Tendencies*, 18-28.
Waugh, Arthur. "John Galsworthy as Novelist." *Bookman* (London), 83 (March 1933), 485.

John Galsworthy, continued

West, Rebecca. *Ending in Ernest*, 129-33.
_____. *The Strange Necessity*, 199-213.
Williamson, Hugh R. "John Galsworthy: Notes at Random." *Bookman* (London), 83 (March 1933), 473-79.
Woolf, Virginia. *Collected Essays*, v. 1, 319-37.
See also: Adcock, *Gods*; Allen, *English*; E. Baker, *History*; Beach, *20th*; A. Collins, *20th*; Cunliffe, *Half-Century, 20th Century*; Daiches, *Novel*; Drew, *Modern*; Edgar, *Art*; Frierson; Gill; J. Gray; Hamilton; Hind, *Authors*; Kettle; Lacon; Lovett, *History*; MacCarthy, *Memories*; McCullough; Mackenzie; Muller, *Modern*; W. Phelps; Pritchett, *Living*; J. Reilly; Richards; Routh; Scott-James, *50*; Swinnerton, *Georgian*; Wagenknecht, *Cavalcade*; Ward, *20th*; Weygandt; V. Woolf, *Contemporary*.

THE FORSYTE SAGA
Aiken, Conrad. "The Last of the Forsytes." *New Republic*, 56 (October 10, 1928), 221-22.
Banerjee, Jacqueline. "Galsworthy's 'Dangerous Experiment'." *AWR*, 24, 52 (1974), 135-43.
Bennett, Arnold. *Books and Persons*, 214-16.
Braybrooke, Patrick. "The Forsyte Saga." *CL&PM*, 252 (December 1929), 446-50.
Chicherin, A. "A Reconsideration of Opinions about *The Forsyte Saga*." *VLM*, 1 (1958), 152-66.
Cohen, Walter, Jan Struther, and Lyman Bryson. "The Forsyte Saga." *Invitation to Learning*. Ed. George D. Crothers, 180-89.
Conrad, Joseph. "A Middle-Class Family." *Outlook*, 17 (March 31, 1906), 449-50.
Cross, Wilbur. "The Forsytes." *YR*, 19 (1930), 527-50.
Dooley, D. J. "Character and Credibility in *The Forsyte Saga*." *DR*, 50 (1970), 373-77.
Duffin, H. C. "The Rehabilitation of Soames Forsyte." *Cornhill*, 141 (1930), 397-406.
Eaker, J. Gordon. "Galsworthy as Thinker in *The Forsyte Saga*." *Phi Kappa Phi Journ.*, 51, 1 (1971), 10-20.
Eaton, Harold T. *Reading Galsworthy's THE FORSYTE SAGA*. New York: Scribner's, 1936.
Grove, Frederick P. "Morality in *The Forsyte Saga*." *UTQ*, 15 (1945), 54-64.
Hamilton, Robert. "The Forsyte Saga." *QR*, 304 (1966), 431-41.
Harris, Wendell V. "Molly's 'Yes': The Transvaluation of Sex in Modern Fiction." *TSLL*, 10 (1968), 107-18.

103

Hart, John E. "Ritual and Spectacle in *The Man of Property.*" *RS*, 40 (1972), 34-43.

Lambert, J. W. "The Galsworthy Saga." *Horizon (N.Y.)*, 4 (Autumn 1968), 106-11.

Marchant, Peter. *"The Forsyte Saga* Reconsidered: The Case of the Common Reader Versus Literary Criticism." *WHR*, 24 (1970), 221-29.

Pike, E. Royston. *Human Documents of the Age of the Forsytes.* London: Allen and Unwin, 1969, 7-12.

Pritchett, V. S. *The Working Novelist*, 49-55.

Thody, Philip. "The Politics of the Family Novel: Is Conservatism Inevitable?" *Mosaic*, 3, 1 (1969), 87-101.

Tilby, A. Wyatt. "The Epic of Property." *Edinburgh*, 241 (1925), 271-85.

Van Egmond, Peter. "Naming Techniques in John Galsworthy's *The Forsyte Saga.*" *Names*, 16 (1968), 371-79.

Wilson, Angus. "Galsworthy's *Forsyte Saga.*" *New Statesman*, 51 (1956), 187.

See also: Bergonzi, *Turn*; Kettle; H. Williams, *Modern*.

DAVID GARNETT

GENERAL STUDIES

Garnett, David, ed. *The White/Garnett Letters*. New York: Viking, 1968.

Heilbrun, Caroline G. *The Garnett Family: The History of a Literary Family*. New York: Macmillan, 1961.

Irwin, W. R. "The Metamorphoses of David Garnett." *PMLA*, 73 (1958), 386-92.

Johnson, Ann S. "Garnett's Amazon from Dahomey: Literary Debts in *The Sailor's Return.*" *ConL*, 14 (1973), 169-85.

See also: Allen, *Tradition*; MacCarthy, *Criticism*; Vines.

RUMER GODDEN

GENERAL STUDIES

Frey, John R. "Past or Present Tense? A Note on the Technique of Narration." *JEGP*, 46 (1947), 205-08.

Hartley, Lois. "The Indian Novels of Rumer Godden." *Mahfil*, 3, 2-3 (1966), 65-75.

Simpson, Hassell A. *Rumer Godden*. New York: Twayne, 1973.

Tindall, William York. "Rumer Godden, Public Symbolist." *CE*, 13 (1952), 297-303.

See also: Prescott.

WILLIAM GOLDING

BIBLIOGRAPHIES

Biles, Jack T. "A William Golding Checklist." *TCL*, 17 (1971), 107-21.
Vann, J. Don. "William Golding: A Checklist of Criticism." *Serif*, 8, 2 (1971), 21-26.

INTERVIEWS

Biles, Jack I. *Talk: Conversations with William Golding*. New York: Harcourt, 1970.
Davis, Douglas M. "Conversation with Golding." *New Republic*, 148 (May 4, 1963), 28-30.
_____. "Golding, the Optimist, Belies His Somber Pictures and Fiction." *National Observer*, 1, 33 (September 17, 1962), 17.
Dick, Bernard F. " 'The Novelist Is a Displaced Person': An Interview With William Golding." *CE*, 26 (1965), 480-82.
Keating, James. "Interview with William Golding." *LORD OF THE FLIES*, by William Golding (Casebook Ed.). Ed. James R. Baker and Arthur P. Ziegler, Jr. New York: Putnam, 1964, 189-95.
Kermode, Frank, and William Golding. "The Meaning of It All." *Books and Bookmen*, 5 (October 1959), 9-10.
Webster, Owen. "Living with Chaos." *Books and Art*, March 1958, 15-16.

SPECIAL ISSUES

Biles, Jack I., ed. "A William Golding Miscellany." *SLitI*, 2, 2 (1969), 1-95.

GENERAL STUDIES

Alcantara-Demalanta, O. "Christian Dimensions in Contemporary Literature." *Unitas*, 46 (1973), 213-23.
Aldridge, John W. "Mr. Golding's Own Story." *NYTBR*, Dec. 10, 1961, 56-57.
Anderson, David. *The Tragic Protest*, 155-79.
Babb, Howard S. "Four Passages from William Golding's Fiction." *MinnR*, 5 (1965), 50-58.
_____. *The Novels of William Golding*. Columbus: Ohio State Univ. Press, 1970.
Baker, James R. *William Golding: A Critical Study*. New York: St. Martin's, 1965.
Biles, Jack I. "Literary Sources and William Golding." *SAB*, 37, 2 (1972), 29-36.

Bowen, John. "One Man's Meat: The Idea of Individual Responsibility." *TLS*, August 7, 1959, xii-xiii.

Broes, Arthur T. "The Two Worlds of William Golding." *Lectures on Modern Novelists*. Ed. Arthur T. Broes, et al., 1-14.

Byczkowska, Ewa. "William Golding's Novels and the Anglo-American Tradition of Allegory in Fiction." *AW*, 2 (1972), 63-74.

Clark, George. "An Illiberal Education: William Golding's Pedagogy." *Seven Contemporary Authors*. Ed. Thomas B. Whitbread, 73-95.

Cockren, Thomas M. "Is Golding Calvinistic?" *America*, 109 (July 6, 1963), 18-20.

Crane, John K. "Golding and Bergson: The Free Fall of Free Will." *BRMMLA*, 26 (1972), 136-41.

——. "Crossing the Bar Twice: Post-Mortem Consciousness in Bierce, Hemingway, and Golding." *SSF*, 6 (1969), 361-76.

Davenport, Guy. "Jungles of the Imagination." *National Review* (N.Y.), 13 (October 1962), 273-74.

Davies, Harold. "Moral Choice in the Novels of William Golding." *ModSp*, 11, 5 (1969), 1-2, 35-45.

Delbaere-Garant, Jeanne. "From the Cellar to the Rock: A Recurrent Pattern in William Golding's Novels." *MFS*, 17 (1971-72), 501-12.

Dick, Bernard F. *William Golding*. New York: Twayne, 1967.

Duncan, Kirby L. "William Golding and Vardis Fisher: A Study in Parallels and Extensions." *CE*, 27 (1965), 232-35.

Egan, John M. "Golding's View of Man." *America*, 108 (January 26, 1963), 140-41.

Elmen, Paul. *William Golding: A Critical Study*. Grand Rapids, Mich.: Erdmans, 1967.

Ely, Sister M. Amanda, O.P. "The Adult Image in Three Novels of Adolescent Life." *EJ*, 56 (1967), 1127-31.

Fox, Dorothy. "William Golding's Microcosms of Evil." *Innisfree*, 1 (1974), 30-37.

Freedman, Ralph. "The New Realism: The Fancy of William Golding." *Per*, 10 (1958), 118-28.

Gindin, James. " 'Gimmick' and Metaphor in the Novels of William Golding." *MFS*, 6 (1960), 145-52.

Goldberg, Gerald J. "The Search for the Artist in Some Recent British Fiction." *SAQ*, 62 (1963), 387-401.

Grande, Luke M. "The Appeal of Golding." *Cweal*, 77 (1962), 457-59.

Green, Martin. "Distaste for the Contemporary." *Nation*, 190 (1960), 451-54.

Green, Peter. "The World of William Golding." *REL*, 1, 2 (1960), 62-72; Royal Soc. of Lit. of the U. K., London. *Essays by Divers Hands*, v. 32, 37-57.

Gregor, Ian, and Mark Kinkead-Weekes. "The Strange Case of Mr. Golding and His Critics." *TC*, 167 (1960), 115-25.
Herndl, George C. "Golding and Salinger: A Clear Choice." *WR*, 502 (1964), 309-22.
Hodson, Leighton. *Golding*. Edinburgh: Oliver and Boyd, 1969.
Hollinger, Alexander. "Human Condition in W. Golding's Novels." *AUB-LG*, 22 (1973), 177-82.
Hynes, Samuel. "Novels of a Religious Man." *Cweal*, 71 (1960), 673-75.
_____. *William Golding*. New York: Columbia Univ. Press, 1964.
Irwin, Joseph J. "The Serpent Coiled Within." *Motive*, 23 (May 1963), 1-5.
Josipovici, Gabriel. *The World and the Book*, 236-51.
Kearns, Francis E. "Salinger and Golding: Conflict on the Campus." *America*, 108 (January 26, 1963), 136-39.
_____, and Luke M. Grande. "The Appeal of Golding: An Exchange of Views." *Cweal*, 77 (1963), 569-71.
Kennard, Jean E. *Number and Nightmare*, 176-202.
Kermode, Frank. "The Novels of William Golding." *ILA*, 3 (1961), 11-29.
Kinkead-Weekes, Mark, and Ian Gregor. *William Golding: A Critical Study*. London: Faber and Faber, 1967; New York: Harcourt, 1968.
Kvam, Ragnar. "William Golding." *Vinduet*, 13 (1959), 292-98.
MacLure, Millar. "William Golding's Survivor Stories." *TamR*, 5 (1957), 60-67.
MacShane, Frank. "The Novels of William Golding." *DR*, 42 (1962), 171-83.
Malin, Irving. "The Elements of William Golding." *Contemporary British Novelists*. Ed. Charles Shapiro, 36-47.
Marcus, Steven. "The Novel Again." *PR*, 29, 2 (1962), 171-95.
Marsden, Arthur. "The Novels of William Golding." *Delta*, 10 (1956), 26-29.
Mitchell, Juliet. "Concepts and Technique in William Golding." *NewLR*, 15 (May-June 1962), 63-71.
Mužina, Matej. "William Golding: The World of Perception and the World of Cognition." *SRAZ*, 27-28 (1969), 107-27.
_____. "William Golding: Novels of Extreme Situations." *SRAZ*, 27-28 (1969), 43-66.
Nossen, Evon. "The Beast-Man Theme in the Work of William Golding." *BSUF*, 9, 2 (1968), 60-69.
Oldsey, Bernard S., and Stanley Weintraub. *The Art of William Golding*. New York: Harcourt, 1965; Bloomington: Indiana Univ. Press, 1968.

William Golding, continued

"Origins of the Species." *TLS*, November 5, 1971, 1381.
Pemberton, Clive. *William Golding*. London: Longmans, Green, 1969.
Pendry, E. D. "William Golding and 'Mankind's Essential Illness'."
    MSpr, 55 (1961), 1-7.
Peter, John. "The Fables of William Golding." *KR*, 19 (1957), 577-92.
Pittock, Malcolm, and J. G. Roberts. "Michael Roberts and William
    Golding." *ES*, 52 (1971), 442-43.
Pritchett, V. S. "God's Folly." *New Statesman*, 67 (1964), 562-63.
———. *The Working Novelist*, 56-61.
Rexroth, Kenneth. "William Golding." *Atlantic*, 215 (May 1965), 96-98.
Steiner, George. *Language and Silence*, 289-94.
Stinson, John J. "Trying to Exorcise the Beast: The Grotesque in the
    Fiction of William Golding." *Cithara*, 2, 1 (1971), 3-30.
Sullivan, Walter. "William Golding: The Fables and the Art." *SR*, 71
    (1963), 660-64.
Thomson, George H. "The Real World of William Golding." *Alphabet*,
    9 (1964), 26-33.
———. "William Golding: Between God-Darkness and God-Light."
    Cresset, 32, 7 (1969), 8-12.
Tiger, Virginia. *William Golding: The Dark Fields of Discovery*. Lon-
    don: Calder and Boyars, 1975.
Wain, John. "Lord of the Agonies." *Aspect*, 3 (1963), 56-67.
Walker, Marshall. "William Golding: From Paradigm to Pyramid."
    SLitI, 2, 2 (1969), 67-82.
Walters, Margaret. "Two Fabulists: Golding and Camus." *MCR*, 4
    (1961), 18-29.
Wasserstrom, William. "Reason and Reverence in Art and Science."
    L&P, 12 (1962), 2-5.
See also: Allen, *Tradition*; Karl; Kermode; Pritchett, *Living*.

FREE FALL
Aarseth, Inger. "Golding's Journey to Hell: An Examination of Pre-
    figurations and Archetypal Pattern in *Free Fall*." *ES*, 56 (1975),
    322-33.
Báti, Lászlo. "William Golding's *Free Fall*: A Case of Introspection."
    Studies in English and American, v. 2. Ed. Erzsébet Perényi and
    Tibor Frank, 155-70.
Boyle, Ted E. "The Denial of the Spirit: An Explication of William
    Golding's *Free Fall*." *WascanaR*, 1, 1 (1966), 3-10.
Henry, Avril. "The Structure of Golding's *Free Fall*." *SoRA*, 8 (1975),
    95-124.
Mizener, Arthur. "Some Kinds of Modern Novel." *SR*, 69 (1961), 153-64.

West, Anthony. "Footloose and Fancy-Free." *NY*, 36 (April 30, 1960), 170-76.

See also: Buckley.

THE INHERITORS

Adriaens, Mark. "Style in W. Goldring's *The Inheritors*." *ES*, 51 (1970), 16-30.

Ali, Masood Amjad. "*The Inheritors*: An Experiment in Technique." *Venture*, 5 (1969), 123-31.

Bufkin, E. C. "The Ironic Art of William Golding's *The Inheritors*." *TSLL*, 9 (1968), 567-78.

Fackler, Herbert V. "Paleontology and Paradise Lost: A Study of Golding's Modifications of Fact in *The Inheritors*." *BSUF*, 10, 3 (1969), 64-66.

Halliday, M. A. K. "Linguistic Function and Literary Style: An Inquiry into the Language of William Golding's *The Inheritors. Literary Style: A Symposium*. Ed. Seymour Chatman, 330-65. [See also 365-68]

Hurt, James R. "Grendel's Point of View: *Beowulf* and William Golding." *MFS*, 13 (1967), 264-65.

Sternlicht, Sanford. "Songs of Innocence and Songs of Experience in *Lord of the Flies* and *The Inheritors*." *MQ*, 9 (1968), 383-90.

LORD OF THE FLIES

Baker, James R. "The Decline of *Lord of the Flies*." *SAQ*, 69 (1970), 446-60.

――――. "Why It's No Go: A Study of William Golding's *Lord of the Flies*." *ArQ*, 19 (1963), 293-305.

Banaag, Concepcion B. "Evil and Redemption in *Lord of the Flies*." *FJS*, 3 (1970), 1-13.

Biles, Jack I. "Piggy: *Apologia Pro Vita Sua*." *SLitI*, 1, 2 (1968), 83-109.

Braybrooke, Neville. "Two William Golding Novels: Two Aspects of His Work." *QQ*, 76 (1969), 92-100.

Bufkin, E. C. "*Lord of the Flies*: An Analysis." *GaR*, 19 (1965), 40-57.

Capey, A. C. " 'Will' and 'Idea' in *Lord of the Flies*." *Use of English*, 24 (1972), 99-107.

Cox, C. B. "*Lord of the Flies*." *CritQ*, 2 (1960), 112-17.

Ditlevsen, Torben. "Civilization and Culture, or *Pro Civitate Dei*: William Golding's *Lord of the Flies*." *Lang&L*, 1, 3 (1972), 20-38.

Drew, Philip. "Second Reading." *CambR*, 78 (1956), 79-84.

Epstein, E. L. "Biographical and Critical Note." William Golding, *Lord of the Flies*. New York: Capricorn Books, 1955, 249-55.

Fleck, A. D. "The Golding Bough: Aspects of Myth and Ritual in *The Lord of the Flies. On the Novel.* Ed. Benedikt S. Benedikz, 189-205.

Gallagher, Michael P. "The Human Image in William Golding." *Studies,* 54 (1965), 197-216.

Gaskin, J. C. A. "Beelzebub." *HJ,* 66 (1968), 58-61.

Golding, William. *"The Hot Gates" and Other Occasional Pieces.* New York: Harcourt, 1966, 85-101.

Gordon, Robert C. "Classical Themes in *Lord of the Flies." MFS,* 11 (1966), 424-27.

Gulbin, Suzanne. "Parallels and Contrasts in *Lord of the Flies* and *Animal Farm." EJ,* 55 (1966), 86-90, 92.

Hollahan, Eugene. "Running in Circles: A Major Motif in *Lord of the Flies." SNNTS,* 2 (1970), 22-30.

Lederer, Richard H. "Student Reactions to *Lord of the Flies." EJ,* 53 (1964), 575-79.

Levitt, Leon. "Trust the Tale: A Second Reading of *Lord of the Flies." EJ,* 58 (1969), 521-22.

MacLure, Millar "Allegories of Innocence." *DR,* 40 (1960), 145-56.

Michel-Michot, Paulette. "The Myth of Innocence." *RLV,* 28 (1962), 510-20.

Mitchell, Charles. *"The Lord of the Flies* and the Escape from Freedom." *ArQ,* 22 (1966), 27-40.

Moody, Philippa. *A Critical Commentary on William Golding's LORD OF THE FLIES.* London: Macmillan, 1966.

Mueller, William R. "An Old Story Well Told." *ChC,* 80 (October 2, 1963), 1203-6.

Nelson, William, ed. *William Golding's LORD OF THE FLIES: A Source Book.* New York: Odyssey, 1963.

Niemeyer, Carl. "The Coral Island Revisited." *CE,* 22 (1961), 241-45.

O'Hara, J. D. "Mute Choirboys and Angelic Pigs: The Fable in *Lord of the Flies." TSLL,* 7 (1966), 411-20.

Oldsey, Bernard S., and Stanley Weintraub. *"Lord of the Flies*: Beelzebub Revisited." *CE,* 25 (1963), 90-99.

Page, Norman. *"Lord of the Flies." Use of English,* 16 (1964), 44-45, 57.

Richter, David H. *Fable's End,* 60-83.

Rippier, Joseph S. *Some Postwar English Novelists,* 46-69.

Rosenberg, Bruce A. "Lord of the Fire-Flies." *CentR,* 11 (1967), 128-39.

Rosenfield, Claire. " 'Men of a Smaller Growth': A Psychological Analysis of William Golding's *Lord of the Flies." L&P,* 11 (1961), 93-101. [See also "Reply by Miss Rosenfield." *L&P,* 12 (1962), 11-12]

Ruotolo, Lucio P. *Six Existential Heroes*, 101-18.
Smith, Eric. *Some Versions of the Fall*, 163-202.
Spitz, David. "Power and Authority: An Interpretation of Golding's *Lord of the Flies.*" *AR*, 30 (1970), 21-33.
Stern, Joseph. P. *On Realism*, 20-27.
Sternlicht, Sanford. "Songs of Innocence and Songs of Experience in *Lord of the Flies* and *The Inheritors.*" *MQ*, 9 (1968), 383-90.
———. "A Source for Golding's *Lord of the Flies*: Peter Pan?" *EngR*, 14 (1963), 41-42.
Talon, Henri. "Irony in *Lord of the Flies.*" *EIC*, 18 (1968), 296-309.
Taylor, Harry H. "The Case Against William Golding's Simon-Piggy." *ContempR*, 209 (1966), 155-60.
Townsend, R. C. "*Lord of the Flies*: Fool's Gold?" *JGE*, 16 (1964), 153-60.
Veidemanis, Gladys. "*Lord of the Flies* in the Classroom—No Passing Fad." *EJ*, 53 (1964), 569-74.
Warner, Oliver. "Mr. Golding and Marryat's *Little Savage.*" *REL*, 5, 1 (1964), 51-55.
Watson, Kenneth. "A Reading of *Lord of the Flies.*" *English*, 15 (1964), 2-7.
White, Robert J. "Butterfly and Beast in *Lord of the Flies.*" *MFS*, 10 (1964), 163-70.

PINCHER MARTIN

Babb, Howard S. "On the Ending of *Pincher Martin.*" *EIC*, 14 (1964), 106-8.
Biles, Jack I., and Carl R. Kropf. "The Cleft Rock of Conversion: 'Robinson Crusoe' and 'Pincher Martin'." *SLitI*, 2, 2 (1969), 17-43.
Braybrooke, Neville. "The Return of Pincher Martin." *Cweal*, 89 (1968), 115-18.
———. "Two William Golding Novels: Two Aspects of His Work." *QQ*, 76 (1969), 92-100.
Bufkin, E. C. "William Golding's Morality Play." *SLitI*, 2, 2 (1969), 5-16.
Cox, C. B. "William Golding's *Pincher Martin.*" *Listener*, 71 (1964), 430-31.
Delbaere-Garant, Jeanne. "William Golding's *Pincher Martin.*" *ES*, 51 (1970), 538-44.
Harvey, W. J. "The Reviewing of Contemporary Fiction." *EIC*, 8 (1958), 182-87.
LaChance, Paul R. "*Pincher Martin*: The Essential Dilemma of Modern Man." *Cithara*, 8, 2 (1969), 55-60.

Mizener, Arthur. "The Historical Romance and Twentieth-Century Sensibility: Ford's 'Fifth Queen'." *SR*, 78 (1970), 563-77.

Pearson, Anthony. "H. G. Wells and *Pincher Martin.*" *N&Q*, 12 (1965), 275-76.

Quinn, Michael. "An Unheroic Hero: William Golding's Pincher Martin." *CritQ*, 4 (1962), 247-56.

Robinson, John. "Pincher's Rock." *RMS*, 19 (1975), 129-39.

Russell, Kenneth C. "The Free Fall of William Golding's *Pincher Martin.*" *SRC*, 5 (1975), 267-74.

Ryan, J. S. "The Two Pincher Martins: From Survival Adventure to Golding's Myth of Dying." *Australian Universities Language and Literature Assn.* Ed. J. R. Ellis, 156-58. [Also in *ES*, 55 (1974), 140-51]

Sasso, Laurence J., Jr. "A Note on the Dwarf in *Pincher Martin.*" *MSE*, 1 (1968), 66-68.

Sternlicht, Sanford. *"Pincher Martin*: A Freudian Crusoe." *EngR*, 15 (1965), 2-4.

Whitehead, Lee M. "The Moment Out of Time: Golding's *Pincher Martin.*" *ConL*, 12 (1971), 18-41.

See also: Fleishman.

THE PYRAMID

Dick, Bernard F. *"The Pyramid*: Mr. Golding's 'New' Novel." *SLitI*, 2, 2 (1969), 83-95.

"Down to Earth." *TLS*, June 1, 1967, 481.

Henry, Avril. "William Golding: *The Pyramid.*" *SoRA*, 3 (1968), 5-31.

Johnston, Arnold. "Innovation and Rediscovery in Golding's *The Pyramid.*" *Crit*, 14, 2 (1972), 97-112.

Sheed, Wilfred. *The Morning After*, 280-82.

Trickett, Rachel. "Recent Novels: Craftsmanship in Violence and Sex." *YR*, 57 (1968), 438-52.

Whitehead, John. "A Conducted Tour to the Pyramid." *LonM*, n.s. 7, 3 (June 1967), 100-04.

THE SPIRE

Carmichael, D. "A God in Ruins." *Quadrant*, 9, 1 (January 1965), 72-74.

"The Cost of a Vision." *TLS*, April 16, 1964, 310.

Crompton, D. W. *"The Spire.*" *CritQ*, 9 (1967), 63-79.

Delbaere-Garant, Jeanne. "The Evil Plant in William Golding's *The Spire.*" *RLV*, 35 (1969), 623-31.

Dick, Bernard F., and Raymond J. Porter. "Jocelin and Oedipus." *Cithara*, 6, 1 (1966), 43-48.

Freehof, Solomon B. "Nostalgia for the Middle Ages: William Golding's *The Spire.*" *Carnegie,* 39 (January 1965), 13-16.

Furbank, P. N. "Golding's 'Spire'." *Encounter,* 22 (May 1964), 59-61.

Hyman, Stanley E. *Standards: A Chronicle of Books for Our Time,*
219-23.

Kort, Wesley. "The Groundless Glory of Golding's Spire." *Renascence,*
20 (1968), 75-78.

Kunkel, Francis L. *Passion and The Passion,* 57-74.

Livingston, James C. *William Golding's THE SPIRE.* New York:
Seabury, 1967.

Lodge, David. "William Golding." *Spectator,* 212 (April 10, 1964),
489-90.

Roper, Derek. "Allegory and Novel in Golding's *The Spire.*" *WSCL,* 8
(1967), 19-30.

Skilton, David. "Golding's *The Spire.*" *SLitI,* 2, 2 (1969), 45-56.

Sternlicht, Sanford. "The Sin of Pride in Golding's *The Spire.*" *MinnR,*
5 (1965), 59-60.

―――. "Two Views of the Builder in Graham Green's *A Burnt-Out
Case* and William Golding's *The Spire.*" *CalR,* n.s. 1 (1970),
401-04.

Sullivan, Walter. "The Long Chronicle of Guilt: William Golding's *The
Spire.*" *HC,* 1, 3 (1964), 1-12.

Sutherland, Raymond C. "Medieval Elements in *The Spire.*" *SLitI,* 2, 2
(1969), 57-65.

Temple, E. R. A. "William Golding's *The Spire*: A Critique." *Renascence,* 20 (1968), 171-73.

ROBERT GRAVES

BIBLIOGRAPHIES
Pownall, David E. "An Annotated Bibliography on Robert Graves."
Focus, 2 (1973), 17-23.

INTERVIEWS
Buckman, Peter, and William Fifield. "Robert Graves." *Paris Review.
Writers at Work,* 4th ser., 45-65.

Haller, John. "Conversations with Robert Graves." *SWR,* 42 (1957),
237-41.

―――. "Robert Graves in Lecture and Talk." *ArQ,* 15 (1959), 150-56.

Sherman, Arnold. "A Talk with Robert Graves, English Poet in Ma-
jorca." *Commentary,* 22, 4 (October 1956), 364-66.

Sillitoe, Alan. "I Reminded Him of Muggleton." *Shenandoah,* 13, 2
(1962), 47-50.

Robert Graves, continued

SPECIAL ISSUES
Auden, W. H., et al. "A Symposium on Robert Graves." *Shenandoah*, 13, 2 (1962), 5-62.
Malahat Review [MHRev], 35 (July 1975), 5-188.

GENERAL STUDIES
Bergonzi, Bernard. *Heroes' Twilight*, 154-58.
Bogan, Louise. *Selected Criticism*, 316-18.
Canary, Robert H. "History and Fantasy in the Claudius Novels." *Focus*, 1 (1972), 3-8.
———. "Utopian and Fantastic Dualities in Robert Graves' *Watch the North Wind Rise*." *SFS*, 1 (Fall 1974), 248-55.
Cohen, J. M. *Robert Graves*. Edinburgh: Oliver and Boyd, 1960; New York: Grove, 1961.
Enright, D. J. "The Example of Robert Graves." *Shenandoah*, 13, 2 (1962), 13-15.
———. *Robert Graves and the Decline of Modernism*. Singapore: Univ. of Malaya, n.d. [c. 1960]. [Repr. in *EIC*, 11 (1961), 319-36]
Feibleman, James K. *In Praise of Comedy*, 165-67.
Fraser, G. S. "The Reputation of Robert Graves." *Shenandoah*, 13, 2 (1962), 19-32.
Grant, Michael. "The Dark Side of the Moon: Robert Graves as Mythographer." *MHRev*, 35 (July 1975), 143-65.
Gregory, Horace. "Robert Graves: A Parable for Writers." *PR*, 20, 1 (1953), 44-54.
Gunn, Thomas. "In Nobody's Pantheon." *Shenandoah*, 13, 2 (1962), 34-35.
Kirkham, Michael. "Robert Graves' Debt to Laura Riding." *Focus*, 3 (1973), 33-44.
Leiber, Fritz. "Utopia for Poets and Witches." *RQ*, 4 (1970), 194-205.
McKinley, James. "Subject: Robert Graves—Random Notes of a Biographer." *NewL*, 40, 4 (1974), 37-60.
Mehoker, James S. *Robert Graves: Peace-Weaver*. The Hague: Mouton, 1975.
Muir, Edwin. *Transition*, 163-76.
Presley, John W. "Robert Graves: The Art of Revision." *ICarbS*, 2 (1975), 133-45.
Quennell, Peter. *Casanova in London*, 175-86.
Seymour-Smith, Martin. *Robert Graves*. London: Longmans, Green, 1955.
Simon, Myron. "The Georgian Infancy of Robert Graves." *Focus*, 4 (1974), 49-70.

Stade, George. *Robert Graves.* New York: Columbia Univ. Press, 1967.
Steiner, George. "The Genius of Robert Graves." *KR*, 22 (1960), 340-65.
Vickery, John B. *Robert Graves and the White Goddess.* Lincoln: Univ. of Nebraska Press, 1972.
Wilson, Colin. "Some Notes on Graves's Prose." *Shenandoah*, 13, 2 (1962), 55-62.
See also: Enright, *Conspirators*; Swinnerton, *Georgian.*

HENRY GREEN

INTERVIEWS
Breit, Harvey. *The Writer Observed*, 103-06.
Lambourne, David. " 'No Thundering Horses': The Novels of Henry Green." *Shenandoah*, 26, 4 (1975), 57-71.
Ross, Alan. "Green, with Envy: Critical Reflections and an Interview." *LonM*, 6, 4 (April 1959), 18-24.
Southern, Terry. "The Art of Fiction, XXII: Henry Green." *Paris Review*, 19 (1958), 60-77.

GENERAL STUDIES
Allen, Walter. "An Artist of the Thirties." *Folios of New Writing*, 3 (Spring 1941), 149-58.
_____. "Greening." *New Statesman*, 57 (1959), 615-16.
_____. "Henry Green." *Modern British Writing.* Ed. Denys Val Baker, 258-71.
Bain, Bruce. "Henry Green: The Man and His Work." *World Review*, May 1949, 55-58, 80.
Bassoff, Bruce. "Prose Consciousness in the Novels of Henry Green." *Lang&S*, 5 (1972), 276-86.
_____. *Toward LOVING: The Poetics of the Novel and the Practice of Henry Green.* Columbia: Univ. of South Carolina Press, 1975.
Cosman, Max. "The Elusive Henry Green." *Cweal*, 72 (1960), 472-75.
Dennis, Nigel. "The Double Life of Henry Green." *Life*, August 4, 1952, 83-88, 91, 92, 94.
Gill, Brendan. "Something." *NY*, 26 (March 25, 1950), 111-12.
Hall, James. "The Fiction of Henry Greene [sic]: Paradoxes of Pleasure-and-Pain." *KR*, 19 (1957), 76-88.
Hart, Clive. "The Structure and Technique of *Party Going.*" *YES*, 1 (1971), 185-99.
Johnson, Bruce. "Henry Green's Comic Symbolism." *BSUF*, 6, 3 (1965), 29-35.
Jones, Ernest, "Henry Green, Virtuoso." *Nation*, 170 (1950), 328-29.

Mehoke, James S. "Sartre's Theory of Emotion and Three English Novelists: Waugh, Green, and Amis." *WSL*, 3 (1966), 105-11.

Melchiori, Giorgio. *The Tightrope Walkers*, 188-212.

Odom, Keith C. "Symbolism and Diversion: Birds in the Novels of Henry Green." *Descant*, 6 (1962), 30-41.

Phelps, Robert. "The Vision of Henry Green." *HudR*, 5 (1953), 614-20.

Reed, John R. *Old School Ties*, 120-21, 212-17, 246-55.

Ross, Alan. "Green, with Envy: Critical Reflections and an Interview." *LonM*, 6, 4 (April 1959), 18-24.

Russell, John D. *Henry Green: Nine Novels and an Unpacked Bag.* New Brunswick, N.J.: Rutgers Univ. Press, 1960.

――――. "There It Is." *KR*, 26 (1964), 433-65.

Ryf, Robert S. *Henry Green*. New York: Columbia Univ. Press, 1967.

Schorer, Mark. "Introduction to Henry Green's World." *NYTBR*, October 9, 1949, 1, 22.

Shapiro, Stephen A. "Henry Green's *Back*: The Presence of the Past." *Crit*, 7, 1 (1964), 87-96.

Stokes, Edward. "Henry Green, Dispossessed Poet." *AusQ*, 28, 4 (1956), 84-91.

――――. *The Novels of Henry Green*. London: Hogarth, 1959.

Taylor, Donald S. "Catalytic Rhetoric: Henry Green's Theory of the Modern Novel." *Criticism*, 7 (1965), 81-99.

Toynbee, Philip. "The Novels of Henry Green." *PR*, 16, 5 (1949), 487-97.

Turner, Myron. "The Imagery of Wallace Stevens and Henry Green." *WSCL*, 8 (1967), 60-77.

Unterecker, John. "Fiction at the Edge of Poetry: Durrell, Beckett, Green." *Forms of Modern British Fiction*. Ed. Alan Friedman, 165-99.

Weatherhead, A. Kingsley. *A Reading of Henry Green*. Seattle: Univ. of Washington Press, 1961.

――――. "Structure and Texture in Henry Green's Latest Novels." *Accent*, 19 (1959), 111-22.

Weaver, Robert L. "The Novels of Henry Green." *CanF*, 30 (1951), 227-31.

Welty, Eudora. "Henry Green, a Novelist of the Imagination." *TQ*, 4, 3 (1961), 246-56.

See also: Allen, *Tradition*; Gill; Hall, *Tragic*; Karl; Kettle; Prescott; Tindall, *Symbol*.

LOVING

Churchill, Thomas. "*Loving*: A Comic Novel." *Crit*, 4, 2 (1961), 29-38.

Davidson, Barbara. "The World of *Loving*." *WSCL*, 2, 1 (1961), 65-78.

Labor, Earle. "Henry Green's Web of Loving." *Crit*, 4, 1 (1961), 29-40.
Quinton, Anthony. "A French View of *Loving*." *LonM*, 6, 4 (April 1959), 25-35.

GRAHAM GREENE

BIBLIOGRAPHIES

Beebe, Maurice. "Criticism of Graham Greene, with an Index to Studies of Separate Works." *MFS*, 3 (1957), 281-88.
Birmingham, William. "Graham Greene Criticism, a Bibliographical Study." *Thought*, 27 (1952), 72-100.
Vann, J. Don. *Graham Greene: A Checklist of Criticism*. Kent, Ohio: Kent State Univ. Press, 1970.

INTERVIEWS

Kermode, Frank. "The House of Fiction: Interviews with Seven English Novelists." *PR*, 30 (1963), 61-82.
Mookerjee, R. N. "Graham Greene on the Art of Fiction." *RUSEng*, 6 (1972), 91-101.
Osterman, Robert. "Interview with Graham Greene." *CathW*, 170 (1950), 356-61.
Shuttleworth, Martin, and Simon Raven. "The Art of Fiction III: Graham Greene." *Paris Review*, 1 (1953), 24-41.

SPECIAL ISSUES

Literature Film Quarterly [*LFQ*], 2 (1974), 293-387.
"Graham Greene Number." *MFS*, 3, 3 (1957).
Renascence, 12, 1 (1959).
Renascence, 23, 1 (1970).

GENERAL STUDIES

Alcantara-Demalanta, O. "Christian Dimensions in Contemporary Literature." *Unitas*, 46 (1973), 213-23.
Allen, Walter. "Awareness of Evil: Graham Greene." *Nation*, 182 (1956), 344-46.
————. "The Novels of Graham Greene." *Penguin New Writing*, 18 (1943), 148-60.
Allen, W. Gore. "Evelyn Waugh and Graham Greene." *IrM*, 77 (January 1949), 16-22.
————. "The World of Graham Greene." *IrEccRec*, 71 (January 1949), 42-49.

Allott, Kenneth, and Miriam Farris [Allott]. *The Art of Graham Greene.* London: Hamish Hamilton, 1951; New York: Russell and Russell, 1963.

Aoki, Yuzo. *Graham Greene.* Tokyo: Kenkyusha, 1971.

Atkins, John. *Graham Greene.* London: J. Calder, 1957; New York: Roy Publishers, 1958; London: Calder and Boyers, 1966.

Auden, W. H. "The Heresy of Our Time." *Renascence*, 1, 2 (1949), 23-24.

Barnes, Robert J. "Two Modes of Fiction: Hemingway and Greene." *Renascence*, 14 (1962), 193-98.

Barratt, Harold. "Adultery as Betrayal in Graham Greene." *DR*, 45 (1965), 324-32.

Battock, Marjorie. "The Novels of Graham Greene." *Norseman*, 13 (January-February 1955), 45-52.

Beary, Thomas J. "Religion and the Modern Novel." *CathW*, 166 (1947), 203-11.

Bedard, B. J. "Reunion in Havana." *LFQ*, 2 (1974), 352-58.

Boardman, Gwenn R. *Graham Greene: The Aesthetics of Exploration.* Gainesville: Univ. Presses of Florida, 1971.

Boyle, Alexander. "Graham Greene." *IrM*, 77 (November 1949), 519-25.

_____. "The Symbolism of Graham Greene." *IrM*, 80 (March 1952), 98-102.

Braybrooke, Neville. "Graham Greene." *Envoy*, 3 (September 1950), 10-23.

_____. "Graham Greene: A Pioneer Novelist." *CE*, 12 (1950), 1-9.

Brock, D. Heyward, and James M. Welsh. "Graham Greene and the Structure of Salvation." *Renascence*, 27 (1974), 31-39.

Burgess, Anthony. "Politics in the Novels of Graham Greene." *JCH*, 2 (1967), 93-99.

_____. "The Politics of Graham Greene." *Page 2.* Ed. Francis Brown, 284-91.

Calder-Marshall, Arthur. "Graham Greene." *Living Writers.* Ed. Gilbert Phelps, 37-47.

_____. "The Works of Graham Greene." *Horizon*, 1 (January 1940), 367-75.

Cargas, Harry J., ed. *Graham Greene.* St. Louis: Herder, 1969.

Cassis, A. F. "The Dream as Literary Device in Graham Greene's Novels." *L&P*, 24 (1974), 99-108.

Cervo, Nathan A. "The Gargouille Anti-Hero: Victim of Christian Satire." *Renascence*, 22 (1970), 69-77.

Chapman, Raymond. "The Vision of Graham Greene." *Forms of Extremity in the Modern Novel.* Ed. Nathan A. Scott, Jr., 75-94.

Cheney, Lynne. "Joseph Conrad's *The Secret Agent* and Graham

Greene's *It's a Battlefield*: A Study in Structural Meaning." *MFS*, 16 (1970), 117-31.

Clancy, L. J. "Graham Greene's Battlefield." *CR*, 10 (1967), 99-108.

Connolly, Francis X. "Inside Modern Man: The Spiritual Adventures of Graham Greene." *Renascence*, 1, 2 (1949), 16-24.

Cosman, Max. "Disquieted Graham Greene." *ColQ*, 6 (1958), 319-25.

————. "An Early Chapter in Graham Greene." *ArQ*, 11 (1955), 143-47.

"The Cost of Caring." *TLS*, September 14, 1973, 1055-56.

Davidson, Arnold C. "Graham Greene's Spiritual Lepers." *IEY*, 15 (1970), 50-55.

De Hegedus, Adam. "Graham Greene and the Modern Novel." *Tomorrow*, 8 (October 1948), 54-56.

————. "Graham Greene: The Man and His Work." *World Review*, August 1948, 57-61.

Desmond, John F. "Graham Greene and the Eternal Dimension." *ABR*, 20 (1969), 418-27.

DeVitis, A. A. "The Entertaining Mr. Greene." *Renascence*, 14 (1961), 8-24.

————. *Graham Greene*. New York: Twayne, 1964.

————. "Religious Aspects in the Novels of Graham Greene." *The Shapeless God*. Ed. Harry J. Mooney and Thomas F. Staley, 41-65.

Dinkins, Paul. "Graham Greene: The Incomplete Version." *CathW*, 176 (1952), 96-102.

Duffy, Joseph M., Jr. "The Lost World of Graham Greene." *Thought*, 33 (1958), 229-47.

Ellis, William D., Jr. "The Grand Theme of Graham Greene." *SWR*, 41 (1956), 239-50.

Evans, Robert O., ed. *Graham Greene: Some Critical Considerations*. Lexington: Univ. of Kentucky Press, 1963.

Fielding, Gabriel. "Graham Greene: The Religious Englishman." *Listener*, 72 (1964), 465-66.

Fowler, Alastair. "Novelist of Damnation." *Theology*, 56 (July 1953), 259-64.

Fytton, Francis. "Graham Greene: Catholicism and Controversy." *CathW*, 180 (1954), 172-75.

Glicksberg, Charles I. "Graham Greene: Catholicism in Fiction." *Criticism*, 1 (1959), 339-53.

Gregor, Ian, and Brian Nicholas. *The Moral and the Story*, 185-91, 267-70.

Grubbs, Henry A. "Albert Camus and Graham Greene." *MLQ*, 10 (1949), 33-42.

Graham Greene, continued

Hall, James. *The Lunatic Giant in the Drawing Room*, 111-23.

Harkness, Bruce. "Conrad, Graham Greene, and Film." *Joseph Conrad: Theory and World Fiction*. Ed. Wolodymyr T. Zyla and Wendell M. Aycock, 71-87.

Harris, Wendell V. "Molly's 'Yes': The Transvaluation of Sex in Modern Fiction." *TSLL*, 10 (1968), 107-18.

Herling, Gustav. "Two Sanctities: Greene and Camus." *Adam*, 17, 201 (1949), 10-19.

Hortmann, Wilhelm. "Graham Greene: The Burnt-Out Catholic." *TCL*, 10 (1964), 64-76.

Houle, Sister Sheila. "The Subjective Theological Vision of Graham Greene." *Renascence*, 23, 1 (1970), 3-13.

Howes, Jane. "Out of the Pit." *CathW*, 171 (1950), 36-40.

Hughes, Catharine. "Innocence Revisited." *Renascence*, 12, 1 (1959), 29-34.

Hynes, Samuel, ed. *Graham Greene: A Collection of Critical Essays*. Englewood Cliffs, N.J.: Prentice-Hall, 1973.

Jacobsen, Josephine. "A Catholic Quartet." *ChS*, 47 (1964), 139-54.

Jerrold, Douglas. "Graham Greene, Pleasure-Hater." *Harper's*, 205 (August 1952), 50-52.

Jones, Grahame C. "Graham Greene and the Legend of Péguy." *CL*, 21 (1969), 138-45.

Jones, James Land. "Graham Greene and the Structure of the Moral Imagination." *Phoenix*, 2 (1966), 34-56.

Joselyn, Sister M. "Graham Greene's Novels: The Conscience in the World." *Literature and Society*. Ed. Bernice Slote, 153-72.

Kellogg, Gene. *The Vital Tradition*, 111-36.

Kennedy, Alan. *The Protean Self*, 231-49.

Kenny, Herbert A. "Graham Greene." *CathW*, 185 (1957), 326-29.

Keyser, Les. "*England Made Me*." *LFQ*, 2 (1974), 364-72.

King, Bruce. "Graham Greene's Inferno." *EA*, 21 (1968), 35-51.

King, James. "In the Lost Boyhood of Judas: Graham Greene's Early Novels of Hell." *DR*, 49 (1969), 229-36.

Kohn, Lynette. *Graham Greene: The Major Novels*. Stanford, Cal.: Stanford Univ. Press, 1961.

Kort, Wesley. "The Obsession of Graham Greene." *Thought*, 45 (1970), 20-44.

Kulkarni, H. B. "Redemptive Sin in Graham Greene." *PUASAL*, 49, 2 (1972), 36-50.

Kunkel, Frances L. *The Labyrinthine Ways of Graham Greene*. New York: Sheed and Ward, 1959.

Lauder, Robert E. "The Catholic Novel and the 'Insider God'." *Cweal*, 101 (1974), 78-81.

Lees, F. N. "Graham Greene: a Comment." *Scrutiny*, 19 (1952), 31-42.

Lerner, Lawrence. "Graham Greene." *CritQ*, 5 (1963), 217-31.

Lewis, R. W. B. "The Fiction of Graham Greene: Between the Horror and the Glory." *KR*, 19 (1957), 56-75.

———. *The Picaresque Saint*, 220-74.

Lodge, David. *Graham Greene*. New York: Columbia Univ. Press, 1966.

Lohf, Kenneth A. "Graham Greene and the Problem of Evil." *CathW*, 173 (1951), 196-99.

McCormick, John O. "The Rough and Lurid Vision: Henry James, Graham Greene and the International Theme." *JA*, 2 (1957), 158-67.

McDonald, James L. "Graham Greene: A Reconsideration." *ArQ*, 27 (1971), 197-210.

MacSween, R. J. "Exiled from the Garden: Graham Greene." *AntigR*, 1, 2 (1970), 41-48.

"The Man Within: Graham Greene in Retrospect." *TLS*, September 17, 1971, 1101.

Marian, Sister, I.H.M. "Graham Greene's People: Being and Becoming." *Renascence*, 18 (1965), 16-22.

Marković, Vida E. "Graham Greene in Search of God." *TSLL*, 5 (1963), 271-82.

Marshall, Bruce. "Graham Greene and Evelyn Waugh." *Cweal*, 51 (1950), 551-53.

Martin, Graham. "Novelists of Three Decades: Evelyn Waugh, Graham Greene, C. P. Snow." *The Pelican Guide to English Literature*, v. 7. Ed. Boris Ford, 412-32.

Mesnet, Marie-Béatrice. "Graham Greene." *The Politics of Twentieth-Century Novelists*. Ed. George A. Panichas, 100-23.

———. *Graham Greene and the Heart of the Matter*. London: Cresset, 1954.

Miller, J. D. B. "Graham Greene." *Meanjin*, 5 (1946), 193-97.

Milner, Ian. "Values and Irony in Graham Greene." *AUC-PPSE*, 14 (1971), 65-73.

Monroe, N. Elizabeth. "The New Man in Fiction." *Renascence*, 6 (1953), 9-12.

Muller, Charles H. "Graham Greene and the Absurd." *UES*, 10, 2 (1972), 34-44.

———. "Graham Greene and the Justification of God's Ways." *UES*, 10, 1 (1972), 23-35.

———. "Graham Greene: The Melodramatic Character." *UES*, 12, 3 (1974), 31-37.

Murray, Edward. *The Cinematic Imagination*, 244-60.

O'Donnell, Donat [Conor Cruise O'Brien]. "Graham Greene." *Chimera*, 5, 4 (1947), 18-30.

―――. *Maria Cross*, 63-91, 225-59.

Peters, W. "The Concern of Graham Greene." *Month*, 10 (1953), 281-90.

Phillips, Gene D. *Graham Greene: The Films of His Fiction.* New York: Teachers Coll. Press of Columbia Univ., 1974.

Poole, Roger C. "Graham Greene's Indirection." *Blackfriars*, 45 (June 1964), 257-68.

Pryce-Jones, David. *Graham Greene*. New York: Barnes and Noble, 1968.

―――. "Graham Greene's Human Comedy." *Adam*, 31, 301-03 (1966), 21-38.

Puentevella, Renato. "Ambiguity in Greene." *Renascence*, 12, 1 (1959), 35-37.

Reed, John R. *Old School Ties*, 56-57, 67-68, 161-66, 178-81, 187-93.

Reinhardt, Kurt F. *The Theological Novel of Modern Europe*, 170-202.

Rolo, Charles J. "Graham Greene: The Man and the Message." *Atlantic*, 207 (May 1961), 60-65.

Sackville-West, Edward. "The Electric Hare: Some Aspects of Graham Greene." *Month*, 6 (1951), 141-47.

Scott, Nathan A., Jr. "Graham Greene: Christian Tragedian." *VolR*, 1, 1 (1954), 29-42.

Seward, Barbara. "Graham Greene: A Hint of an Explanation." *WestR*, 22 (1958), 83-95.

Sewell, Elizabeth. "Graham Greene." *DubR*, 228 (1954), 12-21.

―――. "The Imagination of Graham Greene." *Thought*, 29 (1954), 51-60.

Sheed, Wilfred. *The Morning After*, 66-75.

Skerrett, Joseph T., Jr. "Graham Greene at the Movies: A Novelist's Experience with Film." *LFQ*, 2 (1974), 293-301.

Smith, A. J. M. "Graham Greene's Theological Thrillers." *QQ*, 68 (1961), 15-33.

Sonnenfeld, Albert. "Children's Faces: Graham Greene." *The Vision Obscured*. Ed. Melvin J. Friedman, 109-28.

Sternlicht, Sanford. "Prologue to the Sad Comedies: Graham Greene's Major Early Novels." *MQ*, 12 (1971), 427-35.

―――. "The Sad Comedies: Graham Greene's Later Novels." *FQ*, 1, 4 (1968), 65-77.

Stewart, Douglas G. *The Ark of God*, 71-98.

Stratford, Philip. *Faith and Fiction: Creative Process in Greene and Mauriac*. Notre Dame, Ind.: Univ. of Notre Dame Press, 1964.

―――. "Graham Greene, Master of Melodrama." *TamR*, 19 (1961), 67-86.

Sullivan, Walter. "Old Age, Death, and Other Modern Landscapes: Good and Indifferent Fables for Our Time." *SR*, 82 (1974), 138-47.

Tracy, Honor. "The Life and Soul of the Party." *New Republic*, 140 (April 20, 1959), 15-16.

Traversi, Derek. "Graham Greene: The Earlier Novels." *TC*, 149 (1951), 231-40; "Graham Greene: The Later Novels." *TC*, 149 (1951), 318-28.

Turnell, Martin. *Graham Greene: A Critical Essay.* Grand Rapids, Mich.: Eerdmans, 1967.

_____. "Graham Greene: The Man Within." *Ramparts*, 4 (June 1965), 54-64.

_____. "The Religious Novel." *Cweal*, 55 (1951), 55-57.

Voorhees, Richard J. "Recent Greene." *SAQ*, 62 (1963), 244-55.

_____. "The World of Graham Greene." *SAQ*, 50 (1951), 389-98.

Wansbrough, John. "Graham Greene: The Detective in the Wasteland." *HarvA*, 126, 2 (1962), 11-13, 29-31.

Wassmer, Thomas A. "Graham Greene: A Look at His Sinners." *Critic*, 18 (December 1959-January 1960), 16-17, 72-74.

_____. "The Problem and the Mystery of Sin in the Works of Graham Greene." *ChS*, 43 (1960), 309-15.

_____. "The Sinners of Graham Greene." *DR*, 39 (1959), 326-32.

Welsh, James M., and Gerald R. Barrett. "Graham Greene's *Ministry of Fear*: The Transformation of an Entertainment." *LFQ*, 2 (1974), 310-23.

West, Anthony. *Principles and Persuasions*, 174-78.

West, Paul. *The Wine of Absurdity*, 174-85.

Why Do I Write? An Exchange of Views Between Elizabeth Bowen, Graham Greene and V. S. Pritchett.

Wichert, Robert A. "The Quality of Graham Greene's Mercy." *CE*, 25 (1963), 99-103.

Wilshere, A. D. "Conflict and Conciliation in Graham Greene." *E&S*, 19 (1966), 122-37.

Wilson, Angus. "Evil in the English Novel." *KR*, 29 (1967), 167-94.

Wilson, Colin. *The Strength to Dream*, 46-60.

Wolfe, Peter. *Graham Greene: The Entertainer.* Carbondale: Southern Illinois Univ. Press, 1972.

Woodcock, George. *The Writer and Politics*, 125-53.

Woodward, Anthony. "Graham Greene: The War Against Boredom." *Seven Studies in English*. Ed. Gildas Roberts, 64-105.

Wyndham, Francis. *Graham Greene*. London: Longmans, Green, 1955.

Zabel, Morton D. "Graham Greene." *Nation*, 157 (July 5, 1943), 18-20; *Forms of Modern Fiction*. Ed. William Van O'Connor, 287-93.

Graham Greene, continued

See also: Allen, *Tradition*; Bradbury, *Possibilities*; A. Collins, *20th*; Eagleton; Enright, *Onion*; Gillie, *Movements*; Karl; Kazin, *Contemporaries*; Kermode; Lodge, *Novelist*; Marković; Maurois; O'Faoláin; Prescott; Webster, *Trauma*; Zabel, *Craft*.

BRIGHTON ROCK

Consolo, Dominick P. "Music as Motif: The Unity of *Brighton Rock*." *Renascence*, 15 (1962), 12-20.

Cox, Gerald H., III. "Graham Greene's Mystical Rose in Brighton." *Renascence*, 23, 1 (1970), 21-30.

Kubal, David L. "Graham Greene's *Brighton Rock*: The Political Theme." *Renascence*, 23, 1 (1970), 46-54.

Lenfest, David S. "*Brighton Rock/Young Scarface*." *LFQ*, 2 (1974), 373-78.

McCall, Dan. "*Brighton Rock*: The Price of Order." *ELN*, 3 (1966), 290-94.

McGowan, F. A. "Symbolism in *Brighton Rock*." *Renascence*, 8 (1955), 25-35.

Ruotolo, Lucio P. "*Brighton Rock*'s Absurd Heroine." *MLQ*, 25 (1964), 425-33.

―――. *Six Existential Heroes*, 39-53.

A BURNT-OUT CASE

Dooley, D. J. "The Suspension of Disbelief: Greene's *A Burnt-Out Case*." *DR*, 43 (1963), 343-52.

Hess, M. Whitcomb. "Graham Greene's Travesty on *The Ring and the Book*." *CathW*, 194 (1961), 37-42.

Kermode, Frank. "Mr. Greene's Eggs and Crosses." *Encounter*, 16 (April 1961), 69-75.

Noxon, James. "Kierkegaard's Stages and *A Burnt-Out Case*." *REL*, 3 1 (1962), 90-101.

Poole, Roger. " 'Those Sad Arguments': Two Novels of Graham Greene." *RMS*, 13 (1969), 148-60.

Sackville-West, Edward. "Time-Bomb." *Month*, 25 (1961), 175-78.

Shor, Ira Neil. "Greene's Later Humanism: *A Burnt-Out Case*." *LitR*, 16 (1973), 397-411.

Simon, John K. "Off the *Voie royale*: The Failure of Greene's *A Burnt-Out Case*." *Symposium (S)*, 18 (1964), 163-70.

Smith, Francis J. "The Anatomy of *A Burnt-Out Case*." *America*, 105 (September 9, 1961), 711-12.

Sternlicht, Sanford. "Two Views of the Builder in Graham Greene's *A Burnt-Out Case* and William Golding's *The Spire*." *CalR*, n.s. 1 (1970), 401-04.

Stratford, Philip. "Chalk and Cheese: A Comparative Study of *A Kiss for the Leper* and *A Burnt-Out Case.*" *UTQ*, 33 (1964), 200-18.

Van Kaam, Adrian, and Kathleen Healy. *The Demon and the Dove*, 259-85.

THE COMEDIANS

Allen, Walter. "*The Comedians.*" *LonM*, n.s. 5, 12 (March 1966), 73-80.

Barker, Paul. "The Masks of Graham Greene: *The Comedians.*" *New Society*, January 27, 1966, 29.

Bedford, Sybille. "Tragic Comedians." *NYRB*, 6 (March 3, 1966), 25-27.

Choudhury, M. K. "The Significance of Caricature in Graham Greene's *The Comedians.*" *PURBA*, 5, 2 (1974), 51-56.

Davenport, John. "The Last Albigensian." *Spectator*, 215 (January 28, 1966), 110-11.

DeVitis, A. A. "Greene's *The Comedians*: Hollower Men." *Renascence*, 18 (1966), 129-36, 146.

Gilman, Richard. "Up from Hell with Graham Greene." *New Republic*, 154 (January 29, 1966), 25-28.

Lodge, David. "Graham Greene's Comedians." *Cweal*, 83 (1966), 604-06.

Routh, Michael. "Greene's Parody of Farce and Comedy in *The Comedians.*" *Renascence*, 26 (1974), 139-51.

THE END OF THE AFFAIR

Arnold, G. L. "Adam's Tree." *TC*, 150 (1951), 337-42.

Bogan, Louise. "Good Beyond Evil." *New Republic*, 125 (December 10, 1951), 29-30.

Braybrooke, Neville. "Graham Greene—The Double Man: An Approach to His Novel *The End of the Affair.*" *DubR*, 226, 1 (1952), 61-73.

————. "The Priest in an Age of Psychology: An Enquiry for Novelists." *Renascence*, 11, 1 (1958), 10-13.

Gardiner, Harold C. *In All Conscience*, 98-102.

Gregor, Ian, and Brian Nicholas. *The Moral and the Story*, 185-208, 213-16, 236-38, 267-70.

Isaacs, Rita. "Three Levels of Allegory in Graham Greene's *The End of the Affair.*" *LNL*, 1, 1 (1975), 29-52.

Lichtheim, George. *Collected Essays*, 477-82.

Lodge, David. "The Use of Key-Words in the Novels of Graham Greene—Love, Hate, and *The End of the Affair.*" *Blackfriars*, 42 (November 1961), 468-74.

See also: A. West, *Principles*.

THE HEART OF THE MATTER

DeVitis, A. A. "The Church and Major Scobie." *Renascence*, 10 (1958), 115-20.

Gordon, Caroline. "Some Readings and Misreadings." *SR*, 61 (1953), 384-407.

Hynes, Joseph. "The 'Facts' at *The Heart of the Matter*." *TSLL*, 13 (1972), 711-26.

Inglis, Fred. *An Essential Discipline*, 192-94.

Jefferson, Mary E. "*The Heart of the Matter*: The Responsible Man." *CarQ*, 9 (1957), 23-31.

Knipp, Thomas R. "Gide and Greene: Africa and the Literary Imagination." *Serif*, 6, 2 (1969), 3-14.

Levin, Gerald. "The Rhetoric of Greene's *The Heart of the Matter*." *Renascence*, 23, 1 (1970), 14-20.

McGugan, Ruth E. "*The Heart of the Matter*." *LFQ*, 2 (1974), 359-63.

Moré, Marcel. "The Two Holocausts of Scobie." *Cross Currents*, 1 (1951), 44-63.

Mueller, William R. *The Prophetic Voice in Modern Fiction*, 136-57.

O'Faoláin, Seán. "The Novels of Graham Greene: *The Heart of the Matter*." *Britain Today*, 148 (August 1948), 32-36.

Orwell, George. *The Collected Essays*, v. 4, 439-43.

Tucker, Martin. *Africa in Modern Literature*, 12-14, 230-35.

Walker, Ronald G. "Seriation as Stylistic Norm in Graham Greene's *The Heart of the Matter*." *Lang&S*, 6 (1973), 161-75.

See also: Kettle.

THE POWER AND THE GLORY

Céleste, Sister Marie, S.C. "Bernanos and Graham Greene on the Role of the Priest." *Culture*, 30 (1969), 287-98.

Cummingham, Lawrence. "The Alter Ego of Greene's 'Whiskey Priest'." *ELN*, 8 (1970), 50-52.

Davies, Horton. *A Mirror of the Ministry in Modern Novels*, 100-10.

Grob, Alan. "*The Power and the Glory*: Graham Greene's Argument from Design." *Criticism*, 11 (1969), 1-30.

Harmer, Ruth Mulvey. "Greene World of Mexico: The Birth of a Novelist." *Renascence*, 15 (1963), 171-82, 194.

Hoggart, Richard. "The Force of Caricature: Aspects of the Art of Graham Greene with Particular Reference to *The Power and the Glory*." *EIC*, 3 (1953), 447-62.

_____. *Speaking to Each Other*, v. 2, 40-55.

McDonnell, Lawrence V. "The Priest-Hero in the Modern Novel." *CathW*, 196 (1963), 306-11.

Michener, Richard L. *"The Plumed Serpent* and *The Power and the Glory." URev*, 34 (1968), 313-16.

Sandra, Sister Mary, S.S.A. "The Priest-Hero in Modern Fiction." *Person*, 46 (1965), 527-42.

Thomas, D. P. "Mr. Tench and Secondary Allegory in *The Power and the Glory." ELN*, 7 (1969), 129-33.

Waugh, Evelyn. "Felix Culpa?" *Cweal*, 48 (1948), 322-25.

Wells, Arvin R. *"The Power and the Glory." Insight II.* Ed. John V. Hagopian and Martin Dolch, 152-64.

White, W. D. "The Power and the Glory: An Apology to the Church." *UPoR*, 21 (Spring 1969), 14-22.

Woodcock, George. "Mexico and the English Novelist." *WestR*, 21 (1956), 21-32.

See also: Allen, *Reading.*

THE QUIET AMERICAN

Elistratova, Anna. "Graham Greene and His New Novel." *SovL*, no. 8 (August 1956), 149-55.

Hinchliffe, Arnold P. "The Good American." *TC*, 168 (1960), 529-39.

Hughes, R. E. *"The Quiet American*: The Case Reopened." *Renascence*, 12, 1 (1959), 41-42, 49.

Lichtheim, George. *Collected Essays*, 490-92.

McMahon, J. "Graham Greene and *The Quiet American." JKUR*, 1 (November 1958), 64-73.

Poole, Roger. " 'Those Sad Arguments': Two Novels of Graham Greene." *RMS*, 13 (1969), 148-60.

Rahv, Philip. "Wicked American Innocence." *Commentary*, 21, 5 (May 1956), 488-90.

Rudman, Harry W. "Clough and Graham Greene's *The Quiet American." VN*, 19 (1961), 14-15.

Trilling, Diane, and Philip Rahv. "America and *The Quiet American." Commentary*, 22, 1 (July 1956), 66-71.

THE THIRD MAN

Alloway, Lawrence. "Symbolism in *The Third Man." World Review*, March 1950, 57-60.

Gomez, Joseph A. *"The Third Man*: Capturing the Visual Essence of Literary Conception." *LFQ*, 2 (1974), 332-40.

VanWert, William F. "Narrative Structure in *The Third Man." LFQ*, 2 (1974), 341-46.

TRAVELS WITH MY AUNT

Chaudhury, M. K. "Graham Greene's *Travels with My Aunt*: A Picaresque Novel." *PURBA*, 3, 2 (1972), 79-85.

Fagin, Steven. "Narrative Design in *Travels with My Aunt.*" *LFQ*, 2 (1974), 379-83.

"Portrait of No Lady." *TLS*, November 11, 1969, 1329.

L. P. HARTLEY

INTERVIEWS

Firchow, Peter. *The Writer's Place*, 163-172.

SPECIAL ISSUES

Adam International Review [Adam], 29, 294-96 (1961).

GENERAL STUDIES

Athos, John. "L. P. Hartley and the Gothic Infatuation." *TCL*, 7 (1962), 172-79.

Bien, Peter. *L. P. Hartley*. London: Chatto and Windus, 1963.

Bloomfield, Paul. "L. P. H.: Short Note on a Great Subject." *Adam*, 29, 294-96 (1961), 5-7.

_____. "L. P. Hartley." *Anthony Powell and L. P. Hartley*, by Paul Bloomfield and Bernard Bergonzi, 5-39.

Grossvogel, David I. "Under the Sign of Symbols: Losey and Hartley." *Diacritics*, 4, 3 (1974), 51-56.

Kitchin, Clifford H. B. "Leslie Hartley—A Personal Angle." *Adam*, 29, 294-96 (1961), 7-12.

Kitchin, Laurence. "Imperial Weekend." *Listener*, 74 (1965), 662-63, 667.

Kreutz, Irving. "L. P. Hartley, Who Are U? or, Luncheon in the Lounge." *KR*, 25 (1963), 150-54.

Melchiori, Giorgio. "The English Novelist and the American Tradition." *SR*, 68 (1960), 502-15.

Moan, Margaret A. "Setting and Structure: An Approach to Hartley's *The Go-Between.*" *Crit*, 15, 2 (1973), 27-36.

Mulkeen, Anne. *Wild Thyme, Winter Lightning: The Symbolic Novels of L. P. Hartley*. Detroit: Wayne State Univ. Press, 1974.

Sørensen, Knud. "Language and Society in L. P. Hartley's *Facial Justice.*" *OL*, 26 (1971), 68-78.

Webster, Harvey Curtis. "The Novels of L. P. Hartley." *Crit*, 4, 2 (1961), 39-51.

See also: Allen, *Tradition*; Hall, *Tragic*; Webster.

RICHARD HUGHES

INTERVIEWS
Firchow, Peter. *The Writer's Place*, 183-208.

GENERAL STUDIES
Bosano, J. "Richard Hughes." *EA*, 16 (1963), 262-69.

Miller, Richard Hugh. "History and Children in Richard Hughes's *The Wooden Shepherdess*." *AntigR*, 22 (1975), 31-35.

Poole, Richard. "Morality and Selfhood in the Novels of Richard Hughes." *AWR*, 25, 55 (1975), 10-29.

Sullivan, Walter. "Old Age, Death, and Other Modern Landscapes: Good and Indifferent Fables for Our Time." *SR*, 82 (1974), 138-47.

Symons, Julian. "Politics and the Novel." *TC*, 170 (1962), 147-54.

Thomas, Peter. "Measuring the Wind: The Early Writings of Richard Hughes." *AWR*, 20, 45 (1971), 36-56.

————. *Richard Hughes*. Cardiff: Univ. of Wales for the Welsh Arts Council, 1973.

See also: Allen, *Tradition*; Swinden.

A HIGH WIND IN JAMAICA
Brown, Daniel R. "*A High Wind in Jamaica*: Comedy of the Absurd." *BSUF*, 9, 1 (1968), 6-12.

Henighan, T. J. "Nature and Convention in *A High Wind in Jamaica*." *Crit*, 9, 1 (1967), 5-18.

Woodward, Daniel H. "The Delphic Voice: Richard Hughes's *A High Wind in Jamaica*." *PLL*, 3 (1967), 57-74.

ALDOUS HUXLEY

BIBLIOGRAPHIES
Clareson, Thomas D., and Carolyn S. Andrews. "Aldous Huxley: A Bibliography, 1960-1964." *Extrapolation*, 6 (1964), 2-21.

Davis, Dennis O. "Aldous Huxley: A Bibliography, 1965-73." *BB*, 31 (1974), 67-70.

Eschelbach, Claire John, and Joyce Lee Shober. *Aldous Huxley: A Bibliography, 1916-1959*. Berkeley: Univ. of California Press, 1961.

————, and Joyce S. Marthaler. "Aldous Huxley: A Bibliography, 1919-64 (A Supplementary Listing)." *BB*, 28 (1971), 114-17.

INTERVIEWS
Beerman, Hans. "An Interview with Aldous Huxley." *MQ*, 5 (1964), 223-30.

Aldous Huxley, continued

Breit, Harvey. *The Writer Observed*, 127-30.
Ratnam, Kamala. "Chilean Writer Meets Aldous Huxley in India." *UA*, 16 (1964), 257-60.
Stokes, Sewell. "Aldous Huxley in London." *Listener*, 58 (1957), 977-78.
Wallace, Mike. "Aldous Huxley on Thought Control: A Television Interview." *Listener*, 60 (1958), 373-74.
Wickes, George, and Ray Frazer. "Aldous Huxley." *Paris Review. Writers at Work*, 2d ser., 193-214. [See also *ClareQ*, 8, 1 (1960), 5-22]

GENERAL STUDIES

Aldington, Richard. *Selected Critical Writings*, 19-23.
Alexander, Henry. "Lawrence and Huxley." *QQ*, 42 (1935), 96-108.
Atkins, John. *Aldous Huxley: A Literary Study*. London: J. Calder, 1955; rev. New York: Orion, 1967.
Baker, Howard. "In Praise of the Novel: The Fiction of Huxley, Steinbeck and Others." *SoR*, 5 (1940), 778-800.
Bald, R. C. "Huxley as a Borrower." *CE*, 11 (1950), 183-87.
Bartlett, Norman. "Aldous Huxley and D. H. Lawrence." *AusQ*, 36, 1 (1964), 76-84.
Bedford, Sybille. *Aldous Huxley: A Biography, I: 1894-1939*. London: Chatto and Windus, Collins, 1973. *II: 1939-1962*. London: Chatto and Windus, Collins, 1974; as one vol., New York: Knopf, Harper, 1974.
Bentley, Joseph. "The Later Novels of Huxley." *YR*, 59 (1970), 507-19.
──────. "Huxley's Ambivalent Responses to the Ideas of D. H. Lawrence." *TCL*, 13 (1967), 139-53.
Bergonzi, Bernard. "Life's Divisions." *Encounter*, 41 (July 1973), 65-68.
Birnbaum, Milton. "Aldous Huxley." *The Politics of Twentieth-Century Novelists*. Ed. George A. Panichas, 65-84.
──────. "Aldous Huxley's Animadversions Upon Sexual Love." *TSLL*, 8 (1966), 285-96.
──────. "Aldous Huxley's Conception of the Nature of Reality." *Person*, 47 (1966), 297-314.
──────. *Aldous Huxley's Quest for Values*. Knoxville: Univ. of Tennessee Press, 1971.
──────. "Aldous Huxley's Quest for Values: A Study in Religious Syncretism." *CLS*, 3 (1966), 169-82.
──────. "Aldous Huxley's Treatment of Nature." *HJ*, 64 (1966), 150-52.
──────. "Aldous Huxley's Views on Education." *XUS*, 6 (1967), 81-91.
Bowering, Peter. *Aldous Huxley: A Study of the Major Novels*. London: Athlone; New York: Oxford Univ. Press, 1969.

Brander, Laurence. *Aldous Huxley: A Critical Study*. Lewisburg, Pa.: Bucknell Univ. Press; London: Hart-Davis, 1970.

Brooke, Jocelyn. *Aldous Huxley*. London: Longmans, Green, 1954.

Browning, Gordon. "Toward a Set of Standards for Anti-Utopian Fiction." *Cithara*, 10, 1 (1970), 18-32.

Buck, Philo M., Jr. *Directions in Contemporary Literature*, 169-91.

Bullough, Geoffrey. "Aspects of Aldous Huxley." *ES*, 30 (1949), 233-43.

Burgum, Edwin B. *The Novel and the World's Dilemma*, 140-56.

Cary, Richard. "Aldous Huxley, Vernon Lee and the *Genius Loci*." *CLQ*, ser. 5 (1960), 128-41.

Chase, Richard. "The Huxley-Heard Paradise." *PR*, 10, 2 (1943), 143-58.

Choudhary, Nora S. "The Huxley-Hero." *RUSEng*, 6 (1972), 70-84.

Church, Margaret. "Aldous Huxley's Attitude toward Duration." *CE*, 17 (1956), 388-91.

————. "Concepts of Time in Novels of Virginia Woolf and Aldous Huxley." *MFS*, 1, 2 (1955), 19-24.

Clark, Ronald W. *The Huxleys*. London: Heinemann; New York: McGraw-Hill, 1968.

Conner, Frederick W. " 'Attention'! Aldous Huxley's Epistemological Route to Salvation." *SR*, 81 (1973), 282-308.

Connolly, Cyril. *Enemies of Promise*, rev. ed., 52-54, 63-64.

————. *The Evening Colonnade*, 247-50.

Dyson, A. E. *The Crazy Fabric*, 166-86.

————. "Aldous Huxley and the Two Nothings." *CritQ*, 3 (1961), 293-309.

Eaton, Gai. *The Richest Vein*, 166-82.

Estrich, Helen W. "Jesting Pilate Tells the Answer: Aldous Huxley." *SR*, 47 (1939), 63-81.

Evans, B. Ifor. *English Literature Between the Wars*, 58-67.

Farmer, David. "A Note on the Text of Huxley's *Crome Yellow*." *PBSA*, 63 (1969), 131-33.

Firchow, Peter E. *Aldous Huxley, Satirist and Novelist*. Minneapolis: Univ. of Minnesota Press, 1972.

Ghose, Sisirkumar. *Aldous Huxley: A Cynical Salvationist*. New York: Asia Pub. House, 1962.

Glicksberg, Charles I. "Aldous Huxley: Arts and Mysticism." *PrS*, 27 (1953), 344-53.

————. "Huxley, the Experimental Novelist." *SAQ*, 52 (1953), 98-110.

————. "The Intellectual Pilgrimage of Aldous Huxley." *DR*, 19 (1939), 165-78.

————. "The Literary Struggle for Selfhood." *Person*, 42 (1961), 52-65.

————. *Modern Literary Perspectivism*, 24-27.

Aldous Huxley, continued

Godfrey, D. R. "The Essence of Aldous Huxley." *ES(A)*, 32 (1951), 97-106.

Greenblatt, Stephen J. *Three Modern Satirists*, 77-101, 105-17.

Gump, Margaret. "From Ape to Man and from Man to Ape." *KFLQ*, 4 (1957), 177-185.

Hacker, A. "Dostoevsky's Disciples: Man and Sheep in Political Theory." *JPol*, 17 (1955), 590-613.

Harris, Wendell V. "Molly's 'Yes': The Transvaluation of Sex in Modern Fiction." *TSLL*, 10 (1968), 107-18.

Hart, Hubert N. "Aldous Huxley." *CathW*, 175 (1952), 204-08.

Hausermann, Hans W. "Aldous Huxley as Literary Critic." *PMLA*, 48 (1933), 908-18.

Hays, Peter L. *The Limping Hero*, 77-84.

Heard, Gerald. "The Poignant Prophet." *KR*, 27 (1965), 49-70.

Henderson, Alexander. *Aldous Huxley.* New York: Harper, 1936; New York: Russell and Russell, 1964.

Hines, Bede. *The Social World of Aldous Huxley.* Loretto, Pa.: Seraphic Press, 1957; Loretto Pa.: Mariale Press, 1962.

Hoffman, Frederick J. "Aldous Huxley and The Novel of Ideas." *CE*, 8 (1946), 129-37; *Forms of Modern Fiction.* Ed. William Van O'Connor, 189-200.

Hoffmann, Charles G. "The Change in Huxley's Approach to the Novel of Ideas." *Person*, 42 (1961), 85-90.

Holmes, Charles M. *Aldous Huxley and the Way to Reality.* Bloomington: Indiana Univ. Press, 1970.

──────. "Aldous Huxley's Struggle with Art." *WHR*, 15 (1961), 149-56.

Houston, P. H. "The Salvation of Aldous Huxley." *AmerR*, 4 (1934), 209-32.

Huxley, Aldous, and John Morgan. "Aldous Huxley on Contemporary Society." *Listener*, 66 (1961), 237-39.

Huxley, Julian, ed. *Aldous Huxley, 1894-1963: A Memorial Volume.* London: Chatto and Windus; New York: Harper, 1965.

Joad, C. E. M. *Return to Philosophy*, 72-88, 109-38, 149-52, 175-78, 188-200.

Jog, D. V. *Aldous Huxley: The Novelist.* Bombay, India: Book Centre Private Ltd., 1960; Folcroft, Pa.: Folcroft Editions, 1969.

Kennedy, Richard S. "Aldous Huxley: The Final Wisdom." *SWR*, 50 (1965), 37-47.

Ketser, G. "Aldous Huxley: A Retrospect." *RLV*, 30 (1964), 179-84.

King, Carlyle. "Aldous Huxley and Music." *QQ*, 70 (1963), 336-51.

──────. "Aldous Huxley's Way to God." *QQ*, 61 (1954), 80-100.

Kirkwood, M. M. "The Thought of Aldous Huxley." *UTQ*, 6 (1937), 189-98.

Kolek, Leszek. "English Novel of Ideas: An Attempt at a Preliminary Definition and Description of the Genre." *ZRL*, 17, 1 (1974), 21-38.

Kuehn, Robert E., ed. *Aldous Huxley: A Collection of Critical Essays.* Englewood Cliffs, N.J.: Prentice-Hall, 1974.

Lebowitz, Martin. "Everlasting Mr. Huxley." *KR*, 7 (1945), 135-38.

LeGates, Charlotte. "Huxley and Brueghel." *WHR*, 29 (1975), 365-71.

Loos, Anita. "Aldous Huxley in California." *Harper's*, 228 (May 1964), 51-55.

Macdermott, Doireann. "The Zoologist of Fiction: Aldous Huxley." *FMod*, 37 (1969), 27-45.

Makino, Seiichi. "An Aspect of Aldous Huxley's Style." *Current Trends in Stylistics.* Ed. Braj B. Kachru and Herbert F. W. Stahlke, 243-50.

Marković, Vida E. "Aldous Huxley." *FP*, 3-4 (1964), 103-18.

Marovitz, Sanford E. "Aldous Huxley and the Visual Arts." *PLL*, 9 (1973), 172-88.

———. "Aldous Huxley's Intellectual Zoo." *PQ*, 48 (1969), 495-507.

Matson, Floyd. "Aldous and Heaven Too: Religion Among the Intellectuals." *AR*, 14 (1953), 293-309.

Matter, William W. "The Utopian Tradition and Aldous Huxley." *SFS*, 2 (1975), 146-51.

May, Keith M. *Aldous Huxley.* London: Elek, 1972.

Maynard, Theodore. "Aldous Huxley, Moralist." *CathW*, 144 (1936), 12-22.

Meckier, Jerome. *Aldous Huxley: Satire and Structure.* London: Chatto and Windus, 1969.

———. "Aldous Huxley: Satire and Structure." *WSCL*, 7 (1966), 284-94.

———. "The Hippopotamian Question: A Note on Aldous Huxley's Unfinished Novel." *MFS*, 16 (1970), 505-14.

———. "Quarles Among the Monkeys: Huxley's Zoological Novels." *MLR*, 68 (1973), 268-82.

———. "Shakespeare and Aldous Huxley." *SQ*, 22 (1971), 129-35.

Misra, G. S. P., and Nora Satin. "The Meaning of Life in Aldous Huxley." *MQ*, 9 (1968), 351-63.

Montgomery, Marion. "Lord Russell and Madame Sesostris." *GR*, 28 (1974), 269-82.

Muir, Edwin. *Transition*, 101-13.

Mužina, Matej. "Reverberations of Jung's *Psychological Types* in the Novels of Aldous Huxley." *SRAZ*, 33-36 (1972-73), 305-34.

Nagarajan, S. "Religion in Three Recent Novels of Aldous Huxley." *MFS*, 5 (1959), 153-65.

Nazareth, Peter. "Aldous Huxley and His Critics." *ESA*, 7 (1964), 65-81.

Aldous Huxley, continued

Neumann, Henry. "Aldous Huxley and H. G. Wells Seek a Religion."
    Standard, 23 (April 1937), 169-74.
New, Melvyn. "Ad Nauseam: A Satiric Device in Huxley, Orwell, and
    Waugh." *SNL*, 8 (1970), 24-28.
Nicholson, Norman. "Aldous Huxley and the Mystics." *Fortnightly*,
    n.s. 161 (1947), 131-35.
———. *Man and Literature*, 87-111.
Noonan, Gerald. "Aldous Huxley and the Critical Path in Canadian
    Literature; or, How Imperious Fashion Screws Up Local Art—
    Everywhere." *JCF*, 2, 1 (1973), 73-76.
Overton, Grant M. *Cargoes for Crusoes*, 97-113.
Patty, James S. "Baudelaire and Aldous Huxley." *SAB*, 33, 4 (1968),
    5-8.
Pinkus, Philip. "Satire and St. George." *QQ*, 70 (1963), 30-49.
Powell, Lawrence C. *California Classics*, 357-70.
Quennell, Peter "Aldous Huxley." *Living Writers*. Ed. Gilbert Phelps,
    128-37.
———. "D. H. Lawrence and Aldous Huxley. "*The English Novelists*.
    Ed. Derek Verschoyle, 267-78.
Quina, James H., Jr. "The Philosophical Phases of Aldous Huxley."
    CE, 23 (1962), 636-41.
Roberts, John H. "Huxley and Lawrence." *VQR*, 13 (1937), 546-57.
Rogers, Winfield H. "Aldous Huxley's Humanism." *SR*, 43 (1935),
    262-72.
Rolo, Charles J. "Aldous Huxley." *Atlantic*, 180 (August 1947), 109-15.
Rose, Steven. "The Fear of Utopia." *EIC*, 24 (1974), 55-70.
Savage, Derek S. "Aldous Huxley and the Dissociation of Personali-
    ty." *SR*, 55 (1947), 537-68.
———. *The Withered Branch*, 129-55.
Schall, J. V. "Buber and Huxley: Recent Developments in Philos-
    ophy." *Month*, 19 (1958), 97-102.
Schmerl, Rudolf B. "Aldous Huxley's Social Criticism." *ChiR*, 13, 1
    (1959), 37-58.
———. "The Two Future Worlds of Aldous Huxley." *PMLA*, 77 (1962),
    328-34.
Simons, John D. "The Grand Inquisitor in Schiller, Dostoevsky and
    Huxley." *NZSJ*, 8 (1971), 20-31.
Slochower, Harry. *No Voice is Wholly Lost*, 32-35.
Smith, Grover, ed. *Letters of Aldous Huxley*. London: Chatto and
    Windus; New York: Harper, 1969.
Spencer, Theodore. "Aldous Huxley: The Latest Phase." *Atlantic*, 165
    (March 1940), 407-09.

Sponberg, Florence L. "Huxley's Perennial Preoccupation." *MSCS*, 3 (1968), 1-18.

Stewart, Douglas G. *The Ark of God*, 44-70.

——. "Significant Modern Writers: Aldous Huxley." *ET*, 71 (1960), 100-03.

Thody, Philip. *Aldous Huxley: A Biographical Introduction.* London: Studio Vista, 1973.

Tindall, William York. "Transcendentalism in Contemporary Literature." *The Asian Legacy and American Life.* Ed. Arthur E. Christy, 175-92.

——. "The Trouble with Aldous Huxley." *ASch*, 11 (1942), 452-64.

Vitoux, Pierre. "Aldous Huxley and D. H. Lawrence: An Attempt at Intellectual Sympathy." *MLR*, 69 (1974), 501-22.

Voorhees, Richard J. "The Perennial Huxley." *PrS*, 23 (1949), 189-92.

Wagner, Linda W. "Satiric Marks: Huxley and Waugh." *SNL*, 3 (1966), 160-62.

Wajc-Tenenbaum, R. "Aesthetics and Metaphysics: Aldous Huxley's Last Novel." *RLV*, 37 (1971), 160-75.

Watkin, Edward. *Men and Tendencies*, 29-48.

Watts, Harold. *Aldous Huxley.* New York: Twayne, 1969.

Waugh, Evelyn, Angus Wilson, Francis Wyndham, John Wain, and Peter Quennell. "A Critical Symposium on Aldous Huxley." *LonM*, 2, 8 (August 1955), 51-64.

Webster, H. T. "Aldous Huxley: Notes on a Moral Evolution." *SAQ*, 45 (1946), 372-83.

Wilson, Colin. "Existential Criticism and the Work of Aldous Huxley." *LonM*, 5, 9 (September 1958), 46-59.

——. *The Strength to Dream*, 213-38.

Wilson, Edmund. *Classics and Commercials*, 209-14.

Woodcock, George. *Dawn and the Darkest Hour: A Study of Aldous Huxley.* New York: Viking, 1972.

——. "Mexico and the English Novelist." *WestR*, 21 (1956), 21-32.

Yoder, Edwin M., Jr. "Aldous Huxley and His Mystics." *VQR*, 42 (1966), 290-94.

See also: Adcock, *Glory*; Aiken, *ABC*; Allen, *Tradition*; Beach, *20th*; Brewster and Burrell; A. Collins, *20th*; Cunliffe, *20th Century*; Daiches, *Novel*; Edgar, *Art*; Frierson; Gill; J. Gray; Hall, *Tragic*; Karl and Magalaner; Lovett, *History*; MacCarthy, McCormick; *Criticism*; Maurois; Muller, *Modern*; O'Faoláin; Overton, *Authors*; Swinnerton, *Figures, Georgian*; Tindall, *Forces*; Vines; Webster.

Aldous Huxley, continued

ANTIC HAY

Collins, Joseph. *Taking the Literary Pulse*, 156-68.

Enroth, Clyde. "Mysticism in Two of Aldous Huxley's Early Novels." *TCL*, 6 (1960), 123-32.

Karl, Frederick R. "The Play Within the Novel in *Antic Hay.*" *Renascence*, 13 (1961), 59-68.

Montgomery, Marion. "Aldous Huxley's Uncomparable Man in *Antic Hay.*" *Discourse*, 3 (1960), 227-32.

BRAVE NEW WORLD

Beauchamp, Gorman L. "Future Words: Language and the Dystopian Novel." *Style*, 8 (1974), 462-76.

Berneri, Mary Louise. *Journey Through Utopia*, 313-17.

Clareson, Thomas D. "The Classic: Aldous Huxley's *Brave New World.*" *Extrapolation*, 2 (1961), 33-40.

Coleman, D. C. "Bernard Shaw and *Brave New World.*" *ShawR*, 10 (1967), 6-8.

Curle, Adam. "Huxley's Brave New World." *New Statesman*, 49 (1955), 508-09.

Elliott, Robert C. *The Shape of Utopia*, 95-97, 146-48.

Enroth, Clyde. "Mysticism in Two of Aldous Huxley's Early Novels." *TCL*, 6 (1960), 123-32.

Firchow, Peter E. "The Satire of Huxley's *Brave New World.*" *MFS*, 12 (1966), 451-60.

———. "Science and Conscience in Huxley's *Brave New World.*" *ConL*, 16 (1975), 301-16.

Grushow, Ira. "*Brave New World* and *The Tempest.*" *CE*, 24 (1962), 42-45.

Howe, Irving. "The Fiction of Anti-Utopia." *New Republic*, 146 (April 23, 1962), 13-16.

Huxley, Aldous. *Brave New World Revisited.* New York: Harper, 1958.

Jones, William M. "The Iago of *Brave New World.*" *WHR*, 15 (1961), 275-78.

Kessler, Martin. "Power and the Perfect State: A Study in Disillusionment as Reflected in Orwell's *Nineteen Eighty-Four* and Huxley's *Brave New World.*" *PSQ*, 72 (1957), 565-77.

LeRoy, Gaylord C. "A.F. 632 to 1984." *CE*, 12 (1950), 135-38.

Miles, O. Thomas. "Three Authors in Search of a Character." *Person*, 46 (1965), 65-72.

Richards, D. "Four Utopias." *SEER*, 40 (1962), 220-28.

Walsh, Chad. *From Utopia to Nightmare*, 92-106, 112-13, 135-47.

Webster, Harvey C. "Facing Futility." *SR*, 42 (1934), 193-208.

Wells, Arvin R. *"Brave New World." Insight II.* Ed. John V. Hagopian and Martin Dolch, 175-85.
Westlake, J. H. J. "Aldous Huxley's *Brave New World* and George Orwell's *Nineteen Eighty-Four*: A Comparative Study." *NS*, 21 (1972), 94-102.
Wilson, Robert H. *"Brave New World* as Shakspere Criticism." *ShAB*, 21 (1946), 99-107.
———. "Versions of *Brave New World." LCUT*, 8, 4 (1968), 28-41.
Wing, George. "The Shakespearean Voice of Conscience in *Brave New World." DR*, 51 (1971), 153-64.
Woodcock, George. "Utopias in Negative." *SR*, 64 (1956), 81-97.

EYELESS IN GAZA
Bentley, Phyllis. "The Structure of *Eyeless in Gaza." EJ*, 26 (1937), 127-32.
Venter, Susan. "The 'dog episode' in Aldous Huxley's *Eyeless in Gaza*: An Exegesis." *Standpunte*, 96 (1971), 16-19.
Vitoux, Pierre. "Structure and Meaning in Aldous Huxley's *Eyeless in Gaza." YES*, 2 (1972), 212-24.

ISLAND
Choudhary, Nora Satin. *"Island*: Huxley's Attempt at Practical Philosophy." *LE&W*, 16 (1972), 1155-67.
Elliott, Robert C. *The Shape of Utopia*, 100-3, 137-53.
Leeper, Geoffrey. "The Happy Utopias of Aldous Huxley and H. G. Wells." *Meanjin*, 24 (1965), 120-24.
McMichael, Charles T. "Aldous Huxley's *Island*: The Final Vision." *SLitI*, 1, 2 (1968), 73-82.
Meckier, Jerome T. "Cancer in Utopia: Positive and Negative Elements in Huxley's *Island." DR*, 54 (1974), 619-33.
Stewart, D. H. "Aldous Huxley's *Island." QQ*, 70 (1963), 326-35.
Watt, Donald J. "Vision and Symbol in Aldous Huxley's *Island." TCL*, 14 (1968), 149-60.

POINT COUNTER POINT
Alexander, Claudia. "Bach, Beethoven, and *Point Counter Point." Innisfree*, 2 (1975), 17-21.
Baker, Robert S. "Spandrell's 'Lydian Heaven': Moral Masochism and the Centrality of Spandrell in Huxley's *Point Counter Point." Criticism*, 16 (1974), 120-35.
Baldanza, Frank. *"Point Counter Point*: Aldous Huxley on 'The Human Fugue'." *SAQ*, 58 (1959), 248-57.

Aldous Huxley, continued

Henderson, Phillip. *The Novel Today*, 118-29.

Keyishian, Harry. "The Martyrology of Nymphomania: Nancy Cunard in *The Green Hat* and *Point Counter Point*." *Proc. of the Sixth Nat'l. Conv. of Popular Culture Ass'n*. Ed. Michael T. Marsden, 292-98.

Kolek, Leszek. "Music in Literature—Presentation of Huxley's Experiment in 'Musicalization of Fiction'." *ZRL*, 14, 2 (1972), 111-22.

Linn, James W., and H. W. Taylor. *A Foreword to Fiction*, 94-98.

Lovett, Robert M. "Vanity Fair Up-to-Date." *New Republic*, 57 (December 5, 1928), 75-76.

O'Brien, Justin. *The French Literary Horizon*, 103-08.

Watson, David S. "*Point Counter Point*: The Modern Satiric Novel a Genre?" *SNL*, 6 (1969), 31-35.

Watt, Donald J. "The Criminal-Victim Pattern in Huxley's *Point Counter Point*." *SNNTS*, 2 (1970), 42-51.

See also: Brewster and Burrell; Kettle.

CHRISTOPHER ISHERWOOD

INTERVIEWS

Breit, Harvey. *The Writer Observed*, 215-17.

Geherin, David J. "An Interview with Christopher Isherwood." *JNT*, 2 (1972), 143-58.

Isherwood, Christopher, and Stanley Poss. "A Conversation on Tape." *LonM*, n.s. 1, 3 (June 1961), 41-58.

Scobie, W. I. "Christopher Isherwood." *Paris Review. Writers at Work*, 4th ser., 211-42.

Solway, Clifford. "An Interview with Christopher Isherwood." *TamR*, 39 (1966), 22-35.

Wickes, George. "An Interview with Christopher Isherwood." *Shenandoah*, 16, 3 (1965), 23-52.

GENERAL STUDIES

Bantock, G. H. "The Novels of Christopher Isherwood." *Focus Four*. Ed. Balachandra Rajan, 46-57.

Connolly, Cyril. *Enemies of Promise*, 70-81.

Dempsey, David. "Connolly, Orwell and Others: An English Miscellany." *AR*, 7 (1947), 142-50.

Dewsnap, Terence. "Isherwood Couchant." *Crit*, 13, 1 (1971), 31-47.

Farrell, James T. *Literature and Morality*, 125-32.

Hampshire, Stuart. "Isherwood's Hell." *Encounter*, 19 (November 1962), 86-88.

Heilbrun, Carolyn G. *Christopher Isherwood*. New York: Columbia Univ. Press, 1970.

Holloway, John. "Narrative Structure and Text Structure: Isherwood's *A Meeting by the River* and Muriel Spark's *The Prime of Miss Jean Brodie.*" *CritI*, 1 (1975), 581-604.

Jebb, Julian. "Down There on a Visit." *LonM*, n.s. 2, 1 (April 1962), 87-89.

Kennedy, Alan. *The Protean Self*, 213-29.

Kermode, Frank. "The Interpretation of the Times." *Encounter*, 15 (September 1960), 71-76.

McLaughlin, Richard. "Isherwood's Arrival and Departure." *SatR*, 30 (December 27, 1947), 14-15.

Maes-Jelinek, Hena. "The Knowledge of Man in the Works of Christopher Isherwood." *RLV*, 26 (1960), 341-60.

Mayne, Richard. "The Novel and Mr. Norris." *CambJ*, 6 (1953), 561-70.

Nagarajan, S. "Christopher Isherwood and the Vedantic Novel: A Study of *A Single Man.*" *ArielE*, 3, 4 (1972), 63-71.

"Naked, Not Unashamed." *TLS*, June 15, 1967, 525.

Pritchett, V. S. "Books in General." *New Statesman*, 44 (1952), 213-14.

———. "Men of the World." *Penguin New Writing*, 30 (1947), 135-41.

Pryce-Jones, David. "Isherwood Reassessed." *T&T*, 41 (1960), 1162-63.

Rosenfeld, Isaac. *An Age of Enormity*, 149-54.

Spender, Stephen. *World Within World*, 91-95, 109-17, 158-59.

Turner, W. J. "Christopher Isherwood." *Living Writers*. Ed. Gilbert Phelps, 48-57.

Whitehead, John. "Christophananda: Isherwood at Sixty." *LonM*, n.s. 5, 4 (July 1965), 90-100.

Wilde, Alan. *Christopher Isherwood*. New York: Twayne, 1971.

———. "Irony and Style: The Example of Christopher Isherwood." *MFS*, 16 (1970), 475-89.

———. "Language and Surface: Isherwood and the Thirties." *ConL*, 16 (1975), 478-91.

Wilson, Angus. "The New and the Old Isherwood." *Encounter*, 3 (August 1954), 62-68.

See also: Allen, *Tradition*; Kermode.

GOODBYE TO BERLIN

Blades, Joe. "The Evolution of *Cabaret.*" *LFQ*, 1 (1973), 226-38.

Jarka, Horst. "Pre-War Austria as Seen by Spender, Isherwood and Lehmann." *PPNCFL*, 15 (1964), 231-40.

Thomas, David P. "*Goodbye to Berlin*: Refocusing Isherwood's Camera." *ConL*, 13 (1972), 44-52.

PAMELA HANSFORD JOHNSON

INTERVIEWS

Firchow, Peter. *The Writer's Place*, 209-22.
Newquist, Roy, ed. *Counterpoint*, 366-73.

GENERAL STUDIES

Quigly, Isabel. *Pamela Hansford Johnson*. London: Longmans, Green, 1968.
Raymond, John. *The Doge of Dover*, 156-63.
Webster, Harvey C. "Farce and Faith." *KR*, 25 (1963), 747-51.
See also: Allen, *Tradition*; Karl; Webster.

JAMES JOYCE

BIBLIOGRAPHIES

Beebe, Maurice, and Walton Litz. "Criticism of James Joyce: A Selected Checklist with an Index to Studies of Separate Works." *MFS*, 4 (1958), 71-99.
Cohn, Alan M. "Joyce Bibliographies: A Survey." *ABC*, 15, 10 (1965), 11-16.
Deming, Robert H. *A Bibliography of James Joyce Studies*. Lawrence: Univ. of Kansas Libraries, 1964; enlarged, Boston: G. K. Hall, 1977.
James Joyce Quarterly [*JJQ*]. (publishes annual bibliography of criticism)
Litz, A. Walton. "Joyce." *The English Novel*. Ed. A. E. Dyson, 349-69.
McLuhan, Marshall. "A Survey of Joyce Criticism." *Renascence*, 4 (1951), 12-18.
Roberts, R. F. "Bibliographical Notes on James Joyce's *Ulysses*." *Colophon*, n.s. 1 (1936), 565-79.
Spoerri, James F. *James Joyce: Books and Pamphlets Relating to the Author and His Works*. Charlottesville: Univ. of Virginia Bibliog. Soc., 1959.
Walker, Brenda M. "James Joyce: A Bibliography." *ManR*, 8 (1958), 151-60.

INTERVIEWS

Borach, Georges. "Conversations with James Joyce." *CE*, 15 (1954), 325-27.
Power, Arthur R. *Conversations with James Joyce*. Ed. Clive Hart. London: Millington; New York: Barnes and Noble, 1974.
————. "Conversations with Joyce." *JJQ*, 3 (1965), 41-49.

SPECIAL ISSUES
Adam International Review [Adam], 29, 297-98 (1961).
Modern Fiction Studies [MFS], 15, 1 (1969).
"Ulysses and *The Waste Land* Fifty Years After." *Mosaic*, 6, 1 (1972), 3-111.
Studies in the Literary Imagination [SLitI], 3, 2 (1970), 1-96.

GENERAL STUDIES
Adams, Robert M. *James Joyce: Common Sense and Beyond*. New York: Vintage, 1966.
_____. "The Operatic Novel: Joyce and D'Annunzio." *New Looks at Italian Opera*. Ed. William W. Austin, 260-81.
Allott, Miriam. "James Joyce: The Hedgehog and the Fox." *On the Novel*. Ed. Benedikt S. Benedikz, 161-77.
Anderson, Chester G. *James Joyce and His World*. London: Thames and Hudson, 1967.
_____. "On the Sublime and Its Anal-Urethral Sources in Pope, Eliot, and Joyce." *Modern Irish Literature*. Ed. Raymond J. Porter and James D. Brophy, 234-49.
Andreasen, N. J. C. "James Joyce: A Portrait of the Artist as a Schizoid." *JAMA*, 224 (1973), 67-71.
Arnold, Allen D. "A Consideration of James Joyce's Aesthetic Theory and His Indebtedness to Gustave Flaubert." *Horizontes*, 25 (1971), 27-35.
Arnold, Armin. *James Joyce*. New York: Ungar, 1969.
Bamborough, J. B. "Joyce and Jonson." *REL*, 2, 4 (1961), 45-50.
Bates, Ronald, and Harry J. Pollock, eds. *Letters from Aloft: Papers Delivered at the Second Canadian James Joyce Seminar, McMaster University*, 1972.
Beebe, Maurice. *Ivory Towers and Sacred Founts*, 260-95.
Beechhold, Henry F. "Joyce's Otherworld." *Eire*, 7, 1 (1972), 103-15.
Begnal, Michael H. "James Joyce and the Mythologizing of History." *Directions in Literary Criticism*. Ed. Stanley Weintraub and Philip Young, 211-19.
Beharriell, Frederick J. "Freud and Literature." *QQ*, 65 (1958), 118-25.
Beja, Morris. "Mau-Mauing the Epiphany Catchers." *PMLA*, 87 (1972), 1131-32.
_____. "The Wooden Sword: Threatener and Threatened in the Fiction of James Joyce." *JJQ*, 2 (1964), 33-41.
Bickerton, Derek. "James Joyce and the Development of Interior Monologue." *EIC*, 18 (1968), 32-46.
Blanche, Jacques-Emile. *More Portraits of a Lifetime*, 278-88.

James Joyce, continued

Block, Haskell M. "The Critical Theory of James Joyce." *JAAC*, 8 (1950), 172-84.

――――. "James Joyce and Thomas Hardy." *MLQ*, 19 (1958), 337-42.

――――. "Theory of Language in Gustave Flaubert and James Joyce." *RLC*, 35 (1961), 197-206.

Bonheim, Helmut. "James Joyce: Nation Versus World." *Proceedings of IVth Congress of the Int'l. Comp. Lit. Ass'n.* Ed. François Jost, 462-66.

――――. *Joyce's Benefictions.* Berkeley: Univ. of California Press, 1964.

Boyle, Alexander. "Joyce's Unjust City." *CathW*, 181 (1955), 6-10.

Boyle, Robert. "Miracle in Black Ink: A Glance at Joyce's Use of His Eucharistic Image." *JJQ*, 10 (1972), 47-60.

Brandabur, Edward. *A Scrupulous Meanness: A Study of Joyce's Early Work.* Urbana: Univ. of Illinois Press, 1971.

Bredin, Hugh T. "Applied Aquinas: James Joyce's Aesthetics." *Eire*, 3, 1 (1968), 61-78.

Brennan, Joseph G. *Three Philosophic Novelists: James Joyce, André Gide, Thomas Mann.* New York: Macmillan, 1964.

Brick, Allan. "The Madman in His Cell: Joyce, Beckett, Nabokov, and the Stereotypes." *MR*, 1 (1959), 40-55.

Brivic, Sheldon R. "From Stephen to Bloom." *Psychoanalysis and Literary Process.* Ed. Frederick C. Crews, 118-62.

Brooke, Jocelyn. "Proust and Joyce: The Case for the Prosecution." *Adam*, 29, 297-98 (1961), 5-8, 34-66.

Brown, Homer O. *James Joyce's Early Fiction: The Biography of a Form.* Cleveland: The Press of Case Western Reserve Univ., 1973.

Brown, Malcolm. *The Politics of Irish Literature*, 224-26, 385-89.

Burgess, Anthony. *Here Comes Everybody: An Introduction to James Joyce for the Ordinary Reader.* London: Faber and Faber; New York: Norton, 1965. [American ed. entitled *Re Joyce*]

――――. *Joysprick: An Introduction to the Language of James Joyce.* London: Deutsch; New York: Academic Press, 1973; New York: Harcourt, 1974.

Campbell, Joseph. "Contransmagnific and-jewbangtantiality." *SLitI*, 3, 2 (1970), 3-18.

Chace, William M., ed. *Joyce: A Collection of Critical Essays.* Englewood Cliffs, N. J.: Prentice-Hall, 1973.

Church, Margaret. *Time and Reality*, 27-66.

Clarke, John. "Joyce and the Blakean Vision." *Criticism*, 5 (1963), 173-80.

Cohn, Ruby. "Joyce and Beckett, Irish Cosmopolitans." *Proceedings*

of the IVth Congress of the Int'l. Comp. Lit. Ass'n. Ed. François
   Jost, 109-13. [Also in *JJQ*, 8 (1971), 385-91]
Coleman, Elliott. "A Note on Joyce and Jung." *JJQ*, 1, 1 (1963), 11-16.
Collins, Norman. *The Facts of Fiction*, 276-84.
Colum, Mary. *From These Roots*, 312-60.
_____, and Padraic Colum. *Our Friend James Joyce*. Garden City,
   N.Y.: Doubleday, 1958.
Connolly, Cyril. *Previous Convictions*, 269-81.
Cope, Jackson I. "James Joyce: Test Case for a Theory of Style." *ELH*,
   21 (1954), 221-36.
Coveney, Peter. *Poor Monkey*, 253-58.
Cronin, John. "The Funnel and the Tundish: Irish Writers and the
   English Language." *WascanaR*, 3, 1 (1968), 80-88.
Cross, Richard K. *Flaubert and Joyce: The Rite of Fiction*. Princeton,
   N. J.: Princeton Univ. Press, 1971.
Curran, Constantine. *James Joyce Remembered*. New York: Oxford
   Univ. Press, 1968.
Dahl, Liisa. "A Comment on Similarities Between Édouard Dujardin's
   monologue intérieur and James Joyce's Interior Monologue."
   NM, 73 (1972), 45-54.
_____. *Linguistic Features of the Stream-of-Consciousness Tech-
   niques of James Joyce, Virginia Woolf and Eugene O'Neill*.
Dahlberg, Edward, and Herbert Read. *Truth is More Sacred*, 11-65.
Daiches, David. "James Joyce: The Artist as Exile." *CE*, 2 (1940), 197-
   206; *Forms of Modern Fiction*. Ed. William Van O'Connor, 67-71.
Davies, Stan Gebler. *James Joyce: A Portrait of the Artist*. London:
   Davis-Poynter, 1975.
Day, Robert Adams. "Joyce, Stoom, King Mark: 'Glorious Name of
   Irish Goose'." *JJQ*, 12 (1975), 211-50.
Deming, Robert H. *James Joyce: The Critical Heritage*. London: Rout-
   ledge and K. Paul; New York: Barnes and Noble, 1970.
Donoghue, Denis. "Joyce and the Finite Order." *SR*, 68 (1960), 256-73.
_____. "Joyce's Landscapes." *Studies*, 46 (1957), 76-90.
Duff, Charles. *James Joyce and the Plain Reader, An Essay*. London:
   Harmsworth, 1932.
Eglinton, John. *Irish Literary Portraits*, 131-58.
Eliot, T. S. "A Message to the Fish." *Golden Horizon*. Ed. Cyril Connol-
   ly, 388-90.
Ellmann, Richard. *Eminent Domain: Yeats among Wilde, Joyce,
   Pound, Eliot, and Auden*. New York: Oxford Univ. Press, 1967,
   29-56.
_____. *Golden Codgers*, 132-54.

James Joyce, continued

———. *James Joyce.* New York: Oxford Univ. Press, 1959.

———. "James Joyce, Irish European." *TriQ*, 8 (1967), 199-204.

———. *Joyce in Love.* Ithaca, N. Y.: Cornell Univ. Press, 1959.

———. "The Limits of Joyce's Naturalism." *SR*, 63 (1955), 567-75.

Epstein, E. L. "James Joyce and *The Way of All Flesh*." *JJQ*, 7 (1969), 22-29.

Ernst, Morris L. *The Best is Yet . . .* , 112-19.

Evans, B. Ifor. *English Literature Between the Wars*, 40-48.

Every, George. "James Joyce." *The New Spirit.* Ed. E. W. Martin, 54-57.

Fanger, Donald. "Joyce and Meredith: A Question of Influence and Tradition." *MFS*, 6 (1960), 125-30.

Farrell, James T. "Joyce and the Tradition of the European Novel." *NYTBR*, January 21, 1945, 4, 18.

———. *Reflections at Fifty*, 66-96.

Feibleman, James K. *In Praise of Comedy*, 230-36.

Fleming, Rudd. "Dramatic Involution: Tate, Husserl, and Joyce." *SR*, 60 (1952), 445-64.

———. "*Quidditas* in the Tragi-Comedy of Joyce." *UKCR*, 15 (1949), 288-296.

Frank, Joseph. *The Widening Gyre*, 14-19.

Friedman, Melvin J. *Stream of Consciousness*, 210-43.

———. "Three Experiences of War: A Triptych." *Promise of Greatness.* Ed. George A. Panichas, 541-55.

Fritz, Helen M. "Joyce and Existentialism." *JJR*, 2, 1-2 (1958), 13-21.

Fuller, Edmund. *Man in Modern Fiction*, 122-32.

Garrett, Peter. *Scene and Symbol from George Eliot to James Joyce*, 214-71.

Gillet, Louis. *Claybook for James Joyce.* Tr. Georges Markow-Totevy. New York: Abelard-Schuman, 1958.

Givens, Sean, ed. *James Joyce: Two Decades of Criticism.* New York: Vanguard, 1948, 1963.

Godwin, Murray. "A Rushlight for the Labyrinth." *PS*, 6 (1952), 84-96.

Goldberg, S. L. *James Joyce.* Edinburgh: Oliver and Boyd, 1962; New York: Grove, 1963.

———. "Joyce and the Artist's Fingernails." *REL*, 2, 2 (1961), 59-73.

Golding, Louis. *James Joyce.* London: Butterworth, 1933.

Goldman, Arnold. *James Joyce.* London: Routledge and K. Paul; New York: Humanities, 1968.

———. *The Joyce Paradox: Form and Freedom in His Fiction.* Evanston, Ill.: Northwestern Univ. Press; London: Routledge and K. Paul, 1966.

Goodheart, Eugene. *The Cult of the Ego*, 183-200.

Gorman, Herbert. *James Joyce: His First Forty Years*. New York: Huebsch, 1924.

Gregory, Horace. *The Dying Gladiators*, 157-64.

Griffin, Gerald. *The Wild Geese*, 22-45.

Grose, Kenneth. *James Joyce*. London: Evans; Totowa, N. J.: Rowman and Littlefield, 1975.

Gross, John J. *James Joyce*. New York: Viking, 1970.

Halper, Nathan. *The Early James Joyce*. New York: Columbia Univ. Press, 1973.

Hampshire, Stuart. "Joyce and Vico: The Middle Way." *NYRB*, 20 (October 18, 1973), 8-21.

Hardy, Barbara. *Tellers and Listeners*, 206-76.

Hart, Clive. "James Joyce's Sentimentality." *PQ*, 46 (1967), 517-26.

Hartley, Lodwick. " 'Swiftly-Sterneward': The Question of Sterne's Influence on Joyce." *SLitI*, 3, 2 (1970), 37-47.

Hawkes, Terry. "Joyce and Speech." *JJR*, 1, 4 (1957), 33-37.

Helsinger, Howard. "Joyce and Dante." *ELH*, 35 (1968), 591-605.

Henderson, Philip. *The Novel Today*, 81-86.

Hendry, Irene. "Joyce's Epiphanies." *SR*, 54 (1946), 449-67.

Higginson, Fred H. "James Joyce, Linguist." *WS*, 31, 5 (1956), 1-3.

Highet, Gilbert. *The Classical Tradition*, 501-19.

———. *Explorations*, 135-46.

Hodgart, Matthew J. C., and Mabel P. Worthington. *Song in the Works of James Joyce*. New York: Columbia Univ. Press for Temple Univ. Pubs., 1959.

Hoffman, Frederick J. *Freudianism and the Literary Mind*, 116-50.

———. *The Imagination's New Beginning*, 22-43.

Howarth, Herbert. *The Irish Writers*, 245-87.

Humphrey, Robert. *Stream of Consciousness Technique*, 15-17, 26-28, 43-48, 52-54, 74-76, 87-99.

Huneker, James G. *Unicorns*, 187-94.

Hutchins, Patricia. *James Joyce's World*. London: Methuen, 1957.

Huxley, Aldous, and Stuart Gilbert. *Joyce the Artificer: Two Studies of Joyce's Method*. [n.p.], 1952.

Isaacs, Neil D. "The Autoerotic Metaphor in Joyce, Sterne, Lawrence, Stevens, and Whitman." *L&P*, 15 (1965), 92-106.

Jameson, F. R. "Seriality in Modern Literature." *BuR*, 18, 1 (1970), 63-80.

Jenkins, William D. "It Seems There Were Two Irishmen." *MFS*, 15, 1 (1969), 63-72.

James Joyce, continued

Johnson, E. Bond, III. "Parody and Myth: Flaubert, Joyce, Nabokov."
   FWF, 1 (1974), 149-73.
Jolas, Maria, ed. *A James Joyce Yearbook*. Paris: Transition, 1949.
Jones, David E. "The Essence of Beauty in James Joyce's Aesthetics."
   JJQ, 10 (1973), 291-311.
Jones, William Powell. *James Joyce and the Common Reader*. Nor-
   man: Univ. of Oklahoma Press, 1955.
Kain, Richard M. "He Who Runes May Rede . . . Joyce as Philolo-
   gist." *Mosaic*, 2, 2 (1969), 74-85.
_____. "James Joyce and the Game of Language." *SLitI*, 3, 2 (1970),
   19-25.
_____. "Problems of Interpreting Joycean Symbolism." *JGE*, 17
   (1965), 227-35.
Kaplan, Harold. *The Passive Voice*, 43-91.
Kazin, Alfred. *The Inmost Leaf*, 3-8.
Kelleher, John V. "The Perceptions of James Joyce." *Atlantic*, 201
   (March 1958), 82-90.
Kelly, Robert G. "James Joyce: A Partial Explanation." *PMLA*, 64
   (1949), 26-39.
Kempf, Roger. "James Job Joyce." *Crit*, 24 (1968), 368-79.
Kenner, Hugh. *Dublin's Joyce*. Bloomington: Indiana Univ. Press,
   1956.
_____. "Joyce and Ibsen's Naturalism." *SR*, 59 (1951), 75-96.
_____. "Prometheus' Diary." *PrS*, 32 (1958), 14-20.
_____. *The Stoic Comedians: Flaubert, Joyce and Beckett*. Boston:
   Beacon, 1962; Berkeley: Univ. of California Press, 1974, 30-66.
_____. "The Trivium in Dublin." *English Institute Essays, 1952*,
   202-227.
Kettle, Arnold. "The Consistency of James Joyce." *The Pelican Guide
   to English Literature*, v. 7. Ed. Boris Ford, 319-32.
Klawitter, Robert. "Henri Bergson and James Joyce's Fictional
   World." *CLS*, 3 (1966), 429-37.
Knuth, Leo. "Joyce's Verbal Acupuncture." *JJQ*, 10 (1972), 61-71.
Kronegger, M. E. "Joyce's Debt to Poe and the French Symbolists."
   RLC, 39 (1965), 243-54.
_____. "The Theory of Unity and Effect in the Works of E. A. Poe and
   James Joyce." *RLC*, 40 (1966), 226-34.
Kumar, Shiv K. *Bergson and the Stream of Consciousness Novel*,
   103-38.
_____. "Joyce and Bergson's *mémoire pure*." *OJES*, 1 (1961), 55-60.
_____. "Joyce's Epiphany and Bergson's *L'intuition philosophique*'."
   MLQ, 20 (1959), 27-30.

Lauer, Christopher. "A Certain Element of Play in Joyce's Work." *JJQ*, 12 (1975), 423-35.

Levin, Harry. *Contexts of Criticism*, 131-39.

――――. "James Joyce." *Atlantic*, 178 (December 1946), 125-29.

――――. *James Joyce: A Critical Introduction*. Norfolk, Conn.: New Directions, 1941; rev., 1960.

Levitt, Morton P. "Shalt Be Accurst? The Martyr in James Joyce." *JJQ*, 5 (1968), 285-96.

Lillyman, W. J. "The Interior Monologue in James Joyce and Otto Ludwig." *CL*, 23 (1971), 45-54.

Litz, A. Walton. *James Joyce*. New York: Twayne, 1966, 1972.

――――. "Vico and Joyce." *Giambattista Vico: An International Symposium*. Ed. Giorgio Tagliacozzo and Hayden V. White. Baltimore: Johns Hopkins Univ. Press, 1969.

Loss, Archie K. "The Pre-Raphaelite Woman, the Symbolist *Femme-Enfant*, and the Girl with Long Flowing Hair in the Earlier Work of Joyce." *JML*, 3 (1973), 3-23.

Lovett, Robert M. *Preface to Fiction*, 113-27.

Lyons, J. B. *James Joyce and Medicine*. Dublin: Dolmen, 1973, New York: Humanities, 1974.

Lyons, John O. "James Joyce and Chaucer's Prioress." *ELN*, 2 (1964), 127-32.

MacLeod, Vivienne K. "The Influence of Ibsen on Joyce." *PMLA*, 60 (1945), 879-98; 62 (1947), 573-80.

McLuhan, Marshall. *The Interior Landscape*, 5-47.

――――. "James Joyce: Trivial and Quadrivial." *Thought*, 28 (1953), 75-98.

――――. "Joyce, Aquinas, and the Poetic Process." *Renascence*, 4 (1951), 3-11.

――――. "Joyce, Mallarmé, and the Press." *SR*, 62 (1954), 38-55.

McMichael, Charles T., and Ted R. Spivey. " 'Chaos—hurray!—is come again': Heroism in James Joyce and Conrad Aiken." *SLitI*, 3, 2 (1970), 65-68.

Magalaner, Marvin. "James Joyce and the Myth of Man." *ArQ*, 4 (1948), 300-09.

――――. "James Joyce and the Uncommon Reader." *SAQ*, 52 (1953), 267-76.

――――, ed. *A James Joyce Miscellany*. New York: The James Joyce Society, 1957; 2d ser. Carbondale: Southern Illinois Univ. Press, 1959; 3d ser. Carbondale: Southern Illinois Univ. Press, 1962.

――――, and Richard M. Kain. *Joyce: The Man, the Work, the Reputation*. New York: New York Univ. Press, 1956.

James Joyce, continued

Mallam, Duncan. "Joyce and Rabelais." *UKCR*, 23 (1956), 99-110.
_____. *Time of Apprenticeship: The Fiction of Young James Joyce.*
London, New York, and Toronto: Abelard-Schuman, 1959.
Marcus, Phillip L. "George Moore's Dublin 'Epiphanies' and Joyce."
JJQ, 5 (1968), 157-61.
Mason, Ellsworth, and Richard Ellmann, eds. *The Critical Writings of
James Joyce.* New York: Viking, 1959.
_____. "James Joyce: Moralist." *TCL*, 1 (1956), 196-206.
_____. "Joyce's Categories." *SR*, 61 (1953), 427-32.
Mayoux, J.-J. "Parody and Self-Mockery in the Work of James Joyce."
English Studies Today, 3d ser. Ed. G. I. Duthie, 187-98.
Melchiori, Giorgio. "Joyce, Eliot and the Nightmare of History." *RLV*,
40 (1974), 582-98.
_____. *The Tightrope Walkers*, 34-52.
Mercanton, Jacques. "The Hours of James Joyce, Part I." *KR*, 24
(1962), 700-30; Part II, *KR*, 25 (1963), 93-118.
Mercier, Vivian. "James Joyce and French Literature." *Cahiers I*, 2-3
(1974), 215-27.
_____. "James Joyce and the French New Novel." *TriQ*, 8 (1967),
205-19.
Mitchell, Breon. "Joyce and Döblin: At the Crossroads of *Berlin Alex-
anderplatz*." *ConL*, 12 (1971), 173-87.
Moore, John Rees. "Artifices for Eternity: Joyce and Yeats." *Eire*, 3, 4
(1968), 66-73.
More, Paul E. "James Joyce." *AmerR*, 5 (1935), 129-57.
_____. *On Being Human*, 69-96.
Morin, Edward. "Joyce as Thomist." *Renascence*, 9 (1957), 127-31.
Morse, J. Mitchell. "Art and Fortitude: Joyce and the *Summa Theolog-
ica*." *JJR*, 1, 1 (1957), 19-30.
_____. "Augustine's Theodicy and Joyce's Aesthetics." *ELH*, 24
(1957), 30-43.
_____. "Baudelaire, Stephen Dedalus, and Shem the Penman." *BuR*,
7, 3 (1958), 187-98.
_____. "The Disobedient Artist: Joyce and Loyola." *PMLA*, 72 (1957),
1018-35.
_____. "Joyce and the Blind Stripling." *MLN*, 71 (1956), 497-501.
_____. "Joyce and the Early Thomas Mann." *RLC*, 36 (1962), 377-85.
_____. *The Sympathetic Alien: James Joyce and Catholicism.* New
York: New York Univ. Press, 1959.
Mosely, Virginia D. *Joyce and the Bible.* De Kalb: Northern Illinois
Univ. Press, 1967.
Moucheron, Andrée. "Joyce and Shakespeare." *RLV*, 30 (1964), 342-46.

Muir, Edwin. *Transition*, 19-45.

Murdoch, Walter. *Collected Essays*, 218-22.

Murillo, J. A. *The Cyclical Night: Irony in James Joyce and Jorge Luis Borges*. Cambridge, Mass.: Harvard Univ. Press, 1970.

Murray, Edward. *The Cinematic Imagination*, 124-41.

Natanson, Maurice. "Being-In-Reality." *PPR*, 20 (1959), 231-37.

Nicholson, Norman. *Man and Literature*, 144-56.

Noon, William T. "God and Man in Twentieth-Century Fiction." *Thought*, 37 (1962), 35-56.

———. "James Joyce and Catholicism." *JJR*, 1, 4 (1957), 3-17.

———. "James Joyce: Unfacts, Fiction, and Facts." *PMLA*, 76 (1961), 254-76.

———. "The Lion and the Honeycomb." *C&L*, 19, 3 (1970), 18-24.

Obler, Paul C. "Joyce's Numerology: A Knot in the Labyrinth." *JJR*, 3, 1-2 (1959), 53-56.

O'Brien, Darcy. *The Conscience of James Joyce*. Princeton, N.J.: Princeton Univ. Press, 1968.

O'Connor, Frank. *The Mirror in the Roadway*, 295-316.

Paul, Elliot. "Farthest North: A Study of James Joyce." *Bookman* (N.Y.), 75 (1932), 156-63.

Peter, John. "Joyce and the Novel." *KR*, 18 (1956), 619-32.

Pittman, Dan C. "James Joyce: Critic of a Dead Society." *SoQ*, 5 (1967), 471-82.

Poss, Stanley H. "A Portrait of the Artist as Beginner " *UKCR*, 26 (1960), 189-96.

Pound, Ezra. *Literary Essays*, 403-17.

———. "Past History." *EJ*, 22 (1933), 349-58.

Praz, Mario. "Notes on James Joyce." *Mosaic*, 6, 1 (1972), 85-100.

Prescott, Joseph. *Exploring James Joyce*. Carbondale: Southern Illinois Univ. Press, 1964.

Preston, Dennis R. "Visibility in Joyce." *KN*, 22 (1975), 407-18.

Priestley, J. B. *Literature and Western Man*, 415-18.

Rader, Ralph W. "Defoe, Richardson, Joyce, and the Concept of Form in the Novel." *Autobiography, Biography, and the Novel*. Ed. William Matthews and Ralph W. Rader, 31-72.

Raisor, Philip. "Grist for the Mill: James Joyce and the Naturalists." *ConL*, 15 (1974), 457-73.

Raleigh, John Henry. "Victorian Morals and the Modern Novel." *PR*, 25, 2 (1958), 241-64.

Read, Forrest, ed. *Pound/Joyce: Letters and Essays*. New York: New Directions, 1967.

Reid, John. "Joyce, Alas." *AntigR*, 16 (1974), 88-99.

James Joyce, continued

Reynolds, Mary T. "Joyce and Nora: The Indispensable Countersign." *SR*, 72 (1964), 29-64.

Roberts, John H. "James Joyce: From Religion to Art. *New Humanist*, 7, 3 (1934), 7-13.

Rodway, Allan. "Expanding Images in the Joycian Universe." *RMS*, 15 (1971), 63-69.

Rosenfeld, Paul. *Men Seen*, 23-42.

Rothman, Nathan L. "Thomas Wolfe and James Joyce: A Study in Literary Influence." *Southern Vanguard*. Ed. Allen Tate, 52-77.

Rubin, Louis D., Jr. "Joyce and Sterne: A Study in Affinity." *HopR*, 3 (1950), 14-22.

———. *The Teller in the Tale*, 141-77.

Rutherford, Andrew. "Joyce's Use of Correspondences." *EIC*, 6 (1956), 123-25.

Ryf, Robert S. "Joyce's Visual Imagination." *TSLL*, 1 (1959), 30-43.

Savage, Derek S. *The Withered Branch*, 156-99.

Scholes, Robert. "In Search of James Joyce." *JJQ*, 11 (1973), 5-16.

———. "Joyce and the Epiphany: The Key to the Labyrinth?" *SR*, 72 (1964), 65-77.

———, and Florence L. Walzl. "The Epiphanies of Joyce." *PMLA*, 82 (1967), 152-54.

Scott, Bonnie K. "Joyce's Schooling in the Field of George Moore," *Eire*, 9, 4 (1974), 117-41.

Scott, Evelyn. "A Contemporary of the Future." *Dial*, 69 (October 1920), 353-67.

Semmler, Clement. *For the Uncanny Man*, 12-132.

———. "Solving the Problem of James Joyce." *Meanjin*, 19 (1960), 78-83.

Senn, Fritz, ed. *New Light on Joyce from the Dublin Symposium*. Bloomington: Indiana Univ. Press, 1972.

Sharpe, Garold. "The Philosophy of James Joyce." *MFS*, 9 (1963), 120-26.

Shechner, Mark. "The Song of the Wandering Aengus: James Joyce and His Mother." *JJQ*, 10 (1972), 72-89.

Silverman, O. A., ed. *Epiphanies, with an Introduction and Notes*. Buffalo: Lockwood Mem. Libr., Univ. of Buffalo, 1956.

Slochower, Harry. *No Voice is Wholly Lost*, 243-48.

Smidt, Kristian. *James Joyce and the Cultic Use of Fiction*. Oslo: Akademiskforlag, 1955; New York: Humanities, 1957.

———. "Joyce and Ibsen: A Study in Literary Influence." *Edda*, 70 (1975), 85-97.

———. "Joyce and Norway." *ES*, 41 (1960), 318-21.

Spencer, John. "A Note on the 'Steady Monologny of the Interiors'." *REL*, 6, 2 (1965), 32-41.

Spiegel, Alan. "Flaubert to Joyce: Evolution of a Cinematographic Form." *Novel*, 6 (1973), 229-43.

Spivey, Ted R. "The Reintegration of Modern Man: An Essay on James Joyce and Hermann Hesse." *SLitI*, 3, 2 (1970), 49-64.

Sporn, Paul. "James Joyce: Early Thoughts on the Subject Matter of Art." *CE*, 24 (1962), 19-24.

Staley, Harry C. "Joyce's Catechisms." *JJQ*, 6 (1968), 137-53.

Staley, Thomas F., ed. *James Joyce Today: Essays on the Major Works*. Bloomington: Indiana Univ. Press, 1966.

Stamirowska, Krystyna. "The Conception of a Character in the Works of Joyce and Beckett." *KN*, 14 (1967), 443-47.

Stephens, James. *James, Seumas, and Jacques*, 147-55.

Stern, James. "James Joyce: A First Impression." *Listener*, 66 (1961), 461-63.

Stewart, Douglas G. *The Ark of God*, 17-43.

Stewart, J. I. M. *Eight Modern Writers*, 422-83.

_____. *James Joyce*. London and New York: Longmans, Green, 1958.

Stoll, John E. "Common Womb Imagery in Joyce and Lawrence." *BSUF*, 11, 2 (1970), 10-24.

Strong, L. A. G. "James Joyce." *The English Novelists*. Ed. Derek Verschoyle, 301-16.

_____. "James Joyce and the New Fiction." *AmerM*, 35 (1935), 433-37.

_____. "James Joyce and Vocal Music." English Association, London. *Essays and Studies*, v. 31 (1945), 95-106.

_____. *Personal Remarks*, 184-89.

_____. *The Sacred River: An Approach to James Joyce*. London: Methuen, 1949; New York: Pellegrini and Cudahy, 1951.

Stuart, Michael. "Mr. Joyce's Word-Creatures." *Symposium*, 2, 4 (1931), 459-67.

Sullivan, Kevin. *Joyce Among the Jesuits*. New York: Columbia Univ. Press, 1958.

Sweeney, James J. "The Word Was His Oyster." *HudR*, 5 (1952), 404-08.

Taylor, Estella Ruth. *The Modern Irish Writers*, 140-44.

Thorn, Eric P. "James Joyce: Early Imitations of Structural Unity." *Costerus*, 9 (1973), 229-38.

Thornton, Weldon. "James Joyce and the Power of the Word." *The Classic British Novel*. Ed. Howard M. Harper, Jr. and Charles Edge, 183-201.

Tindall, William York. "Dante and Mrs. Bloom." *Accent,* 11 (1951), 85-92.

———. "James Joyce and the Hermetic Tradition." *JHI,* 15 (1954), 23-39.

———. *James Joyce: His Way of Interpreting the Modern World.* New York: Scribner's, 1950.

———. *A Reader's Guide to James Joyce.* New York: Noonday, 1959.

———. "The Symbolic Novel." *AD,* 3 (Winter 1952), 56-82.

Tompkins, Phillip K. "The Rhetoric of James Joyce." *QJS,* 54 (1968), 107-14.

Troy, William. *Selected Essays,* 89-109.

Tysdahl, Bjørn J. *Joyce and Ibsen: A Study in Literary Influence.* Oslo: Universitetsforlaget; New York: Humanities, 1968.

———. "Joyce's Use of Norwegian Writers." *ES,* 50 (1969), 261-73.

Untermeyer, Louis. *Makers of the Modern World,* 586-96.

Ussher, Arland. *Three Great Irishmen: Shaw, Yeats, Joyce.* New York: Devin-Adair, 1953; New York: New American Library, 1957, 115-60.

Vickery, John B. *The Literary Impact of THE GOLDEN BOUGH,* 326-423.

Wagner, Geoffrey. "Wyndham Lewis and James Joyce: A Study in Controversy." *SAQ,* 56 (1957), 57-66.

Waldock, Arthur J. A. *James, Joyce, and Others.* London: Williams and Norgate, 1937, 30-52.

Walzl, Florence L. "The Liturgy of the Epiphany Season and the Epiphanies of Joyce." *PMLA,* 80 (1975), 436-50.

Weathers, Winston. "Joyce and the Tragedy of Language." *ForumH,* 4, 12 (1967), 16-21.

Webb, Eugene. *The Dark Dove,* 111-56.

Weir, Lorraine. "Joyce, Myth and Memory." *IUR,* 2, 2 (1972), 172-88.

Wells, H. G. "H. G. Wells on James Joyce." *Novelists on Novelists.* Ed. Louis Kronenberger, 343-46.

Whitaker, Thomas R. "The Drinkers and History: Rabelais, Balzac, and Joyce." *CL,* 11 (1959), 157-64.

White, David A. "The Labyrinth of Language: Joyce and Wittgenstein." *JJQ,* 12 (1975), 294-304.

Wicker, Brian. *The Story-Shaped World,* 134-50.

Wickham, Harvey. *The Impuritans,* 235-90.

Williams, William Carlos. *Selected Essays,* 75-90.

Woodbery, Potter. "The Irrelevance of Stephen Dedalus: Some Reflections on Joyce and the Student Activist Movement." *SLitI,* 3, 2 (1970), 69-78.

Wilson, Robert Anton. "Joyce and Tao." *JJR*, 3, 1-2 (1959), 8-16.
Zyla, Wolodymyr T., ed. *Proceedings of the Comparative Literature Symposium, II: James Joyce: His Place in World Literature.* February 7-8, 1969. Lubbock: Interdepartmental Committee on Comp. Lit., Texas Tech. Coll., 1969.
See also: Beach, *20th*; Beja; Beresford; Bradbury, *Social*; A. Collins, *20th*; J. Collins, *Doctor*; Daiches, *Novel*; Donoghue, *Universe*; Drew, *Modern*; Edel; Edgar, *Art*; Forster, *Aspects*; A. Friedman, *Turn*; Gindin, *Harvest*; Hoare; Karl and Magalaner; Lovett, *History*; Lynd, *Books*; MacCarthy, *Memories*; Macy; Muller, *Modern*; O'Faoláin; Scott-James, *50*; Swinnerton, *Georgian*; Tindall, *Forces*; Vines; Wagenknecht, *Cavalcade*.

FINNEGANS WAKE
Asenjo, F. G. "The General Problem of Sentence Structure: An Analysis Prompted by the Loss of Subject in *Finnegans Wake*." *CentR*, 8 (1964), 398-408.
Atherton, James S. *The Books at the Wake: A Study of Literary Allusion in James Joyce's FINNEGANS WAKE.* New York: Viking; London: Faber and Faber, 1959; Carbondale: Southern Illinois Univ. Press; London: Feffer and Simons, 1974.
———. "A Few More Books at the Wake." *JJQ*, 2 (1965), 142-49.
———. *"Finnegans Wake*: The Gist of the Pantomine." *Accent*, 15 (1955), 14-26.
———. "Islam and the Koran in *Finnegans Wake*." *CL*, 6 (1954), 240-55.
———. "James Joyce and *Finnegans Wake*." *ManR*, 9 (1961), 97-108.
———. "Lewis Carroll and *Finnegans Wake*." *ES*, 33 (1952), 1-15.
Aubert, Jacques. "Notes on the French Element in *Finnegans Wake*." *JJQ*, 5 (1968), 110-24.
Bates, Ronald. "The Feast Is a Flyday." *JJQ*, 2 (1965), 174-87.
Beckett, Samuel, et al. *Our Exagmination Round His Factification for Incamination of Work in Progress.* Paris: Shakespeare and Co., 1929; Norfolk, Conn.: New Directions, 1939.
Beechhold, Henry F. "Finn MacCool and *Finnegans Wake*." *JJR*, 2, 1-2 (1958), 3-12.
Begnal, Michael H. "The Fables of *Finnegans Wake*." *JJQ*, 6 (1969), 357-67.
———. "Mourners at the Wake: The Family and Friends of HCE." *WHR*, 24 (1970), 383-93.
———. "The Narrator of *Finnegans Wake*." *Eire*, 4, 3 (1969), 38-49.
———. "The Prankquean in *Finnegans Wake*." *JJQ*, 1, 3 (1964), 14-18.

———, and Fritz Senn. *A Conceptual Guide to FINNEGANS WAKE.* University Park: Penn. State Univ. Press, 1974.

———, and Grace Eckley. *Narrator and Character in FINNEGANS WAKE.* Lewisburg, Pa.: Bucknell Univ. Press, 1974.

Benstock, Bernard. "Americana in *Finnegans Wake.*" *BuR,* 12, 1 (1964), 64-81.

———. "Every Telling Has a Taling: A Reading of the Narrative of *Finnegans Wake.*" *MFS,* 15, 1 (1969), 3-25.

———. "The Final Apostasy: James Joyce and *Finnegans Wake.*" *ELH,* 28 (1961), 417-37.

———. "Here Comes Everybody: *Finnegans Wake* as Epic." *Nine Essays in Modern Literature.* Ed. Donald E. Stanford, 3-35.

———. *Joyce-again's Wake: An Analysis of FINNEGANS WAKE.* Seattle: Univ. of Washington Press, 1966.

———. "L. Boom as Dreamer in *Finnegans Wake.*" *PMLA,* 82 (1967), 91-97.

———. "A Portrait of the Artist in *Finnegans Wake.*" *BuR,* 4, 4 (1961), 257-71.

———. "The Quiddity of Shem and the Whatness of Shaun." *JJQ,* 1, 1 (1963), 26-33.

Berger, Alfred P. "Wakeful Ad-Venture." *JJQ,* 7 (1969), 52-60.

Bernbaum, Ernest. "The Crucial Question Regarding *Finnegans Wake.*" *CE,* 7 (1945), 151-54.

Bierman, Robert. "The Dreamer and the Dream of *Finnegans Wake.*" *Renascence,* 11, 4 (1959), 197-200.

———. "*Ulysses* and *Finnegans Wake*: The Explicit, the Implicit, and the Tertium Quid." *Renascence,* 11, 1 (1958), 14-19.

———. " 'White and Pink Elephants': *Finnegans Wake* and the Tradition of 'Unintelligibility'." *MFS,* 4 (1958), 62-70.

Bishop, John Peale. *Collected Essays,* 146-65.

———. "*Finnegans Wake.*" *SoR,* 5 (1939), 439-52.

Blish, James. "Formal Music at the Wake, Parts I and II." *WN,* 7, 2 (1970), 19-27, 35-43.

Bogan, Louise. *Selected Criticism,* 142-53.

Boldereff, Frances M. *Hermes to His Son Thoth: Being Joyce's Use of Giordano Bruno in FINNEGANS WAKE.* Woodward, Pa.: Classic Nonfiction Library, 1968.

———. *Reading FINNEGANS WAKE.* Woodward, Pa.: Classic Nonfiction Library, 1959.

Bonheim, Helmut. "The Father in *Finnegans Wake.*" *SN,* 31 (1959), 182-90.

———. "God and the Gods in *Finnegans Wake.*" *SN,* 34 (1962), 294-314.

———. *A Lexicon of the German in FINNEGANS WAKE.* Berkeley: Univ. of California Press, 1967.

———, and Manfred Putz, eds. *"A Wake Newslitter* for the Greeter Glossary of Code: A Finding-List to Wake-Glosses in *A Wake Newslitter* 1962-1971." [*WN* Ten-Year Index (1972), 3-30.]

Broes, Arthur T. "The Bible in *Finnegans Wake.*" *WN*, n.s. 2 (1965), 6, 3-11. [See also 3, 102-05]

———. "More Books at the *Wake.*" *JJQ*, 9 (1971), 189-217.

———. "Shakespeare in *Finnegans Wake.*" *HAB*, 25 (1974), 304-17.

Bruns, Gerald L. *Modern Poetry and the Idea of Language,* 138-63.

Budgen, Frank. "Joyce's Chapters of Going Forth by Day." *Horizon,* 4 (September 1941), 172-91.

Burgum, Edwin B. *The Novel and the World's Dilemma,* 109-19.

Campbell, Joseph, and Henry M. Robinson. *A Skeleton Key to FINNEGANS WAKE.* New York: Harcourt, 1944; New York: Viking, 1961.

Carlson, Marvin. "Henrik Ibsen and *Finnegans Wake.*" *CL,* 12 (1960), 133-41.

Chase, Richard V. "Finnegans Wake: An Anthropological Study." *ASch,* 13 (1944), 418-26.

Christiani, Dounia. "H. C. Earwicker the Ostman." *JJQ,* 2 (1965), 150-57.

———. *Scandinavian Elements of FINNEGANS WAKE.* Evanston, Ill.: Northwestern Univ. Press, 1965.

Coleman, Elliott. "Heliotropical Noughttime: Light and Color in *Finnegans Wake.*" *TQ,* 4, 4 (1961), 162-77.

Colum, Padraic. "From a Work in Progress." *New Republic,* 64 (September 17, 1930), 131-32.

———. "Notes on *Finnegans Wake.*" *YR,* 30 (1941), 640-45.

Connolly, Thomas E., ed. *Scribbledehobble, the Ur-workbook for FINNEGANS WAKE.* Evanston, Ill.: Northwestern Univ. Press, 1961.

Dalton, Jack P., and Clive Hart, eds. *Twelve and a Tilly: Essays on the Occasion of the 25th Anniversary of FINNEGANS WAKE.* London: Faber and Faber; Evanston, Ill.: Northwestern Univ. Press, 1965.

Deutsch, Babette. *Poetry in Our Time,* 312-17.

Dohmen, William F. " 'Chilly Spaces': Wyndham Lewis as Ondt." *JJQ,* 11 (1974), 368-86.

Eckley, Grace. "Eggoarchicism and the Bird Lore of *Finnegans Wake.*" *Literary Monographs,* v. 5. Ed. Eric Rothstein, 139-84.

James Joyce, continued

———. " 'Petween Peas Like Ourselves': The Folklore of the Prank-quean." *JJQ*, 9 (1971), 177-88.

———. "Shem Is a Sham But Shaun Is a Ham, or Samuraising the Twins in *Finnegans Wake*." *MFS*, 20 (1974-75), 469-81.

Edel, Leon. "James Joyce and His New Work." *UTQ*, 9 (1939), 68-81.

Epstein, E. L. "Interpreting *Finnegans Wake*: A Half-Way House." *JJQ*, 3 (1966), 252-71.

Fáj, Attila. "Probable Byzantine and Hungarian Models of *Ulysses* and *Finnegans Wake*." *Arcadia*, 3 (1968), 48-72.

———. "Some Important, Hitherto Unnoticed Sources for *Finnegans Wake*." *WN*, 10 (1973), 3-12.

Fleming, William S. "Formulaic Rhythms in *Finnegans Wake*." *Style*, 6 (1972), 19-37.

Fowlie, Wallace. *Love in Literature*, 80-127.

Frye, Northrop. "Blake and Joyce: Quest and Cycle in *Finnegans Wake*." *JJR*, 1, 1 (1957), 39-47.

———. *Fables of Identity*, 256-64.

Garzilli, Enrico. *Circles Without Center*, 65-74.

Gillet, Louis. "Joyce's Testament: *Finnegans Wake*." *QRL*, 1 (1944), 87-99.

Glasheen, Adaline. *A Census of FINNEGANS WAKE: An Index of the Characters and Their Roles*. Evanston, Ill.: Northwestern Univ. Press, 1956.

———. "*Finnegans Wake* and the Girls from Boston, Mass." *HudR*, 7 (1954), 89-96.

———. "Out of My Census." *Analyst*, 17 (1959), 1-73.

———. "Part of What Thunder Said in *Finnegans Wake*." *Analyst*, 23 (1964), 1-29.

———. *A Second Census of FINNEGANS WAKE: An Index of the Characters and Their Roles*. Evanston, Ill.: Northwestern Univ. Press, 1963.

Glendinning, Alex. "Commentary: *Finnegans Wake*." *NA*, 126 (1939), 73-82.

Goodwin, David. "Hebrew in the *Wake*." *WN*, 9 (1972), 68-75.

Hackett, Francis. *On Judging Books*, 51-60.

Halper, Nathan. "James Joyce and the Russian General." *PR*, 18, 4 (1951), 424-31.

———. "Joyce and Eliot." *WN*, n.s. 2 (1965), 3, 3-10; 4, 17-23; 6, 22-26.

Hart, Clive. *A Concordance to FINNEGANS WAKE*. Minneapolis: Univ. of Minnesota Press, 1963; Mamaroneck, N.Y.: Appel, 1974.

———. "His Good Smetterling of Entymology." *WN*, 4, 1 (1967), 14-24.

——. "Notes on the Text of *Finnegans Wake.*" *JEGP*, 59 (1960), 229-39.

——. *Structure and Motif in FINNEGANS WAKE.* London: Faber and Faber; Evanston, Ill.: Northwestern Univ. Press, 1962.

——, and Fritz Senn, eds. *A Wake Digest.* Sydney: Sydney Univ. Press, 1968.

Hassan, Ihab H. *Paracriticisms*, 77-94.

Hayman, David. "Dramatic Motion in *Finnegans Wake.*" *StudiesE*, 37 (1958), 155-76.

——. "Farcical Themes and Forms in *Finnegans Wake.*" *JJQ*, 11 (1974), 323-42.

——, ed. *A First-Draft Version of FINNEGANS WAKE.* Austin: Univ. of Texas Press, 1963.

——. "From *Finnegans Wake*: A Sentence in Progress." *PMLA*, 73 (1958), 136-54.

——. "Tristan and Isolde in *Finnegans Wake*: A Study of the Sources and Evolution of a Theme." *CLS*, 1 (1964), 93-112.

Henseler, Donna L. " 'Harpsidichord', the Formal Principle of HCE, ALP, and the Cad." *JJQ*, 6 (1968), 53-68.

Higginson, Fred H. *Anna Livia Plurabelle: The Making of a Chapter.* Minneapolis: Univ. of Minnesota Press, 1960.

——. "Notes on the Text of *Finnegans Wake.*" *JEGP*, 55 (1956), 451-56.

Hodgart, M. J. C. "The Earliest Sections of *Finnegans Wake.*" *JJR*, 1, 1 (1957), 3-18.

Howarth, Robert Guy. *Literary Particles*, 42-55.

Jarrell, Mackie L. "Swiftiana in *Finnegans Wake.*" *ELH*, 26 (1959), 271-94.

Johnston, Denis. "Clarify Begins at: The Non-Information of *Finnegans Wake.*" *MR*, 5 (1964), 357-64.

Jolas, Eugene. "The Revolution of the Word." *ModQ*, 5 (1929), 273-92.

——, Paul Elliott, and Robert Sage. "First Aid to the Enemy." *Transition*, 9 (1927), 161-76.

Kelleher, John V. "Identifying the Irish Printed Sources for *Finnegans Wake.*" *IUR*, 1, 2 (1971), 161-77.

Kenner, Hugh. "The Search for Joyce." *PrS*, 36 (1962), 19-24.

Kiralis, Karl. "Joyce and Blake: A Basic Source for *Finnegans Wake.*" *MFS*, 4 (1958), 329-34.

Knuth, Leo. "*Finnegans Wake*: A Product of the Twenties." *JJQ*, 11 (1974), 310-22.

——. "Shem's Riddle of the Universe." *WN*, 9 (1972), 79-88; 11 (1974), 93-103.

Koch, Ronald J. "Giordano Bruno and *Finnegans Wake*: A New Look at Shaun's Objection to the 'Nolanus Theory'." *JJQ*, 9 (1971), 237-49.

Kopper, Edward A., Jr. "Some Additional Christian Allusions in *Wake*." *Analyst*, 24 (1965), 5-24.

Kumar, Shiv K. "Space-Time Polarity in *Finnegans Wake*." *MP*, 54 (1957), 230-33.

Leavis, F. R. "Joyce and the 'Revolution of the Word'." *Scrutiny*, 2, 2 (1933), 193-201.

Levin, Harry. "On First Looking into *Finnegans Wake*." *New Directions in Prose and Poetry, 1939*. Ed. James Laughlin, 253-87.

Litz, A. Walton. *The Art of James Joyce: Method and Design in ULYSSES and FINNEGANS WAKE*. London: Oxford Univ. Press, 1961; rev. New York: Oxford Univ. Press, 1964.

––––––. "The Evolution of Joyce's Anna Livia Plurabelle." *PQ*, 36 (1957), 36-48.

McLuhan, Eric. "The Rhetorical Structure of *Finnegans Wake*." *JJQ*, 11 (1974), 394-404.

McMillan, Dougald. *Transition*, 179-231, 279-84.

Magalaner, Marvin. "The Myth of Man: Joyce's *Finnegans Wake*." *UKCR*, 16 (1950), 265-77.

Malings, Ron. "Cricketers at the Wake." *JJQ*, 7 (1970), 333-49.

Mink, Louis O. "Reading *Finnegans Wake*." *SHR*, 9 (1975), 1-16.

Misra, B. P. "Joyce's Use of Indian Philosophy in *Finnegans Wake*." *IJES*, 1 (1960), 70-78.

Montgomery, Niall. "The Pervigilium Phoenicis." *NMQ*, 23 (1953), 437-72.

Morris, Wright. *The Territory Ahead*, 218-21.

Morse, J. Mitchell. "Cain, Abel, and Joyce." *ELH*, 22 (1955), 48-60.

––––––. "H C E's Chaste Ecstasy." *YR*, 56 (1967), 397-405.

––––––. "Jacob and Esau in *Finnegans Wake*." *MP*, 52 (1954), 123-30.

Norris, Margot C. "The Consequence of Deconstruction: A Technical Perspective of Joyce's *Finnegans Wake*." *ELH*, 41 (1974), 130-48.

––––––. "The Function of Mythic Repetition in *Finnegans Wake*." *JJQ*, 11 (1974), 343-54.

––––––. "The Language of Dream in *Finnegans Wake*." *L&P*, 24 (1974), 4-11.

O'Brien, Darcy C. "The Twins That Tick Homo Vulgaris: A Study of Shem and Shaun." *MFS*, 12 (1966), 183-99.

O'Hehir, Brendan. "Anna Livia Plurabelle's Gaelic Ancestry." *JJQ*, 2 (1965), 158-66.

James Joyce, continued

_____. A Gaelic Lexicon for FINNEGANS WAKE, and Glossary for Joyce's Other Works. Berkeley: Univ. of California Press, 1967.
Peery, William. "Shakhisbeard at Finnegans Wake." StudiesE, 30 (1951), 243-57.
Putz, Manfred. "The Identity of the Reader in Finnegans Wake." JJQ, 11 (1974), 387-93.
Ransom, John Crowe. "The Aesthetic of Finnegans Wake." KR, 1 (1939), 424-28.
Ransom, Timothy. "The P-p-p-p-power of the Words, Words, Words: Finnegans Wake as Words Wake." JJQ, 9 (1971), 259-65.
Reed, Henry. "Joyce's Progress." Orion, 4 (1947), 131-46.
Robinson, Henry M. "The Curious Case of Thornton Wilder." Esquire, 47 (March 1957), 70-71, 124-26.
_____, and Joseph Campbell. "Unlocking the Door to Joyce." SatR, 26 (June 19, 1943), 4-6, 28.
Rodgers, W. R. "Joyce's Wake." Explorations, 5 (1955), 19-29.
Schlauch, Margaret. "The Language of James Joyce." Science and Society, 3 (1939), 482-97.
Semmler, Clement. "Some Notes on the Themes and Language of Finnegans Wake." Southerly, 15 (1954), 156-71.
Senn, Fritz. "Reading in Progress: Words and Letters in Finnegans Wake." LB, 57 (1968), 2-18.
_____, and Clive Hart, eds. A Wake Newslitter. Newcastle, N.S.W.: English Dept. of the Univ. of Newcastle. [A bi-monthly newsletter containing interpretations of brief portions of Finnegans Wake.]
Sherwood, John C. "Joyce and the Empire: Some Thoughts on Finnegans Wake." SNNTS, 1 (1969), 357-63.
Solomon, Margaret C. Eternal Geomater: The Sexual Universe of FINNEGANS WAKE. Carbondale: Southern Illinois Univ. Press; London and Amsterdam: Feffer and Simons, 1969.
Stephens, James. James, Seumas, and Jacques, 160-62.
Stewart, Douglas Alexander. The Flesh and the Spirit, 39-44.
Stoll, E. E. From Shakespeare to Joyce, 350-88.
Svendsen, John. "A Structural Analysis of a Passage from Finnegans Wake." Lang&L, 1, 1 (1971), 75-89.
Swinson, Ward. "Riddles in Finnegans Wake." TCL, 19 (1973), 165-80.
Theall, Donald F. "Sound Sense and the Enveloping Facts: Inspecting the Wit's Waste of an Unheavenly Body." ESC, 1 (1975), 97-110.
Thompson, Francis J. "A Portrait of the Artist Asleep." WestR, 14 (1950), 245-53.

159

James Joyce, continued

Thompson, John H. *"Finnegans Wake." Modern Poetry: British and American.* Ed. Kimon Friar and John Brinnin, 505-19.

Thompson, William Irwin. "The Language of *Finnegans Wake." SR,* 72 (1964), 78-90.

Tindall, William York. *A Reader's Guide to FINNEGANS WAKE.* New York: Farrar, Straus, 1969.

Troy, William. "Notes on *Finnegans Wake." PR,* 6, 4 (1939), 97-110.

Vickery, John B. *"Finnegans Wake* and Sexual Metamorphosis." *ConL,* 13 (1972), 213-42.

Von Phul, Ruth. *"Chamber Music* at the *Wake." JJQ,* 11 (1974), 355-67.

_____. "Who Sleeps at Finnegans Wake?" *JJR,* 1, 2 (1957), 23-38.

Wilder, Thornton. "Giordano Bruno's Last Meal in *Finnegans Wake." HudR,* 16 (1963), 74-79.

Wilson, Edmund. *Classics and Commercials,* 81-86, 182-89.

_____. *The Wound and the Bow,* 198-222.

Wilson, Gary. "The Old Testament Design of the Flood Episode." *WN,* 11 (1974), 48-52.

Worthington, Mabel P. "American Folk Songs in Joyce's *Finnegans Wake." AL,* 28 (1956), 197-210.

_____. "Nursery Rhymes in *Finnegans Wake." JAF,* 70 (1957), 37-48.

See also: Connolly, *Playground;* Spender, *Struggle.*

A PORTRAIT OF THE ARTIST AS A YOUNG MAN and STEPHEN HERO

Anderson, Chester G. "The Sacrificial Butter." *Accent,* 12 (1952), 3-13.

_____. "The Text of James Joyce's *A Portrait of the Artist as a Young Man." MN,* 65 (1964), 160-200.

_____. *A Word-Index to James Joyce's STEPHEN HERO.* Ridgefield, Conn.: Ridgebury, 1958.

Aspell, Joseph. "Fire Symbolism in *A Portrait of the Artist as a Young Man." UDR,* 5, 3 (1968-69), 29-39.

August, Eugene R. "Father Arnall's Use of Scripture in *A Portrait." JJQ,* 4 (1967), 275-79.

Baker, James R. "James Joyce: Esthetic Freedom and Dramatic Art." *WHR,* 5 (1951), 29-40.

Bates, Ronald. "The Correspondence of Birds to Things of the Intellect." *JJQ,* 2 (1965), 281-90.

_____. "The Tradition of the Marketplace: Joyce's Nice Use of Diction." *ESC,* 1 (1975), 203-16.

Beebe, Maurice. "Joyce and Aquinas: The Theory of Aesthetics." *PQ,* 36 (1957), 20-35.

Beja, Morris, ed. *James Joyce, DUBLINERS and A PORTRAIT OF*

THE ARTIST AS A YOUNG MAN: A Selection of Critical Essays. London: Macmillan, 1973.

Booth, Wayne C. *The Rhetoric of Fiction,* 323-36.

Brandabur, Edward. "Stephen's Aesthetic in *A Portrait of the Artist.*" *The Celtic Cross.* Ed. Ray B. Browne, William J. Roscelli, and Richard J. Loftus, 11-21.

Burrows, John. "A Sketch of Joyce's *Portrait.*" *Balcony,* 3 (1965), 23-29.

Byrd, Forrest M. "Unifying Factors in *A Portrait of the Artist as a Young Man.*" *PAPA,* 1, 3 (1975), 1-4.

Carothers, Robert L. "The Hand and Eye in Joyce's *Portrait.*" *Serif,* 4, 1 (1967), 17-29.

Carr, Duane R. "Stephen's Retreat to the Word: A Post-Victorian Fallacy." *WHR,* 28 (1974), 381-84.

Connolly, Thomas E. "Joyce's Aesthetic Theory." *UKCR,* 23 (1956), 47-50.

———, ed. *Joyce's PORTRAIT: Criticisms and Critiques.* New York: Appleton, 1962.

———. "Kinesis and Stasis: Structural Rhythm in Joyce's *Portrait.*" *URev,* 32 (1966), 21-30.

———. "*Stephen Hero* Revised." *JJR,* 3, 1-2 (1959), 40-46.

Dundes, Alan. "Re: Joyce—No In at the Womb." *MFS,* 8 (1962), 137-47.

Egri, Peter. "The Function of Dreams and Visions in *A Portrait* and *Death in Venice.*" *JJQ,* 5 (1968), 86-102.

Ellmann, Richard. "A Portrait of the Artist as Friend." *Society and Self in the Novel.* Ed. Mark Schorer, 60-77; *KR,* 18 (1956), 53-67.

Epstein, Edmund L. *The Ordeal of Stephen Dedalus: The Conflict of the Generations in James Joyce's A PORTRAIT OF THE ARTIST AS A YOUNG MAN.* Carbondale: Southern Illinois Univ. Press, 1973.

Evans, David. "Stephen and the Theory of Literary Kinds." *JJQ,* 11 (1974), 145-49.

Farkas, Paul D. "The Irony of the Artist as a Young Man: A Study in the Structure of Joyce's *Portrait.*" *Thoth,* 11, 3 (1971), 22-32.

Farrell, James T. *League of Frightened Philistines,* 45-59.

Feehan, Joseph, ed. *Dedalus on Crete: Essays on the Implications of Joyce's PORTRAIT.* Los Angeles: St. Thomas More Guild, Immaculate Heart Coll., 1956.

Fenichel, Robert R. "A Portrait of the Artist as a Young Orphan." *L&P,* 9 (1959), 19-22.

Fernando, Lloyd. "Language and Reality in *A Portrait of the Artist*: Joyce and Bishop Berkeley." *ArielE,* 2, 1 (1971), 78-93.

James Joyce, continued

Feshbach, Sidney. "A Dramatic First Step: A Source for Joyce's Interest in the Idea of Daedalus." *JJQ*, 8 (1971), 197-204.

_____. "A Slow and Dark Birth: A Study of the Organization of *A Portrait of the Artist as a Young Man.*" *JJQ*, 4 (1967), 289-300.

Foran, Donald J. "A Mirror Held Up to Stephen." *JJQ*, 4 (1967), 301-09.

Fortuna, Diane. "The Labyrinth as Controlling Image in Joyce's *A Portrait of the Artist as a Young Man.*" *BNYPL*, 76 (1972), 120-80.

French, Warren. "Two Portraits of the Artist: James Joyce's *Young Man*; Dylan Thomas's *Young Dog.*" *UR*, 33 (1967), 261-66.

Gabler, Hans W. "The Christmas Dinner Scene, Parnell's Death, and the Genesis of *A Portrait of the Artist as a Young Man.*" *JJQ*, 13 (1975), 27-38.

_____. "Towards a Critical Text of James Joyce's *A Portrait of the Artist as a Young Man.*" *SB*, 27 (1974), 1-53.

Geckle, George J. "Stephen Dedalus and W. B. Yeats: The Making of the Villanelle." *MFS*, 15, 1 (1969), 87-96.

Gillie, Christopher. *Character in English Literature*, 177-202.

Gordon, William A. "Submission and Autonomy: Identity Patterns in Joyce's *Portrait.*" *PsyR*, 61 4 (1974-75), 535-55.

Grayson, Thomas W. "James Joyce and Stephen Dedalus: The Theory of Aesthetics." *JJQ*, 4 (1967), 310-19.

Hackett, Francis. *Horizons*, 163-68.

_____. *On Judging Books*, 251-54.

Hancock, Leslie. *Word Index to James Joyce's PORTRAIT OF THE ARTIST*. Carbondale: Southern Illinois Univ. Press, 1967.

Harrison, Kate. "The *Portrait* Epiphany." *JJQ*, 8 (1971), 142-50.

Hayman, David. "Daedalian Imagery in *A Portrait of the Artist as a Young Man.*" *Hereditas*. Ed. Frederic Will, 31-54.

_____. "*A Portrait of the Artist as a Young Man* and *l'Education sentimentale*: The Structural Affinites." *OL*, 19 (1964), 161-75.

Helms, Denise M. "A Note on Stephen's Dream in *Portrait.*" *JJQ*, 8 (1971), 151-56.

Hennig, John. "*Stephen Hero* and *Wilhelm Meister*: A Study of Parallels." *GL&L*, 5 (1951), 22-29.

Hueffer [Ford], Ford Madox. "A Haughty and Proud Generation." *YR*, n.s. 11 (1922), 703-17.

Jack, Jane H. "Art and *The Portrait of the Artist.*" *EIC*, 5 (1955), 354-64.

Johnson, Robert G. "The Daedalus Myth in Joyce's *A Portrait of the Artist as a Young Man.*" *SIH*, 3 (1973), 17-19.

Kain, Richard M., and Robert E. Scholes, eds. "The First Version of Joyce's *Portrait*." *YR*, 49 (1960), 355-69.

Karpowitz, Stephen. "A Psychology of the Joycean Artist and Aesthetic." *UWR*, 7, 1 (1971), 56-61.

Kenner, Hugh. "Joyce's *Portrait*—A Reconsideration." *UWR*, 1, 1 (1965), 1-15.

_____. "The *Portrait* in Perspective." *KR*, 10 (1948), 361-81.

Klein, James R. "Lotts, Horse Piss, and Rotted Straw." *CE*, 34 (1973), 952-74.

Kumar, Shiv K. "Bergson and Stephen Dedalus' Aesthetic Theory." *JAAC*, 16 (1957), 124-27.

Leigh, David L. "From the Mists of Childhood: Language as Judgment of the Emerging Artist in Joyce's *A Portrait*." *JJQ*, 12 (1975), 371-79.

Lemon, Lee T. "*A Portrait of the Artist as a Young Man*: Motif as Motivation and Structure." *MFS*, 12 (1966-67), 439-50.

Link, Frederick M. "The Aesthetics of Stephen Dedalus." *PLL*, 2 (1966), 140-49.

Magalaner, Marvin, ed. *Critical Reviews of A PORTRAIT OF THE ARTIST AS A YOUNG MAN*. New York: Pocket Books, 1965.

_____. "The Humanization of Stephen Dedalus." *Mosaic*, 6, 1 (1972), 63-67.

_____. "James Mangan and Joyce's Dedalus Family." *PQ*, 31 (1952), 363-71.

_____. "Reflections on *A Portrait of the Artist*." *JJQ*, 4 (1967), 343-46.

Manso, Peter. "The Metaphoric Style of Joyce's *Portrait*." *MFS*, 13 (1967), 221-36.

Mason, Michael Y. "*Ulysses* the Sequel to *A Portrait*? Joyce's Plans for the Two Works." *ELN*, 8 (1971), 296-300.

Morris, William E., and Clifford A. Nault, eds. *Portraits of an Artist*. New York: Odyssey, 1962.

Moseley, Virginia D. "James Joyce's 'Grave of Boyhood'." *Renascence*, 13 (1960), 10-20.

_____. "Stephen Hero: 'The Last of the First'." *JJQ*, 3 (1966), 278-87.

Mueller, William R. *The Prophetic Voice in Modern Fiction*, 27-55.

Naremore, James. "Style As Meaning in *A Portrait of the Artist*." *JJQ*, 4 (1967), 331-42.

Noon, William T. "Three Young Men in Rebellion." *Thought*, 38 (1963), 559-77.

O'Dea, Richard J. "The Young Artist as Archangel." *SoR*, n.s. 3 (1967), 106-14.

James Joyce, continued

Paliwal, B. "The Artist as Creator in *A Portrait of the Artist as a Young Man.*" *LCrit*, 10, 1 (1971), 44-49.

Pascal, Roy. "The Autobiographical Novel and the Autobiography," *EIC*, 9 (1959), 134-50.

Poss, Stanley. "A Portrait of the Artist as Hard-Boiled Messiah." *MLQ*, 27 (1966), 68-79.

———. "Stephen's Words, Joyce's Attitude." *RS*, 28 (1960), 156-61.

Prescott, Joseph. "James Joyce's *Stephen Hero.*" *JEGP*, 53 (1954), 214-23.

Ranald, Margaret Loftus. "Stephen Dedalus' Vocation and the Irony of Religious Ritual." *JJQ*, 2 (1965), 97-102.

Reddick, Bryan. "The Importance of Tone in the Structural Rhythm of Joyce's *Portrait.*" *JJQ*, 6 (1969), 201-18.

Redford, Grant H. "The Role of Structure in Joyce's *Portrait.*" *MFS*, 4 (1958), 21-30.

Robinson, K. E. "The Stream of Consciousness Technique and the Structure of Joyce's *Portrait.*" *JJQ*, 9 (1971), 63-84.

Rossman, Charles. "Stephen Dedalus and the Spiritual-Heroic Refrigerating Apparatus: Art and Life in Joyce's *Portrait.*" *Forms of Modern British Fiction.* Ed. Alan W. Friedman, 101-31.

———. "Stephen Dedalus' Villanelle." *JJQ*, 12 (1975), 281-93.

Ryf, Robert S. *A New Approach to Joyce: THE PORTRAIT OF THE ARTIST as a Guidebook.* Berkeley: Univ. of California Press, 1962.

Scholes, Robert E. "Stephen Dedalus: *Eiron* and *Alazon.*" *TSLL*, 3 (1961), 8-15.

———. "Stephen Dedalus, Poet or Esthete?" *PMLA*, 79 (1964), 484-89.

———, and Richard M. Kain, eds. *The Workshop of Daedalus: James Joyce and the Raw Materials for A PORTRAIT OF THE ARTIST AS A YOUNG MAN.* Evanston, Ill.: Northwestern Univ. Press, 1965.

Schutte, William, ed. *A PORTRAIT OF THE ARTIST AS A YOUNG MAN: A Collection of Critical Essays.* Englewood Cliffs, N.J.: Prentice-Hall, 1968.

Scotto, Robert M. " 'Visions' and 'Epiphanies': Fictional Technique in Pater's *Marius* and Joyce's *Portrait.*" *JJQ*, 11 (1973), 41-50.

Seward, Barbara. "The Artist and the Rose." *UTQ*, 26 (1957), 180-90.

Sharpless, F. Parvin. "Irony in Joyce's *Portrait*: The Stasis of Pity." *JJQ*, 4 (1967), 320-30.

Singh, V. D. "Versions of Joyce's *Portrait.*" *RUSEng*, 5 (1971), 59-67.

Smith, John B. "Image and Imagery in Joyce's *Portrait*: A Computer-Assisted Analysis." *Directions in Literary Criticism.* Ed. Stanley Weintraub and Philip Young, 220-27.

Sole, J. L. "Structure in Joyce's *A Portrait*." *Serif*, 5, 4 (1968), 9-13.

Spencer, Theodore. *"Stephen Hero*: The Unpublished Manuscript of James Joyce's *Portrait of the Artist as a Young Man*." *SoR*, 7 (1941), 174-86.

Sprinchorn, Evert. "A Portrait of the Artist as Achilles." *Approaches to the Twentieth-Century Novel*. Ed. John Unterecker, 9-50.

Squire, John C. *Books in General*, 1st ser., 225-30.

Stern, Richard G. "Proust and Joyce Underway: *Jean Santeuil* and *Stephen Hero*." *KR*, 18 (1956), 486-96.

Tarbox, Raymond. "Auditory Experience in Joyce's *Portrait*." *AI*, 27 (1970), 301-28.

Tobin, Patricia. "A Portrait of the Artist as Autobiographer: Joyce's *Stephen Hero*." *Genre*, 6 (1973), 189-203.

Turaj, Frank. " 'Araby' and *Portrait*: Stages of Pagan Conversion." *ELN*, 7 (1970), 209-13.

Van Laan, Thomas F. "The Meditative Structure of Joyce's *Portrait*." *JJQ*, 1, 3 (1964), 3-13.

Waith, Eugene M. "The Calling of Stephen Dedalus." *CE*, 18 (1957), 256-61.

Walsh, Ruth M. "That Pervasive Mass—In *Dubliners* and *A Portrait of The Artist As A Young Man*." *JJQ*, 8 (1971), 205-20.

Wasson, Richard. "Stephen Dedalus and the Imagery of Sight: A Psychological Approach." *L&P*, 15 (1965), 195-209.

Wells, H. G. "James Joyce." *New Republic*, 10 (March 10, 1917), 158-60.

Wilds, Nancy G. "Style and Auctorial Presence in *A Portrait of the Artist as a Young Man*." *Style*, 7 (1973), 39-55.

Woodward, A. G. "Technique and Feeling in James Joyce's *The Portrait of the Artist as a Young Man*." *ESA*, 4 (1961), 39-53.

See also: Buckley; Drew, *Novel*; Mueller, *Celebration*; Van Ghent.

ULYSSES

Adams, Robert M. *Surface and Symbol: The Consistency of James Joyce's ULYSSES*. New York: Oxford Univ. Press, 1962.

Ahearn, Edward J. "Religious Values in Joyce's *Ulysses*." *ChS*, 44 (1961), 139-45.

Albert, Leonard. *"Ulysses*, Cannibals, and Freemasons." *AD*, 2 (Autumn 1951), 265-83.

Aldaz, Anna-Marie. "James Joyce's *Ulysses*: A Perspective." *IH*, 11 (1975), 133-58.

Aldington, Richard. *Literary Studies and Reviews*, 192-207.

Anderson, Chester G. "Leopold Bloom as Dr. Sigmund Freud." *Mosaic*, 6, 1 (1972), 23-43.

Baker, James R. "James Joyce: Affirmation after Exile." *MLQ*, 18 (1957), 275-81.

Bard, Joseph. "Tradition and Experiment." Royal Soc. of Lit. of the U. K., London. *Essays by Divers Hands*, v. 21, 103-24.

Bauerle, Ruth. "A Sober Drunken Speech: Stephen's Parodies in 'The Oxen of the Sun'." *JJQ*, 5 (1967), 40-46.

Beach, Sylvia. *Ulysses in Paris*. New York: Harcourt, 1956.

Beausang, Michael. "Seeds for the Planting of Bloom." *Mosaic*, 6, 1 (1972), 11-22.

Beebe, Maurice. "James Joyce: Barnacle Goose and Lapwing." *PMLA*, 71 (1956), 302-20.

———. "*Ulysses* and the Age of Modernism." *JJQ*, 10 (1972), 172-88.

Begnal, Michael H. "The Mystery Man of *Ulysses*." *JML*, 2 (1972), 565-68.

Bellow, Saul. "Literature in the Age of Technology." *Technology and the Frontiers of Knowledge*, 1-22.

Benjamin, Judy-Lynn, ed. *The Celtic Bull: Essays on James Joyce's ULYSSES by Students of the Honors Seminar in ULYSSES, Hunter College*. Tulsa, Okla.: Univ. of Tulsa Press, 1967.

Bennett, Arnold. *Things That Have Interested Me*, 2d ser., 191-201.

Bennett, John Z. "Unposted Letter: Joyce's Leopold Bloom." *BuR*, 14, 1 (1966), 1-13.

Benstock, Bernard. "*Ulysses* Without Dublin." *JJQ*, 10 (1972), 90-117.

Benstock, Shari. "*Ulysses* as Ghoststory." *JJQ*, 12 (1975), 396-413.

Bierman, Robert. "*Ulysses* and *Finnegans Wake*: The Explicit, the Implicit, and the Tertium Quid." *Renascence*, 11, 1 (1958) 14-19.

Biro, Diana. "Leopold in Noman's Land: The 5:00 Chapter of *Ulysses*." *Thoth*, 11, 3 (1971), 9-21.

Blackmur, R. P. "The Jew in Search of a Son." *VQR*, 24 (1948), 96-116.

———. *A Primer of Ignorance*, 59-80.

Blamires, Harry. *The Bloomsday Book: A Guide Through Joyce's ULYSSES*. London: Methuen, 1966.

Blodgett, Harriet. "Joyce's Time Mind in *Ulysses*: A New Emphasis." *JJQ*, 5 (1967), 22-29.

Bowen, Zack. "The Bronzegold Sirensong: A Musical Analysis of the Sirens Episode in Joyce's *Ulysses*." *Literary Monographs*, v.1.Ed. Eric Rothstein and Thomas K. Dunseath, 247-98, 319-20.

Boyd, Elizabeth F. "James Joyce's Hell-Fire Sermons." *MLN*, 75 (1960), 561-71.

Boyle, Robert. "*Ulysses* as Frustrated Sonata Form." *JJQ*, 2 (1965), 247-54.

Briand, Paul L., Jr. "The Catholic Mass in James Joyce's *Ulysses*." *JJQ*, 5 (1968), 312-22.

Brivic, Sheldon R. "Time, Sexuality and Identity in Joyce's *Ulysses*." *JJQ*, 7 (1969), 30-51.

Brooks, Cleanth. "Joyce's *Ulysses*: Symbolic Poem, Biography, or Novel?" *Imagined Worlds*. Ed. Maynard Mack and Ian Gregor, 419-39.

Brown, Alec. "Joyce's *Ulysses* and the Novel." *DM*, 9 (January-March 1934), 41-50.

Bryer, Jackson R. "Joyce, *Ulysses*, and the *Little Review*." *SAQ*, 66 (1967), 148-64.

Budgen, Frank. *James Joyce and the Making of ULYSSES*. London: Grayson, 1934, 1937; New York: Harrison Smith and Robert Haas, 1934; Bloomington: Indiana Univ. Press, 1960; London: Oxford Univ. Press, 1972.

Burgess, Anthony. "The *Ulysses* Sentence." *JJQ*, 9 (1972), 423-35.

Burgum, Edwin B. *The Novel and the World's Dilemma*, 95-108.

_____. " 'Ulysses' and the Impasse of Individualism." *VQR*, 17 (1941), 561-73.

Busch, Frederick. "The Friction of Fiction: a *Ulysses* Omnirandum." *ChiR*, 26, 4 (1975), 5-17.

Byrd, Don. "Joyce's Method of Philosophic Fiction." *JJQ*, 5 (1967), 9-21.

Canby, Henry S. *American Estimates*, 170-77.

Card, James Van Dyck. " 'Contradicting': The Word for Joyce's 'Penelope'." *JJQ*, 11 (1973), 17-26.

Carver, Craig. "Moly: Bloom's Preservative; Correspondence and Function in *Ulysses*." *JJQ*, 12 (1975), 414-22.

Cole, David W. "Fugal Structure in the Sirens Episode of *Ulysses*." *MFS*, 19 (1973), 221-26.

Cope, Jackson I. "The Rhythmic Gesture: Image and Gesture in Joyce's *Ulysses*." *ELH*, 29 (1962), 67-89.

_____. "*Ulysses*: Joyce's Kabbalah." *JJQ*, 7 (1970), 93-113.

Cronin, Anthony. "A Question of Modernity." *XR*, 1 (1960), 283-92.

_____. *A Question of Modernity*, 58-96.

Curtius, Ernst R. *Essays on European Literature*, 327-54.

_____. "Technique and Thematic Development in James Joyce." *Transition*, 16-17 (1929), 310-25.

Cwiakala, Jadwiga. "Homeric Parody in James Joyce's *Ulysses*." *KN*, 18 (1971), 57-68.

Dahl, Liisa. "The Linguistic Presentation of the Interior Monologue in James Joyce's *Ulysses*." *JJQ*, 7 (1970), 114-19.

James Joyce, continued

Daiches, David. *New Literary Values*, 69-82.

Dalton, Jack P. "The Text of *Ulysses.*" *Eire*, 7, 2 (1972), 67-83.

Davidson, Donald. "Decorum in the Novel." *ModA*, 9 (1964-65), 34-48.

Day, R. A. "Joyce's Waste Land and Eliot's Unknown God." *Literary Monographs* v. 4. Ed. Eric Rothstein, 137-206.

DiBernard, Barbara. "Parallax as Parallel: Paradigm and Paradox in *Ulysses.*" *Eire*, 10, 1 (1975), 69-84.

Duncan, Edward. "Unsubstantial Father: A Study of the *Hamlet* Symbolism in Joyce's *Ulysses.*" *UTQ*, 19 (1950), 126-40.

Duncan, Joseph E. "The Modality of the Audible in Joyce's *Ulysses.*" *PMLA*, 72 (1957), 286-95.

Edwards, Calvin R. "The Hamlet Motif in Joyce's *Ulysses.*" *WestR*, 15 (1950), 5-13.

Egri, Peter. *Avantgardism and Modernity: A Comparison of James Joyce's ULYSSES with Thomas Mann's DER ZAUBERBERG and LOTTE IN WEIMAR*. Tr. Paul Aston. Budapest: Akad. Kiado; Tulsa, Okla.: Univ. of Tulsa Press, 1972.

_____. *"Natura naturans*: An Approach to the Poetic Reflection of Reality—The Aspect of Poetry in the Proteus Episode of James Joyce's *Ulysses.*" *ALitASH*, 15 (1973), 379-417.

Eliot, T. S. "*Ulysses*, Order, and Myth." *Dial*, 75 (November 1923), 480-83.

Ellmann, Richard. "The Backgrounds of *Ulysses.*" *KR*, 16 (1954), 337-86.

_____. "James Joyce's *Ulysses.*" *Inventario*, 17, 1 (1962), 22-33.

_____. "Ulysses, the Divine Nobody." *YR*, 47 (1957), 56-71; *Twelve Original Essays on Great English Novels*. Ed. Charles Shapiro, 233-51.

Empson, William. "The Theme of *Ulysses.*" *KR*, 18 (1956), 26-52.

Evans, William A. "Wordagglutinations in Joyce's *Ulysses.*" *SLitI*, 3, 2 (1970), 27-36.

Fáj, Attila. "Probable Byzantine and Hungarian Models of *Ulysses* and *Finnegans Wake.*" *Arcadia*, 3 (1968), 48-72.

Ferris, William R., Jr. "*Ulysses*: A Reexamination of Artistic Rebellion." *JSCR*, 4, 1 (1972), 1-12.

Fiedler, Leslie. "Bloom on Joyce; or, Jokey for Jacob." *JML*, 1 (1970), 19-29.

Finholt, Richard D. "Method in the Cyclops Episode: Joyce on the Nature of Epic Heroes in the Modern World." *UDR*, 9, 1 (1972), 3-13.

Fitzpatrick, William P. "The Myth of Creation: Joyce, Jung, and *Ulysses.*" *JJQ*, 11 (1974), 123-44.

Fleishman, Avrom. "Science in Ithaca." *WSCL*, 8 (1967), 377-91.

Foran, Donald J. "A Mirror Held Up to Stephen." *JJQ*, 4 (1967), 301-09.

Ford, Ford Madox. "*Ulysses* and the Handling of Indecencies." *ER*, 35 (1922), 538-48.

Ford, Hugh D. *Published in Paris*, 3-33.

Geckle, George L. "Stephen Dedalus as Lapwing: A Symbolic Center of *Ulysses*." *JJQ*, 6 (1968), 104-14.

Gifford, Don, with Robert J. Seidman. *Notes for Joyce: An Annotation of James Joyce's ULYSSES*. New York: Dutton, 1974.

Gilbert, Stuart. *James Joyce's ULYSSES: A Study*. London: Faber and Faber; New York: Knopf, 1930, 1934, rev. 1952.

Gill, Richard. "The 'Corporal Works of Mercy' as a Moral Pattern in Joyce's *Ulysses*." *TCL*, 9 (1963), 17-21.

Goldberg, S. L. "Art and Freedom: the Aesthetic of *Ulysses*." *ELH*, 24 (1957), 44-64.

―――. *The Classical Temper: A Study of James Joyce's ULYSSES*. London: Chatto and Windus; New York: Barnes and Noble, 1961.

―――. "The Conception of History in Joyce's *Ulysses*." *Present Opinion*, 2 (1947), 62-65.

Goldknopf, David. "Realism in the Novel." *YR*, 60 (1970), 69-84.

Goodwin, Murray. "Three Wrong Turns in 'Ulysses'." *WestR*, 15 (1951), 221-25.

Greenway, John. "A Guide Through James Joyce's *Ulysses*." *CE*, 17 (1955), 67-78.

Groden, Michael. " 'Cyclops' in Progress, 1919." *JJQ*, 12 (1975), 123-68.

Gross, Harvey. "From Barabas to Bloom: Notes on the Figure of the Jew." *WHR*, 11 (1957), 149-56.

Grossvogel, David I. *Limits of the Novel*, 256-99.

Hall, Vernon, and Gene Arnold Rister. "Joyce's *Ulysses* and Homer's *Odyssey*." *Complit-Litcomp*, 1 (1973), 12-58.

Hamalian, Leo. "The 'Gift of Guilt' in *Ulysses*." *Renascence*, 19 (1966), 21-29.

Hanley, Miles L. (with the assistance of Martin Joos, Theresa Fein, and others). *Word Index to James Joyce's ULYSSES*. Madison: Univ. of Wisconsin Press, 1937, 1951.

Hardy, Anne. "A Fugal Analysis of the Siren Episode in Joyce's *Ulysses*." *MSE*, 2, 3 (1970), 59-67.

Hardy, Barbara. "Form as End and Means in *Ulysses*." *OL*, 19 (1964), 194-200.

Harkness, Marguerite. " 'Circe': The Mousetrap of *Ulysses*." *JJQ*, 12 (1975), 259-72.

Harris, Wendell V. "Molly's 'Yes': The Transvaluation of Sex in Modern Fiction." *TSLL*, 10 (1968), 107-18.

James Joyce, continued

Hart, Clive. *James Joyce's ULYSSES*. University Park: Penn. State Univ. Press; Sydney, Australia: Sydney Univ. Press; London: Methuen, 1968.

———, and David Hayman, eds. *James Joyce's ULYSSES: Critical Essays*. Berkeley: Univ. of California Press, 1974.

———, and Leo Knutt. *A Topographical Guide to James Joyce's ULYSSES*, 2 vol. Colchester, Eng.: Wake Newslitter Press, 1975.

Hayman, David. "Forms of Folly in Joyce: A Study of Clowning in *Ulysses*." *ELH*, 34 (1967), 260-83.

———. *ULYSSES: The Mechanics of Meaning*. Englewood Cliffs, N.J.: Prentice-Hall, 1970.

Henig, Suzanne. "*Ulysses* in Bloomsbury." *JJQ*, 10 (1973), 203-08.

Henke, Suzette A. "Joyce's Bloom: Beyond Sexual Possessiveness." *AI*, 32 (1975), 329-34.

Heppenstall, Rayner. *The Fourfold Tradition*, 131-59.

Herring, Phillip F. "The Bedsteadfastness of Molly Bloom." *MFS*, 15, 1 (1969), 49-62.

———. "Experimentation with a Landscape: Pornotopography in *Ulysses*—The Phallocy of Imitative Form." *MFS*, 20 (1974), 371-78.

Higgins, Bertram. "The Natural Pander: Leopold Bloom and the Others." *CalML*, 1 (1925), 139-46.

Huddleston, Sisley. *Articles de Paris*, 41-47.

Iser, Wolfgang. *The Implied Reader*, 179-233.

———. "Indeterminacy and the Reader's Response in Prose Fiction." *Aspects of Narrative*. Ed. J. Hillis Miller, 33-39.

Jenkins, Ralph. "Theosophy in 'Scylla and Charybdis'." *MFS*, 15, 1 (1969), 35-48.

Jerrell, Mackie L. "Joyce's Use of Swift's *Polite Conversation* in the 'Circe' Episode of *Ulysses*." *PMLA*, 72 (1957), 545-54.

Jones, Alun. "Portrait of the Artist as Himself." *CritQ*, 2 (1960), 40-46.

Jones, W. Powell. "The Common Reader and James Joyce's *Ulysses*." *ASch*, 21 (1952), 161-71.

Jung, C. G. "*Ulysses*: A Monologue" [1932]. *Nimbus* (London), 2, 1 (1952), 7-20; rpt. in *The Spirit of Man, Art, and Literature*, by C. G. Jung. Tr. R. F. C. Hull. Princeton, N.J.: Princeton Univ. Press, 1966, 109-34.

Kain, Richard. *Fabulous Voyager*. Chicago: Univ. of Chicago Press, 1947; rev. New York: Viking, 1959.

———. "The Significance of Stephen's Meeting Bloom: A Survey of Interpretations." *JJQ*, 10 (1972), 147-60.

———. "*Ulysses* as a Classic: Some Anniversary Reconsiderations." *Mosaic*, 6, 1 (1972), 57-62.

Kelly, H. A. "Consciousness in the Monologues of *Ulysses.*" *MLQ*, 24 (1963), 3-12.

Kenner, Hugh. "Baker Street to Eccles Street: The Odyssey of a Myth" *HudR*, 1 (1949), 481-99.

———. "Joyce's *Ulysses*: Homer and Hamlet." *EIC*, 2 (1952), 85-104.

———. "Molly's Masterstroke." *JJQ*, 10 (1972), 19-28.

Killham, John. " 'Ineluctable Modality' in Joyce's *Ulysses.*" *UTQ*, 34 (1965), 269-89.

Kimball, Jean. "The Hypostasis in *Ulysses.*" *JJQ*, 10 (1973), 422-38.

Kimpel, Ben D. "The Voices of *Ulysses.*" *Style*, 9 (1975), 283-319.

Klein, A. M. "The Black Panther." *Accent*, 10 (1950), 139-55.

———. "The Oxen of the Sun." *Here and Now*, 1 (1949), 28-48.

Knight, Douglas. "The Reading of *Ulysses.*" *ELH*, 19 (1952), 64-80.

Knight, G. Wilson. *Neglected Powers*, 148-55.

———. "Lawrence, Joyce, and Powys." *EIC*, 11 (1961), 403-17.

Knuth, Leo. "A Bathymetric Reading of Joyce's *Ulysses*, Chapter X." *JJQ*, 9 (1972), 405-22.

———. "James Joyce's *Ulysses*, Chapter X: *Wandering Rocks.*" *Lang&L*, 1, 2 (1972), 30-54.

Koch, Vivienne. "An Approach to the Homeric Content of Joyce's *Ulysses.*" *MarQ*, 1 (1944), 119-30.

Kopper, Edward A., Jr. "*Ulysses* and James Joyce's Use of Comedy." *Mosaic*, 6, 1 (1972), 45-55.

Kuehn, Robert E. "Mr. Bloom and Mr. Joyce: A Note on 'Heroism' in *Ulysses.*" *WSCL*, 4 (1963), 209-15.

Lane, Mervin. "A Synecdochic Reading of 'Wandering Rocks' in *Ulysses.*" *WHR*, 28 (1974), 125-40.

Lee, Robin. "Patterns of Sympathy and Judgement in *Ulysses.*" *ESA*, 14 (1971), 37-48.

Leithauser, Gladys G., and Paul Sporn. "Hypsospadia: Linguistic Guidepost to the Themes of the 'Circe' Episode of *Ulysses.*" *JML*, 4 (1974), 109-14.

Lennam, T. "The Happy Hunting Ground." *UTQ*, 29 (1960), 386-97.

LeRoy, Gaylord C., and Ursula Beitz, eds. *Preserve and Create*, 96-99.

Levenston, E. A. "Narrative Technique in *Ulysses*: A Stylistic Comparison of 'Telemachus' and 'Eumaeus'." *Lang&S*, 5 (1972), 260-75.

Leventhal, A. J. "The Jew Errant." *Dubliner*, 2 (1963), 11-24.

Levin, Lawrence L. "The Sirens Episode as Music: Joyce's Experiment in Prose Polyphony." *JJQ*, 3 (1965), 12-24.

Levitt, Morton P. "A Hero for Our Time: Leopold Bloom and the Myth of *Ulysses.*" *JJQ*, 10 (1972), 132-46.

Lewis, Wyndham. *Time and Western Man*, 91-130.

Linn, James W., and H. W. Taylor. *A Foreword to Fiction*, 103-6.

Littmann, Mark E., and Charles A. Schweighauser. "Astronomical Allusions, Their Meaning and Purpose in *Ulysses*." *JJQ*, 2 (1965), 238-46.

Litz, A. Walton. *The Art of James Joyce: Method and Design in ULYSSES and FINNEGANS WAKE*. London: Oxford Univ. Press, 1961; rev. New York: Oxford Univ. Press, 1964.

_____. "Early Vestiges of Joyce's *Ulysses*." *PMLA*, 71 (1956), 51-60.

_____. "The Genre of *Ulysses*." *The Theory of the Novel*. Ed. John Halperin, 109-20.

_____. "Joyce's Notes for the Last Episodes of *Ulysses*." *MFS*, 4 (1958), 3-20.

_____. "The Last Adventure of *Ulysses*." *PULC*, 28 (1967), 63-75.

_____. "Pound and Eliot on *Ulysses*: The Critical Tradition." *JJQ*, 10 (1972), 5-18.

Loehrich, Rolf R. *The Secret of ULYSSES: An Analysis of James Joyce's ULYSSES*. McHenry, Ill.: Compass, 1953.

Loeppert, Elsberth. "The Prophecy of *Ulysses*." *Cresset*, 35, 5 (1972), 10-12.

Lorch, Thomas M. "The Relationship Between *Ulysses* and *The Waste Land*." *TSLL*, 6 (1964), 123-33.

Lord, George de F. "The Heroes of *Ulysses* and Their Homeric Proto- types." *YR*, 62 (1972), 43-58.

McAleer, Edward C. "The Ignorance of Mr. Bloom." *Studies in Honor of Hodges and Thaler*. Ed. Richard Beale Davis and John L. Lievsay, 121-29.

McCarroll, David L. "Stephen's Dream—and Bloom's." *JJQ*, 6 (1968), 174-76.

McCarthy, Patrick A. "The Riddle in Joyce's *Ulysses*." *TSLL*, 17 (1975), 193-205.

McCole, Camille. "*Ulysses*." *CathW*, 138 (1934), 722-28.

McDonald, James L., and Norman G. McKendrick. "The Family in the *Odyssey* and *Ulysses*." *IFR*, 2 (1975), 143-49.

McMillan, Dougald. "Influences of Gerhardt Hauptmann in Joyce's *Ulysses*." *JJQ*, 4 (1967), 107-19.

McNelly, Willis E. "Liturgical Deviations in *Ulysses*." *JJQ*, 2 (1965), 291-98.

Maddox, James H., Jr. " 'Eumaeus' and the Theme of Return in *Ulysses*." *TSLL*, 16 (1974), 211-20.

Madtes, Richard E. "Joyce and the Building of Ithaca." *ELH*, 31 (1964), 443-59.

Magalaner, Marvin. "Leopold Bloom Before *Ulysses*." *MLN*, 68, 3 (1953), 110-12.

Marre, K. E. "Experimentation with a Symbol from Mythology: The Courses of the Comets in the 'Ithaca' Chapter of *Ulysses.*" *MFS*, 20 (1974), 385-90.

Mason, Michael. *James Joyce: ULYSSES.* London: E. Arnold, 1972.

──────. "*Ulysses* the Sequel to *A Portrait*? Joyce's Plans for the Two Works." *ELN*, 8 (1971), 296-300.

Meagher, J. A. "A Dubliner Reads *Ulysses.*" *AusQ*, 17, 2 (1945), 74-86.

Melchiori, Giorgio. "The Wandering Rocks, or, The Rejection of Stephen Dedalus." English Association, London. *Essays and Studies*, n.s., v. 28 (1975), 58-75.

──────. "*The Waste Land* and *Ulysses.*" *ES*, 35 (1954), 56-68.

Milner, Ian. "The Heroic and the Mock-Heroic in James Joyce's *Ulysses.*" *PP*, 2 (1959), 37-45.

Morse, J. Mitchell. "Augustine, Ayenbite, and *Ulysses.*" *PMLA*, 70 (1955), 1143-59.

Mosely, Virginia. "The Martha-Mary Theme in *Ulysses.*" *MQ*, 4 (1963), 165-78.

Murry, J. Middleton. "The Break-up of the Novel." *YR*, n.s. 12 (1923), 288-304.

Nassar, Eugene P. *The Rape of Cinderella*, 59-70.

Noon, William T. " 'Song the Syrens Sang'." *Mosaic*, 6, 1 (1972), 77-83.

Novak, Jane. "Verisimilitude and Vision: Defoe and Blake as Influences on Joyce's Molly Bloom." *Carrell*, 8, 1 (1967), 7-20.

Parr, Mary. *James Joyce: The Poetry of Conscience, A Study of ULYSSES.* Milwaukee: Inland, 1961.

Paterakis, Deborah T. "Keylessness, Sex and the Promised Land: Associated Themes in *Ulysses.*" *Eire*, 8, 1 (1973), 97-108.

Pearce, Richard. "Experimentation with the Grotesque: Comic Collisions in the Grotesque World of *Ulysses.*" *MFS*, 20 (1974), 378-84.

Peery, William. "The Hamlet of Stephen Dedalus." *StudiesE*, 31 (1952), 109-19.

Peradotto, John J. "A Liturgical Pattern in *Ulysses.*" *MLN*, 75 (1960), 321-26.

Pinsker, Sanford. "*Ulysses* and the Post-Modern Temper." *MQ*, 15 (1974), 406-16.

Poss, Stanley. "*Ulysses* and the Comedy of the Immobilized Act." *ELH*, 24 (1957), 65-83.

Prescott, Joseph. "The Characterization of Stephen Dedalus in *Ulysses.*" *LM*, 9 (1959), 145-63.

──────. "Homer's *Odyssey* and Joyce's *Ulysses.*" *MLQ*, 3 (1942), 427-44.

──────. "James Joyce: A Study in Words." *PMLA*, 54 (1939), 304-15.

James Joyce, continued

——. "Local Allusions in Joyce's *Ulysses*." *PMLA*, 68 (1953), 1223-28.

——. "Notes on Joyce's *Ulysses*." *MLQ*, 13 (1952), 149-62.

Radford, F. L. " 'Christfox in Leather Trews': The Quaker in the Library in *Ulysses*." *ELH*, 39 (1972), 441-58.

Rankin, H. D. "James Joyce's Satyr-Play: The 'Cyclops' Episode in *Ulysses*." *Agora*, 2, 2 (1973), 3-12.

Raspa, Richard. "The 'Wandering Rocks' of *Ulysses*." *LHY*, 16, 1 (1975), 131-52.

Richardson, Robert O. "Molly's Last Words." *TCL*, 12 (1967), 177-85.

Rogers, Howard E. "Irish Myth and the Plot of *Ulysses*." *ELH*, 15 (1948), 306-27.

Rogers, William G., William York Tindall, and Lyman Bryson. "*Ulysses*." *Invitation to Learning*. Ed. George D. Crothers, 198-207.

Russell, H. K. "The Incarnation in *Ulysses*." *MFS*, 4 (1958), 53-61.

Russell, Stanley C. "A Baedeker to Bloom." *JJQ*, 3 (1966), 226-35.

Sayler, Oliver M. "Long Day's Journey into 'Nighttown'." *TAr*, 43 (January 1959), 57-61.

Scholes, Robert. "*Ulysses*: A Structuralist Perspective." *JJQ*, 10 (1972), 161-71.

Schutte, William M. *Joyce and Shakespeare: A Study in the Meaning of ULYSSES.* New Haven: Yale Univ. Press, 1957.

——. "Leopold Bloom: A Touch of the Artist." *JJQ*, 10 (1972), 118-31.

Schwartsman, Myron. "The V.A.8 Copybook: An Early Draft of the 'Cyclops' Chapter of *Ulysses* with Notes on Its Development." *JJQ*, 12 (1975), 64-122.

Schwartz, Lewis M. "Eccles Street and Canterbury: An Approach to Molly Bloom." *TCL*, 15 (1969), 155-65.

Senn, Fritz. "Book of Many Turns." *JJQ*, 10 (1972), 29-46.

——. "Seven Against *Ulysses*." *JJQ*, 4 (1967), 170-93.

Seward, Barbara. "The Artist and the Rose." *UTQ*, 26 (1957), 180-90.

Shapiro, Stephen A. "Leopold Bloom and Gulley Jimson: The Economics of Survival." *TCL*, 10 (1964), 3-11.

Shechner, Mark. *Joyce in Nighttown: A Psychoanalytic Inquiry into ULYSSES.* Berkeley: Univ. of California Press, 1974.

Silverstein, Norman. "Magic on the Notesheets of the Circe Episode." *JJQ*, 1, 4 (1964), 19-26.

Smith, Don N. "Musical Form and Principles in the Scheme of *Ulysses*." *TCL*, 18 (1972), 79-92.

Smith, Paul J. *A Key to the ULYSSES of James Joyce.* New York: Covici, 1934.

James Joyce, continued

Staley, Harry C. "The Spheretual Exercises of Dedalus and Bloom."
JJQ, 10 (1973), 209-14.
Staley, Thomas F. "The Irish Exile in Paris: James Joyce and George
Moore." *ULYSSES: Cinquante ans Après*. Ed. Louis Bonnerot,
with Jean Jacquot and Claude Jaquet, 15-22.
_____. "*Ulysses*: Fifty Years in the Joycean Conundrum." *Mosaic*, 6, 1
(1972), 69-76.
_____, ed. *ULYSSES: Fifty Years*. Bloomington: Indiana Univ. Press,
1974.
_____, and Bernard Benstock, eds. *Approaches to ULYSSES: Ten
Essays*. Pittsburgh: Univ. of Pittsburgh Press, 1970.
Stanford, W. B. *The Ulysses Theme: A Study in the Adaptability of a
Traditional Hero*. Oxford: Blackwell, 1954, 211-25.
Stavrou, C. N. "Mr. Bloom and Nikos' Odysseus." *SAQ*, 62 (1963),
107-18.
Stein, Sol. "The Aesthetics of James Joyce's *Ulysses*." *UKCR*, 18
(1952), 241-54.
Steinberg, Erwin R. "A Book with a Molly in It." *JJR*, 2, 1-2 (1958),
55-62.
_____. "Introducing the Stream-of-Consciousness Technique in
Ulysses." *Style*, 2 (1968), 49-58.
_____. " 'Lestrygonions,' A Pale 'Proteus'?" *MFS*, 15, 1 (1969), 73-86.
_____. "The Proteus Episode: Signature of Stephen Dedalus." *JJQ*, 5
(1968), 187-98.
_____. "Rogue's Rum Lingo: The Language of Stephen, Bloom, and
Molly." *A Modern Miscellany*. Ed. David P. Demarest, Jr., et al.,
21-30.
_____. *The Stream of Consciousness and Beyond in ULYSSES*. Pitts-
burgh: Univ. of Pittsburgh Press, 1973.
Stephens, James. *James, Seumas, and Jacques*. 156-59.
Stern, Frederick C. "Pyrrhus, Fenians and Bloom." *JJQ*, 5 (1968),
211-28.
Sternfeld, Frederick W. "Poetry and Music: Joyce's *Ulysses*." *Sound
and Poetry*. Ed. Northrop Frye, 16-54.
Stewart, Douglas Alexander. *The Flesh and the Spirit*, 45-52.
Sultan, Stanley. *The Argument of ULYSSES*. Columbus: Ohio State
Univ. Press, 1965.
_____. "Joyce's Irish Politics: The Seventh Chapter of *Ulysses*." *MR*, 2
(1961), 549-56.
_____. "The Sirens at the Ormond Bar: *Ulysses*." *UKCR*, 26 (1959),
83-92.

Summerhayes, Don. "Joyce's *Ulysses* and Whitman's 'Self': A Query." *WSCL*, 4 (1963), 216-24.

Survant, Joseph. "The Idea of History in James Joyce's *Ulysses*." *PCL*, 1, 2 (1975), 3-19.

Swanson, Roy A. "Edible Wandering Rocks: The Pun as Allegory in Joyce's 'Lestrygonians'." *Genre*, 5 (1972), 385-403.

Thornton, Weldon. "An Allusion List for James Joyce's *Ulysses*." *JJQ*, 1, 1 (1963), 17-25; 1, 2 (1964), 2-9; 1, 3 (1964), 25-41; 1, 4 (1964), 7-13.

————. *Allusions in ULYSSES: An Annotated List.* Chapel Hill: Univ. of North Carolina Press, 1968.

Thrane, James R. "Joyce's Sermon on Hell: Its Source and Its Backgrounds." *MP*, 57 (1960), 172-98.

Timpe, Eugene F. "*Ulysses* and the Archetypal Feminine." *Perspectives in Literary Symbolism.* Ed. Joseph Strelka, 199-213.

Tindall, William York. "Mosaic Bloom." *Mosaic*, 6, 1 (1972), 3-9.

Tolomeo, Diane. "The Final Octagon of *Ulysses*." *JJQ*, 10 (1973), 439-54.

Tomasi, Barbara R. "The Fraternal Theme in Joyce's *Ulysses*." *AI*, 30 (1973), 177-91.

Tompkins, Phillip K. "James Joyce and the Enthymeme: The Seventh Episode of *Ulysses*." *JJQ*, 5 (1968), 199-205.

Tracy, Robert. "Leopold Bloom Fourfold: A Hungarian-Hebraic-Hellenic-Hibernian Hero." *MR*, 6 (1965), 523-38.

Troy, William. "Stephen Dedalus and James Joyce." *Nation*, 138 (1934), 187-88.

van der Vat, D. G. "Paternity in *Ulysses*." *ES*, 19 (1937), 145-58.

Visser, Gerald J. "James Joyce's *Ulysses* and Anglo-Irish." *ES*, 24 (1942), 45-56, 79-90.

Vogel, Jane. "The Consubstantial Family of Stephen Dedalus." *JJQ*, 2 (1965), 109-32.

Von Abele, Rudolph. "*Ulysses*: The Myth of Myth." *PMLA*, 69 (1954), 358-64.

Von Phul, Ruth. "The Boast of Heraldry in the 'Proteus' Episode of *Ulysses*." *JML*, 1 (1971), 399-405.

Walcott, William. "Notes by a Jungian Analyst on the Dreams in *Ulysses*." *JJQ*, 9 (1971), 37-48.

Walsh, Ruth M. "In the Name of the Father and of the Son . . . Joyce's Use of the Mass in *Ulysses*." *JJQ*, 6 (1969), 321-47.

Wasserstrom, William. "In Gertrude's Closet: Incest-Patterns in Recent Literature." *YR*, 48 (1958), 245-65.

Watson, Edward A. "Stoom-Bloom: Scientific Objectivity versus Romantic Subjectivity in the Ithaca Episode of Joyce's *Ulysses*." *UWR*, 2, 1 (1966), 11-25.
Weinstein, Arnold L. *Vision and Response in Modern Fiction*, 167-90.
West, Alick. *Crisis and Criticism*, 143-80.
West, Rebecca. *The Strange Necessity*, 20-58.
Whaley, Helen R. "The Role of the Blind Piano Tuner in Joyce's *Ulysses*." *MFS*, 16 (1971), 531-35.
White, John. "*Ulysses*: The Metaphysical Foundations and Grand Design." *MFS*, 15, 1 (1969), 27-34.
White, Patrick. "The Key in *Ulysses*." *JJQ*, 9 (1971), 10-25.
_____. "Vico's Institution of Burial in *Ulysses*." *BSUF*, 14, 4 (1973), 59-68.
Wilson, Edmund. *Axel's Castle*, 191-236.
Woolsey, John M. "United States of America v. One Book Called *Ulysses*." *Voices in Court*. Ed. William H. Davenport, 218-23.
Worthington, Mabel P. "Irish Folk Songs in Joyce's *Ulysses*." *PMLA*, 71 (1956), 321-39.
Wykes, David. "*The Odyssey* in *Ulysses*." *TSLL*, 10 (1968), 301-16.
Zhantieva, B. G. "Joyce's *Ulysses*." *Preserve and Create*. Ed. Gaylord C. LeRoy and Ursula Beitz, 138-72.
See also: Brewster and Burrell; Karl and Magalaner; Kettle; MacCarthy, *Criticism*; Tillyard, *Epic*.

D. H. LAWRENCE

BIBLIOGRAPHIES
Beebe, Maurice, and Anthony Tommasi. "Criticism of D. H. Lawrence: A Selected Checklist with an Index to Studies of Separate Works." *MFS*, 5 (1959), 83-98.
D. H. Lawrence Review [*DHLR*]. (publishes an annual bibliography of criticism)
Spilka, Mark. "Lawrence." *The English Novel*. Ed. A. E. Dyson, 334-48.
White, William. "D. H. Lawrence: A Checklist, 1931-1948." *BB*, 19 (1949), 174-77, 207-11, 235-39.
_____. *D. H. Lawrence: A Checklist of Writings, 1931-50*. Detroit: Wayne State Univ. Press, 1950.

INTERVIEWS
Patmore, Brigit. "Conversations with Lawrence." *LonM*, 4, 6 (June 1957), 31-45.

D. H. Lawrence, continued

SPECIAL ISSUES
Literature Film Quarterly [LFQ], 1 (1973), 3-70.
Modern Fiction Studies [MFS], 5, 1 (1959).

GENERAL STUDIES
Adamowski, T. H. "Character and Consciousness: D. H. Lawrence, Wilhelm Reich, and Jean-Paul Sartre." *UTQ*, 43 (1974), 311-34.

Aldington, Richard. *Artifex*, 209-23.

———. *D. H. Lawrence: An Indiscretion.* Seattle: Univ. of Washington Book Store, 1927.

———. "D. H. Lawrence: Ten Years After." *SatR*, 20 (June 24, 1939), 3-4, 14.

———. *Selected Critical Writings*, 130-37.

Alexander, Edward. "Thomas Carlyle and D. H. Lawrence: A Parallel." *UTQ*, 37 (1968), 248-67.

Alexander, Henry. "Lawrence and Huxley." *QQ*, 42 (1935), 96-108.

Alexander, John C. "D. H. Lawrence and Teilhard de Chardin: A Study in Agreements." *DHLR*, 2 (1969), 138-56.

Alldritt, Keith. *The Visual Imagination of D. H. Lawrence.* Evanston, Ill.: Northwestern Univ. Press; London: E. Arnold, 1971.

Alves, Leonard. "The Relevance of D. H. Lawrence." *ELLS*, 10 (1973), 83-108.

Andrews, Wyndham T., ed. *Critics on D. H. Lawrence.* Coral Gables, Fla.: Univ. of Miami Press, 1971.

Arnold, Armin. *D. H. Lawrence and America.* London: Linden Press, 1958; New York: Philosophical Library, 1959.

———. "D. H. Lawrence and Thomas Mann." *CL*, 13 (1961), 33-38.

———. "D. H. Lawrence, the Russians, and Giovanni Verga." *CLS*, 2 (1965), 249-57.

Auden, W. H. *The Dyer's Hand*, 278-95.

Baim, Joseph. "D. H. Lawrence's Social Vision." *In Honor of Austin Wright*. Ed. Joseph Baim, Ann L. Hayes, and Robert J. Gangewere, 1-9.

Baldanza, Frank. "D. H. Lawrence's Song of Songs." *MFS*, 7 (1961), 106-14.

Barry, J. "Oswald Spengler and D. H. Lawrence." *ESA*, 12 (1969), 151-61.

Bartlett, Norman. "Aldous Huxley and D. H. Lawrence." *AusQ*, 36, 1 (1964), 76-84.

Beal, Anthony. *D. H. Lawrence.* Edinburgh: Oliver and Boyd, 1961.

Bedient, Calvin. *Architects of the Self*, 117-53, 172-82.

Beebe, Maurice. *Ivory Towers and Sacred Founts*, 101-13.

Beharriell, Frederick J. "Freud and Literature." *QQ*, 65 (1958), 118-25.

Bentley, Eric. *A Century of Hero-Worship: A Study of the Idea of Heroism in Carlyle and Nietzsche, with notes on Wagner, Spengler, Stefan George, and D. H. Lawrence*, rev. ed. Boston: Beacon, 1957, 215-36. [Originally published in 1944 by Lippincott; published in Great Britain as *The Cult of Superman* by Robert Hale, 1947]

Bentley, Joseph. "Huxley's Ambivalent Responses to the Ideas of D. H. Lawrence." *TCL*, 13 (1967), 139-53.

Bersani, Leo. "Lawrentian Stillness." *YR*, 65 (1975), 38-60.

Bishop, John Peale. *Collected Essays*, 233-40.

Blanchard, Lydia. "Love and Power: A Reconsideration of Sexual Politics in D. H. Lawrence." *MFS*, 21 (1975), 431-43.

Blanche, Jacques-Emile. *More Portraits of a Lifetime*, 65-67, 93-95.

Blissett, William. "D. H. Lawrence, D'Annunzio, Wagner." *WSCL*, 7 (1966), 21-46.

Boadella, David. *The Spiral Flame*. Nottingham: Ritter Press, 1956.

Bobbitt, Joan. "Lawrence and Bloomsbury: The Myth of a Relationship." *ELUD*, 1, 3 (1973), 31-43.

Bramley, J. A. "The Significance of D. H. Lawrence." *ContempR*, 195 (1959), 304-07.

Broembsen, F. von. "Mythic Identification and Spatial Inscendence: The Cosmic Vision of D. H. Lawrence." *WHR*, 29 (1975), 137-54.

Bynner, Witter. *Journey With Genius*. New York: Day, 1951.

Canby, Henry S. *American Estimates*, 281-87.

_____. *Definitions*, ser. 2, 113-22.

Carroll, La von B. "Syzgy: A Study of the Light-Dark Imagery in Five of the Novels of D. H. Lawrence." *PUASAL*, 44, 1 (1967), 139-49.

Carswell, Catherine. *The Savage Pilgrimage*. New York: Harcourt, 1932; rev. London: Secker and Warburg, 1951.

Carter, Frederick. *D. H. Lawrence and the Body Mystical*. London: Denis Archer, 1932.

_____. *The Dragon of Revelation*. London: Harmsworth, 1931.

Caudwell, Christopher. *Studies in a Dying Culture*, 44-72.

Cavitch, David. *D. H. Lawrence and the New World*. New York: Oxford Univ. Press, 1969.

_____. "Solipsism and Death in D. H. Lawrence's Late Works." *MR*, 7 (1966), 495-508.

Chevalley, Abel. *The Modern English Novel*, 236-38.

Clarke, Colin. *River of Dissolution: D. H. Lawrence and English Romanticism*. London: Routledge and K. Paul; New York: Barnes and Noble, 1969.

D. H. Lawrence, continued

Collins, Norman. *The Facts of Fiction*, 237-48.
Connolly, Cyril. *Previous Convictions*, 262-69.
Cook, Albert S. *The Meaning of Fiction*, 167-78.
Coombes, Henry, ed. *D. H. Lawrence: A Critical Anthology*. Harmondsworth, Middlesex: Penguin, 1973.
Corke, Helen. *D. H. Lawrence: The Croydon Years*. Austin: Univ. of Texas Press, 1965.
_____. "D. H. Lawrence: The Early Stage." *DHLR*, 4 (1971), 111-21.
Cornwell, Edith F. *The "Still Point,"* 208-41.
Coveney, Peter. *Poor Monkey*, 266-81.
Cowan, James C. *D. H. Lawrence's American Journey: A Study in Literature and Myth*. Cleveland: Case Western Reserve Univ. Press, 1970.
Craig, David. *The Real Foundations*, 17-38, 143-67.
Craig, G. Armour. "D. H. Lawrence on Thinghood and Selfhood." *MR*, 1 (1959), 56-60.
Dahlberg, Edward, and Herbert Read. *Truth is More Sacred*, 69-117.
Daleski, H. M. "The Duality of Lawrence." *MFS*, 5, 1 (1959), 3-18.
_____. *The Forked Flame: A Study of D. H. Lawrence*. Evanston, Ill.: Northwestern Univ. Press, 1965.
Dawson, E. W. "Lawrence's Pollyanalytic Esthetic for the Novel." *Paunch*, 26 (1966), 60-68.
Delavenay, Emile. *D. H. Lawrence and Edward Carpenter: A Study in Edwardian Transition*. New York: Taplinger, 1971.
_____. "D. H. Lawrence and Sacher-Masoch." *DHLR*, 6 (1973), 119-48.
_____. *D. H. Lawrence: The Man and His Work—The Formative Years*. Tr. Katherine M. Delavenay. London: Heinemann; Carbondale: Southern Illinois Univ. Press, 1972.
Ditsky, John M. " 'Dark, Darker Than Fire': Thematic Parallels in Lawrence and Faulkner." *SHR*, 8 (1974), 497-505.
Dobrée, Bonamy. *The Lamp and the Lute*, 86-106.
Doheny, John. "The Novel Is the Book of Life: D. H. Lawrence and a Revised Version of Polymorphous Perversity." *Paunch*, 26 (1966), 40-59.
Donoghue, Denis. *Thieves of Fire*, 111-39.
Drain, Richard L. *Tradition and D. H. Lawrence*. Groningen: J. B. Wolters, 1960.
Draper, Ronald P. *D. H. Lawrence*. New York: Twayne, 1964.
_____, ed. *D. H. Lawrence: The Critical Heritage*. New York: Barnes and Noble; London: Routledge and K. Paul, 1970.
_____. "Satire as a Form of Sympathy: D. H. Lawrence as a Satirist." *Renaissance and Modern Essays*. Ed. G. R. Hibbard, 189-97.

_____. "The Sense of Reality in the Work of D. H. Lawrence." *RLV*, 33 (1967), 461-70.

Ehrstine, John W. "The Dialectic in D. H. Lawrence." *RS*, 33 (1965), 11-26.

Eliot, T. S. "London Letter." *Dial*, 73 (September 1922), 329-31.

Elsbree, Langdon. "D. H. Lawrence, *Homo Ludens*, and the Dance." *DHLR*, 1 (1968), 1-30.

_____, ed. "On the Teaching of D. H. Lawrence: A Forum." *DHLR*, 8 (1975), 63-79.

_____. "The Purest and Most Perfect Form of Play: Some Novelists and the Dance." *Criticism*, 14 (1972), 361-72.

Engel, Monroe. "The Continuity of Lawrence's Short Novels." *HudR*, 11 (1958), 201-09.

"E. T." [Jessie Chambers]. *D. H. Lawrence: A Personal Record.* London: J. Cape, 1935; 2d ed. Ed. J. D. Chambers. New York: Barnes and Noble, 1965.

Evans, B. Ifor. *English Literature Between the Wars*, 49-58.

Every, George. "D. H. Lawrence." *The New Spirit*. Ed. E. W. Martin, 58-65.

Faas, Egbert. "Charles Olson and D. H. Lawrence: Aesthetics of the 'Primitive Abstract'." *Boundary*, 2 (1973-74), 113-26.

Fairbanks, N. David. " 'Strength through Joy' in the Novels of D. H. Lawrence." *L&I*, 8 (1971), 67-78.

Fay, Eliot. *Lorenzo in Search of the Sun: D. H. Lawrence in Italy, Mexico and the American Southwest.* New York: Bookman, 1953; London: Vision, 1955.

Fergusson, Francis. "D. H. Lawrence's Sensibility." *Hound & Horn*, April-June 1933, 447-63; *Forms of Modern Fiction*. Ed. William Van O'Connor, 72-79.

Ford, Ford Madox. *Portraits from Life*, 70-89.

Ford, George H. *Double Measure: A Study of the Novels and Stories of D. H. Lawrence.* New York: Holt, 1965.

Freeman, Mary. *D. H. Lawrence: A Basic Study of his Ideas.* Gainesville, Fla.: Univ. of Miami Press, 1955.

Friedman, Alan W. "The Other Lawrence." *PR*, 37 (1970), 239-53.

Garcia, Reloy. "The Quest for Paradise in the Novels of D. H. Lawrence." *DHLR*, 3 (1970), 93-114.

_____. *Steinbeck and D. H. Lawrence: Fictive Voices and the Ethical Imperative.* Muncie, Ind.: Steinbeck Soc. of America, 1972.

_____, and James Karabatsos, eds. *A Concordance to the Short Fiction of D. H. Lawrence.* Lincoln: Univ. of Nebraska Press, 1972.

Garnett, Edward. *Friday Nights*, 145-60.

Garrett, Peter. *Scene and Symbol from George Eliot to James Joyce,*
181-213.

Gass, William H. *Fiction and the Figures of Life,* 212-21.

Gatti, Hilary. "D. H. Lawrence and the Idea of Education." *EM,* 21
(1970), 209-31.

George, Walter L. *Literary Chapters,* 74-86.

Gerard, D. E., comp. "Glossary of Eastwood Dialect Words Used by D.
H. Lawrence in His Poems, Plays, and Fiction." *DHLR,* 1 (1968),
215-37.

Gifford, Henry. "Anna, Lawrence, and 'The Law'." *Russian Literature
and Modern English Fiction.* Ed. Donald Davie, 148-52; "Further
Notes on 'Anna Karenina'," 160-63.

Gilbert, Sandra. *Acts of Attention.* Ithaca, N. Y.: Cornell Univ. Press,
1972.

Gindin, James J. "Society and Compassion in the Novels of D. H.
Lawrence." *CentR,* 12 (1968), 355-74.

Glicksberg, Charles I. "D. H. Lawrence and Science." *Scientific
Monthly,* 73 (1951), 99-104.

Goodheart, Eugene. *The Cult of the Ego,* 161-82.

―――. "Lawrence and the Critics." *ChiR,* 16, 3 (1963), 127-37.

―――. *The Utopian Vision of D. H. Lawrence.* Chicago: Univ. of Chicago Press, 1963.

Goodman, Richard. *Footnote to Lawrence.* London: White Owl Press,
1932.

Gordon, David J. *D. H. Lawrence as Literary Critic.* New Haven,
Conn.: Yale Univ. Press, 1966.

―――. "D. H. Lawrence's Quarrel with Tragedy." *Per,* 13 (1964),
135-50.

―――. "Two Anti-Puritan Puritans: Bernard Shaw and D. H. Lawrence." *YR,* 56 (1966), 76-90.

Grant, Douglas. "Hands Up, America!" *REL,* 4, 4 (1963), 11-17.

Gray, Ronald. *The German Tradition in Literature,* 340-54.

Green, Eleanor H. "Blueprints for Utopia: The Political Idea of
Nietzsche and D. H. Lawrence." *RMS,* 18 (1974), 141-61.

―――. "Schopenhauer and D. H. Lawrence on Sex and Love." *DHLR,*
8 (1975), 329-45.

―――. "The *Wille zur Macht* and D. H. Lawrence." *MSE,* 5, 2 (1975),
25-30.

Greene, Thomas. "Lawrence and the Quixotic Hero." *SR,* 59 (1951),
559-73.

Gregory, Horace. *D. H. Lawrence: Pilgrim of the Apocalypse—A Critical Study.* New York: Viking, 1933; rev. New York: Grove, 1957.

———. "D. H. Lawrence: The Posthumous Reputation." *Literary Opinion in America*, rev. ed. Ed. Morton Dauwen Zabel, 370-75.

———. *Spirit of Time and Place*, 180-85.

Grigson, Geoffrey. *The Contrary View*, 112-18.

Guttmann, Allen. "D. H. Lawrence: The Politics of Irrationality." *WSCL*, 5 (1964), 151-63.

Haegert, John W. "Brothers and Lovers: D. H. Lawrence and the Theme of Friendship." *SoRA*, 8 (1975), 39-50.

Hall, Margaret A. "The Impact of Exotic Cultures on D. H. Lawrence and E. M. Forster." Doshisha Women's College of Liberal Arts. *Annual Reports of Studies*, v. 22, 246-61.

Hamalian, Leo, ed. *D. H. Lawrence: A Collection of Criticism*. New York: McGraw-Hill, 1973.

Hardy, Barbara. *The Appropriate Form*, 1-4, 122-4, 132-73, 174-81.

Harris, Wendell V. "Molly's 'Yes': The Transvaluation of Sex in Modern Fiction." *TSLL*, 10 (1968), 107-18.

Harrison, John R. *The Reactionaries*, 163-92.

Hays, Peter L. *The Limping Hero*, 35-39, 77-80.

Henderson, Philip. *The Novel Today*, 60-72.

Henig, Suzanne. "D. H. Lawrence and Virginia Woolf." *DHLR*, 2 (1969), 265-71.

Highet, Gilbert. *People, Places, and Books*, 37-44.

Hinz, Evelyn J. "D. H. Lawrence's Clothes Metaphor." *DHLR*, 1 (1968), 87-113.

Hochman, Baruch. *Another Ego: The Changing View of Self and Society in the Work of D. H. Lawrence*. Columbia: Univ. of South Carolina Press, 1970.

Hoffman, Frederick J., and Harry T. Moore, eds. *The Achievement of D. H. Lawrence*. Norman: Univ. of Oklahoma Press, 1953.

———. *Freudianism and the Literary Mind*, 151-76.

Hogan, Robert. "The Amorous Whale: A Study in the Symbolism of D. H. Lawrence." *MFS*, 5, 1 (1959), 39-46.

Hough, Graham. *The Dark Sun, A Study of D. H. Lawrence*. New York: Macmillan, 1956.

———. *Image and Experience*, 133-59.

———. *Two Exiles: Lord Byron and D. H. Lawrence*. Nottingham: Univ. of Nottingham Press, 1956.

Howarth, Herbert. "Impersonal Aphrodite." *Mosaic*, 1, 2 (1968), 74-86.

Hoyles, John. "D. H. Lawrence and the Counter-Revolution: An Essay in Socialist Aesthetics." *DHLR*, 6 (1973), 173-200.

Hueffer [Ford], Ford Madox. "A Haughty and Proud Generation." *YR*, n.s. 11 (1922), 703-17.

D. H. Lawrence, continued

Hugger, Ann-Grete. "The Dichotomy Between Private and Public Sphere: Sex Roles in D. H. Lawrence's Novels." *L&L*, 2, 2 (1973), 127-36.

Humma, John B. "D. H. Lawrence as Friedrich Nietzsche." *PQ*, 53 (1974), 110-20.

Huxley, Aldous. "Aldous Huxley on D. H. Lawrence." *Novelists on Novelists*. Ed. Louis Kronenberger, 306-29.

———. *Collected Essays*. New York: Harper, 1959, 115-29.

———. *Music at Night*, 153-62.

———. *Olive Tree*, 203-42.

Inniss, Kenneth. *D. H. Lawrence's Bestiary: A Study of His Use of Animal Trope and Symbol*. The Hague: Mouton, 1971.

Isaacs, Neil D. "The Autoerotic Metaphor in Joyce, Sterne, Lawrence, Stevens, and Whitman." *L&P*, 15 (1965), 92-106.

Ivker, Barry. "Schopenhauer and D. H. Lawrence." *XUS*, 11, 2 (1972), 22-36.

Jacobson, Dan. "D. H. Lawrence and Modern Society." *JCH*, 2 (1967), 81-92.

Joad, C. E. M. *Return to Philosophy*, 142-91, 197-200.

Johnston, Walter E. "The Shepherdess in the City." *CL*, 26 (1974), 124-41.

Jones, William M. "Growth of a Symbol: The Sun in Lawrence and Eudora Welty." *UKCR*, 26 (1959), 68-73.

Joost, Nicholas, and Alvin Sullivan. *D. H. Lawrence and "The Dial."* Carbondale: Southern Illinois Univ. Press, 1970.

Juta, Jan. "Portrait in Shadow: D. H. Lawrence." *CLC*, 18 (1969), 2-16.

Kaplan, Harold. *The Passive Voice*, 159-85.

Kay, Wallace G. "The Cortege of Dionysus: Lawrence and Giono." *SoQ*, 4 (1966), 159-71.

———. "Dionysus, D. H. Lawrence, and Jean Giono: Further Considerations." *SoQ*, 6 (1968), 394-414.

Kazin, Alfred. *The Inmost Leaf*, 98-102.

Keith, W. J. "Spirit of Place and *Genus Loci*: D. H. Lawrence and Rolf Gardiner." *DHLR*, 7 (1974), 127-38.

Kendle, Burton S. "D. H. Lawrence: The Man Who Misunderstood Gulliver." *ELN*, 2 (1964), 42-46.

Kenmare, Dallas [pseud.]. *Fire-bird: A Study of D. H. Lawrence*. London: Barrie, 1951.

Kermode, Frank. "Lawrence and the Apocalyptic Types." *CritQ*, 10 (1968), 14-38.

Kessler, Jascha. "D. H. Lawrence's Primitivism." *TSLL*, 5 (1964), 467-88.

Kinkead-Weekes, Mark. "Eros and Metaphor: Sexual Relationships in the Fiction of D. H. Lawrence." *TCS*, 1 (1969), 3-19.
_____. "The Marble and the Statue: The Exploratory Imagination of D. H. Lawrence." *Imagined Worlds*, Ed. Maynard Mack and Ian Gregor, 371-418.
Kissane, Leedice. "D. H. Lawrence, Ruth Suckow, and 'Modern Marriage'." *Rendezvous*, 4, 1 (1969), 39-45.
Klein, Robert C. "I, Thou, and You in Three Lawrencian Relationships." *Paunch*, 31 (1968), 52-70.
Kleinbard, David J. "D. H. Lawrence and Ontological Insecurity." *PMLA*, 89 (1974), 154-63.
_____. "Laing, Lawrence, and the Maternal Cannibal." *PsyR*, 58, 1 (1971), 5-13.
Knight, G. Wilson. *Neglected Powers*, 142-55, 399-402.
Kohler, Dayton. "D. H. Lawrence." *SR*, 39 (1931), 25-38.
Lavrin, Janko. *Aspects of Modernism from Wilde to Pirandello*, 141-59.
Leaver, Florence B. "The Man-Nature Relationship in D. H. Lawrence's Novels." *UKCR*, 19 (1953), 241-48.
Leavis, F. R. *The Common Pursuit*, 233-63.
_____. *D. H. Lawrence*. Cambridge: Minority Press, 1930.
_____. *D. H. Lawrence, Novelist*. London: Chatto and Windus, 1955; New York: Knopf, 1956; New York: Simon and Schuster, 1970.
_____. *For Continuity*, 111-59.
_____. "Lawrence and Class." *SR*, 62 (1954), 535-62.
Lee, Brian. "America, My America." *Renaissance and Modern Essays*, Ed. G. R. Hibbard, 181-88.
Lee, Robin. "The 'Strange Reality of Otherness': D. H. Lawrence's Social Attitudes." *Standpunte*, 102 (1972), 3-10.
Lerner, Laurence. *The Truthtellers: Jane Austen, George Eliot, D. H. Lawrence*. New York: Schocken; London: Chatto and Windus, 1967.
McCurdy, Harold Crier. "Literature and Personality: Analysis of the Novels of D. H. Lawrence." *Character and Personality*, 8 (1940), 182-97.
Magalaner, Marvin. "D. H. Lawrence Today." *Cweal*, 70 (1959), 275-76.
Malraux, Andre. "D. H. Lawrence and Eroticism." Tr. Bert M-P. Leefman. *From the N.R.F.* Ed. Justin O'Brien, 194-98.
Martin, W. B. J. "Significant Modern Writers: D. H. Lawrence." *ET*, 71 (1960), 174-76.

D. H. Lawrence, continued

Mather, Rodney. "Patrick White and Lawrence: A Contrast." *CR*, 13 (1970), 34-50.

Maud, Ralph N. "D. H. Lawrence: True Emotion as the Ethical Control in Art." *WHR*, 9 (1955), 233-40.

Mauriac, Francois. *Second Thoughts*, 122-25.

Mayhall, Jane. "D. H. Lawrence: The Triumph of Texture." *WHR*, 19 (1965), 161-74.

Mégroz, R. L. "D. H. Lawrence." *Post-Victorians*, by Various Authors, 315-28.

_____. *Five Novelist Poets of Today*, 189-235.

Mendel, Sydney. "Shakespeare and D. H. Lawrence: Two Portraits of the Hero." *WascanaR*, 3, 2 (1968), 49-60.

Mercier, Vivian. "James Joyce and an Irish Tradition." *Society and Self in the Novel*. Ed. Mark Schorer, 78-116; *Studies*, 45 (1956), 194-218.

Merivale, Patricia. "D. H. Lawrence and the Modern Pan Myth." *TSLL*, 6 (1964), 297-305.

Meyers, Jeffrey. "D. H. Lawrence and Homosexuality." *LonM*, 13, 4 (October-November 1973), 68-98.

_____. *Painting and the Novel*, 46-82.

Miles, Kathleen M. *The Hellish Meaning: The Demonic Motif in the Works of D. H. Lawrence*. Carbondale: Southern Illinois Univ. Press, 1970.

Miller, Henry. "The Apocalyptic Lawrence." *SWR*, 31 (1946), 254-56.

Moore, Harry T., and Warren Roberts. *D. H. Lawrence and His World*. London: Thames and Hudson; New York: Viking, 1966.

_____. "D. H. Lawrence and the Flicks." *LFQ*, 1 (1973), 3-11.

_____, ed. *A D. H. Lawrence Miscellany*. Carbondale: Southern Illinois Univ. Press, 1959.

_____. *The Intelligent Heart: The Story of D. H. Lawrence*. New York: Grove, 1955; rev., *The Priest of Love: A Life of D. H. Lawrence*, London: Heinemann; New York: Viking, 1974.

_____. *The Life and Works of D. H. Lawrence*. New York: Twayne, 1951; rev., *D. H. Lawrence: His Life and Works*, New York: Twayne, 1964.

Morris, Wright. *The Territory Ahead*, 221-28.

Moynahan, Julian. *The Deed of Life: The Novels and Tales of D. H. Lawrence*. Princeton, N. J.: Princeton Univ. Press, 1963.

Muir, Edwin. *Transition*, 49-63.

Murry, J. Middleton. "The Living Dead—I: D. H. Lawrence." *LonM*, 3, 5 (May 1956), 57-63.

_____. *Love, Freedom, and Society*, 23-123.

———. *Selected Criticism*, 55-58, 290-302.

Myers, Walter L. *The Later Realism*, 53-54, 63-70, 82-92, 118-19.

Nahal, Chaman. *D. H. Lawrence: An Eastern View.* New York: A. S. Barnes, 1970.

Nehls, Edward, ed. *D. H. Lawrence: A Composite Biography*, 3 vol. Madison: Univ. of Wisconsin Press, 1957-59.

Newman, Paul B. "D. H. Lawrence and *The Golden Bough.*" *KM*, 1962, 79-86.

Nicholson, Norman. *Man and Literature*, 64-86.

Nin, Anais. *D. H. Lawrence: An Unprofessional Study.* Paris: E. W. Titus, 1932; Denver: Swallow, 1964.

Noon, William T. "God and Man in Twentieth-Century Fiction." *Thought*, 37 (1962), 35-56.

O'Connor, Frank. *The Mirror in the Roadway*, 270-79.

Orwell, George. *The Collected Essays*, v. 4, 30-33.

Pachmuss, Temira. "Dostoevsky, D. H. Lawrence, and Carson McCullers: Influences and Confluences." *GSlav*, 4 (1974), 59-68.

Panichas, George A. *Adventures in Consciousness: The Meaning of D. H. Lawrence's Religious Quest.* The Hague: Mouton, 1964.

———. "D. H. Lawrence and the Ancient Greeks." *EM*, 16 (1965), 195-214.

———. "E. M. Forster and D. H. Lawrence: Their Views on Education." *Renaissance and Modern Essays.* Ed. G. R. Hibbard, 199-213.

———. "The End of the Lamplight." *ModA*, 14 (1970), 65-74.

———. "F. M. Dostoevsky and D. H. Lawrence: Their Vision of Evil." *RMS*, 5 (1961), 49-75.

———. *The Reverent Discipline*, 135-69, 205-28, 335-50.

Patmore, Derek. *D. H. Lawrence and the Dominant Male.* London: Covent Garden Press, 1970.

Peterson, Richard F. "Steinbeck and D. H. Lawrence." *Steinbeck's Literary Dimension.* Ed. Tetsumaro Haysahi, 67-82.

Phelps, Gilbert. *The Russian Novel in English Fiction*, 180-87.

Pinto, Vivian de Sola. "D. H. Lawrence." *The Politics of Twentieth-Century Novelists.* Ed. George A. Panichas, 30-50.

———. *D. H. Lawrence: Prophet of the Midlands.* Nottingham: Univ. of Nottingham Press, 1951.

———. "William Blake and D. H. Lawrence." *William Blake: Essays for S. Foster Damon.* Providence, R. I.: Brown Univ. Press, 1969, 84-106.

Porter, Katherine Anne. *The Days Before*, 262-67.

Potter, Stephen. *D. H. Lawrence: A First Study.* London: J. Cape, 1930.

D. H. Lawrence, continued

Powell, Dilys. *Descent from Parnassus*, 1-54.

Powell, Lawrence C. *Books in My Baggage*, 37-43.

———. *Southwest Classics: The Creative Literature of the Arid Lands —Essays on the Books and Their Writers.* Los Angeles: Ward Ritchie, 1974, 81-92.

Pratt, Annis. "Women and Nature in Modern Fiction." *ConL*, 13 (1972), 476-90.

Priestley, J. B. "The Younger Novelists." *EJ*, 14 (1925), 435-43.

Pritchard, Ronald E. *D. H. Lawrence: Body of Darkness*. Pittsburgh: Univ. of Pittsburgh Press, 1971.

Pritchard, William. "Lawrence and Lewis." *Agenda*, 7, 3-8, 1 (1970), 140-47.

———. "Wyndham Lewis and Lawrence." *IowaR*, 2, 2 (1971), 91-96.

Pugh, Bridget. *The Country of My Heart: A Local Guide to D. H. Lawrence*. Nottingham: Nottingham Local Hist. Council, 1972.

Quennell, Peter C. "D. H. Lawrence and Aldous Huxley." *The English Novelists*. Ed. Derek Verschoyle, 267-78.

Rahv, Philip. *Literature and the Sixth Sense*, 289-306.

Raleigh, John Henry. "Victorian Morals and the Modern Novel." *PR*, 25, 2 (1958), 241-64.

Rascoe, Burton. *Prometheans: Ancient and Modern*, 221-38.

Read, Herbert. "On D. H. Lawrence." *TC*, 165 (1959), 556-66.

Rees, Richard. *Brave Men: A Study of D. H. Lawrence and Simone Weil*. London: Gollancz, 1958.

Remsbury, John. " 'Real Thinking': Lawrence and Cézanne." *CQ*, 2 (1967), 117-47.

Rieff, Philip. "Two Honest Men." *Listener*, 62 (1960), 794-96.

Roberts, John H. "Huxley and Lawrence." *VQR*, 13 (1937), 546-57.

———. "The Religion of D. H. Lawrence." *New Humanist*, 5 (1932), 29-34.

Roberts, Mark. *The Tradition of Romantic Morality*, 322-48.

Roberts, Walter. "After the Prophet: The Reputation of D. H. Lawrence." *Month*, 27 (1962), 237-40.

Rosenfeld, Paul. *Men Seen*, 45-62.

Ross, Charles L. "Art and 'Metaphysic' in D. H. Lawrence's Novels." *DHLR*, 7 (1974), 206-17.

Rossman, Charles. " 'You Are the Call and I Am the Answer': D. H. Lawrence and Women." *DHLR*, 8 (1975), 255-328.

Russell, Bertrand. *Portraits from Memory*, 111-16.

Ruthven, K. K. "The Savage God: Conrad and Lawrence." *CritQ*, 10 (1968), 39-54.

Sagar, Keith. *The Art of D. H. Lawrence.* Cambridge: Cambridge Univ. Press, 1966, 1975.
Sale, Roger. "D. H. Lawrence, 1912-1916." *MR*, 6 (1965), 467-80.
———. *Modern Heroism*, 11-108, 246-55.
Salter, K. W. "Lawrence, Hardy, and 'The Great Tradition'." *English*, 22 (1973), 60-65.
Sanders, Scott. *D. H. Lawrence: The World of Five Major Novels.* New York: Viking, 1974.
Savage, D. S. "Lewis and Lawrence." *TCV*, 6/7 (November/December 1937), 142.
Schneider, Daniel J. "The Symbolism of the Soul: D. H. Lawrence and Some Others." *DHLR*, 7 (1974), 107-26.
Schorer, Mark. *D. H. Lawrence.* New York: Dell, 1968.
———. "Lawrence and the Spirit of Place." *Poste Restante: A Lawrence Travel Calendar.* Ed. Harry T. Moore. Berkeley: Univ. of California Press, 1956, 1-18.
Scott, Nathan A., Jr. *Rehearsals of Discomposure: Alienation and Reconciliation in Modern Literature—Franz Kafka, Ignazio Silone, D. H. Lawrence, T. S. Eliot.* New York: King's Crown Press of Columbia Univ. Press, 1952, 112-177.
Seligman, H. J. *D. H. Lawrence: An American Interpretation.* New York: Seltzer, 1924.
Shanks, Edward. *Second Essays on Literature*, 62-83.
Sherman, Stuart P. *Critical Woodcuts*, 18-31.
Sinzell, Claude. *The Geographical Background of the Early Works of D. H. Lawrence.* Paris: Didier, 1964.
Sitwell, Osbert. *Penny Foolish*, 293-97.
Slade, Tony. *D. H. Lawrence.* London: Evans Bros.; New York: Arco, 1970.
Slochower, Harry. *No Voice is Wholly Lost*, 136-43.
Spender, Stephen. *D. H. Lawrence: Novelist, Poet, Prophet.* London: Weidenfeld and Nicolson; New York: Harper, 1973.
Spilka, Mark. "D. H. Lawrence." *UKCR*, 21 (1955), 291-99.
———, ed. *D. H. Lawrence: A Collection of Critical Essays.* Englewood Cliffs, N. J.: Prentice-Hall, 1963.
———. "Lawrence's Quarrel with Tenderness." *CritQ*, 9 (1968), 363-77.
———. "Lawrence Up-Tight, or The Anal Phase Once Over." *Novel,* 4 (1971), 252-67; reply, George Ford, Frank Kermode, Colin Clarke, Mark Spilka. "On 'Lawrence Up-Tight': Four Tail-Pieces." *Novel*, 5 (1971), 54-70.
———. "Lessing and Lawrence: The Battle of the Sexes." *ConL*, 16 (1975), 218-40.

D. H. Lawrence, continued

_____. *The Love Ethic of D. H. Lawrence*. Bloomington: Indiana Univ. Press, 1955; London: Dobson, 1958.

Squires, Michael. *The Pastoral Novel: Studies in George Eliot, Thomas Hardy, and D. H. Lawrence*. Charlottesville: Univ. Press of Virginia, 1974, 174-212.

Stavrou, Constantine N. "D. H. Lawrence's 'Psychology' of Sex." *L&P*, 6 (1956), 90-95.

_____. "William Blake and D. H. Lawrence." *UKCR*, 22 (1956), 235-40.

Steinbauer, H. "Eros and Psyche: A Nietzschean Motif in Anglo-American Literature." *MLN*, 64 (1949), 217-28.

Stewart, J. I. M. *Eight Modern Writers*, 484-593.

Stoehr, Taylor. " 'Mentalized Sex' in D. H. Lawrence." *Novel*, 8 (1975), 101-22.

Stoll, John E. "Common Womb Imagery in Joyce and Lawrence." *BSUF*, 11, 2 (1970), 10-24.

_____. *The Novels of D. H. Lawrence: A Search for Integration*. Columbia: Univ. of Missouri Press, 1971.

Stonier, G. W. *Gog Magog*, 70-87.

Suckow, Ruth. "Modern Figures of Destiny: D. H. Lawrence and Frieda Lawrence." *DHLR*, 3 (1970), 1-30.

Swigg, Richard. *Lawrence, Hardy, and American Literature*. London and New York: Oxford Univ. Press, 1972.

Tedlock, E. W., Jr. *D. H. Lawrence, Artist and Rebel: A Study of Lawrence's Fiction*. Albuquerque: Univ. of New Mexico Press, 1963.

Tenenbaum, Louis. "Two Views of the Modern Italian: D. H. Lawrence and Sean O'Faolain." *Italica*, 37 (1960), 118-25.

Terry, C. J. "Aspects of D. H. Lawrence's Struggle with Christianity." *DR*, 54 (1974), 112-29.

Tetsumura, Haruo. "D. H. Lawrence's Mysticism: What the Moon Signifies." *HSELL*, 9, 1-2 (1963), 51-65.

Thompson, Alan R. "D. H. Lawrence: Apostle of the Dark God." *Bookman* (N. Y.), 72 (1931), 492-99.

Thompson, Leslie M. "D. H. Lawrence and Judas." *DHLR*, 4 (1971), 1-19.

Tindall, William York. *D. H. Lawrence and Susan His Cow*. New York: Columbia Univ. Press, 1939.

_____. "D. H. Lawrence and the Primitive." *SR*, 45 (1935), 198-211.

_____. "Transcendentalism in Contemporary Literature." *The Asian Legacy and American Life*. Ed. Arthur E. Christy, 175-92.

Tiverton, William [Martin Jarrett-Kerr]. *D. H. Lawrence and Human Existence*. London: Rockliff, 1951; London: SCM, 1961.

Travis, Leigh. "D. H. Lawrence: The Blood-Conscious Artist." *AI*, 25 (1968), 163-90.

Trease, Geoffrey. *D. H. Lawrence: The Phoenix and the Flame.* London: Macmillan, 1973.

Trilling, Diana. "Lawrence: Creator and Dissenter." *SRL*, 29 (December 7, 1946), 17-18, 82-84.

Trilling, Lionel. "D. H. Lawrence: A Neglected Aspect." *Symposium*, 1, 3 (1930), 361-70.

Troy, William. "The Lawrence Myth." *PR*, 4, 2 (1937), 3-13.

_____. *Selected Essays*, 110-33.

Turnell, Martin. *Modern Literature and Christian Faith*, 25-45.

Undset, Sigrid. *Men, Women, and Places*, 33-53.

Untermeyer, Louis. *Makers of the Modern World*, 632-42.

Vaskeel, H. J. "D. H. Lawrence: Social Theorist and Mystic." *VQ*, 26 (1960), 24-44.

Vickery, John B. *The Literary Impact of THE GOLDEN BOUGH*, 280-325.

Vitoux, Pierre. "Aldous Huxley and D. H. Lawrence: An Attempt at Intellectual Sympathy." *MLR*, 69 (1974), 501-22.

Vivas, Eliseo. *D. H. Lawrence: The Failure and Triumph of Art.* Evanston, Ill.: Northwestern Univ. Press, 1960.

_____. "Lawrence's Problems." *KR*, 3 (1941), 83-94.

_____. "The Two Lawrences." *BuR*, 7, 3 (1958), 113-32.

Waldron, Philip. "The Education of D. H. Lawrence." *AUMLA*, 24 (1965), 239-52.

Walsh, William. "D. H. Lawrence and the Genetic Approach." *EA*, 26 (1973), 327-30.

_____. *The Use of Imagination*, 163-74, 199-228.

Waugh, Arthur. *Tradition and Change*, 131-37.

Weatherby, H. L. "Old-Fashioned Gods: Eliot on Lawrence and Hardy." *SR*, 75 (1967), 301-16.

Weiss, Daniel A. *Oedipus in Nottingham: D. H. Lawrence.* Seattle: Univ. of Washington Press, 1962.

Werner, Alfred. "Lawrence and Pascin." *KR*, 23 (1961), 217-28.

West, Alick. *Crisis and Criticism*, 259-82.

West, Anthony. *D. H. Lawrence.* London: Barker, 1951.

West, Paul. *The Wine of Absurdity*, 19-38.

West, Rebecca. *D. H. Lawrence.* London: Secker, 1930.

_____. *Ending in Ernest*, 257-80.

Wicker, Brian. *The Story-Shaped World*, 120-33.

Wickham, Anna. "The Spirit of the Lawrence Women: A Posthumous Memoir." *TQ*, 9, 3 (1966), 31-50.

D. H. Lawrence, continued

Wickham, Harvey. *The Impuritans*, 235-90.

Widmer, Kingsley. *The Art of Perversity: D. H. Lawrence's Shorter Fictions*. Seattle: Univ. of Washington Press, 1962.

———. "D. H. Lawrence and the Art of Nihilism." *KR*, 20 (1958), 604-16.

———. "Lawrence and the Fall of Modern Woman." *MFS*, 5, 1 (1959), 47-56.

Williams, Charles. *Image of the City and Other Essays*, 68-75.

Williams, Joy and Raymond, eds. *D. H. Lawrence on Education*. Harmondsworth, Middlesex: Penguin, 1973.

Williams, Raymond. *Culture and Society*, 199-215.

———. "Lawrence and Tolstoy." *CritQ*, 2 (1960), 33-39; *Russian Literature and Modern English Fiction*. Ed. Donald Davie, 152-60; *Modern Tragedy*, 121-38.

———. "Tolstoy, Lawrence, and Tragedy." *KR*, 25 (1963), 633-50.

Wilson, Colin. *The Strength to Dream*, 180-86.

Winegarten, Renée. *Writers and Revolution*, 248-60.

Winter, Ella. *D. H. Lawrence*. Carmel, Cal.: The Carmelite, 1930.

Wright, Raymond. "Lawrence's Non-Human Analogues." *MLN*, 76 (1961), 426-32.

Young, Kenneth. *D. H. Lawrence*. London: Longmans, Green, 1951.

Yudhishtar, M. *Conflict in the Novels of D. H. Lawrence*. Edinburgh: Oliver and Boyd; New York: Barnes and Noble, 1969.

Zytaruk, George J. "D. H. Lawrence's Reading of Russian Literature." *DHLR*, 2 (1969), 120-37.

———. *D. H. Lawrence's Response to Russian Literature*. The Hague: Mouton, 1971.

———. "The Phallic Vision: D. H. Lawrence and V. V. Rozanov." *CLS*, 4 (1967), 283-97.

———, ed. *The Quest for Rananium: D. H. Lawrence's Letters to S. S. Koteliansky, 1914-1930*. Montreal: McGill-Queen's Univ. Press, 1970.

See also: Aiken, *ABC*; Allen, *Tradition*; Beach, *20th*; Beresford; Bowen, *Impressions*; A. Collins, *20th*; J. Collins, *Doctor*; Cunliffe, *Half-Century, 20th Century*; Daiches, *Novel*; Drew, *Modern*; Eagleton; Edgar, *Art*; Forster, *Aspects*; A. Friedman, *Turn*; Gillie, *Movements*; Goldring, *Reputations*; Hoare; R. Johnson, *Men*; Karl and Magalaner; Lacon; Lovett, *History*; MacCarthy, *Criticism*; McCormick; Macy; Maurois; Muller, *Modern*; Pritchett, *Living*; Scott-James, *50*; Spender, *Creative, Destructive, Love-Hate, Struggle*; Swinden; Swinnerton, *Georgian*; Tindall, *Forces*; Vines; Wagenknecht, *Cavalcade*; R. Williams, *Novel*.

AARON'S ROD

Barry, Sandra. "Singularity of Two; the Plurality of One." *Paunch*, 26 (1966), 34-39.

Orr, Christopher. "Lawrence after the Deluge: The Political Ambiguity of *Aaron's Rod*." *BWVACET*, 1, 2 (1974), 1-14.

Wagner, Jeanie. "A Botanical Note on *Aaron's Rod*." *DHLR*, 4 (1971), 287-90.

THE CAPTAIN'S DOLL

Bordinat, Philip. "Poetic Image in D. H. Lawrence's *The Captain's Doll*." *WVUPP*, 19 (1972), 45-49.

Dawson, Eugene W. "Love Among the Mannikins: *The Captain's Doll*." *DHLR*, 1 (1968), 137-48.

THE FOX

Boren, James L. "Commitment and Futility in 'The Fox'." *UR*, 31 (1965), 301-04.

Brayfield, Peg. "Lawrence's 'Male and Female Principles' and the Symbolism of 'The Fox'." *Mosaic*, 4, 3 (1971), 41-51.

Burns, Wayne, et al. "A Seminar on D. H. Lawrence's *The Fox*." *RecL*, 4, 2 (1975), 5-47.

Crump, G. B. "*The Fox* on Film." *DHLR*, 1 (1968), 238-44.

Davis, Patricia C. "Chicken Queen's Delight: D. H. Lawrence's 'The Fox'." *MFS*, 19 (1973), 565-71.

Draper, R. P. "The Defeat of Feminism: D. H. Lawrence's *The Fox* and 'The Woman Who Rode Away'." *SSF*, 3 (1966), 186-98.

Fulmer, O. Bryan. "The Significance of the Death of the Fox in D. H. Lawrence's *The Fox*." *SSF*, 5 (1968), 275-82.

Gregor, Ian. "*The Fox*: A Caveat." *EIC*, 9 (1959), 10-21.

Levin, Gerald. "The Symbolism of Lawrence's *The Fox*." *CLAJ*, 11 (1967), 135-41.

Mellen, Joan. "Outfoxing Lawrence: Novella into Film." *LFQ*, 1 (1973), 17-27.

Miller, Hillis. "The Fox and the Perspective Glass: D. H. Lawrence." *HarvA*, 126, 2 (1962), 14-16, 26-28.

Rossi, Patrizio. "Lawrence's Two *Foxes*: A Comparison of the Texts." *EIC*, 22 (1972), 265-78.

Shields, E. F. "Broken Vision in Lawrence's 'The Fox'." *SSF*, 9 (1972), 353-63.

Sobchack, Thomas. "*The Fox*: The Film and the Novel." *WHR*, 23 (1969), 73-78.

D. H. Lawrence, continued

KANGAROO

Alexander, John. "D. H. Lawrence's *Kangaroo*: Fantasy, Fact or Fiction?" *Meanjin*, 24 (1965), 179-97.

Atkinson, Curtis. "Was There Fact in D. H. Lawrence's *Kangaroo*?" *Meanjin*, 24 (1965), 358-59.

Draper, R. P. "Authority and The Individual: A Study of D. H. Lawrence's *Kangaroo*." *CritQ*, 1 (1959), 208-15.

Gurko, Leo. "*Kangaroo*: D. H. Lawrence in Transit." *MFS*, 10 (1965), 349-58.

Heuzenroeder, John. "D. H. Lawrence's Australia." *ALS*, 4 (1970), 319-33.

Hope, A. D. "D. H. Lawrence's *Kangaroo*: How It Looks to an Australian." *The Australian Experience: Critical Essays on Australian Novels*. Ed. W. S. Ramson. Canberra: Australian National Univ., 1974, 157-73.

Maud, Ralph. "The Politics in *Kangaroo*." *Southerly*, 17 (1956), 67-71.

Samuels, Marilyn S. "Water, Ships, and the Sea: Unifying Symbols in Lawrence's *Kangaroo*." *UR*, 37 (1970), 46-57.

Sepčić, Višnja. "The Category of Landscape in D. H. Lawrence's *Kangaroo*." *SRAZ*, 27-28 (1969), 129-52.

Wilding, Michael. "*Kangaroo* and the Form of the Political Novel." *ALS*, 4 (1970), 334-48.

————. " 'A New Show': The Politics of *Kangaroo*." *Southerly*, 30 (1970), 20-40.

LADY CHATTERLEY'S LOVER

Balakian, Nona. "The Prophetic Vogue of the Anti-Heroine." *SWR*, 47 (1962), 134-41.

Bedford, Sybille. "The Last Trial of Lady Chatterley." *Esquire*, 55 (April 1961), 132-55.

Bedient, Calvin. "The Radicalism of *Lady Chatterley's Lover*." *HudR*, 19 (1966), 407-16.

Black, Michael. "That Which Is Perfectly Ourselves (IV): Connie Chatterley." *Human World*, 8 (1972), 45-54.

Brophy, Brigid. *Don't Never Forget*, 101-05.

Burns, Wayne. "*Lady Chatterley's Lover*: A Pilgrim's Progress for Our Time." *Paunch*, 26 (1966), 16-33.

Davidson, Donald. "Decorum in the Novel." *ModA*, 9 (1964-65), 34-48.

Donald, D. R. "The First and Final Versions of *Lady Chatterley's Lover*." *Theoria*, 22 (1964), 85-97.

Empson, William. "Lady Chatterley Again." *EIC*, 13 (1963), 101-04.

Gill, Stephen. "The Composite World: Two Versions of *Lady Chatterley's Lover*." *EIC*, 21 (1971), 347-64.

Gregor, Ian, and Brian Nicholas. *The Moral and the Story*, 217-48, 251-53, 267-70.

Hall, Stuart. "*Lady Chatterley's Lover*: The Novel and Its Relationship to Lawrence's Work." *NewLR*, 6 (November-December 1960), 32-35.

Harkin, M. " 'For the Public Good': A Summary of the *Lady Chatterley's Lover* Controversy." *ManR*, 9 (1960), 91-93.

Holbrook, David. *The Quest for Love*, 192-344.

"The Immorality of Lady Chatterley." *TLS*, April 27, 1973, 471-72.

Kauffmann, Stanley. "*Lady Chatterley* at Last." *New Republic*, 140 (May 5, 1959), 13-16; *Meanjin*, 18 (1959), 450-55.

Kazin, Alfred. "Lady Chatterley in America." *Atlantic*, 204 (July 1959), 33-36.

Knight, G. Wilson. "Lawrence, Joyce, and Powys." *EIC*, 11 (1961), 403-17.

Knoepflmacher, U. C. "The Rival Ladies: Mrs. Ward's *Lady Connie* and Lawrence's *Lady Chatterley's Lover*." *VS*, 4 (1960), 141-58.

Lawrence, D. H. *Sex, Literature and Censorship: Essays, Including Lawrence's Own Defense of LADY CHATTERLEY'S LOVER*. Ed. Harry T. Moore. New York: Twayne, 1953; New York: Viking, 1959.

McHenry, G. B. "Carrying On." *MCR*, 10 (1967), 46-62.

McIntosh, Angus. "A Four-Letter Word in 'Lady Chatterley's Lover'." *Patterns of Language*. Ed. Angus McIntosh and M. A. K. Halliday, 151-64.

MacLennan, Hugh. "The Defense of Lady Chatterley." *CanL*, 6 (1960), 18-23.

Mandel, Oscar. "Ignorance and Privacy." *ASch*, 29 (1960), 509-19.

Morris, James. "Reflections on the Chatterley Case." *NYTM*, December 4, 1960, 24-25, 123, 126.

Moynahan, Julian. "*Lady Chatterley's Lover*: The Deed of Life." *ELH*, 26 (1959), 66-90.

Porter, Katherine Anne. "A Wreath for the Gamekeeper." *Shenandoah*, 11, 1 (1959), 3-12.

Rembar, Charles. *The End of Obscenity: The Trials of Lady Chatterley, Tropic of Cancer, and Fanny Hill*. New York: Random House, 1968.

Reuben, Elaine. "Feminist Criticism in the Classroom, or, 'What Do You Mean *We*, White Man?' " *WS*, 1 (1973), 315-25.

D. H. Lawrence, continued

Rolph, C. H., ed. *The Trial of Lady Chatterley*. Baltimore: Penguin, 1961.

Rudikoff, Sonya. "D. H. Lawrence and Our Life Today: Re-reading *Lady Chatterley's Lover*." *Commentary*, 28, 5 (November 1959), 408-13.

Schorer, Mark. "On *Lady Chatterley's Lover*." *EvR*, 1, 1 (1957), 149-78.

Scott, James F. "The Emasculation of *Lady Chatterley's Lover*." *LFQ*, 1 (1973), 37-45.

Sepčić, Višnja. "The Dialogue in *Lady Chatterley's Lover*." *Mirko Deanovic octagenario in honorem. SRAZ*, 29-32 (1970-71), 461-80.

Sheerin, John B. "Sane Censorship and Lady Chatterley." *CathW*, 189 (1959), 412-16.

Shonfield, Andrew. "Lawrence's Other Censor." *Encounter*, 17 (September 1961), 63-64.

Sparrow, John. "Regina v. Penguin Books Ltd." *Encounter*, 18 (February 1962), 35-43.

Spilka, Mark. "On *Lady Chatterley's Lover*." *Folio*, 20 (1955), 29-38.

Squires, Michael. "Pastoral Patterns and Pastoral Variants in *Lady Chatterley's Lover*." *ELH*, 39 (1972), 129-46.

Strickland, Geoffrey. "The First *Lady Chatterley's Lover*." *Encounter*, 36 (January 1971), 44-52.

Taube, Myron. "Fanny and the Lady: The Treatment of Sex in *Fanny Hill* and *Lady Chatterley's Lover*." *LHR*, 15 (1974), 37-40.

Thody, Philip. "*Lady Chatterley's Lover*: A Pyrrhic Victory." *Threshold*, 5, 2 (1961-62), 36-49.

Way, Brian. "Sex and Language." *NewLR*, 27 (September-October 1964), 66-80.

Weiss, Daniel. "D. H. Lawrence's Great Circle: From *Sons and Lovers* to *Lady Chatterley*." *PsyR*, 50, 3 (1963), 112-38.

Welch, Colin. "Black Magic, White Lies." *Encounter*, 16 (February 1961), 75-79.

―――, and E. L. Mascall. "Chatterley and the Law." *Encounter*, 16 (April 1961), 85.

Welker, Robert H. "Advocate for Eros: Notes on D. H. Lawrence." *ASch*, 30 (1961), 191-202.

West, Rebecca, et al. "*Chatterley*, the Witnesses, and the Law." *Encounter*, 16 (March 1961), 52-56.

Widmer, Kingsley. "The Pertinence of Modern Pastoral: The Three Versions of *Lady Chatterley's Lover*." *SNNTS*, 5 (1973), 298-313.

Williams, Raymond. "The Law and Literary Merit." *Encounter*, 17 (September 1961), 66-69.

Wilson, Edmund. *The Shores of Light*, 403-07.

Yoshida, Tetsuo. "The Broken Balance and the Negative Victory in *Lady Chatterley's Lover." SELL*, 24 (1974), 117-29.
See also: Fuller, *Books*; Gill; Kazin, *Contemporaries*.

THE LOST GIRL
Delbaere-Garant, Jeanne. "The Call of the South: *Where Angels Fear to Tread* and *The Lost Girl." RLV*, 29 (1963), 336-57.
Gurko, Leo. "*The Lost Girl*: D. H. Lawrence as a 'Dickens of the Midlands'." *PMLA*, 78 (1963), 601-05.
Hafley, James. "*The Lost Girl*—Lawrence Really Real." *ArQ*, 10 (1954), 312-22.
Heywood, C. "D. H. Lawrence's *The Lost Girl* and Its Antecedents by George Moore and Arnold Bennett." *ES*, 47 (1966), 131-34.

THE MAN WHO DIED
Cowan, James C. "D. H. Lawrence's Quarrel with Christianity." *Literature and Theology*. Ed. Thomas F. Staley and Lester F. Zimmerman, 32-43.
Fiderer, Gerald. "D. H. Lawrence's *The Man Who Died*: The Phallic Christ." *AI*, 25 (1968), 91-96.
Goodheart, Eugene. "Lawrence and Christ." *PR*, 31 (1964), 42-59.
Kay, Wallace G. "*Women in Love* and 'The Man Who Had Died': Resolving Apollo and Dionysus." *SoQ*, 10 (1972), 325-39.
Kunkel, Francis L. *Passion and the Passion*, 37-57.
LeDoux, Larry V. "Christ and Isis: The Function of the Dying and Reviving God in *The Man Who Died." DHLR*, 5 (1972), 132-47.
Miller, Milton. "Definition by Comparison: Chaucer, Lawrence and Joyce." *EIC*, 3 (1953), 369-81.
Panichas, George A. "D. H. Lawrence's Concept of the Risen Lord." *ChS*, 47 (1964), 56-65.
Rieff, Philip. "A Modern Mythmaker." *Myth and Mythmaking*. Ed. Henry A. Murray, 240-75.
Sturm, Ralph D. "Lawrence: Critic of Christianity." *CathW*, 208 (1968), 75-79.
Thompson, Leslie M. "The Christ Who Didn't Die: Analogues to D. H. Lawrence's *The Man Who Died." DHLR*, 8 (1975), 19-30.

THE PLUMED SERPENT
Baldwin, Alice. "The Structure of the Coatl Symbol in *The Plumed Serpent." Style*, 5 (1971), 138-50.
Brotherston, J. G. "Revolution and the Ancient Literature of Mexico for D. H. Lawrence and Antonin Artaud." *TCL*, 18 (1972), 181-89.

D. H. Lawrence, continued

Clark, L. D. *Dark Night of the Body: D. H. Lawrence's THE PLUMED SERPENT.* Austin: Univ. of Texas Press, 1964.

Cowan, James C. "The Symbolic Structure of *The Plumed Serpent.*" *TSE*, 14 (1965), 75-96.

Martin, Dexter. "D. H. Lawrence and Pueblo Religion: An Inquiry into Accuracy." *ArQ*, 9 (1953), 219-34.

Meyers, Jeffrey. "The Plumed Serpent and the Mexican Revolution." *JML*, 4 (1974), 55-72.

Michener, Richard L. "Apocalyptic Mexico: *The Plumed Serpent* and *The Power and the Glory.*" *UR*, 34 (1968), 313-16.

Porter, Katherine Anne. *The Collected Essays*, 421-25.

Tedlock, E. W., Jr. "Lawrence's Annotations of Ouspensky's *Tertium Organum.*" *TSLL*, 2 (1960), 206-18.

Vickery, John B. *"The Plumed Serpent* and the Eternal Paradox." *Criticism*, 5 (1963), 119-34.

————. *"The Plumed Serpent* and the Reviving God." *JML*, 2 (1972), 505-32.

Villiers, B. "D. H. Lawrence in Mexico." *SWR*, 15 (1930), 425-33.

Woodcock, George. "Mexico and the English Novelist." *WestR*, 21 (1956), 21-32.

THE RAINBOW

Adam, Ian. "Lawrence's Anti-symbol: The Ending of *The Rainbow.*" *JNT*, 3 (1973), 77-84.

Adamowski, T. H. *"The Rainbow* and 'Otherness'." *DHLR*, 7 (1974), 58-77.

Alinei, Tamara. "Imagery and Meaning in D. H. Lawrence's *The Rainbow.*" *YES*, 2 (1972), 205-11.

Brandabur, A. M. "The Ritual Corn Harvest Scene in *The Rainbow.*" *DHLR*, 6 (1973), 284-302.

Brown, Homer O. " 'The Passionate Struggle into Conscious Being': D. H. Lawrence's *The Rainbow.*" *DHLR*, 7 (1974), 275-90.

Burns, Robert. "The Novel as a Metaphysical Statement: Lawrence's *The Rainbow.*" *SoRA*, 4 (1970), 139-60.

Butler, Gerald J. "Sexual Experience in D. H. Lawrence's *The Rainbow.*" *RecL*, 2 (Fall-Winter 1973), 1-92.

Carter, John. *"The Rainbow* Prosecution." *TLS*, February 27, 1969, 216. [See also *TLS*, April 17, 1969, 414; April 24, 1969, 440; September 4, 1969, 979.]

Chapple, J. A. V. *Documentary and Imaginative Literature*, 72-80.

Chavis, Geraldine Giebel. "Ursula Brangwen: Toward Self and Selflessness." *Thoth*, 12, 1 (1971), 18-28.

198

Chrisman, Reva Wells. "Ursula Brangwen in the University: D. H. Lawrence's Rejection of Authority in *The Rainbow.*" *KPAB,* 1974, 9-16.

Clarke, Colin, ed. *THE RAINBOW and WOMEN IN LOVE: A Casebook.* London: Macmillan, 1969.

Clements, A. L. "The Quest for Self: D. H. Lawrence's *The Rainbow.*" *Thoth,* 3, 2 (1962), 90-100.

Cross, Barbara. "Lawrence and the Unbroken Circle." *Per,* 11 (1959), 81-89.

Cushman, Keith. " 'I Am Going through a Transition Stage': 'The Prussian Officer' and *The Rainbow.*" *DHLR,* 8 (1975), 176-97.

Delany, Paul. "Lawrence and E. M. Forster: Two Rainbows." *DHLR,* 8 (1975), 54-62.

Dougherty, Adelyn. "The Concept of Person in D. H. Lawrence's *The Rainbow.*" *C&L,* 21, 4 (1972), 15-22.

Engelberg, Edward. "Escape From the Circles of Experience: D. H. Lawrence's *The Rainbow* as a Modern *Bildungsroman.*" *PMLA,* 78 (1963), 103-13.

Goldberg, S. L. "*The Rainbow*: Fiddle-Bow and Sand." *EIC,* 11 (1961), 418-34.

Heilbrun, Carolyn G. *Towards a Recognition of Androgyny,* 102-10.

Heldt, Lucia Henning. "Lawrence on Love: The Courtship and Marriage of Tom Brangwen and Lydia Lensky." *DHLR,* 8 (1975), 358-70.

Hill, Ordelle G., and Potter Woodbery. "Ursula Brangwen of *The Rainbow*: Christian Saint or Pagan Goddess?" *DHLR,* 4 (1971), 274-79.

Hyde, Virginia. "Will Brangwen and Paradisal Vision in *The Rainbow* and *Women in Love.*" *DHLR,* 8 (1975), 346-57.

Idema, James M. "The Hawk and the Plover: 'The Polarity of Life' in the 'Jungle Aviary' of D. H. Lawrence's Mind in *Sons and Lovers* and *The Rainbow.*" *ForumH,* 3, 7 (1961), 11-14.

Inglis, Fred. *An Essential Discipline,* 240-51.

Kay, Wallace G. "Lawrence and *The Rainbow*: Apollo and Dionysus in Conflict." *SoQ,* 10 (1972), 209-22.

Kesava Menon, K. P. "The Impact of Symbolism on Story and Character in D. H. Lawrence's *The Rainbow.*" *Literary Studies.* Ed. K. P. Kesava Manon, M. Manuel, and K. Ayyappa Paniker, 23-33.

Kinkead-Weekes, Mark, ed. *THE RAINBOW: A Collection of Critical Essays.* Englewood Cliffs, N.J.: Prentice-Hall, 1971.

Lainoff, Seymour. "*The Rainbow*: the Shaping of Modern Man." *MFS,* 1, 4 (1955), 23-27.

D. H. Lawrence, continued

Latta, William. "Lawrence's Debt to Rudolph, Baron Von Hube." *DHLR*, 1 (1968), 60-62.

Leavis, F. R. "The Novel as Dramatic Poem: *The Rainbow*." *Scrutiny*, 18 (1952), 197-210; 18 (1952), 273-87; 19 (1952), 15-30.

Lee, R. H. "A True Relatedness: Lawrence's View of Mortality." *ESA*, 10 (1967), 178-85.

Meyers, Jeffrey. "*The Rainbow* and Fra Angelico." *DHLR*, 7 (1974), 139-55.

Mori, Haruhide. "Lawrence's Imagistic Development in *The Rainbow* and *Women in Love*." *ELH*, 31 (1964), 460-81.

Obler, Paul. "D. H. Lawrence's World of *The Rainbow*." *DUS*, 8 (1955), 3-23.

Raddatz, Volker. "Lyrical Elements in D. H. Lawrence's *The Rainbow*." *RLV*, 40 (1974), 235-42.

Raina, M. L. "The Wheel and the Centre: An Approach to *The Rainbow*." *LCrit*, 9, 2 (1970), 41-55.

Sager, Keith. "The Genesis of *The Rainbow* and *Women in Love*." *DHLR*, 1 (1968), 179-99.

Sale, Roger. "The Narrative Technique of *The Rainbow*." *MFS*, 5, 1 (1959), 29-38.

Schneider, Daniel J. "Techniques of Cognition in Modern Fiction." *JAAC*, 26 (1968), 317-28.

Sepčić, Višnja. "A Link Between D. H. Lawrence's *The Trespasser* and *The Rainbow*." *SRAZ*, 24 (1967), 113-26.

Sharma, Radhe S. "D. H. Lawrence's *The Rainbow*: A Note on the Contextuality of the Symbol." *OJES*, 9, 1 (1972), 21-25.

Smith, Frank G. *D. H. Lawrence: THE RAINBOW*. London: E. Arnold, 1971.

Spilka, Mark. "The Shape of an Arch: A Study of Lawrence's *The Rainbow*." *MFS*, 1, 2 (1955), 30-38.

Squires, Michael. "Recurrence as a Narrative Technique in *The Rainbow*." *MFS*, 21 (1975), 230-36.

———. "Scenic Construction and Rhetorical Signals in Hardy and Lawrence." *DHLR*, 8 (1975), 125-46.

Stroupe, John S. "D. H. Lawrence's Portrait of Ben Franklin in *The Rainbow*." *IEY*, No. 11 (1966), 64-68.

Wasson, Richard. "Comedy and History in *The Rainbow*." *MFS*, 13 (1967), 465-77.

See also: Kettle; Mueller, *Celebration*.

SONS AND LOVERS

Alinei, Tamara. "Three Times Morel: Recurrent Structure in *Sons and Lovers*." *DQR*, 5 (1975), 39-53.

Baldanza, Frank. "*Sons and Lovers*: Novel to Film as a Record of Cultural Growth." *LFQ*, 1 (1973), 64-70.

Beards, Richard D. "*Sons and Lovers* as *Bildungsroman*." *CollL*, 1 (1974), 204-17.

Beebe, Maurice. "Lawrence's Sacred Fount: The Artist Theme of *Sons and Lovers*." *TSLL*, 4 (1962), 539-52.

Bramley, J. A. "D. H. Lawrence and 'Miriam'." *Cornhill*, 171 (1960), 241-49.

Buckley, Jerome Hamilton. "Autobiography in the English *Bildungsroman*." *The Interpretation of Narrative*. Ed. Morton W. Bloomfield, 93-104.

Burwell, Rose Marie. "Schopenhauer, Hardy, and Lawrence: Toward a New Understanding of *Sons and Lovers*." *WHR*, 28 (1974), 105-17.

DiMaggio, Richard. "A Note on *Sons and Lovers* and Emerson's 'Experience'." *DHLR*, 6 (1973), 214-16.

Draper, R. P. "D. H. Lawrence on Mother-Love." *EIC*, 8 (1958), 285-89.

Eichrodt, John M. "Doctrine and Dogma in *Sons and Lovers*." *ConnR*, 4, 1 (1970), 18-32.

Farr, Judith, ed. *SONS AND LOVERS: A Collection of Critical Essays*. Englewood Cliffs, N.J.: Prentice-Hall, 1970.

Fraiberg, Louis. "The Unattainable Self: D. H. Lawrence's *Sons and Lovers*." *Twelve Original Essays on Great English Novels*. Ed. Charles Shapiro, 175-201.

Gose, Elliott B., Jr. "An Expense of Spirit." *NMQ*, 25 (1956), 358-63.

Hinz, Evelyn J. "*Sons and Lovers*: The Archetypal Dimensions of Lawrence's Oedipal Tragedy." *DHLR*, 5 (1972), 26-53.

Hornick, Edward J., Harry T. Moore, and George D. Crothers. "*Sons and Lovers*." *Invitation to Learning*. Ed. George D. Crothers, 190-97.

Idema, James M. "The Hawk and the Plover: 'The Polarity of Life' in the 'Jungle Aviary' of D. H. Lawrence's Mind in *Sons and Lovers* and *The Rainbow*." *ForumH*, 3, 7 (1961), 11-14.

Jeffries, Christie. "Metaphor in *Sons and Lovers*." *Person*, 29 (1948), 287-92.

Kazin, Alfred. "Sons, Lovers and Mothers." *PR*, 29, 3 (1962), 373-85.

Kittner, Alfred Booth. "*Sons and Lovers*: A Freudian Appreciation." *PsyR*, 3 (1916), 295-317.

Littlewood, J. C. F. "Son and Lover." *CQ*, 4 (1969), 323-61.

Melchiori, Barbara. " 'Objects in the powerful light of emotion'." *ArielE*, 1, 1 (1970), 21-30.

Mortland, Donald E. "The Conclusion of *Sons and Lovers*: A Reconsideration." *SNNTS*, 3 (1971), 305-15.

D. H. Lawrence, continued

Moseley, Edwin M. *Pseudonyms of Christ in the Modern Novel*, 69-86.
New, William H. "Character as Symbol: Annie's Role in *Sons and Lovers*." *DHLR*, 1 (1968), 31-43.
Panken, Shirley. "Some Psychodynamics in *Sons and Lovers*: A New Look at the Oedipal Theme." *PsyR*, 61, 4 (1974-75), 571-89.
Pascal, Roy. "The Autobiographical Novel and the Autobiography." *EIC*, 9 (1959), 134-50.
Reddick, Bryan. "*Sons and Lovers*: The Omniscient Narrator." *Thoth*, 7 (1966), 68-75.
Rossman, Charles. "The Gospel According to D. H. Lawrence: Religion in *Sons and Lovers*." *DHLR*, 3 (1970), 31-41.
Salgado, Gamini. *D. H. Lawrence: SONS AND LOVERS*. London: E. Arnold, 1961.
Sepčić, Višnja. "Realism Versus Symbolism: The Double Patterning of *Sons and Lovers*." *SRAZ*, 33-36 (1972-73), 185-208.
Smith, Grover, Jr. "The Doll-Burners: D. H. Lawrence and Louisa Alcott." *MLQ*, 19 (1958), 28-32.
"*Sons and Lovers*." *Paunch*, 35 (1972), 26-31.
Spilka, Mark. "The Floral Pattern in *Sons and Lovers*." *NMQ*, 25 (1955), 44-56.
Taylor, John A. "The Greatness in *Sons and Lovers*." *MP*, 71 (1974), 380-87.
Tedlock, E. W., Jr., ed. *D. H. Lawrence and SONS AND LOVERS: Sources and Criticism*. New York: New York Univ. Press, 1965.
Tomlinson, T. B. "Lawrence and Modern Life: *Sons and Lovers*, *Women in Love*." *CR*, 8 (1965), 3-18.
Van Tassel, Daniel E. "The Search for Manhood in D. H. Lawrence's *Sons and Lovers*." *Costerus*, 3 (1972), 197-210.
Vredenburgh, Joseph L. "Further Contributions to a Study of the Incest Object." *AI*, 16 (1959), 263-68.
Weiss, Daniel. "D. H. Lawrence's Great Circle: From *Sons and Lovers* to *Lady Chatterley*." *PsyR*, 50, 3 (1963), 112-38.
————. "Oedipus in Nottinghamshire." *L&P*, 7 (1957), 33-42.
Wise, James N. "Emerson's 'Experience' and *Sons and Lovers*." *Costerus*, 6 (1972), 179-221.
Woolf, Virginia. *Collected Essays*, v. 1, 352-55.
See also: Brewster and Burrell; Buckley; Pritchett, *Living*; Van Ghent.

ST. MAWR

Craig, David, and T. W. Thomas. "The Critical Forum: Mr. Liddell and Dr. Leavis." *EIC*, 5 (1955), 64-80.
Gidley, Mick. "Antipodes: D. H. Lawrence's *St. Mawr*." *ArielE*, 5, 1 (1974), 25-41.

Leavis, F. R. "The Novel as Dramatic Poem: *St. Mawr.*" *Scrutiny,* 17 (1950), 38-53.
Liddell, Robert. "Lawrence and Dr. Leavis: The Case of *St. Mawr.*" *EIC,* 4 (1954), 321-27.
Ragussis, Michael. "The False Myth of *St. Mawr*: Lawrence and the Subterfuge of Art." *PLL,* 11 (1975), 186-96.
Scholtes, M. "*St. Mawr*: Between Degeneration and Regeneration." *DQR,* 5 (1975), 253-69.
Smith, Bob L. "D. H. Lawrence's *St. Mawr*: Transposition of Myth." *ArQ,* 24 (1968), 197-208.
Wasserman, Jerry. "*St. Mawr* and the Search for Community." *Mosaic,* 5, 2 (1972), 113-23.
Wilde, Alan. "The Illusion of St. Mawr: Technique and Vision in D. H. Lawrence's Novel." *PMLA,* 79 (1964), 164-70.

THE TRESPASSER

Corke, Helen. "The Writing of *The Trespasser.*" *DHLR,* 7 (1974), 227-39.
Gurko, Leo. "*The Trespasser*: D. H. Lawrence's Neglected Novel." *CE,* 24 (1962), 29-35.
Hinz, Evelyn J. "*The Trespasser*: Lawrence's Wagnerian Tragedy and Divine Comedy." *DHLR,* 4 (1971), 122-41.
Howarth, Herbert. "D. H. Lawrence from Island to Glacier." *UTQ,* 37 (1968), 215-29.
Millett, Robert. "Great Expectations: D. H. Lawrence's *The Trespasser.*" *Twenty-Seven to One.* Ed. Bradford B. Broughton, 125-32.
Sepčić, Višnja. "A Link Between D. H. Lawrence's *The Trespasser* and *The Rainbow.*" *SRAZ,* 24 (1967), 113-26.
Sharpe, Michael C. "The Genesis of D. H. Lawrence's *The Trespasser.*" *EIC,* 11 (1961), 34-39.

THE VIRGIN AND THE GIPSY

Crump, G. B. "Gopher Prairie or Papplewick? *The Virgin and the Gipsy* as Film." *DHLR,* 4 (1971), 142-53.
Gutierrez, Donald. "Lawrence's *The Virgin and the Gipsy* as Ironic Comedy." *LitQ,* 8 (1972-73), 61-69.
Meyers, Jeffrey. " 'The Voice of Water': *The Virgin and the Gipsy.*" *EM,* 21 (1970), 199-207.
Smith, Julian. "Vision and Revision: *The Virgin and the Gipsy* as Film." *LFQ,* 1 (1973), 28-36.

D. H. Lawrence, continued

THE WHITE PEACOCK

Gajdusek, Robert E. "A Reading of 'A Poem of Friendship': A Chapter in Lawrence's *The White Peacock.*" *DHLR*, 3 (1970), 47-62.

Ghiselin, Brewster. "D. H. Lawrence and the Peacocks of Atrani." *MQR*, 14 (1975), 119-34.

Hinz, Evelyn J. "Juno and *The White Peacock*: Lawrence's English Epic." *DHLR*, 3 (1970), 115-35.

Keith, W. J. "D. H. Lawrence's *The White Peacock*: An Essay in Criticism." *UTQ*, 37 (1968), 230-47.

Orr, Christopher. "D. H. Lawrence and E. M. Forster: From *The White Peacock* to *Maurice.*" *BWVACET*, 2, 2 (1975), 22-28.

Osgerby, J. R. "Set Books: D. H. Lawrence's *The White Peacock.*" *Use of English*, 13 (1962), 256-61.

Sepčić, Višnja. "*The White Peacock* Reconsidered." *SRAZ*, 38 (1974), 105-14.

Squires, Michael. "Lawrence's *The White Peacock*: A Mutation of Pastoral." *TSLL*, 12 (1970), 263-83.

Stanford, Raney. "Thomas Hardy and Lawrence's *The White Peacock.*" *MFS*, 5, 1 (1959), 19-28.

WOMEN IN LOVE

Adamowski, T. H. "Being Perfect: Lawrence, Sartre, and *Women in Love.*" *CritI*, 2 (1975), 345-68.

Barber, David S. "Can a Radical Interpretation of *Women in Love* Be Adequate?" *DHLR*, 3 (1970), 168-74.

_____. "Community in *Women in Love.*" *Novel*, 5 (1971), 32-41.

Beker, Miroslav. " 'The Crown,' 'The Reality of Peace,' and *Women in Love.*" *DHLR*, 2 (1969), 254-64.

Bickerton, Derek. "The Language of *Women in Love.*" *REL*, 8, 2 (1967), 56-67.

Branda, Eldon S. "Textual Changes in *Women in Love.*" *TSLL*, 6 (1964), 306-21.

Chamberlain, Robert L. "Pussum, Minette, and the Africo-Nordic Symbol in Lawrence's *Women in Love.*" *PMLA*, 78 (1963), 407-16.

Chavis, Geraldine G. "Ursula Brangwen: Toward Self and Selflessness." *Thoth*, 12, 1 (1971), 18-28.

Clark, Colin, ed. *THE RAINBOW and WOMEN IN LOVE: A Casebook.* London: Macmillan, 1969.

Clark, L. D. "The Contravened Knot." *Approaches to the Twentieth-Century Novel.* Ed. John Unterecker, 51-78.

Crump, G. B. "*Women in Love*: Novel and Film." *DHLR*, 4 (1971), 28-41.

204

Davis, Herbert. "*Women in Love*: A Corrected Typescript." *UTQ*, 27 (1957), 34-53.

Erlich, Richard D. "Catastrophism and Coition: Universal and Individual Development in *Women in Love*." *TSLL*, 9 (1967), 117-28.

Ford, George H. "An Introductory Note to D. H. Lawrence's Prologue to *Women in Love*." *TQ*, 6, 1 (1963), 92-97.

———. "Shelley or Schiller? A Note on D. H. Lawrence at Work." *TSLL*, 4 (1962), 154-56.

———. " 'The Wedding' Chapter of D. H. Lawrence's *Women in Love*." *TSLL*, 6 (1964), 134-47.

Gerber, Stephen. "Character, Language, and Experience in 'Water Party'." *Paunch*, 36-37 (1973), 3-29.

Goldknopf, David. "Realism in the Novel." *YR*, 60 (1970), 69-84.

Gregor, Ian. "Towards a Christian Literary Criticism." *Month*, 33 (1965), 239-49.

Hall, William F. "The Image of the Wolf in Chapter XXX of D. H. Lawrence's *Women in Love*." *DHLR*, 2 (1969), 272-74.

Harper, Howard M. "*Fantasia* and the Psychodynamics of *Women in Love*." *The Classic British Novel*. Ed. Howard M. Harper, Jr. and Charles Edge, 202-19.

Hyde, Virginia. "Will Brangwen and Paradisal Vision in *The Rainbow* and *Women in Love*." *DHLR*, 8 (1975), 346-57.

Jacobson, Sibyl. "The Paradox of Fulfillment: A Discussion of *Women in Love*." *JNT*, 3 (1973), 53-65.

Joffe, Phil. "*Women in Love*: The Minor Characters." *Bolt*, 1, 3 (1970), 3-8, 45-46.

Kay, Wallace G. "*Women in Love* and 'The Man Who Had Died': Resolving Apollo and Dionysus." *SoQ*, 10 (1972), 325-39.

Kestner, Joseph. "Sculptural Character in Lawrence's *Women in Love*." *MFS*, 21 (1975), 543-53.

Krieger, Murray. *The Tragic Vision*, 37-49.

Langman, F. H. "*Women in Love*." *EIC*, 17 (1967), 183-206.

Lawrence, D. H. "Prologue to *Women in Love*. (Unpublished)." *TQ*, 6, 1 (1963), 98-111.

Leavis, F. R. "The Novel as Dramatic Poem: *Women in Love*." *Scrutiny*, 17 (1950), 203-20; 17 (1951), 318-30; 18 (1951), 18-31.

Lee, Robin. "Darkness and 'A Heavy Gold Glamour': Lawrence's *Women in Love*." *Theoria*, 42 (1974), 57-64.

Martin, W. R. " 'Freedom Together' in D. H. Lawrence's *Women in Love*." *ESA*, 8 (1965), 111-20.

Miko, Stephen J. *Toward WOMEN IN LOVE: The Emergence of a Lawrentian Aesthetic*. New Haven: Yale Univ. Press, 1971.

D. H. Lawrence, continued

———, ed. *WOMEN IN LOVE: A Collection of Critical Essays.* Englewood Cliffs, N.J.: Prentice-Hall, 1969.

Moody, H. L. B. "African Sculpture Symbols in a Novel by D. H. Lawrence." *Ibadan*, 26 (1969), 73-77.

Mori, Haruhide. "Lawrence's Imagistic Development in *The Rainbow* and *Women in Love.*" *ELH*, 31 (1964), 460-81.

Newman, Paul B. "The Natural Aristocrat in Letters." *UR*, 31 (1964), 23-31.

Rachman, Shalom. "Art and Value in D. H. Lawrence's *Women in Love.*" *DHLR*, 5 (1972), 1-25.

Raskin, Jonah. *The Mythology of Imperialism*, 252-56.

Reddick, Bryan D. "Point of View and Narrative Tone in *Women in Love*: The Portrayal of Interpsychic Space." *DHLR*, 7 (1974), 156-71.

Remsbury, John. "*Women in Love* as a Novel of Change." *DHLR*, 6 (1973), 149-72.

Robson, W. W. "D. H. Lawrence and *Women in Love.*" *The Pelican Guide to English Literature*, v. 7. Ed. Boris Ford, 298-318.

Ross, Charles L. "The Composition of *Women in Love*: A History, 1913-1919." *DHLR*, 8 (1975), 198-212.

———. "A Problem of Textual Transmission in the Typescripts of *Women in Love.*" *Library*, 29 (1974), 197-205.

———, and George J. Zytaruk. "*Goats and Compasses* and/or *Women in Love*: An Exchange." *DHLR*, 6 (1973), 33-46.

Rudrum, Alan. "Philosophical Implication in Lawrence's *Women in Love.*" *DR*, 51 (1971), 240-50.

Sagar, Keith. "The Genesis of *The Rainbow* and *Women in Love.*" *DHLR*, 1 (1968), 179-99.

———. "*Goats and Compasses* and *Women in Love* Again." *DHLR*, 6 (1973), 303-08.

Schorer, Mark. "*Women in Love* and Death." *HudR*, 6 (1953), 34-47.

Sepčić, Višnja. "Notes on the Structure of *Women in Love.*" *SRAZ*, 21-22 (1966), 289-304.

Sharma, Radhe S. "The Symbol as Archetype: A Study of Symbolic Mode in D. H. Lawrence's *Women in Love.*" *OJES*, 8, 2 (1971), 31-53.

Simon, John I. *Movies into Film*, 57-62.

Smailes, T. A. "The Mythical Bases of *Women in Love.*" *DHLR*, 1 (1968), 129-36.

Spilka, Mark. "Star-Equilibrium in *Women in Love.*" *CE*, 17 (1955), 79-83.

Stroupe, John H. "Ruskin, Lawrence, and Gothic Naturalism." *BSUF*, 11, 2 (1970), 3-9.

Tomlinson, T. B. "Lawrence and Modern Life: *Sons and Lovers, Women in Love.*" *CR*, 8 (1965), 3-18.

Van Doren, Carl. *Roving Critic*, 209-11.

Vivas, Eliseo. "The Substance of *Women in Love.*" *SR*, 66 (1958), 588-632.

Weiss, Daniel. "Oedipus in Nottinghamshire." *L&P*, 7 (1957), 33-42.

Worthen, John. "Sanity, Madness, and *Women in Love.*" *Trivium*, 10 (1975), 125-36.

Zambrano, Ana Laura. "*Women in Love*: Counterpoint on Film." *LFQ*, 1 (1973), 46-54.

See also: Drew, *Novel.*

ROSAMOND LEHMANN

GENERAL STUDIES

Balakian, Nona. "Three English Novels." *KR*, 15 (1953), 490-96.

Blanche, Jacques-Emile. *More Portraits of a Lifetime*, 68-73.

Bowen, Elizabeth. "The Modern Novel and the Theme of Love." *New Republic*, 128 (May 11, 1953), 18-19.

Coopman, Tony. "Symbolism in Rosamond Lehmann's *The Echoing Grove.*" *RLV*, 40 (1974), 116-21.

Dangerfield, George. "Rosamond Lehmann and the Perilous Enchantment of Things Past." *Bookman* (N.Y.), 76 (1933), 172-76.

Dorosz, Wiktoria. *Subjective Vision and Human Relationships in the Novels of Rosamond Lehmann*. Stockholm: Almqvist and Wiksell, 1975.

Fremantle, Anne. "Whose Fountains are Within." *Cweal*, 42 (1945), 72-75.

Gindin, James J. "Rosamond Lehmann: A Revaluation." *ConL*, 15 (1974), 203-11.

Jarka, Horst. "Pre-War Austria as Seen by Spender, Isherwood and Lehmann." *PPNCFL*, 15 (1964), 231-40.

Kaplan, Sydney Janet. *Feminine Consciousness in the Modern British Novel*, 110-35.

LeStourgeon, Diana E. *Rosamond Lehmann*. New York: Twayne, 1965.

Millett, Fred B. "Feminine Fiction." *Cornhill*, 155 (1937), 225-35.

Pendry, E. D. *The New Feminism of English Fiction*, 153-72.

Raven, Simon. "The Cause that Nobody Wins: The Novels of Rosamond Lehmann." *LonM*, n.s. 3, 1 (April 1963), 59-64.

Shuman, R. Baird. "Personal Isolation in the Novels of Rosamond Lehmann." *RLV*, 26 (1960), 76-80.

Rosamond Lehmann, continued

Thornton, Lawrence. "Rosamond Lehmann, Henry James, and the Temporal Matrix of Fiction." *VWQ*, 1, 3 (1973), 66-75.
See also: Allen, *Tradition*; McCormick.

DORIS LESSING

BIBLIOGRAPHIES
Burkom, Selma R. *Doris Lessing: A Checklist of Primary and Secondary Sources.* Troy, N.Y.: Whitston, 1973.
_____. "A Doris Lessing Checklist." *Crit*, 11, 1 (1969), 69-81.
Ipp, C. *Doris Lessing.* Johannesburg: Univ. of the Witwatersrand Dept. of Bibliography, Librarianship and Typography, 1967.
Krouse, Agate N. "A Doris Lessing Checklist." *ConL*, 14 (1973), 590-97.

INTERVIEWS
Driver, C. J. "Profile 8: Doris Lessing." *New Review*, 1 (1974), 17-23.
Howe, Florence. "A Conversation with Doris Lessing." *ConL*, 14 (1973), 418-36.
_____. "A Talk with Doris Lessing." *Nation*, 204 (1967), 311-13.
Newquist, Roy, ed. *Counterpoint*, 414-24.
Oates, Joyce Carol. "A Visit with Doris Lessing." *SoR*, n.s. 9 (1973), 873-82.
Raskin, Jonah. "Doris Lessing at Stony Brook: An Interview." *New American Review 8*. New York: New American Library, 1970, 166-179.
Webb, Marilyn. "Feminism and Doris Lessing: Becoming the Men We Wanted to Marry." *Village Voice*, Jan. 4, 1973, 1, 14-17, 19.
Wiseman, Thomas. "Mrs. Lessing's Kind of Life." *T&T*, 42 (April 12, 1962), 26-29.

SPECIAL ISSUES
Contemporary Literature [*ConL*], 14 (1973).
"Special Section on Doris Lessing." *Anonymous*, 1 (1974), 47-81.
World Literature Written in English [*WLWE*], 12, 2 (1973).

GENERAL STUDIES
Barnouw, Dagmar. "Disorderly Company: From *The Golden Notebook* to *The Four-Gated City*." *ConL*, 14 (1973), 491-514.
Bergonzi, Bernard. "In Pursuit of Doris Lessing." *NYRB*, 2 (February 11, 1965), 12-14.
Brewer, Joseph E. "The Anti-Hero in Contemporary Literature." *IEY*, 12 (1967), 55-60.
Brewster, Dorothy. *Doris Lessing.* New York: Twayne, 1965.

Brown, Lloyd W. "The Shape of Things: Sexual Images and the Sense of Form in Doris Lessing's Fiction." *WLWE*, 14 (1975), 176-86.

Burkom, Selma R. " 'Only Connect': Form and Content in the Works of Doris Lessing." *Crit*, 11, 1 (1969), 51-68.

Drabble, Margaret. "Doris Lessing: Cassandra in a World Under Siege." *Ramparts*, February 10, 1972, 50-54.

Graves, Nora C. "Doris Lessing's Two Antheaps." *NConL*, 2, 3 (1972), 6-8.

Hardin, Nancy S. "Doris Lessing and the Sufi Way." *ConL*, 14 (1973), 565-81.

Howe, Florence. "Doris Lessing's Free Women." *Nation*, 200 (1965), 34-37.

Joyner, Nancy. "The Underside of the Butterfly: Lessing's Debt to Woolf." *JNT*, 4 (1974), 204-11.

Kaplan, Sydney Janet. *Feminine Consciousness in the Modern British Novel*, 136-72.

―――. "The Limits of Consciousness in the Novels of Doris Lessing." *ConL*, 14 (1973), 536-49.

Karl, Frederick R. "Doris Lessing in the Sixties: The New Anatomy of Melancholy." *ConL*, 13 (1972), 15-33.

Lebowitz, Naomi. *Humanism and the Absurd*, 130-36.

Lefcowitz, Barbara F. "Dream and Action in Lessing's *The Summer Before the Dark*." *Crit*, 17, 2 (1975), 107-20.

Lessing, Doris. *A Small Personal Voice: Essays, Reviews, and Interviews by Doris Lessing*. Ed. Paul Schlueter. New York: Knopf, 1974.

McDowell, Frederick P. W. "The Fiction of Doris Lessing: An Interim View." *ArQ*, 21 (1965), 315-45.

Marchino, Lois A. "The Search for Self in the Novels of Doris Lessing." *SNNTS*, 4 (1972), 252-61.

Markow, Alice B. "The Pathology of Feminine Failure in the Fiction of Doris Lessing." *Crit*, 16, 1 (1974), 88-100.

O'Fallon, Kathleen. "Quest for a New Vision." *WLWE*, 12, 2 (1973), 180-89.

Owen, Roger. "A Good Man Is Hard to Find." *Commentary*, 39, 4 (April 1965), 79-82.

Pratt, Annis. "Women and Nature in Modern Fiction." *ConL*, 13 (1972), 476-90.

―――, and L. S. Dembo, eds. *Doris Lessing: Critical Studies*. Madison: Univ. of Wisconsin Press, 1974.

Rapping, Elayne Antler. "Unfree Women: Feminism in Doris Lessing's Novels." *WS*, 3 (1975), 29-44.

Doris Lessing, continued

Rose, Ellen Cronan. "The Eriksonian Bildungsroman: An Approach Through Doris Lessing." *HSL*, 7 (1975), 1-17.
Rubenstein, Roberta. "Outer Space, Inner Space: Doris Lessing's Metaphor of Science Fiction." *WLWE*, 14, 1 (1975), 187-97.
Ryf, Robert S. "Beyond Ideology: Doris Lessing's Mature Vision." *MFS*, 21 (1975), 193-201.
Schlueter, Paul. "Doris Lessing: The Free Woman's Commitment." *Contemporary British Novelists*. Ed. Charles Shapiro, 48-61.
_____. *The Novels of Doris Lessing*. Carbondale: Southern Illinois Univ. Press, 1973.
Seligman, Dee. "The Sufi Quest." *WLWE*, 12, 2 (1973), 190-206.
Silva, Nancy Neufield. "Doris Lessing's Ideal Reconciliation." *Anonymous*, 1 (1974), 72-81.
Spacks, Patricia M. "Free Women." *HudR*, 24 (1971), 559-73.
Spilka, Mark. "Lessing and Lawrence: The Battle of the Sexes." *ConL*, 16 (1975), 218-40.
Stein, Karen F. "Reflections in a Jagged Mirror: Some Metaphors of Madness." *Aphra*, 6, 2 (1975), 2-11.
Sudrann, Jean. "Hearth and Horizon: Changing Concepts of the 'Domestic' Life of the Heroine." *MR*, 14 (1973), 235-50.
Sukenick, Lynn. "Feeling and Reason in Doris Lessing's Fiction." *ConL*, 14 (1973), 515-35.
Thorpe, Michael. *Doris Lessing*. Harlow: Longmans, Green, 1973.
Tiger, Virginia. "Advertisements for Herself." *CUF*, 3, 2 (1974), 15-16, 18-19.
Tucker, Martin. *Africa in Modern Literature*, 175-83.
Zak, Michele W. "*The Grass Is Singing*: A Little Novel About the Emotions." *ConL*, 14 (1973), 481-90.
See also: Bergonzi, *Situation*; Gindin, *Postwar*.

BRIEFING FOR A DESCENT INTO HELL
Ahearn, Marie. "Science Fiction in the Mainstream Novel: Doris Lessing." *Proceedings of the Fifth National Convention of the Popular Culture Association*, ed. Michael T. Marsden, 1277-96.
Bolling, Douglass. "Structure and Theme in *Briefing for a Descent into Hell*." *ConL* 14 (1973), 550-65.
Richey, Clarence W. "Professor Watkins' 'Sleep of Necessity': A Note on the Parallel Between Doris Lessing's *Briefing for a Descent into Hell* and the G. I. Gurdjieff-P. D. Ouspensky System of Esoteric Psychology." *NConL*, 2, 2 (1972), 9-11.

CHILDREN OF VIOLENCE
[MARTHA QUEST, A PROPER MARRIAGE, A RIPPLE
FROM THE STORM, LANDLOCKED, THE FOUR-GATED
CITY]
Aycock, Linnea. "The Mother/Daughter Relationship in the *Children of Violence* Series." *Anonymous*, 1 (1974), 48-55.
Lewis, M. Susan. "Conscious Evolution in *The Four-Gated City*." *Anonymous*, 1 (1974), 56-71.
Porter, Nancy. "Silenced History: *Children of Violence* and *The Golden Notebook*." *WLWE*, 12, 2 (1973), 161-79.
Steele, M. C. *CHILDREN OF VIOLENCE and Rhodesia: A Study of Doris Lessing as Historical Observer*. Salisbury: Central Africa Hist. Assoc., 1974.
"The Wrong Members in Control." *TLS*, July 3, 1969, 720.
See also: Enright, *Onion*; R. Morris, *Continuance*.

THE GOLDEN NOTEBOOK
Brooks, Ellen W. "The Image of Woman in Lessing's *The Golden Notebook*." *Crit*, 15, 1 (1973), 101-09.
Carey, John L. "Art and Reality in *The Golden Notebook*." *ConL*, 14 (1973), 437-56.
Craig, Joanne. "*The Golden Notebook*: The Novelist as Heroine." *UWR*, 10, 1 (1974), 55-66.
Hinz, Evelyn J., and John J. Teunissen. "The Pietà as Icon in *The Golden Notebook*." *ConL*, 14 (1973), 457-70.
Hynes, Joseph. "The Construction of *The Golden Notebook*." *IowaR*, 4, 3 (1973), 100-13.
Lessing, Doris. "On the Golden Notebook." *PR*, 40 (1973), 14-30.
Libby, Marion V. "Sex and the New Woman in *The Golden Notebook*." *IowaR*, 5 (1974), 106-20.
Lightfoot, Marjorie J. "Breakthrough in *The Golden Notebook*." *SNNTS*, 7 (1975), 277-84.
Morgan, Ellen. "Alienation of the Woman Writer in *The Golden Notebook*." *ConL*, 14 (1973), 471-80.
Mulkeen, Anne M. "Twentieth-Century Realism: The 'Grid' Structure of *The Golden Notebook*." *SNNTS*, 4 (1972), 262-74.
Mutti, Giuliana. "Female Roles and the Function of Art in *The Golden Notebook*." *MSE*, 3, 3 (1972), 78-83.
Porter, Dennis. "Realism and Failure in *The Golden Notebook*." *MLQ*, 35 (1974), 56-65.

Porter, Nancy. "Silenced History: *Children of Violence* and *The Golden Notebook.*" *WLWE*, 12, 2 (1973), 161-79.

Pratt, Annis. "The Contrary Structure of Doris Lessing's *The Golden Notebook.*" *WLWE*, 12, 2 (1973), 150-60.

Rubenstein, Roberta. "Doris Lessing's *The Golden Notebook*: The Meaning of Its Shape." *AI*, 32 (1975), 40-58.

Spencer, Sharon. " 'Femininity' and the Woman Writer: Doris Lessing's *The Golden Notebook* and the *Diary* of Anais Nin." *WS*, 1 (1973), 247-57.

C. S. LEWIS

BIBLIOGRAPHIES

Christopher, Joe R., and Joan K. Ostling, eds. *C. S. Lewis: An Annotated Checklist of Writings About Him and His Works.* Kent, Ohio: Kent State Univ. Press, 1973.

INTERVIEWS

Wrong, Charles. "Meeting with C. S. Lewis in Broad St., Oxford, This Afternoon (August 8, 1959)." *CSLBull*, 4, 4 (1973), 6-8.

GENERAL STUDIES

Adey, Lionel. "The Barfield-Lewis 'Great War'." *CSLBull*, 6, 10 (1975), 10-14.

Arnott, Anne. *The Secret Country of C. S. Lewis.* London: Hodder and Stoughton, 1974.

Babbage, Stuart B. "C. S. Lewis and the Humanitarian Theory of Punishment." *CSR*, 2 (1972), 224-35.

Carnell, Corbin S. *Bright Shadow of Reality: C. S. Lewis and the Feeling Intellect.* Grand Rapids, Mich.: Eerdmans, 1974.

_____. "C. S. Lewis: An Appraisal." *Mythlore*, 1, 4 (1969), 18-20.

_____. "C. S. Lewis on Eros as a Means of Grace." *Imagination and the Spirit.* Ed. Charles A. Huttar, 341-51.

Frost, Naomi. "Life after Death: Visions of Lewis and Williams." *CSLBull*, 6, 6 (1975), 2-6.

Gardner, Helen. *Clive Staples Lewis, 1898-1963.* London: Oxford Univ. Press, 1966.

_____. "Clive Staples Lewis, 1898-1963." *PBA*, 51 (1965), 417-28.

Gibb, Jocelyn, ed. *Light on C. S. Lewis.* London: Bles, 1965; New York: Harcourt, 1966.

Gilbert, Douglas. *C. S. Lewis: Images of His World.* Grand Rapids, Mich.: Eerdmans, 1974.

Green, Roger L., and Walter Hooper. *C. S. Lewis: A Biography.* New York: Harcourt, 1974.

GoodKnight, Glen. "A Comparison of Cosmological Geography in the Works of J. R. R. Tolkien, C. S. Lewis, and Charles Williams." *Mythlore*, 1, 3 (1969), 18-22.

———. "The Social History of the Inklings, J. R. R. Tolkien, C. S. Lewis, and Charles Williams." *Mythlore*, 2, 1 (1970), 7-9.

Haldane, J. B. S. "Auld Hornie, F. R. S." *ModQ*, n.s. 1 (1946), 32-40.

Hannay, Margaret. "C. S. Lewis' Theory of Mythology." *Mythlore*, 1, 1 (1969), 14-24.

———. "C. S. Lewis and Homosexuality." *CSLBull*, 5, 1 (1973), 2-5.

———. "Orual: The Search for Justice." *Mythlore*, 2, 3 (1971), 5-6.

Highet, Gilbert. *People, Places, and Books*, 130-37.

Hutton, Muriel. ". . . and I Quote." *CSLBull*, 3, 11 (1972), 5-16.

Keefe, Carolyn, ed. *C. S. Lewis: Speaker and Teacher.* Grand Rapids, Mich.: Zondervan, 1971.

Kilby, Clyde S. *The Christian World of C. S. Lewis.* Grand Rapids, Mich.: Eerdmans, 1964.

———. "Tolkien, Lewis, and Williams." *Mythcon I: Proceedings.* Ed. Glen GoodKnight, 3-4.

———, and Linda J. Evans. "C. S. Lewis and Music." *CSR*, 4 (1974), 1-15.

Kimball, William C. "The Christian Commitment: C. S. Lewis and the Defense of Doctrine." *BYUS*, 12 (1972), 185-208.

Kirkpatrick, Hope. "Hierarchy in C. S. Lewis." *CSLBull*, 6, 4 (1975), 1-6.

———. "The Humanitarian Theory of Punishment." *CSLBull*, 5, 2 (1973), 1-6.

———. "Lewis *contra* Freud." *CSLBull*, 4, 4 (1973), 2-6.

———. "Some Preliminary Thoughts on Lewis and Freud." *CSLBull*, 3, 11 (1972), 2-4.

Kirkpatrick, Mary. "Lewis and MacDonald." *CSLBull*, 5, 7 (1974), 2-4.

Kranz, Gisbert. "Dante in the Work of C. S. Lewis." *CSLBull*, 4, 10 (1973), 1-8.

Kreeft, Peter. *C. S. Lewis: A Critical Essay.* Grand Rapids, Mich.: Eerdmans, 1969.

Kuhn, Daniel K. "The Joy of the Absolute: A Comparative Study of the Romantic Visions of William Wordsworth and C. S. Lewis." *Imagination and the Spirit.* Ed. Charles A. Huttar, 189-214.

Lewis, C. S. *Of Other Worlds.* Ed. Walter Hooper. London: Bles, 1966; New York: Harcourt, 1967.

C. S. Lewis, continued

Lindskoog, Kathryn. "Farewell to Shadowlands: C. S. Lewis on Death." *Mythcon I: Proceedings.* Ed. Glen GoodKnight, 10-12.

McGovern, Eugene. "Obstinacy in Belief at the Socratic Club." *CSLBull*, 4, 1 (1973), 2-5.

Milward, Peter. "C. S. Lewis on Allegory." *EigoS*, 114 (1968), 227-32.

Moorman, Charles. *Arthurian Triptych*, 102-26.

Myers, Doris T. "Brave New World: The Status of Women According to Tolkien, Lewis, and Williams." *CimR*, 17 (1971), 13-19.

Nott, Kathleen. *Emperor's Clothes*, 253-98.

Pittenger, W. Norman. "Apologist vs. Apologist: A Critique of C. S. Lewis as 'Defender of the Faith'." *ChCen*, 75, October 1, 1958, 1104-07 and December 24, 1958, 1485-86.

Plank, Robert. "Can Lewis and Freud Be Reconciled?" *CSLBull*, 4, 5 (1973), 5-7.

Purcell, James M. "Lewis vs. Empson: Was Eden Plato's or OGPU's?" *CSLBull*, 4, 6 (1973), 6-8.

Purtill, Richard. *Lord of the Elves and Eldils*, 15-211.

Reilly, Robert J. *Romantic Religion*, 98-147.

Robson, W. W. "C. S. Lewis." *CQ*, 1 (1966), 252-72.

Rose, Lois, and Stephen Rose. *The Shattered Ring*, 60-64.

Routley, Erik. "The Prophet Lewis." *CSLBull*, 4, 1 (1973), 5-7.

Sale, Roger. "England's Parnassus: C. S. Lewis, Charles Williams, and J. R. R. Tolkien." *HudR*, 17 (1964), 203-25.

Samaan, Angele Botros. "C. S. Lewis: The Utopist and His Critics." *CairoSE*, 1963-66, 137-66.

Stahl, John T. "Austin Farrer on C. S. Lewis as 'The Christian Apologist'." *CSR*, 4 (1975), 231-37.

Sundaram, P. S. "C. S. Lewis: Literary Critic." *Quest*, 60 (1969), 58-66.

Thompson, Claude H. "The Unmaking of an Atheist." *EUQ*, 12 (October 1956), 148-56.

Tripp, Raymond P., Jr., ed. *Man's "Natural Powers": Essays for and about C. S. Lewis.* [London?]: Soc. for New Lang. Study, 1975.

Urang, Gunnar. *Shadows of Heaven*, 5-50.

Utley, Francis L. "Anglicanism and Anthropology: C. S. Lewis and John Speirs." *SFQ*, 31 (1967), 1-11.

Wain, John. "C. S. Lewis." *Encounter*, 22 (May 1964), 51-53, 56.

Walsh, Chad. "C. S. Lewis and the Christian Life." *CathW*, (1949), 370-75.

———. "C. S. Lewis: Apostle to the Skeptics." *Atlantic*, 178 (September 1946), 115-19.

———. *C. S. Lewis: Apostle to the Skeptics.* New York: Macmillan, 1949.

_____. "C. S. Lewis: The Man and the Mystery." *Shadows of Imagination*. Ed. Mark R. Hillegas, 1-14.

Weatherby, H. L. "Two Medievalists: Lewis and Eliot on Christianity and Literature." *SR*, 78 (1970), 330-47.

Weinig, Sister Mary Anthony. "Images of Affirmation: Perspectives on the Fiction of Charles Williams, C. S. Lewis, J. R. R. Tolkien." *UPoR*, 20, 1 (1968), 43-46.

West, Richard C. "Contemporary Medieval Authors." *Orcrist*, 3 (1969), 9-10, 15.

White, William L. *The Image of Man in C. S. Lewis*. Nashville, Tenn.: Abingdon, 1969.

Wright, Marjorie E. "The Vision of Cosmic Order in the Oxford Myth-makers." *Imagination and the Spirit*. Ed. Charles A. Huttar, 259-76.

Wrong, Charles. "Christianity and Progress." *CSLBull*, 6, 10 (1975), 19-24.

See also: Fuller, *Books*.

THE CHRONICLES OF NARNIA
[THE LION, THE WITCH AND THE WARDROBE, PRINCE CASPIAN, THE VOYAGE OF THE "DAWN TREADER," THE SILVER CHAIR, THE HORSE AND HIS BOY, THE MAGICIAN'S NEPHEW, THE LAST BATTLE]

Another Clerk [pseud.]. "Narnia: The Journey and Garden Symbols in *The Magician's Nephew* and *The Horse and His Boy*." *CSLBull*, 3, 8 (1972), 5-8.

Aymard, Eliane. "On C. S. Lewis and the *Narnian Chronicles*." *Caliban*, 5 (1968), 129-45.

Brady, Charles A. "Finding God in Narnia." *America*, 46 (October 27, 1956), 103-05.

Christopher, Joe R. "An Introduction to Narnia. Part I: The Chronology of the Chronicles." *Mythlore*, 2, 2 (1970), 23-25.

_____. "An Introduction to Narnia, Part II: The Geography of the Chronicles." *Mythlore*, 2, 3 (1971), 12-16, 27.

_____. "An Introduction to Narnia: Part IV: The Literary Classification of the Chronicles." *Mythlore*, 3, 1 (1973), 12-15, 27.

Ellwood, Gracia F. "A High and Lonely Destiny." *Mythcon I: Proceedings*. Ed. Glen GoodKnight, 23-27.

Hooper, Walter. "Narnia: The Author, the Critics, and the Tale." *Children's Literature: The Great Excluded*, v. 3. Ed. Francelia Butler and Bennett A. Brockman, 12-22.

C. S. Lewis, continued

_____. "Past Watchful Dragons: The Fairy Tales of C. S. Lewis." *Imagination and the Spirit.* Ed. Charles A. Huttar, 277-339.

Lindskoog, Kathryn A. *The Lion of Judah in Never-Never Land: The Theology of C. S. Lewis Expressed in His Fantasies for Children.* Grand Rapids, Mich.: Eerdmans, 1973.

Narnia Conference Proceedings. Maywood, Cal.: Mythopoeic Society, 1970.

Smith, L. H. "News from Narnia." *Only Connect.* Ed. Sheila Egoff, G. Stubbs, T. and L. F. Ashley, 170-75.

SPACE TRILOGY
[OUT OF THE SILENT PLANET, PERELANDRA, THAT HIDEOUS STRENGTH]

Aquino, John. "Shaw and C. S. Lewis's *Space Trilogy.*" *ShawR*, 18 (1975), 28-32.

Callahan, Patrick J. "The Two Gardens in C. S. Lewis's *That Hideous Strength.*" *Science Fiction: The Other Side of Realism.* Ed. Thomas D. Clareson, 147-56.

Como, James. "Myth and Belief in *Perelandra.*" *CSLBull*, 4, 2 (1972), 2-7.

Deasy, Philip. "God, Space, and C. S. Lewis." *Cweal*, 68 (1958), 421-23.

Green, Roger Lancelyn. *Into Other Worlds: Space-Flight in Fiction from Lucian to Lewis.* London and New York: Abelard-Schuman, 1958.

Grennan, Margaret R. "The Lewis Trilogy: A Scholar's Holiday." *CathW*, 167 (1948), 337-44.

Hamm, Victor M. "Mr. Lewis in Perelandra." *Thought*, 20 (1945), 271-90.

Hannay, Margaret. "Arthurian and Cosmic Myth in *That Hideous Strength.*" *Mythlore*, 2, 2 (1970), 7-9.

_____. "The Mythology of *Out of the Silent Planet.*" *Mythlore*, 1, 4 (1969), 11-14.

_____. "The Mythology of *Perelandra.*" *Mythlore* 2, 1 (1970), 14-16.

Haynes, Jack. "Eros in *That Hideous Strength.*" *CSLBull*, 5, 6 (1974), 2-4.

Hillegas, Mark R. "*Out of the Silent Planet* as Cosmic Voyage." *Shadows of Imagination.* Ed. Mark R. Hillegas, 41-58.

Hodgens, Richard. "The Planetology of C. S. Lewis: In Summary." *CSLBull*, 3, 9 (1972), 2-5.

Hume, Kathryn. "C. S. Lewis' Trilogy: A Cosmic Romance." *MFS*, 20 (1974-75), 505-17.

216

Irwin, W. R. "There and Back Again: The Romances of Williams, Lewis, and Tolkien." *SR*, 69 (1961), 566-78.

Jeanes, Geoff. " 'Other Worlds' in Fiction: Reflections on a Body of Literature." *CSLBull*, 6, 8 (1975), 1-4.

Lieb, Laurie. "Body and Mind in *That Hideous Strength*." *CSLBull*, 5, 11 (1974), 10-12.

Lobdell, Jared C. "C. S. Lewis, Distributist: His Economics as Seen in *That Hideous Strength*." *Orcrist*, 6 (1971-72), 20-21.

———. "That Hideous Strength." *CSLBull*, 4, 5 (1973), 1-5.

Manlove, Colin N. *Modern Fantasy*, 99-151.

Moorman, Charles. " 'Now Entertain Conjecture of a Time': The Fictive Worlds of C. S. Lewis and J. R. R. Tolkien." *Shadows of Imagination*. Ed. Mark R. Hillegas, 59-69.

———. *The Precincts of Felicity*, 65-85, 97-99.

———. "Space Ships and Grail: The Myths of C. S. Lewis." *CE*, 18 (1957), 401-05.

Neulieb, Janice. "Technology and Theocracy: The Cosmic Voyages of Wells and Lewis." *Extrapolation*, 16 (1975), 130-36.

Nolan, Charles J., Jr. "The Child Motif in *That Hideous Strength*." *CSLBull*, 5, 10 (1974), 5-7.

Norwood, W. D., Jr. "C. S. Lewis, Owen Barfield, and the Modern Myth." *MQ*, 8 (1967), 279-91.

———. "Unifying Themes in C. S. Lewis' Trilogy." *Crit*, 9, 2 (1967), 67-80.

Phelan, John M. "Men and Morals in Space." *America*, 113 (October 9, 1965), 405-07.

Philmus, Robert M. "C. S. Lewis and the Fictions of 'Scientism'." *Extrapolation*, 13 (1972), 92-101.

Plank, Robert. "Some Psychological Aspects of Lewis's Trilogy." *Shadows of Imagination*. Ed. Mark R. Hillegas, 26-40.

Rothberg, Ellen. "The 'hnau' Creatures of C. S. Lewis." *Mythcon I: Proceedings*. Ed. Glen GoodKnight, 49-53.

Schmerl, Rudolf B. "Fantasy as Technique." *VQR*, 43 (1967), 644-56.

Shumaker, Wayne. "The Cosmic Trilogy of C. S. Lewis." *HudR*, 8 (1955), 240-54.

Spacks, Patricia Meyer. "The Myth-Maker's Dilemma: Three Novels by C. S. Lewis." *Discourse*, 2 (1959), 234-44.

Vidal, Jaime. "The Ubiquitous Center in Bonaventure and Lewis: With Application to the Great Dance on Perelandra." *CSLBull*, 6, 5 (1974), 1-4.

Wallis, Ethel. "Surprising Joy: C. S. Lewis' Deep Space Trilogy." *Mythcon I: Proceedings*. Ed. Glen GoodKnight, 21-23.

Watt, Donald. "The View from Malacandra." *CSLBull*, 6, 8 (1975), 5-7.

C. S. Lewis, continued

TILL WE HAVE FACES

Braude, Nan. "Sion and Parnassus: Three Approaches to Myth." *Mythlore*, 1, 1 (1969), 6-8.

Christopher, Joe R. "The Labors of Psyche: A Sorting of Events." *CSLBull*, 7, 1 (1975), 7-10.

Como, James. "*Till We Have Faces*: A Preface to Comprehension." *CSLBull*, 7, 1 (1975), 1-3.

Keefe, Carolyn. "Mystic Experience in *Till We Have Faces*." *CSLBull*, 7, 1 (1975), 4-7.

Norwood, W. D., Jr. "C. S. Lewis' Portrait of Aphrodite." *SoQ*, 8 (1970), 237-72.

Warren, Eugene. "Venus Redeemed." *Orcrist*, 6 (1971-72), 14-16.

WYNDHAM LEWIS

INTERVIEWS

Murphy, J. Stanley. "Wyndham Lewis at Windsor." *CanL*, 35 (1968), 9-19.

Symons, Julian. "Meeting Wyndham Lewis." *LonM*, 4, 10 (October 1957), 47-53.

SPECIAL ISSUES

Agenda, 7, 3-8, 1 (1970).

Canadian Literature [CanL], 35 (1968), 9-73.

Shenandoah, 4, 2-3 (1953), 3-88.

Twentieth Century Verse [TCV], 6/7 (November/December 1937), 104-48.

GENERAL STUDIES

Allen, Walter. "Lonely Old Volcano: The Achievement of Wyndham Lewis." *Encounter*, 21 (September 1963), 63-70.

————. "The Roaring Queen." *Encounter*, 41 (August 1973), 41-47.

————, and Michael Ayrton. "Wyndham Lewis." *Meanjin*, 16 (1957), 189-95.

Armstrong, Terrence I. F. *Apes, Japes, and Hitlerism: A Study and Bibliography of Wyndham Lewis*. London: Unicorn, 1932.

Chapman, Robert T. *Wyndham Lewis: Fictions and Satires*. New York: Barnes and Noble, 1973.

Cox, Kenneth. "Dualism and les Autres." *Agenda*, 7, 3-8, 1 (1970), 134-39.

Currie, Robert. *Genius: An Ideology in Literature*, 116-42.

Dale, Peter. "*The Revenge for Love*." *Agenda*, 7, 3-8, 1 (1970), 71-77.

————. "*Self Condemned*." *Agenda*, 7, 3-8, 1 (1970), 31-36.

Dohmen, William F. " 'Chilly Spaces': Wyndham Lewis as Ondt." *JJQ*, 11 (1974), 368-86.

Eliot, T. S. "The Lion and the Fox." *TCV*, 6/7 (November/December 1937), 109-12.

―――. "A Note on *Monstre Gai.*" *HudR*, 7 (1955), 522-26.

―――. "Wyndham Lewis." *HudR*, 10 (1957), 167-70.

―――. "Wyndham Lewis: Two Views." *Shenandoah*, 4, 2-3 (1953), 64-71.

Fjelde, Rolf. "Time, Space, and Wyndham Lewis." *WestR*, 15 (1951), 201-12.

Fox, C. J. "The Wild Land: A Celebration of Globalism." *CanL*, 35 (1968), 29-36.

Fraser, G. S. "Wyndham Lewis: An Energy of Mind." *TC*, 161 (1957), 386-92.

Friedman, Melvin J. "Three Experiences of the War: A Triptych." *Promise of Greatness*. Ed. George A. Panichas, 541-55.

Frye, Northrop. "Neo-Classical Agony." *HudR*, 10 (1958), 592-98.

Gregory, Horace. *The Dying Gladiators*, 21-28.

Grigson, Geoffrey. *A Master of Our Time: A Study of Wyndham Lewis*. London: Methuen, 1951.

―――. "Recollections of Wyndham Lewis." *Listener*, 57 (1957), 785-86.

―――. "Wyndham Lewis." *Living Writers*. Ed. Gilbert Phelps, 70-78.

Handley-Read, Charles, ed. *The Art of Wyndham Lewis*. London: Faber and Faber, 1951.

Harrison, John R. *The Reactionaries*, 77-110.

Holloway, John. *The Charted Mirror*, 118-36.

―――. "From Between the Dragon's Teeth." *CritQ*, 13 (1971), 367-76.

―――. "Wyndham Lewis: The Massacre and the Innocents." *HudR*, 10 (1957), 171-88.

Holroyd, Michael. "Damn and 'Blast!': The Friendship of Wyndham Lewis and Augustus John." Royal Soc. of Lit. of the U. K., London. *Essays by Divers Hands*, v. 38, 48-57.

Jameson, Frederic. "Wyndham Lewis as Futurist." *HudR*, 26 (1973), 295-329.

Kenner, Hugh. "Excerpts from *The Man of the World.*" *Agenda*, 7, 3 - 8, 1 (1970), 181-83.

―――. *Gnomon*, 215-41.

―――. "The Last European." *CanL*, 36 (1968), 5-13.

―――. "The Revenge of the Void." *HudR*, 6 (1953), 382-97.

―――. "The War with Time." *Shenandoah*, 4, 2-3 (1953), 18-49.

―――. *Wyndham Lewis*. Norfolk, Conn.: New Directions, 1954.

Kermode, Frank. "The New Apocalyptists." *PR*, 33 (1966), 339-61.

Wyndham Lewis, continued

Kirk, Russell. "Wyndham Lewis' First Principles." *YR*, 44 (1955), 520-34.
Leavis, F. R. *The Common Pursuit*, 240-47.
McLuhan, Marshall. *The Interior Landscape*, 83-94.
————. "Wyndham Lewis: His Theory of Art and Communication." *Shenandoah*, 4, 2-3 (1953), 77-88.
————. "Wyndham Lewis: Lemuel in Lilliput." *SLUSHSTA*, 2 (1944), 58-72.
Materer, Timothy. "Wyndham Lewis: Satirist of the Machine Age." *SNL*, 10 (1973), 9-18.
Mayne, Richard. "Wyndham Lewis." *Encounter*, 38 (February 1972), 42-51.
Mudrick, Marvin. "The Double-Artist and the Injured Party." *Shenandoah*, 4, 2-3 (1953), 54-64.
Murphy, J. Stanley. "Wyndham Lewis at Windsor." *CanL*, 35 (1968), 9-19.
Newton, Eric. "Emergence of Mr. Wyndham Lewis." *Listener*, 41, 1060 (May 19, 1949), 852; *In My View*, 248-51.
Parker, David H. "The Vorticist, 1914: The Artist as a Predatory Savage." *SoRA*, 8 (1975), 3-21.
Parsons, D. S. J. "Roy Campbell and Wyndham Lewis." *PLL*, 7 (1971), 406-21.
Porteus, Hugh Gordon. "Anthologies of Lewis." *Agenda*, 7, 3-8, 1 (1970), 93-96.
————. "A Man Apart." *Agenda*, 7, 3-8, 1 (1970), 172-80.
————. *Wyndham Lewis: A Discursive Exposition*. London: Harmsworth, 1932.
Pound, Ezra. "Augment of the Novel." *Agenda*, 7, 3-8, 1 (1970), 49-56.
————. *Literary Essays*, 423-30.
————. "On Wyndham Lewis." *Shenandoah*, 4, 2-3 (1953), 17.
————. "Vorticism." *Fortnightly*, n.s. 96 (1914), 461-71.
Pritchard, William. "Lawrence and Lewis." *Agenda*, 7, 3-8, 1 (1970), 140-47.
————. *Wyndham Lewis*. New York: Twayne, 1968. London: Routledge and K. Paul, 1972.
————. "Wyndham Lewis and Lawrence." *IowaR*, 2, 2 (1971), 91-96.
Regnery, Henry. "Eliot, Pound and Lewis: A Creative Friendship." *ModA*, 16 (1972), 146-60.
Richards, I. A. "A Talk on *The Childermass*." *Agenda*, 7, 3-8, 1 (1970), 16-21.
Roberts, William. *The Resurrection of Vorticism and the Apotheosis of Wyndham Lewis at the Tate*. London: Favil, 1956.

_____. "Wyndham Lewis, the Vorticist." *Listener*, 57 (1957), 470.

Rose, W. K. "Exile's Letters." *CanL*, 35 (1968), 64-73.

_____. "Ezra Pound and Wyndham Lewis: The Crucial Years." *SoR*, n.s. 4 (1968), 72-89.

_____. "Pound and Lewis." *Agenda*, 7, 3-8, 1 (1970), 117-33.

Russell, Peter. "Wyndham Lewis Today." *Shenandoah*, 4, 2-3 (1953), 72-76.

Sala, Annamaria. "Vorticism and Futurism." *Agenda*, 7, 3-8, 1 (1970), 156-62.

Savage, D. S. "Lewis and Lawrence." *TCV*, 6/7 (November/December 1937), 142.

Seymour-Smith, Martin. "Zero and the Impossible." *Encounter*, 9 (November 1957), 38-51.

_____. "Wyndham Lewis as an Imaginative Writer." *Agenda*, 7, 3-8, 1 (1970), 9-15.

"Shodbutt is Staggered." *TLS*, August 3, 1973, 893.

Sisson, C. H. "The Politics of Wyndham Lewis." *Agenda*, 7, 3-8, 1 (1970), 109-16.

Stanford, Derek. "Percy Wyndham Lewis: A Valedictory." *Month*, 17 (1957), 320-24.

_____. "Wyndham Lewis." *ContempR*, 191 (1957), 209-11.

Stone, Geoffrey. "The Ideas of Wyndham Lewis." *AmerR*, 1 (1933), 578-99; 2 (1934), 82-96.

Stonier, G. W. *Gog Magog*, 88-95.

_____. "That Taxi-Driver." *TCV*, 6/7 (November/December 1937), 125-27.

Symons, A. J. A. "The Novelist." *TCV*, 6/7 (November/December 1937), 121-24.

Symons, Julian. "The Thirties Novels." *Agenda*, 7, 3-8, 1 (1970), 37-48.

Tomlin, E. W. F. "The Philosopher-Politician." *TCV*, 6/7 (November/December 1937), 135-39.

_____. *Wyndham Lewis*. London: Longmans, Green, 1955.

_____. "Wyndham Lewis Reconsidered." *EigoS*, 116 (1970), 202-03.

Wagner, Geoffrey. "*The Wild Body*: A Sanguine of the Enemy." *Nine*, 4, 1 (1954), 18-27.

_____. "Wyndham Lewis." *The Politics of Twentieth-Century Novelists*. Ed. George A. Panichas, 51-64.

_____. "Wyndham Lewis and Catholic Thought." *CathW*, 178 (1954), 284-87.

_____. "Wyndham Lewis and James Joyce: A Study in Controversy." *SAQ*, 56 (1957), 57-66.

Wyndham Lewis, continued

_____. "Wyndham Lewis and the Vorticist Aesthetic." *JAAC*, 13 (1954), 1-17.

_____. *Wyndham Lewis: A Portrait of the Artist as Enemy*. London: Routledge and K. Paul; New Haven, Conn.: Yale Univ. Press, 1957.

Wees, William C. "England's Avant-Garde: The Futurist-Vorticist Phase." *WHR*, 21 (1967), 117-28.

Wickham, Harvey. *The Impuritans*, 84-95.

Wiebe, Dallas E. "Wyndham Lewis and the Picaresque Novel." *SAQ*, 62 (1963), 587-96.

Woodcock, George. *Odysseus Ever Returning*, 50-55.

See also: Aiken, *ABC*; Allen, *Tradition*; Bergonzi, *Turn*; Bradbury, *Possibilities, Social*; Goldring, *Reputations*; McCormick; Orage, *Readers*; Pritchett, *Books*; Spender, *Destructive*; Swinnerton, *Georgian*; Vines.

THE APES OF GOD

Aldington, Richard. *Selected Critical Writings*, 24-31

Chapman, Robert T. "Satire and Aesthetics in Wyndham Lewis' *Apes of God*." *ConL*, 12 (1971), 133-45.

Henderson, Philip. *The Novel Today*, 97-102.

Lewis, Wyndham. *Men Without Art*, 115-28.

Materer, Timothy. "*The Apes of God*." *Agenda*, 7, 3-8, 1 (1970), 57-66.

Pound, Ezra. "Augment of the Novel." *New Directions in Prose and Poetry, 1941*. Ed. James Laughlin, 705-13.

THE HUMAN AGE

Bridson, D. G. "The Making of *The Human Age*." *Agenda*, 7, 3-8, 1 (1970), 163-71.

Carter, Thomas. "Rationalist in Hell." *KR*, 18 (1956), 326-36.

Kenner, Hugh. "The Devil and Mr. Lewis." *Shenandoah*, 8 (1955), 15-30.

Palmer, Penelope. "*The Human Age*." *Agenda*, 7, 3-8, 1 (1970), 22-30.

Wagner, Geoffrey. "Wyndham Lewis's Inhuman Tetralogy: An Introduction to *The Human Age*." *MFS*, 2 (1956), 221-27.

TARR

Parker, David H. "*Tarr* and Wyndham Lewis's War-Time Stories." *SoRA*, 8 (1975), 166-81.

West, Rebecca. "*Tarr*." *Agenda*, 7, 3-8, 1 (1970), 67-70.

ROSE MACAULEY

GENERAL STUDIES

Bensen, Alice R. "The Ironic Aesthete and the Sponsoring of Causes: A Rhetorical Quandary in Novelistic Technique." *ELT*, 9, 1 (1966), 39-45.

———. *Rose Macauley.* New York: Twayne, 1969.

———. "The Skeptical Balance: A Study of Rose Macauley's *Going Abroad.*" *PMASAL*, 48 (1963), 675-83.

Chase, Mary Ellen. "Five Literary Portraits." *MR*, 3 (1962), 511-16.

Hollis, Christopher. "Rose Macauley." *Spectator*, 201 (November 7, 1958), 603-04.

Inglisham, John. "Rose Macauley." *Bookman* (London), 72 (1927), 107-10.

Irwin, W. R. "Permanence and Change in *The Edwardians* and *Told by an Idiot.*" *MFS*, 2 (1956), 63-67.

Lawrence, Margaret. *The School of Femininity*, 203-08.

Lockwood, William J. "Rose Macauley." *Minor British Novelists*. Ed. Charles A. Hoyt, 135-56.

Mansfield, Katherine. *Novels and Novelists*, 5-8, 200-01.

Millett, Fred B. "Feminine Fiction." *Cornhill*, 155 (1937), 225-35.

Nicholson, Harold, and Rosamund Lehmann, Alan Pryce-Jones, Dwight Macdonald, Patrick Kinross, C. V. Wedgwood, Mark Bonham Carter, Anthony Powell, William Plomer, Diana Cooper. "The Pleasures of Knowing Rose Macauley." *Encounter*, 12 (March 1959), 23-31.

Pendry, E. D. *The New Feminism of English Fiction*, 63-65.

Pryce-Jones, Alan. "Introduction." *Orphan Island*, by Rose Macauley. London: Collins, 1960.

Sherman, Stuart P. *Critical Woodcuts*, 83-93.

Smith, Constance Babington. "Rose Macauley in Her Writings." Royal Soc. of Lit. of the U. K., London. *Essays by Divers Hands*, v. 38, 143-58.

Stewart, Douglas G. *The Ark of God*, 99-128.

Swinnerton, Frank. "Rose Macauley." *KR*, 29 (1967), 591-608.

Taylor, Griffin. "What Does It Profit a Man. . . ?" *SR*, 66 (1958), 132-46.

See also: Swinnerton, *Georgian*; Vines; Webster.

COMPTON MACKENZIE

INTERVIEWS

Freeman, John. "Sir Compton Mackenzie 'Face to Face'." *Listener*, 67 (1962), 165-67.

Compton Mackenzie, continued

GENERAL STUDIES

Adcock, A. St. John. *Gods of Modern Grub Street*, 183-90.

Boyle, Alexander. "Compton Mackenzie—Humorist." *IrM*, 78 (December 1950), 558-61.

Chevalley, Abel. *The Modern English Novel*, 225-27.

Dooley, David J. *Compton Mackenzie*. New York: Twayne, 1974.

Eliot, T. S. "London Letter." *Dial*, 73 (September 1922), 329-31.

Freeman, John. *English Portraits and Essays*, 197-222.

———. "The Novels of Mr. Compton Mackenzie." *London Mercury*, 1 (1920), 448-57.

Fytton, Francis. "Compton Mackenzie: Romance versus Realism." *CathW*, 182 (1956), 358-63.

Guedalla, Philip. *A Gallery*, 153-55.

James, Henry. "The Younger Generation." *TLS*, March 19, 1914, 133-34; April 2, 1914, 157-58.

McLaren, Moray. "Compton Mackenzie." *John O'London's Weekly*, 4 (April 6, 1961), 375-76.

———. *Compton Mackenzie: A Panegyric for his Eightieth Birthday*. Edinburgh: MacDonald, 1963.

Mansfield, Katherine. *Novels and Novelists*, 88-91, 185-87.

Priestley, J. B. "The Younger Novelists." *EJ*, 14 (1925), 435-43.

Proctor, Mortimer R. *The English University Novel*, 154-75, 197-98.

Robertson, Leo. *Compton Mackenzie: An Appraisal of His Literary Work*. London: Richards, 1954.

Sanderson, Stewart F. "The Four Winds of Love." *ArielE*, 2, 3 (1971), 7-15.

Strong, L. A. G. "Books and Writers." *Spectator*, 187 (September 14, 1951), 336.

Tynemouth, W. "Compton Mackenzie." *Bookguide*, 1 (September 1957), 9-11.

West, Rebecca. "Poor Relations." *New Republic*, 21 (February 18, 1920), 362-63.

Wilson, Angus. "Broken Promise." *Listener*, 45 (1951), 575-76.

Wilson, Edmund. *The Bit Between My Teeth*, 540-41.

Young, Kenneth. *Compton Mackenzie*. London: Longmans, Green, 1968.

See also: Adcock, *Gods*; Cunliffe, *Half-Century*; Gould; Goldring, *Reputations*; R. Johnson, *Men*; Mais, *Books*; Marble; Swinnerton, *Background, Georgian*; H. Williams, *Modern*; V. Woolf, *Contemporary*.

W. SOMERSET MAUGHAM

BIBLIOGRAPHIES

Sanders, Charles. *W. Somerset Maugham: An Annotated Bibliography of Writings About Him.* DeKalb: Northern Illinois Univ. Press, 1970.

_____. "W. Somerset Maugham: A Supplementary Bibliography." *ELT*, 15, 2 (1972), 168-73.

Tate, Marie T. "W. Somerset Maugham." *ELT*, 6, 2 (1963), 108-17.

INTERVIEWS

Breit, Harvey. *The Writer Observed*, 147-49.

Rascoe, Burton. *A Bookman's Daybook*, 148-53.

_____. *We Were Interrupted*, 288-90.

Rees, Leslie. "A Meeting with Somerset Maugham." *Meanjin*, 26 (1967), 452-56.

Van Gelder, Robert. *Writers and Writing*, 138-41.

GENERAL STUDIES

Adcock, A. St. John. *Gods of Modern Grub Street*, 213-20.

Aldington, Richard. *Selected Critical Writings*, 32-38.

Bason, Fred T. "Postscript to Maugham." *The Saturday Book*, 26, 185-88.

Beavan, John. "Maugham: A 'Free Man' at 85." *NYTM*, January 25, 1959, 14, 34-35, 37.

Boothby, Lord [Robert John Graham]. *My Yesterday, Your Tomorrow*, 224-28.

Brander, Laurence. *Somerset Maugham: A Guide.* Edinburgh: Oliver and Boyd, 1963.

Brophy, John. *Somerset Maugham.* London: Longmans, Green, 1952.

Brown, Ivor. *W. Somerset Maugham.* London: International Textbook, 1970.

Calder, Robert L. *W. Somerset Maugham and the Quest for Freedom.* Garden City, N. Y.: Doubleday, 1973.

Chapple, J. A. V. *Documentary and Imaginative Literature*, 132-34.

Colburn, William E. "Dr. Maugham's Prescription for Success." *EUQ*, 19 (1963), 14-21.

Connolly, Cyril. *Enemies of Promise*, rev. ed., 66-69, 76-81, 89-93.

Cordell, Richard A. *Somerset Maugham: A Biographical and Critical Study.* London: Heinemann, 1961; Bloomington: Indiana Univ. Press, 1961.

_____. "Somerset Maugham at Eighty." *CE*, 15 (1954), 201-07.

W. Somerset Maugham, continued

_____. "Somerset Maugham: Lucidity Versus Cunning." *EFT*, 1, 3 (1958), 30-32.

_____. *W. Somerset Maugham*. London and New York: Nelson, 1937.

Cosman, Max. "Mr. Maugham as Footnote." *PS*, 10 (1956), 64-69.

_____. "A Pattern of Doubt." *ArQ*, 9 (1953), 246-57.

Curtis, Anthony. *The Pattern of Maugham: A Critical Portrait*. London: Hamilton; New York: Taplinger, 1974.

Dickie, Francis. "From Forest Fire to France: Somerset Maugham and His Moorish Mansion." *ABC*, 9, 7 (1959), 7-13.

Doner, Dean. "Spinoza's *Ethics* and Maugham." *UKCR*, 21 (1955), 261-69.

Gordon, Caroline. "Notes on Chekhov and Maugham." *SR*, 57 (1949), 401-10.

Haddo, Oliver [Edward Alexander Crowley]. "How to Write a Novel! After W. S. Maugham." *Vanity Fair*, December 30, 1908, 838-40.

Haire, David B., and Dennis E. Hensley. "A Comparative Look at W. S. Maugham and Jack London." *JLN*, 8 (1975), 114-18.

Heywood, C. "Somerset Maugham's Debt to *Madame Bovary* and Miss Braddon's *The Doctor's Wife*." *EA*, 19 (1966), 64-69.

_____. "Two Printed Texts of Somerset Maugham's *Mrs. Craddock*." *ELN*, 5 (1967), 39-46.

Highet, Gilbert. *Talents and Geniuses*, 150-53.

Hoch, Claire. "Georges Duhamel and W. Somerset Maugham." *RLC*, 46 (1972), 261-71.

Jensen, Sven A. *William Somerset Maugham: Some Aspects of the Man and His Work*. Oslo: Universitetsford, 1957.

Jonas, Klaus W., ed. *The Maugham Enigma*. New York: Citadel, 1954.

_____. "W. Somerset Maugham: An Appreciation." *BA*, 33 (1959), 20-23.

_____, ed. *The World of Somerset Maugham: An Anthology*. New York: British Book Centre, 1959.

Keating, P. J. *The Working Classes in Victorian Fiction*, 186-91.

Krim, Seymour. "Maugham the Artist." *Cweal*, 61 (1954), 284-87.

Lehmann, John. "A Very Old Party." *New Republic*, 154 (January 8, 1966), 23-24.

MacCarthy, Desmond. *W. Somerset Maugham, The English Maupassant*. London: Heinemann, 1934.

Mais, Stuart P. B. *Some Modern Authors*, 115-28.

Mansfield, Katherine. *Novels and Novelists*, 17-20.

Marlow, Louis [Louis Wilkinson]. *Seven Friends*, 142-70.

_____. "Somerset Maugham." *Writers of Today*, 2. Ed. Denys Val Baker, 37-52.

Maugham, Robin. *Somerset and All the Maughams.* London: Longmans; London: Heinemann; New York: New American Library, 1966.

Maugham, W. Somerset. *Selected Prefaces and Introductions of W. Somerset Maugham.* Garden City, N. Y.: Doubleday, 1963.

Menard, Wilmon. "Somerset Maugham and Paul Gauguin." *MQR*, 7 (1968), 227-32.

Naik, M. K. *W. Somerset Maugham.* Norman: Univ. of Oklahoma Press, 1966.

Nichols, Beverley. *A Case of Human Bondage.* London: Secker and Warburg, 1966.

Pfeiffer, Karl G. *W. Somerset Maugham: A Candid Portrait.* New York: Norton, 1959.

Pollock, John. "Somerset Maugham and His Work." *QR*, 304 (1966), 365-78.

Ross, Woodburn O. "W. Somerset Maugham: Theme and Variations." *CE*, 8 (1946), 113-22.

Scully, Frank. *Rogues' Gallery*, 15-36.

Spencer, Theodore. "Somerset Maugham." *CE*, 2 (1940), 1-10.

Swinnerton, Frank A. "Maugham at Eighty." *SatR*, 37 (January 23, 1954), 13-14, 70-72.

Viswanath, G. V. "The Novels of Somerset Maugham." *Quest*, 23 (1959), 50-52.

Viswanathan, K. *India in English Fiction*, 217-42.

Ward, Richard H. *W. Somerset Maugham.* London: Bles, 1937.

Wells, James M. "The Artist in the English Novel, 1850-1919." *PhilS*, 4 (1943), 77-80.

Wescott, Glenway. "Somerset Maugham and Posterity." *Harper's*, 195 (October 1947), 302-11. [Expanded in Wescott, Glenway. *Images of Truth*, 59-85]

Wilson, Edmund. *The Bit Between My Teeth*, 276-77, 540-41.

Yevish, Irving A. "In Defense of Mr. Maugham." *MQR*, 12 (1973), 72-80.

Zlobina, Maya. "The Surprises in Somerset Maugham." *SovR*, 3, 6 (1962), 3-9.

See also: Adcock, *Gods*; Bowen, *Impressions*; Drew, *Modern*; Edgar, *Art*; Frierson; J. Gray; Greene; MacCarthy, *Memories*; Marble; Muller, *Modern*; Overton, *Authors*; Routh; Swinnerton, *Figures, Georgian*; Walcutt; H. Williams, *Modern*; Zabel, *Craft*.

W. *Somerset Maugham, continued*

CAKES AND ALE
Brown, Allen B. "Substance and Shadow: The Originals of the Characters in *Cakes and Ale.*" *PMASAL*, 45 (1959 meeting; pub. 1960), 439-46.
See also: A. West, *Principles.*

THE MOON AND SIXPENCE
Collins, Joseph. *Idling in Italy*, 148-58.
Paul, David. "Maugham and Two Myths: Shown in *The Moon and Sixpence* and *The Razor's Edge.*" *Cornhill*, 162 (1946), 143-48.

OF HUMAN BONDAGE
Archer, Stanley. "Artists and Paintings in Maugham's *Of Human Bondage.*" *ELT*, 14, 3 (1971), 181-89.
Davies, Horton. *A Mirror of the Ministry in Modern Novels*, 113-22.
Dreiser, Theodore. "As a Realist Sees It." *New Republic*, 5 (December 25, 1915), 202-04.
Harris, Wendell V. "Molly's 'Yes': The Transvaluation of Sex in Modern Fiction." *TSLL*, 10 (1968), 107-18.
Reed, John R. *Old School Ties*, 182-85.
Spence, R. "Maugham's 'Of Human Bondage': The Making of a Masterpiece." *LCUP*, 17 (1951), 104-14.
Webster, H. T. "Possible Influence of George Gissing's *Workers in the Dawn* on Maugham's *Of Human Bondage.*" *MLQ*, 7 (1946), 315.
See also: Brewster and Burrell; Buckley.

THE RAZOR'S EDGE
Paul, David. "Maugham and Two Myths: Shown in *The Moon and Sixpence* and *The Razor's Edge.*" *Cornhill*, 162 (1946), 143-48.
See also: Connolly, *Playground.*

BRIAN MOORE

INTERVIEWS
Dahlie, Hallvard. "Brian Moore: An Interview." *TamR*, 46 (1968), 7-29.
Fulford, Robert. "Robert Fulford Interviews Brian Moore." *TamR*, 23 (1962), 5-18.

GENERAL STUDIES
Dahlie, Hallvard. *Brian Moore.* Toronto: Copp Clark, 1969.
_____. "Brian Moore's Broader Vision: *The Emperor of Ice Cream.*" *Crit*, 9 (1967), 43-55.

Foster, John Wilson. "Crisis and Ritual in Brian Moore's Belfast Novels." *Eire*, 3, 3 (1968), 66-74.

French, Philip. "The Novels of Brian Moore." *LonM*, n.s. 5, 1 (February 1966), 86-91.

Gallagher, Michael Paul. "The Novels of Brian Moore." *Studies*, 60 (1971), 180-94.

Hornyansky, Michael. "Countries of the Mind." *TamR*, 26 (1963), 58-68.

Kersnowski, Frank L. "Exit the Anti-Hero." *Crit*, 10, 3 (1968), 60-71.

Ludwig, Jack. "Brian Moore: Ireland's Loss, Canada's Novelist." *Crit*, 5, 1 (1962), 5-14.

———. "Exile from the Emerald Isle." *Nation*, 200 (1965), 287-88.

———. "Fiction for the Majors." *TamR*, 17 (1960), 65-71.

———. "A Mirror of Moore." *CanL*, 7 (1961), 18-23.

Prosky, Murry. "The Crisis of Identity in the Novels of Brian Moore." *Eire*, 6, 3 (1971), 106-18.

Ricks, Christopher. "The Simple Excellence of Brian Moore." *New Statesman*, 71 (1966), 227-28.

Taranath, Rajeev. "Deepening Experience: A Note on *The Emperor of Ice-Cream*." *LCrit*, 6, 4 (1965), 68-72.

Woodcock, George. *Odysseus Ever Returning*, 40-49.

GEORGE MOORE

BIBLIOGRAPHIES

Blakey, Barbara. "George Moore." *ELT*, 15, 1 (1972), 85-90.

Gerber, Helmut E. "George Moore: An Annotated Bibliography of Writings About Him." *EFT*, 2, 2 (1959), 1-91; "Supplement I," 3, 2 (1960), 34-46; "Supplement II," *ELT*, 4, 2 (1961), 30-42; "Supplement," 9, 4 (1966), 225-28.

Korg, Jacob. "George Moore." *Victorian Fiction: A Guide to Research.* Ed. Lionel Stevenson, 389-401.

O'Malley, Charles et al. "George Moore." *ELT*, 14, 1 (1971), 75-83.

Robbins, Mary. "George Moore." *ELT*, 18, 1 (1975), 63-70.

INTERVIEWS

Archer, William. *Real Conversations.* London: Heinemann, 1904, 85-106.

Balderston, John Lloyd. "The Freedom of the Pen: A Conversation with George Moore." *Fortnightly*, n.s. 102 (1917), 539-51.

Goodwin, Geraint. *Conversations with George Moore.* London: Benn, 1929; New York: Knopf, 1930; London: Cape, 1937.

Nichols, Beverley. *Are They the Same at Home?*, 7-9, 220-24.

Phelps, William Lyon. "Conversations with George Moore." *YR*, 18 (1929), 558-65.

GENERAL STUDIES

Aitken, W. F. "George Moore." *Bookman* (London), 83 (March 1933), 488.

Anglin, Norman. "George Moore, Juvenal and Johnson." *ManchQ*, 11 (1921), 30-48.

Armstrong, Martin. "The Spoken Word: More on Moore." *Listener*, 47 (1952), 399.

Battock, Marjorie. "George Moore." *DM*, 27 (April-June 1952), 27-31.

Beerbohm, Max. "George Moore." *Atlantic*, 186 (December 1950), 34-39.

Bennett, Arnold. *Fame and Fiction*, 233-68.

Blanche, Jacques-Emile. *More Portraits of a Lifetime*, 86-95, 170-72, 250-59, 278-82.

———. *Portraits of a Lifetime*, 136-52, 290-98.

Blissett, William F. "George Moore and Literary Wagnerism." *CL*, 13 (1961), 52-71.

Bowra, C. M. "George Moore." *New Oxford Outlook*, 1 (May 1933), 43-51.

Boyd, Ernest A. *Ireland's Literary Renaissance*, 289-308, 380-85.

———. *Portraits*, 227-35.

Brown, Malcolm. *George Moore: A Reconsideration.* Seattle: Univ. of Washington Press, 1955.

———. *The Politics of Irish Literature*, 260-61, 272-74.

Burdett, Osbert. "George Moore." *London Mercury*, 27 (1933), 415-26.

Cargill, Oscar. *Intellectual America*, 77-82.

Cary, Meredith. "George Moore's *Roman Expérimental*." *Eire*, 9, 4 (1974), 142-50.

Cave, Richard. "The Quest of George Moore." *CambR*, 90 (1968), 186-89.

Chaikin, Milton. "The Composition of *A Modern Lover*." *CL*, 7 (1955), 259-64.

———. "A French Source for George Moore's *A Mere Accident*." *MLN*, 71 (1956), 28-30.

Chesterton, G. K. *Heretics*, 128-34.

Chew, Samuel C. "Mr. Moore and Mr. Chew." *AmerM*, 1 (January 1924), 39-47.

Clark, Barrett H. "George Moore at Work." *AmerM*, 4 (1925), 202-09.

———. *Intimate Portraits*, 57-153.

Clutton-Brock, Arthur. *Essays on Literature and Life*, 168-81.
Colby, Robert A. " 'How it Strikes a Contemporary': The *Spectator* as Critic." *NCF*, 11 (1956), 182-206.
Collins, Norman. *The Facts of Fiction*, 249-57.
Cooper, Douglas. "George Moore and Modern Art." *Horizon (L)*, 11 (February 1945), 113-30.
Cordasco, Francesco. "George Moore and Edouard Dujardin." *MLN*, 62 (1947), 244-51.
Cunard, Nancy. *GM: Memories of George Moore*. London: Hart-Davis, 1956; New York: Macmillan, 1957.
Cunliffe, J. W. *English Literature During the Last Half-Century*, 2d ed., 263-69.
Decker, Clarence. *The Victorian Conscience*, 49-61, 82-99.
Dunleavy, Janet E. *George Moore: The Artist's Vision, the Story-teller's Art*. Lewisburg, Pa.: Bucknell Univ. Press, 1973.
Eglinton, John. *Irish Literary Portraits*, 85-127.
Ellis, Havelock. *From Marlowe to Shaw*, 314-16.
———. *My Confessional*, 208-11.
Ellis, Stewart M. *Mainly Victorian*, 257-60.
Elwin, Malcolm. *Old Gods Falling*, 46-106.
Ernst, Morris L., and William Seagle. *To the Pure*, 92-95.
Ervine, St. John G. *Some Impressions of My Elders*, 161-88.
Ferguson, Walter D. *The Influence of Flaubert on George Moore*. Philadelphia: Univ. of Pennsylvania Press, 1934.
Ford, Ford Madox. *It Was The Nightingale*, 32-43.
———. "John Galsworthy and George Moore." *EngRev*, 57 (1933), 130-42.
Freeman, John. "Mr. George Moore." *London Mercury*, 2 (1920), 281-91.
———. *A Portrait of George Moore in a Study of His Work*. London: Laurie, 1922.
Frierson, William C. "The English Controversy Over Realism in Fiction, 1885-1895." *PMLA*, 43 (1928), 533-50.
———. "George Moore Compromised with the Victorians." *Trollopian*, 1, 4 (March 1947), 37-44.
Furst, Lilian G. "George Moore, Zola, and the Question of Influence." *CRCL*, 1 (1974), 138-55.
Garnett, David. "Some Writers I Have Known: Galsworthy, Forster, Moore, and Wells." *TQ*, 4, 3 (1961), 190-202.
Gaunt, William. *The Aesthetic Adventure*, 69-75, 79-86, 112-17, 120-23, 133-35, 147-48, 190-95, 213-14.

George Moore, continued

Gerber, Helmut E., ed. *George Moore in Transition: Letters to T. Fisher Unwin and Lena Milman, 1894-1910.* Detroit: Wayne State Univ. Press, 1968.
Gettmann, Royal A. "George Moore's Revisions of *The Lake, The Wild Goose,* and *Esther Waters.*" *PMLA,* 59 (1944), 540-55.
_____. *Turgenev in England and America,* 148-53.
Gosse, Edmund W. *More Books on the Table,* 325-32.
Gregory, Horace. *The Dying Gladiators,* 125-40.
_____. *The Shield of Achilles,* 119-35.
Griffin, Gerald. *The Wild Geese,* 46-65.
H., J. [Joseph Hone?]. "George Moore: The Making of a Writer." *TLS,* February 29, 1952, 149-50.
Heywood, C., "Flaubert, Miss Braddon, and George Moore." *CL,* 12 (1960), 151-58.
Hicks, Granville. *Figures of Transition,* 203-17.
Hone, Joseph M. *The Life of George Moore.* London: Gollancz; New York: Macmillan, 1936.
Hough, Graham. "George Moore and the Nineties." *Edwardians and Late Victorians.* Ed. Richard Ellmann, 1-27.
_____. *Image and Experience,* 179-210.
Howarth, Herbert. *The Irish Writers,* 32-82.
Hughes, Douglas A., ed. *The Man of Wax: Critical Essays on George Moore.* New York: New York Univ. Press, 1971.
Huneker, James G. *Pathos of Distance,* 16-48.
_____. *Variations,* 20-29.
Jean-Aubry, G. "George Moore and Emile Zola." *Bookman's Journal and Print Collector,* n.s. 11 (1924), 98-100.
Jeffares, A. Norman. *George Moore.* London and New York: Longmans, Green, 1965.
Jernigan, Jay. "A Protean Self-Study of the Artist *Manqué*: George Moore's *Vain Fortune.*" *KanQ,* 7, 4 (1975), 31-39.
Josephson, Matthew. *Zola and His Time.* London: Gollancz; New York: Macaulay, 1928, 273-76, 479.
Keating, P. J. *The Working Classes in Victorian Fiction,* 133-36.
Knight, Grant C. *The Novel in English,* 287-98.
Lynch, Thomas J. "George Moore." *Cweal,* 17 (1933), 629-31.
Lyons, F. S. L. "George Moore and Edward Martyn." *Hermathena,* 98 (1964), 9-32.
MacCarthy, Desmond. *Portraits,* v. 1, 192-203.
McGreevy, T. "George Moore." *Scrutinies.* Ed. Edgell Rickword, 109-30.
Mitchell, Susan L. *George Moore.* Dublin and London: Maunsell; New York: Dodd, Mead, 1916.

Monahan, Michael. *Adventures in Life and Letters.* New York and London: Kennerly, 1912; rev. New York: Frank-Maurice, 1925, 58-66.

Montague, G. H. "Mr. George Moore." *HarvM,* 32 (1901), 146-58.

Morgan, Charles. *An Epitaph on George Moore.* New York: Macmillan, 1935.

———. "Epitaph on George Moore." *AmerM,* 36 (1935), 176-86.

———. "George Moore: A Centenary Appreciation." *Listener,* 47 (1952), 349-51.

Nejdefors-Frisk, Sonja. *George Moore's Naturalistic Prose.* Lund: Carl Bloms Boktrykeri A.B., 1952; Cambridge, Mass.: Harvard Univ. Press, 1952.

Newton, William. "Hardy and the Naturalists: Their Use of Physiology." *MP,* 49 (1951), 28-41.

Niess, Robert J. "George Moore and Emile Zola Again." *Symposium(S),* 20 (1966), 43-49.

Nye, Francis L. "George Moore's Use of Sources in *Héloise and Abélard.*" *ELT,* 18, 3 (1975), 161-80.

O'Faoláin, Seán. "Pater and Moore." *London Mercury,* 34 (1936), 330-38.

Owens, Graham, ed. *George Moore's Mind and Art.* London: Oliver and Boyd, 1968; New York: Barnes and Noble, 1970.

Peck, Harry Thurston. *The Personal Equation,* 89-132.

Phelps, Gilbert. *The Russian Novel in English Fiction,* 96-109, 144-45, 157-58.

———. "Russian Realism and English Fiction." *CambJ,* 3 (1950), 277-91.

Quiller-Couch, Arthur Thomas. *Adventures in Criticism,* 2d ed., 195-200.

Rascoe, Burton. *Titans of Literature,* 472-77.

Reid, Forrest. "The Novels of George Moore." *WestmR,* 172 (1909), 200-08.

Roberts, R. Ellis. "George Moore." *NC,* 113 (1933), 369-83.

Schwab, Arnold T. "Irish Author and American Critic: George Moore and James Huneker." *NCF,* 8 (1954), 256-71; 9 (1954), 22-37.

Scott, Bonnie K. "Joyce's Schooling in the Field of George Moore." *Eire,* 9, 4 (1974), 117-41.

Sechler, Robert P. *George Moore: A Disciple of Walter Pater.* Philadelphia: Univ. of Pennsylvania Press, 1931.

Seinfelt, Frederick W. *George Moore: Ireland's Unconventional Realist.* Philadelphia: Dorrance, 1975.

———. "Wagnerian Elements in the Writing of George Moore." *SIH,* 1 (1969), 38-49.

George Moore, continued

Seymour-Smith, Martin. "Rediscovering George Moore." *Encounter*, 35 (December 1970), 58-67.
Shawe-Taylor, Desmond. "The Achievement of George Moore." *The Life of George Moore*, by Joseph Hone. London: Gollancz; New York: Macmillan, 1936, 465-92.
Sherman, Stuart P. *On Contemporary Literature*, 120-68.
Squire, John C. *Books in General*, 2d ser., 53-57.
_____. *Books Reviewed*, 63-69.
Staley, Thomas F. "The Irish Exile in Paris: James Joyce and George Moore." *ULYSSES: Cinquante ans Après*. Ed. Louis Bonnerot, with Jean Jacquot and Claude Jaquet, 15-22.
Starkie, Enid. *From Gautier to Eliot*, 70-80.
Stephens, James. *James, Seumas, and Jacques*, 163-67.
Stevenson, Lionel. "George Moore: Romantic, Naturalist, Aesthete." *EA*, 21 (1968), 362-66.
Steward, S. M. "J.-K. Huysmans and George Moore." *RR*, 25 (1934), 197-206.
Stone, Donald David. *Novelists in a Changing World*, 35-38, 58-66.
Taylor, Estella Ruth. *The Modern Irish Writers*, 19-21, 51-55, 91-97.
Temple, Ruth Z. *The Critic's Alchemy*, 231-71.
Ure, Peter. "George Moore as Historian of Consciences." *Imagined Worlds*. Ed. Maynard Mack and Ian Gregor, 257-76.
Watson, Sara Ruth. "George Moore and the Dolmetsches." *ELT*, 6, 2 (1963), 65-75.
Weaver, Jack W. "An Exile Returned: Moore and Yeats in Ireland." *Eire*, 3, 1 (1968), 40-47.
Wolfe, Humbert. *Dialogues and Monologues*, 3-25.
_____. "George Moore." *Post-Victorians*, by Various Authors, 411-23.
_____. *George Moore*. New York: Oxford Univ. Press, 1932.
Woolf, Leonard. *Essays on Literature, History, Politics, etc.*, 86-90.
Woolf, Virginia. *Collected Essays*, v. 1, 338-41.
Young, George M. *Daylight and Champaign*, 178-79, 187-88.
See also: Aiken, *ABC*; Allen, *English*; E. Baker, *History*; Beach, *20th*; Beresford; Bowen, *Impressions*; Cunliffe, *Half-Century, Leaders, 20th Century*; Edgar, *Art*; Frierson; Hind, *Authors*; Hoare; Lovett, *History*; McCullough; Macy; Marble; Muller, *Modern*; W. Phelps; Richards; Routh; Swinnerton, *Georgian*; Wagenknecht, *Cavalcade*; Weygandt.

THE BROOK KERITH
Bell, Archie. "Which Side of Jordan is *The Brook Kerith*?" *Bookman* (N. Y.), 45 (1917), 61-63.

Brooks, Michael W. "George Moore, Schopenhauer, and the Origins of *The Brook Kerith*." *ELT*, 12, 1 (1969), 21-31.
Gilman, Lawrence. "Mary Hunter's Bible." *NoAmR*, 204 (1916), 932-37.
Graves, Robert. *Five Pens in Hand*, 123-28.
———. "Jewish Jesus, Gentile Christ." *New Republic*, 135 (October 15, 1956), 25-27.
Harris, Frank. *Contemporary Portraits*, 2d ser., 107-40.
Phillips, Duncan. "George Moore." *YR*, n.s. 6 (1917), 342-57.
Richards, I. A. "Jesus' Other Life." *NYRB*, 15 (December 3, 1970), 47-49.
Sarkar, Eileen. " 'Wonderful Meeting': George Moore's Saint Paul and Jesus." *Eire*, 10, 3 (1975), 38-45.

A DRAMA IN MUSLIN
Chaikin, Milton. "Balzac, Zola, and George Moore's *A Drama in Muslin*." *RLC*, 29 (1955), 540-43.
Fernando, Lloyd. "The Radical Ideology of the 'New Woman'." *SoRA*, 2 (1967), 206-22.
Jeffares, A. Norman. "*A Drama in Muslin*." *Essays Presented to Amy G. Stock*. Ed. R. K. Kaul, 137-54.
Marcus, Phillip L. "George Moore's Dublin 'Epiphanies' and Joyce." *JJQ*, 5 (1968), 157-61.
Sporn, Paul. "Marriage and Class Conflict: The Subversive Link in George Moore's *A Drama in Muslin*." *ClioW*, 3 (1973), 7-20.

ESTHER WATERS
Atkinson, F. G. "George Moore and *Esther Waters*." *N&Q*, 19 (1972), 421-23.
Bartlett, Lynn C. "*Maggie*: A New Source for *Esther Waters*." *ELT*, 9, 1 (1966), 18-20.
Jernigan, Jay. "The Forgotten Serial Version of George Moore's *Esther Waters*." *NCF*, 23 (1968), 99-103.
Mansfield, Katherine. "*Esther Waters* Revisited." *Athenaeum*, August 6, 1920, 176.
———. *Novels and Novelists*, 233-37.
Morton, Donald E. "Lyrical Form and the World of *Esther Waters*." *SEL*, 13 (1973), 688-700.
Nicholas, Brian. "The Case of Esther Waters." *The Moral and the Story*. Ed. Ian Gregor and Brian Nicholas, 98-122.
Ohmann, Carol. "George Moore's *Esther Waters*." *NCF*, 25 (1970), 174-87.

George Moore, continued

Sporn, Paul. *"Esther Waters*: The Sources of the Baby-Farm Episode."
 ELT, 11, 1 (1968), 39-42.
Stevenson, Lionel. "Introduction." *Esther Waters*, by George Moore.
 Boston: Houghton Mifflin, 1963, v-xxiv.
See also: V. Woolf, *Contemporary.*

EVELYN INNES
Archer, William. *Study and Stage*, 198-204.
Fitzpatrick, Kathleen. "A Plea for *Evelyn Innes." Southerly*, 9 (1948),
 198-203.
Huneker, James G. *Overtones*, 188-99.

THE LAKE
Cordonnier, Max E. "Siegfried in Ireland: A Study of Moore's *The
 Lake." DM*, 6 (1967), 3-12.
Cronin, John. "George Moore's *The Lake*: A Possible Source." *Eire*, 6, 3
 (1971), 12-14.
Kennedy, Eileen. "Design in George Moore's *The Lake." Modern Irish
 Literature.* Ed. Raymond J. Porter and James D. Brophy, 53-66.

A MUMMER'S WIFE
Austin, L. F. "Mr. George Moore and the 'Mummers'; or, The Real
 Against the Realistic." *Time*, n.s. 8 (November 1888), 524-33.
Chaikin, Milton. "George Moore's *A Mummer's Wife* and Zola." *RLC*,
 31 (1957), 85-88.
Heywood, C. "D. H. Lawrence's *The Lost Girl* and Its Antecedents by
 George Moore and Arnold Bennett." *ES*, 47 (1966), 131-34.
Jernigan E. Jay. "The Bibliographical and Textual Complexities of
 George Moore's *A Mummer's Wife." BNYPL*, 74 (1970), 396-410.
Knight, Grant C. *Superlatives*, 153-66.

SISTER THERESA
Brown, Calvin S. "Balzac as a Source of George Moore's *Sister Tere-
 sa." CL*, 11 (1959), 124-30.
Huneker, James G. *Overtones*, 199-213.
Newton, William. "Chance as Employed by Hardy and the Natural-
 ists." *PQ*, 30 (1951), 154-75.

IRIS MURDOCH

BIBLIOGRAPHIES
Civin, Laraine. *Iris Murdoch: A Bibliography.* Johannesburg: Univ. of

Witwatersrand, Dept. of Bibliography, Librarianship, and Typography, 1968.
Widmann, R. L. "An Iris Murdoch Checklist." *Crit*, 10, 1 (1968), 17-29.

INTERVIEWS
Heyd, Ruth. "An Interview with Iris Murdoch." *UWR*, 1, 1 (1965), 138-43.
Kermode, Frank. "The House of Fiction: Interviews with Seven English Novelists." *PR*, 30 (1963), 61-82.
Rose, W. K. "An Interview with Iris Murdoch." *Shenandoah*, 19, 2 (1968), 3-22.

SPECIAL ISSUES
Modern Fiction Studies [MFS], 15, 3 (1969).

GENERAL STUDIES
Allsop, Kenneth. *The Angry Decade*, 96-103.
Baldanza, Frank. *Iris Murdoch*. Boston: Twayne, 1974.
———. "Iris Murdoch and the Theory of Personality." *Criticism*, 7 (1965), 176-89.
Berthoff, Warner. *Fictions and Events*, 118-54.
———. "Fortunes of the Novel: Muriel Spark and Iris Murdoch." *MR*, 8 (1967), 301-32.
Bowen, John. "One Man's Meat: The Idea of Individual Responsibility." *TLS*, August 7, 1959, xii-xiii.
Byatt, Antonia S. *Degrees of Freedom: The Novels of Iris Murdoch*. London: Chatto and Windus; New York: Barnes and Noble, 1965.
Clayre, Alasdair. "Common Cause: A Garden in the Clearing." *TLS*, August 7, 1959, xxx-xxxi.
Culley, Ann. "Theory and Practice: Characterization in the Novels of Iris Murdoch." *MFS*, 3 (1969), 335-46.
Dick, Bernard F. "The Novels of Iris Murdoch: A Formula for Enchantment." *BuR*, 14, 2 (1966), 66-81.
Emerson, Donald. "Violence and Survival in the Novels of Iris Murdoch." *TWA*, 57 (1969), 21-28.
Felheim, Marvin. "Symbolic Characterization in the Novels of Iris Murdoch." *TSLL*, 2 (1960), 189-97.
Fraser, G. S. "Iris Murdoch: The Solidity of the Normal." *ILA*, 2 (1959), 37-54.
German, Howard. "Allusions in the Early Novels of Iris Murdoch." *MFS*, 15, 3 (1969), 361-78.

Iris Murdoch, continued

_____. "The Range of Allusions in the Novels of Iris Murdoch." *JML*, 2 (1971), 57-85.

Gerstenberger, Donna. *Iris Murdoch*. Lewisburg, Pa.: Bucknell Univ. Press, 1975.

Gindin, James. "Ethical Structure in John Galsworthy, Elizabeth Bowen, and Iris Murdoch." *Forms of Modern Fiction*. Ed. Alan W. Friedman, 15-41.

_____. "Images of Illusion in the Work of Iris Murdoch." *TSLL*, 2 (1960), 180-88.

Goldberg, Gerald Jay. "The Search for the Artist in Some Recent British Fiction." *SAQ*, 62 (1963), 387-401.

Goshgarian, Gary. "Feminist Values in the Novels of Iris Murdoch." *RLV*, 40 (1974), 519-27.

Hall, James. "Blurring the Will: The Growth of Iris Murdoch." *ELH*, 32 (1965), 256-73.

_____. *The Lunatic Giant in the Drawing Room*, 181-212.

Hall, William. " 'The Third Way': The Novels of Iris Murdoch." *DR*, 46 (1966), 306-18.

Hauerwas, Stanley. "The Significance of Vision: Toward an Aesthetic Ethic." *SRC*, 2 (1972), 36-49.

Hoffman, Frederick J. "Iris Murdoch: The Reality of Persons." *Crit*, 7, 1 (1964) 48-57.

_____. "The Miracle of Contingency: The Novels of Iris Murdoch." *Shenandoah*, 17, 1 (1965), 49-56.

Hope, Francis. "The Novels of Iris Murdoch." *LonM*, n.s. 1, 5 (August 1961), 84-87.

Jacobson, Dan. "Farce, Totem and Taboo." *New Statesman*, 61 (1961), 956-57.

Kaufmann, R. J. "The Progress of Iris Murdoch." *Nation*, 188 (1959), 255-56.

Kennard, Jean E. *Number and Nightmare*, 155-75.

Kermode, Frank. "Myth, Reality, and Fiction." *Listener*, 68 (1962), 311-13.

Kogan, Pauline. "Beyond Solipsism to Irrationalism: A Study of Iris Murdoch's Novels." *L&I*, 2 (1969), 47-69.

Kriegel, Leonard. "Iris Murdoch: Everybody Through the Looking-Glass." *Contemporary British Novelists*. Ed. Charles Shapiro, 62-80.

Kuehl, Linda. "Iris Murdoch: The Novelist as Magician/The Magician as Novelist." *MFS*, 15, 3 (1969), 347-60.

"Letting Others Be." *TLS*, February 23, 1973, 197.

McCabe, Bernard. "The Guises of Love." *Cweal*, 83 (1965), 270-73.

McDowell, Frederick P. W. " 'The Devious Involutions of Human Character and Emotions': Reflections on Some Recent British Novels." *WSCL*, 4 (1963), 355-59.

Maes-Jelinek, Hena. "A House for Free Characters: The Novels of Iris Murdoch." *RLV*, 29 (1963), 45-69.

Majdiak, Daniel. "Romanticism in the Aesthetics of Iris Murdoch." *TSLL*, 14 (1972), 359-75.

Martin, Graham. "Iris Murdoch and the Symbolist Novel." *BJA*, 5 (1965), 296-300.

Martz, Louis L. "Iris Murdoch: The London Novels." *Twentieth-Century Literature in Retrospect.* Ed. Reuben A. Brower, 65-86.

Miller, Vincent. "Unofficial Roses." *National Review* (N. Y.), 13 (September 1962), 194-96.

Miner, Earl. "Iris Murdoch: The Uses of Love." *Nation*, 194 (1962), 498-99.

Morrell, Roy. "Iris Murdoch: The Early Novels." *CritQ*, 9 (1967), 272-82.

Obumselu, Ben. "Iris Murdoch and Sartre." *ELH*, 42 (1975), 296-317.

O'Connor, William Van. "Iris Murdoch: The Formal and the Contingent." *Crit*, 3, 2 (1960), 34-46.

O'Sullivan, Kevin. "Iris Murdoch and the Image of Liberal Man." *Yale Literary Mag.*, 131, 2 (1962), 27-36.

Palmer, Tony. "Artistic Privilege." *LonM*, n.s. 8, 2 (May 1968), 47-52.

Pearson, Gabriel. "Iris Murdoch and the Romantic Novel." *NewLR*, 13-14 (January-April 1962), 137-45.

Pondrom, Cyrena N. "Iris Murdoch: An Existentialist?" *CLS*, 5 (1968), 403-19.

Rabinovitz, Rubin. *Iris Murdoch*. New York: Columbia Univ. Press, 1968.

Raymond, John. *The Doge of Dover*, 179-84.

───. "The Unclassifiable Image." *New Statesman*, 56 (1958), 697-98.

Rippier, Joseph S. *Some Postwar English Novelists*, 70-105.

Souvage, J. "The Novels of Iris Murdoch." *SGG*, 4 (1962), 225-52.

Stubbs, Patricia. "Two Contemporary Views on Fiction: Iris Murdoch and Muriel Spark." *English*, 23 (1974), 102-10.

Taylor, Griffin. "What Does It Profit a Man . . . ?" *SR*, 66 (1958), 132-46.

Weatherhead, A. K. "Backgrounds with Figures in Iris Murdoch." *TSLL*, 10 (1969), 635-48.

Whitehorn, Katharine. "Three Women." *Encounter*, 21 (December 1963), 78-82.

Whiteside, George. "The Novels of Iris Murdoch." *Crit*, 7, 1 (1964), 27-47.

Wolfe, Peter. *The Disciplined Heart: Iris Murdoch and Her Novels.* Columbia: Univ. of Missouri Press, 1966.

See also: Allen, *Tradition*; Fraser; O'Connor, *New*; Swinden.

THE BELL

Jones, Dorothy. "Love and Morality in Iris Murdoch's *The Bell.*" *Meanjin*, 26 (1967), 85-90.

Kaehele, Sharon, and Howard German. "The Discovery of Reality in Iris Murdoch's *The Bell.*" *PMLA*, 82 (1967), 554-63.

Kimber, John. "*The Bell*: Iris Murdoch." *Delta*, 18 (1959), 31-34.

McCarthy, Margot. "Dualities in *The Bell.*" *ContempR*, 213 (1968), 313-17.

Souvage, Jacques. "Symbol as Narrative Device: An Interpretation of Iris Murdoch's *The Bell.*" *ES*, 43 (1962), 81-96.

Wall, Stephen. "The Bell in *The Bell.*" *EIC*, 13 (1963), 265-73.

BRUNO'S DREAM

Hall, William F. "*Bruno's Dream*: Technique and Meaning in the Novels of Iris Murdoch." *MFS*, 15, 3 (1969), 429-44.

Thomson, P. W. "Iris Murdoch's Honest Puppetry: The Characters of *Bruno's Dream.*" *CritQ*, 11 (1969), 277-83.

A FAIRLY HONOURABLE DEFEAT

Hoskins, Robert. "Iris Murdoch's Midsummer Nightmare." *TCL*, 18 (1972), 191-98.

"Re-run for the Enchanter." *TLS*, January 29, 1970, 101.

Watrin, Jany. "Iris Murdoch's *A Fairly Honourable Defeat.*" *RLV*, 38 (1972), 46-64.

THE FLIGHT FROM THE ENCHANTER

Meidner, Olga McDonald. "Reviewer's Bane: A Study of Iris Murdoch's *The Flight from the Enchanter.*" *EIC*, 11 (1961), 435-47.

Souvage, Jacques. "Theme and Structure in Iris Murdoch's *The Flight from the Enchanter.*" *SHVBVGG*, 3 (1960-61), 73-88.

Sullivan, Zohreh Tawakuli. "Enchantment and the Demonic in Iris Murdoch: *The Flight from the Enchanter.*" *MQ*, 16 (1975), 276-97.

THE ITALIAN GIRL

Bronzwaer, W. J. M. *Tense in the Novel*, 83-116.

Furbank, P. N. "Gowned Mortality." *Encounter*, 23 (November 1964), 88-90.

Tracy, Honor. "Misgivings about Miss Murdoch." *New Republic*, 151 (October 10, 1964), 21-22.

THE NICE AND THE GOOD
Baldanza, Frank. *"The Nice and the Good." MFS*, 15, 3 (1969), 417-28.
"Characters in Love." *TLS*, January 25, 1968, 77.

THE RED AND THE GREEN
Kemp, Peter. "The Fight Against Fantasy: Iris Murdoch's *The Red and the Green." MFS*, 15, 3 (1969), 403-16.
Ricks, Christopher. "A Sort of Mystery Novel." *New Statesman*, 70 (1965), 604-05.
Rome, Joy. "A Respect for the Contingent: A Study of Iris Murdoch's Novel *The Red and the Green." ESA*, 14 (1971), 87-98.
Sheed, Wilfred. *The Morning After*, 296-98.
Tucker, Martin. "The Odd Fish in Iris Murdoch's Kettle." *New Republic*, 154 (February 5, 1966), 26-28.

A SEVERED HEAD
Baldanza, Frank. "The Manuscript of Iris Murdoch's *A Severed Head." JML*, 3 (1973), 75-90.
Gregor, Ian. "Towards a Christian Literary Criticism." *Month*, 33 (1965), 239-49.
Kane, Patricia. "The Furnishings of a Marriage: An Aspect of Characterization in Iris Murdoch's *A Severed Head." NConL*, 2, 5 (1972), 4-5.
Kenney, Alice P. "The Mythic History of *A Severed Head." MFS*, 15, 3 (1969), 387-402.
O'Connor, William Van. "Iris Murdoch: *A Severed Head." Crit*, 5, 1 (1962), 74-77.

UNDER THE NET
Batchelor, Billie. "Revision in Iris Murdoch's *Under the Net." BI*, 8 (1968), 30-36.
Bradbury, Malcolm. "Iris Murdoch's *Under the Net." CritQ*, 4 (1962), 47-54.
DeMott, Benjamin. "Dirty Words?" *HudR*, 18 (1965), 31-44.
Fitzsimmons, Thomas. "World of Love." *SR*, 63 (1955), 323-30.
Meidner, Olga M. "The Progress of Iris Murdoch." *ESA*, 4 (1961), 17-38.
Porter, Raymond J. "Leitmotiv in Iris Murdoch's *Under the Net." MFS*, 15, 3 (1969), 379-86.
Souvage, Jacques. "The Unresolved Tension: An Interpretation of Iris Murdoch's *Under the Net." RLV*, 26 (1960), 420-30.

Iris Murdoch, continued

Vickery, John B. "The Dilemmas of Language: Sartre's *La Nausée* and Iris Murdoch's *Under the Net*." *JNT*, 1 (1971), 69-76.

Widmann, R. L. "Murdoch's *Under the Net*: Theory and Practice of Fiction." *Crit*, 10, 1 (1968), 5-16.

See also: Bradbury, *Possibilities.*

THE UNICORN

Bradbury, Malcolm. "Under the Symbol." *Spectator*, 211 (September 6, 1963), 295.

Detweiler, Robert. *Iris Murdoch's THE UNICORN.* New York: Seabury, 1969.

Grigson, Geoffrey. *The Contrary View*, 30-33.

Hebblethwaite, Peter. "Out Hunting Unicorns." *Month*, 30 (1963), 224-28.

Pondrom, Cyrena N. "Iris Murdoch: *The Unicorn*." *Crit*, 6, 1 (1963-64), 177-80.

Scholes, Robert. *The Fabulators*, 106-32.

L. H. MYERS

GENERAL STUDIES

Bantock, G. H. "L. H. Myers and Bloomsbury." *The Pelican Guide to English Literature*, v. 7. Ed. Boris Ford, 288-97.

Bottrall, Ronald. "L. H. Myers." *REL*, 2, 2 (1960), 47-58.

Eaton, Gai. *The Richest Vein*, 146-65.

Gupta, B. S. "L. H. Myers's Treatment of Buddhism in *The Near and the Far*." *RLV*, 37 (1971), 64-74.

Raskin, Jonah. *The Mythology of Imperialism*, 271-85.

Strong, L. A. G. *Personal Remarks*, 201-04.

Viswanathan, K. *India in English Fiction*, 171-216.

Wilson, Colin. *Eagle and Earwig*, 171-90.

P. H. NEWBY

INTERVIEWS

Balakian, Nona. "Talk with P. H. Newby." *NYTBR*, April 19, 1953, 18.

LeFranc, Bolivar. " 'We're Weak Animals in a Cold and Hostile Universe'." *Books and Bookmen*, 14 (July 1969), 30-32.

GENERAL STUDIES

Balakian, Nona. "Three English Novels." *KR*, 15 (1953), 490-96.

Bufkin, E. C. "Quest in the Novels of P. H. Newby." *Crit*, 8, 1 (1965), 51-62.

_____. *P. H. Newby.* Boston: Twayne, 1975.
Dickerson, Lucia. "Portrait of the Artist as a Jung Man." *KR*, 21 (1959), 58-83.
Fraser, G. S. *P. H. Newby.* London: Longmans, Green, 1975.
Halpern, Ben. "The Wisdom of Blindness." *Midstream*, 3 (Winter 1957), 104-07.
Mathews, Francis X. "Newby on the Nile." *TCL*, 14 (1968), 3-16.
_____. "Witness to Violence: The War Novels of P. H. Newby." *TSLL*, 12 (1970), 121-35.
"A Novelist on His Own." *TLS*, April 6, 1962, 232.
Poss, Stanley. "Manners and Myths in the Novels of P. H. Newby." *Crit*, 12, 1 (1970), 5-19.
Watts, Harold H. "P. H. Newby: Experience as Farce." *Per*, 10 (1958), 106-17.
See also: Allen, *Tradition*; Fraser; Karl; McCormick.

GEORGE ORWELL

BIBLIOGRAPHIES
McDowell, M. Jennifer. "George Orwell: Bibliographical Addenda." *BB*, 23, 10 (1963), 224-29; 24, 1 (1963), 19-24; 24, 2 (1963), 36-40.
Meyers, Jeffrey. "George Orwell: A Bibliography." *BB*, 31, 3 (1974), 117-21.
Willison, I. R. and Ian Angus. "George Orwell: Bibliographical Addenda." *BB*, 23, 5 (1965), 180-87.
Zeke, Zoltan G. and William White. "George Orwell: A Selected Bibliography." *BB*, 23, 5 (1961), 110-14; "Orwelliana," *BB*, 23, 6 (1961), 140-44; 23, 7 (1962), 166-68.

SPECIAL ISSUES
Modern Fiction Studies [*MFS*], 21, 1 (1975).
World Review, June 1950, 3-61.

GENERAL STUDIES
Alldritt, Keith. *The Making of George Orwell: An Essay in Literary History.* London: E. Arnold, 1969; New York: St. Martin's, 1970.
Alver, Leonard. "The Relevance of George Orwell." *ELLS*, 8 (1971), 65-79.
Atkins, John A. *George Orwell: A Literary and Biographical Study.* New York: Ungar, 1954; London: J. Calder, 1954; London: Calder and Boyers, 1971. [British ed. entitled *George Orwell: A Literary Study*]

Beadle, Gordon. "George Orwell and Charles Dickens: Moral Critics of Society." *JHS*, 2 (1969-70), 245-55.

──────. "George Orwell and the Death of God." *ColQ*, 23 (1974), 51-63.

Brander, Lawrence. *George Orwell*. London: Longmans, Green, 1954.

Braybrooke, Neville. "George Orwell." *Fortnightly*, n.s. 169 (51), 403-09.

Browning, Gordon. "Toward a Set of Standards for Anti-Utopian Fiction." *Cithara*, 10, 1 (1970), 18-32.

Byrne, Katharine. "George Orwell and the American Character." *Cweal*, 100 (1974), 135-37.

Calder, Jenni. *Chronicles of Conscience: A Study of George Orwell and Arthur Koestler*. Pittsburgh: Univ. of Pittsburgh Press; London: Secker and Warburg, 1968.

Carnall, Geoffrey. "Saints and Human Beings: Orwell, Osborne & Gandhi." *Essays Presented to Amy G. Stock*. Ed. R. K. Kaul, 168-77.

Colquitt, Betsy Feagan. "Orwell: Traditionalist in Wonderland." *Discourse*, 8 (1965), 370-83.

Connolly, Cyril. *Enemies of Promise*, rev. ed., 163-65.

──────. *The Evening Colonnade*, 335-49.

──────. *Previous Convictions*, 317-19.

Cook, Richard. "Rudyard Kipling and George Orwell." *MFS*, 7 (1961), 125-35.

Cosman, Max. "George Orwell and the Autonomous Individual." *PS*, 9 (1955), 74-84.

──────. "Orwell's Terrain." *Person*, 35 (1954), 41-49.

Crompton, Donald. "False Maps of the World: George Orwell's Autobiographical Writings and the Early Novels." *CritQ*, 16 (1974), 149-69.

Cruise O'Brien, Conor. *Writers and Politics*, 31-37.

Dooley, D. J. "The Limitations of George Orwell." *UTQ*, 28 (1959), 291-300.

Elevitch, Bernard. "Identity and Biology." *BUJ*, 22, 1 (1974), 3-8.

Elliott, George P. "A Failed Prophet." *HudR*, 10 (1957), 149-54.

Espey, David B. "George Orwell vs. Christopher Caudwell." *Ill. Quart.*, 36, 4 (1974), 46-60.

Fiderer, Gerald. "Masochism as Literary Strategy: Orwell's Psychological Novels." *L&P*, 20, 1 (1970), 3-21.

Fitzgerald, John J. "George Orwell's Social Compassion." *Discourse*, 9 (1966), 219-26.

Fixler, Michael. "George Orwell and the Instrument of Language." *IEY*, No. 9 (1964), 46-54.

Foley, Joseph, and James Ayer. "Orwell in English and Newspeak: A Computer Translation." *CCC*, 17 (1966), 15-18.

Forster, E. M. *Two Cheers for Democracy*, 60-63.

Forsyth, R. A. "Robert Buchanan and the Dilemma of the Brave New Victorian World." *SEL*, 9 (1969), 647-57.

Fyvel, T. R. "George Orwell and Eric Blair: Glimpses of a Dual Life." *Encounter*, 13 (July 1959), 60-65.

Glicksberg, Charles I. "The Literary Contribution of George Orwell." *ArQ*, 10 (1954), 234-45.

Greenblatt, Stephen J. *Three Modern Satirists*, 35-73, 105-17.

Griffin, C. W. "Orwell and the English Language." *Audience*, 7 (1960), 63-76.

Gross, Miriam, ed. *The World of George Orwell*. London: Weidenfeld and Nicolson, 1971; New York: Simon and Schuster, 1972.

Highet, Gilbert. *Clerk of Oxenford*, 62-68.

Hobbs, Albert H. "Welfarism and Orwell's Reversal." *Intercollegiate Rev.* (Bryn Mawr), 6, 3 (1970), 105-12.

Hollis, Christopher. *A Study of George Orwell, the Man and His Works*. Chicago: Regnery, 1955.

Hopkinson, Tom. *George Orwell*. London: Longmans, Green, 1953, 1962.

Ingle, Stephen J. "The Politics of George Orwell: A Reappraisal." *QQ*, 80 (1973), 22-33.

Jain, Jasbir. "Orwell and Imperialism." *BP*, 16 (1971), 1-7.

————. "Orwell: The Myth of a Classless Society." *Quest*, 72 (1971), 95-100.

————. "The Vision of Orwell." *RUSEng*, 5 (1971), 68-86.

Kalechofsky, Roberta. *George Orwell*. New York: Ungar, 1973.

King, Carlyle. "The Politics of George Orwell." *UTQ*, 26 (1956), 79-91.

Kirk, Russell. "George Orwell's Despair." *Intercollegiate Rev.* (Bryn Mawr), 5, 1 (1968), 21-25.

Koestler, Arthur. *The Trail of the Dinosaur*, 102-05.

Kubal, David L. "George Orwell: The Early Novelist." *ArQ*, 27 (1971), 59-73.

————. *Outside the Whole: George Orwell's Art and Politics*. Notre Dame, Ind.: Notre Dame Univ. Press, 1972.

Lee, Robert A. *Orwell's Fiction*. Notre Dame, Ind.: Univ. of Notre Dame Press, 1969.

Lewis, Wyndham. *The Writer and the Absolute*, 153-93.

Lief, Ruth Ann. *Homage to Oceania: The Prophetic Vision of George Orwell*. Columbus: Ohio State Univ. Press, 1969.

Lutman, Stephen. "Orwell's Patriotism." *JCH*, 2 (1967), 149-58.

George Orwell, continued

Mander, John. *The Writer and Commitment*, 71-110.
Mellichamp, Leslie. "George Orwell and the Ethics of Revolutionary Politics." *ModA*, 9 (1965), 272-78.
Meyers, Jeffrey, ed. *George Orwell: The Critical Heritage*. London: Routledge and K. Paul, 1975.
———. "Orwell's Painful Childhood." *ArielE*, 3, 1 (1972), 54-61.
———. *A Reader's Guide to George Orwell*. London: Thames and Hudson, 1975.
Mudrick, Marvin. *On Culture and Literature*, 15-28.
Nair, K. N. "Orwell's Guilt Complex and the Submersion-Reversion Pattern in His Writings." *Literary Studies*. Ed. K. P. Kesava Menon, M. Manuel, and K. Ayyappa Paniker, 119-25.
New, Melvyn. "Ad nauseum: A Satiric Device in Huxley, Orwell, and Waugh." *SNL*, 8 (1970), 24-28.
O'Donnell, Donat [Conor Cruise O'Brien]. "Orwell Looks at the World." *New Statesman*, 61 (1961), 837-38.
O'Flinn, J. P. "Orwell on Literature and Society." *CE*, 31 (1970), 603-12.
Ono, Kyoichi. *George Orwell*. Tokyo: Kenkyusha, 1970.
Oxley, B. T. *George Orwell*. London: Evans Bros., 1967.
Parrinder, Patrick. "George Orwell and the Detective Story." *JPC*, 6 (1973), 692-97.
Pinkus, Philip. "Satire and St. George." *QQ*, 70 (1963), 30-49.
Potts, Paul. *Dante Called You Beatrice*, 71-87.
———. "Don Quixote on a Bicycle: In Memorian, George Orwell, 1903-1950." *LonM*, 4, 3 (March 1957), 39-47.
Pritchett, V. S. "George Orwell." *Living Writers*. Ed. Gilbert Phelps, 106-15.
Quintana, Ricardo. "George Orwell: The Satiric Resolution." *WSCL*, 2, 1 (1961), 31-38.
Raskin, Jonah. *The Mythology of Imperialism*, 46-52.
Reed, John R. *Old School Ties*, 88-90, 155-60, 177-79, 193-95, 220-56.
Rees, Richard. "George Orwell." *The Politics of Twentieth-Century Novelists*. Ed. George A. Panichas, 85-99.
———. *George Orwell: Fugitive from the Camp of Victory*. London: Secker and Warburg, 1961; Carbondale: Southern Illinois Univ. Press, 1962.
Rieff, Philip. "George Orwell and the Post-Liberal Imagination." *KR*, 16 (1954), 49-70.
Rovere, Richard H., ed. *Orwell Reader: Fiction, Essays, and Reportage*. New York: Harcourt, 1956.
Russell, Bertrand. "George Orwell." *World Review*, June 1950, 5-7.

Sandison, Alan. *The Last Man in Europe: An Essay on George Orwell.* New York: Barnes and Noble, 1974.

Schmerl, Rudolf B. "Fantasy as Technique." *VQR*, 43 (1967), 644-56.

Shapiro, Marjorie. "George Orwell's Criticism." *ConnR*, 6, 2 (1973), 70-75.

Shibata, Toshihiko. "The Road to Nightmare: An Essay on George Orwell." *SELL*, No. 12 (1962), 41-53.

Small, Christopher. *The Road of Miniluv: George Orwell, the State and God.* London: Gollancz, 1975.

Smith, W. D. "George Orwell." *ContempR*, 189 (1956), 283-86.

Smyer, Richard I. "Orwell's *A Clergyman's Daughter.*" *MFS*, 21, 1 (1975), 31-48.

Stansky, Peter, and William Abrahams. *The Unknown Orwell.* London: Constable; New York: Knopf, 1972.

Strachey, John. *The Strangled Cry*, 23-32.

Swingewood, Alan. "George Orwell, Socialism and the Novel." *The Sociology of Literature.* Ed. Diana T. Laurenson and Alan Swingewood, 249-75.

Thody, Philip. "The Curiosity of George Orwell." *ULR*, 12 (1969), 69-80.

Thomas, Edward M. *George Orwell.* Edinburgh: Oliver and Boyd, 1965.

Thompson, Frank H., Jr. "Orwell's Image of the Man of Good Will." *CE*, 22 (1961), 235-40.

Trilling, Lionel. "George Orwell and the Politics of Truth." *Commentary*, 13, 3 (March 1952), 218-37.

Trocchi, Alexander. "A Note on George Orwell." *EvR*, 2, 6 (1958), 150-55.

Voorhees, Richard J. "George Orwell: Rebellion and Responsibility." *SAQ*, 53 (1954), 556-65.

———. *The Paradox of George Orwell.* Lafayette, Ind.: Purdue Research Foundation, 1961.

Wadsworth, Frank. "Orwell as Novelist." *UKCR*, 22 (1955), 93-99; 22 (1956), 189-94.

———. "Orwell's Later Work." *UKCR*, 22 (1956), 285-90.

Wain, John. *A House for the Truth*, 43-66.

———. "Orwell & the Intelligentsia." *Encounter*, 31 (December 1968), 72-80.

———. "Orwell in Perspective." *New World Writing*, 12 (1957), 84-96.

Walsh, James. "An Appreciation of an Individualist Writer: George Orwell." *MarxQ*, 3, 1 (1956), 3-9.

George Orwell, continued

Warncke, Wayne. "George Orwell's Critical Approach to Literature."
    SHR, 2 (1968), 484-98.

———. "The Permanence of Orwell." *UR*, 33 (1967), 189-96.

Watson, George. "Orwell and the Spectrum of European Politics."
    JES, 1 (1971), 191-97.

Way, Brian. "George Orwell: The Political Thinker We Might Have
    Had." *Gemini/Dialogue*, 3 (1960), 8-18.

Williams, Raymond. *Culture and Society*, 285-94.

———, ed. *George Orwell: A Collection of Critical Essays*. Englewood
    Cliffs, N. J.: Prentice-Hall, 1974.

———. *Orwell*. London: Fontana; New York: Viking, 1971.

Willison, Ian. "Orwell's Bad Good Books." *TC*, 157 (1955), 354-66.

Winegarten, Renée. *Writers and Revolution*, 294-313.

Wollheim, Richard. "Orwell Reconsidered." *PR*, 27, 1 (1960), 82-97.

Woodcock, George. *The Crystal Spirit: A Study of George Orwell*. Bos-
    ton: Little, Brown, 1966.

———. *The Writer and Politics*, 111-24.

Wulfsberg, Frederik. *George Orwell*. Oslo: Universitetsforlaget, 1968.

Yorks, Samuel A. "George Orwell: Seer Over His Shoulder." *BuR*, 9, 1
    (1960), 32-45.

Zwerdling, Alex. *Orwell and the Left*. New Haven, Conn.: Yale Univ.
    Press, 1974.

See also: Eagleton; Gillie, *Movements*; Karl; Prescott; Spender, *Crea-
    tive, Love-Hate*; A. West, *Principles*.

ANIMAL FARM

Brown, Spencer. "Strange Doings at *Animal Farm*." *Commentary*, 19,
    2 (February 1955), 155-61.

Cooper, Nancy M. "*Animal Farm*: An Explication for Teachers of Or-
    well's Novel." *CEJ*, 4 (1968), 59-69.

Davis, Robert M. "Politics in the Pig-Pen." *JPC*, 2 (1968), 314-20.

Dempsey, David. "Connolly, Orwell and Others: An English Miscel-
    lany." *AR*, 7 (1947), 142-50.

Gulbin, Suzanne. "Parallels and Contrasts in *Lord of the Flies* and
    Animal Farm." *EJ*, 55 (1966), 86-90, 92.

Hoggart, Richard. *Speaking to Each Other*, v. 2, 106-10.

Hopkinson, Tom. "*Animal Farm*." *World Review*, June 1950, 54-57.

Lee, Robert A. "The Uses of Form: A Reading of *Animal Farm*." *SSF*, 6
    (1969), 557-73.

Meyers, Jeffrey. "Orwell's Bestiary: The Political Allegory of *Animal
    Farm*." *SITC*, 8 (1971), 65-84.

Osgerby, J. R. "Set Books: *Animal Farm* and *1984*." *Use of English*, 17 (1966), 237-43.

Smyer, Richard I. *"Animal Farm*: The Burden of Consciousness." *ELN*, 9 (1971), 55-59.

BURMESE DAYS

Knapp, John V. "Dance to a Creepy Minuet: Orwell's *Burmese Days*, Precursor of *Animal Farm*." *MFS*, 21, 1 (1975), 11-30.

Lee, Robert A. "Symbol and Structure in *Burmese Days*: A Revaluation." *TSLL*, 11 (1969), 819-35.

Lewis, Robin J. "Orwell's *Burmese Days* and Forster's *A Passage to India*: Two Novels of Human Relations in the British Empire." *MSE*, 4, 3 (1974), 1-36.

Meyers, Jeffrey. "The Ethics of Responsibility: Orwell's *Burmese Days*." *UR*, 35 (1968), 83-87.

———. "Orwell in Burma." *AN&Q*, 11 (1972), 52-54.

Muggeridge, Malcolm. *"Burmese Days."* *World Review*, June 1950, 45-48.

Nakaji, Hiromichi. "Nats in the Novels of Burma by Orwell and Takeyama." Kyoritsu Women's Junior College, Tokyo. *Collected Essays by the Members of the Faculty*, 115-26.

Stevens, A. Wilber. "George Orwell and Southeast Asia." *YCGL*, 11 (1962), 133-41.

COMING UP FOR AIR

Fink, Howard. *"Coming up for Air*: Orwell's Ambiguous Satire on the Wellsian Utopia." *SLitI*, 6, 2 (1973), 51-60.

Meyers, Jeffrey. "Orwell's Apocalypse: *Coming Up for Air*." *MFS*, 21, 1 (1975), 69-80.

Van Dellen, Robert J. "George Orwell's *Coming Up For Air*: The Politics of Powerlessness." *MFS*, 21, 1 (1975), 57-68.

DOWN AND OUT IN PARIS AND LONDON

Kubal, David L. *"Down and Out in Paris and London*: The Conflict of Art and Politics." *MQ*, 12 (1971), 199-209.

Ross, William T. " 'My Theme is Poverty': Orwell's *Down and Out in Paris and London*." *MSLC*, 1, 2 (1974), 31-39.

Smyer, Richard I. "Loss of Innocence in George Orwell's *Down and Out in Paris and London*." *SDR*, 8, 4 (1970), 75-83.

249

George Orwell, continued

HOMAGE TO CATALONIA

Beadle, Gordon B. "George Orwell and the Spanish Civil War." *Duquesne Rev.*, 16 (1971), 3-16.

Edrich, Emanuel. "Naiveté and Simplicity in Orwell's Writing: *Homage to Catalonia.*" *UKCR*, 27 (1961), 289-97.

Meyers, Jeffrey. " 'An Affirming Flame': Orwell's *Homage to Catalonia.*" *ArQ*, 27 (1971), 5-22.

Spender, Stephen. *"Homage to Catalonia."* *World Review*, June 1950, 51-54.

Sperber, Murray A. " 'Marx: G.O.'s Dog': A Study of Politics and Literature in George Orwell's *Homage to Catalonia.*" *DR*, 52 (1972), 226-36.

Trilling, Lionel. *The Opposing Self*, 151-72.

KEEP THE ASPIDISTRA FLYING

Guild, Nicholas. "In Dubious Battle: George Orwell and the Victory of the Money-God." *MFS*, 21, 1 (1975), 49-56.

Kubal, David L. "George Orwell and the Aspidistra." *UR*, 37 (1970), 61-67.

NINETEEN EIGHTY-FOUR

Aldiss, Brian W. *Billion Year Spree*, 254-56.

Bakker, J. "George Orwell's Newspeak in Light of *A Philosophy In a New Key.*" *LT*, 242 (1967), 674-83.

Barr, Alan. "The Paradise Behind *1984.*" *EM*, 19 (1968), 197-203.

Beauchamp, Gorman. "Future Words: Language and the Dystopian Novel." *Style*, 8 (1974), 462-76.

———. "Of Man's Last Disobedience: Zamiatin's *We* and Orwell's *1984.*" *CLS*, 10 (1973), 285-301.

Connors, James. " 'Do It to Julia': Thoughts on Orwell's *1984.*" *MFS*, 16 (1970), 463-73.

———. "Zamyatin's *We* and the Genesis of *1984.*" *MFS*, 21, 1 (1975), 107-24.

Deutscher, Isaac. *Heretics and Renegades*, 35-50.

———. *Russia in Transition*, 230-45.

Dyson, A. E. *The Crazy Fabric*, 197-219.

Edrich, Emanuel. "George Orwell and the Satire in Horror." *TSLL*, 4 (1962), 96-108.

Elsbree, Langdon. "The Structured Nightmare of *1984.*" *TCL*, 5 (1959), 135-41.

Ferguson, Alfred R. "Newspeak, the First Edition: Tyranny and the Decay of Language." *MQR*, 14 (1975), 445-53.

Fink, Howard. "Newspeak: The Epitome of Parody Techniques in *Nineteen Eighty-Four.*" *CritS*, 5 (1971), 155-63.

Geering, R. G. "*Darkness at Noon* and *Nineteen Eighty Four*: A Comparative Study." *AusQ*, 30, 3 (1958), 90-96.

Gleckner, Robert F. "1984 or 1948?" *CE*, 18 (1956), 95-99.

Hamilton, Kenneth M. "G. K. Chesterton and George Orwell: A Contrast in Prophecy." *DR*, 31 (1951), 198-205.

Harris, Harold J. "Orwell's Essays and *1984.*" *TCL*, 4 (1959), 154-61.

Howe, Irving. "The Fiction of Anti-Utopia." *New Republic*, 146 (April 23, 1962), 13-16.

―――. "Orwell: History as Nightmare." *ASch*, 25 (1956), 193-207.

―――, ed. *Orwell's NINETEEN EIGHTY-FOUR: Text, Sources, Criticism.* New York: Harcourt, 1963.

Hynes, Samuel, ed. *1984: A Collection of Critical Essays.* Englewood Cliffs, N. J.: Prentice-Hall, 1971.

Kessler, Martin. "Power and the Perfect State: A Study in Disillusionment as Reflected in Orwell's *Nineteen Eighty-Four* and Huxley's *Brave New World.*" *PSQ*, 72 (1957), 565-77.

LeRoy, Gaylord C. "A.F. 632 to 1984." *CE*, 12 (1950), 135-38.

Lyons, John O. "George Orwell's Opaque Glass in *1984.*" *WSCL*, 2, 3 (1961), 39-46.

Maddison, Michael. "*1984*: A Burnhamite Fantasy." *PolQ*, 32 (January 1961), 71-79.

Meyers, Jeffrey. "The Evolution of *1984.*" *EM*, 23 (1972), 247-61.

New, Melvyn. "Orwell and Antisemitism: Toward *1984.*" *MFS*, 21, 1 (1975), 81-106.

Nott, Kathleen. "Orwell's *1984.*" *The Listener*, 70 (1963), 687-88.

Osgerby, J. R. "Set Books: *Animal Farm* and *1984.*" *Use of English*, 17 (1966), 237-43.

Philmus, Robert M. "The Language of Utopia." *SLitI*, 6, 2 (1973), 61-78.

Rahv, Philip. "The Unfuture of Utopia." *PR*, 16, 7 (1949), 743-49.

Ranald, Ralph A. "George Orwell and the Mad World: The Anti-Universe of *1984.*" *SAQ*, 66 (1967), 544-53.

Rankin, David. "Orwell's Intention in *1984.*" *ELN*, 12 (1975), 188-92.

Read, Herbert. "*1984.*" *World Review*, June 1950, 58-59.

Richards, D. "Four Utopias." *SEER*, 40 (1962), 220-28.

Russell, Bertrand. *Portraits from Memory*, 221-28.

Schmerl, Rudolf B. "Orwell as Fantasist." *Cresset*, 25, 8 (1962), 8-13.

Siegel, Paul N. "The Cold War: *1984* Twenty-five Years After." *Confrontation*, 8 (1974), 148-56.

Slater, Joseph. "The Fictional Values of *1984.*" *Essays on Literary History Presented to J. Milton French.* Ed. Rudolf Kirk and Charles F. Main, 249-64.

Smith, Marcus. "The Wall of Blackness: A Psychological Approach to *1984.*" *MFS*, 14 (1968), 423-33.

Smyer, Richard I. "*1984*: The Search for the Golden Country." *ArQ*, 27 (1971), 41-52.

Steinhoff, William. *George Orwell and the Origins of 1984.* Ann Arbor: Univ. of Michigan Press; London: Weidenfeld and Nicolson, 1975. [British ed. entitled *The Road to 1984*]

Struc, Roman S. "George Orwell's *Nineteen Eighty-Four* and Dostoevsky's 'Underground Men'." *Proceedings: Pacific Northwest Conference on Foreign Languages.* Ed. Walter C. Kraft, 217-20.

Thale, Jerome. "Orwell's Modest Proposal." *CritQ*, 4 (1962), 365-68.

Voorhees, Richard J. "*Nineteen Eighty-Four*: No Failure of Nerve." *CE*, 18 (1956), 101-02.

Walsh, Chad. *From Utopia to Nightmare*, 97-98, 106-14, 140-47, 157-58.

Westlake, J. H. J. "Aldous Huxley's *Brave New World* and George Orwell's *Nineteen Eighty-Four*: A Comparative Study." *NS*, 21 (1972), 94-102.

Wicker, Brian. "An Analysis of Newspeak." *Blackfriars*, 43 (June 1962), 272-85.

Woodcock, George. "Utopias in Negative." *SR*, 64 (1956), 81-97.

See also: Mueller, *Celebration*; Spender, *Creative*.

THE ROAD TO WIGAN PIER

Beavan, John. "*The Road to Wigan Pier*." *World Review*, June 1950, 48-51.

Hoggart, Richard. "George Orwell and *The Road to Wigan Pier*." *CritQ*, 7 (1965), 72-85.

_____. *Speaking to Each Other*, v. 2, 111-28.

Macdonald, Dwight. "Varieties of Political Experience." *NY*, 35 (March 28, 1959), 135-51.

ANTHONY POWELL

INTERVIEWS

"Anthony Powell: A *Summary* Interview." *Summary*, 1, 1 (1970), 129-39.

Davis, Douglas M. "An Interview with Anthony Powell, Frome, England, June 1962." *CE*, 24 (1963), 533-36.

SPECIAL ISSUES

"Anthony Powell: A Symposium." *Summary*, 1, 1 (1970), 34-139.

GENERAL STUDIES

Amis, Kingsley. "Afternoon World." *Spectator*, 194 (May 13, 1955), 69-20.

Antonini, Giacomo. "Anthony Powell and True Modernation." *Summary*, 1, 1 (1970), 106-110.

Atkins, John. "Widening Sympathies: Reflections on the Work of Anthony Powell." *KN*, 22 (1975), 191-205.

Bailey, Paul. "Sniffing the Scandal." *LonM*, 11, 3 (August-September 1971), 147-50.

Bergonzi, Bernard. *Anthony Powell*. London and New York: Longmans, Green, 1962; rev. ed., by Ian Scott-Kilvert, Harlow: Longmans, Green, 1971.

———. "Anthony Powell." *Anthony Powell and L. P. Hartley*, by Paul Bloomfield and Bernard Bergonzi, 24-40.

———. "Anthony Powell: 9/12." *CritQ*, 11 (1969), 76-86.

Bliven, Naomi. "The Credibility of Nicholas Jenkins." *Summary*, 1, 1 (1970), 84-86.

Brennan, Neil F. *Anthony Powell*. New York: Twayne, 1974.

Brooke, Jocelyn. "Anthony Powell." *Unilit*, May 1964, 41-43.

———. "From Wauchop to Widmerpool." *LonM*, 7, 9 (September 1960), 60-64.

Cooper, Jilly. "Start of an Addiction." *Summary*, 1, 1 (1970), 44-46.

"Dancing in the Dark." *TLS*, October 17, 1968, 1170.

"Degrees of Decay." *TLS*, June 22, 1973, 709.

Duffy, Joseph M. "The Dancer and the Dance: Anthony Powell's *The Music of Time*." *Summary*, 1, 1 (1970), 74-81.

Fuller, Roy. "Comedy, Realism, and Poetry in *The Music of Time*." *Summary*, 1, 1 (1970), 47-53.

Gant, Roland. "A *Marche Militaire* in *The Music of Time*." *Summary*, 1, 1 (1970), 87-90.

Glazebrook, Mark. "The Art of Horace Isbister, E. Bosworth Deacon, and Ralph Barnby." *LonM*, n.s. 7, 8 (November 1967), 76-82.

Gutierrez, Donald. "The Discrimination of Elegance: Anthony Powell's *A Dance to the Music of Time*." *MHRev*, 34 (April 1975), 126-41.

———. "Power in *A Dance to the Music of Time*." *ConnR*, 6, 2 (1973), 50-60.

Hall, James. "The Uses of Polite Surprise: Anthony Powell." *EIC*, 12 (1962), 167-83.

Hartley, L. P. "Good Dog, Good Dog." *T&T*, 43 (June 28, 1962), 21-22.

Herring, H. D. "Anthony Powell: A Reaction Against Determinism." *BSUF*, 9, 1 (1968), 17-21.

Anthony Powell, continued

Hillman, Serrell. "Powell from the Other Side." *Summary*, 1, 1 (1970), 120-24.

Hynes, Sam. "Novelist of Society." *Cweal*, 70 (1959), 396-97.

Janeway, Elizabeth. "Anthony Powell: The Serial Novel." *Summary*, 1, 1 (1970), 54-57.

Karl, Frederick R. "Sisyphus Descending: Mythical Patterns in the Novels of Anthony Powell." *Mosaic*, 4, 3 (1971), 13-22.

Kermode, Frank. "The Interpretation of the Times." *Encounter*, 15 (September 1960), 71-76.

Lambourne, David. "Understanding the Past: Anthony Powell's Classicism." *Summary*, 1, 1 (1970), 111-16.

Lurie, Alison. "Up Jenkins." *Summary*, 1, 1 (1970), 82-83.

Martin, W. R. "Style as Achievement in Anthony Powell's *The Music of Time*." *ESA*, 14 (1971), 73-86.

McCall, Raymond G. "Anthony Powell's Gallery." *CE*, 27 (1965), 227-32.

McDowell, Frederick P. W. " 'The Devious Involutions of Human Characters and Emotions': Reflections on Some Recent British Novels." *WSCL*, 4 (1963), 362-65.

McLeod, Dan. "Anthony Powell: Some Notes on the Art of the Sequence Novel." *SNNTS*, 3 (1971), 44-63.

Mizener, Arthur. "A Dance to the Music of Time: The Novels of Anthony Powell." *KR*, 22 (1960), 79-92.

_____. *The Sense of Life in the Modern Novel*, 79-103.

_____. "Some Kinds of Modern Novels." *SR*, 69 (1961), 153-64.

Moore, John Rees. "Anthony Powell's England: A Dance to the Music of Time." *HC*, 8, 4 (1971), 1-16.

Morris, Robert K. "Mars Mercurial: Anthony Powell's War Trilogy." *Summary*, 1, 1 (1970), 91-105.

_____. *The Novels of Anthony Powell*. Pittsburgh: Univ. of Pittsburgh Press, 1968.

"Nick Goes to War." *TLS*, March 5, 1964, 189.

Powell, Anthony. "Anthony Powell: Some Questions Answered." *AWR*, 14, 33 (1964), 77-79.

_____. "Taken from Life." *TC*, 170 (1961), 50-53.

Pritchett, V. S. *The Working Novelist*, 172-80.

Quesenbery, W. D., Jr. "Anthony Powell: The Anatomy of Decay." *Crit*, 7, 1 (1964), 5-26.

Radner, Sanford. "Powell's Early Novels: A Study in Point of View." *Renascence*, 16 (1964), 194-200.

_____. "The World of Anthony Powell." *ClareQ*, 10, 2 (1963), 41-57.

Ruoff, Gene W. "Social Mobility and the Artist in *Manhattan Transfer* and the *Music of Time*." *WSCL*, 5 (1964), 64-76.

Russell, John D. *Anthony Powell: A Quintet, Sextet, and War.* Bloomington: Indiana Univ. Press, 1970.

———. "Humour and the Early Novels." *Summary,* 1, 1 (1970), 38-43.

———. "Quintet from the 30s: Anthony Powell." *KR,* 27 (1965), 698-726.

———. "The War Trilogies of Anthony Powell and Evelyn Waugh." *ModA,* 16 (1972), 289-300.

Schlesinger, Arthur, Jr. "Anthony Powell: The Prosopographer as Novelist." *Summary,* 1, 1 (1970), 66-73.

Shapiro, Charles. "Widmerpool and 'The Music of Time'." *Contemporary British Novelists.* Ed. Charles Shapiro, 80-94.

Sions, Harry. "The Relevance of Anthony Powell." *Summary,* 1, 1 (1970), 34-37.

"Time Marches On." *TLS,* Feb. 19, 1971, 199.

Vaizey, John. "Notes on the Structure of *The Music of Time.*" *Summary,* 1, 1 (1970), 58-65.

Vinson, James. "Anthony Powell's *Music of Time.*" *Per,* 10 (1958), 146-52.

Voorhees, Richard J. "Anthony Powell: The First Phase." *PrS,* 28 (1954), 337-44.

———. "*The Music of Time*: Themes and Variations." *DR,* 42 (1962), 313-21.

Waugh, Evelyn. "Marriage à la Mode—1936." *Spectator,* 204 (June 24, 1960), 919.

Weidman, Jerome. "A Note About Anthony Powell." *Summary,* 1, 1 (1970), 125-28.

West, Anthony. "Wry Humor." *NY,* 28 (December 13, 1952), 170-78.

Woodward, A. G. "The Novels of Anthony Powell." *ESA,* 10 (1967), 117-28.

Zigerell, James J. "Anthony Powell's *Music of Time*: Chronicle of a Declining Establishment." *TCL,* 12 (1966), 138-46.

Ziman, H. D. "The Private and the Public Powell." *Summary,* 1, 1 (1970), 117-19.

See also: Allen, *Tradition*; Bergonzi, *Situation*; Hall, *Tragic*; Karl; McCormick; R. Morris, *Continuance*; Pritchett, *Living*; Walcutt.

J. C. POWYS

BIBLIOGRAPHIES

Anderson, Arthur J. "John Cowper Powys: A Bibliography." *BB,* 25, (1967), 73-78, 94.

Carter, Kenneth, ed. *The Powys Family: A Catalogue of Books by and about the Powys Family in Dorset County Library*. Dorchester, Dorset, Eng.: Dorset County Library, 1972.

Langridge, Derek W. *John Cowper Powys: A Record of Achievement*. London: Library Ass'n., 1966.

INTERVIEWS

de Wet, Oloff. *A Visit to John Cowper Powys*. London: Village Press, 1974.

_____. "Visit to John Cowper Powys." *TQ*, 11, 3 (1968), 91-116.

Hopkins, Kenneth. "A Visit to John Cowper Powys." *Philobiblon*, 8 (Winter 1966), 23-25.

SPECIAL ISSUES

Philobiblon, 8 (Winter 1966), 1-34.

Review of English Literature (Leeds) [*REL*], 4, 1 (1963).

GENERAL STUDIES

Aury, Dominique. "Reading Powys." *REL*, 4, 1 (1967), 33-57.

Brebner, John A. *The Demon Within: A Study of John Cowper Powys's Novels*. New York: Barnes and Noble, 1973.

Cavaliero, Glen. *John Cowper Powys: Novelist*. Oxford: Clarendon, 1973.

Chaning-Pearce, Melville. *The Terrible Crystal*, 179-93.

Churchill, Reginald C. *The Powys Brothers*. London: Longmans, Green, 1962.

Collins, H. P. *John Cowper Powys: Old Earth-man*. London: Barrie and Rockliff, 1966.

Cook, David A. "Between Two Worlds: A Reading of *Weymouth Sands*." *PowysN*, 3 (1972-73), 18-24.

Coombes, Harry. "John Cowper Powys: A Modern Merlin?" *SoR*, n.s. 11 (1975), 779-93.

Durant, Will. *Adventures in Genius*, 301-15.

Elwin, Malcolm. "John Cowper Powys." *Writers of To-day, 2*. Ed. Denys Val Baker, 117-34.

_____. "John Cowper Powys: Publishing His Later Work." *Philobiblon*, 8 (Winter 1966), 27-29.

Gillis, James M. *This Our Day*, 188-95, 348-54.

Govan, Gilbert E. "The Powys Family." *SR*, 46 (1938), 74-90.

Greenwald, Michael. "The Second Novel: *Rodmoor*." *PowysN*, 3 (1972-73), 8-17.

Gregory, Alyse. "A Famous Family." *LonM*, 5, 3 (March 1958), 44-53.

Hanbury, Michael. "John Cowper Powys and Some Catholic Contacts." *Month*, 30 (1963), 299-303.

Hanley, James. "The Man in the Corner." *John O'London's Weekly*, 63 (September 3, 1954), 877-78.

Hentschel, Cedric. "John Cowper Powys and the 'Gretchen-Cult'." *SN*, 15 (1942), 91-104.

Hooker, Jeremy. *John Cowper Powys*. Cardiff: Univ. of Wales Press, 1973.

Hopkins, Kenneth. *The Powys Brothers: A Biographical Appreciation*. Rutherford, N.J.: Fairleigh Dickinson Univ. Press, 1967.

Humfrey, Belinda, ed. *Essays on John Cowper Powys*. Cardiff: Univ. of Wales Press; Mystic, Conn.: Very, 1972.

Jones, Bernard. *John Cowper Powys*. Dorchester: Dorset Natural History and Archaeological Society, 1962.

Jordan-Smith, Paul. *For the Love of Books*, 101-10.

Knight, G. Wilson. *Neglected Powers*, 67-69, 153-227, 399-415, 430-40.

―――. "Preface." *Rodmoor: A Romance*, by John Cowper Powys, new ed. London: Macdonald, 1974.

―――. *Saturnian Quest: A Chart of the Prose Works of John Cowper Powys*. London: Methuen; New York: Barnes and Noble, 1964.

Langridge, Derek W. *John Cowper Powys: A Record of Achievement*. London: Library Ass'n., 1966.

Mahanti, J. C. "Beyond Yes and No: The Novels of John Cowper Powys." *IFR*, 2 (1975), 77-79.

Marlow, Louis [Louis Wilkinson]. *Seven Friends*, 65-85.

―――. *Welsh Ambassadors*. London: Chapman and Hall, 1936, 114-60.

Miller, Henry. *The Books in My Life*, 134-39, 248-52.

―――. "The Immortal Bard." *REL*, 4, 1 (1963), 21-24.

Priestley, J. B. "The Happy Introvert." *REL*, 4, 1 (1963), 25-32.

Pritchett, V. S. "The Mysteries of John Cowper Powys." *New Statesman*, 69 (1965), 534-35.

Robillard, Douglas. "Landscape with Figures: The Early Fiction of John Cowper Powys." *SLitI*, 1, 2 (1968), 51-58.

Saalbach, Robert P. "Dreiser and the Powys Family." *Dreiser Newsl.*, 6, 2 (1975), 10-16.

Van Doren, Mark. *The Private Reader*, 201-04.

Ward, Richard Heron. *The Powys Brothers*. London: Bodley Head, 1935.

Wilkinson, Louis. "The Brothers Powys." *Philobiblon*, 8 (Winter 1966), 16-17.

―――. "The Brothers Powys." Royal Soc. of Lit. of the U. K., London. *Essays by Divers Hands*, v. 24, 40-62.

J. C. Powys, continued

Wilson, Angus. "Evil in the English Novel." *KR*, 29 (1967), 167-94.

———. "Introduction." *Weymouth Sands*, by John Cowper Powys. Cambridge: Rivers, 1973.

———. " 'Mythology' in John Cowper Powys' Novels." *REL*, 4, 1 (1963), 9-20.

Wilson, Colin. *Eagle and Earwig*, 113-21.

See also: Aiken, *ABC*; Allen, *Tradition*; J. Collins, *20th*.

A GLASTONBURY ROMANCE

Brooke, Jocelyn. "On Rereading *A Glastonbury Romance*." *LonM*, 3, 4 (April 1956), 44-51.

Cook, David A. "John Cowper Powys' *A Glastonbury Romance*: A Modern Mystery Play." *ConL*, 13 (1972), 341-60.

Delafield, E. M. "Romantic Glastonbury; or, Happy Haunts for Summer Holidays." *Essays of the Year, 1933-1934*, by Various Authors, 61-67.

Knight, G. Wilson. "Lawrence, Joyce, and Powys." *EIC*, 11 (1961), 403-17.

Reid, Margaret J. C. *The Arthurian Legend*, 150, 154-57.

OWEN GLENDOWER

Brebner, John A. "Owen Glendower: The Pursuit of the Fourth Dimension." *AWR*, 18, 42 (1970), 207-16.

Knight, G. Wilson. "Owen Glendower." *REL*, 4, 1 (1963), 41-52.

PORIUS

Blackmore, R. L. "The Matter of Porius." *PowysN*, 4 (1974-75), 4-6.

Powys, J. C. "The Characters of the Book." *PowysN*, 4 (1974-75), 14-21.

———. "Preface (or Anything You Like) to *Porius*." *PowysN*, 4 (1974-75), 7-13.

Slater, Joseph. "*Porius* Restauratus." *PowysN*, 4 (1974-75), 22-44.

———. "The Stones of Porius." *PowysN*, 3 (1972-73), 25-29.

WOLF SOLENT

Cook, David A. "The Creation of Self in John Cowper Powys: A Reading of *Wolf Solent*." *EAS*, 4 (1975), 23-44.

Sadleir, Michael. "Long Novels." *Essays of the Year, 1929-1930*, by Various Authors, 229-51.

T. F. POWYS

BIBLIOGRAPHIES

Riley, Peter. *A Bibliography of T. F. Powys*. Hastings, Middlesex: Brimmell, 1967.

INTERVIEWS
"Why I Have Given Up Writing." *John O'London's Weekly*, 36 (October 23, 1936), 145-46, 152.

GENERAL STUDIES
Boulton, J. A. "Evening for T. F. Powys." *N&Q*, 19 (1972), 338-40.

_____. " 'The Moods of God': An Early Version of 'Mr. Tasker's Gods'." *N&Q*, 19 (1972), 56-59.

Buning, M. "Folly Down Revisited: Some New Light on T. F. Powys." *ES*, 50 (1969), 588-97.

Carr, W. I. "T. F. Powys: A Comment." *English*, 15 (1964), 8-12.

Churchill, R. C. "The Path of T. F. Powys." *Critic*, 1 (Spring 1947), 25-31.

Coombes, H. *T. F. Powys*. London: Barrie and Rockliff, 1960.

Hopkins, Kenneth. "The Second Brother: A Note on T. F. Powys." *REL*, 4, 1 (1963), 59-67.

Hunter, William. *The Novels and Stories of T. F. Powys*. Cambridge: Frazer, 1931.

Jordan-Smith, Paul. *For the Love of Books*, 101-10.

MacCampbell, Donald. "The Art of T. F. Powys." *SR*, 42 (1934), 461-73.

Marlow, Louis. [Louis Wilkinson] "T. F. Powys." *Living Writers*. Ed. Gilbert Phelps, 151-57.

_____. *Seven Friends*, 86-107.

_____. *Welsh Ambassadors*. London: Chapman and Hall, 1936, 161-210.

Nicholson, Norman. *Man and Literature*, 144-56.

Riley, A. P. "The Original Ending of *Mr. Weston's Good Wine*." *REL*, 8, 2 (1967), 49-55.

Saalbach, Robert P. "Dreiser and the Powys Family." *Dreiser Newsl.*, 6, 2 (1975), 10-16.

Sewell, Brocard, ed. *Theodore: Essays on T. F. Powys by Neville Braybrooke (and Others) with a Story by T. F. Powys, "The Useless Woman," And Some Letters of T. F. Powys to Littleton C. Powys and Elizabeth Meyers*. Aylesford, Kent: St. Albert's, 1964.

Steinmann, Martin, Jr. "The Symbolism of T. F. Powys." *Crit*, 1, 2 (1957), 49-63.

_____. "Water and Animal Symbolism in T. F. Powys." *ES*, 41 (1960), 359-65.

Van Kranendonk, A. G. "Theodore Powys." *ES(A)*, 26 (1944-1945), 97-107.

Warren, C. "The Novels of T. F. Powys." *Criterion*, 7, 4 (1928), 134-37.

See also: Entries under "J. Powys"; Allen, *Tradition*; A. Collins, *20th.*

J. B. PRIESTLEY

BIBLIOGRAPHIES

Day, Alan E. "J. B. Priestley: A Checklist." *BB*, 28 (1971), 42-48.

INTERVIEWS

Braine, John. "Lunch with J. B. Priestley." *Encounter*, 10 (June 1958), 8-14.

Breit, Harvey. *The Writer Observed*, 191-93.

GENERAL STUDIES

Brown, Ivor. *J. B. Priestley*. London: Longmans, Green, 1957.

Collins, Norman. *The Facts of Fiction*, 258-75.

Cooper, Susan. *J. B. Priestley: Portrait of an Author*. London: Heinemann, 1970; New York: Harper, 1970.

"The Dark Truster in God and the Thwarted Believer in Man." *TLS*, March 13, 1969, 257-58.

Deakin, Nicholas. "J. B. Priestley's Anglo-Saxon Attitudes." *T&T*, 42 (1961), 1159-61.

Hughes, David. *J. B. Priestley: An Informal Study of His Work*. London: Hart-Davis, 1958.

Lindsay, Jack. "J. B. Priestley." *Writers of To-Day*. Ed. Denys Val Baker, 72-82.

MacRae, D. G., ed. *The World of J. B. Priestley*. London: Heinemann, 1967.

Mann, Dorothea L. "J. B. Priestley: Servant of the Comic Spirit." *Bookman* (N.Y.), 73 (1931), 241-46.

Mercier, Vivian. "Priestley on Literature: A Reader's Guide." *Cweal*, 73 (1960), 40-45.

Smith, Grover, Jr. "Time Alive: J. W. Dunne and J. B. Priestley." *SAQ*, 56 (1957), 224-33.

Steel, Johannes. *Men Behind the War*, 58-64.

West, Alick. *The Mountain in the Sunlight*, 155-84.

Whidden, R. W. "Priestley and his Novels." *QQ*, 48 (1941), 57-62.

See also: A. Collins, *20th*; Spender, *Love-Hate*; Swinnerton, *Georgian*; Vines.

V. S. PRITCHETT

INTERVIEWS

Firchow, Peter. *The Writer's Place*, 276-84.

GENERAL STUDIES

Sheed, Wilfred. *The Morning After*, 66-75.

Solotaroff, Theodore. *The Red Hot Vacuum*, 286-90.

Why Do I Write? An Exchange of Views Between Elizabeth Bowen, Graham Greene and V. S. Pritchett.

See also: McCormick.

HERBERT READ

SPECIAL ISSUES

Malahat Review [*MHRev*], 9 (January 1969), 7-264.

GENERAL STUDIES

Bergonzi, Bernard. *Heroes' Twilight*, 72-79, 147-50.

Harder, Worth T. "Crystal Source: Herbert Read's *The Green Child*." *SR*, 81 (1973), 714-38.

Knight, G. Wilson. "Herbert Read and Byron." *MHRev*, 9 (January 1969), 130-34.

————. *Neglected Powers*, 481-85.

Raine, Kathleen. "Herbert Read as a Literary Critic." *MHRev*, 9 (January 1969), 135-57.

Tate, Allen. *Essays of Four Decades*, 372-81.

Wasson, Richard. "*The Green Child*: Herbert Read's Ironic Fantasy." *PMLA*, 77 (1962), 645-51.

West, Alick. *Crisis and Criticism*, 47-53.

Woodcock, George. "The Philosopher of Freedom." *MHRev*, 9 (January 1969), 68-87.

See also: Green; Spender, *Struggle*; Vines.

MARY RENAULT

GENERAL STUDIES

Burns, Landon C., Jr. "Men Are Only Men: The Novels of Mary Renault." *Crit*, 6, 3 (1963-64), 102-21.

Casey, Bill. "Nurse Novels." *SWR*, 49, 4 (1964), 332-41.

Dick, Bernard F. *The Hellenism of Mary Renault*. Carbondale: Southern Illinois Univ. Press, 1972.

Herbert, Kevin. "The Theseus Theme: Some Recent Versions." *CJ*, 55 (1960), 173-85.

Renault, Mary. "History in Fiction." *TLS*, March 23, 1973, 315.

————. "Notes on *The King Must Die*." *Afterwords*. Ed. Thomas McCormack, 80-87.

Mary Renault, continued

Wills, Garry. "The Autosexual Novel." *National Review* (N.Y.), 7 (July 1959), 186-87.
Wolfe, Peter. *Mary Renault*. New York: Twayne, 1969

JEAN RHYS

GENERAL STUDIES
Mellown, Elgin W. "Character and Themes in the Novels of Jean Rhys." *ConL*, 13 (1972), 458-75.
Wyndham, Francis. "Introduction to Jean Rhys." *LonM*, 7, 1 (January 1960), 15-18.

DOROTHY RICHARDSON

BIBLIOGRAPHIES
Gliken, Gloria. "Dorothy M. Richardson: An Annotated Bibliography of Writings About Her." *ELT*, 8, 1 (1965), 12-35; 14, 1 (1971), 84-88; [as Gloria Glikin Fromm] 18, 1 (1975), 70-72.

INTERVIEWS
Brome, Vincent. "A Last Meeting with Dorothy Richardson." *LonM*, 6, 6 (June 1959), 26-32.
Morgan, Louise. "How Writers Work: Dorothy Richardson." *Everyman*, October 22, 1931, 395-96, 400.

SPECIAL ISSUES
Adam International Review [*Adam*], 31, 310-12 (1966), 16-48.

GENERAL STUDIES
Blake, Caesar R. *Dorothy Richardson*. Ann Arbor: Univ. of Michigan Press, 1960.
Bliven, Naomi. "Memoirs of a Travelling Woman." *NY*, 44 (May 4, 1968), 181-86.
Bowling, Lawrence Edward. "What is the Stream of Consciousness Technique?" *PMLA*, 65 (1950), 333-45.
Bryher, [Winifred]. "Dorothy Richardson." *Adam*, 31, 310-12 (1966), 22-23.
Chevalley, Abel. *The Modern English Novel*, 249-51.
Church, Richard. "An Essay in Estimation of Dorothy Richardson's *Pilgrimage*." *PILGRIMAGE, the Life Work of Dorothy Richardson*. [Publisher's brochure] London: Dent and Cresset, 1938, 3-11.
———. "The Poet and the Novel." *Fortnightly*, n.s. 144 (1938), 593-604.
Cross, Wilbur. "Some Novels of 1920." *YR*, n.s. 10 (1921), 396-411.

Donovan, Josephine. "Feminist Style Criticism." *Images of Women in Fiction*. Ed. Susan Koppelman Cornillon, 341-52.

Eagleson, Harvey. "Pedestal for Statue: The Novels of Dorothy M. Richardson." *SR*, 42 (1934), 42-53.

Edel, Leon. "Dorothy Richardson, 1882-1957." *MFS*, 4 (1958), 165-68.

———. "Novelists of Influence-VII. Dorothy Richardson, Feminine Realist." *TES(L)*, June 1, 1956, 743.

Fitzgerald, Ellen. "Dorothy M. Richardson." *Life and Letters*, 17, 10 (1937), 37-39.

Friedman, Melvin J. *Stream of Consciousness*, 178-209.

Fromm, Gloria Glikin. "The Misfortunes of Dorothy Richardson: A Review Essay." *MSLC*, 1, 3 (1974-75), 59-64.

Glikin, Gloria. "Dorothy M. Richardson: The Personal 'Pilgrimage'." *PMLA*, 78 (1963), 586-600.

———. "The 'I' and the 'She'." *Adam*, 31, 310-12 (1966), 41-44.

———. "Through the Novelist's Looking-Glass." *KR*, 31 (1969), 297-319.

———. "Variations on a Method." *JJQ*, 2 (1964), 42-49.

Grabo, Carl H. *The Technique of the Novel*, 276-81, 291-92, 296-97.

Gregory, Horace. "An Adventure in Self-Discovery." *Adam*, 31, 310-12 (1966), 45-47.

———. *Dorothy Richardson: An Adventure in Self-Discovery*. New York: Holt, 1967.

———. "Dorothy Richardson Reviewed." *Life and Letters*, 21, 19 (1939), 36-45.

Grindea, Miron. "A Neglected Pioneer." *Adam*, 31, 310-12 (1966), 16-19.

Hawkins, Ethel Wallace. "The Stream of Consciousness Novel." *Atlantic*, 138 (September 1926), 356-60.

Hueffer [Ford], Ford Madox. "A Haughty and Proud Generation." *YR*, n.s. 11 (1922), 703-17.

Humphrey, Robert. *Stream of Consciousness Technique*, 9-12, 34-35, 78-80.

Hyde, Lawrence. "The Work of Dorothy Richardson." *Adelphi*, 2 (1924), 508-17.

Kaplan, Sydney Janet. " 'Featureless Freedom' or Ironic Submission: Dorothy Richardson and May Sinclair." *CE*, 32 (1971), 914-17.

———. *Feminine Consciousness in the Modern British Novel*, 8-46.

Kelly, Robert G. "The Strange Philosophy of Dorothy M. Richardson." *PS*, 8 (1954), 76-82.

Kumar, Shiv K. *Bergson and the Stream of Consciousness Novel*, 36-63.

———. "Dorothy Richardson and Bergson's *Durée*." *IJES*, 1 (1960), 12-17.

Dorothy Richardson, continued

———. "Dorothy Richardson and Bergson's *Mémoire par Excellence*."
N&Q, 6 (1959), 14-19.

———. "Dorothy Richardson and the Dilemma of 'Being versus Becoming'." *MLN*, 74 (1959), 494-501.

Lawrence, D. H. "Surgery for the Novel—Or a Bomb." *LDIBR*, 1 (April
1923), 3-6, 63.

Mais, Stuart P. B. *Books and Their Writers*, 75-86.

Maisel, E. M. "Dorothy M. Richardson's *Pilgrimage*." *CanF*, 19 (1939),
89-92.

Mansfield, Katherine. *Novels and Novelists*, 1-4, 137-40.

Millett, Fred B. "Feminine Fiction." *Cornhill*, 155 (1937), 225-35.

Murry, J. Middleton. "The Break-up of the Novel." *YR*, n.s. 12 (1923),
288-304.

Myers, Walter L. *The Later Realism*, 73-77, 84-85, 119-22, 135-37, 149-
53, 158-59.

"The Novel in Disintegration." *TLS*, August 28, 1953, xii.

Powys, John Cowper. *Dorothy M. Richardson*. London: Joiner and
Steele, 1931.

Priestley, J. B. "Proust, Joyce, and Miss Richardson." *Spectator*, 130
(June 30, 1923), 1084-85.

Rose, Shirley. "Dorothy Richardson's Focus on Time." *ELT*, 17, 3
(1974), 163-72.

———. "Dorothy Richardson's Theory of Literature: The Writer as
Pilgrim." *Criticism*, 12 (1970), 20-37.

———. "Dorothy Richardson: The First Hundred Years, A Retrospec-
tive View." *DR*, 53 (1973), 92-96.

———. "The Unmoving Center: Consciousness in Dorothy Richardson's *Pilgrimage*." *ConL*, 10 (1969), 366-82.

Rosenberg, John. *Dorothy Richardson: The Genius They Forgot: A
Critical Biography*. London: Duckworth; New York: Knopf,
1973. [American ed. entitled *Dorothy Richardson*]

Rourke, Constance. "Dorothy M. Richardson." *New Republic*, 20 (November 26, 1919), 14-15.

Scott, Evelyn. "A Contemporary of the Future." *Dial*, 69 (October
1920), 353-67.

Sinclair, Frederick. "A Poet's World in Woburn Walk." *SPJ*, December
1948, 124-27.

Sinclair, May. "The Novels of Dorothy Richardson." *LittleR*, 4 (1918),
3-11; *Egoist*, 5 (April 1918), 57-59.

Staley, Thomas. "A Strange Anachronism." *Adam*, 31, 310-12 (1966),
48-50.

Stanford, Derek. "Dorothy Richardson's Novels." *ContempR*, 192
(1957), 86-89.

Stern, G. B. "Saga Novels and Miss Richardson." *NYHTB*, March 11, 1928, 1, 6-7.

Tomkinson, Grace. "Dorothy M. Richardson, Pioneer." *DR*, 38 (1959), 465-71.

Trickett, Rachel. "The Living Dead—V: Dorothy Richardson." *LonM*, 6, 6 (June 1959), 20-25.

Wilson, Angus. "Sexual Revolution." *Listener*, 80 (1968), 457-60.

See also: Aiken, *ABC*; Beach, *20th*; Beresford; J. Collins, *Doctor*; Drew, *Modern*; Edel; Edgar, *Art*; Greene; R. Johnson, *Women*; Lovett, *History*; Marble; Scott-James, *50*; Swinnerton, *Georgian*; Tindall, *Forces*; Vines; Wagenknecht, *Cavalcade*; V. Woolf, *Contemporary*.

V. SACKVILLE-WEST

GENERAL STUDIES

Baldanza, Frank. "*Orlando* and the Sackvilles." *PMLA*, 70 (1955), 274-79.

Hicks, Granville. "Talent Without Courage." *New Republic*, 64 (September 24, 1930), 158-59.

Irwin, W. R. "Permanence and Change in *The Edwardians* and *Told By An Idiot*." *MFS*, 2 (1956), 63-67.

Lawrence, Margaret. *The School of Femininity*, 305-10.

Mais, Stuart P. B. *Some Modern Authors*, 142-44.

Mansfield, Katherine. *Novels and Novelists*, 29-32.

Millett, Fred B. "Feminine Fiction." *Cornhill*, 155 (1937), 225-35.

Pendry, E. D. *The New Feminism of English Fiction*, 56-59.

Stevens, Michael. *V. Sackville-West: A Critical Biography*. London: Joseph, 1973; New York: Scribner's, 1974.

Trautmann, Joanne. *The Jessamy Brides*.

Walpole, Hugh. "V. Sackville-West." *Bookman* (N.Y.), 72 (1930), 21-26.

Watson, Sara R. *V. Sackville-West*. New York: Twayne, 1972.

Will, J. S. "The New Writers, 21." *CanF*, 11 (1931), 462-63.

Young, George M. *Daylight and Champaign*, 280-84.

See also: Gill; Marble; Overton, *Authors*; Swinnerton, *Georgian*.

WILLIAM SANSOM

INTERVIEWS

Firchow, Peter. *The Writer's Place*, 285-93.

GENERAL STUDIES

Mason, Ronald. "William Sansom." *Modern British Writing*. Ed. Denys Val Baker, 281-91.

William Sanson, continued

Michel-Michot, P. "Franz Kafka and William Sansom Reconsidered." *RLV*, 37 (1971), 712-18.
Vickery, John B. "William Sansom and Logical Empiricism." *Thought*, 36 (1961), 231-45.
See also: Allen, *Tradition*; Karl.

DOROTHY SAYERS

BIBLIOGRAPHIES
Christopher, Joe R. "A Sayers Bibliography, Part 4." *Unicorn*, 2, 5 (1973), 28-30.
―――. "A Sayers Bibliography, Part 5." *Unicorn*, 3 (1974), 51-52.

GENERAL STUDIES
Auerbach, Nina. "Dorothy Sayers and the Amazons." *Feminist Studies*, 3, 1-2 (1975), 54-62.
Chase, Mary Ellen. "Five Literary Portraits." *MR*, 3 (1962), 511-16.
Harrison, Barbara Grizutti. "Dorothy L. Sayers and the Tidy Art of Detective Fiction." *Ms.*, 5 (November 1974), 66-69, 84-89.
Heilbrun, Carolyn G. "Sayers, Lord Peter and God." *ASch*, 37 (1968), 324-34.
Hitchman, Janet. *Such a Strange Lady: An Introduction to Dorothy L. Sayers, 1893-1957*. London: New English Library; New York: Harper, 1975.
Moorman, Charles. *The Precincts of Felicity*, 113-36.
Peters, Margot, and Agate N. Krouse. "Women and Crime: Sexism in Allingham, Sayers, and Christie." *SWR*, 59 (1974), 144-52.
Ray, Laura K. "The Mysteries of *Gaudy Night*: Feminism, Faith, and the Depths of Character." *MDAC*, 4 (1973), 272-85.
Rickman, H. P. "From Detection to Theology: The Work of Dorothy Sayers." *HJ*, 60 (1962), 290-96.
Rockow, Karen. "Blowing the Whistle on Dorothy Sayers and Lord Peter." *Unicorn*, 3 (1974), 37-38, 45.
Webster, Deborah. "Reinterpreter: Dorothy L. Sayers." *CathW*, 169 (1949), 330-35.

ALAN SILLITOE

INTERVIEWS
Lefranc, Michel. "Alan Sillitoe: An Interview." *EA*, 26 (1973), 35-48.
Wood, Ramsay. "Alan Sillitoe: The Image Shedding the Author." *Four Quarters*, 21, 1 (1971), 3-10.

GENERAL STUDIES
Aldridge, John W. *Time to Murder and Create*, 239-44.
Atherton, Stanley S. "Alan Sillitoe's Battleground." *DR*, 48 (1968), 324-31.
Denny, N. "The Achievement of the Long-Distance Runner." *Theoria*, 24 (1965), 1-12.
Dixon, Terrell F. "Expostulation and a Reply: The Character of Clegg in Fowles and Sillitoe." *NConL*, 4, 2 (1974), 7-9.
Gindin, James J. "Alan Sillitoe's Jungle." *TSLL*, 4 (1962), 35-48.
Gray, Nigel. *The Silent Majority*, 101-32.
Haller, Robert S. "The Crux of Merging Deltas: A Note on Alan Sillitoe." *PrS*, 48 (1974), 351-58.
Hurrell, John Dennis. "Alan Sillitoe and the Serious Novel." *Crit*, 4, 1 (1961), 3-16.
Klotz, Günther. "Alan Sillitoe's Heroes." *Essays in Honour of William Gallacher*. Ed. Erika Lingner, et al., 259-63.
Maloff, Saul. "The Eccentricity of Alan Sillitoe." *Contemporary British Novelists*. Ed. Charles Shapiro, 95-113.
Meckier, Jerome. "Looking Back at Anger: The Success of a Collapsing Stance." *DR*, 52 (1972), 47-58.
Nardella, Anna R. "The Existential Dilemmas of Alan Sillitoe's Working-Class Heroes." *SNNTS*, 5 (1973), 469-82.
Penner, Allen R. *Alan Sillitoe*. New York: Twayne, 1972.
———. *"The General*: Exceptional Proof of a Critical Rule." *SHR*, 4 (1970), 135-43.
———. "Illusory Deluge: Alan Sillitoe's 'Noah's Art.' " *CLAJ*, 12 (1968), 134-41.
Rippier, Joseph S. *Some Postwar English Novelists*, 178, 193-206.
Rosselli, John. "A Cry from the Brick Streets." *Reporter*, 23 (November 10, 1960), 37-42.
Shestakov, Dmitri. "Alan Sillitoe from Nottingham." *SovL*, no. 9 (September 1963), 176-79.
———. "Fifteen Million Prototypes." *InoL*, 11 (November 1964), 226-35.
Sillitoe, Alan. *Raw Material*. New York: Scribner's, 1972.
Simmons, Michael K. "The 'In-Laws' and 'Out-Laws' of Alan Sillitoe." *BSUF*, 14, 1 (1973), 76-78.
Stéphane, Nelly. "Alan Sillitoe." *Europe*, 417-418 (1964), 289-93.
Wilding, Michael. "Alan Sillitoe's Political Novels." *Cunning Exiles*. Ed. Don Anderson and Stephen Knight, 129-64.
See also: Gindin, *Postwar*; Karl.

THE DEATH OF WILLIAM POSTERS

Kermode, Frank. "Rammel." *New Statesman*, 69 (1965), 765-66.

Penner, Allen R. "The Political Prologue and Two Parts of a Trilogy: *The Death of William Posters* and *A Tree on Fire*." *UR*, 35 (1968), 11-20.

KEY TO THE DOOR

McDowell, Frederick P. W. "Self and Society: Alan Sillitoe's *Key to the Door*." *Crit*, 6, 1 (1963), 116-23.

Penner, Allen R. "Dantesque Allegory in Sillitoe's *Key to the Door*." *Renascence*, 20 (1968), 79-85, 103.

THE LONELINESS OF THE LONG DISTANCE RUNNER

Penner, Allen R. "Human Dignity and Social Anarchy: Sillitoe's 'The Loneliness of the Long-Distance Runner'." *ConL*, 10 (1969), 253-65.

Updike, John. *Assorted Prose*, 227-30.

SATURDAY NIGHT AND SUNDAY MORNING

Coleman, John. "The Unthinkables." *New Statesman*, 62 (1961), 610-12.

Craig, David. *The Real Foundations*, 270-85.

Osgerby, J. R. "Alan Sillitoe's *Saturday Night and Sunday Morning*." *Renaissance and Modern Essays Presented to Vivian de Sola Pinto*. Ed. G. R. Hibbard, 215-30.

Prince, Rod. "*Saturday Night and Sunday Morning*." *NewLR*, 6 (November-December 1960), 14-17.

Staples, Hugh B. "*Saturday Night and Sunday Morning*: Alan Sillitoe and the White Goddess." *MFS*, 10 (1964), 171-81.

West, Anthony. "On the Inside Looking In." *NY*, 35 (September 5, 1959), 103-04.

A START IN LIFE

"A Naturalist No More." *TLS*, September 18, 1970, 1026.

Watrin, Jany. "Alan Sillitoe's *A Start in Life*." *RLV*, 38 (1972), 508-16.

MAY SINCLAIR

BIBLIOGRAPHIES

Robb, Kenneth A. "May Sinclair: An Annotated Bibliography of Writings About Her." *ELT*, 16, 3 (1973), 177-231.

GENERAL STUDIES

Adcock, A. St. John. *Gods of Modern Grub Street*, 273-80.

Boll, T. E. M. "May Sinclair and the Medico-Psychological Clinic of London." *PAPS*, 106 (August 1962), 310-26.

_____. *Miss May Sinclair, Novelist: A Biographical and Critical Introduction*. Rutherford, N.J.: Fairleigh Dickinson Univ. Press, 1973.

_____. "The Mystery of Charlotte Mew and May Sinclair: An Inquiry." *BNYPL*, 74 (1970), 445-53.

Bosschère, Jean de. "Charity and Grace in the Work of May Sinclair." *Egoist*, 5 (September 1918), 109-11.

_____. "Charity in the Work of May Sinclair." *YR*, n.s. 14 (1925), 82-94.

Braybrooke, Patrick. *Novelists: We Are Seven*, 33-53.

Cecil, Eleanor. "The Cant of Unconventionality." *Living Age*, 255 (December 7, 1907), 579-89.

Chevalley, Abel. *The Modern English Novel*, 198-207.

Cooper, Frederic T. *Some English Story Tellers*, 352-79.

Cross, Wilbur. "Some Novels of 1920." *YR*, n.s. 10 (1921), 396-411.

Davidow, Mary C. "The Charlotte Mew-May Sinclair Relationship: A Reply." *BNYPL*, 75 (1971), 295-300.

Eliot, T. S. "London Letter." *Dial*, 73 (September 1922), 329-31.

Elwin, Malcolm. *Old Gods Falling*, 313-15.

Ford, Ford Madox. *It Was The Nightingale*, 185-88.

Gaines, Clarence H. "Some Philosophers in Fiction." *NoAmR*, 220 (1924), 375-84.

Gorsky, Susan. "The Gentle Doubters: Images of Women in Englishwomen's Novels, 1840-1920." *Images of Women in Fiction*. Ed. Susan Koppelman Cornillon, 28-54.

Howarth, Herbert. *Notes on Some Figures Behind T. S. Eliot*, 272-77.

_____. "T. S. Eliot's *Criterion*: The Editor and his Contributors." *CL*, 11 (1959), 97-110.

"jh" [Jane Heaps]. "Eat 'em Alive!" *LittleR*, 6 (December 1919), 30-32.

Kaplan, Sydney Janet. " 'Featureless Freedom' or Ironic Submission: Dorothy Richardson and May Sinclair." *CE*, 32 (1971), 914-17.

_____. *Feminine Consciousness in the Modern British Novel*, 47-75.

Kenton, Edna. "May Sinclair's *Mary Olivier*." *LittleR*, 6 (December 1919), 29-30.

Lawrence, Margaret. *The School of Femininity*, 268-72.

Lovett, Robert M. "Miss Sinclair's Later Work." *Dial*, 71 (December 1921), 699-703.

Loving, Pierre. "Tolstoi and May Sinclair." *LittleR*, 6 (March 1920), 51-54.

May Sinclair, continued

Mansfield, Katherine. *Novels and Novelists*, 40-43, 274-79.
Mayer, Frederick P. "Craftsmanship in Some Modern Novels." *VQR*, 3 (1927), 463-74.
Millett, Fred B. "Feminine Fiction." *Cornhill*, 155 (1937), 225-35.
Myers, Walter L. *The Later Realism*, 44-53, 61-63, 86-87, 117-18.
Pratt, Annis. "Women and Nature in Modern Fiction." *ConL*, 13 (1972), 476-90.
Scott, C. A. Dawson. "May Sinclair." *Bookman* (N.Y.), 52 (1920), 246-49.
Scott, Evelyn. "A Contemporary of the Future." *Dial*, 69 (October 1920), 353-67.
Strangnell, Sylvia. "Critical Review: A Study in Sublimations." *PsyR*, 10 (1923), 209-13.
Underhill, Evelyn. " 'The Cant of Unconventionality': A Rejoinder to Lady Robert Cecil." *Living Age*, 256 (February 8, 1908), 323-29.
Wellington, Amy. "An Artist of the Supernormal." *Dial*, 63 (September 1917), 195-98.
West, Rebecca. "Notes on Novels." *New Statesman*, 20 (1922), 270-72.
See also: Adcock, *Gods*; Allen, *Tradition*; P. Braybrooke, *Philosophies*; Brewster and Burrell; Buckley; Drew, *Modern*; Frierson; Gould; R. Johnson, *Women*; Lovett, *History*; Mackenzie; Marble; W. Phelps; Stevenson, *History*; Swinnerton, *Georgian*; Vines; H. Williams, *Modern*.

C. P. SNOW

INTERVIEWS
"Interview with C. P. Snow." *REL*, 3, 3 (1962), 91-108.
Kermode, Frank. "The House of Fiction: Interviews with Seven English Novelists." *PR*, 30 (1963), 61-82.
Muggeridge, Malcolm, and C. P. Snow. "Appointment with C. P. Snow." *Encounter*, 18 (February 1962), 90-93.
Newquist, Roy, ed. *Counterpoint*, 554-61

GENERAL STUDIES
Adams, Robert. "Pomp and Circumstance: C. P. Snow." *Atlantic*, 214 (November 1964), 95-98.
Ashton, Thomas L. "Realism and the Chronicle: C. P. Snow's *Cinéma Vérité*." *SAQ*, 72 (1973), 516-27.
Bergonzi, Bernard. "The World of Lewis Eliot." *TC*, 167 (1960), 214-25.
Bernard, Kenneth. "C. P. Snow and Modern Literature." *UR*, 31 (1965), 231-33.

Bonnet, Jacky. "Last Things: Snow's Refusal of Man's Tragic Individual Condition." *LanM*, 66 (1972), 302-04.

Burgess, Anthony. "Powers That Be." *Encounter*, 24 (January 1965), 71-76.

Cooper, William [Harry Summerfield Hoff]. *C. P. Snow.* London: Longmans, Green, 1959; rev. 1971.

———. "The World of C. P. Snow." *Nation*, 184 (1957), 104-05.

Davis, Robert Gorham. *C. P. Snow.* New York: Columbia Univ. Press, 1965.

Dobrée, Bonamy. "The Novels of C. P. Snow." *LHY*, 2 (1961), 28-34.

Finkelstein, Sidney. "The Art and Science of C. P. Snow." *Mainstream*, 14, 9 (1961), 31-57.

Fison, Peter. "A Reply to Bernard Bergonzi's 'The World of Lewis Eliot'." *TC*, 167 (1960), 568-71.

Fraser, G. S. "C. P. Snow." *The Politics of Twentieth-Century Novelists.* Ed. George A. Panichas, 124-33.

Gardner, Helen. "The World of C. P. Snow." *New Statesman*, 55 (1958), 409-10.

Graves, Nora C. "Literary Allusions in *Last Things*." *NConL*, 1, 1 (1971), 7-8.

———. *The Two Cultures Theory in C. P. Snow's Novels.* Hattiesburg: Univ. and Coll. Press of Mississippi, 1972.

Greacen, Robert. "The World of C. P. Snow." *TQ*, 4, 3 (1961), 266-74.

———. *The World of C. P. Snow.* New York: London House and Maxwell, 1963.

Halio, Jay L. "C. P. Snow's Literary Limitations." *NWR*, 5 (1962), 97-102.

Hall, James. *The Lunatic Giant in the Drawing Room*, 128-32.

Hall, William F. "The Humanism of C. P. Snow." *WSCL*, 4 (1963), 199-208.

Hamilton, Kenneth. "C. P. Snow and Political Man." *QQ*, 69 (1962), 416-27.

Heppenstall, Rayner. *The Fourfold Tradition*, 213-48.

Ivasheva, V. "Illusion and Reality about the Work of Charles P. Snow." *InoL*, 6 (June 1960), 198-203.

Jaffa, Herbert C. "C. P. Snow, Portrait of Man as an Adult." *Humanist*, 24 (September-October 1964), 148-50.

Johnson, Pamela Hansford. "Three Novelists and the Drawing of Character: C. P. Snow, Joyce Cary, and Ivy Compton-Burnett." English Association, London. *Essays and Studies*, n.s., v. 3 (1950), 82-99.

C. P. Snow, continued

Karl, Frederick R. "C. P. Snow: The Unreason of Reason." *Contemporary British Novelists*. Ed. Charles Shapiro, 114-24.
_____. *The Politics of Conscience: The Novels of C. P. Snow*. Carbondale: Southern Illinois Univ. Press, 1963.
Kazin, Alfred. "A Gifted Boy from the Midlands." *Reporter*, 20 (February 5, 1959), 37-39.
Ketels, Violet B. "Shaw, Snow, and the New Men." *Person*, 47 (1966), 520-31.
Leavis, F. R. *Nor Shall My Sword*, 39-74.
Lehan, Richard. "The Divided World: *The Masters* Examined." *Six Contemporary Novels*. Ed. William O. S. Sutherland, 46-57.
Macdonald, Alastair. "The Failure of Success." *DR*, 44 (1964), 494-500.
_____. "Imagery in C. P. Snow." *UR*, 32 (1966), 303-06; 33 (1966), 33-38.
Mandel, E. W. "Anarchy and Organization." *QQ*, 70 (1963), 131-41.
_____. "C. P. Snow's Fantasy of Politics." *QQ*, 69 (1962), 24-37.
Martin, Graham. "Novelists of Three Decades: Evelyn Waugh, Graham Greene, C. P. Snow." *The Pelican Guide to English Literature*, v. 7. Ed. Boris Ford, 412-32.
Mayne, Richard. "The Club Armchair." *Encounter*, 21 (November 1963), 76-82.
Millar, Ronald. "The Play of the Book." *TLS*, September 19, 1968, 1053.
Millgate, Michael. "Strangers and Brothers." *Commentary*, 30, 1 (July 1960), 76-79.
_____. "Structure and Style in the Novels of C. P. Snow." *REL*, 1, 2 (1960), 34-41.
Miner, Earl. "C. P. Snow and the Realistic Novel." *Nation*, 190 (1960), 554-55.
"Monsters at Bay." *TLS*, October 31, 1968, 1217.
Muggeridge, Malcolm. "Oh No, Lord Snow." *New Republic*, 151 (November 28, 1964), 27-29.
Murray, Byron O. "C. P. Snow: Grounds for Reappraisal." *Person*, 47 (1966), 91-101.
Nelson, Bryce E. "The Affair." *Audit*, 1 (March 1961), 11-15.
Noon, William T. "Satire: Poison and the Professor." *EngR*, 11 (1960), 53-56.
Nott, Kathleen. "The Type to Which the Whole Creation Moves?" *Encounter*, 18 (February 1962), 87-88, 94-97.
Olsen, F. Bruce. "*The Masters*." *Insight II*. Ed. John V. Hagopian and Martin Dolch, 330-36.
Putt, S. Gorley. "Technique and Culture: Three Cambridge Portraits." *E&S*, 14 (1961), 17-34.

Rabinovitz, Rubin. "C. P. Snow vs. the Experimental Novel." *CUF*, 10, 3 (1967), 37-41.

"The Realism of the Worldly." *TLS*, November 5, 1964, 993.

Shestakov, Dmitri. "What C. P. Snow Means to Us." *SovL*, no. 1 (January 1966), 174-79.

Smith, LeRoy W. "C. P. Snow as Novelist: A Delimitation." *SAQ*, 64 (1965), 316-31.

Stanford, Derek. "C. P. Snow: The Novelist as Fox." *Meanjin*, 19 (1960), 236-51.

———. "A Disputed Master: C. P. Snow and His Critics." *Month*, 29 (1963), 91-94.

Stanford, Raney. "The Achievement of C. P. Snow." *WHR*, 16 (1962), 43-52.

———. "Personal Politics in the Novels of C. P. Snow." *Crit*, 2, 1 (1958), 16-28.

Thale, Jerome. *C. P. Snow*. Edinburgh and London: Oliver and Boyd, 1964; New York: Scribner's, 1965.

———. "C. P. Snow: The Art of Worldliness." *KR*, 22 (1960), 621-34.

Turner, Ian. "Above the Snow-Line: The Sociology of C. P. Snow." *Overland*, 18 (1960), 42-43.

Vogel, Albert W. "The Academic World of C. P. Snow." *TCL*, 9 (1963), 143-52.

Wagner, Geoffrey. "Writer in the Welfare State." *Cweal*, 65 (1956), 49-50.

Wall, Stephen. "The Novels of C. P. Snow." *LonM*, n.s. 4, 1 (April 1964), 68-74.

Watson, Kenneth. "C. P. Snow and *The New Man*." *English*, 15 (1965), 134-39.

Webster, Harvey C. "The Sacrifices of Success." *SatR*, 41 (July 12, 1958), 8-10, 34.

Weintraub, Stanley, ed. *C. P. Snow: A Spectrum*. New York: Scribner's, 1963.

———. "*Last Things*: C. P. Snow Eleven Novels After." *Mosaic*, 4, 3 (1971), 135-41.

Widdowson, Peter J. "C. P. Snow's *Strangers and Brothers Sequence*: Lewis Eliot and the Failure of Realism." *RMS*, 19 (1975), 112-28.

Wilson, Edmund. *The Bit Between My Teeth*, 534-36.

See also: Allen, *Reading, Tradition*; Bradbury, *Possibilities*; Enright, *Conspirators*; Fuller, *Books*; Gindin, *Postwar*; Karl; Kazin, *Contemporaries*; Kermode; R. Morris, *Continuance*; Rabinovitz; Webster.

MURIEL SPARK

INTERVIEWS

Kermode, Frank. "The House of Fiction: Interviews with Seven English Novelists." *PR*, 30 (1963), 61-82.

GENERAL STUDIES

Baldanza, Frank. "Muriel Spark and the Occult." *WSCL*, 6 (1965), 190-203.

Berthoff, Warner. "Fortunes of the Novel: Muriel Spark and Iris Murdoch." *MR*, 8 (1967), 301-32.

Bradbury, Malcolm. "Muriel Spark's Fingernails." *CritQ*, 14 (1972), 241-50.

Casson, Alan. "Muriel Spark's *The Girls of Slender Means*." *Crit*, 7, 3 (1965), 94-96.

Davison, Peter. "The Miracles of Muriel Spark." *Atlantic*, 222 (October 1968), 139-42.

Dobie, Ann B. "Muriel Spark's Definition of Reality." *Crit*, 12, 1 (1970), 20-27.

———, and Carl Wooton. "Spark and Waugh: Similarities by Coincidence." *MQ*, 13 (1972), 423-34.

Gable, Sister Mariella. "Prose Satire and the Modern Christian Temper." *ABR*, 11 (1960), 29-30, 33.

Greene, George. "A Reading of Muriel Spark." *Thought*, 43 (1968), 393-407.

Grosskurth, Phyllis. "The World of Muriel Spark: Spirits or Spooks?" *TamR*, 39 (1966), 62-67.

Hoyt, Charles A. "Muriel Spark: The Surrealist Jane Austen." *Contemporary British Novelists*. Ed. Charles Shapiro, 125-43.

Hynes, Joseph. "After Marabar: Reading Forster, Robbe-Grillet, Spark." *IowaR*, 5, 1 (1974), 120-26.

Hynes, Samuel. "The Prime of Muriel Spark." *Cweal*, 75 (1962), 562-68.

Jacobsen, Josephine. "A Catholic Quartet." *ChS*, 47 (1964), 139-54.

Kemp, Peter. *Muriel Spark*. London: Elek, 1974; New York: Barnes and Noble, 1975.

Kennedy, Alan. *The Protean Self*, 151-211.

Keyser, Barbara. "Muriel Spark's Gargoyles." *Descant*, 20, 1 (Fall 1975), 32-39.

Malin, Irving. "The Deceptions of Muriel Spark." *The Vision Obscured*. Ed. Melvin J. Friedman, 95-107.

Malkoff, Karl. "Demonology and Dualism: The Supernatural in Isaac

Singer and Muriel Spark." *Critical Views of Isaac Bashevis Singer*. Ed. Irving Malin. New York: New York Univ. Press, 1969, 149-68.

_____. *Muriel Spark*. New York: Columbia Univ. Press, 1968.

Mayne, Richard. "Fiery Particle: On Muriel Spark." *Encounter*, 25 (December 1965), 61-68.

Murphy, Carol. "A Spark of the Supernatural." *Approach*, 60 (Summer 1966), 26-30.

Ohmann, Carol B. "Muriel Spark's *Robinson*." *Crit*, 8, 1 (1965), 70-84.

Potter, Nancy A. J. "Muriel Spark: Transformer of the Commonplace." *Renascence*, 17 (1965), 115-20.

Richmond, Velma B. "The Darkening Vision of Muriel Spark." *Crit*, 15, 1 (1973), 71-85.

Ricks, Christopher. "Extreme Distances." *NYRB*, 11 (December 19, 1968), 31-32.

Schneider, Harold W. "A Writer in Her Prime: The Fiction of Muriel Spark." *Crit*, 5, 2 (1962), 28-45.

"Shallowness Everywhere." *TLS*, June 13, 1968, 612.

Soule, George. "Must a Novelist Be an Artist?" *CarlM*, 5 (1964), 92-98.

Stanford, Derek. *Muriel Spark: A Biographical and Critical Study*. Fontwell, Eng.: Centaur, 1963.

_____. "The Work of Muriel Spark: An Essay on Her Fictional Method." *Month*, 28 (1962), 92-99.

Stubbs, Patricia. *Muriel Spark*. Harlow: Longmans, Green, 1973.

_____. "Two Contemporary Views on Fiction: Iris Murdoch and Muriel Spark." *English*, 23 (1974), 102-10.

Sudrann, Jean. "Hearth and Horizon: Changing Concepts of the 'Domestic' Life of the Heroine." *MR*, 14 (1973), 235-55.

Updike, John. "Creatures of the Air." *NY*, 37 (September 30, 1961), 161-67.

Whitehorn, Katharine. "Three Women." *Encounter*, 21 (December 1963), 78-82.

Wildman, John Hazard. "Translated by Muriel Spark." *Nine Essays in Modern Literature*. Ed. Donald E. Stanford, 129-44.

See also: Bradbury, *Possibilities*; Enright, *Onion*; Swinden.

THE BALLAD OF PECKHAM RYE

Dierickx, J. "A Devil-figure in a Contemporary Setting: Some Aspects of Muriel Spark's *The Ballad of Peckham Rye*." *RLV*, 33 (1967), 576-87.

Lanning, George. "Silver Fish in the Plumbing." *KR*, 23 (1961), 173-81.

THE MANDELBAUM GATE
Berthoff, Warner. *Fictions and Events*, 118-54.
Cohen, Gerda L. "Tilting the Balance." *Midstream*, 12 (January 1966), 68-70.
Enright, D. J. "Public Doctrine and Private Judging: *The Mandelbaum Gate*." *New Statesman*, 70 (1965), 563-66.
Kermode, Frank. "The Novel as Jerusalem: Muriel Spark's *Mandelbaum Gate*." *Atlantic*, 216 (October 1965), 92-98.
"Talking about Jerusalem." *TLS*, October 14, 1965, 913.

THE PRIME OF MISS JEAN BRODIE
Dobie, Ann B. "*The Prime of Miss Jean Brodie*: Muriel Spark Bridges the Credibility Gap." *ArQ*, 25 (1969), 217-28.
Holloway, John. "Narrative Structure and Text Structure: Isherwood's *A Meeting by the River* and Muriel Spark's *The Prime of Miss Jean Brodie*." *CritI*, 1 (1975), 581-604.
Kermode, Frank. "The Prime of Miss Muriel Spark." *New Statesman*, 66 (1963), 397-98.
Laffin, Garry S. "Muriel Spark's Portrait of the Artist as a Young Girl." *Renascence*, 24 (1972), 213-23.
Lodge, David. "The Uses and Abuses of Omniscience: Method and Meaning in Muriel Spark's *The Prime of Miss Jean Brodie*." *CritQ*, 12 (1970), 235-57.
See also: Lodge, *Novelist*.

DAVID STOREY

GENERAL STUDIES
Churchill, Thomas. "Waterhouse, Storey, and Fowles: Which Way Out of the Room?" *Crit*, 10, 3 (1968), 72-87.
Gray, Nigel. *The Silent Majority*, 132-59.
McGuiness, Frank. "The Novels of David Storey." *LonM*, n.s. 3, 12 (March 1964), 79-83.
Storey, David. "Writers on Themselves: Journey Through a Tunnel." *Listener*, 70 (1963), 159-61.
Taylor, John Russell. *David Storey*. Harlow: Longmans, Green, 1974.
See also: Gindin, *Postwar*; O'Connor, *New*.

ELIZABETH TAYLOR

GENERAL STUDIES
Austen, Richard. "The Novels of Elizabeth Taylor." *Cweal*, 62 (1955), 258-59.

Boll, Ernest. "*At Mrs. Lippincote's* and *Tristram Shandy.*" *MLN*, 65 (1950), 119-21.
Liddell, Robert. "The Novels of Elizabeth Taylor." *REL*, 1, 2 (April 1960), 54-61.
Toulson, Michael. "The Sensibility Angle." *Isis*, January 28, 1959.

J. R. R. TOLKIEN

BIBLIOGRAPHIES

West, Richard C. "An Annotated Bibliography of Tolkien Criticism." *Orcrist*, 1 (1966-67), 32-55; 2 (1967-68), 40-54; 3 (1969), 22-23; *Orcrist*, 5 - *Tolkien Journal*, 14 [combined issue] (1971), 14-31.
———. "An Annotated Bibliography of Tolkien Criticism." *Extrapolation*, 10 (1968), 17-45.
———. *Tolkien Criticism: An Annotated Checklist*. Kent, Ohio: Kent State Univ. Press, 1970.

SPECIAL ISSUES

Mankato State College Studies [*MSCS*], 2 (February 1967).

GENERAL STUDIES

Aldiss, Brian W. *Billion Year Spree*, 265-69.
Allen, James. "Tolkien and Recovery." *Mythlore*, 3, 2 (1975), 12-13.
Bisenieks, Dainis. "Reading and Misreading Tolkien." *MSCS*, 2 (February 1967), 98-100.
Blackmun, Kathryn. "Translation from the Elvish." *MSCS*, 2 (February 1967), 95-97.
Boswell, George W. "Tolkien as *Littérateur*." *SCB*, 32 (1972), 188-97.
Braude, Nan. "Sion and Parnassus: Three Approaches to Myth." *Mythlore*, 1, 1 (1969), 6-8.
———. "Tolkien and Spenser." *Mythlore*, 1, 3 (1969), 8-13.
Callahan, Patrick J. "Tolkien, *Beowulf*, and the Barrow-Wights." *NDEJ*, 7, 2 (1972), 4-13.
Carter, Lin. "Howendile: A Link Between Cabell and Tolkien." *Kalki*, 3, 3 (1969), 85-87.
Castell, Daphne. "The Realms of Tolkien." *New Worlds*, 50 (November 1966), 143-54.
Ellwood, Gracia Fay. "The Good Guys and the Bad Guys." *Tolkien Journal*, 10 (1969), 9-11.
Epstein, E. L. "The Novels of J. R. R. Tolkien and the Ethnology of Medieval Christendom." *PQ*, 48 (1969), 517-25.
Evans, Robley. *J. R. R. Tolkien*. New York: Warner Paperback Library, 1972.

J. R. R. Tolkien, continued

Fifield, Merle. "Fantasy in the Sixties." *EJ*, 55 (1966), 841-44.
GoodKnight, Glen. "A Comparison of Cosmological Geography in the Works of J. R. R. Tolkien, C. S. Lewis, and Charles Williams." *Mythlore*, 1, 3 (1969), 18-22.
––––––. "The Social History of the Inklings. J. R. R. Tolkien, C. S. Lewis, and Charles Williams." *Mythlore*, 2, 1 (1970), 7-9.
Helms, Randel. *Tolkien's World*. London: Thames and Hudson; Boston: Houghton Mifflin, 1974.
Howard, Claire. "The Vented Spleen." *Mythlore*, 2, 3 (1971), 9-11.
Irwin, W. R. "There and Back Again: The Romances of Williams, Lewis, and Tolkien." *SR*, 69 (1961), 566-78.
Kilby, Clyde S. "The Lost Myth." *ASoc*, 6 (1969), 155-63.
––––––. "Tolkien and Coleridge." *Orcrist*, 3 (1969), 16-19.
––––––. "Tolkien, Lewis, and Williams." *Mythcon 1: Proceedings*. Ed. Glen GoodKnight, 3-4.
Koelle, Barbara S. "Oz and Middle Earth." *BaumB*, 15, 1 (1971), 17-19.
Monsman, Gerald. "The Imaginative World of J. R. R. Tolkien." *SAQ*, 69 (1970), 264-78.
Moorman, Charles. " 'Now Entertain Conjecture of a Time': The Fictive Worlds of C. S. Lewis and J. R. R. Tolkien." *Shadows of Imagination*. Ed. Mark R. Hillegas, 59-69.
––––––. *The Precincts of Felicity*, 86-100.
Morris, John S. "Fantasy in a Mythless Age." *Children's Literature: The Great Excluded*, v. 2. Ed. Francelia Butler, 77-86.
Myers, Doris T. "Brave New World: The Status of Women According to Tolkien, Lewis, and Williams." *CimR*, 17 (1971), 13-19.
O'Hare, Colman. "On the Reading of an 'Old Book'." *Extrapolation*, 14 (1972), 59-63.
Parker, Douglass. "Hwaet, We Holbytla." *HudR*, 9 (1957), 598-609.
Pfotenhauer, Paul. "Christian Themes in Tolkien." *Cresset*, 32, 3 (1969), 13-15.
Purtill, Richard. *Lord of the Elves and Eldils*, 15-211.
Randolph, Burr. "The Singular Incompetence of the Volar." *Tolkien Journal*, 9 (1968), 11-13.
Rang, Jack C. "Two Servants." *MSCS*, 2 (February 1967), 84-94.
Ready, William. "The Tolkien Relation." *CanLib*, 25 (September 1968), 128-36.
––––––. *The Tolkien Relation: A Personal Inquiry*. Chicago: Regnery, 1968.
Reckford, Kenneth J. "Some Trees in Virgil and Tolkien." *Perspectives of Roman Poetry: A Classics Symposium*. Ed. G. Karl Galinsky. Austin: Univ. of Texas Press, 1974, 57-91.

Robinson, James. "The Wizard and History: Saruman's Vision of a New Order." *Orcrist*, 1 (1966-67), 13-17.

Ryan, J. S. "German Mythology Applied: The Extension of the Literary Folk Memory." *Folklore*, 77 (1966), 45-59.

Sale, Roger. "England's Parnassus: C. S. Lewis, Charles Williams, and J. R. R. Tolkien." *HudR*, 17 (1964), 203-25.

_____. *Modern Heroism*, 11-15, 193-240, 250-55.

Sirridge, Mary. "J. R. R. Tolkien and Fairy Tale Truth." *BJA*, 15 (1975), 81-92.

Stein, Ruth M. "The Changing Style in Dragons." *ElemE*, 45 (February 1968), 181-83.

Stevens, Cj. "Sound Systems of the Third Age of Middle Earth." *QJS*, 54 (1968), 232-40.

Stimpson, Catharine R. *J. R. R. Tolkien*. New York: Columbia Univ. Press, 1969.

Tolkien, J. R. R. "Tolkien on Tolkien." *Diplomat*, 18 (October 1966), 39.

Urang, Gunnar. *Shadows of Heaven*, 93-130.

_____. "Tolkien's Fantasy: The Phenomenology of Hope." *Shadows of Imagination*. Ed. Mark R. Hillegas, 97-110.

Webster, Deborah C. "Good Guys, Bad Guys: A Clarification on Tolkien." *Orcrist*, 2 (1967-68), 18-23.

Weinig, Sister Mary Anthony. "Images of Affirmation: Perspectives of the Fiction of Charles Williams, C. S. Lewis, J. R. R. Tolkien." *UPoR*, 20, 1 (1968), 43-46.

West, Richard C. "Contemporary Medieval Authors." *Orcrist*, 3 (1969), 9-10, 15.

Wilson, Colin. *The Strength to Dream*, 145-49.

_____. *Tree by Tolkien*. London: Covent Garden, 1973; Santa Barbara, Cal.: Capra, 1974.

Wojcik, Jan. "Tolkien and Coleridge: Remaking of the 'Green Earth'." *Renascence*, 20 (1968), 134-39, 146.

Wright, Marjorie E. "The Vision of Cosmic Order in the Oxford Mythmakers." *Imagination and the Spirit*. Ed. Charles A. Huttar, 259-76.

See also: Fuller, *Books*.

FARMER GILES OF HAM

Green, William H. "Legendary and Historical Time in Tolkien's *Farmer Giles of Ham*." *NConL*, 5, 3 (1975), 14-15.

Johnson, J. A. "*Farmer Giles of Ham*: What Is It?" *Orcrist*, 7 (1973), 21-24.

J. R. R. Tolkien, continued

THE HOBBIT
Bisenieks, Dainis. "The Hobbit Habit in the Critic's Eye." *Tolkien Journal*, 15 (1972), 14-15.

Christensen, Bonniejean M. "Report from the West: Exploitation of *The Hobbit*." *Orcrist*, 4 (1969), 15-16.

_____. "Tolkien's Creative Technique: *Beowulf* and *The Hobbit*." *Orcrist*, 7 (1973), 16-20.

Cox, C. B. "The World of the Hobbits." *Spectator*, 217 (December 30, 1966), 844.

Davie, Donald. *Thomas Hardy and British Poetry*, 93-98.

Duriez, Colin. "Leonardo, Tolkien, and Mr. Baggins." *Mythlore*, 1, 2 (1969), 18-28.

Ellmann, Mary. "Growing Up Hobbitic." *New American Review, No. 2*. New York: New American Library, 1968, 217-29.

Ellwood, Robert. "The Japanese *Hobbit*." *Mythlore*, 1, 3 (1969), 14-17.

Hodgart, Matthew. "Kicking the Hobbit." *NYRB*, 8 (May 4, 1967), 10-11.

Menen, Aubrey. "Learning to Love the Hobbits." *Diplomat*, 18 (October 1966), 32-34, 37-38.

Miller, David M. "Hobbits: Common Lens for Heroic Experience." *Orcrist*, 3 (1969), 11-15.

Norman, Philip. "The Prevalence of Hobbits." *NYTM*, January 15, 1967, 30-31, 97, 100, 102.

Watson, J. R. "The Hobbits and the Critics." *CritQ*, 13 (1971), 252-58.

Woods, Samuel H., Jr. "J. R. R. Tolkien and the Hobbits." *CimR*, 1, 1 (1967), 44-52.

THE LORD OF THE RINGS
[THE FELLOWSHIP OF THE RING, THE TWO TOWERS, THE RETURN OF THE KING]
Allen, James. "Genesis of *The Lord of the Rings*: A Study in Saga Development." *Mythlore*, 3, 1 (1973), 3-9.

Auden, W. H. "At the End of the Quest, Victory." *NYTBR*, January 22, 1956, 5.

_____. "Good and Evil in *The Lord of the Rings*." *CritQ*, 10 (1968), 138-42.

_____. "The Hero is a Hobbit." *NYTBR*, October 31, 1954, 37.

_____. "The Quest Hero." *Perspectives in Contemporary Criticism*. Ed. Sheldon N. Grebstein, 370-81.

_____. "A World Imaginary, But Real." *Encounter*, 3 (November 1954), 59-62.

Ballif, Sandra. "A Sindarin-Quenya Dictionary, More or Less, Listing

All Elvish Words Found in *The Lord of the Rings, The Hobbit*, and *The Road Goes Ever On* by J. R. R. Tolkien." *Mythlore*, 1, 1 (1969), 41-44; 1, 2 (1969), 33-36; 1, 4 (1969), 23-26.

Barber, Dorothy K. "The Meaning of *The Lord of the Rings*." *MSCS*, 2 (February 1967), 38-50.

Barbour, Douglas. " 'The Shadow of the Past': History in Middle Earth." *UWR*, 8, 1 (1972), 35-42.

Basney, Lionel. "The Place of Myth in a Mythical Land: Two Notes (Converging)." *Mythlore*, 3, 2 (1975), 15-17.

Beagle, Peter S. "Tolkien's Magic Ring." *Holiday*, 39 (June 1966), 128, 130, 133-34.

Beatie, Bruce A. "Folk Tale, Fiction, and Saga in J. R. R. Tolkien's *The Lord of the Rings*." *MSCS*, 2 (February 1967), 1-17.

Begg, Ean C. M. *The LORD OF THE RINGS and the Signs of the Times*. London: Guild of Pastoral Psychology, 1975.

Bell, Judy W. "The Language of J. R. R. Tolkien in *The Lord of the Rings*." *Mythcon 1: Proceedings*. Ed. Glen GoodKnight, 35-40.

Bisenieks, Dainis. "Power and Poetry in Middle-Earth." *Mythlore*, 3, 2 (1975), 20-24.

Blissett, William. "The Despots of the Rings." *SAQ*, 58 (1959), 448-56.

Boswell, George W. "Proverbs and Phraseology in Tolkien's *Lord of the Rings* Complex." *UMSE*, 10 (1969), 59-65.

———. "Tolkien's Riddles in *Lord of the Rings*." *TFSB*, 25 (1969), 44-49.

Bradley, Marion Z. "Men, Halfling, and Hero Worship." *Niekas*, 16 (June 30, 1966), 25-44.

Callahan, Patrick J. "Animism and Magic in Tolkien's *The Lord of the Rings*." *RQ*, 4 (1971), 240-49.

———. "Tolkien's Dwarfs and the Eddas." *Tolkien Journal*, 15 (1972), 20.

Carter, Lin. *Tolkien: A Look Behind THE LORD OF THE RINGS*. New York: Ballantine, 1969.

Clausen, Christopher. "*Lord of the Rings* and '*The Ballad of the White Horse*'." *SAB*, 39, 2 (1974), 10-16.

Dabney, Virginia. "On the Natures and Histories of the Great Rings." *Mythcon 1: Proceedings*. Ed. Glen GoodKnight, 8-10.

Ellwood, Gracia F. *Good News from Tolkien's Middle Earth: Two Essays on the "Applicability" of THE LORD OF THE RINGS*. Grand Rapids, Mich.: Eerdmans, 1970.

Evans, W. D. Emrys. "*The Lord of the Rings*." *The School Librarian*, 16 (December 1968), 284-88.

Friedman, Barton R. "Fabricating History: Narrative Strategy in *The Lord of the Rings*." *ClioW*, 2 (1973), 123-44.

Glover, Willis B. "The Christian Character of Tolkien's Invented World." *Criticism*, 13 (1971), 39-53.

GoodKnight, Glen. " 'Death and the Desire for Deathlessness': The Counsel of Elrond." *Mythlore*, 3, 2 (1975), 19.

_____. "The White Tree." *Mythcon 1: Proceedings*. Ed. Glen Good-Knight, 56-58.

Gottlieb, Stephen A. "An Interpretation of Gollum." *Orcrist*, 5 - *Tolkien Journal*, 14 [combined issue] (1971), 11-12.

Halle, Louis J. "History Through the Mind's Eye." *SatR*, 39 (January 28, 1956), 11-12.

Hayes, Noreen, and Robert Renshaw. "Of Hobbits: *The Lord of the Rings*." *Crit*, 9, 2 (1967), 58-66.

Helms, Randel. "Orc: The Id in Blake and Tolkien." *L&P*, 20, 1 (1970), 31-35.

_____. "The Structure and Aesthetic of Tolkien's *Lord of the Rings*." *Mythcon 1: Proceedings*. Ed. Glen GoodKnight, 1971, 5-8.

Hope, Francis. "Welcome to Middle Earth." *New Statesman*, 72 (1966), 701-02.

Hughes, Daniel. "Pieties and Giant Forms in *The Lord of the Rings*." *Shadows of Imagination*. Ed. Mark R. Hillegas, 81-96.

Huxley, Francis. "The Endless Worm." *New Statesman*, 50 (1955), 587-88.

Isaacs, Neil D., and Rose A. Zimbardo, eds. *Tolkien and the Critics: Essays on J. R. R. Tolkien's THE LORD OF THE RINGS*. Notre Dame, Ind.: Univ. of Notre Dame Press, 1968.

Juhren, Marcella. "The Ecology of Middle Earth." *Mythlore*, 2, 1 (1970), 4-6, 9.

Kilby, Clyde S. "Meaning in *The Lord of the Rings*." *Shadows of Imagination*. Ed. Mark R. Hillegas, 70-80.

Kirk, Elizabeth D. " 'I Would Rather Have Written in Elvish': Language, Fiction and *The Lord of the Rings*." *Novel*, 5 (1971), 5-18.

Kocher, Paul H. *Master of Middle-Earth: The Fiction of J. R. R. Tolkien*. Boston: Houghton Mifflin, 1972.

Levitin, Alexis. "The Genre of *The Lord of the Rings*." *Orcrist*, 3 (1969), 4-8, 23.

_____. "The Hero in J. R. R. Tolkien's *The Lord of the Rings*." *MSCS*, 2 (February 1967), 25-37.

_____. "The Lure of the Ring." *Mythcon 1: Proceedings*. Ed. Glen GoodKnight, 20-21.

_____. "Power in *The Lord of the Rings*." *Orcrist*, 4 (1969), 11-14.

Lewis, C. S. "The Gods Return to Earth." *T&T*, 35 (1954), 1082-83.

Lobdell, Jared C. "Words That Sound Like Castles." *National Review* (N. Y.), 19 (September 1967), 972-74.

Manlove, Colin N. *Modern Fantasy*, 152-206.

Mathewson, Joseph. "The Hobbit Habit." *Esquire,* 66 (September 1966), 130-31, 221-22.

Miesel, Sandra. "Some Motifs and Sources for *Lord of the Rings.*" *RQ,* 3 (1968), 125-28.

———. "Some Religious Aspects of *Lord of the Rings.*" *RQ,* 3 (1968), 209-13.

Miller, David M. "The Moral Universe of J. R. R. Tolkien." *MSCS,* 2 (February 1967), 51-62.

Moorman, Charles W. "Heroism in *The Lord of the Rings.*" *SoQ,* 11 (1972), 29-39.

Nored, Gary. "*The Lord of the Rings*: A Textual Inquiry." *PBSA,* 68 (1974), 71-74.

Norwood, W. D. "Tolkien's Intention in *The Lord of the Rings.*" *MSCS,* 2 (February 1967), 18-24.

O'Connor, Gerard. "Why Tolkien's *The Lord of the Rings* Should *Not* Be Popular Culture." *Extrapolation,* 13 (1971), 48-55.

Pauline, Sister, C.S.M. "Mysticism in The Ring." *Tolkien Journal,* 10 (1969), 12-14.

"The Peril of the World." *Tolkien Journal,* 15 (1972), 16-17.

Perret, Marion. "Rings Off Their Fingers: Hands in *The Lord of the Rings.*" *ArielE,* 6, 4 (1975), 52-66.

Randolph, Burt. "The Singular Incompetence of Valar." *Tolkien Journal,* 9 (1968), 11-13.

Ratliff, William E., and Charles G. Flinn. "The Hobbit and the Hippie." *ModA,* 12 (1968), 142-46.

Ready, William. *Understanding Tolkien and THE LORD OF THE RINGS.* New York: Paperback Library, 1969.

Reilly, Robert J. *Romantic Religion,* 190-211.

———. "Tolkien and the Fairy Story." *Thought,* 38 (1963), 89-106.

Reinken, Donald L. "J. R. R. Tolkien's *The Lord of the Rings*: A Christian Refounding of the Political Order." *ChrPer,* Winter 1966, 16-23.

Ring, David. "*Ad Valar Defendendi.*" *Tolkien Journal,* 15 (1972), 18, 22.

Roberts, Mark. "Adventure in English." *EIC,* 6 (1956), 450-59.

Rockow, Karen. "Funeral Customs in Tolkien's Trilogy." *Unicorn,* 3, 1 (1973), 22-30.

Ruskin, Laura A. "Three Good Mothers: Galadriel, Psyche, and Sybil Coningsby." *Mythcon 1: Proceedings.* Ed. Glen GoodKnight, 12-14.

Schroth, Raymond A. "Lord of the Rings." *America,* 116 (February 18, 1967), 254.

Scott, Nan C. "War and Pacifism in *The Lord of the Rings.*" *Tolkien Journal*, 15 (1972), 23-30.

Spacks, Patricia Meyer. " 'Ethical Patterns' in *The Lord of the Rings.*" *Crit*, 3, 1 (1959), 30-42.

Straight, Michael. "Fantastic World of Professor Tolkien." *New Republic*, 134 (January 16, 1956), 24-26.

Taylor, William L. "Frodo Lives: J. R. R. Tolkien's *The Lord of the Rings.*" *EJ*, 56 (1967), 818-21.

Thomson, George H. "*The Lord of the Rings*: The Novel as Traditional Romance." *WSCL*, 8 (1967), 43-59.

Traversi, Derek. "The Realm of Gondor." *Month*, 15 (1956), 370-71.

Van de Bogart, Doris. "Some Comments on the *Lord of the Rings* by J. R. R. Tolkien." *Dialogue*, 1, 4 (1973), 33-42.

West, Richard C. "The Interlace and Professor Tolkien: Medieval Narrative Technique in *The Lord of the Rings.*" *Orcrist*, 1 (1966-67), 19-31.

Wilson, Colin. *The Strength to Dream*, 145-49.

Wilson, Edmund. "Oo, Those Awful Orcs!" *Nation*, 182 (1956), 312-14; *The Bit Between My Teeth*, 326-32.

Winter, Karen C. "Grendel, Gollum, and the Un-Man." *Orcrist*, 2 (1967-68), 28-37.

Wojcik, Jan. "Samwise—Halfwise? or Who Is the Hero of *The Lord of the Rings?*" *Tolkien Journal*, 3, 2 (1967), 16-18.

Zgorzelski, Andrzej. "Time Setting in J. R. R. Tolkien's *The Lord of the Rings.*" *ZRL*, 13, 2 (1971), 91-100.

JOHN WAIN

INTERVIEWS

Firchow, Peter. *The Writer's Place*, 313-30.

Kermode, Frank. "The House of Fiction: Interviews with Seven English Novelists." *PR*, 30 (1963), 61-82.

GENERAL STUDIES

Allsop, Kenneth. *The Angry Decade*, 66-76.

Bluestone, George. "John Wain and John Barth: The Angry and the Accurate." *MR*, 1 (1960), 582-89.

Cox, Charles B. *The Free Spirit*, 157-61.

Davenport, Guy. "Jungles of the Imagination." *National Review* (*N.Y.*), 13 (October 1962), 273-74.

Dixon, Terrell F. "The Use of Literary History in *Hurry on Down.*" *NConL*, 2, 2 (1972), 6-7.

Gindin, James J. "The Reassertion of the Personal." *TQ*, 1, 4 (1958), 126-34.

Glicksberg, Charles I. "The Literature of the Angry Young Men." *ColQ*, 8 (1960), 293-303.

Gorer, Geoffrey. "The Perils of Hypergamy." *New Statesman*, 53 (1957), 566-68.

Heppenstall, Rayner. *The Fourfold Tradition*, 213-48.

Holloway, John. "Tank in the Stalls: Notes on the 'School of Anger'." *HudR*, 10 (1957), 424-29.

Lehmann, John. "The Wain-Larkin Myth." *SR*, 66 (1958), 578-87.

McGovern, Eugene. "Obstinacy in Belief at the Socratic Club." *CSLBull*, 4, 1 (1973), 2-5.

Meckier, Jerome. "Looking Back at Anger: The Success of a Collapsing Stance." *DR*, 52 (1972), 47-58.

Mellown, Elgin W. "Steps Toward Vision: The Development of Technique in John Wain's First Seven Novels." *SAQ*, 68 (1969), 330-42.

O'Connor, William Van. "John Wain: The Will to Write." *WSCL*, 1, 1 (1960), 35-49.

―――. "The New University Wits." *KR*, 20 (1958), 38-50.

Reed, John R. *Old School Ties*, 275-78.

Rippier, Joseph S. *Some Postwar English Novelists*, 138, 139, 159-77.

Ross, Theodore J. "A Good Girl Is Hard to Find." *New Republic*, 141 (September 21, 1959), 17-19.

Scott, J. D. "Britain's Angry Young Men." *SatR*, 40 (July 27, 1957), 8-11.

Wain, John. "The New Puritanism, the New Academism, the New, the New . . . " *CritQ*, 14 (1972), 7-18.

Walzer, Michael. "John Wain: The Hero in Limbo." *Per*, 10 (1958), 137-45.

See also: Allen, *Tradition*; Gindin, *Postwar*; Hall, *Tragic*; O'Connor, *New*.

HUGH WALPOLE

BIBLIOGRAPHIES
Steele, Elizabeth. "Hugh Walpole: An Annotated Bibliography of Writings About Him." *ELT*, 19, 3 (1976), 150-233.

INTERVIEWS
Crozier, Gladys Beattie. "Hugh Walpole, An Interview." *Strand*, 64 (April 1924), 357-62.

Morgan, Louise. "Hugh Walpole Finds Himself." *Everyman*, June 4, 1931, 587-89.

GENERAL STUDIES
Adcock, A. St. John. *Gods of Modern Grub Street*, 293-300.
Bain, James S. *A Bookseller Looks Back*, 247-60.
Beach, Joseph Warren. "The English Sentimentalists." *NoAmR*, 216 (1922), 89-101.
————. *Outlook for American Prose*, 132-36.
Bennett, Arnold. "Hugh Walpole, A Familiar Sketch." *Book News Monthly*, 32 (April 1914), 371-73.
Bidwell, Edward J. "A Twentieth Century Trollope?" *QQ*, 30 (1923), 363-71.
Birkmyre, Robert. "Hugh Walpole." *Bookman* (London), 52 (1917), 136-37.
Boynton, H. W. "Ideals and Allegiances in Current Fiction." *Bookman* (N. Y.), 46 (1918), 598-604.
Braybrook, Patrick. *Novelists: We Are Seven*, 77-95.
Bullett, Gerald W. *Modern English Fiction*, 121-23.
Burnett, Richard G. "The Courage of Hugh Walpole." *LonQR*, 166 (1941), 463-66.
Chevalley, Abel. *The Modern English Novel*, 219-22.
Coveney, Peter. *Poor Monkey*, 210-19.
Dane, Clemence [Winifred Ashton]. *Tradition and Hugh Walpole*. Garden City, N. Y.: Doubleday, 1929.
Dutton, George B. "Romance and Mr. Walpole." *SR*, 31 (1923), 178-86.
Edel, Leon. "Hugh Walpole and Henry James: The Fantasy of *The Killer and the Slain*." *AI*, 8 (1951), 351-69.
Hart-Davis, Rupert. *Hugh Walpole, A Biography*. London and New York: Macmillan, 1952.
Hergesheimer, Joseph. *Hugh Walpole, An Appreciation*. New York: Doran, 1919.
James, Henry. "The Younger Generation." *TLS*, March 19, 1914, 133-34; April 2, 1914, 157-58.
Knickerbocker, William S. "Analysis of Hugh Walpole's *Rogue Herries*." *Creative Reading*, 4 (1930), 366-80.
Lewis, Sinclair, ed. *Hugh Walpole, Master Novelist*. New York: Doran, 1915; rev. 1930.
Lowndes, Marie Belloc. "Hugh Walpole." *Book News Monthly*, 32 (April 1914), 372-73.
McAlpin, Edwin A. *Old and New Books as Life Teachers*, 66-79.
Mais, Stuart P. B. *Some Modern Authors*, 137-41.

Mansfield, Katherine. *Novels and Novelists*, 61-63, 269-72.

Melville, Lewis. "The Reader, Hugh Walpole." *Bookman* (London), 56 (1919), 6-9.

Murry, John Middleton. "The Case of Mr. Hugh Walpole." *Nation and Athenaeum*, 29 (July 16, 1921), 584-85.

Overton, Grant, ed. *Hugh Walpole: Appreciations.* New York: Doran, 1923.

Paul, David Blackwood. "Some Thoughts on Hugh Walpole and the Popular Novel." *TLR*, 12 (1954), 3-20.

Priestley, J. B. "Hugh Walpole." *EJ*, 17 (1928), 529-36.

――――. "Hugh Walpole, Novelist." *Bookman* (New York), 64 (1927), 684-92; rev. *Fortnightly*, n.s. 122 (1927), 753-63.

――――. "The Younger Novelists." *EJ*, 14 (1925), 435-43.

Steele, Elizabeth. *Hugh Walpole.* New York: Twayne, 1972.

Steen, Marguerite. *Hugh Walpole: A Study.* London: Nicholson and Watson; Garden City, N. Y.: Doubleday, 1933.

Strong, Leonard A. G. "Hugh Walpole: The Making of a Novelist." *John O'London's Weekly*, 44 (December 20, 1940), 305-06.

――――. *Personal Remarks*, 222-25.

Wall, Arnold. *Sir Hugh Walpole and His Writings.* Wellington, N. Z.: Turnbull Library, 1947.

Waugh, Alec. "The Nail in the Coffin: The Curious Fate of Hugh Walpole." *Harper's*, 207 (July 1953), 32-37.

Waugh, Arthur. "The New Realism." *Fortnightly*, n.s. 99 (1916), 849-58.

West, Anthony. *Principles and Persuasions*, 143-49.

――――. "Waiting for Mr. Right." *NY*, 28 (August 23, 1952), 79-84.

Wilson, A. C. "Hugh Walpole's Novels." *PMLC*, 53 (1927), 171-88.

See also: Beach, *20th*; P. Braybrooke, *Philosophies*; Cunliffe, *20th Century, Half-Century*; Frierson; Goldring, *Reputations*; Hind, *Authors*; R. Johnson, *Men*; Lacon; Marble; Overton, *Authors*; Routh; Swinnerton, *Background, Figures, Georgian*; Weygandt; H. Williams, *Modern*; V. Woolf, *Contemporary*.

REX WARNER

SPECIAL ISSUE

Rajan, Balachandra, and Andrew Pearse, eds. *Focus One: Symposium on Kafka and Rex Warner.* London: Dobson, 1945, 5-65.

GENERAL STUDIES

Atkins, John. "On Rex Warner." *Focus One*. Ed. Balachandra Rajan and Andrew Pearse, 33-37.

Churchill, Thomas. "Rex Warner: Homage to Necessity." *Crit*, 10, 1 (1968), 30-44.

Davenport, John. "Re-assessment: The Air Marshall's Story." *Spectator*, 215 (June 24, 1966), 796.

DeVitis, A. A. "Rex Warner and the Cult of Power." *TCL*, 6 (1960), 107-16.

Drenner, Don V. R. "Kafka, Warner, and the Cult of Power." *KM*, 1952, 62-64.

Enright, D. J. "The Use and Misuse of Symbolism." *Focus One*. Ed. Balachandra Rajan and Andrew Pearse, 30-39.

Flynn, James. "Rex Warner's *The Aerodrome*: A Study in the Politics of Twentieth-Century Fiction." *RecL*, 4, 3 (1975), 27-44.

Harris, Henry. "The Symbol of the Frontier in the Social Allegory of the Thirties." *ZAA*, 14 (1966), 127-40.

Harrison, Tom. "Rex Warner's Writing." *Focus One*. Ed. Balachandra Rajan and Andrew Pearse, 39-41.

Howarth, Herbert. "Pieces of History." *Crit*, 2, 1 (1958), 54-64.

McLeod, Alan Lindsey, ed. *The Achievement of Rex Warner*. Sydney: Wentworth, 1965.

_____. *Rex Warner: Writer*. Sydney: Wentworth, 1960.

Maini, Darshan Singh. "Rex Warner's Political Novels: An Allegorical Crusade Against Fascism." *IJES*, 2 (1961), 91-107.

Pritchett, V. S. "Rex Warner." *Modern British Writing*. Ed. Denys Val Baker, 304-09.

Rajan, Balachandra. "Kafka: A Comparison with Rex Warner." *Focus One*. Ed. Balachandra Rajan and Andrew Pearse, 7-14.

Stonier, G. W. "The New Allegory." *Focus One*. Ed. Balachandra Rajan and Andrew Pearse, 26-29.

Woodcock, George. "Kafka and Rex Warner." *Focus One*. Ed. Balachandra Rajan and Andrew Pearse, 59-65.

_____. *The Writer and Politics*, 197-206.

See also: Allen, *Tradition*; Fraser; Karl; McCormick.

KEITH WATERHOUSE

GENERAL STUDIES

Churchill, Thomas. "Waterhouse, Storey, and Fowles: Which Way Out of the Room?" *Crit*, 10, 3 (1968), 72-87.

Corbett, Martyn. "First Person Singular." *Delta*, 35 (1965), 9-16.

Gray, Nigel. *The Silent Majority*, 47-72.

See also: Gindin, *Postwar*; O'Connor, *New*.

EVELYN WAUGH

BIBLIOGRAPHIES

Davis, Robert M., Paul A. Doyle, Heinz Kosok, and Charles E. Linck, Jr., eds. *Evelyn Waugh: A Checklist of Primary and Secondary Materials*. Troy, N. Y.: Whitston, 1972.

Evelyn Waugh Newsletter [EWN]. (annually publishes "The Year's Work in Waugh Studies" and regularly publishes "Supplementary Checklists of Criticism")

Kosok, Heinz. "Evelyn Waugh: A Checklist of Criticism." *TCL*, 11 (1966), 211-15.

INTERVIEWS

Breit, Harvey. *The Writer Observed*, 43-46, 147-49.

Jebb, Julian. "Evelyn Waugh." *Paris Review. Writers at Work*, 3d ser., 103-14.

GENERAL STUDIES

Allen, W. Gore. "Evelyn Waugh and Graham Greene." *IrM*, 77 (January 1949), 16-22.

Auden, W. H. *Forewords and Afterwords*, 492-524.

Bell, Alan. "General Cruttwell's Emporium." *TLS*, October 25, 1974, 1197.

Benedict, Stewart H. "The Candide Figure in the Novels of Evelyn Waugh." *PMASAL*, 48 (1963), 685-90.

Bergonzi, Bernard. "Evelyn Waugh's Gentleman." *CritQ*, 5 (1963), 23-36.

Betjeman, John. "Evelyn Waugh." *Living Writers*. Ed. Gilbert Phelps, 137-50.

Bogaards, Winnifred M. "Evelyn Waugh, Oscar Wilde and Irish Folklore." *EWN*, 7, 1 (1973), 1-5.

Borrello, Alfred. "Evelyn Waugh and Erle Stanley Gardner." *EWN*, 4, 3 (1970), 1-3.

Boyle, Alexander. "Evelyn Waugh." *IrM*, 78 (February 1950), 75-81.

Bradbury, Malcolm. *Evelyn Waugh*. Edinburgh: Oliver and Boyd, 1964.

Braybrooke, Neville. "Evelyn Waugh." *Fortnightly*, 171 (1952), 197-202.

Brophy, Brigid. *Don't Never Forget*, 156-58.

Browning, Gordon. "Silenus' Wheel: Static and Dynamic Characters in the Satiric Fiction of Evelyn Waugh." *Cithara*, 14, 1 (1974), 13-24.

Evelyn Waugh, continued

Carens, James F. *The Satiric Art of Evelyn Waugh.* Seattle: Univ. of Washington Press, 1966.

Clark, John R. "*Verboten* Passage: Strategy in Early Waugh." *EWN*, 7, 2 (1973), 5-9.

Cook, William J. *Masks, Modes and Morals: The Art of Evelyn Waugh.* Rutherford, N. J.: Fairleigh Dickinson Univ. Press, 1971.

Corr, Patricia. "Evelyn Waugh: Sanity and Catholicism." *Studies*, 51 (1962), 388-99.

Cosman, Max. "The Nature and Work of Evelyn Waugh." *ClasQ*, 4 (1956), 428-41.

Davis, Robert M., comp. *Evelyn Waugh.* St. Louis: Herder, 1969.

———. "Evelyn Waugh on the Art of Fiction." *PLL*, 2 (1966), 243-52.

———. "Evelyn Waugh's Early Work: The Formation of a Method." *TSLL*, 7 (1965), 97-108.

———. "The Mind and Art of Evelyn Waugh." *PLL*, 3 (1967), 270-87.

———. "Social History in a *Black Mischief* Revision." *EWN*, 7, 3 (1973), 8-9.

———. "Textual Problems in the Novels of Evelyn Waugh." *PBSA*, 62 (1968), 259-63; 63 (1969), 41-46.

Dennis, Nigel. "Evelyn Waugh: The Pillar of Anchorage House." *PR*, 10, 4 (1943), 350-61.

DeVitis, A. A. *Roman Holiday: The Catholic Novels of Evelyn Waugh.* New York: Bookman, 1955.

Dobie, Ann B., and Carl Wooton. "Spark and Waugh: Similarities by Coincidence." *MQ*, 13 (1972), 423-34.

Donaldson, Frances. *Evelyn Waugh: Portrait of a Country Neighbour.* London: Weidenfeld and Nicolson, 1967.

Dooley, D. J. "The Council's First Victim." *Triumph*, 5, 6 (1970), 33-35.

———. "Waugh and Black Humor." *EWN*, 2, 2 (1968), 1-3.

Doyle, Paul A. *Evelyn Waugh: A Critical Essay.* Grand Rapids, Mich.: Eerdmans, 1969.

———. "The Politics of Waugh." *Renascence*, 11 (1959), 171-74, 221.

Dyson, A. E. *The Crazy Fabric*, 187-96.

———. "Evelyn Waugh and the Mysteriously Disappearing Hero." *CritQ*, 2 (1960), 72-79.

Farr, D. Paul. "The Edwardian Golden Age and Nostalgic Truth." *DR*, 50 (1970), 378-93.

———. "Evelyn Waugh: Tradition and a Modern Talent." *SAQ*, 68 (1969), 506-19.

———. "Waugh's Conservative Stance: Defending 'The Standards of Civilization'." *PQ*, 51 (1972), 471-84.

Fielding, Gabriel. "Evelyn Waugh and the Cross of Satire." *Critic,* 23 (February-March 1965), 52-56.

――――. "Evelyn Waugh: The Price of Satire." *Listener,* 72 (1964), 541-42.

Fytton, Francis. "Waughfare." *CathW,* 181 (1955), 349-55.

Gardiner, Harold C. *In All Conscience,* 89-96.

Gleason, James. "Evelyn Waugh and the Stylistics of Commitment." *WSL,* 2 (1965), 70-74.

Grace, William J. "Evelyn Waugh as a Social Critic." *Renascence,* 1, 2 (1949), 28-40.

Green, Martin. "British Comedy and the British Sense of Humour: Shaw, Waugh, and Amis." *TQ,* 4, 3 (1961), 217-27.

Greenblatt, Stephen J. *Three Modern Satirists,* 1-33, 105-17.

Greene, George. "Scapegoat with Style: The Status of Evelyn Waugh." *QQ,* 71 (1965), 485-93.

Griffiths, Joan. "Waugh's Problem Comedies." *Accent,* 9 (1949), 165-70.

Hall, James. "The Other Post-War Rebellion: Evelyn Waugh Twenty-Five Years After." *ELH,* 28 (1961), 187-202.

Heath, Jeffrey. "Evelyn Waugh: Afraid of the Shadow." *EWN,* 9, 3 (1975), 1-4.

Highet, Gilbert. *The Anatomy of Satire,* 193-95, 204-05.

Hinchcliffe, Peter. "Fathers and Children in the Novels of Evelyn Waugh." *UTQ,* 35 (1966), 293-310.

Hines, Leo. "Waugh and His Critics." *Cweal,* 76 (1962), 60-63.

Hollis, Christopher. *Evelyn Waugh.* London: Longmans, Green, 1966.

Howarth, Herbert. "Quelling the Riot: Evelyn Waugh's Progress." *The Shapeless God.* Ed. Harvey J. Mooney, Jr. and Thomas F. Staley, 67-89.

Hugo, Howard. "Evelyn Waugh: Candide in Wonderland." *HarvA,* 126, 2 (1952), 23-25, 36.

Hynes, Joseph. "Varieties of Death Wish: Evelyn Waugh's Central Theme." *Criticism,* 14 (1972), 65-77.

Johnson, Robert V. "The Early Novels of Evelyn Waugh." *Approaches to the Novel.* Ed. John Colmer, 78-89.

Kellogg, Gene. *The Vital Tradition,* 101-10.

Kernan, Alvin B. *The Plot of Satire,* 154-67.

――――. "The Wall and the Jungle: The Early Novels of Evelyn Waugh." *YR,* 53 (1964), 199-220.

Kleine, Don W. "The Cosmic Comedies of Evelyn Waugh." *SAQ,* 61 (1962), 533-39.

Evelyn Waugh, continued

Linklater, Eric. *The Art of Adventure*, 44-58.
Lodge, David. "The Arrogance of Evelyn Waugh." *Critic*, 30, 5 (May-June 1972), 62-70.
―――. *Evelyn Waugh*. New York: Columbia Univ. Press, 1971.
Macaulay, Rose. "The Best and Worst, II.: Evelyn Waugh." *Horizon(L)*, 14 (December 1946), 360-76; *Writers of To-day, 2.* Ed. Denys Val Baker, 135-52.
Marcus, Steven. "Evelyn Waugh and the Art of Entertainment." *PR*, 23, 3 (1956), 348-57.
―――. *Representations*, 88-101.
Marshall, Bruce. "Graham Greene and Evelyn Waugh." *Cweal*, 51 (1950), 551-53.
Martin, Graham. "Novelists of Three Decades: Evelyn Waugh, Graham Greene, C. P. Snow." *The Pelican Guide to English Literature*, v. 7. Ed. Boris Ford, 412-32.
Meckier, Jerome. "Evelyn Waugh: Satire and Symbol." *GaR*, 27 (1973), 166-74.
Mehoke, James S. "Sartre's Theory of Emotion and Three English Novelists: Waugh, Green, and Amis." *WSL*, 3 (1966), 105-11.
Menen, Aubrey. "The Baroque and Mr. Waugh." *Month*, 5 (1951), 226-37.
Meyer, Heinrich. "Evelyn Waugh (1903-66)." *BA*, 40 (1966), 410-11.
New, Melvyn. "Ad nauseum: A Satiric Device in Huxley, Orwell, and Waugh." *SNL*, 8 (1970), 24-28.
Nichols, James W. "Romantic and Realistic: The Tone of Evelyn Waugh's Early Novels." *CE*, 24 (1962), 46, 51-56.
O'Donnell, Donat [Conor Cruise O'Brien]. *Maria Cross*, 119-34, 225-59.
―――. "The Pieties of Evelyn Waugh." *Bell*, 13 (December 1946), 38-49; *KR*, 9 (1947), 400-11.
Pritchett, V. S. "Books in General." *New Statesman*, 37 (1949), 473-74.
Pryce-Jones, David, ed. *Evelyn Waugh and His World*. London: Weidenfeld and Nicolson; Boston: Little, Brown, 1973.
Quennell, Peter. *Casanova in London*, 163-68.
―――. "Evelyn Waugh." *Page 2.* Ed. Francis Brown, 260-64.
Raymond, John. *The Doge of Dover*, 148-55.
Reed, John R. *Old School Ties*, 84-85, 90-93, 196-201, 207-11, 244-46.
Rees, John O. " 'What Price Dotheboys Hall?': Some Dickens Echoes in Waugh." *KanQ*, 7, 4 (1975), 14-18.
Reinhardt, Kurt F. *The Theological Novel of Modern Europe*, 203-16.
Rolo, Charles J. "Evelyn Waugh: the Best and the Worst." *Atlantic*, 194 (October 1954), 80-86.
―――. *The World of Evelyn Waugh*. Boston: Little, Brown, 1958.

Savage, Derek S. "The Innocence of Evelyn Waugh." *WestR*, 14 (1950), 197-206.
Sheehan, Edward R. F. "Evelyn Waugh Runs a Fair." *Harper's*, 220 (January 1960), 30-37.
Staley, Thomas F. "Waugh the Artist." *Cweal*, 84 (1966), 280-82.
Stopp, Frederick J. *Evelyn Waugh: Portrait of an Artist.* London: Chapman and Hall; Boston: Little, Brown, 1958.
———. "Waugh: End of an Illusion." *Renascence*, 9 (1956), 59-67, 76.
Sykes, Christopher, et al. "A Critique of Waugh." *Listener*, 78 (1967), 267-69.
Tucker, Martin. *Africa in Modern Literature*, 141-48, 250-53.
Tysdahl, Björn. "The Bright Young Things in the Early Novels of Evelyn Waugh." *Edda*, 62 (1962), 98-103.
Ulanov, Barry. "The Ordeal of Evelyn Waugh." *The Vision Obscured.* Ed. Melvin J. Friedman, 79-93.
Van Zeller, Hubert. "Evelyn Waugh." *Month*, 36 (1966), 69-71.
Voorhees, Richard J. "Evelyn Waugh Revisited." *SAQ*, 48 (1949), 270-80.
Wagner, Linda W. "Satiric Marks: Huxley and Waugh." *SNL*, 3 (1966), 160-62.
Walsh, Chad. *From Utopia to Nightmare*, 79-81.
Waugh, Alec. *My Brother Evelyn and Other Profiles.*
Waugh, Auberon. "Waugh's World." *NYTM*, October 7, 1973, 20-21, 100-02, 106.
Waugh, Evelyn. "Fan-Fare." *Life*, April 8, 1946, 53-60.
West, Rebecca. *Ending in Ernest*, 217-26.
Wicker, Brian. *The Story-Shaped World*, 151-68.
Wilson, Colin. *The Strength to Dream*, 42-55.
Wilson, Edmund. *The Bit Between My Teeth*, 536-38.
———. *Classics and Commercials*, 298-305.
Woodcock, George. "Evelyn Waugh: The Man and His Work." *World Review*, March 1949, 51-56.
See also: Allen, *Tradition*; Bergonzi, *Situation*; Bradbury, *Possibilities*; Eagleton; Gill; Hall, *Tragic*; Karl; Kermode; McCormick; O'Faoláin; Prescott; Spender, *Creative*; Webster.

BRIDESHEAD REVISITED
Beary, Thomas J. "Religion and the Modern Novel." *CathW*, 166 (1947), 203-11.
Canney, Daniel J. "The Kingfisher Image in *Brideshead*." *EWN*, 7, 3 (1973), 6-7.

Evelyn Waugh, continued

Churchill, Thomas. "The Trouble with *Brideshead Revisited.*" *MLQ*, 28 (1967), 213-28.

Cogley, John. "Revisiting Brideshead." *Cweal*, 80 (1964), 103-06.

Cohen, Martin S. "Allusive Conversation in *A Handful of Dust* and *Brideshead Revisited.*" *EWN*, 5, 2 (1971), 1-6.

———. "*Brideshead Revisited* and *Jasper Tristram.*" *EWN*, 5, 3 (1971), 6-8.

Davis, Robert M. "Serial Version of *Brideshead Revisited.*" *TCL*, 15 (1969), 35-43.

Delasanta, Rodney, and Mario L. D'Avanzo. "Truth and Beauty in *Brideshead Revisited.*" *MFS*, 11 (1965), 140-52.

Greene, Donald. "The Wicked Marquess: Disraeli to Thackeray to Waugh." *EWN*, 7, 2 (1973), 1-5.

Harty, E. R. "*Brideshead* Re-read: A Discussion of Some of the Themes of Evelyn Waugh's *Brideshead Revisited.*" *UES*, 3 (1967), 66-74.

Heck, Francis S. "*Brideshead*, or Proust and Gide Revisited." *EWN*, 9, 2 (1975), 4-7.

Heilman, Robert B. "Sue Brideshead Revisited." *Accent*, 7 (1947), 123-26.

LaFrance, Marston. "Context and Structure of Evelyn Waugh's *Brideshead Revisited.*" *TCL*, 10 (1964), 12-18.

Mahon, John W. "Charles Ryder and Evelyn Waugh." *EWN*, 6, 1 (1972), 2-3.

Martindale, C. C. "Back Again to *Brideshead.*" *TC(A)*, 2 (1948), 26-33.

Stopp, Frederick J. "Grace in Reins: Reflections on Mr. Waugh's *Brideshead* and *Helena.*" *Month*, 10 (August 1953), 69-84.

Vredenburgh, Joseph. "The Character of the Incest Object: A Study of Alternation between Narcissism and Object Choice." *AI*, 14 (1957), 45-52.

———. "Further Contributions to a Study of the Incest Object." *AI*, 16 (1959), 263-68.

Wooton, Carl. "Evelyn Waugh's *Brideshead Revisited*: War and Limited Hope." *MQ*, 10 (1969), 359-75.

See also: J. Hardy.

DECLINE AND FALL

Doyle, P. A. "*Decline and Fall*: Two Versions." *EWN*, 2 (1967), 4-5.

Farr, D. Paul. "The Success and Failure of *Decline and Fall.*" *EA*, 24 (1971), 257-70.

Friedmann, Thomas. "*Decline and Fall* and the Satirist's Responsibility." *EWN*, 6, 2 (1972), 3-8.

294

McAleer, Edward C. *"Decline and Fall* as Imitation." *EWN,* 7, 3 (1973), 1-4.

A HANDFUL OF DUST

Burbridge, Roger T. "The Function of Gossip, Rumor, and Public Opinion in Evelyn Waugh's *A Handful of Dust.*" *EWN,* 4, 1 (1970), 3-5.

Cohen, Martin S. "Allusive Conversation in *A Handful of Dust* and *Brideshead Revisited.*" *EWN,* 5, 2 (1971), 1-6.

Davis, Robert M. *"Harper's Bazaar* and *A Handful of Dust.*" *PQ,* 48 (1969), 508-16.

———. "Title and Theme in *A Handful of Dust.*" *EWN,* 6, 2 (1972), 1.

Firchow, Peter E. "In Search of *A Handful of Dust:* The Literary Background of Evelyn Waugh's Novel." *JML,* 2 (1972), 406-16.

Green, Peter. *"Du Côté de Chez Waugh.*" *REL,* 2, 2 (1961), 89-100.

Kearful, Frank J. "Tony Last and Ike McCaslin: The Loss of a Usable Past." *UWR,* 3, 2 (1968), 45-52.

Wasson, Richard. *"A Handful of Dust:* Critique of Victorianism." *MFS,* 7 (1961), 327-37.

THE LOVED ONE

Connolly, Cyril. "Introduction to *The Loved One.*" *Horizon(L),* 17 (February 1948), 76-77.

Davis, Robert M. *"The Loved One:* Text and Context." *TQ,* 15, 4 (1972), 100-07.

Powers, J. F. "Waugh Out West." *Cweal,* 48 (1948), 326-27.

Wecter, Dixon. "On Dying in Southern California." *Pacific Spectator,* 2 (1948), 375-87.

THE ORDEAL OF GILBERT PINFOLD

Duer, Harriet W. "Pinfold's Pinfold." *EWN,* 8, 1 (1974), 3-6.

Gallagher, D. S. "Pinfold Unfolded." *EWN,* 6, 1 (1972), 1-2.

Heath, Jeffrey M. "Apthorpe Placatus?" *ArielE,* 5, 1 (1974), 5-24.

SCOOP

Blayac, Alain. "Technique and Meaning in *Scoop:* Is *Scoop* a Modern Fairy-Tale?" *EWN,* 6, 3 (1972), 1-8.

Davis, Robert M. "Some Textual Variants in *Scoop.*" *EWN,* 2 (1967), 1-3.

Farr, D. Paul. "The Novelist's Coup: Style as Satiric Norm in *Scoop.*" *ConnR,* 8, 2 (1975), 42-54.

Evelyn Waugh, continued

SWORD OF HONOUR
[MEN AT ARMS, OFFICERS AND GENTLEMEN,
THE END OF THE BATTLE
(UNCONDITIONAL SURRENDER)]

Amis, Kingsley. "Crouchback's Regress." *Spectator*, 207 (October 27, 1961), 581-82.

Bergonzi, Bernard. "Evelyn Waugh's *Sword of Honour*." *Listener*, 71 (1964), 306-07.

Bogaards, Winnifred M. "The Conclusion of Waugh's Trilogy: Three Variants." *EWN*, 4, 2 (1970), 6-7.

Braybrooke, Neville. "Evelyn Waugh and Blimp." *Blackfriars*, 38 (December 1952), 508-12.

Coppieters, R. "A Linguistic Analysis of a Corpus of Quoted Speech in Evelyn Waugh's Novel *The Sword of Honour*." *SGG*, 11 (1969), 87-153.

Costello, Patrick. "An Idea of Comedy and Waugh's *Sword of Honour*." *KanQ*, 1, 3 (1969), 41-50.

Delbaere-Garant, J. " 'Who shall inherit England?': A Comparison Between *Howards End*, *Parade's End* and *Unconditional Surrender*." *ES*, 50 (1969), 101-05.

Didion, Joan. "Gentlemen in Battle." *National Review* (N. Y.), 12 (March 1962), 215-17.

LaFrance, Marston. "*Sword of Honour*: The Ironist Placatus." *DR*, 55 (1975), 23-53.

O'Donovan, Patrick. "Evelyn Waugh's Opus of Disgust." *New Republic*, 146 (February 12, 1962), 21-22.

Parker, Kenneth. "Quantitative Judgements Don't Apply." *ESA*, 9 (1966), 192-201.

Russell, John. "The War Trilogies of Anthony Powell and Evelyn Waugh." *ModA*, 16 (1972), 289-300.

Rutherford, Andrew. "Waugh's *Sword of Honour*." *Imagined Worlds*. Ed. Maynard Mack and Ian Gregor, 441-60.

Scheideman, J. W. "Miss Vavasour Remembered." *EWN*, 9, 3 (1975), 4-9.

Semple, H. E. "Evelyn Waugh's Modern Crusade." *ESA*, 11 (1968), 47-59.

Stopp, Frederick J. "The Circle and the Tangent: An Interpretation of Mr. Waugh's *Men At Arms*." *Month*, 12 (July 1954), 18-34.

Voorhees, Richard J. "Evelyn Waugh's War Novels: A Toast to Lost Causes." *QQ*, 65 (1958), 53-63.

Wilson, B. W. "*Sword of Honour*: The Last Crusade." *English*, 23 (1974), 89-93.

VILE BODIES

Heath, Jeffrey M. "*Vile Bodies*: A Revolution in Film Art." *EWN*, 8, 3 (1974), 2-9.

Isaacs, Neil D. "Evelyn Waugh's Restoration Jesuit." *SNL*, 2 (1965), 91-94.

Jervis, Steven A. "Evelyn Waugh, *Vile Bodies*, and the Younger Generation." *SAQ*, 66 (1967), 440-48.

Linck, Charles E., Jr., and Robert M. Davis. "The Bright Young People in *Vile Bodies*." *PLL*, 5 (1969), 80-90.

MARY WEBB

BIBLIOGRAPHIES

Sanders, Charles. "Mary Webb: An Annotated Bibliography of Writings About Her." *ELT*, 9, 3 (1966), 119-36.

GENERAL STUDIES

Addison, Hilda. *Mary Webb*. London: Cecil Palmer, 1931.

Armstrong, Martin. "Introduction." *The Essential Mary Webb*. London: J. Cape, 1949.

Bentley, Phyllis. *The English Regional Novel*, 34-35.

Bury, Adrian. "An Impression of Mary Webb." *Sufi*, 7 (June 1931), 11-13.

Byford-Jones, W. *Shropshire Haunts of Mary Webb*. Shrewsbury: Wilding and Son, 1948.

Chapman, Grace. "Mary Webb." *London Mercury*, 23 (1931), 364-71.

Chappell, W. Reid. *The Shropshire of Mary Webb*. London: Cecil Palmer, 1930.

Collard, Lorna. "Mary Webb." *ContempR*, 143 (1933), 455-64.

Collins, Joseph. *Taking the Literary Pulse*, 207-18.

Evans, Caradoc. "Mary Webb." *Colophon*, n.s. 3 (1938), 63-66.

Hannah, Barbara. *Striving Towards Wholeness*, 73-104.

Hawkins, Ethel Wallace. "The Books of Mary Webb." *Atlantic*, 144 (August 1929), 12, 14.

Jordan-Smith, Paul. *For the Love of Books*, 76-81.

Lawrence, Margaret. *The School of Femininity*, 331-38.

McNeil, W. K. "The Function of Legend, Belief, and Custom in *Precious Bane*." *Folklore*, 82 (1972), 132-46.

Marshall, H. P. "Mary Webb." *Edinburgh*, 249 (1929), 315-27.

Moult, Thomas. *Mary Webb: Her Life and Works*. London: J. Cape, 1932.

Newton, Alfred E. *End Papers*, 36-46.

Parsons, Alice Beal. "Mary Webb." *Nation*, 129 (1929), 145-46.
Peake, Gladys E. "The Religious Teaching of Mary Webb." *ConQ*, 11 (1933), 41-50.
Pitfield, Robert L. "The Shropshire Lass and Her Goitre: Some Account of Mary Meredith Webb and Her Works." *AMH*, 3d ser., 4 (July 14, 1942), 284-93.
Pugh, Edwin. "Mary Webb." *Bookman* (London), 64 (1923), 7-8; 74 (1928), 193-96.
Reade, Arthur R. *Main Currents in Modern Literature*, 197-213.
Sanders, Charles. "*The Golden Arrow*: Mary Webb's 'Apocalypse of Love'." *ELT*, 10, 1 (1967), 1-8.
―――. "Mary Webb: An Introduction." *ELT*, 9, 3 (1966), 115-18.
Sedgwick, Ellery. *The Happy Profession*, 192-95.
Wrenn, Dorothy P. H. *Goodbye to Morning*. Shrewsbury, Eng.: Wilding and Son, 1964.
See also: Adcock, *Glory*; E. Baker, *History*; Stevenson, *Panorama*; Swinnerton, *Georgian*; Tindall, *Forces*; Wagenknecht, *Cavalcade*.

H. G. WELLS

BIBLIOGRAPHIES
Borrello, Alfred. "H. G. Wells." *ELT*, 11, 1 (1968), 56-64; 12, 1 (1969), 49-54; 14, 2 (1971), 146-48; 15, 1 (1972), 94-98; 16, 2 (1973), 168-70.
Lauterbach, E. S. "H. G. Wells." *EFT*, 5, 4 (1962), 36-43; *ELT*, 6, 2 (1963), 119-23; 6, 4 (1963), 238-41.
Weeks, Robert P. "H. G. Wells." *EFT*, 1, 1 (1957), 37-42.
H. G. Wells Society. *H. G. Wells: A Comprehensive Bibliography*. London: H. G. Wells Society, 1966.

INTERVIEWS
Van Gelder, Robert. *Writers and Writing*, 127-31.

SPECIAL ISSUES
University of Windsor Review [UWR], 2, 2 (1967), 1-77.

GENERAL STUDIES
Aldiss, Brian W. *Billion Year Spree*, 113-33.
Armytage, W. H. "Superman and the System, Part I." *RQ*, 2 (1966), 232-42.
Arnot, R. P. "Retrospect on H. G. Wells." *ModQ*, 2 (1947), 194-207.
Bailey, J. C. "Is Science-Fiction Art? A Look at H. G. Wells." *Extrapolation*, 2 (1960), 17-19.

Bartlett, Robert M. *They Dared to Live*, 71-75.
Baylen, Joseph O. "W. T. Stead and the Early Career of H. G. Wells, 1895-1911." *HLQ*, 38 (1974), 53-79.
Becker, Carl L. *Everyman His Own Historian*, 169-90.
Belgion, Montgomery. *H. G. Wells*. London: Longmans, Green, 1953.
―――. "Men Like Ants." *Essays of the Year, 1933-1934*, by Various Authors, 366-78.
Bellamy, William. *The Novels of Wells, Bennett, and Galsworthy*, 51-143, 211-16.
Bennett, Arnold. *Books and Persons*, 109-16, 294-99.
Bergonzi, Bernard. *The Early H. G. Wells: A Study of the Scientific Romances*. Manchester: Univ. of Manchester Press; Toronto: Univ. of Toronto Press, 1961.
―――. "H. G. Wells." *The Politics of Twentieth-Century Novelists*. Ed. George A. Panichas, 3-14.
Bland, D. S. "An Early Estimate of H. G. Wells." *EFT*, 5, 4 (1962), 21-22.
Borges, Jorges Luis. *Other Inquisitions*, 86-88.
Borrello, Alfred. *H. G. Wells: Author in Agony*. Carbondale: Southern Illinois Univ. Press, 1972.
Braybrooke, Patrick. *Peeps at the Mighty*, 9-25, 95-112.
Brome, Vincent. *H. G. Wells*. London: Longmans, Green, 1951.
―――. "H. G. Wells as a Controversialist." *UWR*, 2, 2 (1967), 31-46.
Brown, E. K. "Two Formulas for Fiction: Henry James and H. G. Wells." *CE*, 8 (1946), 7-17.
Bullett, Gerald W. *Modern English Fiction*, 18-33.
Burt, Maxwell S. *The Other Side*, 83-132.
Camberton, Roland. "The Vision of H. G. Wells." *Humanist* (London), 72, 4 (1957), 11-13.
Canby, Henry S. *American Estimates*, 79-89.
―――. *Definitions*, ser. 2, 179-82.
―――. "The Superjournalist." *SatR*, 29 (August 31, 1946), 10-11.
Caudwell, Christopher. *Studies in a Dying Culture*, 73-95.
Chapple, J. A. V. *Documentary and Imaginative Literature*, 263-78.
Chesterton, G. K. *Avowals and Denials*, 213-18.
―――. *Fancies Versus Fads*, 117-23.
―――. *Heretics*, 68-91.
―――. "Patriot of the Planet." *Essays Toward Truth*, 2d ser. Ed. Kenneth A. Robinson, 232-46.
Clarke, Ignatius F. "Science Fiction: Past and Present." *QR*, 295 (1957), 260-70.
―――. *Voices Prophesying War*, 91-103.
Collins, Norman. *The Facts of Fiction*, 258-75.

H. G. Wells, continued

Connes, George A. *A Dictionary of the Characters and Scenes in the Novels, Romances and Short Stories of H. G. Wells.* Dijon: M. Darantiere, 1926; New York: Haskell House, 1971.

Costa, Richard H. "Edwardian Intimations of the Shape of Fiction to Come: Mr. Britling/Job Huss as Wellsian Central Intelligences." *ELT*, 18, 4 (1975), 229-42.

_____. *H. G. Wells.* New York: Twayne, 1967.

_____. "H. G. Wells: Literary Journalist." *JQ*, 28 (1951), 63-68.

_____. "Wells and the Cosmic Despair." *Nation*, 203 (1966), 222-24.

Cross, Wilbur L. *Four Contemporary Novelists*, 157-93.

_____. "The Mind of H. G. Wells." *YR*, 16 (1927), 298-315.

Crowley, C. P. "Failure of Nerve: H. G. Wells." *UWR*, 2, 2 (1967), 1-8.

Dataller, Roger [A. A. Eaglestone]. *The Plain Man and the Novel*, 101-06, 174-75.

Davis, Elmer H. "Notes on the Failure of a Mission." *SatR*, 29 (August 31, 1946), 6-8.

Dewey, John. *Characters and Events*, 78-82.

Dickson, Lovat. *H. G. Wells: His Turbulent Life and Times.* New York: Atheneum, 1969.

Donaghy, Henry J. "Love and Mr. Wells: A Shelleyan Search for the Epipsyche." *SLitI*, 1, 2 (1968), 41-50.

Drinkwater, F. H. "H. G. Wells and War." *Cweal*, 73 (December 30, 1960), 362-64.

Edel, Leon, and Gordon N. Ray, eds. *Henry James and H. G. Wells: A Record of Their Friendship, Their Debate on the Art of Fiction, and Their Quarrel.* Urbana: Univ. of Illinois Press; London: Hart-Davis, 1958.

Ellis, Havelock. *From Marlowe to Shaw*, 297-302.

_____. *Views and Reviews*, 1st ser., 204-12.

Ervine, St. John G. *Some Impressions of My Elders*, 240-63.

Fadiman, Clifton. "The Passing of a Prophet." *SatR*, 29 (August 31, 1946), 3-6.

Flandrau, Charles Macomb. *Prejudices*, 185-203.

Ford, Ford Madox. "H. G. Wells." *AmerM*, 38 (May 1936), 48-58.

_____. *Portraits from Life*, 107-23.

Garnett, David. "Some Writers I Have Known: Galsworthy, Forster, Moore, and Wells." *TQ*, 4, 3 (1961), 190-202.

Gillis, James M. *False Prophets*, 20-44.

Glikin, Gloria. "Through the Novelist's Looking-Glass." *KR*, 31 (1969), 297-319.

Glover, Willis B. "Religious Orientations of H. G. Wells: A Case Study in Scientific Humanism." *HTR*, 65 (1972), 117-35.

Grabo, Carl H. "H. G. Wells: Chronicler, Philosopher and Seer." *New Humanist*, 7, 4 (1934), 1-7.

Gregory, Horace. *The Dying Gladiators*, 113-24.

―――. "H. G. Wells: A Wreath for the Liberal Tradition." *New World Writing*, 11 (1957), 100-10.

Guedalla, Philip. *A Gallery*, 54-61.

"H. G. and G. B. S.: Varied Reflections on Two Edwardian Polymaths." *TLS*, November 27, 1969, 1349.

Hackett, Francis. *Horizons*, 101-38.

―――. "Shaw—and Wells." *Atlantic*, 187 (May 1951), 73-76.

Hamill, Paul. "Conrad, Wells, and the Two Voices." *PMLA*, 89 (1974), 581-82.

Harris, Frank. *Contemporary Portraits*, 3d ser., 1-13.

Harris, Mason. "Science Fiction as Dream and Nightmare of Progress." *WCR*, 9, 4 (1973), 3-9.

Heard, Gerald. "H. G. Wells: The End of a Faith." *SRL*, 31 (March 13, 1948), 9-10, 31.

Henderson, Philip. *The Novel Today*, 103-09.

Hillegas, Mark R. "Cosmic Pessimism in H. G. Wells's Scientific Romances." *PMASAL*, 46, 655-63.

―――. *The Future as Nightmare: H. G. Wells and the Anti-Utopians*. New York: Oxford Univ. Press, 1967.

Holms, John. "H. G. Wells." *Scrutinies*. Ed. Edgell Rickword, 145-60.

Hughes, David Y. "H. G. Wells: Ironic Romancer." *Extrapolation*, 6 (1965), 32-38.

―――. "H. G. Wells and the Charge of Plagiarism." *NCF*, 21 (1966), 85-90.

Hyde, William J. "The Socialism of H. G. Wells in the Early Twentieth Century." *JHI*, 17 (1956), 217-34.

Ingle, Stephen J. "The Political Writing of H. G. Wells." *QQ*, 81 (1974), 396-411.

Jacobs, Robert G. "H. G. Wells, Joseph Conrad, and the Relative Universe." *Conradiana*, 1, 1 (1968), 51-55.

Kagarlitski, J. *The Life and Thought of H. G. Wells*. Tr. Moura Budberg. London: Sidgwick and Jackson, 1966.

Karl, Frederick R. "Conrad, Wells, and the Two Voices." *PMLA*, 88 (1973), 1049-65.

Kauffmann, Stanley. "Wells and the New Generation: The Decline of a Leader of Youth." *CE*, 1 (1940), 573-82.

Kazin, Alfred. "H. G. Wells, America and 'The Future'." *ASch*, 37 (1968), 137-44.

Knight, Grant C. *The Novel in English*, 320-26.

H. G. Wells, continued

Krutch, Joseph Wood. "The Loss of Confidence." *ASch*, 22 (1953), 141-53.
Lemire, Eugene D. "H. G. Wells and the World of Science Fiction." *UWR*, 2, 2 (1967), 59-66.
Lerner, Max. *Actions and Passions*, 16-18.
Lewis, Sinclair. "Our Friend, H.G." *A Sinclair Lewis Reader: The Man from Main Street*. New York: Random House, 1953, 246-53.
Light, Martin. "H. G. Wells and Sinclair Lewis: Friendship, Literary Influence, and Letters." *EFT*, 5, 4 (1962), 1-20.
Lodge, David. "Assessing H. G. Wells." *Encounter*, 28 (January 1967), 54-61.
McFarland, Michael. "Wells's Early Fiction: The Seeds of Utopian Nightmare." *Interp*, 5 (1973), 44-50.
Mackenzie, Norman, and Jeanne Mackenzie. *H. G. Wells: A Biography*. New York: Simon and Schuster, 1973.
McNamara, Eugene. "H. G. Wells as Novelist." *UWR*, 2, 2 (1967), 21-30.
Masur, Gerhard. *Prophets of Yesterday*, 285-91.
Maugham, W. Somerset. "Remembrances of H. G. Wells." *SatR*, 36 (April 11, 1953), 17-19, 68.
———. *The Vagrant Mood*, 209-20.
Mellersh, H. E. L. "H. G. Wells: An Episode." *ContempR*, 224 (1974), 306-12.
Mencken, H. L. *Prejudices*, 1st ser., 22-35.
Moore, Patrick. *Science and Fiction*, 63-70.
Moskowitz, Sam. *Explorers of the Infinite*, 128-41.
Mullen, Richard D. "H. G. Wells and Victor Rousseau Emmanuel: *When the Sleeper Wakes* and *The Messiah of the Cylinder*." *Extrapolation*, 8 (1967), 31-63.
———. "H. G. Wells: The Old Orthodoxy and the New." *RQ*, 3 (1967), 66-68.
Murphy, Dorothy. "Time and the Modern Novel." *WaterR*, 1 (1958), 30-40.
Myers, Walter L. *The Later Realism*, 128-31, 146-48.
Neulieb, Janice. "Technology and Theocracy: The Cosmic Voyages of Wells and Lewis." *Extrapolation*, 16 (1975), 130-36.
Neumann, Henry. "Aldous Huxley and H. G. Wells Seek a Religion." *Standard*, 23 (April 1937), 169-74.
Newbolt, Henry J. *Studies, Green and Gray*, 102-34.
Newell, Kenneth B. *Structure in Four Novels by H. G. Wells*. The Hague: Mouton, 1968.
Nicholson, Norman. *H. G. Wells*. Denver: Swallow, 1950.
———. *Man and Literature*, 49-61.

Nickerson, C. C. "A Note on Some Neglected Opinions of H. G. Wells." *EFT*, 5, 5 (1962), 27-30.

Orwell, George. *Dickens, Dali, and Others*, 115-23.

———. "Wells, Hitler and the World State." *Horizon(L)*, 4 (August 1941), 133-39.

Parr, J. Gordon. "H. G. Wells: His Significance in 1966." *UWR*, 2, 2 (1967), 67-76.

Parrinder, Patrick. *H. G. Wells*. Edinburgh: Oliver and Boyd, 1970.

———, ed. *H. G. Wells: The Critical Heritage*. London: Routledge and K. Paul, 1972.

———. "Imagining the Future: Zamyatin and Wells." *SFS*, 1 (Spring 1973), 17-26.

Philmus, Robert M. "Wells and Borges and the Labyrinths of Time." *SFS*, 1 (1974), 237-48.

Platzner, Robert L. "H. G. Wells' 'Jungle Book': The Influence of Kipling on *The Island of Dr. Moreau*." *VN*, 36 (1969), 19-22.

Priestley, J. B. *Literature and Western Man*, 344-48.

———. "Wells: Light in a Thousand Dark Places." *Horizon(N.Y.)*, 8, 1 (Winter 1966), 32-37.

Quennell, Peter. *The Singular Preference*, 167-81.

Raknem, Ingvald. *H. G. Wells and His Critics*. Oslo: Universitetsforl., 1962.

Ray, Gordon N. *H. G. Wells and Rebecca West*.

———. "H. G. Wells Tries to Be a Novelist." *Edwardians and Late Victorians*. Ed. Richard Ellmann, 106-59.

Raymond, John. "Alive and Kicking." *New Statesman*, 57 (1959), 46.

Rexroth, Kenneth. *Assays*, 114-17.

———. *The Elastic Retort*, 120-23.

———. "The Screw Turns on Mr. James." *Nation*, 187 (August 16, 1958), 76-77.

Rose, Lois, and Stephen Rose. *The Shattered Ring*, 31-39.

Russell, Bertrand. *Portraits from Memory*, 81-85.

Salter, J. A. *Personality in Politics*, 120-37.

Scheik, William J. "If not a Window, At Least a Peephole." *ELT*, 13, 1 (1970), 86-88.

———. "Reality and the Word: The Last Books of H. G. Wells." *ELT*, 12, 3 (1969), 151-54.

———. "The Thing That Is and the Speculative If: The Pattern of Several Motifs in Three Novels by H. G. Wells." *ELT*, 11, 2 (1968), 67-78.

———. "The Womb of Time: Spengler's Influence on Wells's *Apropos of Dolores*." *ELT*, 18, 4 (1975), 217-28.

H. G. Wells, continued

Schonfield, Hugh. "H. G. Wells: Prophet and Seer." *John O'London's Weekly*, 5 (September 28, 1961), 346-47.
Shanks, Edward. *First Essays on Literature*, 148-71.
Sherman, Stuart P. *Critical Woodcuts*, 94-107.
———. "H. G. Wells and the Victorians." *Bookman* (*N. Y.*), 74 (1931), 230-37.
———. *On Contemporary Literature*, 50-84, 104-11.
Slosson, Edwin E. *Six Major Prophets*, 56-128.
Smith, H. "The Mind of the Race." *American Criticism, 1926*. Ed. William A. Drake, 243-50.
Smith, Page. "The Millennial Vision of H. G. Wells." *JHS*, 2 (1969), 23-24.
Snow, C. P. *Variety of Men*, 63-85.
Speare, Morris Edmund. *The Political Novel*, 268-86.
Squire, John C. *Books in General*, 2d ser., 238-43.
Starr, William T. "Romain Rolland and H. G. Wells." *FR*, 30 (1957), 195-200.
Steinberg, M. W. "H. G. Wells as a Social Critic." *UWR*, 2, 2 (1967), 9-20.
Sussman, Herbert L. *Victorians and the Machine*, 162-93.
Suvin, Darko. "Wells as the Turning Point for the SF Tradition." *MinnR*, n.s. 4 (1975), 106-15.
Swan, Michael. *A Small Part of Time*, 173-204.
Swinnerton, Frank A. *Tokefield Papers*, 121-23.
Sykes, W. J. "Is Wells Also Among the Prophets?" *QQ*, 49 (1942), 233-45.
Taylor, A. J. P. "The Man Who Tried to Work Miracles." *Listener*, 76 (1966), 81-84.
Thompson, Edward R. *Portraits of the New Century*, 41-46.
Timko, Michael. "H. G. Wells and 'The Most Unholy Trade'." *ELN*, 1 (1964) 280-84.
Untermeyer, Louis. *Makers of the Modern World*, 345-51.
Vernier, Jean-Pierre. *Wells at the Turn of the Century: From Science Fiction to Anticipation*. Dagenham, Essex: H. G. Wells Society, 1973.
Wagar, W. Warren. "H. G. Wells and the Radicalism of Despair." *SLitI*, 6, 2 (1973), 1-10.
———. *H. G. Wells and the World State*. New Haven, Conn.: Yale Univ. Press, 1961.
———, ed. *H. G. Wells: Journalism and Prophecy, 1893-1946—An Anthology*. Boston: Houghton Mifflin, 1964; London: Bodley Head, 1965.
Walsh, Chad. *From Utopia to Nightmare*, 35-36, 52-57, 89-90.

Watkin, Edward. *Men and Tendencies*, 1-17.

Weeks, Robert P. "Disentanglement as a Theme in H. G. Wells' Fiction." *PMASAL*, 39 (1954), 439-44.

West, Anthony. "The Dark World of H. G. Wells." *Harper's*, 214 (May 1957), 68-73.

_____. "H. G. Wells." *Encounter*, 8 (February 1957), 52-59.

_____. *Principles and Persuasions*, 4-20.

West, Rebecca. *The Strange Necessity*, 199-213.

Whittemore, Reed. *The Fascination of the Abomination*, 129-66.

Williamson, Jack. "H. G. Wells, Critic of Progress." *RQ*, 3 (1967), 6-31, 96-117; *RQ*, 3 (1968), 187-207, 272-93; *RQ*, 4 (1969), 24-33.

_____. *H. G. Wells: Critic of Progress*. Baltimore: Mirage, 1973.

Wilson, Colin. *The Strength to Dream*, 97-100, 111-17, 189-200.

Wilson, Harris, ed. *Arnold Bennett and H. G. Wells: A Record of a Personal and a Literary Friendship*. Urbana: Univ. of Illinois Press; London: Hart-Davis, 1960.

Woodcock, George. "The Darkness Violated by Light: A Revisionist View of H. G. Wells." *MHRev*, 26 (April 1973), 144-60.

Woolf, Virginia. *Collected Essays*, v. 1, 319-37.

"The World of Wells and Bennett." *TLS*, August 28, 1953, xxvi.

Young, George M. *Daylight and Champaign*, 156-58.

Zamyatin, Yevgeny. "H. G. Wells." *Midway*, 10, 1 (1969), 97-126.

_____. *A Soviet Heretic*, 259-90.

See also: Adcock, *Gods*; Beach, *20th*; Beresford; Bergonzi, *Turn*; Bradbury, *Social*; P. Braybrooke, *Philosophies*; Buckley; A. Collins, *20th*; Cunliffe, *Half-Century, 20th Century*; Drew, *Modern*; Eagleton; Edgar, *Art*; Follett and Follett; Forster, *Aspects*; Frierson; Gill; Gillie, *Movements*; Goldring, *Reputations*; J. Gray; Hamilton; Hind, *Authors*; Hynes, *Edwardian*; Lacon; Lodge, *Novelist*; Lovett, *History*; Lynd, *Books*; MacCarthy, *Memories*; Mackenz; W. Phelps; Pritchett, *Living*; Richards; Routh; Scott-James, Macy; Marble; Maugham; Maurois; Orage, *Essays 50, Personality*; Swinnerton, *Background, Georgian*; Wagenknecht, *Cavalcade*; Ward, *20th*; Weygandt; H. Williams, *Modern*; R. Williams, *Novel*; V. Woolf, *Contemporary*.

THE HISTORY OF MR. POLLY

Dessner, Lawrence J. "H. G. Wells, *Mr. Polly*, and the Uses of Art." *ELT*, 16, 2 (1973), 121-34.

Fido, Martin. "Mr. Biswas and Mr. Polly." *ArielE*, 5, 4 (1974), 30-37.

Shenfield, Margaret. "Mr. Biswas and Mr. Polly." *English*, 23 (1974), 95-100.

H. G. Wells, continued

Watson, John Gillard. "The Role of the Writer." *HJ*, 56 (1958), 371-76.
See also: Eagleton.

KIPPS
Newell, Kenneth B. *"Kipps* and the Masterman Episode." *PMLA*, 86 (1971), 1035-36.
Wilson, Harris. "The Death of Masterman: A Repressed Episode in H. G. Wells's *Kipps.*" *PMLA*, 86 (1971), 63-69.

MEN LIKE GODS and
A MODERN UTOPIA
Berneri, Marie Louise. *Journey Through Utopia*, 293-308.
Collins, Christopher. "Zamyatin, Wells and the Utopian Literary Tradition." *SEER*, 44 (1966), 351-60.
Fink, Howard. "Coming up for Air: Orwell's Ambiguous Satire on the Wellsian Utopia." *SLitI*, 6, 2 (1973), 51-60.
Hillegas, Mark R. "Introduction." *A Modern Utopia*, by H. G. Wells [1905]. Lincoln: Univ. of Nebraska Press, 1967, v-xxiv.
Huxley, Julian S. *Essays in Popular Science.* New York: Knopf, 1927, 70-78.
Kaempffert, Waldemar. "Evangelist of Utopia." *SatR*, 29 (August 31, 1946), 8-9.
Leeper, Geoffrey. "The Happy Utopias of Aldous Huxley and H. G. Wells." *Meanjin*, 24 (1965), 120-24.
Westmeyer, Russell E. *Modern Economic and Social Systems*, 90-93.

THE TIME MACHINE
Bergonzi, Bernard. "The Publication of *The Time Machine*, 1894-1895." *Science Fiction: The Other Side of Realism.* Ed. Thomas D. Clareson, 204-15.
―――. *"The Time Machine*: An Ironic Myth." *CritQ*, 2 (1960), 293-305.
Connelly, Wayne C. "H. G. Wells's *The Time Machine*: It's [sic] Neglected Mythos." *RQ*, 5 (1972), 178-91.
Eisenstein, Alex. "Very Early Wells: Origins of Some Major Physical Motifs in *The Time Machine* and *The War of the Worlds.*" *Extrapolation*, 13 (1972), 119-26.
Jacobs, Robert G. "H. G. Wells, Joseph Conrad, and the Relative Universe." *Conradiana*, 1, 1 (1968), 51-55.
Philmus, Robert M. *"The Time Machine*; or, The Fourth Dimension as Prophecy." *PMLA*, 84 (1969), 530-35.
Suvin, Darko. *"The Time Machine* versus *Utopia* as a Structural Model for Science Fiction." *CLS*, 10 (1973), 334-52.

TONO-BUNGAY

Harson, Robert R. "H. G. Wells: The Mordet Island Episode." *Costerus*, 8 (1973), 65-76.

Herbert, Lucille. "*Tono-Bungay*: Tradition and Experiment." *MLQ*, 33 (1972), 140-55.

Lodge, David. *Language of Fiction*, 214-42.

Newell, Kenneth B. "The Structure of H. G. Wells' *Tono-Bungay*." *EFT*, 4, 2 (1961), 1-8.

Poston, Lawrence, III. "*Tono-Bungay*: Wells's Unconstructed Tale." *CE*, 26 (1965), 433-38.

Rogal, Samuel J. "The Biographical Elements in *Tono-Bungay*." *IEY*, 13 (1968), 51-56.

Webb, Max A. "The Missing Father and the Theme of Alienation in H. G. Wells's *Tono-Bungay*." *ELT*, 18, 4 (1975), 243-47.

See also: Kettle.

WAR OF THE WORLDS

Eisenstein, Alex. "Very Early Wells: Origins of Some Major Physical Motifs in *The Time Machine* and *The War of the Worlds*." *Extrapolation*, 13 (1972), 119-26.

Hillegas, Mark. "The First Invasion from Mars." *MAQR*, 66 (1960), 107-12.

Hughes, David Y. "*The War of the Worlds* in the Yellow Press." *JQ*, 43 (1966), 639-46.

THE WORLD OF WILLIAM CLISSOLD

Gillis, James M. *This Our Day*, 83-92.

Keynes, J. M. *Essays in Persuasion*, 349-57.

_____. "One of Wells's Worlds." *New Republic*, 49 (February 2, 1927), 301-03.

Lawrence, D. H. *Selected Literary Criticism*, 133-38.

REBECCA WEST

GENERAL STUDIES

Braybrooke, Patrick. *Novelists: We Are Seven*, 141-56.

Ellmann, Mary. "The Russians of Rebecca West." *Atlantic*, 218 (December 1966), 68-71.

Hutchinson, George E. *Itinerant Ivory Tower*, 241-55.

"In Communion with Reality." *TLS*, December 21, 1973, 1553-55.

Kobler, Turner S. "The Eclecticism of Rebecca West." *Crit*, 13, 2 (1971), 30-49.

Myers, Walter L. *The Later Realism*, 54-57.

Pendry, E. D. *The New Feminism of English Fiction*, 49-50.

Rainer, Dachine. "Rebecca West: Disturber of the Peace." *Cweal*, 88 (1968), 227-30.

Ransom, John Crowe. *World's Body*, 266-69.

Ray, Gordon N. *H. G. Wells and Rebecca West.*

West, Rebecca. "Dame Rebecca West and Marshall McLuhan." *TLS*, July 10, 1969, 754.

————. "Women and Literature, I: And They All Lived Unhappily Ever After." *TLS*, July 26, 1974, 779.

Wolfe, Peter. *Rebecca West: Artist and Thinker.* Carbondale: Southern Illinois Univ. Press, 1971.

See also: Adcock, *Glory*; Allen, *Tradition*; P. Braybrooke, *Philosophies*; J. Collins, *Doctor*; Overton, *Authors*; Swinnerton, *Georgian*; Vines.

T. H. WHITE

GENERAL STUDIES

Cameron, J. R. "T. H. White in Camelot: The Matter of Britain Revitalized." *HAB*, 16, 1 (1965), 45-48.

Crane, John K. *T. H. White.* New York: Twayne, 1974.

Dunn, Stephen P. "Mr. White, Mr. Williams, and the Matter of Britain." *KR*, 24 (1962), 363-71.

Floyd, Barbara. "A Critique of T. H. White's *The Once and Future King*." *RQ*, 1 (1965), 175-80; 2 (1966), 54-57, 127-33, 210-13.

Garnett, David, ed. *The White/Garnett Letters.* New York: Viking, 1968.

High-Jones, Siriol. "A Visible Export: T. H. White, Merlyn's Latest Pupil." *TLS*, August 7, 1959, ix.

Molin, Sven E. "Appraisals: T. H. White, 1906-1964." *JIL*, 2, 2-3 (1973), 142-50.

Swanson, Donald R. "The Uses of Tradition: King Arthur in the Modern World." *CEA*, 36, 3 (1974), 19-21.

Warner, Sylvia T. *T. H. White: A Biography.* London: J. Cape with Chatto and Windus, 1967; New York: Viking, 1968.

West, Richard. "Contemporary Medieval Authors." *Orcrist*, 3 (1969), 9-10, 15.

CHARLES WILLIAMS

GENERAL STUDIES

Auden, W. H. "Charles Williams: A Review Article." *ChC*, 73 (May 2, 1956), 552-54.

Beaumont, Ernest. "Charles Williams and the Power of Eros." *DubR*, 233 (1959), 61-74.

Boies, J. J. "Existential Exchange in the Novels of Charles Williams." *Renascence*, 26 (1974), 219-29.

Bolling, Douglass. "Imagery of Light and Darkness in Charles Williams' *Many Dimensions.*" *BSUF*, 14, 4 (1973), 69-73.

Borrow, Antony. "The Affirmation of Images: An Examination of the Novels of Charles Williams." *Nine*, 3, 4 (1952), 325-54.

Carmichael, Douglas. "Love and Rejection in Charles Williams." *Universitas*, 2 (1964), 14-22.

Cavaliero, Glen. "The Way of Affirmation: A Study of the Writing of Charles Williams." *CQR*, 157 (1956), 19-28.

Conquest, Robert. "The Art of the Enemy." *EIC*, 7 (1957), 42-55.

Dawson, Lawrence R., Jr. "Reflections of Charles Williams on Fiction." *BSTCF*, 5, 1 (1964), 23-29.

Dunn, Stephen P. "Mr. White, Mr. Williams, and the Matter of Britain." *KR*, 24 (1962), 363-71.

Frost, Naomi. "Life after Death: Visions of Lewis and Williams." *CSLBull*, 6, 6 (1975), 2-6.

GoodKnight, Glen. "A Comparison of Cosmological Geography in the Works of J. R. R. Tolkien, C. S. Lewis, and Charles Williams." *Mythlore*, 1, 3 (1969), 18-22.

————. "The Social History of the Inklings, J. R. R. Tolkien, C. S. Lewis, and Charles Williams." *Mythlore*, 2, 1 (1970), 7-9.

Hadfield, Alice Mary. *An Introduction to Charles Williams.* London: Robert Hale, 1959.

————. "The Relationship of Charles Williams' Working Life to His Fiction." *Shadows of Imagination.* Ed. Mark R. Hillegas, 125-38.

Hartley, L. P. "The Novels of Charles Williams." *T&T*, 27 (1947), 628-30.

Heath-Stubbs, John. *Charles Williams.* London: Longmans, Green, 1955.

Heppenstall, Rayner. "The Works of Charles Williams." *New Statesman*, 37 (1949), 532, 534.

Holder, Robert C. "Art and the Artist in the Fiction of Charles Williams." *Renascence*, 27 (1975), 81-87.

Huttar, Charles A. "Charles Williams, Novelist and Prophet." *GorR*, 10 (1967), 51-75.

Irwin, W. R. "Christian Doctrine and the Tactics of Romance: The Case of Charles Williams." *Shadows of Imagination.* Ed. Mark R. Hillegas, 139-49.

————. "There and Back Again: The Romances of Williams, Lewis, and Tolkien." *SR*, 69 (1961), 566-78.

Kilby, Clyde S. "Tolkien, Lewis, and Williams." *Mythcon 1: Proceedings.* Ed. Glen GoodKnight, 3-4.

Lewis, C. S. , ed. *Essays Presented to Charles Williams.* London: Oxford Univ. Press, 1947; Grand Rapids, Mich.: Eerdmans, 1966.

Moorman, Charles. *Arthurian Triptych*, 38-101.

_____. "Myth in the Novels of Charles Williams." *MFS*, 3 (1957), 321-27.

_____. *The Precincts of Felicity*, 19-64.

Morris, John S. "Fantasy in a Mythless Age." *Children's Literature: The Great Excluded*, v. 2. Ed. Francelia Butler, 77-86.

Myers, Doris T. "Brave New World: The Status of Women According to Tolkien, Lewis, and Williams." *CimR*, 17 (1971), 13-19.

Parsons, Geoffrey. "The Spirit of Charles Williams." *Atlantic*, 184 (November 1949), 77-79.

Peoples, Galen. "The Agnostic in the Whirlwind: The Seven Novels of Charles Williams." *Mythlore*, 2, 2 (1970), 10-15.

Pitt, Valerie. "Charles Williams: The Affirmation of Images." *Mandrake*, 3 (May 1946), 27-33.

Purtill, Richard. *Lord of the Elves and Eldils*, 208-11.

Reilly, Robert J. *Romantic Religion*, 148-89.

Ridler, Anne B. "Introduction." *Image of the City and Other Essays*, by Charles Williams, ix-lxxii.

Sale, Roger. "England's Parnassus: C. S. Lewis, Charles Williams, and J. R. R. Tolkien." *HudR*, 17 (1964), 203-25.

Shideler, Mary McDermott. *Charles Williams: A Critical Essay.* Grand Rapids, Mich.: Eerdmans, 1966.

_____. *The Theology of Romantic Love: A Study of the Writings of Charles Williams.* New York: Harper, 1962.

Spacks, Patricia M. "Charles Williams: A Novelist's Pilgrimage." *Religion in Life*, 29 (1960), 277-88.

_____. "Charles Williams: The Fusions of Fiction." *Shadows of Imagination.* Ed. Mark R. Hillegas, 150-59.

Spanos, William V. "Charles Williams' *Judgement at Chelmsford*: A Study in the Aesthetic of Sacramental Time." *ChS*, 45 (1962), 107-17.

_____. "Charles Williams' *Seed of Adam*: The Existential Flight from Death." *ChS*, 49 (1966), 105-18.

Trowbridge, Clinton W. "The Beatricean Character in the Novels of Charles Williams." *SR*, 79 (1971), 335-43.

Urang, Gunnar. *Shadows of Heaven*, 51-92.

Versinger, Georgette. "Charles Williams." *EA*, 18 (1965), 285-95.

Wandall, Frederick S. "Charles Williams." *Minor British Novelists.* Ed. Charles A. Hoyt, 121-34.

Winship, George P., Jr. "The Novels of Charles Williams." *Shadows of Imagination.* Ed. Mark R. Hillegas, 111-24.

―――. "This Rough Magic: The Novels of Charles Williams." *YR,* 40 (1950), 285-96.

Wright, Marjorie E. "The Vision of Cosmic Order in the Oxford Mythmakers." *Imagination and the Spirit.* Ed. Charles A. Huttar, 259-76.

See also: Fuller, *Books.*

ALL HALLOWS' EVE
Davidson, Clifford. "Williams' *All Hallows' Eve*: The Way of Perversity." *Renascence,* 20 (1968), 86-93.

Sellery, J'nan. "Fictive Modes in Charles Williams' *All Hallows' Eve.*" *Genre,* 1 (1968), 316-31.

DESCENT INTO HELL
Crowley, Cornelius P. "The Structural Pattern of Charles Williams' *Descent into Hell.*" *PMASAL,* 39 (1953), 421-28.

LaLande, Sister M., S.S.N.D. "Williams' Pattern of Time in *Descent Into Hell.*" *Renascence,* 15 (1963), 88-95.

McMichael, Barbara. "Hell Is Oneself: An Examination of the Concept of Damnation in Charles Williams' *Descent into Hell.*" *SLitI,* 1, 2 (1968), 59-71.

THE GREATER TRUMPS
Hinz, Evelyn J. "An Introduction to *The Greater Trumps.*" *ESC,* 1 (1975), 217-29.

Thrash, Lois G. "A Source for the Redemption Theme in *The Cocktail Party.*" *TSLL,* 9 (1968), 547-53.

ANGUS WILSON

INTERVIEWS
Biles, Jack I. "A *Studies in the Novel* Interview: An Interview in London with Angus Wilson." *SNNTS,* 2 (1970), 76-87.

Drescher, Horst W. "Angus Wilson: An Interview." *NS,* 17 (1968), 351-56.

Firchow, Peter. *The Writer's Place,* 331-52.

Kermode, Frank. "The House of Fiction: Interviews with Seven English Novelists." *PR,* 30 (1963), 61-82.

McDowell, Frederick P. W. "An Interview with Angus Wilson." *IowaR,* 3, 4 (1972), 77-105.

Millgate, Michael. "Angus Wilson." *Paris Review. Writers at Work,* 1st ser., 251-66.

Angus Wilson, continued

Narita, Seiju. "A Reformer, not a Revolutionary." *EigoS*, 115 (1969) 752-59.
Poston, Lawrence, III. "A Conversation with Angus Wilson." *BA*, 40 (1966), 29-31.

GENERAL STUDIES

Bowen, John. "One Man's Meat: The Idea of Individual Responsibility." *TLS*, August 7, 1959, xii-xiii.
Burgess, Anthony. "Powers That Be." *Encounter*, 24 (January 1965), 71-76.
Cockshut, A. O. J. "Favoured Sons: The Moral World of Angus Wilson." *EIC*, 9 (1959), 50-60.
Cox, Charles B. *The Free Spirit*, 117-53.
———. "The Humanism of Angus Wilson: A Study of *Hemlock and After*." *CritQ*, 3 (1961), 227-37.
Edelstein, Arthur. "Angus Wilson: The Territory Behind." *Contemporary British Novelists*. Ed. Charles Shapiro, 144-61.
Gindin, James J. "The Reassertion of the Personal." *TQ*, 1, 4 (1958), 126-34.
Gransden, Karl W. *Angus Wilson*. London: Longmans, Green, 1969.
"The Green and Brown Revolution." *TLS*, June 1, 1973, 605.
Halio, Jay. *Angus Wilson*. Edinburgh: Oliver and Boyd, 1964.
———. "The Novels of Angus Wilson." *MFS*, 8 (1962), 171-81.
Katona, Anna. "Angus Wilson's Fiction and its Relation to the English Tradition." *ALitASH*, 10 (1968), 111-27.
Kermode, Frank. "Mr. Wilson's People." *Spectator*, 201 (November 21, 1958), 705-06.
———. "Myth, Reality, and Fiction." *Listener*, 68 (1962), 311-13.
Mander, John. *The Writer and Commitment*, 111-52.
Oakland, John. "Angus Wilson and Evil in the English Novel." *Renascence*, 26 (1973), 24-36.
Riddell, Edwin. "The Humanist Character in Angus Wilson." *English*, 21 (1972), 45-53.
Rippier, Joseph S. *Some Postwar English Novelists*, 19-45.
Scott-Kilvert, Ian. "Angus Wilson." *REL*, 1, 2 (1960), 42-53.
Smith, William J. "Angus Wilson's England." *Cweal*, 82 (1965), 18-21.
Taylor, Griffin. "What Does It Profit a Man. . . ?" *SR*, 66 (1958), 132-46.
Wilson, Edmund. *The Bit Between My Teeth*, 270-74.
See also: Allen, *Tradition*; Bergonzi, *Situation*; Fraser; Gindin, *Postwar, Harvest*; Karl; Kermode; McCormick; Rabinovitz.

THE MIDDLE AGE OF MRS. ELIOT

Fletcher, John. "Women in Crises: Louise and Mrs. Eliot." *CritQ*, 15 (1973), 157-70.

Raymond, John. *The Doge of Dover*, 170-78.

Shaw, Valerie A. "*The Middle Age of Mrs. Eliot* and *Late Call*: Angus Wilson's Traditionalism." *CritQ*, 12 (1970), 9-27.

See also: Kermode.

NO LAUGHING MATTER

Gillie, Christopher. "The Shape of Modern Fiction: Angus Wilson's *No Laughing Matter*." *Delta*, 43 (1968), 18-23.

Kums, Guido. "Reality in Fiction: *No Laughing Matter*." *ES*, 53 (1972), 523-31.

Parrinder, Patrick. "Pastiche and After." *CambR*, 89A (1967), 66-67.

"Playing the Game." *TLS*, October 5, 1967, 933.

Servotte, Herman. "A Note on the Formal Characteristics of Angus Wilson's *No Laughing Matter*." *ES*, 50 (1969), 58-64.

Sudrann, Jean. "The Lion and the Unicorn: Angus Wilson's Triumphant Tragedy." *SNNTS*, 3 (1971), 390-400.

Trickett, Rachel. "Recent Novels: Craftsmanship in Violence and Sex." *YR*, 57 (1968), 438-52.

See also: Bradbury, *Possibilities*.

THE OLD MEN AT THE ZOO

Halio, Jay L. "Angus Wilson: *The Old Men at the Zoo*." *Crit*, 5, 1 (1962), 77-82.

Lindberg, Margaret. "Angus Wilson: *The Old Men at the Zoo* as Allegory." *IEY*, 14 (1969), 44-48.

Pritchett, V. S. "Bad-Hearted Britain." *New Statesman*, 62 (1961), 429-30.

Symons, Julian. "Politics and the Novel." *TC*, 170 (1962), 147-54.

COLIN WILSON

GENERAL STUDIES

Allsop, Kenneth. *The Angry Decade*, 156-92.

Campion, Sidney. *The World of Colin Wilson*. London: Muller, 1963.

Dillard, R. H. W. "Toward an Existential Realism: The Novels of Colin Wilson." *HC*, 4, 4 (1967), 1-12.

Kegel, Charles H. "Shelley and Colin Wilson." *KSJ*, 9 (1960), 125-30.

Malcolm, Donald. "First, Get Yourself Crucified." *New Republic*, 135 (November 5, 1956), 18-19.

Glicksberg, Charles I. "The Literature of the Angry Young Men."
    ColQ, 8 (1960), 293-303.
Priestley, J. B. "Thoughts on *The Outsider*." *New Statesman*, 52
    (1956), 10-11.
Weigel, John A. *Colin Wilson*. Boston: Twayne, 1975.
Widmer, Kingsley. *The Literary Rebel*, 164-67, 173-74, 240-41.
Wilson, Colin. "Beyond the Outsider." *Declaration*. Ed. Tom Masch-
    ler, 29-59.
––––––. *Voyage to a Beginning: An Intellectual Autobiography*. New
    York: Crown, 1969.
––––––. "The Writer and Publicity." *Encounter*, 13 (November 1959),
    8-13.
See also: Gindin, *Postwar*.

VIRGINIA WOOLF

BIBLIOGRAPHIES

Weiser, Barbara. "Criticism of Virginia Woolf from 1956 to the Pres-
    ent: A Selected Checklist with an Index to Studies of Separate
    Works." *MFS*, 18 (1972), 477-86.

SPECIAL ISSUES

Adam International Review [*Adam*], 37, 364-66 (1972).
Modern Fiction Studies [*MFS*], 2, 1 (1956).
Modern Fiction Studies [*MFS*], 18, 3 (1972).

GENERAL STUDIES

Alexander, Jean. *Venture of Form in the Novels of Virginia Woolf*.
    Port Washington, N.Y.: Kennikat, 1974.
Alves, Leonard. "The Relevance of Virginia Woolf." *ELLS*, 12 (1975),
    31-65.
Ariail, Jacqueline A. "An Elegy for Androgyny." *IEY*, 24, 3 (1974),
    13-20.
Batchelor, J. B. "Feminism in Virginia Woolf." *English*, 17 (1968), 1-7.
Bazin, Nancy T. *Virginia Woolf and the Androgynous Vision*. New
    Brunswick, N.J.: Rutgers Univ. Press, 1973.
––––––. "Virginia Woolf's Quest for Equilibrium." *MLQ*, 32 (1971),
    305-19.
Beach, Joseph Warren. "Virginia Woolf." *EJ*, 26 (1937), 603-12.
Beck, Warren. "For Virginia Woolf." *American Prefaces*, 7, 4 (1942),
    316-27; *Forms of Modern Fiction*. Ed. William Van O'Connor,
    243-53.

Beede, Margaret. "Virginia Woolf: Romantic." *NDQ*, 27, 1 (1959), 21-29.

Beja, Morris. "Matches Struck in the Dark: Virginia Woolf's Moments of Vision." *CritQ*, 6 (1964), 137-52.

Bell, Millicent. "Virginia Woolf Now." *MR*, 14 (1973), 655-87.

Bell, Quentin. *Virginia Woolf: A Biography*. New York: Harcourt, 1972.

Bennett, Joan. *Virginia Woolf: Her Act as a Novelist*. Cambridge: Cambridge Univ. Press, 1945, 1964.

Blackstone, Bernard. *Virginia Woolf*. London: Longmans, Green, 1962.

―――. *Virginia Woolf: A Commentary*. London: Hogarth; New York: Harcourt, 1949.

Bowen, Elizabeth. "The Achievement of Virginia Woolf." *Highlights of Modern Literature*. Ed. Francis Brown, 109-13.

Brace, Marjorie. "Worshipping Solid Objects: The Pagan World of Virginia Woolf." *ACCENT Anthology*. Ed. Kerker Quinn and Charles Shattuck, 489-95.

Bradbrook, Frank W. "Virginia Woolf: The Theory and Practice of Fiction." *The Pelican Guide to English Literature*, v. 7. Ed. Boris Ford, 275-87.

Bradbrook, M. C. "Notes on the Style of Virginia Woolf." *Scrutiny*, 1 (1932), 33-38.

Brewster, Dorothy. *Virginia Woolf*. New York: New York Univ. Press, 1962.

Brogan, Howard O. "Science and Narrative Structure in Austen, Hardy and Woolf." *NCF*, 11 (1957), 276-87.

Brophy, Brigid. *Don't Never Forget*, 182-85.

Brower, Reuben A. "The Novel as Poem: Virginia Woolf—Exploring a Critical Metaphor." *The Interpretation of Narrative*. Ed. Morton W. Bloomfield, 229-47.

Brown, Robert Curtis. "Laurence Sterne and Virginia Woolf: A Study in Literary Continuity." *UKCR*, 26 (1959), 153-59.

Burgum, Edwin B. *The Novel and the World's Dilemma*, 120-39.

Cecil, David. *Poets and Storytellers*, 160-80.

Chambers, R. L. *The Novels of Virginia Woolf*. London: Oliver and Boyd, 1947; New York: Russell and Russell, 1971.

Chapman, Robert T. "The 'Enemy' vs. Bloomsbury." *Adam*, 37, 364-66 (1972), 81-84.

Church, Margaret. "Concepts of Time in Novels of Virginia Woolf and Aldous Huxley." *MFS*, 1, 2 (1955), 19-24.

―――. *Time and Reality*, 67-101.

Virginia Woolf, continued

Cornwell, Edith F. *The "Still Point,"* 159-207.
Coveney, Peter. *Poor Monkey,* 259-66.
Cox, Charles B. *The Free Spirit,* 103-16.
———. "The Solitude of Virginia Woolf." *CritQ,* 1 (1959), 329-34.
Dahl, Liisa. *Linguistic Features of the Stream-of-Consciousness Techniques of James Joyce, Virginia Woolf and Eugene O'Neill.*
Daiches, David. *Virginia Woolf.* Norfolk, Conn.: New Directions, 1942.
Deiman, Werner J. "History, Pattern, and Continuity in Virginia Woolf." *ConL,* 15 (1974), 49-66.
Doner, Dean. "Virginia Woolf: The Service of Style." *MFS,* 2, 1 (1956), 1-12.
Eliot, T. S. "Virginia Woolf: I." *Horizon,* 3 (May 1941), 313-16.
Empson, William. "Virginia Woolf." *Scrutinies,* v. 2. Ed. Edgell Rickword, 203-16.
Enright, Dennis J. *The Apothecary's Shop,* 168-86.
Evans, B. Ifor. *English Literature Between the Wars,* 68-74.
Farwell, Marilyn R. "Virginia Woolf and Androgyny." *ConL,* 16 (1975), 433-51.
Fischer, Greti K. "Edward Albee and Virginia Woolf." *DR,* 49 (1969), 196-207.
Fishman, Solomon. "Virginia Woolf on the Novel." *SR,* 51 (1943), 321-40.
Fleishman, Avrom. *Virginia Woolf: A Critical Study.* Baltimore: Johns Hopkins Press, 1975.
———. "Virginia Woolf: Tradition and Modernity." *Forms of Modern British Fiction.* Ed. Alan W. Friedman, 133-63.
———. "Woolf and McTaggart." *ELH,* 36 (1969), 719-38.
Forster, E. M. *Abinger Harvest,* 106-15.
———. "E. M. Forster on Virginia Woolf." *Novelists on Novelists.* Ed. Louis Kronenberger, 242-58.
———. *Two Cheers for Democracy,* 242-58.
———. *Virginia Woolf.* Cambridge: Cambridge Univ. Press, 1942.
Francis, Herbert E., Jr. "Virginia Woolf and 'The Moment'." *EUQ,* 16 (1960), 139-51.
Franks, Gabriel. "Virginia Woolf and the Philosophy of G. E. Moore." *Person,* 50 (1969), 222-40.
Freedman, Ralph. *The Lyrical Novel: Studies in Hermann Hesse, André Gide, and Virginia Woolf.* Princeton, N.J.: Princeton Univ. Press, 1963, 185-270.
Friedman, Melvin J. *Stream of Consciousness,* 178-209.
———. "Three Experiences of the War: A Triptych." *Promise of Greatness.* Ed. George A. Panichas, 541-55.

Friedman, Norman. "Criticism and the Novel: Hardy, Hemingway, Crane, Woolf, and Conrad." *AR*, 18 (1958), 343-70.

Garnett, David. "Virginia Woolf." *ASch*, 34 (Summer 1965), 371-86.

Gillespie, Diane F. "Virginia Woolf and the 'Reign of Error'." *RS*, 43 (1975), 222-34.

Goldman, Mark. "Virginia Woolf and E. M. Forster: A Critical Dialogue." *TSLL*, 7 (1966), 387-400.

———. "Virginia Woolf and the Critic as Reader." *PMLA*, 80 (1965), 275-84.

Graham, John. "A Negative Note on Bergson and Virginia Woolf." *EIC*, 6 (1956), 70-74.

———. "Time in the Novels of Virginia Woolf." *UTQ*, 18 (1949), 186-201.

Grant, Duncan. "Virginia Woolf." *Horizon*, 3 (June 1941), 402-06; *Golden Horizon*. Ed. Cyril Connolly, 390-94.

Gregory, Horace. *Spirit of Time and Place*, 175-79.

Grindea, Miron. "The Stuff of Which Legends Are Made." *Adam*, 37, 364-66 (1972), 2-14.

Gruber, Ruth. *Virginia Woolf: A Study*. Leipzig: Tauchnitz, 1935.

Guiguet, Jean. *Virginia Woolf and Her Works*. Tr. Jean Stewart. London: Hogarth; New York: Harcourt, 1965.

Hafley, James. *The Glass Roof: Virginia Woolf as a Novelist. UCPES*, 9 (1954).

Hale, Nancy. "Half-Glimpses of Genius." *VQR*, 49 (1973), 309-12.

Hardwick, Elizabeth. *Seduction and Betrayal*, 125-39.

Hartman, Geoffrey H. "Virginia's Web." *ChiR*, 14, 4 (1961), 20-32.

Hawkins, Ethel Wallace. "The Stream of Consciousness Novel." *Atlantic*, 138 (September 1926), 356-60.

Heffmann, Charles F. " 'From Lunch to Dinner': Virginia Woolf's Apprenticeship." *TSLL*, 10 (1969), 609-27.

Heine, Elizabeth. "The Significance of Structure in the Novels of E. M. Forster and Virginia Woolf." *ELT*, 16 (1973), 289-306.

Henderson, Philip. *The Novel Today*, 87-96.

Henig, Suzanne. "D. H. Lawrence and Virginia Woolf." *DHLR*, 2 (1969), 265-71.

———. "Virginia Woolf and Lady Murasaki." *LE&W*, 11 (1967), 421-23.

Hildick, Wallace. "In That Solitary Room." *KR*, 27 (1965), 302-17.

Holtby, Winifred. *Virginia Woolf*. London: Wishart, 1932.

Humphrey, Robert. *Stream of Consciousness Technique*, 12-14, 31-33, 54-56, 99-104.

Virginia Woolf, continued

Hyman, Virginia R. "The Metamorphosis of Leslie Stephen: 'Those are pearls that were his eyes'." *VWQ*, 2, 1-2 (1975), 48-65.

Hynes, Samuel. "The Whole Contention Between Mr. Bennett and Mrs. Woolf." *Novel*, 1 (1967), 34-44.

Johnson, Manly. *Virginia Woolf*. New York: Ungar, 1973.

Johnstone, J. K. "World War I and the Novels of Virginia Woolf." *Promise of Greatness*. Ed. George A. Panichas, 528-40.

Jones, E. B. C. "E. M. Forster and Virginia Woolf." *The English Novelists*. Ed. Derek Verschoyle, 281-97.

Josephson, Matthew. "Virginia Woolf and the Modern Novel." *New Republic*, 66 (April 15, 1931), 239-41.

Joyner, Nancy. "The Underside of the Butterfly: Lessing's Debt to Woolf." *JNT*, 4 (1974), 204-11.

Kaplan, Sydney Janet. *Feminine Consciousness in the Modern British Novel*, 76-109.

Kelley, Alice van Buren. *The Novels of Virginia Woolf: Fact and Vision*. Chicago: Univ. of Chicago Press, 1973.

Kreutz, Irving. "Mr. Bennett and Mrs. Woolf." *MFS*, 8 (1962), 103-15.

Kumar, Shiv K. *Bergson and the Stream of Consciousness Novel*, 64-102.

———. "Virginia Woolf and Bergson's *'memoire par excellence'*." *ES*, 41 (1960), 313-18.

Lakshmi, Vijay. "The Solid and the Intangible: Virginia Woolf's Theory of the Androgynous Mind." *LCrit*, 10, 1 (1971), 28-34.

———. "The Unviewed Room: An Interpretation of the Room Analogy in Virginia Woolf's Critical Writings." *RUSEng*, 6 (1972), 64-69.

———. "Virginia Woolf and E. M. Forster: A Study of Their Critical Relations." *LHY*, 12, 2 (1971), 39-49; "Virginia Woolf and E. M. Forster: A Study in Inter-Criticism." *BP*, 16 (1971), 8-18.

Latham, Jacqueline E. M., ed. *Critics on Virginia Woolf: Readings in Literary Criticism*. Coral Gables, Fla.: Univ. of Miami Press; London: Allen and Unwin, 1970.

Lawrence, Margaret. *The School of Femininity*, 373-82.

Lehmann, John. *The Open Night*, 23-33.

———. "Virginia Woolf." *Writers of To-day, 2*. Ed. Denys Val Baker, 73-85.

———. *Virginia Woolf and Her World*. London: Thames and Hudson, 1975.

Lewis, Thomas, ed. *Virginia Woolf: A Collection of Criticism*. New York: McGraw-Hill, 1975.

Lewis, Wyndham. *Men Without Art*, 158-71.

Lorberg, Aileen D. "Virginia Woolf, Benevolent Satirist." *Person*, 33 (1952), 148-58.

Lund, Mary Graham. "The Androgynous Moment: Woolf and Eliot." *Renascence*, 12 (1960), 74-78.

Macauley, Rose. "Virginia Woolf: II." *Horizon*, 3 (May 1941), 316-18; *Golden Horizon*. Ed. Cyril Connolly, 394-96.

McIntyre, Clara F. "Is Virginia Woolf a Feminist?" *Person*, 41 (1960), 176-84.

McLaurin, Allen. *Virginia Woolf: The Echoes Enslaved*. New York: Cambridge Univ. Press, 1973.

Majumdar, Robin. "Virginia Woolf and Thoreau." *TSB*, 109 (1969), 4-5.

_____, and Allen McLaurin, eds. *Virginia Woolf: The Critical Heritage*. London: Routledge and K. Paul, 1975.

Manuel, M. "Virginia Woolf as the Common Reader." *LCrit*, 7, 2 (1966), 28-32.

Marder, Herbert. *Feminism and Art: A Study of Virginia Woolf*. Chicago: Univ. of Chicago Press, 1968.

_____. "Virginia Woolf's 'System That Did Not Shut Out'." *PLL*, 4 (1968), 106-11.

Melchiori, Giorgio. *The Tightrope Walkers*, 175-87.

Mellers, W. H. "Virginia Woolf: The Last Phase." *KR*, 4 (1942), 381-87.

Mendez, Charlotte W. "I Need a Little Language." *VWQ*, 1, 1 (1972), 87-105.

Millett, Fred B. "Feminine Fiction." *Cornhill*, 155 (1937), 225-35.

Monroe, N. Elizabeth. "The Inception of Mrs. Woolf's Art." *CE*, 2 (1940), 217-30.

_____. *The Novel and Society*, 188-224.

Moody, Anthony D. *Virginia Woolf*. Edinburgh: Oliver and Boyd; New York: Grove, 1963.

Moore, Geoffrey. "The Significance of Bloomsbury." *KR*, 17 (1955), 119-29.

Muir, Edwin. *Transition*, 67-82.

Muller, Herbert J. "Virginia Woolf and Feminine Fiction." *SatR*, 15 (February 6, 1937), 3-4, 14, 16.

Naremore, James. "A World Without a Self: The Novels of Virginia Woolf." *Novel*, 5 (1972), 122-34.

_____. *The World Without a Self: Virginia Woolf and the Novel*. New Haven, Conn.: Yale Univ. Press, 1973.

Newton, Deborah. *Virginia Woolf*. Melbourne: Melbourne Univ. Press, 1946.

Noble, Joan R., ed. *Recollections of Virginia Woolf*. New York: Morrow, 1972.

Novak, Jane. *The Razor Edge of Balance: A Study of Virginia Woolf*. Coral Gables, Fla.: Univ. of Miami Press, 1974.

Oates, Joyce Carol. *New Heaven, New Earth*, 9-36.

Virginia Woolf, continued

O'Connor, William Van. "Toward a History of Bloomsbury." *SWR*, 40 (1955), 36-52.

Olson, Stanley. "North from Richmond, South from Bloomsbury." *Adam*, 37, 364-66 (1972), 70-74.

Pachmuss, Temira. "Dostoevsky, Werfel, and Virginia Woolf: Influences and Confluences." *CLS*, 9 (1972), 416-28.

Painter, George. "Proust and Virginia Woolf." *Adam*, 37, 364-66 (1972), 17-23.

Pendry, E. D. *The New Feminism of English Fiction*, 27-45.

Phelps, Gilbert. *The Russian Novel in English Fiction*, 132-37.

Pippett, Aileen. *The Moth and the Star: A Biography of Virginia Woolf*. Boston: Little, Brown, 1955.

Plomer, William. "Virginia Woolf: IV." *Horizon*, 3 (May 1941), 323-27.

Porter, Katherine Anne. *The Collected Essays*, 68-71.

Pratt, Annis. "Women and Nature in Modern Fiction." *ConL*, 13 (1972), 476-90.

Rahv, Philip. *Image and Idea*, 139-43.

――――. *Literature and the Sixth Sense*, 326-30.

Ramsay, Warren. "The Claims of Language: Virginia Woolf as Symbolist." *EFT*, 4, 1 (1961), 12-17.

Rantavaara, Irma. *Virginia Woolf and Bloomsbury*. Helsinki: Suomalainen Tiediakatemia, 1953.

Richter, Harvena. *Virginia Woolf: The Inward Voyage*. Princeton, N.J.: Princeton Univ. Press, 1970.

Ridley, Hilda. "Leslie Stephen's Daughter." *DR*, 33 (1953), 65-72.

Roberts, John H. "Towards Virginia Woolf." *VQR*, 10 (1934), 587-602.

――――. " 'Vision and Design' in Virginia Woolf." *PMLA*, 61 (1946), 835-47.

Rogat, Ellen H. "A Form of One's Own." *Mosaic*, 8, 1 (1975), 77-90.

――――. "The Virgin in the Bell Biography." *TCL*, 20 (1974), 96-113.

Rosenbaum, S. P. "The Philosophical Realism of Virginia Woolf." *English Literature and British Philosophy*. Ed. S. P. Rosenbaum, 316-56.

Rubenstein, Roberta. "The Evolution of an Image: Virginia Woolf and the 'Globe of Life'." *AntigR*, 15 (1973), 43-50.

――――. "Virginia Woolf and the Russian Point of View." *CLS*, 9 (1972), 196-206.

――――. "Virginia Woolf, Chekhov, and *The Rape of the Lock*." *DR*, 54 (1974), 429-35.

Sackville-West, V. "Virginia Woolf: III." *Horizon*, 3 (May 1941), 318-23.

Sakamoto, Tadanobu. " 'Modern Novels' and 'Modern Fiction': A Study of Some Discrepancies." *SELit*, 43 (1967), 215-28.

Samuelson, Ralph. "More Than One Room of Her Own: Virginia Woolf's Critical Dilemmas." *WHR*, 19 (1965), 249-56.

Savage, Derek S. *The Withered Branch*, 70-105.

Schaefer, Joseph O'Brien. *The Three-Fold Nature of Reality in the Novels of Virginia Woolf*. The Hague: Mouton, 1965.

Schneider, Daniel J. *Symbolism: The Manichean Vision*, 119-51.

Scott, Nathan A., Jr. "The Bias of Comedy and the Narrow Escape into Faith." *ChS*, 44 (1961), 9-39.

Shoukri, Doris E.-C. "The Nature of Being in Woolf and Duras." *ConL*, 12 (1971), 317-28.

Showalter, Elaine. "Killing the Angel in the House: The Autonomy of Women Writers." *AR*, 32 (1973), 339-53.

Simon, Irene. "Some Aspects of Virginia Woolf's Imagery." *ES*, 41 (1960), 180-96.

Smart, J. A. E. "Virginia Woolf." *DR*, 21 (1941), 37-50.

Smith, J. Oates. "Henry James and Virginia Woolf: The Art of Relationships." *TCL*, 10 (1964), 119-29.

Sprague, Claire, ed. *Virginia Woolf: A Collection of Critical Essays*. Englewood Cliffs, N.J.: Prentice-Hall, 1971.

Stamirowska, Krystyna. "Virginia Woolf's Concept of Reality and Some Theories of Her Time." *KN*, 22 (1975), 207-17.

Steele, Philip L. "Virginia Woolf's Spiritual Autobiography." *Topic*, 18 (1969), 64-74.

Steinberg, Erwin R. "Freudian Symbolism and Communication." *L&P*, 3, 2 (1953), 2-5.

Sugiyama, Yoku. *Rainbow and Granite: A Study of Virginia Woolf*. Tokyo: Hokuseido, 1973.

Thakur, N. C. *The Symbolism of Virginia Woolf*. New York: Oxford Univ. Press, 1965.

Toynbee, Philip. "The Best and the Worst, I: Virginia Woolf—A Study of Three Experimental Novels." *Horizon*, 14 (November 1946), 290-304.

Trautmann, Joanne. *The Jessamy Brides*.

Trilling, Diana. *Claremont Essays*, 87-104.

Troy, William. "Virginia Woolf: The Poetic Method" and "Virginia Woolf: The Poetic Style." *Symposium*, 3, 1 (1932), 53-63; 3, 2 (1932), 153-66.

Turnell, Martin. *Modern Literature and Christian Faith*, 25-45.

Watt, Donald J. "G. E. Moore and the Bloomsbury Group." *ELT*, 12, 3 (1969), 119-34.

West, Rebecca. *Ending in Earnest*, 208-13.

Wilson, Angus. "Sexual Revolution." *Listener*, 80 (1968), 457-60.

Wilson, James S. "Time and Virginia Woolf." *VQR*, 18 (1942), 267-76.
Woodring, Carl. *Virginia Woolf*. New York: Columbia Univ. Press, 1966.
Woolf, Leonard. *Downhill All the Way: An Autobiography of the Years 1919-1939*. London: Hogarth; New York: Harcourt, 1967.
Worrell, Elizabeth. "The Unspoken Word." *Studies in Interpretation*. Ed. Esther M. Doyle and Virginia Hastings Floyd, 191-203.
See also: Aiken, *ABC*; Allen, *Tradition*; Beach, *20th*; Beja; Bowen, *Impressions*; Brewster and Burrell; A. Collins, *20th*; J. Collins, *Doctor*; Cunliffe, *20th Century*; Daiches, *Novel*; Drew, *Modern*; Eagleton; Edel; Edgar, *Art*; Fleishman; Forster, *Aspects*; Gindin, *Harvest*; Hoare; R. Johnson, *Women*; Karl and Magalaner; Lovett, *History*; Marble; Markovic; Maurois; Muller, *Modern*; O'Faoláin; Scott-James, *50*; Swinnerton, *Georgian*; Tindall, *Forces*; Vines; Wagenknecht, *Cavalcade*.

BETWEEN THE ACTS

Basham, C. "*Between the Acts*." *DUJ*, 21 (1960), 87-94.
Fox, Stephen D. "The Fish Pond as Symbolic Center in *Between the Acts*." *MFS*, 18, 3 (1972), 467-73.
Gibson, Susan M. "Our Part Is to Be the Audience: Virginia Woolf's *Between the Acts*." *GyS*, 2, 1 (1974), 5-12.
Hafley, James. "A Reading of *Between the Acts*." *Accent*, 13 (1953), 178-87.
Leavis, F. R. "After *To the Lighthouse*." *Scrutiny*, 10 (1942), 295-98.
Naremore, James. "The 'Orts and Fragments' in *Between the Acts*." *BSUF*, 14, 1 (1973), 59-69.
Quick, Jonathan R. "The Shattered Moment: Form and Crisis in *Mrs. Dalloway* and *Between the Acts*." *Mosaic*, 7, 3 (1974), 127-36.
Shanahan, Mary S. "*Between the Acts*: Virginia Woolf's Final Endeavor in Art." *TSLL*, 14 (1972), 123-38.
Summerhayes, Don. "Society, Morality, Analogy: Virginia Woolf's World *Between the Acts*." *MFS*, 9 (1964), 329-37.
Watkins, Renée. "Survival in Discontinuity: Virginia Woolf's *Between the Acts*." *MR*, 10 (1969), 356-76.
Wilkinson, Ann Yanko. "A Principle of Unity in *Between the Acts*." *Criticism*, 8 (1966), 53-63.
Zorn, Marilyn. "The Pageant in *Between the Acts*." *MFS*, 2, 1 (1956), 31-35.

JACOB'S ROOM

Carew, Dudley. "Virginia Woolf." *Living Age*, 330 (July 1926), 47-54.
Grabo, Carl H. *The Technique of the Novel*, 297-305.

Morgenstern, Barry S. "The Self-Conscious Narrator in *Jacob's Room.*" *MFS*, 18, 3 (1972), 351-61.
See also: Buckley.

MRS. DALLOWAY

Ames, Kenneth J. "Elements of Mock-Heroic in Virginia Woolf's *Mrs. Dalloway.*" *MFS*, 18, 3 (1972), 363-74.

Baldanza, Frank. "Clarissa Dalloway's 'Party Consciousness'." *MFS*, 2, 1 (1956), 24-30.

Becker, Miroslav. "London as a Principle of Structure of *Mrs. Dalloway.*" *MFS*, 18, 3 (1972), 375-85.

Benjamin, Anna S. "Towards an Understanding of the Meaning of Virginia Woolf's *Mrs. Dalloway.*" *WSCL*, 6 (1965), 214-27.

Blanchard, Margaret. "Socialization in *Mrs. Dalloway.*" *CE*, 34 (1972), 287-305.

Brower, Reuben A. *The Fields of Light*, 123-37.

Fortin, René E. "Sacramental Imagery in *Mrs. Dalloway.*" *Renascence*, 18 (1965), 23-31.

Gamble, Isabel. "The Secret Sharer in *Mrs. Dalloway.*" *Accent*, 16 (1956), 235-51.

Gelfant, Blanche. "Love and Conversion in *Mrs. Dalloway.*" *Criticism*, 8 (1966), 229-45.

Ghiselin, Brewster. "Virginia Woolf's Party." *SR*, 80 (1972), 47-50.

Gillen, Francis. " 'I Am This, I Am That': Shifting Distance and Movement in *Mrs. Dalloway.*" *SNNTS*, 4 (1972), 484-93.

Graves, Nora C. "The Case of Mrs. Dalloway." *VWQ*, 1, 3 (1973), 51-59.

Harper, Howard M. "Mrs. Woolf and Mrs. Dalloway." *The Classic British Novel*. Ed. Howard M. Harper, Jr. and Charles Edge, 220-39.

Hawthorn, Jeremy. *Virginia Woolf's MRS. DALLOWAY: A Study in Alienation*. London: Chatto and Windus, 1975.

Heilbrun, Carolyn G. *Towards a Recognition of Androgyny*, 151-67.

Higdon, David L., and Jean Wyatt. "*Mrs. Dalloway* Revisited [an Exchange]." *PMLA*, 89 (1974), 178-80.

Hoffmann, Charles G. "From Short Story to Novel: The Manuscript Revisions of Virginia Woolf's *Mrs. Dalloway.*" *MFS*, 14 (1968), 171-86.

———. "The 'Real' Mrs. Dalloway." *UKCR*, 22 (1956), 204-08.

Hollingsworth, Keith. "Freud and the Riddle of *Mrs. Dalloway.*" *Studies in Honor of John Wilcox*. Ed. A. Dayle Wallace and Woodburn O. Ross, 239-50.

Hulcoop, John F. "McNichol's Mrs. Dalloway: Second Thoughts." *Virginia Woolf Misc.*, 3 (1975), 3-4, 7.

Hungerford, Edward A. " 'My Tunneling Process': The Method of *Mrs. Dalloway*." *MFS*, 3 (1957), 164-67.

Latham, Jacqueline E. M. "Archetypal Figures in *Mrs. Dalloway*." *NM*, 71 (1970), 480-88.

———. "The Manuscript Revisions of Virginia Woolf's *Mrs. Dalloway*: A Postscript." *MFS*, 18, 3 (1972), 475-76.

Lewis, A. J. "From 'The Hours' to *Mrs. Dalloway*." *BMQ*, 28 (1964), 15-18.

Miller, David N. "Authorial Point of View in Virginia Woolf's *Mrs. Dalloway*." *JNT*, 2 (1972), 125-32.

Miller, J. Hillis. "Virginia Woolf's All Souls' Day: The Omniscient Narrator in *Mrs. Dalloway*." *The Shaken Realist*. Ed. Melvin Friedman and John B. Vickery, 100-27.

Miroiu, Mihai. "Unity and Coherence in Mrs. Dalloway." *AUB-LUC*, 19, 1 (1970), 117-21.

Mollach, Francis L. "Thematic and Structural Unity in *Mrs. Dalloway*." *Thoth*, 5, 2 (1964), 62-73.

Moody, A. D. "The Unmasking of Clarissa Dalloway." *REL*, 3, 1 (1962), 67-79.

Page, Alex. "A Dangerous Day: Mrs. Dalloway Discovers Her Double." *MFS*, 7 (1961), 115-24.

Penner, Catherine S. "The Sacred Will in *Mrs. Dalloway*." *Thoth*, 12, 2 (1972), 3-20.

Philipson, Morris. "Mrs. Dalloway, 'What's the Sense of Your Parties?' " *CritI*, 1 (1974), 123-48.

Quick, Jonathan R. "The Shattered Moment: Form and Crisis in *Mrs. Dalloway* and *Between the Acts*." *Mosaic*, 7, 3 (1974), 127-36.

Rachman, Shalom. "Clarissa's Attic: Virginia Woolf's *Mrs. Dalloway* Reconsidered." *TCL*, 18 (1972), 3-18.

Roll-Hansen, Diderik. "Peter Walsh's Seven-League Boots: A Note on *Mrs. Dalloway*." *ES*, 50 (1969), 301-04.

Rosenberg, Stuart. "The Match in the Crocus: Obtrusive Art in Virginia Woolf's *Mrs. Dalloway*." *MFS*, 13 (1967), 211-20.

Ruotolo, Lucio P. *Six Existential Heroes*, 13-35.

Sakamoto, Tadanobu. "Virginia Woolf: 'Mrs. Dalloway in Bond Street' and *Mrs. Dalloway*." *SELit*, 50 (1974), 75-88.

Samuels, Marilyn S. "The Symbolic Functions of the Sun in *Mrs. Dalloway*." *MFS*, 18, 3 (1972), 387-99.

Samuelson, Ralph. "The Theme of *Mrs. Dalloway*." *ChiR*, 11, 4 (1958), 57-76.

Schlack, Beverly Ann. "A Freudian Look at *Mrs. Dalloway*." *L&P*, 23 (1973), 49-58.

Schoff, Francis G. "Mrs. Dalloway and Mrs. Ramsay." *IEY*, No. 9 (1964), 54-60.

Sharma, O. P. "Feminism as Aesthetic Vision: A Study of Virginia Woolf's *Mrs. Dalloway*." *PURBA*, 2, 2 (1971), 1-10, [Rpt. in *WS*, 3 (1975), 61-73]

Shields, E. F. "The American Edition of *Mrs. Dalloway*." *SB*, 27 (1974), 157-75.

————. "Death and Individual Values in *Mrs. Dalloway*." *QQ*, 80 (1973), 79-89.

Snow, Lotus. "The Heat of the Sun: The Double in *Mrs. Dalloway*." *RS*, 41 (1973), 75-83.

Swanston, Hamish F. G. "Virginia Woolf and the Corinthians." *New Blackfriars*, 54 (1973), 360-65.

Wright, Nathalia. "*Mrs. Dalloway*: A Study in Composition." *CE*, 5 (1944), 351-58.

Wyatt, Jean M. "*Mrs. Dalloway*: Literary Allusion as Structural Metaphor." *PMLA*, 88 (1973), 440-51.

See also: Mueller, *Celebration*; Walcutt.

NIGHT AND DAY

Cumings, Melinda F. "*Night and Day*: Virginia Woolf's Visionary Synthesis of Reality." *MFS*, 18, 3 (1972), 339-49.

Mansfield, Katherine. *Novels and Novelists*, 107-11.

Zuckerman, Joanne P. "Anne Thackeray Ritchie as the Model for Mrs. Hilbery in Virginia Woolf's *Night and Day*." *VWQ*, 1, 3 (1973), 32-46.

See also: Mais, *Why*.

ORLANDO

Baldanza, Frank. "*Orlando* and the Sackvilles." *PMLA*, 70 (1955), 274-79.

Bowen, Elizabeth. *Seven Winters*, 130-39.

German, Howard, and Sharon Kaehele. "The Dialectic of Time in *Orlando*." *CE*, 24 (1962), 35-41.

Graham, John. "The 'Caricature Value' of Parody and Fantasy in *Orlando*." *UTQ*, 30 (1961), 345-66.

Hoffmann, Charles G. "Fact and Fantasy in *Orlando*: Virginia Woolf's Manuscript Revisions." *TSLL*, 10 (1968), 435-44.

Mendilow, A. A. *Time and the Novel*, 228-31.

Morgan, Ellen. "Humanbecoming: Form and Focus in the Neo-Feminist Novel." *Images of Women in Fiction*. Ed. Susan Koppelman Cornillon, 189-92.

Virginia Woolf, continued

Rubenstein, Roberta. "*Orlando*: Virginia Woolf's Improvisations on a Russian Theme." *FMLS*, 9 (1973), 166-69.
Sakamoto, Tadanobu. "*Orlando*: What Happened in It." *HSELL*, 19, 1 (1972), 22-33.
Samuelson, Ralph. "Virginia Woolf, *Orlando*, and the Feminist Spirit." *WHR*, 15 (1961), 51-58.
Stewart, Jack F. "Historical Impressionism in *Orlando*." *SNNTS*, 5 (1973), 71-85.

TO THE LIGHTHOUSE

Aiken, Conrad. "The Novel as Work of Art." *Dial*, 83 (July 1927), 41-44.
Auerbach, Erich. *Mimesis*, 525-53.
Baldanza, Frank. "*To the Lighthouse* Again." *PMLA*, 70 (1955), 548-52.
Beja, Morris, ed. *Virginia Woolf, TO THE LIGHTHOUSE: A Casebook*. London: Macmillan, 1970.
Bell, Quentin. "The Biographer, the Critic, and the Lighthouse." *ArielE*, 2, 1 (1971), 94-101.
Bennett, Arnold. *The Savour of Life*, 312-13.
Blotner, Joseph. "Mythic Patterns in *To the Lighthouse*." *PMLA*, 71 (1956), 547-62.
Brown, E. K. *Rhythm in the Novel*, 64-70.
Cohn, Ruby. "Art in *To the Lighthouse*." *MFS*, 8 (1962), 127-36.
Corsa, Helen S. "*To the Lighthouse*: Death, Mourning, and Transfiguration." *L&P*, 21 (1971), 115-31.
Derbyshire, S. H. "An Analysis of Mrs. Woolf's *To the Lighthouse*." *CE*, 3 (1942), 353-60.
Donovan, Josephine. "Feminist Style Criticism." *Images of Women in Fiction*. Ed. Susan Koppelman Cornillon, 341-52.
Friedman, Norman. "The Waters of Annihilation: Double Vision in *To the Lighthouse*." *ELH*, 22 (1955), 61-79.
Fromm, Harold. "*To the Lighthouse*: Music and Sympathy." *EM*, 19 (1968), 181-95.
Hashmi, Shahnaz, "Indirect Style in *To the Lighthouse*." *IJES*, 2 (1961), 112-20.
Henke, Suzette. "Virginia Woolf's *To the Lighthouse*: In Defense of the Woman Artist." *VWQ*, 2, 1-2 (1975), 39-47.
Hoffmann, A. C. "Subject and Object and the Nature of Reality: The Dialectic of *To the Lighthouse*." *TSLL*, 13 (1972), 691-703.
Jeffrey, David K. "*To the Lighthouse*: A Bergsonian Reading." *NDQ*, 42, 2 (1974), 5-15.
Kaehele, Sharon, and Howard German. "*To the Lighthouse*: Symbol and Vision." *BuR*, 10, 4 (1962), 328-46.

Lavin, J. A. "The First Editions of Virginia Woolf's *To the Light-house." Proof*, 2 (1972), 185-211.
Leaska, Mitchell A. *Virginia Woolf's LIGHTHOUSE: A Study in Critical Method.* London: Hogarth, 1970.
Liberto, Sarah. "The 'Perpetual Pageant' of Art and Life in *To the Lighthouse." Descant*, 9 (Winter 1965), 35-43.
Little, Judith. "Heroism in *To the Lighthouse." Images of Women in Fiction.* Ed. Susan Koppelman Cornillon, 237-42.
May, Keith M. "The Symbol of 'Painting' in Virginia Woolf's *To the Lighthouse." REL*, 8, 2 (1967), 91-98.
Osgerby, J. R. "Virginia Woolf's *To the Lighthouse." Use of English*, 15 (1963), 116-24.
Overcarsh, F. L. "The Lighthouse, Face to Face." *Accent*, 10 (1950), 107-23.
Pedersen, Glenn. "Vision in *To the Lighthouse." PMLA*, 73 (1958), 585-600.
Pratt, Annis. "Sexual Imagery in *To the Lighthouse*: A New Feminist Approach." *MFS*, 18, 3 (1972), 417-31.
Proudfit, Sharon W. "Lily Briscoe's Painting: A Key to Personal Relationships in *To the Lighthouse." Criticism*, 13 (1971), 26-38.
Rose, Phyllis. "Mrs. Ramsay and Mrs. Woolf." *WS*, 1 (1973), 199-216.
Sagiyama, Yoko. "A Study of *To The Lighthouse." KGUAS*, 17 (1968), 21-37.
Seltzer, Alvin J. *Chaos in the Novel*, 120-40.
Sharma, O. P. "Feminism as Aesthetic Vision and Transcendence: A Study of Virginia Woolf's *To the Lighthouse." PURBA*, 3, 1 (1972), 1-8.
Spacks, Patricia Meyer. "Taking Care: Some Women Novelists." *Novel*, 6 (1972), 36-51.
Vogler, Thomas A., ed. *TO THE LIGHTHOUSE: A Collection of Critical Essays.* Englewood Cliffs, N.J.: Prentice-Hall, 1970.
Warner, John M. "Symbolic Patterns of Retreat and Reconciliation in *To the Lighthouse." Discourse*, 12 (1969), 376-92.
Whitehead, Lee M. "The Shawl and the Skull: Virginia Woolf's 'Magic Mountain'." *MFS*, 18, 3 (1972), 401-15.
See also: Drew, *Novel*; Gill; Kettle; Tindall, *Symbol*.

THE VOYAGE OUT
Blanche, Jacques-Emile. *More Portraits of a Lifetime*, 45-57, 285-89.
Hafley, James. "Another Note on Rachel and Beethoven in *The Voyage Out." Virginia Woolf Misc.*, 4 (1975), 4.
Kelly, George. "Virginia Woolf's Voyage Out." *HarvA*, 126, 2 (1952), 17-19, 31-33.

Virginia Woolf, continued

Leaska, Mitchell A. "Virginia Woolf's *The Voyage Out*: Character Deduction and the Function of Ambiguity." *VWQ*, 1, 2 (1973), 18-41.

THE WAVES

Bevis, Dorothy. "*The Waves*: A Fusion of Symbol, Style, and Thought in Virginia Woolf." *TCL*, 2 (1956), 5-20.

Collins, Robert G. *Virginia Woolf's Black Arrows of Sensation: THE WAVES*. Ilfracombe, Eng.: A. H. Stockwell, 1962.

Dobrée, Bonamy. *Modern Prose Style*, 51-55.

Gorsky, Susan. " 'The Central Shadow': Characterization in *The Waves*." *MFS*, 18, 3 (1972), 449-66.

Graham, John W. "Editing a Manuscript: Virginia Woolf's *The Waves*." *Editing Twentieth Century Texts*. Ed. Francess G. Halpenny, 77-92.

―――. "Point of View in *The Waves*: Some Services of the Style." *UTQ*, 39 (1970), 193-211.

Hampshire, Stuart N. *Modern Writers*, 38-46.

Havard-Williams, Peter, and Margaret Havard-Williams. "*Bateau Ivre*: The Symbol of the Sea in Virginia Woolf's *The Waves*." *ES*, 34 (1953), 9-17.

―――. "Mystical Experience in Virginia Woolf's *The Waves*." *EIC*, 4 (1954), 71-84.

―――. "Perceptive Contemplation in the Work of Virginia Woolf." *ES*, 35 (1954), 97-116.

Heine, Elizabeth. "The Evolution of the Interludes in *The Waves*." *VWQ*, 1, 1 (1972), 60-80.

King, Merton P. "*The Waves* and the Androgynous Mind." *UKCR*, 30 (1963), 128-34; "The Androgynous Mind and *The Waves*." *UKCR*, 30 (1964), 221-24.

McConnell, Frank D. " 'Death Among the Apple Trees': *The Waves* and the World of Things." *BuR*, 16, 3 (1968), 23-39.

Payne, Michael. "The Eclipse of Order: The Ironic Structure of *The Waves*." *MFS*, 15 (1969), 209-18.

Rantavaara, Irma. " 'Ing'-forms in the Service of Rhythm and Style in Virginia Woolf's *The Waves*." *NM*, 61 (1960), 79-97.

―――. "On Romantic Imagery in Virginia Woolf's *The Waves*, with Special Reference to Antithesis." *NM*, 60 (1959), 72-89.

―――. *Virginia Woolf's THE WAVES*. Helsinki: Societas Scientiarum Fennica, 1960.

Richardson, Robert O. "Point of View in Virginia Woolf's *The Waves*." *TSLL*, 14 (1973), 691-709.

Shanahan, Mary Steussy. "The Artist and the Resolution of *The Waves.*" *MLQ*, 36 (1975), 54-74.

Snow, Lotus. "The Wreckful Siege: Disorder in *The Waves.*" *RS*, 42 (1974), 71-80.

Stewart, Jack F. "Existence and Symbol in *The Waves.*" *MFS*, 18, 3 (1972), 433-47.

Stewart, J. I. M. "Notes for a Study of *The Waves.*" *On the Novel.* Ed. Benedikt S. Benedikz, 93-112.

Swanston, Hamish F. G. "Virginia Woolf and the Corinthians." *New Blackfriars*, 54 (1973), 360-65.

Webb, Igor M. " 'Things in Themselves': Virginia Woolf's *The Waves.*" *MFS*, 17 (1971-72), 570-73.

THE YEARS

Hartley, Lodwick. "Of Time and Mrs. Woolf." *SR*, 47 (1939), 235-41.

Hoffmann, Charles G. "Virginia Woolf's Manuscript Revisions of *The Years.*" *PMLA*, 84 (1969), 79-89.

Marder, Herbert. "Beyond the Lighthouse: *The Years.*" *BuR*, 15, 1 (1967), 61-70.

Mellers, W. H. "Mrs. Woolf and Life." *Scrutiny*, 6 (1937), 71-75.

Proudfit, Sharon L. "Virginia Woolf: Reluctant Feminist in *The Years.*" *Criticism*, 17 (1975), 59-73.

Radin, Grace. " 'I Am Not a Hero': Virginia Woolf and the First Version of *The Years.*" *MR*, 16 (1975), 195-208.

Roberts, John Hawley. "The End of the English Novel?" *VQR*, 13 (1937), 437-39.

Van Doren, Mark. *The Private Reader*, 262-66.

PART II: BOOKS CITED AND GENERAL
BIBLIOGRAPHY

GENERAL STUDIES

Abernethy, Peter L., et al. *English Novel Explication: Supplement I.* Hamden, Conn.: Shoe String, 1976.

Adcock, A. St. John. *Gods of Modern Grub Street: Impressions of Contemporary Authors.* London: Low, Marton; New York: Stokes, 1923.

_____. *The Glory that Was Grub Street: Impressions of Contemporary Authors.* London: Low, Marton; New York: Stokes, 1928.

Adelman, Irving, and Rita Dworkin, eds. *The Contemporary Novel: A Checklist of Critical Literature on the British and American Novel Since 1945.* Metuchen, N.J.: Scarecrow, 1972.

Agate, James E. *Alarums and Excursions.* London: Richards; Garden City, N.Y.: Doubleday, 1922.

Ahle, Augustus H. "A Short View of Contemporary Fiction." *Delaware Notes,* 21st ser. (1948), 19-35.

Aiken, Conrad P. *Reviewer's ABC: Collected Criticism of Conrad Aiken, from 1916 to the Present.* New York: Meridian Books, 1958; London: Allen, 1961.

Aitken, A. J., Angus McIntosh, and Hermann Pálsson, eds. *Edinburgh Studies in English and Scots.* London: Longmans, Green, 1971.

Aldington, Richard. *Artifex: Sketches and Ideas.* London: Chatto and Windus, 1935.

_____. *Literary Studies and Reviews.* London: Allen and Unwin; New York: Dial, 1924.

Aldiss, Brian W. *Billion Year Spree: The True History of Science Fiction.* Garden City, N.Y.: Doubleday, 1973.

Aldridge, John W., ed. *Critiques and Essays on Modern Fiction, 1920-1951.* New York: Ronald, 1952.

_____. *Time to Murder and Create: The Contemporary Novel in Crisis.* New York: McKay, 1966.

Alexander, Calvert. *The Catholic Literary Revival: Three Phases in its Development from 1845 to the Present.* Milwaukee: Bruce, 1935.

Allen, Walter. *The English Novel: A Short Critical History.* London: Phoenix House, 1954; New York: Dutton, 1957.

_____. *The Novel Today.* London: Longmans, Green, 1955; rev. 1960.

_____. *Reading a Novel.* London: Phoenix House, 1956.

_____. *Six Great Novelists.* London: Hamilton, 1955.

_____. *Tradition and Dream: The English and American Novel from the Twenties to Our Time.* London: Phoenix House, 1964; New York: Dutton, 1965. [American ed. entitled *The Modern Novel in Britain and the United States*]

Allott, Miriam, ed. *Novelists on the Novel.* London: Routledge and K. Paul, 1959; New York: Columbia Univ. Press, 1962.

Allsop, Kenneth. *The Angry Decade: A Survey of the Cultural Revolt of the Nineteen-Fifties.* London: Peter Owen, 1958; New York: British Book Centre, 1959.

Alter, Robert. *Rogue's Progress: Studies in the Picaresque Novel.* Cambridge, Mass.: Harvard Univ. Press, 1964.

Alvarez, Alfred. *Stewards of Excellence: Studies in Modern English and American Poets.* New York: Scribner's, 1958.

Anderson, David. *The Tragic Protest: A Christian Study of Some Modern Literature.* London: SCM; Richmond, Va.: John Knox, 1969.

Anderson, Don, and Stephen Knight, eds. *Cunning Exiles: Studies of Modern Prose Writers.* Sydney: Angus and Robertson, 1974.

Anderson, James. *British Novels of the Twentieth Century.* Cambridge: Cambridge Univ. Press, 1959.

Andreach, Robert J. *The Slain and Resurrected God: Conrad, Ford and the Christian Myth.* New York: New York Univ. Press; London: Univ. of London Press, 1970.

Archer, William. *Study and Stage: A Year Book of Criticism.* London: Richards, 1899.

Attwater, Donald, ed. *Modern Christian Revolutionaries.* New York: Devin-Adair, 1947.

Auden, W. H. *The Dyer's Hand and Other Essays.* New York: Random House, 1962.

———. *Forewords and Afterwords, Selected by Edward Mendelson.* New York: Random House, 1973.

Auerbach, Erich. *Mimesis: The Representation of Reality in Western Literature.* Princeton, N.J.: Princeton Univ. Press, 1953.

Austin, William W., ed. *New Looks at Italian Opera: Essays in Honor of Donald J. Grout.* Ithaca, N.Y.: Cornell Univ. Press, 1968.

Bailhache, Jean. "Angry Young Men." *LanM,* 2 (1958), 31-46.

Baim, Joseph, Ann L. Hayes, and Robert J. Gangewere. *In Honor of Austin Wright* (Carnegie Series in English 12). Pittsburgh: Carnegie-Mellon Univ. Press, 1972.

Bain, James S. *A Bookseller Looks Back: The Story of the Bains.* London: Macmillan, 1940.

Baker, Denys Val, ed. *Modern British Writing.* New York: Vanguard, 1947.

———. *Writers of To-day.* London: Sidgwick and Jackson, 1946.

———. *Writers of To-day, 2.* London: Sidgwick and Jackson, 1948.

Baker, Ernest A. *The History of the English Novel,* 10 vol. London:

Witherby, 1924-38; New York: Barnes and Noble, 1957. [v. 11 ed. Lionel Stevenson]

Bartlett, Robert M. *They Dared to Live.* New York: Association Press, 1937.

Barzun, Jacques. "Our Non-Fiction Novelists." *Atlantic,* 178 (July 1946), 129-32.

Bateson, F. W., and George Watson, eds. *The Cambridge Bibliography of English Literature,* 5 vol. Cambridge: Cambridge Univ. Press, 1940, 1957. [v. 6, on the modern period, by I. R. Willison, R. J. Roberts, and Charles Corney]

Baugh, Albert C., et al. *A Literary History of England.* New York: Appleton, 1948.

Beach, Joseph Warren. *Outlook for American Prose.* Chicago: Univ. of Chicago Press, 1926.

———. *The Twentieth Century Novel: Studies in Technique.* New York: Appleton, 1932.

Becker, Carl L. *Everyman His Own Historian.* New York: Crofts, 1935.

Bedient, Calvin. *Architects of the Self: George Eliot, D. H. Lawrence, and E. M. Forster.* Berkeley: Univ. of California Press, 1972.

Beebe, Maurice. *Ivory Towers and Sacred Founts: The Artist as Hero in Fiction from Goethe to Joyce.* New York: New York Univ. Press, 1964.

Beja, Morris. *Epiphany in the Modern Novel.* Seattle: Univ. of Washington Press, 1971.

Bell, Inglis F., and Donald Baird. *The English Novel: A Checklist of Twentieth Century Criticism.* Denver: Swallow, 1958; Hamden, Conn.: Shoe String, 1974.

Bellamy, William. *The Novels of Wells, Bennett, and Galsworthy: 1890-1910.* London: Routledge and K. Paul; New York: Barnes and Noble, 1971.

Benedikz, Benedikt S., ed. *On the Novel: A Present for Walter Allen on His 60th Birthday from His Friends and Colleagues.* London: Dent, 1971.

Bennett, Arnold. *Books and Persons: Being Comments on a Past Epoch, 1908-1911.* London: Chatto and Windus; New York: Doran, 1917.

———. *Fame and Fiction: An Enquiry Into Certain Popularities.* London: Richards; New York: Dutton, 1901.

———. *The Savour of Life: Essays in Gusto.* Garden City, N.Y.: Doubleday, 1928.

———. *Things That Have Interested Me,* 2d ser. London: Chatto and Windus; New York: Doran, 1923.

Books Cited and General Bibliography

Bentley, Phyllis. *The English Regional Novel.* London: Allen and Unwin, 1941.

Beresford, J. D. "Experiment in the Novel." *Tradition and Experiment in Present-Day Literature,* by City Literary Institute, London. London: Oxford Univ. Press, 1929.

Bergonzi, Bernard. *Heroes' Twilight: A Study of the Literature of the Great War.* London: Constable, 1965; New York: Coward-McCann, 1966.

––––––. *The Situation of the Novel.* London: Macmillan; Pittsburgh: Univ. of Pittsburgh Press, 1970.

––––––. *The Turn of a Century: Essays on Victorian and Modern English Literature.* New York: Barnes and Noble, 1973.

Berneri, Mary Louise. *Journey Through Utopia.* London: Routledge and K. Paul, 1950; Boston: Beacon, 1951.

Berthoff, Warner. *Fictions and Events: Essays in Criticism and Literary History.* New York: Dutton, 1971.

Bishop, John Peale. *Collected Essays.* New York: Scribner's, 1948.

Björkman, Edwin August. *Voices of To-morrow: Critical Studies of the New Spirit in Literature.* New York and London: Kennerley, 1913.

Blackmur, R. P. *A Primer of Ignorance.* Ed. Joseph Frank. New York: Harcourt, 1967.

Blanche, Jacques-Emile. *More Portraits of a Lifetime: 1918-1938.* Tr. and ed. Walter Clement. London: Dent, 1939.

––––––. *Portraits of a Lifetime.* Tr. and ed. Walter Clement. London: Dent, 1937; New York: Coward-McCann, 1938.

Bloomfield, Morton W., ed. *The Interpretation of Narrative: Theory and Practice.* Cambridge, Mass.: Harvard Univ. Press, 1970.

Bloomfield, Paul, and Bernard Bergonzi. *Anthony Powell and L. P. Hartley.* London: Longmans, Green, 1962.

Bloor, R. H. U. *The English Novel from Chaucer to Galsworthy.* London: Nicholson and Watson, 1935.

Blotner, Joseph I. *The Political Novel.* Garden City, N.Y.: Doubleday, 1955.

Bode, Carl. "The Redbrick Cinderellas." *CE,* 20 (1959), 331-37.

Bogan, Louise. *Selected Criticism: Prose, Poetry.* New York: Noonday, 1955.

Boll, Ernest. "A Rationale for the Criticism of the Realistic Novel." *MLQ,* 9 (1948), 208-15.

Bonnerot, Louis, with Jean Jacquot and Claude Jaquet, eds. *ULYSSES: Cinquante ans Après.* Paris: Didier, 1974.

Booth, Wayne C. *The Rhetoric of Fiction.* Chicago: Univ. of Chicago Press, 1961.

Boothby, Lord [Robert John Graham]. *My Yesterday, Your Tomorrow.* London: Hutchinson, 1962.

Borges, Jorges Luis. *Other Inquisitions, 1937-1952.* Tr. Ruth L. C. Simms. Austin: Univ. of Texas Press, 1964.

Bowen, Elizabeth. *Collected Impressions.* London: Longmans, Green; New York: Knopf, 1950.

——. "English Novelists." *The Romance of English Literature.* Ed. Walter J. Turner. New York: Hastings House, 1945, 227-70.

——. *Seven Winters: Memories of a Dublin Childhood and After-Thoughts—Pieces on Writing.* New York: Knopf, 1962.

Boyd, Ernest A. *Ireland's Literary Renaissance.* Dublin and London: Maunsell, 1916; rev. New York: Knopf, 1922.

——. *Portraits: Real and Imaginary.* New York: Doran, 1924.

Brace, Gerald Warner. *The Age of the Novel.* Boston: Boston Univ. Press, 1957.

Bradbury, Malcolm. *Possibilities: Essays on the State of the Novel.* London: Oxford Univ. Press, 1973.

——. *The Social Context of Modern English Literature.* New York: Schocken, 1971.

Brady, Charles A. "The British Novel Today." *Thought,* 34 (1959), 518-46.

Braybrooke, Patrick. *Novelists: We Are Seven.* London: C. W. Daniel; Philadelphia: Lippincott, 1926.

——. *Peeps at the Mighty.* Philadelphia: Lippincott, 1927.

——. *Philosophies in Modern Fiction.* London: C. W. Daniel, 1929.

——. *Some Catholic Novelists: Their Art and Outlook.* London: Burns, Oates, and Washbourne, 1931.

——. *Some Goddesses of the Pen.* London: C. W. Daniel, 1928.

——. *Some Victorian and Georgian Catholics: Their Art and Outlook.* London: Burns, Oates and Washbourne, 1932.

Breit, Harvey. *The Writer Observed.* Cleveland: World, 1956.

Brewer, D. S. *Proteus: Studies in English Literature.* Tokyo: Kenkyusha, 1958.

Brewster, Dorothy, and Angus Burrell. *Modern Fiction.* New York: Columbia Univ. Press, 1934.

Brickell, Herschel. "The Present State of Fiction." *VQR,* 25 (1949), 92-98.

Bridges, Horace J. *Criticisms of Life: Studies in Faith, Hope and Despair.* Boston: Houghton Mifflin, 1915.

——. *The God of Fundamentalism and Other Studies.* Chicago: Covici, 1925.

Broes, Arthur T., et al., eds. *Lectures on Modern Novelists.* Pittsburgh: Department of English, Carnegie Institute of Technology, 1963.

Books Cited and General Bibliography

Bronzwaer, W. J. M. *Tense in the Novel: An Investigation of Some Potentialities of Linguistic Criticism.* Groningen: Wolters-Noordhoff, 1970.

Brophy, Brigid. *Don't Never Forget: Collected Views and Reviews.* New York: Holt, 1966.

Broughton, Bradford B., ed. *Twenty-Seven to One: A Potpourri of Humanistic Material Presented to Dr. Donald Gale Stillman on the Occasion of his Retirement from Clarkson College of Technology by Members of the Liberal Studies-Humanities Department Staff, 1949-1970.* Ogdensburg, N.Y.: Ryan, 1970.

Brower, Reuben A. *The Fields of Light: An Experience in Critical Reading.* New York: Oxford Univ. Press, 1951.

————., ed. *Twentieth-Century Literature in Retrospect.* Cambridge, Mass.: Harvard Univ. Press, 1971.

Brown, E. K. *Rhythm in the Novel.* Toronto: Univ. of Toronto Press, 1950.

Brown, Francis, ed. *Highlights of Modern Literature.* New York: New American Library, 1954.

————. *Page 2: The Best of "Speaking of Books" from THE NEW YORK TIMES BOOK REVIEW.* New York: Holt, 1969.

Brown, Malcolm. *The Politics of Irish Literature.* Seattle: Univ. of Washington Press, 1972.

Browne, Ray B., William J. Roscelli, and Richard J. Loftus. *The Celtic Cross: Studies in Irish Culture and Literature.* Lafayette, Ind.: Purdue Univ. Studies, 1964.

Bruns, Gerald L. *Modern Poetry and the Idea of Language: A Critical and Historical Study.* New Haven, Conn.: Yale Univ. Press, 1974.

Buck, Philo M., Jr. *Directions in Contemporary Literature.* London: Oxford Univ. Press, 1942.

Buckley, Jerome Hamilton. *Season of Youth: The Bildungsroman from Dickens to Golding.* Cambridge, Mass.: Harvard Univ. Press, 1974.

Bufkin, E. C. *The Twentieth-Century Novel in English: A Checklist.* Athens: Univ. of Georgia Press, 1967.

Bullett, Gerald W. *Modern English Fiction: A Personal View.* London: Herbert Jenkins, 1926.

Burgess, Anthony. *English Literature: A Survey for Students,* new ed. London: Longmans, Green, 1974.

————. *The Novel Now: A Student's Guide to Contemporary Fiction.* London: Faber and Faber; New York: Norton, 1967. [American ed. entitled *The Novel Now: A Guide to Contemporary Fiction*]

———. *The Novel Today.* (Bibliographical Series of Supplements to *British Book News.*) London: Longmans, Green, 1963.

———. *Urgent Copy: Literary Studies.* New York: Norton, 1968.

Burgum, Edwin B., ed. *New Criticism: An Anthology of Modern Aesthetics and Literary Criticism.* New York: Prentice-Hall, 1930.

———. *The Novel and the World's Dilemma.* New York: Oxford Univ. Press, 1947.

Burke, Kenneth. *Language as Symbolic Action.* Berkeley: Univ. of California Press, 1966.

Burns, Martin. "The English Novel Since 1900." *DR*, 15 (1935), 213-18.

Burt, Maxwell S. *The Other Side.* New York: Scribner's, 1928.

Butler, Francelia, ed. *Children's Literature: The Great Excluded*, v. 2. Butler, Francelia, and Bennett A. Brockman, eds., v. 3. Storrs, Conn.: Children's Literature Ass'n., 1973; 1974.

Butler, Gerald J. "On a Certain Emptiness in Modern British Fiction." *RecL*, 4, 3 (1975), 5-26.

Canby, Henry S. *American Estimates.* New York: Harcourt, 1929.

———. *Definitions: Essays in Contemporary Criticism*, ser. 1-2. New York: Harcourt, 1922-24.

———. *Seven Years' Harvest: Notes on Contemporary Literature.* New York: Farrar, Rinehart, 1936.

Cargill, Oscar. *Intellectual America: Ideas on the March.* New York: Macmillan, 1941.

Caudwell, Christopher [Christopher St. John Sprigg]. *Studies in a Dying Culture.* London: Lane; New York: Dodd, Mead, 1938.

Cecil, David. *Fine Art of Reading.* Indianapolis: Bobbs-Merrill, 1957.

———. *Poets and Storytellers: A Book of Critical Essays.* New York: Macmillan, 1949.

Chakrabarti, Dipendu, ed. *Essays Presented to Prof. Amalendu Bose. Bulletin of the Department of English, 8, 2 (1972-73).* Calcutta: Calcutta Univ., 1973.

Chaning-Pearce, Melville. *The Terrible Crystal: Studies in Kierkegaard and Modern Christianity.* New York: Oxford Univ. Press, 1941.

Chapple, J. A. V. *Documentary and Imaginative Literature, 1880-1920.* New York: Barnes and Noble, 1970.

Charques, Richard D. *Contemporary Literature and Social Revolution.* London: Secker and Warburg, 1933.

Chatman, Seymour, ed. and tr. *Literary Style: A Symposium.* New York: Oxford Univ. Press, 1971.

Chattopadhyaya, Sisir. *The Technique of the Modern English Novel.* Calcutta: K. L. Mukhopadhyay, 1959.

Chesterton, G. K. *Avowals and Denials: A Book of Essays.* New York: Dodd, Mead, 1935.

————. *Fancies Versus Fads.* New York: Dodd, Mead, 1923.

————. *Heretics.* London and New York: Lane, 1905.

Chevalley, Abel. *The Modern English Novel.* Tr. Ben Ray Redman. New York: Knopf, 1925.

Christy, Arthur E., ed. *The Asian Legacy and American Life: Essays.* New York: John Day, 1945.

Chubb, Edwin W. *Stories of Authors, British and American.* New York: Macmillan, 1926.

Church, Margaret. *Time and Reality: Studies in Contemporary Fiction.* Chapel Hill: Univ. of North Carolina Press, 1963.

Clareson, Thomas D., ed. *Science Fiction: The Other Side of Realism—Essays on Modern Fantasy and Science Fiction.* Bowling Green, Ohio: Bowling Green Univ. Popular Press, 1971.

Clark, Barrett H. *Intimate Portraits: Being Recollections of Maxim Gorky, John Galsworthy, Edward Sheldon, George Moore, Sidney Howard, and Others.* New York: Dramatists Play Service, 1951.

Clarke, David Waldo. *Modern English Writers.* London: Essential Eng. Lib., 1947.

Clarke, Ignatius F. *Voices Prophesying War: 1763-1984.* London and New York: Oxford Univ. Press, 1966.

Clutton-Brock, Arthur. *Essays on Literature and Life.* New York: Dutton, 1927.

Cohn, Ruby. "The Contemporary English Novel." *Per,* 10 (1958), 103-05.

Collins, Arthur S. *English Literature of the Twentieth Century.* London: University Tutorial Press, 1951 ff.

Collins, Joseph. *Doctor Looks at Literature: Psychological Studies of Life and Letters.* New York: Doran, 1923.

————. *Idling in Italy: Studies of Literature and Life.* New York: Scribner's, 1920.

————. *Taking the Literary Pulse: Psychological Studies of Life and Letters.* New York: Doran, 1924.

Collins, Norman. *The Facts of Fiction.* London: Gollancz, 1932; New York: Dutton, 1933.

Colmer, John, ed. *Approaches to the Novel.* Edinburgh and London: Oliver and Boyd, 1966.

Colum, Mary. *From these Roots: The Ideas that Have Made Modern Literature.* New York: Scribner's, 1937.

Comfort, Alex. *The Novel and Our Time.* London: Phoenix House; Denver: Swallow, 1948.

Connolly, Cyril. *The Condemned Playground: Essays, 1927-1944.* London: Routledge and K. Paul; New York: Macmillan, 1946.

———. *Enemies of Promise.* London: Routledge and K. Paul, 1938; Boston: Little, Brown, 1939; rev. New York: Macmillan, 1948.

———. *The Evening Colonnade.* New York: Harcourt, 1975.

———, ed. *Golden Horizon.* London: Weidenfeld and Nicolson, 1953.

———. *The Modern Movement: One Hundred Key Books from England, France, and America, 1880-1950.* New York: Atheneum, 1966.

———. *Previous Convictions: Selected Writings of a Decade.* New York: Harper, 1963.

Conrad, Joseph. *Last Essays.* Garden City, N. Y.: Doubleday, 1926.

Cook, Albert S. *The Meaning of Fiction.* Detroit: Wayne State Univ. Press, 1960.

Cooper, Frederic T. *Some English Story Tellers: A Book of the Younger Novelists.* New York: Holt, 1912.

Cornillon, Susan Koppelman, ed. *Images of Women in Fiction: Feminist Perspectives.* Bowling Green, Ohio: Bowling Green Univ. Popular Press, 1972; rev. 1973.

Cornwell, Edith F. *The "Still Point": Theme and Variation in the Writings of T. S. Eliot, Coleridge, Yeats, Henry James, Virginia Woolf, and D. H. Lawrence.* New Brunswick, N. J.: Rutgers Univ. Press, 1962.

Coveney, Peter. *Poor Monkey.* London: Rockliff, 1957.

Cox, Charles B. *The Free Spirit: A Study of Liberal Humanism in the Novels of George Eliot, Henry James, E. M. Forster, Virginia Woolf, and Angus Wilson.* London: Oxford Univ. Press, 1963.

———, and A. E. Dyson, eds. *The Twentieth-Century Mind: History, Ideas, and Literature in Britain,* v. 2. London: Oxford Univ. Press, 1972.

Craig, David. "The British Working-Class Novel Today." *ZAA,* 11 (1963), 29-41.

———. *The Real Foundations: Literature and Social Change.* London: Oxford Univ. Press, 1974.

Crescent and Green: A Miscellany of Writings on Pakistan. London: Cassell; New York: Philosophical Library, 1955.

Crews, Frederick C. *Out of My System: Psychoanalysis, Ideology, and Critical Method.* New York: Oxford Univ. Press, 1975.

———, ed. *Psychoanalysis and Literary Process.* Cambridge: Winthrop, 1970.

Cronin, Anthony. *A Question of Modernity.* London: Secker and Warburg, 1966.

Books Cited and General Bibliography

Cross, Wilbur L. *Four Contemporary Novelists.* New York: Macmillan, 1930.

Crothers, George D., ed. *Invitation to Learning: English and American Novels.* New York: Basic Books, 1966.

Cruise O'Brien, Conor. *Writers and Politics.* New York: Pantheon, 1965.

Cumberland, Gerald [Charles F. Kenyon]. "Some Considerations of the Modern Novel." *Written in Friendship: A Book of Reminiscences.* New York: Brentano's, 1924, 127-41.

Cunliffe, J. W. *English Literature During the Last Half-Century*, 2d ed. New York: Macmillan, 1927.

———. *English Literature in the Twentieth Century.* New York: Macmillan, 1933.

———. *Leaders of the Victorian Revolution.* New York: Appleton, 1934.

Curle, Richard. *Caravansary and Conversation.* London: J. Cape; New York: Stokes, 1937.

Currie, Robert. *Genius: An Ideology in Literature.* London: Chatto and Windus; New York: Schocken, 1974.

Curtius, Ernst R. *Essays on European Literature.* Tr. Michael Kowal. Princeton, N. J.: Princeton Univ. Press, 1973.

Dahl, Liisa. *Linguistic Features of the Stream-of-Consciousness Techniques of James Joyce, Virginia Woolf and Eugene O'Neill.* Annales Universitatis Turkuensis, Series B, 116. Turku, Finland: Turun Yliopisto, 1970.

Dahlberg, Edward, and Herbert Read. *Truth Is More Sacred: A Critical Exchange on Modern Literature: James Joyce, D. H. Lawrence, Henry James, Robert Graves, T. S. Eliot, Ezra Pound.* New York: Horizon, 1961.

Daiches, David. *A Critical History of English Literature*, 2 vol. New York: Ronald, 1960.

———. *New Literary Values: Studies in Modern Literature.* Edinburgh: Oliver and Boyd, 1936.

———. *The Novel and the Modern World.* Chicago: Univ. of Chicago Press, 1939, 1960.

———. *The Present Age: After 1920.* London: Cresset; Bloomington: Indiana Univ. Press, 1958. [American ed. entitled *The Present Age in British Literature*] (v. 5 of *Introduction to English Literature*) [Replacement of Edwin Muir, *The Present Age: 1941.* London: Cresset, 1939]

Dataller, Roger [A. A. Eaglestone]. *The Plain Man and the Novel.* London and New York: Nelson, 1940.

Davenport, William H., ed. *Voices in Court: A Treasury of the Bench, the Bar, and the Courtroom.* New York: Macmillan, 1958.

Davie, Donald, ed. *Russian Literature and Modern English Fiction: A Collection of Critical Essays.* Chicago: Univ. of Chicago Press, 1965.

———. *Thomas Hardy and British Poetry.* New York: Oxford Univ. Press, 1972; London: Routledge and K. Paul, 1973.

Davies, Horton. *A Mirror of the Ministry in Modern Novels.* New York: Oxford Univ. Press, 1959.

Davies, Hugh Sykes, and George Watson, eds. *The English Mind: Studies in the English Moralists Presented to Basil Willey.* Cambridge: Cambridge Univ. Press, 1964.

Davies, Richard Beale, and John L. Lievsay, eds. *Studies in Honor of John C. Hodges and Alvin Thaler.* Knoxville: Univ. of Tennessee Press, 1961.

Dawson, S. W. "Precarious Complacency: A Note on the Contemporary Novel." *The Black Rainbow: Essays on the Present Breakdown of Culture.* Ed. Peter Abbs. London: Heinemann, 1975, 55-62.

Decker, Clarence. *The Victorian Conscience.* New York: Twayne, 1952.

de la Mare, Walter. *Private View.* London: Faber and Faber, 1953.

Demarest, David P., Jr., et al., eds. *A Modern Miscellany* (Carnegie Series in English 11). Pittsburgh: Carnegie-Mellon Univ. Press, 1970.

Deutsch, Babette. *Poetry in our Time: A Critical Survey of Poetry in the English-Speaking World, 1900-1960.* New York: Holt, 1952; New York: Columbia Univ. Press, 1956, 1958; rev. Garden City, N.Y.: Doubleday, 1963.

Deutscher, Isaac. *Heretics and Renegades.* London: Hamilton, 1955.

———. *Russia in Transition.* New York: Coward-McCann, 1957.

Devoe, Alan. "The Riddle of Modern Writing." *CathW,* 141 (1935), 403-08.

Dewey, John. *Characters and Events: Popular Essays in Social and Political Philosophy,* 2 vol. New York: Holt, 1929.

Dobrée, Bonamy. *The Lamp and the Lute: Studies in Six Modern Authors.* Oxford: Clarendon, 1929.

———. *Modern Prose Style.* Oxford: Clarendon, 1934, 1964.

———. "The Novel: Has It a Function Today?" Royal Society of Literature of the United Kingdom, London. *Essays by Divers Hands,* v. 13. London: Oxford Univ. Press, 1934, 57-76.

Donoghue, Denis. *The Ordinary Universe: Soundings in Modern Literature.* New York: Macmillan, 1968.

Books Cited and General Bibliography

———. *Thieves of Fire*. New York: Oxford Univ. Press, 1975.

Doshisha Women's College of Liberal Arts. *Annual Reports of Studies*, v. 21, 22. Kyoto: Doshisha Women's College, 1970, 1971.

Downer, Alan S., ed. *English Institute Essays, 1952*. New York: Columbia Univ. Press, 1954.

Doyle, Esther M., and Virginia Hastings Floyd, eds. *Studies in Interpretation*, v. 1. Amsterdam: Rodopi N.V., 1972.

Drake, William A., ed. *American Criticism, 1926*. New York: Harcourt, 1926.

Drew, Elizabeth. *The Modern Novel: Some Aspects of Contemporary Fiction*. New York: Harcourt, 1926.

———. *The Novel: A Modern Guide to Fifteen English Masterpieces*. New York: Norton, 1963.

D'Souza, Frank, and Jagdish Shivpuri, eds. *Siddha III*. Bombay: Siddharth College of Arts and Science, 1968.

Durant, Will. *Adventures in Genius*. New York: Simon and Schuster, 1931.

Duthie, George I., ed. *English Studies Today*, 3d ser. Edinburgh: Edinburgh Univ. Press, 1964.

Dyson, A. E. *The Crazy Fabric: Essays in Irony*. New York: St. Martin's, 1965.

———, ed. *The English Novel: Select Bibliographical Guides*. London: Oxford Univ. Press, 1974.

Eagleton, Terry. *Exiles and Émigrés: Studies in Modern Literature*. New York: Schocken, 1970.

Eastwood, Wilfred, and J. T. Good. *Signposts: A Guide to Modern English Literature*. Cambridge: Cambridge Univ. Press, 1960.

Eaton, Gai. *The Richest Vein: Eastern Tradition and Modern Thought*. London: Faber and Faber, 1949.

Edel, Leon A. *The Psychological Novel, 1900-1950*. Philadelphia: Lippincott, 1955; rev. ed., *The Modern Psychological Novel*, New York: Grosset and Dunlap, 1964.

Edgar, Pelham. *The Art of the Novel from 1700 to the Present Time*. New York: Macmillan, 1933.

———. "The Drift of Modern Fiction." *UTQ*, 1 (1931), 123-39.

Eglinton, John [William K. Magee]. *Irish Literary Portraits*. London: Macmillan, 1935.

Egoff, Sheila, G. T. Stubbs, and L. F. Ashley, eds. *Only Connect: Readings in Children's Literature*. New York: Oxford Univ. Press, 1969.

Ehrstine, John W., John R. Elwood, and Robert C. McLean, eds. *On Stage and Off: Eight Essays in English Literature*. Pullman: Washington State Univ. Press, 1968.

Elliott, Robert C. *The Shape of Utopia: Studies in a Literary Genre.* Chicago: Univ. of Chicago Press, 1970.

Ellis, Geoffrey Uther. *Twilight on Parnassus: A Survey of Post-War Fiction and Pre-War Criticism.* London: M. Joseph, 1939.

Ellis, Havelock. *From Marlowe to Shaw: The Studies 1876-1936 in English Literature of Havelock Ellis.* Ed. John Gawsworth. London: Williams and Norgate, 1950.

―――. *My Confessional: Questions of Our Day.* Boston: Houghton Mifflin, 1934.

―――. *The Philosophy of Conflict and Other Essays in War-Time,* 2d ser. London: Constable; Boston: Houghton Mifflin, 1919.

―――. *Views and Reviews: A Selection of Uncollected Articles, 1884-1932,* 1st - 2d ser. Boston: Houghton Mifflin, 1932.

Ellis, Stewart M. *Mainly Victorian.* New York: Hutchinson, 1925.

Ellmann, Richard, ed. *Edwardians and Late Victorians: English Institute Essays, 1959.* New York: Columbia Univ. Press, 1960.

―――. *Golden Codgers: Biographical Speculations.* New York: Oxford Univ. Press, 1973.

Elwin, Malcolm. *Old Gods Falling.* London: Macmillan, 1939.

Endicott, N. J. "The Novel in England Between the Wars." *UTQ,* 12 (1942), 18-31.

Engelberg, Edward. *The Unknown Distance: From Consciousness to Conscience, Goethe to Camus.* Cambridge, Mass.: Harvard Univ. Press, 1972.

English Association, London. *Essays and Studies by Members of the Association.* v. 6, London: Oxford Univ. Press, 1920; v. 31, London: Oxford Univ. Press, 1945; n.s. v. 3, London: Transatlantic, 1950; n.s. v. 28, Atlantic Highlands, N.J.: Humanities, 1975.

Enright, Dennis J. *The Apothecary's Shop: Essays on Literature.* London: Secker and Warburg, 1957.

―――. *Conspirators and Poets.* Chester Springs, Pa.: Dufour; London: Chatto and Windus, 1966.

―――. *Man is an Onion: Reviews and Essays.* La Salle, Ill.: Open Court, 1973.

Ernst, Morris L. *The Best is Yet. . . .* New York: Harper, 1945.

―――, and William Seagle. *To the Pure: A Study of Obscenity and the Censor.* New York: Viking, 1928.

Ervine, St. John G. *Some Impressions of My Elders.* New York: Macmillan, 1922.

Essays in Memory of Barrett Wendell, by his Assistants. Cambridge: Cambridge Univ. Press, 1926.

Essays of the Year, 1929-1930, by Various Authors. London: Argonaut, 1930.

Books Cited and General Bibliography

Essays of the Year, 1930-31, by Various Authors. London: Argonaut, 1931.

Essays of the Year, 1933-1934, by Various Authors. London: Argonaut, 1934.

Evans, B. Ifor. *English Literature Between the Wars*. London: Methuen, 1949.

Farrell, James T. *League of Frightened Philistines*. New York: Vanguard, 1945.

———. *Literature and Morality*. New York: Vanguard, 1947.

———. *Reflections at Fifty and Other Essays*. New York: Vanguard, 1954.

Feibleman, James K. *In Praise of Comedy: A Study in its Theory and Practice*. New York: Macmillan, 1939.

Feldman, Gene, and Max Gartenberg, eds. *The Beat Generation and the Angry Young Men*. New York: Citadel, 1958.

Fernandez, Ramon. *Messages*. Tr. M. Belgion. New York: Harcourt, 1927.

Firchow, Peter. *The Writer's Place: Interviews on the Literary Situation in Contemporary Britain*. Minneapolis: Univ. of Minnesota Press, 1974.

Flandrau, Charles Macomb. *Prejudices*. New York and London: Appleton, 1913.

Fleishman, Avrom. *The English Historical Novel: Walter Scott to Virginia Woolf*. Baltimore: Johns Hopkins Univ. Press, 1971.

Fletcher, Ian, ed. *Romantic Mythologies*. London: Routledge and K. Paul; New York: Barnes and Noble, 1967.

Follett, Helen T., and Wilson J. Follett. *Some Modern Novelists: Appreciations and Estimates*. New York: Holt, 1918.

Ford, Boris, ed. *The Pelican Guide to English Literature, v. 7: The Modern Age*. Harmondsworth, Middlesex: Penguin, 1961, 1963; rev. 1964, 1973.

Ford, Ford Madox. *It Was The Nightingale*. Philadelphia: Lippincott, 1933.

———. *Portraits from Life: Memories and Criticisms*. Boston: Houghton Mifflin, 1937.

Ford, Hugh D. *Published in Paris: American and British Writers, Printers, and Publishers in Paris, 1920-39*. New York: Macmillan, 1975.

Forster, E. M. *Abinger Harvest*. London: E. Arnold; New York: Harcourt, 1936.

———. *Aspects of the Novel and Related Writings*. London: E. Arnold; New York: Harcourt, 1927.

———. *The Development of English Prose Between 1918 and 1939*. Glasgow: Jackson, 1945.

———. *Two Cheers for Democracy*. New York: Harcourt, 1951.

Fowlie, Wallace. *Love in Literature: Studies in Symbolic Expression*. Bloomington: Indiana Univ. Press, 1965. [originally *The Clown's Grail: A Study of Love in Its Literary Expression*. Denver: Swallow, 1948]

Fox, Ralph W. *The Novel and the People*. London: Lawrence and Wishart; New York: International Publishers, 1937.

Frank, Joseph. *The Widening Gyre: Crisis and Mastery in Modern Literature*. New Brunswick, N.J.: Rutgers Univ. Press, 1963.

Fraser, G. S. *The Modern Writer and His World*. London: Derek Verschoyle, 1953; New York: Criterion, 1955; rev. ed. Baltimore: Penguin, 1964.

Frederick, John T. "New Techniques in the Novel." *EJ*, 24 (1935), 355-63.

Freeman, John. *English Portraits and Essays*. London: Hodder and Stoughton, 1924.

———. *The Moderns: Essays in Literary Criticism*. London: Scott, 1916; New York: Crowell, 1917.

Friar, Kimon, and John Brinnin, eds. *Modern Poetry: British and American*. New York: Appleton, 1951.

Friedman, Alan W., ed. *Forms of Modern British Fiction*. Austin: Univ. of Texas Press, 1975.

———. *The Turn of the Novel*. New York: Oxford Univ. Press, 1966.

Friedman, Melvin J., and John B. Vickery, eds. *The Shaken Realist: Essays in Modern Literature in Honor of Frederick J. Hoffman*. Baton Rouge: Louisiana State Univ. Press, 1970.

———. *Stream of Consciousness: A Study in Literary Method*. New Haven, Conn.: Yale Univ. Press, 1955.

———, ed. *The Vision Obscured: Perceptions of Some Twentieth-Century Catholic Novelists*. New York: Fordham Univ. Press, 1970.

Frierson, William C. *The English Novel in Transition, 1885-1940*. Norman: Oklahoma Univ. Press, 1942.

Frye, Northrop. *Fables of Identity: Studies in Poetic Mythology*. New York: Harcourt, 1963.

———, ed. *Sound and Poetry: English Institute Essays, 1956*. New York: Columbia Univ. Press, 1957.

Fuchs, Carolyn. "Words, Action and the Modern Novel." *Kerygma*, 4 (1964), 3-11.

Fuller, Edmund. *Books with Men Behind Them.* New York: Random House, 1962.

————. *Man in Modern Fiction: Some Minority Opinions of Contemporary American Writing.* New York: Random House, 1958.

Gardiner, Alfred G. *Many Furrows.* New York: Dutton, 1924.

————. *Portraits and Portents.* New York: Harper, 1926.

Gardiner, Harold C. *In All Conscience: Reflections on Books and Culture.* Garden City, N.Y.: Hanover House, 1959.

Garnett, Edward. *Friday Nights: Literary Criticisms and Appreciations,* 1st ser. New York: Knopf, 1922.

Garrett, Peter. *Scene and Symbol from George Eliot to James Joyce: Studies in Changing Fictional Mode.* New Haven, Conn.: Yale Univ. Press, 1969.

Garzilli, Enrico. *Circles Without Center: Paths to the Discovery and Creation of Self in Modern Literature.* Cambridge, Mass.: Harvard Univ. Press, 1972.

Gass, William H. *Fiction and the Figures of Life.* New York: Knopf, 1971.

Gaunt, William. *The Aesthetic Adventure.* London: J. Cape, 1945.

George, Walter L. *Literary Chapters.* Boston: Little, Brown; London: Collins, 1918. [British ed. entitled *A Novelist on Novels*]

————. "A Painter's Literature." *EngRev,* 30 (1920), 223-34.

Gerber, Richard. *Utopian Fantasy: A Study of English Utopian Fiction Since the End of the Nineteenth Century.* London: Routledge and K. Paul, 1955.

Gerould, Gordon H. *Patterns of English and American Fiction.* Boston: Little, Brown, 1942.

Gerould, Katharine Fullerton. "British Novelists, Ltd." *YR,* n.s. 7 (1917), 161-85.

————. "Stream of Consciousness." *SRL,* 4 (October 22, 1927), 233-35.

Gettmann, R. A. *Turgenev in England and America.* Urbana: Univ. of Illinois Press, 1941.

Gill, Richard. *Happy Rural Seat: The English Country House and the Literary Imagination.* New Haven: Yale Univ. Press, 1972.

Gillie, Christopher. *Character in English Literature.* London: Chatto and Windus, 1965.

————. *Movements in Modern English Literature, 1900-1940.* Cambridge: Cambridge Univ. Press, 1975.

Gillis, James M. *False Prophets.* New York: Macmillan, 1925, 1930.

————. *This, Our Day: Approvals and Disapprovals.* New York: Paulist Press, 1933.

Gindin, James J. "Comedy in Contemporary British Fiction." *PMA-SAL*, 44 (1959), 389-97.

_____. "The Fable Begins to Break Down." *WSCL*, 8 (1967), 1-18.

_____. *Harvest of a Quiet Eye: The Novel of Compassion.* Bloomington: Indiana Univ. Press, 1971.

_____. *Postwar British Fiction: New Accents and Attitudes.* Berkeley: Univ. of California Press, 1962.

_____. "Well Beyond Laughter: Directions from Fifties' Comic Fiction." *SNNTS*, 3 (1971), 357-64.

Glicksberg, Charles I. "Anti-Utopianism in Modern Literature." *SWR*, 37 (1952), 221-28.

_____. *The Ironic Vision in Modern Literature.* The Hague: Martinus Nijhoff, 1969.

_____. "The Lost Generation of Literature." *SWR*, 38 (1953), 211-18.

_____. *Modern Literary Perspectivism.* Dallas: Southern Methodist Univ. Press, 1970.

_____. *The Self in Modern Literature.* University Park: Penn. State Univ. Press, 1963.

Goldring, Douglas. *Reputations: Essays in Criticism.* New York: Seltzer, 1920.

_____. *South Lodge: Reminiscences of Violet Hunt, Ford Madox Ford, and the English Review Circle.* London: Constable, 1943.

Goodheart, Eugene. *The Cult of the Ego: The Self in Modern Literature.* Chicago: Univ. of Chicago Press, 1968.

Goodin, George V., ed. *The English Novel in the Nineteenth Century: Essays on the Literary Mediation of Human Values.* Urbana: Univ. of Illinois Press, 1972.

GoodKnight, Glen, ed. *Mythcon I: Proceedings.* Los Angeles: Mythopoeic Soc., 1971.

Gose, Elliott B. *Imagination Indulged: The Irrational in the Nineteenth-Century Novel.* Montreal: McGill-Queen's Univ. Press, 1972.

Gosse, Edmund W. *More Books on the Table.* New York: Scribner's; London: Heinemann, 1923.

Gould, Gerald. *The English Novel of Today.* London: Castle, 1924; New York: MacVeagh, 1925.

Grabo, Carl H. *The Technique of the Novel.* New York: Scribner's, 1928.

Gransden, K. W. "Thoughts on Contemporary Fiction." *REL*, 1, 2 (1960), 7-17.

Graves, Robert. *Five Pens in Hand.* Garden City, N.Y.: Doubleday, 1958.

Gray, James. *On Second Thought.* Minneapolis: Univ. of Minnesota Press, 1946.

Gray, Nigel. *The Silent Majority: A Study of the Working Class in Post-War British Fiction.* London: Vision; New York: Barnes and Noble, 1973.

Gray, Ronald. *The German Tradition in Literature, 1871-1945.* Cambridge: Cambridge Univ. Press, 1967.

Grebstein, Sheldon N., ed. *Perspectives in Contemporary Criticism: A Collection of Recent Essays by American, English, and European Literary Critics.* New York: Harper, 1968.

Greenberg, Alvin. "The Death of the Psyche: A Way to the Self in Contemporary Fiction." *Criticism,* 8 (1966), 1-18.

Greenblatt, Stephen J. *Three Modern Satirists: Waugh, Orwell and Huxley.* New Haven, Conn.: Yale Univ. Press, 1965.

Greene, Graham. *Collected Essays.* London: Bodley Head; New York: Viking, 1969.

Gregor, Ian, and Brian Nicholas. *The Moral and the Story.* London: Faber and Faber, 1962.

Gregory, Horace. *The Dying Gladiators and Other Essays.* New York: Grove, 1961.

———. *The Shield of Achilles: Essays on Beliefs in Poetry.* New York: Harcourt, 1944.

———. *Spirit of Time and Place: The Collected Essays of Horace Gregory.* New York: Norton, 1973.

Griffin, Gerald. *The Wild Geese: Pen Portraits of Famous Irish Exiles.* London: Jarrolds, 1938.

Grigson, Geoffrey. *The Contrary View: Glimpses of Fudge and Gold.* Totowa, N.J.: Rowman and Littlefield, 1974.

Grosshans, Henry, ed. *To Find Something New: Studies in Contemporary Literature.* Pullman: Washington State Univ. Press, 1969.

Grossvogel, David I. *Limits of the Novel: Evolutions of a Form from Chaucer to Robbe-Grillet.* Ithaca, N.Y.: Cornell Univ. Press, 1968.

Guedalla, Philip. *A Gallery.* London: Constable; New York: Putnam, 1924.

———. *Masters and Men.* New York: Putnam, 1923.

Hackett, Francis. *Horizons: A Book of Criticism.* New York: Huebsch, 1918.

———. *On Judging Books, In General and In Particular.* New York: Day, 1947.

Hadfield, John, ed. *The Saturday Book, 24-27,* 4 vol. New York: Macmillan, 1964-1967.

Hagopian, John V., and Martin Dolch, eds. *Insight II: Analysis of Modern British Literature.* Frankfurt am Main: Hirschgraben-Verlag, 1964.

Haines, George IV. "Forms of Imaginative Prose: 1900-1940." *SoR*, 7 (1942), 755-75.

Haines, Helen E. *What's in a Novel?* New York: Columbia Univ. Press, 1942.

Hale, Nancy. *The Realities of Fiction: A Book About Writing.* Boston: Little, Brown, 1962.

Hall, James. *The Lunatic Giant in the Drawing Room: The British and American Novel Since 1930.* Bloomington: Indiana Univ. Press, 1968.

———. *The Tragic Comedians: Seven Modern British Novelists.* Bloomington: Indiana Univ. Press, 1963.

Hall, James Norman. *Under a Thatched Roof.* Boston: Houghton Mifflin, 1942.

Halpenny, Francess G., ed. *Editing Twentieth Century Texts.* Toronto: Univ. of Toronto Press, 1972.

Halperin, John, ed. *The Theory of the Novel: New Essays.* New York: Oxford Univ. Press, 1974.

Hamill, Elizabeth. *These Modern Writers.* Melbourne: Georgian House, 1946.

Hamilton, Cosmo. *People Worth Talking About.* New York: Robert McBride, 1933.

Hamilton, Kenneth M. "Theological Bearings in Modern Literature." *DR*, 32 (1952), 121-30.

Hampshire, Stuart N. *Modern Writers and Other Essays.* London: Chatto and Windus, 1969; New York: Knopf, 1970.

Handy, William J. *Modern Fiction: A Formalist Approach.* Carbondale: Southern Illinois Univ. Press, 1971.

Hannah, Barbara. *Striving Towards Wholeness.* New York: Putnam, 1971.

Hansen, Agnes C. *Twentieth Century Forces in European Fiction.* Chicago: American Library Ass'n., 1934.

Hardwick, Elizabeth. *Seduction and Betrayal: Women and Literature.* New York: Random House; London: Weidenfeld and Nicolson, 1974.

Hardy, Barbara. *The Appropriate Form: An Essay on the Novel.* London: Athlone, 1964.

———. *Tellers and Listeners: The Narrative Imagination.* London: Athlone; Atlantic Highlands, N.J.: Humanities, 1975.

Hardy, John Edward. *Man in the Modern Novel.* Seattle: Univ. of Washington Press, 1964.

Harkness, Bruce. "The Lucky Crowd: Contemporary British Fiction." *EJ*, 47 (1958), 387-97.

Harmon, Maurice. *Modern Irish Literature, 1800-1967: A Reader's Guide.* Dublin: Dolmen, 1967; Chester Springs, Pa.: Dufour, 1968.

Harper, Howard M., Jr., and Charles Edge, eds. *The Classic British Novel.* Athens: Univ. of Georgia Press, 1972.

Harris, Frank. *Contemporary Portraits,* 1st - 4th ser. New York: Brentano's, 1915-23.

Harrison, John R. *The Reactionaries: Yeats, Lewis, Pound, Eliot, Lawrence—A Study of the Anti-Democratic Intelligentsia.* New York: Schocken, 1967.

Harvey, W. T. "Have You Anything to Declare? or, Angry Young Men: Facts and Fictions." *International Literary Annual No. 1,* ed. John Wain. London: John Calder, 1958, 47-59.

Harward, Timothy Blake, ed. *European Patterns: Contemporary Patterns in European Writing—A Series of Essays by Bruce Arnold and Others.* Chester Springs, Pa.: Dufour, 1967.

Harwood, H. C. "Recent Tendencies of Modern Fiction." *QR*, 252 (1929), 321-38.

Hassan, Ihab H. "The Anti-Hero in Modern British and American Fiction." *Comparative Literature: Proceedings of the Second Congress of the International Comparative Literature Association,* 2 vol. Ed. Werner P. Friederich. Chapel Hill: Univ. of North Carolina Press, 1959, 309-23.

———. *The Dismemberment of Orpheus: Toward a Post-modern Literature.* New York: Oxford Univ. Press, 1971.

———. *Paracriticisms: Seven Speculations of the Times.* Urbana: Univ. of Illinois Press, 1975.

Hayashi, Tetsumaro, ed. *Steinbeck's Literary Dimension: A Guide to Comparative Studies.* Metuchen, N.J.: Scarecrow, 1973.

Hays, Peter L. *The Limping Hero: Grotesques in Literature.* New York: New York Univ. Press, 1971.

Heilbrun, Carolyn G. *Towards a Recognition of Androgyny.* New York: Knopf, 1973.

———. "The Woman as Hero." *TQ*, 8, 4 (1965), 132-41.

Henderson, Philip. *The Novel Today: Studies in Contemporary Attitudes.* London: Lane, 1936.

Heppenstall, Rayner. *The Fourfold Tradition: Notes on the French and English Literatures, with Some Ethnological and Historical Asides.* London: Barrie and Rockliff; New York: New Directions, 1961.

Hewett, R. P. *Reading and Response: An Approach to the Criticism of Literature.* London: Harrap, 1960.

Hibbard, G. R., with George A. Panichas and Allan Rodway, eds. *Renaissance and Modern Essays Presented to Vivian de Sola Pinto in Celebration of His Seventieth Birthday*. London: Routledge and K. Paul; New York: Barnes and Noble, 1966.

Hicks, Granville. *Figures of Transition: A Study of British Literature at the End of the Nineteenth Century*. New York: Macmillan 1939.

Highet, Gilbert. *The Anatomy of Satire*. Princeton, N.J.: Princetor Univ. Press, 1962.

———. *The Classical Tradition*. New York: Oxford Univ. Press, 1949.

———. *Clerk of Oxenford: Essays in Literature and Life*. New York: Oxford Univ. Press, 1954.

———. *Explorations*. New York: Oxford Univ.Press, 1971.

———. *People, Places, and Books*. New York: Oxford Univ. Press, 1953.

———. *Talents and Geniuses: The Pleasures of Appreciation*. New York: Oxford Univ. Press, 1957.

Hilfer, Anthony Channel. *The Revolt from the Village, 1915-1930*. Chapel Hill: Univ. of North Carolina Press, 1969.

Hillegas, Mark R., ed. *Shadows of Imagination: The Fantasies of C. S. Lewis, J. R. R. Tolkien, and Charles Williams*. Carbondale: Southern Illinois Univ. Press, 1969.

Hind, Charles L. *Authors and I*. London: Lane, 1921.

———. *More Authors and I*. London: Lane, 1922.

Hoare, Dorothy Mackenzie. *Some Studies in the Modern Novel*. London: Chatto and Windus, 1938; Litchfield, Conn.: Prospect, 1940; Philadelphia: Dufour, 1953.

Hoffman, Frederick J. *Freudianism and the Literary Mind*. Baton Rouge: Louisiana State Univ. Press, 1945, 1957.

———. *The Imagination's New Beginning*. Notre Dame, Ind.: Univ. of Notre Dame Press, 1967.

———. *The Mortal No: Death and the Modern Imagination*. Princeton, N.J.: Princeton Univ. Press, 1964.

Hoggart, Richard. *Speaking to Each Other: Essays*, 2 vol. New York: Oxford Univ. Press; London: Chatto and Windus, 1970.

———. "The Unsuspected Audience." *New Statesman*, 56 (1958), 308-10.

Holbrook, David. *The Quest for Love*. University: Univ. of Alabama Press, 1965.

Holloway, John. *The Charted Mirror: Literary and Critical Essays*. London: Routledge and K. Paul, 1960.

Holroyd, Stuart. *Emergence from Chaos*. London: Gollancz; Boston: Houghton Mifflin, 1957.

Hopper, Stanley R., ed. *Spiritual Problems in Contemporary Literature.* New York: Harper, 1957.

Hough, Graham. *Image and Experience: Reflections on a Literary Revolution.* London: Duckworth; Lincoln: Univ. of Nebraska Press, 1960.

Howarth, Herbert. *The Irish Writers, 1880-1940.* New York: Hill and Wang, 1959.

———. *Notes on Some Figures Behind T. S. Eliot.* Boston: Houghton Mifflin, 1964.

Howarth, Robert Guy. *Literary Particles.* Sydney: Angus and Robertson, 1946.

Howe, Irving. *Politics and the Novel.* New York: Horizon, 1957.

Howe, Susanne. *Novels of Empire.* New York: Columbia Univ. Press, 1949.

Hoyt, Charles A., ed. *Minor British Novelists.* Carbondale: Southern Illinois Univ. Press, 1967.

Huddleston, Sisley. *Articles de Paris: A Book of Essays.* London: Methuen; New York: Macmillan, 1928.

Humphrey, Robert. *Stream of Consciousness Technique: A Study of James Joyce, Virginia Woolf, Dorothy Richardson, William Faulkner and Others.* Berkeley: Univ. of California Press, 1954.

Huneker, James G. *Ivory Apes and Peacocks.* New York: Scribner's, 1915.

———. *Overtones: A Book of Temperaments.* New York: Scribner's, 1904.

———. *Pathos of Distance: A Book of a Thousand and One Moments.* New York: Scribner's, 1913.

———. *Unicorns.* New York: Scribner's, 1917.

———. *Variations.* New York: Scribner's, 1921.

Hutchinson, George E. *The Itinerant Ivory Tower: Scientific and Literary Essays.* New Haven: Yale Univ. Press, 1953.

Huttar, Charles A., ed. *Imagination and the Spirit: Essays in Literature and the Christian Faith Presented to Clyde S. Kilby.* Grand Rapids, Mich.: Eerdmans, 1971.

Huxley, Aldous. *Music at Night and Other Essays.* Garden City, N.Y.: Doubleday, 1931.

———. *Olive Tree.* New York: Harper, 1937.

Hyman, Stanley E. *Standards: A Chronicle of Books for our Time.* New York: Horizon, 1966.

Hynes, Samuel. *Edwardian Occasions: Essays on English Writing in the Early Twentieth Century.* London: Routledge and K. Paul; New York: Oxford Univ. Press, 1972.

———. "The 'Poor Sod' as Hero." *Cweal*, 64 (1956), 51-53.

Illinois, University of, Department of English. *Studies by Members of the English Department, in Memory of John Jay Parry.* Urbana: Univ. of Illinois Press, 1955.

Inglis, Fred. *An Essential Discipline.* London: Methuen, 1968.

Isaacs, Jacob. *An Assessment of Twentieth Century Literature.* London: Secker and Warburg, 1951.

Iser, Wolfgang. *The Implied Reader: Patterns of Communication in Prose Fiction from Bunyan to Beckett.* Baltimore: Johns Hopkins Univ. Press, 1974.

Joad, C. E. M. *Return to Philosophy.* London: Faber and Faber, 1935; New York: Dutton, 1936.

Johnson, Pamela Hansford. "Literature." *The Baldwin Age.* Ed. John Raymond. Chester Springs, Pa.: Dufour, 1961, 179-88.

Johnson, Reginald Brinley. *Some Contemporary Novelists: Men.* London: Leonard Parsons, 1922.

———. *Some Contemporary Novelists: Women.* London: Leonard Parsons, 1920.

Johnstone, J. K. *The Bloomsbury Group: A Study of E. M. Forster, Lytton Strachey, Virginia Woolf, and their Circle.* London: Secker and Warburg; New York: Noonday, 1954.

Jones, Claude E. "Modern Books Dealing with the Novel in English: A Check List." *BB*, 22 (1957), 85-87.

Jordan-Smith, Paul. *For the Love of Books: The Adventures of an Impecunious Collector.* New York: Oxford Univ. Press, 1934.

Josipovici, Gabriel. *The World and the Book: A Study of Modern Fiction.* Stanford, Cal.: Stanford Univ. Press, 1971.

Jost, François, ed. *Proceedings of the IVth Congress of the International Comparative Literature Association, Fribourg, 1964.* The Hague: Mouton, 1966.

Jump, John D. "The Recent British Novel." *Memoirs and Proceedings of the Manchester Literary and Philosophical Society*, 10 (1958-1959), 23-28.

Kachru, Braj B., and Herbert F. W. Stahlke, eds. *Current Trends in Stylistics.* Edmonton, Alberta and Champaign, Ill.: Linguistic Research, Inc., 1972.

Kaplan, Harold. *The Passive Voice: An Approach to Modern Fiction.* Athens: Ohio Univ. Press, 1966.

Kaplan, Sydney Janet. *Feminine Consciousness in the Modern British Novel.* Urbana: Univ. of Illinois Press, 1975.

Karl, Frederick R. *The Contemporary English Novel.* New York: Farrar, Straus, 1962.

————, and Marvin Magalaner. *A Reader's Guide to Great Twentieth Century English Novels.* New York: Noonday, 1959.

Kaul, Raj K., ed. *Essays Presented to Amy G. Stock, Professor of English, Rajasthan University, 1961-65.* Jaipur: Rajasthan Univ. Press, 1965.

Kazin, Alfred. *Contemporaries.* Boston: Little, Brown, 1962.

————. *The Inmost Leaf.* New York: Harcourt, 1955.

Keating, P. J. *The Working Classes in Victorian Fiction.* New York: Barnes and Noble, 1971.

Kellett, Ernest E. *Reconsiderations: Literary Essays.* Cambridge: Cambridge Univ. Press, 1928.

Kellogg, Gene. *The Vital Tradition: The Catholic Novel in a Period of Convergence.* Chicago: Loyola Univ. Press, 1970.

Kennard, Jean E. *Number and Nightmare: Forms of Fantasy in Contemporary Fiction.* Hamden, Conn.: Archon, 1975.

Kennedy, Alan. *The Protean Self: Dramatic Action in Contemporary Fiction.* New York: Columbia Univ. Press, 1974.

Kenner, Hugh. *Gnomon: Essays on Contemporary Literature.* New York: McDowell, Obolensky, 1958.

Kermode, Frank. "Myth, Reality, and Fiction." *Listener,* 68 (1962), 311-13.

————. *Puzzles and Epiphanies: Essays and Reviews, 1958-1961.* New York: Chilmark, 1962.

Kernan, Alvin B. *The Plot of Satire.* New Haven, Conn.: Yale Univ. Press, 1965.

Kerr, Elizabeth. *Bibliography of the Sequence Novel.* Minneapolis: Univ. of Minnesota Press, 1950, 11-38.

Kesava Menon, K. P., M. Manuel, and K. Ayyappa Paniker, eds. *Literary Studies: Homage to Dr. A. Sivaramasubramonia Aiyer.* Trivandrum: St. Joseph's, 1973.

Kettle, Arnold. *An Introduction to the English Novel,* 2 vol. London: Hutchinson, 1951-53.

Keynes, John Maynard. *Essays in Persuasion.* London: Macmillan, 1931; New York: Harcourt, 1932; London: Hart-Davis, 1951.

Kiely, Benedict. *Modern Irish Fiction: A Critique.* Dublin: Golden Eagle, 1950.

Killam, G. D. *Africa in English Fiction, 1874-1939.* Ibadan: Ibadan Univ. Press, 1968.

Kirk, Rudolf, and Charles F. Main, eds. *Essays on Literary History Presented to J. Milton French.* New Brunswick, N.J.: Rutgers Univ. Press, 1960.

Kitchin, Laurence. "Imperial Weekend." *Listener,* 74 (1965), 662-63, 667.

Knight, G. Wilson. *Neglected Powers: Essays on Nineteenth and Twentieth Century Literature.* New York: Barnes and Noble, 1971.

Knight, Grant C. *The Novel in English.* New York: R. R. Smith, 1931.

———. *Superlatives.* New York: Knopf, 1925.

Knoepflmacher, U. C. *Laughter and Despair: Readings in Ten Novels of the Victorian Era.* Berkeley: Univ. of California Press, 1971.

Koestler, Arthur. *The Trail of the Dinosaur, and Other Essays.* New York: Macmillan, 1955.

Kohler, Dayton. "Time in the Modern Novel." *CE,* 10 (1948), 15-24.

Kostelanetz, Richard, ed. *On Contemporary Literature.* New York: Avon, 1964.

Kraft, Walter C., ed. *Proceedings: Pacific Northwest Conference on Foreign Languages, Twenty-Fourth Annual Meeting, May 4-5, 1973, Western Washington State College, v. 24.* Corvallis: Oregon State Univ., 1973.

Krieger, Murray. *The Play and Place of Criticism.* Baltimore: Johns Hopkins Univ. Press, 1967.

———. *The Tragic Vision: Variations on a Theme in Literary Interpretation.* New York: Holt, 1960.

Kronenberger, Louis, ed. *Novelists on Novelists: An Anthology.* Garden City, N.Y.: Doubleday, 1962.

Kumar, Shiv K. *Bergson and the Stream of Consciousness Novel.* New York: New York Univ. Press, 1963.

Kunitz, Stanley J., and Howard Haycraft, eds. *Twentieth Century Authors.* New York: Wilson, 1942; *First Supplement,* New York: Wilson, 1955.

Kunkel, Francis L. *Passion and The Passion: Sex and Religion in Modern Literature.* Philadelphia: Westminster, 1975.

Kyoritsu Women's Junior College. *Collected Essays by the Members of the Faculty in Commemoration of the 20th Anniversary,* No. 17. Tokyo: Kyoritsu Women's Junior College, 1973.

Lacon [pseud.]. *Lectures to Living Authors.* Boston: Houghton Mifflin, 1925.

Langbaum, Robert W. *The Modern Spirit: Essays on the Continuity of Nineteenth- and Twentieth-Century Literature.* New York: Oxford Univ. Press, 1970.

Larrett, William. *The English Novel from Thomas Hardy to Graham Greene.* Frankfurt am Main: Diesterweg, 1967.

357

Books Cited and General Bibliography

Laughlin, James, ed. *New Directions in Prose and Poetry, 1939, 1941, 1942.* Norfolk, Conn.: New Directions, 1939, 1941, 1942.

Laurenson, Diana T., and Alan Swingewood. *The Sociology of Literature.* London: MacGibbon and Kee, 1971; New York: Schocken, 1972.

Lavrin, Janko. *Aspects of Modernism, from Wilde to Pirandello.* London: S. Nott, 1935.

Law, Hugh Alexander. *Anglo-Irish Literature.* Dublin and Cork: Talbot, 1926.

Lawrence, D. H. *Selected Literary Criticism.* Ed. Anthony Beal. New York: Viking, 1956.

Lawrence, Margaret. *The School of Femininity.* New York: Stokes, 1936.

Leavis, F. R. *The Common Pursuit.* London: Chatto and Windus; New York: Stewart, 1952; Harmondsworth, Middlesex: Penguin, 1963.

———. *For Continuity.* Cambridge: G. Fraser, The Minority Press, 1933.

———. *The Great Tradition: George Eliot, Henry James, Joseph Conrad.* London: Chatto and Windus; New York: Stewart, 1948; Garden City, N.Y.: Doubleday, 1954.

———. *Nor Shall My Sword: Discourses on Pluralism, Compassion and Social Hope.* New York: Barnes and Noble, 1972.

Lebowitz, Naomi. *Humanism and the Absurd in the Modern Novel.* Evanston, Ill.: Northwestern Univ. Press, 1971.

Leclaire, Lucien. *A General Analytical Bibliography of the Regional Novelists of the British Isles: 1800-1950.* Paris: Société d'Edition "Les Belles Lettres," 1954.

Lehmann, John, ed. *The Craft of Letters in England: A Symposium.* London: Cresset, 1956; Boston: Houghton Mifflin, 1957.

———. *The Open Night.* New York: Harcourt, 1952.

Lerner, Max. *Actions and Passions: Notes on the Multiple Revolution of our Time.* New York: Simon and Schuster, 1949.

LeRoy, Gaylord C., and Ursula Beitz, eds. *Preserve and Create: Essays in Marxist Literary Criticism.* New York: Humanities, 1973.

Levin, Harry. *Contexts of Criticism.* Cambridge, Mass.: Harvard Univ. Press, 1957.

Lewis, R. W. B. *The Picaresque Saint: Representative Figures in Contemporary Fiction.* Philadelphia: Lippincott, 1959.

Lewis, Wyndham. *Men Without Art.* London: Cassell, 1934.

———. *Time and Western Man.* London: Chatto and Windus, 1927.

———. *The Writer and the Absolute.* London: Methuen, 1952.

Lichtheim, George. *Collected Essays.* New York: Viking, 1973.

Liddell, Robert. *A Treatise on the Novel.* London: J. Cape, 1947.

Lindsay, Jack. *After the 'Thirties': The Novel in Britain and Its Future.* London: Lawrence and Wishart, 1956.

Lingner, Erika, et al., eds. *Essays in Honour of William Gallacher.* Berlin: Humboldt Univ., 1966.

Linklater, Eric. *The Art of Adventure.* New York: Macmillan, 1947.

Linn, James W., and H. W. Taylor. *A Foreword to Fiction.* New York: Appleton, 1935.

Littlejohn, David. *Interruptions.* New York: Grossman, 1970.

Lodge, David. *Language of Fiction: Essays in Criticism and Verbal Analysis of the English Novel.* New York: Columbia Univ. Press, 1966.

———. *The Novelist at the Crossroads, and Other Essays on Fiction and Criticism.* Ithaca, N.Y.: Cornell Univ. Press, 1971.

Long, Richard A., and Iva G. Jones. "Toward a Definition of 'The Decadent Novel'." *CE,* 22 (1961), 245-49.

Longaker, Mark, and Edwin C. Bolles. *Contemporary English Literature.* New York: Appleton, 1953.

Lovett, Robert M. *Preface to Fiction: A Discussion of Great Modern Novels.* Chicago: Rockwell, 1931.

———, and Helen S. Hughes. *The History of the Novel in England.* Boston: Houghton Mifflin, 1932.

Lunn, Arnold H. M. *Roman Converts.* London: Chapman, 1924.

Lynd, Robert. *Books and Authors.* New York: Putnam, 1923.

———. *Old and New Masters.* London: Unwin; New York: Scribner's, 1919.

McAlpin, Edwin A. *Old and New Books as Life Teachers.* Garden City, N.Y.: Doubleday, 1928.

Macaulay, Rose, V. S. Pritchett, et al. "The Future of Fiction." *New Letters and Daylight, 1946.* London: John Lehmann, 1946, 71-97.

MacCarthy, Desmond. *Criticism.* New York: Putnam, 1932.

———. *Memories.* Oxford: Oxford Univ. Press, 1953.

———. *Portraits.* New York: Putnam, 1931.

McCarthy, Mary. *The Writing on the Wall, and Other Literary Essays.* New York: Harcourt, 1970.

McCormack, Thomas, ed. *Afterwords: Novelists on their Novels.* New York: Harper, 1968.

McCormick, John. *Catastrophe and Imagination: An Interpretation of the Recent English and American Novel.* London and New York: Longmans, Green, 1957.

McCullough, Bruce M. *Representative English Novelists: Defoe to Conrad.* New York: Harper, 1946.

McDowell, Frederick P. W. " 'The Devious Involutions of Human Character and Emotions': Reflections on Some Recent British Novels." *WSCL*, 4 (1963), 339-66.

———. "Recent British Fiction: Some Established Writers." *ConL*, 11 (1970), 401-31.

McFee, William. *Harbours of Memory.* Garden City, N.Y.: Doubleday, 1921.

———. *Swallowing the Anchor.* Garden City, N.Y.: Doubleday, 1925.

McIntosh, Angus, and M. A. K. Halliday. *Patterns of Language: Papers in General, Descriptive, and Applied Linguistics.* Bloomington: Indiana Univ. Press, 1967.

McIntyre, John P. "The Modes of Disillusionment: Irony in Modern Fiction." *Renascence*, 17, 1 (1964), 70-76, 96.

Mack, Maynard, and Ian Gregor, eds. *Imagined Worlds: Essays on Some English Novels and Novelists in Honour of John Butt.* London: Methuen, 1968.

Mackenzie, Compton. *Literature in My Time.* London: Rich and Cowan, 1933.

McLuhan, Marshall. *The Interior Landscape: The Literary Criticism of Marshall McLuhan, 1943-1962.* Ed. Eugene McNamara. New York: McGraw-Hill, 1969.

McMillan, Dougald. *Transition: The History of a Literary Era, 1927-1938.* New York: Braziller, 1975.

Macy, John A. *The Critical Game.* New York: Boni and Liveright, 1922.

Madden, David, ed. *Rediscoveries: Informal Essays in Which Well-Known Novelists Rediscover Neglected Works of Fiction by One of Their Favorite Authors.* New York: Crown, 1971.

Mair, G. H. *Modern English Literature.* Oxford: Oxford Univ. Press, 1911; rev. 1960.

Mais, Stuart P. B. *Books and Their Writers.* London: Richards; New York: Dodd, Mead, 1920.

———. *Some Modern Authors.* New York: Dodd, Mead; London: Richards, 1923, 1930.

———. *Why We Should Read.* New York: Dodd, Mead; London: Richards, 1921.

Mander, John. *The Writer and Commitment.* London: Secker and Warburg, 1961; Chester Springs, Pa.: Dufour, 1962.

Manheim, Leonard F., and Eleanor B. Manheim, eds. *Hidden Patterns: Studies in Psychoanalytic Literary Criticism.* New York: Macmillan, 1966.

Manlove, Colin N. *Modern Fantasy: Five Studies.* Cambridge and New York: Cambridge Univ. Press, 1975.

Manly, John Matthews, and Edith Rickert. *Contemporary British Literature: Bibliographies and Study Outlines.* New York: Harcourt, 1921; rev. ed. entitled *Contemporary British Literature: Outlines for Study, Indexes, Bibliographies.* New York: Harcourt, 1928. [Subsequently revised by Fred B. Millett]

Mann, Thomas. *Past Masters and Other Papers.* London: Secker and Warburg; New York: Knopf, 1933.

Mannheimer, Monica Lauritzen. "The Individual and Society in Contemporary British Fiction." *MSpr,* 68 (1974), 322-25.

Mansfield, Katherine. *Novels and Novelists.* Ed. J. Middleton Murry. London: Constable; New York: Knopf, 1930.

Marble, Annie R. *A Study of the Modern Novel, British and American, Since 1900.* New York: Appleton, 1928.

Marcu, Valeriu. *Men and Forces of Our Time.* Tr. E. and C. Paul. New York: Viking, 1931.

Marcus, Steven. *Representations: Essays on Literature and Society.* New York: Random House, 1975.

Marković, Vida E. *The Changing Face: Disintegration of Personality in the Twentieth Century British Novel, 1900-1950.* Carbondale: Southern Illinois Univ. Press, 1970.

Marlow, Louis [Louis Wilkinson]. *Seven Friends.* London: Richards, 1953.

Marriott, J. W., ed. *Modern Essays and Sketches.* New York and London: Nelson, 1935.

Marsden, Michael T., ed. *Proceedings of the Fifth National Convention of the Popular Culture Association, St. Louis, Mo., March 20-22, 1975.* Bowling Green, Ohio: Bowling Green State Univ. Popular Press, 1975.

———, ed. *Proceedings of the Sixth National Convention of the Popular Culture Association, Chicago, Illinois, April 22-24, 1976.* Bowling Green, Ohio: Bowling Green State Univ. Popular Press, 1976.

Martin, E. W., ed. *The New Spirit.* London: Dobson, 1946.

Maschler, Tom, ed. *Declaration.* London: MacGibbon and Kee, 1957.

Masur, Gerhard. *Prophets of Yesterday: Studies in European Culture, 1890-1914.* New York: Macmillan, 1961.

Matthews, William, and Ralph W. Rader, eds. *Autobiography, Biography, and the Novel: Papers Read at a Clark Library Seminar, May 13, 1972.* Los Angeles: Wm. Andrews Clark Mem. Lib., U.C.L.A., 1973.

Maugham, W. Somerset. *The Vagrant Mood: Six Essays.* London: Heinemann, 1952; Garden City, N.Y.: Doubleday, 1953.

Mauriac, François. *Second Thoughts: Reflections on Literature and on Life.* Cleveland: World, 1961.

Maurois, André. *Points of View, from Kipling to Graham Greene.* New York: Ungar, 1968; London: Muller, 1970. [Expanded version of *Prophets and Poets.* Tr. H. Miles. New York: Harper, 1935]

Mégroz, R. L. *Five Novelist Poets of Today.* London: Joiner and Steele, 1933.

Melchiori, Giorgio. *The Tightrope Walkers: Studies of Mannerism in Modern English Literature.* London: Routledge and K. Paul, 1956.

Mencken, H. L. *Book of Prefaces.* New York: Knopf, 1917.

———. *Prejudices,* 1st - 6th ser., 6 vol. New York: Knopf, 1919-27.

Mendilow, A. A. *Time and the Novel.* London: Peter Nevill, 1952.

Meyers, Jeffrey. *Painting and the Novel.* New York: Barnes and Noble; Manchester: Manchester Univ. Press, 1975.

Michel, Laurence. *The Thing Contained: Theory of the Tragic.* Bloomington: Indiana Univ. Press, 1970.

Miles, Rosalind. *The Fiction of Sex: Themes and Functions of Sex Difference in the Modern Novel.* New York: Barnes and Noble, 1974.

Miller, Henry. *The Books in My Life.* New York: New Directions, 1957; London: Peter Owen, 1961.

Miller, James E., Jr. *Myth and Method: Modern Theories of Fiction.* Lincoln: Univ. of Nebraska Press, 1960.

Miller, J. Hillis, ed. *Aspects of Narrative.* New York: Columbia Univ. Press, 1971.

———. *Poets of Reality: Six Twentieth-Century Writers.* Cambridge, Mass.: Belknap Press of Harvard Univ. Press, 1965.

Millett, Fred B. "Contemporary British Literature." *Contemporary Literary Scholarship: A Critical Review.* Ed. Lewis Leary. New York: Appleton, 1958, 187-200.

———. *Contemporary British Literature: A Critical Survey and 232 Author-Bibliographies,* 3d rev. and enlarged ed. based on 2d ed. by John M. Manly and Edith Rickert, 1935. New York: Harcourt, 1928; rev. ed. entitled *Contemporary British Literature: Bibliographies and Outlines.* New York: Harcourt, 1948.

Mizener, Arthur. *The Sense of Life in the Modern Novel.* Boston: Houghton Mifflin, 1964.

Monroe, N. Elizabeth. *The Novel and Society: A Critical Study of the Modern Novel.* Chapel Hill: Univ. of North Carolina Press, 1941.

Moody, Philippa. "In the Lavatory of the Athenaeum—Post-War English Novels." *MCR,* 6 (1963), 83-92.

Mooney, Harry J., Jr., and Thomas F. Staley, eds. *The Shapeless God: Essays on Modern Fiction.* Pittsburgh: Univ. of Pittsburgh Press, 1968.

Moore, Patrick. *Science and Fiction.* London: Harrap, 1957.

Moorman, Charles. *Arthurian Triptych: Mythic Materials in Charles Williams, C. S. Lewis, and T. S. Eliot.* Berkeley: Univ. of California Press, 1960.

_____. *The Precincts of Felicity: The Augustinian City of the Oxford Christians.* Gainesville: Univ. of Florida Press, 1966.

More, Paul E. *On Being Human (New Shelburne Essays,* v. 3). Princeton, N.J.: Princeton Univ. Press; London: Oxford Univ. Press, 1936.

Morgan, Stewart S., and William H. Thomas, eds. *Opinions and Attitudes in the Twentieth Century.* New York: Nelson, 1934.

Morley, Christopher. *Internal Revenue.* Garden City, N. Y.: Doubleday, 1933.

_____. *Powder of Sympathy.* Garden City, N. Y.: Doubleday, 1923.

_____. *Romany Stain.* Garden City, N. Y.: Doubleday, 1926.

_____. *Shandygaff.* Garden City, N. Y.: Doubleday, 1918.

Morris, Robert K. *Continuance and Change: The Contemporary British Novel Sequence.* Carbondale: Southern Illinois Univ. Press, 1971.

Morris, Wright. *The Territory Ahead: Critical Interpretations in American Literature.* New York: Atheneum, 1961.

Morton, Arthur L. *The Matter of Britain: Essays on a Living Culture.* London: Laurence and Wishart, 1966.

Moseley, Edwin M. *Pseudonyms of Christ in the Modern Novel: Motifs and Methods.* Pittsburgh: Univ. of Pittsburgh Press, 1962.

Moskowitz, Sam. *Explorers of the Infinite: Shapers of Science Fiction.* Cleveland: World, 1963.

Mudrick, Marvin. *On Culture and Literature.* New York: Horizon, 1970.

Mueller, William R. *Celebration of Life: Studies in Modern Fiction.* New York: Sheed and Ward, 1972.

_____. *The Prophetic Voice in Modern Fiction.* New York: Association Press, 1959.

Muir, Edwin. *Latitudes.* New York: Viking, 1924.

_____. *The Structure of the Novel.* London: L. and V. Woolf, 1928.

_____. *Transition: Essays on Contemporary Literature.* New York: Viking, 1926.

Muller, Herbert J. *In Pursuit of Relevance.* Bloomington: Indiana Univ. Press, 1971.

———. *Modern Fiction: A Study of Values.* New York and London: Funk and Wagnalls, 1937.

Murdoch, Walter. *Collected Essays.* Sydney: Angus and Robertson, 1938.

Murray, Edward. *The Cinematic Imagination: Writers and the Motion Picture.* New York: Ungar, 1972.

Murray, Henry A., ed. *Myth and Mythmaking.* New York: Braziller, 1960.

Murry, J. Middleton. *Love, Freedom, and Society.* London: J. Cape, 1957.

———. *Selected Criticism, 1916-1957.* New York: Oxford Univ. Press, 1960.

Myers, Walter L. *The Later Realism: A Study of Characterization in the British Novel.* Chicago: Univ. of Chicago Press, 1927.

Nassar, Eugene P. *The Rape of Cinderella.* Bloomington: Indiana Univ. Press, 1970.

Nathan, George Jean, et al., eds. *The American Spectator Year Book.* New York: Stokes, 1934.

Neill, S. Diana. *A Short History of the English Novel.* London and New York: Jarrolds, 1951; New York: Macmillan, 1952, rev. 1964.

Newbolt, Henry J. *Studies, Green and Gray.* London and New York: Nelson, 1926.

Newby, P. H. *The Novel, 1945-50.* London: Longmans, Green, 1951.

Newquist, Roy, ed. *Counterpoint.* Chicago: Rand McNally, 1964.

Newton, Alfred E. *End Papers: Literary Recreations.* Boston: Little, Brown, 1933.

Newton, Eric. *In My View.* London and New York: Longmans, Green, 1950.

Nichols, Beverley. *Are They the Same at Home?* London: J. Cape; New York: Doran, 1927.

Nicholson, Norman. *Man and Literature.* London: SCM, 1943.

Nott, Kathleen. *The Emperor's Clothes.* London: Heinemann, 1953; Bloomington: Indiana Univ. Press, 1958.

Oates, Joyce Carol. *New Heaven, New Earth: The Visionary Experience in Literature.* New York: Vanguard, 1974.

O'Brien, Justin. *The French Literary Horizon.* New Brunswick, N. J.: Rutgers Univ. Press, 1967.

———, ed. *From the N.R.F.: An Image of the Twentieth Century from the Pages of the NOUVELLE REVUE FRANCAISE.* New York: Farrar, Straus, 1958.

O'Connor, Frank [Michael O'Donovan]. *The Mirror in the Roadway: A Study of the Modern Novel.* New York: Knopf, 1956.

O'Connor, William Van, ed. *Forms of Modern Fiction.* Minneapolis: Univ. of Minnesota Press, 1948.

———. *The New University Wits and the End of Modernism.* Carbondale: Southern Illinois Univ. Press, 1963.

———. "Two Types of 'Heroes' in Post-War British Fiction." *PMLA*, 77 (1962), 168-74.

O'Donnell, Donat [Conor Cruise O'Brien]. *Maria Cross: Imaginative Patterns in a Group of Modern Catholic Writers.* New York: Oxford Univ. Press, 1952; London: Chatto and Windus, 1953.

O'Faoláin, Seán. *The Vanishing Hero: Studies of the Hero in the Modern Novel.* Boston: Little, Brown, 1957.

Oliphant, Robert. "Public Voices and Wise Guys." *VQR*, 37 (1961), 522-37.

Orage, Alfred R. *Readers and Writers, 1917-1921.* London: Allen and Unwin, 1922.

———. *Selected Essays and Critical Writings.* Ed. Herbert Read and Denis Saurat. London: Nott, 1933.

Orwell, George. *The Collected Essays, Journalism and Letters of George Orwell,* 4 vol. Ed. Sonia Orwell and Ian Angus. New York: Harcourt; London: Secker and Warburg, 1968.

———. *Dickens, Dali, and Others.* New York: Reynal and Hitchcock, 1946.

Overton, Grant M. *Authors of the Day: Studies in Contemporary Literature.* Garden City, N. Y.: Doubleday, 1924.

———. *Cargoes for Crusoes.* New York: Appleton, 1924.

Palmer, Helen H., and Anne Jane Dyson. *English Novel Explication: Criticisms to 1972.* Hamden, Conn.: Shoe String, 1973.

Panichas, George A., ed. *The Politics of Twentieth-Century Novelists.* New York: Hawthorn, 1971.

———, ed. *Promise of Greatness: The War of 1914-1918.* New York: Day, 1968.

———. *The Reverent Discipline: Essays in Literary Criticism and Culture.* Knoxville: Univ. of Tennessee Press, 1974.

Paris Review. Writers at Work: The PARIS REVIEW Interviews, 1st-4th ser. New York: Viking, 1958-1974.

Parry, Benita. *Delusions and Discoveries: Studies on India in the British Imagination, 1880-1930.* London: Lane, 1972.

Peck, Harry Thurston. *The Personal Equation.* New York and London: Harper, 1898.

Pendry, E. D. *The New Feminism of English Fiction: A Study of Contemporary Women-Novelists.* Tokyo: Kenkyusha, 1956.

Penguin New Writing. Harmondsworth, Middlesex: Penguin, 1940.

Perényi, Erzsébet, and Tibor Frank. *Studies in English and American,* v. 2. Budapest: Dept. of Eng., L. Eötvös Univ., 1975.

Pfleger, Karl. *Wrestlers with Christ.* Tr. E. I. Watkin. New York: Sheed and Ward, 1936.

Phelps, Gilbert, ed. *Living Writers: Being Critical Studies Broadcast in the B.B.C. Third Programme.* London: Sylvan, 1947.

———. "The Novel Today." *The Pelican Guide to English Literature,* v. 7: *The Modern Age.* Ed. Boris Ford, 490-530.

———. *The Russian Novel in English Fiction.* London: Hutchinson's Univ. Library, 1956.

Phelps, William Lyon. *The Advance of the English Novel.* New York: Dodd, Mead, 1916.

Plomer, William. *At Home: Memoirs.* London: J. Cape, 1958.

Porter, Katherine Anne. *The Collected Essays and Occasional Writings of Katherine Anne Porter.* New York: Delacorte, 1970.

———. *The Days Before.* New York: Harcourt, 1952.

Porter, Raymond J., and James D. Brophy, eds. *Modern Irish Literature: Essays in Honor of William York Tindall.* New York: Iona Coll. Press and Twayne, 1972.

The Post-Victorians, by Various Authors. London: Nicholson and Watson, 1933.

Potts, Paul. *Dante Called You Beatrice.* London: Eyre and Spottiswoode, 1960.

Pound, Ezra. *Literary Essays.* New York: New Directions; London: Faber and Faber, 1954.

Powell, Dilys. *Descent from Parnassus.* London: Cresset; New York: Macmillan, 1934.

Powell, Lawrence C. *Books in My Baggage: Adventures in Reading and Collecting.* Cleveland: World, 1960.

———. *California Classics: The Creative Literature of the Golden State.* Los Angeles: Ward Ritchie, 1971.

———. *The Little Package: Pages on Literature and Landscape from a Traveling Bookman's Life.* Cleveland: World, 1964.

Prescott, Orville. *In My Opinion: An Inquiry into the Contemporary Novel.* Indianapolis: Bobbs-Merrill, 1952.

Priestley, J. B. *Figures in Modern Literature.* London: Lane; New York: Dodd, Mead, 1924.

———. *Literature and Western Man.* New York: Harper, 1960.

Pritchett, V. S. *Books in General.* London: Chatto and Windus; New York: Harcourt, 1953.

_____. *The Living Novel and Later Appreciations.* New York: Random House, 1964.

_____. *The Working Novelist.* London: Chatto and Windus, 1965.

Proctor, Mortimer R. *The English University Novel.* Berkeley: Univ. of California Press, 1957.

Purtill, Richard. *Lord of the Elves and Eldils: Fantasy and Philosophy in C. S. Lewis and J. R. R. Tolkien.* Grand Rapids, Mich.: Zondervan, 1974.

Putt, S. Gorley. *Scholars of the Heart: Essays in Criticism.* London: Faber and Faber, 1962.

Quennell, Peter. *Casanova in London.* New York: Stein and Day, 1971.

_____. *The Singular Preference: Portraits and Essays.* London: Collins, 1952; New York: Viking, 1953.

Quiller-Couch, Arthur Thomas. *Adventure in Criticism.* London: Cassell; New York: Scribner's, 1896; 2d ed. New York: Putnam's, 1925.

Quinn, Kerker, and Charles Shattuck, eds. *ACCENT Anthology: Selections from ACCENT, a Quarterly of New Literature, 1940-1945.* New York: Harcourt, 1946.

Quinton, Anthony, et al. "The New Novelists: An Enquiry." *LonM,* 5, 11 (November 1958), 13-31.

Raban, Jonathan. *The Technique of Modern Fiction: Essays in Practical Criticism.* London: E. Arnold; Notre Dame, Ind.: Univ. of Notre Dame Press, 1968.

Rabinovitz, Rubin. *The Reaction Against Experiment in the English Novel, 1950-1960.* New York: Columbia Univ. Press, 1967.

Rahv, Philip. *Image and Idea.* New York: New Directions, 1949.

_____. *Literature and the Sixth Sense.* Boston: Houghton Mifflin, 1969.

Rajan, Balachandra, ed. *Focus Four: The Novelist as Thinker.* London: Dobson, 1945, 1947.

Raleigh, John Henry. *Time, Place, and Idea: Essays on the Novel.* Carbondale: Southern Illinois Univ. Press, 1968.

_____. "Victorian Morals and the Modern Novel." *PR,* 25, 2 (1958), 241-64.

Ransom, John Crowe. *World's Body.* New York: Scribner's, 1938.

Raphael, Alice. *Goethe, the Challenger.* New York: J. Cape and R. Ballou, 1932.

Rascoe, Burton. *A Bookman's Daybook.* New York: Liveright, 1929.

————. *Prometheans: Ancient and Modern.* New York: Putnam, 1933.

————. *Titans of Literature, from Homer to the Present.* New York: Putnam, 1932.

————. *We Were Interrupted.* Garden City, N. Y.: Doubleday, 1947.

Raskin, Jonah. *The Mythology of Imperialism: Rudyard Kipling, Joseph Conrad, E. M. Forster, D. H. Lawrence, and Joyce Cary.* New York: Random House, 1971.

Rathburn, Robert C., and Martin Steinmann, Jr., eds. *From Jane Austen to Joseph Conrad: Essays Collected in Memory of James T. Hillhouse.* Minneapolis: Univ. of Minnesota Press, 1958.

Ray, Gordon. *H. G. Wells and Rebecca West.* London: Macmillan; New Haven, Conn.: Yale Univ. Press, 1974.

Raymond, John. *The Doge of Dover, and Other Essays.* London: Mac-Gibbon and Kee, 1960.

Reade, Arthur R. *Main Currents in Modern Literature.* London: Nicholson and Watson, 1935.

Reck, Rima D., ed. *Explorations of Literature.* Baton Rouge: Louisiana State Univ. Press, 1966.

Reed, Henry. *The Novel Since 1939.* London: Longmans, Green, 1946.

Reed, John R. *Old School Ties: The Public Schools in British Literature.* Syracuse, N. Y.: Syracuse Univ. Press, 1964.

Reid, Margaret J. C. *The Arthurian Legend.* Edinburgh: Oliver and Boyd, 1938; New York: Barnes and Noble, 1961.

Reilly, Joseph J. *Of Books and Men.* New York: Messner, 1942.

Reilly, Robert J. *Romantic Religion: A Study of Barfield, Lewis, Williams, and Tolkien.* Athens: Univ. of Georgia Press, 1971.

Reinhardt, Kurt F. *The Theological Novel of Modern Europe: An Analysis of Masterpieces by Eight Authors.* New York: Ungar, 1969.

Rexroth, Kenneth. *Assays.* New York: New Directions, 1962.

————. *The Elastic Retort: Essays in Literature and Ideas.* New York: Seabury, 1973.

Richards, Grant. *Author Hunting.* New York: Coward-McCann, 1934.

Richter, David H. *Fable's End: Completeness and Closure in Rhetorical Fiction.* Chicago: Univ. of Chicago Press, 1975.

Rickword, Edgell, ed. *Scrutinies,* 2 vol. London: Wishart, 1928, 1930.

Rippier, Joseph S. *Some Postwar English Novelists.* Frankfurt am Main: Diesterweg, 1965.

Roberts, Gildas, ed. *Seven Studies in English: for Dorothy Cavers.* Cape Town and London: Purnell and Sons, 1971.

Roberts, Mark. *The Tradition of Romantic Morality.* London: Macmillan, 1973.

Robinson, Kenneth A., et al., eds. *Essays Toward Truth: Studies in Orientation, Selected by K. A. Robinson, W. B. Pressey, J. I. McCallum*, 1st-2d ser., 2 vol. New York: Holt, 1924-29.

Robson, W. W. *Modern English Literature.* London and New York: Oxford Univ. Press, 1970.

Rogers, Robert. *A Psychoanalytic Study of the Double in Literature.* Detroit: Wayne State Univ. Press, 1970.

Romberg, Bertil. *Studies in the Narrative Technique of the First-Person Novel.* Stockholm: Almquist and Wiksell, 1962.

Rosa, Alfred F., and Paul A. Escholz. *Contemporary Fiction in America and England, 1950-1970: A Guide to Information Services.* Detroit: Gale Research, 1976.

Rose, Lois, and Stephen Rose. *The Shattered Ring: Science Fiction and the Quest for Making.* Richmond, Va.: John Knox, 1970.

Rosenbaum, Stanford P., ed. *The Bloomsbury Group: A Collection of Memoirs, Commentary and Criticism.* London: Croom Helm; Toronto: Univ. of Toronto Press, 1975.

_____, ed. *English Literature and British Philosophy: A Collection of Essays.* Chicago: Univ. of Chicago Press, 1971.

Rosenberg, Harold. *Tradition of the New.* New York: Horizon, 1959; London: Thames and Hudson, 1962.

Rosenfeld, Isaac. *An Age of Enormity: Life and Writing in the Forties and Fifties.* Ed. Theodore Solotaroff. Cleveland: World, 1962.

Rosenfeld, Paul. *By Way of Art: Criticisms of Music, Literature, Painting, Sculpture and the Dance.* New York: Coward-McCann, 1928.

_____. *Men Seen: Twenty-Four Modern Authors.* New York: Dial, 1925.

Rothstein, Eric, and Thomas K. Dunseath, eds. *Literary Monographs*, v. 1. Madison: Univ. of Wisconsin Press, 1967. Rothstein, Eric, ed. *Literary Monographs*, v. 4 and 5. Madison: Univ. of Wisconsin Press, 1971, 1972.

Rouse, H. Blair, et al. "A Selective and Critical Bibliography of Studies in Prose Fiction. . . . " *JEGP*, 48 (1949), 259-84; 49 (1950), 358-87; 50 (1951), 376-407; 51 (1952); 364-92.

Routh, H. V. *English Literature and Ideas in the Twentieth Century: An Inquiry into Present Difficulties and Future Prospects.* London: Methuen, 1946; New York: Longmans, Green, 1948.

_____. *Towards the Twentieth Century: Essays in the Spiritual History of the Nineteenth.* New York: Macmillan, 1937; Cambridge: Cambridge Univ. Press, 1937.

Rowse, Alfred L. *The English Spirit: Essays in History and Literature.* London: Macmillan, 1944.

Books Cited and General Bibliography

Royal Society of Literature of the United Kingdom, London. *Essays by Divers Hands*, v. 21, 24, 32, 36, 38. London: Oxford Univ. Press, 1944, 1948, 1963, 1970, 1975.

Rubin, Louis D., Jr. *The Teller in the Tale*. Seattle: Univ. of Washington Press, 1967.

Rueckert, William H. *Kenneth Burke and the Drama of Human Relations*. Minneapolis: Univ. of Minnesota Press, 1963.

Ruotolo, Lucio P. *Six Existential Heroes: The Politics of Faith*. Cambridge, Mass.: Harvard Univ. Press, 1973.

Sackville-West, Edward. *Inclinations*. London: Secker and Warburg, 1949.

Sale, Roger. *Modern Heroism: Essays on D. H. Lawrence, William Empson, and J. R. R. Tolkien*. Berkeley: Univ. of California Press, 1973.

Salter, J. A. *Personality in Politics: Studies of Contemporary Statesmen*. London: Faber and Faber, 1947.

Sampson, George. *The Concise Cambridge History of English Literature*. Cambridge: Cambridge Univ. Press, 1941, 1961.

Sandison, Alan. *The Wheel of Empire: A Study of the Imperial Idea in Some Late Nineteenth and Early Twentieth Century Fiction*. London: Macmillan; New York: St. Martin's, 1967.

Sarason, Bertram D. *Hemingway and THE SUN Set*. Washington, D. C.: NCR Microcard Eds., 1972.

Sarraute, Nathalie. *The Age of Suspicion: Essays on the Novel*. Tr. Marie Jolas. New York: Braziller, 1963.

Savage, Derek S. *The Withered Branch: Six Studies in the Modern Novel*. London: Eyre and Spottiswoode, 1950; New York: Pelligrini and Cudahy, 1952.

Schelling Anniversary Papers, by his Former Students. New York: Appleton, 1923.

Schneider, Daniel J. *Symbolism: The Manichean Vision: A Study in the Art of James, Conrad, Woolf, and Stevens*. Lincoln: Univ. of Nebraska Press, 1975.

Scholes, Robert. *The Fabulators*. New York: Oxford Univ. Press, 1967.

————, and Robert Kellogg. *The Nature of Narrative*. New York: Oxford Univ. Press, 1966.

Schorer, Mark. "The Chronicle of Doubt." *VQR*, 18 (1942), 200-15.

————, ed. *Modern British Fiction: Essays in Criticism*. New York: Oxford Univ. Press, 1961.

————, ed. *Society and Self in the Novel: English Institute Essays, 1955*. New York: Columbia Univ. Press, 1956.

_____. *The World We Imagine: Selected Essays.* New York: Farrar, Straus, 1968.

Scott, Nathan A., Jr., ed. *Forms of Extremity in the Modern Novel.* Richmond, Va.: John Knox, 1965.

_____. *Rehearsals of Discomposure.* New York: King's Crown, 1952.

Scott, Robert Ian. "Modern Theories of Communication and Types of Literature." *JJR,* 1, 4 (1958), 18-32.

Scott-James, Rolfe A. *Fifty Years of English Literature, 1900-1950.* London: Longmans, Green, 1951; 2d ed., with postscript, 1956.

_____. *Personality in Literature, 1913-1931.* New York: Holt, 1932.

Scully, Frank. *Rogues' Gallery: Profiles of My Eminent Contemporaries.* Hollywood, Cal.: Murray and Gee, 1943.

Sedgwick, Ellery. *The Happy Profession.* Boston: Little, Brown, 1946.

Seltzer, Alvin J. *Chaos in the Novel: The Novel in Chaos.* New York: Schocken, 1974.

Semmler, Clement. *For the Uncanny Man: Essays, Mainly Literary.* Melbourne: F. W. Cheshire; London: Angus and Robertson, 1963.

Shalvi, Alice, and A. A. Mendilow, eds. *Studies in English Language and Literature.* Jerusalem: Hebrew Univ., 1966.

Shanks, Edward. *First Essays on Literature.* London: Collins, 1923.

_____. *Second Essays on Literature.* London: Collins, 1927.

Shapiro, Charles, ed. *Contemporary British Novelists.* Carbondale: Southern Illinois Univ. Press, 1965.

_____, ed. *Twelve Original Essays on Great English Novels.* Detroit: Wayne State Univ. Press, 1960.

Shapiro, Stephen A. "The Ambivalent Animal: Man in the Contemporary British and American Novel." *CentR,* 12 (1968), 1-22.

Shaw, G. Bernard. *Selected Prose.* Ed. Diarmuid Russell. New York: Dodd, Mead, 1952.

Sheed, Wilfred. *The Morning After: Selected Essays and Reviews.* New York: Farrar, Straus, 1971.

Sherman, Stuart P. *Critical Woodcuts.* New York: Scribner's, 1926.

_____. *Emotional Discovery of America, and Other Essays.* New York: Farrar, Straus, 1932.

_____. *On Contemporary Literature.* New York: Holt, 1917.

Simon, Irene. "Bloomsbury and Its Critics." *RLV,* 23 (1957), 385-414.

Simon, John. *Movies into Film: Film Criticism, 1967-1970.* New York: Dial, 1971.

Singh, Bhupal. *A Survey of Anglo-Indian Fiction.* London: Oxford Univ. Press, 1934; London: Curzon, 1975.

Sitwell, Osbert. *Noble Essences.* Boston: Little, Brown, 1950.

———. *Penny Foolish: A Book of Tirades and Panegyrics.* New York: Macmillan, 1935.

Slochower, Harry. *No Voice is Wholly Lost: Writers and Thinkers in War and Peace.* New York: Creative Age, 1945.

Slosson, Edwin E. *Six Major Prophets.* Boston: Little, Brown, 1917.

Slote, Bernice, ed. *Literature and Society, by Germaine Brée and Others: A Selection of Papers Delivered at the Joint Meeting of the Midwest Modern Language Association and the Central Renaissance Conference, 1963.* Lincoln: Univ. of Nebraska Press, 1964.

Smith, Eric. *Some Versions of the Fall: The Myth of the Fall of Man in English Literature.* London: Croom Helm, 1973.

Snow, C. P. "The English Realistic Novel, 1957." *MSpr,* 51 (1957), 265-70.

———. *Variety of Men.* New York: Scribner's, 1967.

Solotaroff, Theodore. *The Red Hot Vacuum, and Other Pieces on the Writing of the 60's.* New York: Atheneum, 1970.

Speare, Morris Edmund. *The Political Novel.* New York: Oxford Univ. Press, 1924.

Spender, Stephen. "Anglo-Saxon Attitudes." *PR,* 25, 1 (1958), 110-16.

———. *The Creative Element: A Study of Vision, Despair and Orthodoxy Among Some Modern Writers.* London: Hamilton, 1953.

———. *The Destructive Element: A Study of Modern Writers and Beliefs.* London: J. Cape, 1935, 1953; Boston: Houghton Mifflin, 1936; Philadelphia: Saifer, 1953.

———. *Love-Hate Relations: English and American Sensibilities.* New York: Random House, 1974.

———. "Movements and Influences in English Literature, 1927-1952." *BA,* 27 (1953), 5-32.

———. *The Struggle of the Modern.* Berkeley: Univ. of California Press, 1963.

———. *World Within World.* New York: Harcourt, 1951.

Squire, John C. *Books in General,* 1st-3d ser., 3 vol. London: Heinemann, 1919-21.

———. *Books Reviewed.* London: Hodder and Stoughton; New York: Doran, 1922.

———. *Life and Letters.* London: Hodder and Stoughton, 1920; New York: Doran, 1921.

Staley, Thomas F., and Lester F. Zimmerman, eds. *Literature and Theology.* Tulsa: Univ. of Tulsa Press, 1969.

Stanford, Derek. "Beatniks and Angry Young Men." *Meanjin,* 17 (1958), 413-19.

———. "Thoughts on Contemporary Literature." *ContempR*, 191 (1957), 234-38.

Stanford, Donald E., ed. *Nine Essays in Modern Literature*. Baton Rouge: Louisiana State Univ. Press, 1965.

Starkie, Enid. *From Gautier to Eliot: The Influence of France on English Literature, 1851-1939*. London: Hutchinson; New York: Humanities, 1960.

Starrett, Agnes L., ed. *If By Your Art: Testament to Percival Hunt*. Pittsburgh: Univ. of Pittsburgh Press, 1948.

Stauzel, Frank K. *Narrative Situations in the Novel*. Bloomington: Indiana Univ. Press, 1971.

Steel, Johannes. *Men Behind the War: A "Who's Who" of our Time*. New York: Sheridan House, 1943.

Steiner, George. *Language and Silence: Essays on Language, Literature, and the Inhuman*. New York: Atheneum, 1967.

Stephens, James. *James, Seumas, and Jacques: Unpublished Writings of James Stephens*. New York: Macmillan, 1964.

Stern, Joseph P. *On Realism*. London: Routledge and K. Paul, 1973.

Stevenson, Lionel. *The English Novel: A Panorama*. Boston: Houghton Mifflin, 1960.

———. *The History of the English Novel*, v. 11 (*Yesterday and After*) [v. 1-10 by Earnest A. Baker]. New York: Barnes and Noble, 1967.

———, ed. *Victorian Fiction: A Guide to Research*. Cambridge, Mass.: Harvard Univ. Press, 1964.

Stewart, Douglas Alexander. *The Flesh and the Spirit: An Outlook on Literature*. Sydney: Angus and Robertson, 1948.

Stewart, Douglas G. *The Ark of God: Studies in Five Modern Novelists —James Joyce, Aldous Huxley, Graham Greene, Rose Macaulay, Joyce Cary*. London: Carey Kingsgate, 1961.

Stewart, J. I. M. *Eight Modern Writers*. V. 12 of *Oxford History of English Literature*. Oxford: Clarendon, 1963.

Stoll, E. E. *From Shakespeare to Joyce: Authors and Critics, Literature and Life*. Garden City, N.Y.: Doubleday, 1944.

Stone, Donald David. *Novelists in a Changing World: Meredith, James, and the Transformation of English Fiction in the 1880's*. Cambridge, Mass.: Harvard Univ. Press, 1972.

Stonier, George W. *Gog Magog, and Other Critical Essays*. London: Dent, 1933.

Strachey, John. *The Strangled Cry*. London: Bodley Head, 1962.

Strelka, Joseph, ed. *Perspectives in Literary Symbolism*. University Park: Penn. State Univ. Press, 1968.

Strong, L. A. G. *Personal Remarks.* London: Peter Nevill; New York: Liveright, 1953.

Sudrann, Jean. "The Necessary Illusion: A Letter from London." *AR*, 18 (1958), 236-44.

Sussman, Herbert L. *Victorians and the Machine: The Literary Response to Technology.* Cambridge, Mass.: Harvard Univ. Press, 1968.

Sutherland, William O. S., ed. *Six Contemporary Novels: Six Introductory Essays in Modern Fiction.* Austin: Univ. of Texas Press, 1962.

Swan, Michael. *A Small Part of Time: Essays on Literature, Art, and Travel.* London: J. Cape; Chester Springs, Pa.: Dufour, 1961.

Swinden, Patrick. *Unofficial Selves: Character in the Novel from Dickens to the Present Day.* London: Macmillan; New York: Barnes and Noble, 1973.

Swinnerton, Frank A. *Authors I Never Met.* London: Allen and Unwin, 1956.

––––––. *Background with Chorus: A Footnote to Changes in English Literary Fashion Between 1901 and 1917.* New York: Farrar, Straus; London: Hutchinson, 1956.

––––––. "Eclipse of the Novel." *ContempR*, 189 (1956), 333-38.

––––––. *Figures in the Foreground: Literary Reminiscences, 1917-1940.* London: Hutchinson, 1963; Garden City, N.Y.: Doubleday, 1964.

––––––. *The Georgian Scene: A Literary Panorama.* New York: Farrar and Rinehart, 1934; London: Heinemann, 1935; London: Hutchinson, 1969. [1969 ed. entitled *The Georgian Literary Scene: 1910-1935*]

––––––. *Tokefield Papers, Old and New.* Garden City, N.Y.: Doubleday, 1949.

Symons, Arthur. *Dramatis Personae.* Indianapolis: Bobbs-Merrill, 1923.

Tate, Allen. *Essays of Four Decades.* Chicago: Swallow, 1969.

––––––, ed. *A Southern Vanguard.* New York: Prentice-Hall, 1947.

––––––. "Techniques of Fiction." *SR*, 52 (1944), 210-25.

Taylor, Estella Ruth. *The Modern Irish Writers: Cross Currents of Criticism.* Lawrence: Univ. of Kansas Press, 1954.

Taylor, Rachel Annand. "The Post-War English Novel." *SocR*, 20 (1928), 177-96.

Technology and the Frontiers of Knowledge. Garden City, N.Y.: Doubleday, 1975.

Temple, Ruth Z. *The Critic's Alchemy: A Study of the Introduction of French Symbolism Into English.* New York: Twayne, 1953.

———, and Martin Tucker. *Twentieth Century British Literature: A Reference Guide and Bibliography.* New York: Ungar, 1968.

Thompson, Edward R. [E. T. Raymond]. *Portraits of the New Century: The First Ten Years.* London: Allen and Unwin, 1928.

Thorburn, David, and Geoffrey Hartman, eds. *Romanticism: Vistas, Instances, Continuities.* Ithaca, N.Y.: Cornell Univ. Press, 1973.

Thorp, Willard, and M. F. Thorp, eds. *Modern Writing.* New York: American Book, 1944.

Tillotson, Geoffrey. *Criticism and the Nineteenth Century.* London: Athlone, 1951.

Tillyard, E. M. W. *The Epic Strain in the English Novel.* London: Chatto and Windus; Fairlawn, N.J.: Essential Books, 1958.

———. *Essays, Literary and Educational.* New York: Barnes and Noble, 1962.

Times Literary Supplement. Essays and Reviews, 15 vol. London: Oxford Univ. Press, 1962-1976.

Tindall, William York. *Forces in Modern British Literature: 1885-1956.* New York: Knopf, 1947, 1956.

———. *The Literary Symbol.* New York: Columbia Univ. Press, 1955.

Trautmann, Joanne. *The Jessamy Brides: The Friendship of Virginia Woolf and V. Sackville-West.* University Park: Penn. State Univ. Press, 1973.

Trilling, Diana. *Claremont Essays.* New York: Harcourt, 1964.

Trilling, Lionel. *A Gathering of Fugitives.* Boston: Beacon, 1956.

———. *The Opposing Self.* New York: Viking, 1955.

Troy, William. *Selected Essays.* Ed. Stanley E. Hyman. New Brunswick, N.J.: Rutgers Univ. Press, 1967.

Tucker, Martin. *Africa in Modern Literature: A Survey of Contemporary Writing in English.* New York: Ungar, 1967.

Tully, Jim. *A Dozen and One.* Hollywood, Cal.: Murray and Gee, 1943.

Turnell, Martin. *Modern Literature and Christian Faith.* London: Darton, Longmans and Todd; Westminster, Md.: Newman, 1961.

Tyrmand, Leopold, ed. *Kultura Essays.* New York: Free Press, 1970.

Undset, Sigrid. *Men, Women, and Places.* Tr. A. G. Chater. New York: Knopf, 1939.

Unterecker, John, ed. *Approaches to the Twentieth-Century Novel.* New York: Crowell, 1965.

Untermeyer, Louis. *Makers of the Modern World.* New York: Simon and Schuster, 1955.

Updike, John. *Assorted Prose.* New York: Knopf, 1965.

Urang, Gunnar. *Shadows of Heaven: Religion and Fantasy in the Writing of C. S. Lewis, Charles Williams and J. R. R. Tolkien.* Philadelphia: Pilgrim, 1971.

Books Cited and General Bibliography

Urwin, G. G., ed. *A Taste for Living: Young People in the Modern Novel.* London: Faber and Faber, 1967.

Van Doren, Carl. *Roving Critic.* New York: Knopf, 1923.

Van Doren, Mark. *The Private Reader: Selected Articles and Reviews.* New York: Holt, 1942.

Van Gelder, Robert. *Writers and Writing.* New York: Scribner's, 1946.

Van Ghent, Dorothy. *The English Novel: Form and Function.* New York: Rinehart, 1953.

Van Kaam, Adrian, and Kathleen Healy. *The Demon and the Dove: Personality Growth Through Literature.* Pittsburgh: Duquesne Univ. Press, 1967.

Van Patten, Nathan. *An Index to Bibliographies and the Bibliographical Contributions Relating to the Work of American and British Authors, 1923-1932.* Stanford, Cal.: Stanford Univ. Press, 1934.

Vernon, John E. *The Garden and the Map: Schizophrenia in Twentieth Century Literature and Culture.* Urbana: Univ. of Illinois Press, 1973.

Verschoyle, Derek, ed. *The English Novelists: A Survey of the Novel by Twenty Contemporary Novelists.* New York: Harcourt, 1936.

Vickery, John B. *The Literary Impact of THE GOLDEN BOUGH.* Princeton, N.J.: Princeton Univ. Press, 1973.

Vines, Sherard. *Movements in Modern English Poetry and Prose.* Oxford: Oxford Univ. Press; Tokyo: Ohkayama, 1927.

Viswanathan, K. *India in English Fiction.* Waltair: Andhra Univ. Press, 1971.

Wagenknecht, Edward C. *Cavalcade of the English Novel.* New York: Holt, 1943.

Wagner, Geoffrey. "The Minority Writer in England." *HudR,* 7 (1954), 427-35.

Wain, John. *Essays on Literature and Ideas.* London: Macmillan, 1963.

———. *A House for the Truth: Critical Essays.* New York: Viking, 1973.

———, ed. *International Literary Annual No. 1.* London: John Calder, 1958.

———. *Preliminary Essays.* London: Macmillan; New York: St. Martin's, 1957.

Walcutt, Charles Child. *Man's Changing Mask: Modes and Methods of Characterization in Fiction.* Minneapolis: Univ. of Minnesota Press, 1966.

Walkley, Arthur B. *More Prejudice.* New York: Knopf, 1923.

Wallace, A. Dayle, and Woodburn O. Ross, eds. *Studies in Honor of John Wilcox, by Members of the English Department, Wayne State University.* Detroit: Wayne State Univ. Press, 1958.

Wallace, Archer. *Religious Faith of Great Men.* New York: Round Table Press, 1934.

Walpole, Hugh, et al. *Tendencies of the Modern Novel.* London: Allen and Unwin, 1934.

Walsh, Chad. *From Utopia to Nightmare.* New York: Harper, 1963.

Walsh, William. *The Use of Imagination: Educational Thought and the Literary Mind.* London: Chatto and Windus, 1959.

Ward, A. C. *The Nineteen-Twenties: Literature and Ideas in the Post-War Decade.* London: Methuen, 1930, 1933.

———. *Twentieth Century Literature: The Age of Interrogation, 1901-1925.* London: Methuen, 1928; rev. ed., *Twentieth Century Literature, 1901-1940,* London: Longmans, Green, 1940; 3d ed., *Twentieth Century Literature, 1901-1950,* London: Methuen; New York: Barnes and Noble, 1956; rev. ed., *Twentieth Century English Literature, 1901-1960,* New York: Barnes and Noble, 1964.

Warren, Austin. *Rage for Order: Essays in Criticism.* Chicago: Univ. of Chicago Press, 1948.

Washburn, Claude C. *Opinions.* New York: Dutton, 1926.

Watkin, Edward. *Men and Tendencies.* New York: Sheed and Ward, 1937.

Watson, George, ed. *The Concise Cambridge Bibliography of English Literature, 600-1950.* Cambridge: Cambridge Univ. Press, 1958.

Waugh, Alec. *My Brother Evelyn and Other Profiles.* London: Cassell; New York: Farrar, Straus and Giroux, 1968. [American edition titled *My Brother Evelyn and Other Portraits*]

Waugh, Arthur. *Tradition and Change: Studies in Contemporary Literature.* New York: Dutton, 1919.

Weaver, Robert. "England's Angry Young Men." *QQ,* 65 (1958), 183-94.

Webb, Eugene. *The Dark Dove: The Sacred and Secular in Modern Literature.* Seattle: Univ. of Washington Press, 1975.

Weber, Brom, ed. *Sense and Sensibility in Twentieth-Century Writing: A Gathering in Memory of William Van O'Connor.* Carbondale: Southern Illinois Univ. Press, 1970.

Webster, Harvey Curtis. *After the Trauma: Representative British Novelists Since 1920.* Lexington: Univ. Press of Kentucky, 1970.

Weinstein, Arnold L. *Vision and Response in Modern Fiction.* Ithaca, N.Y.: Cornell Univ. Press, 1974.

Weintraub, Stanley, and Philip Young, eds. *Directions in Literary Criticism: Contemporary Approaches to Literature.* University Park: Penn. State Univ. Press, 1973.

West, Alick. *Crisis and Criticism, and Selected Literary Essays.* London: Lawrence and Wishart, 1975.

———. *The Mountain in the Sunlight: Studies in Conflict and Unity.* London: Lawrence and Wishart, 1958.

West, Anthony. *Principles and Persuasions: The Literary Essays of Anthony West.* London: Eyre and Spottiswood, 1958.

West, Paul. *The Modern Novel,* 2 vol. London: Hutchinson, 1963, 1965, 59-153.

———. *The Wine of Absurdity.* University Park: Penn. State Univ. Press, 1966.

West, Rebecca. *Ending in Earnest: A Literary Log.* Garden City, N.Y.: Doubleday, 1931.

———. *The Strange Necessity.* Garden City, N.Y.: Doubleday, 1928.

Westmeyer, Russell E. *Modern Economic and Social Systems.* New York: Farrar, Straus, 1940.

Weygandt, Cornelius. *Century of the English Novel.* New York: Appleton, 1925.

Whitbread, Thomas B., ed. *Seven Contemporary Authors: Essays on Cozzens, Miller, West, Golding, Heller, Albee and Powers.* Austin: Univ. of Texas Press, 1966.

Whiting, B. J. "Historical Novels, 1949-1950." *Speculum,* 27 (1951), 337-67.

Whittemore, Reed. *The Fascination of the Abomination: Poems, Stories, and Essays.* New York: Macmillan, 1963.

Why Do I Write? An Exchange of Views Between Elizabeth Bowen, Graham Greene and V. S. Pritchett. London: Marshall, 1948.

Wicker, Brian. *The Story-Shaped World: Fiction and Metaphysics, Some Variations on a Theme.* Notre Dame, Ind.: Notre Dame Univ. Press, 1975.

Wickham, Harvey. *The Impuritans.* New York: Dial, 1929.

Widmer, Kingsley. *The Literary Rebel.* Carbondale: Southern Illinois Univ. Press, 1965.

Wiley, Paul L. *The British Novel: Conrad to the Present.* (Goldentree Bibliography). Northbrook, Ill.: AHM, 1973.

Will, Frederic, ed. *Hereditas: Seven Essays on the Modern Experience of the Classical.* Austin: Univ. of Texas Press, 1964.

Williams, Charles. *Image of the City and Other Essays.* London: Oxford Univ. Press, 1958.

Williams, Harold H. *Modern English Writers: Being a Study of Imaginative Literature, 1890-1914.* London: Sidgwick and Jackson, 1918; New York: Knopf, 1919.

Williams, Raymond. *Culture and Society, 1780-1950.* New York: Columbia Univ. Press, 1958.

_____. *The English Novel from Dickens to Lawrence*. New York: Oxford Univ. Press; London: Chatto and Windus, 1970.

_____. *Modern Tragedy*. London: Chatto and Windus; Stanford, Cal.: Stanford Univ. Press, 1966.

_____. "Realism and the Contemporary Novel." *PR*, 26, 2 (1959), 200-13.

Williams, William Carlos. *Selected Essays*. New York: Random House, 1954.

Wilson, Angus. "Evil in the English Novel." [1, "Richardson and Jane Austen." 2, "George Eliot to Virginia Woolf." 3, "Outside the Central Tradition." 4, "Evil and the Novelist Today."] *Listener*, 68 (1962), 1079-80; 69 (1963), 15-16; 69 (1963), 63-65; 69 (1963), 115-17.

_____. "Mood of the Month III." *LonM*, 5, 4 (April 1958), 40-44.

Wilson, Colin. *The Strength to Dream: Literature and the Imagination*. Boston: Houghton Mifflin, 1962.

_____. *Eagle and Earwig*. London: Baker, 1965.

Wilson, Edmund. *Axel's Castle: A Study of the Imaginative Literature of 1870-1930*. New York: Scribner's, 1931.

_____. *The Bit Between My Teeth: A Literary Chronicle of 1950-1965*. New York: Farrar, Straus, 1965.

_____. *Classics and Commercials: A Literary Chronicle of the Forties*. New York: Farrar, Straus, 1950.

_____. *The Shores of Light: A Literary Chronicle of the Twenties and Thirties*. New York: Farrar, Straus, 1952.

_____. *The Wound and the Bow: Seven Studies in Literature*. New York: Oxford Univ. Press, 1959.

Wilson, James S. "The Changing Novel." *VQR*, 10 (1934), 42-52.

Winegarten, Renée. *Writers and Revolution: The Fatal Lure of Action*. London and New York: New Viewpoints, 1974.

Winther, Sophus K. *The Realistic War Novel*. Seattle: Univ. of Washington Chapbooks, No. 35, 1930.

Wolfe, Bernard. "Angry at What?" *Nation*, 187 (1958), 316-22.

Wolfe, Humbert. *Dialogues and Monologues*. New York: Knopf, 1929.

Woodcock, George. *Odysseus Ever Returning: Essays on Canadian Writers and Writing*. Toronto: McClelland and Stewart, 1970.

_____. *The Writer and Politics*. London: Porcupine, 1948.

Woodruff, Douglas, ed. *For Hilaire Belloc: Essays in Honor of His 71st Birthday*. New York: Sheed and Ward, 1942.

Woolf, Leonard. *Essays on Literature, History, Politics, etc*. London: Hogarth; New York: Harcourt, 1927.

Woolf, Samuel Johnson. *Drawn From Life*. New York: McGraw-Hill; New York and London: Whittlesey House, 1932.

Woolf, Virginia. *Collected Essays*, 4 vol. Ed. Leonard Woolf. London: Hogarth; New York: Harcourt, 1966-67.
_____. *Contemporary Writers*. London: Hogarth, 1965; New York: Harcourt, 1966.
Young, George M. *Daylight and Champaign: Essays*. London: J. Cape, 1937; London: Hart-Davis, 1948.
Zabel, Morton Dauwen. *Craft and Character: Texts, Methods and Vocation in Modern Fiction*. New York: Viking, 1957.
_____, ed. *Literary Opinion in America: Essays Illustrating the Status, Methods, and Problems of Criticism in the United States in the Twentieth Century.* New York: Harper, 1937, 1951, 3d rev. ed. 1962.
Zamyatin, Yevgeny I. *A Soviet Heretic: Essays by Yevgeny Zamyatin.* Ed. and Tr. Mirra Ginsburg. Chicago: Univ. of Chicago Press, 1970.
Zyla, Wolodymyr T., and Wendell M. Aycock, eds. *Joseph Conrad: Theory and World Fiction: Proceedings of the Comp. Lit. Symposium, v. 7, January 23, 24, and 25, 1974*. Lubbock: Inter. Dept. Comm. on Comp. Lit., Texas Tech Univ., 1974.